Half-title

Design, Typography, etc.
A Handbook

Acknowledgements
Damien and Claire Gautier would especially like to thank the designers and authors for graciously granting permission to publish their work in this book.
Furthermore, thanks are due to the following people:
Anne-Catherine Céard, Jean-Marie Courant, Colette Delongvert, Roland Dumarsky, Éric Durif-Varambon, Yvan Gauthier, Julien Guinand, Paul and Maguie Jacquin, Thomas Leblond, Sylvain Levrouw, Élodie and Lionel Michée, Sandrine Picherit, Pauline Restoux, Béranger and Cécile Rialland for the time that they gave us, and for their constructive criticism, Pierre Roesch for his rigorous precision and his perceptive comments, Alan Marshall, Maëlle Lebois and Patrice Lecomte from the Musée de l'Imprimerie et de la Communication graphique in Lyon for their kind collaboration, Siegfried Marque for his valuable help, Michel Philippe for his advice, Anne-Élisabeth Carcano and Michel Lepetitdidier for their hospitality and the wonderful time that we spent with them, and our children Jean, Lou, Lisa, Ella, Émy for their patience.

Imprint

Body copy and headlines were set in the typeface Foundry Journal, which was designed in 1997 by David Quay and Freda Sack. This font is distributed by TheFoundry: www.foundrytypes.co.uk

The text uses the pronoun "he" or "his" to refer to both genders for simplicity.

Authors
Damien and Claire Gautier

Concept and design
Damien Gautier

Translation
Brian Switzer

Proofreading
Robert L. Switzer, Sophie Steybe, Nele Kröger

Cover image
Falk von Traubenberg

www.niggli.ch
ISBN 978-3-7212-0977-8

Title

Design, Typography, etc. A Handbook

Authors

Damien and Claire Gautier

Publisher

Niggli

Foreword

Thomas Huot-Marchand
Director of the Atelier National de Recherche Typographique, ANRT (French National Atelier for Typographic Research)

Among other things, typography sets standards. Under its influence writing, spelling, punctuation and the whole graphic ensemble of book design have been gradually defined. Because it made the text more readable, the type more harmonious, and was more practical, a growing number of practices became conventions and rules. Yet, depending on the sensibilities of the era and country, these rules are occasionally contradictory or inadequate for contemporary use.

Today layout has become "liquid", and the very idea of the page is challenged by the ubiquity of digital content. And yet, Damien and Claire Gautier's book seems more necessary than ever: because it makes it possible to understand the rules of graphic design and their range of possible interpretations. It invites us to continue questioning, to validate or contradict the rules, and to constantly search for new solutions.

Peter Keller, who led the National Atelier for Typographic Research between 1990 and 2006, wrote: *"Structural discipline should not [...] be considered a limitation, but rather a dynamic, expressive and liberating tool used to animate and order. The extremist uses of structure and anti-structure are both dangerous: if imposed dogmatically grids can be oppressive or, conversely, a lack of order impedes communication. Between these two extremes there are infinite possibilities for typographic experimentation."*

All terms set in *italics* are explained in the glossary (pages 266 to 270). The entries list the page numbers where that term is used in the book.

Damien and Claire Gautier

Can a single book cover everything that the vast topic of layout has to offer? Can it explain all the necessary fundamentals? This book does not attempt to do so. Instead, its description of the effective parameters intends to provide you with a well-structured overview and a practical tool.
After reading it your knowledge of the subject will certainly have increased, but your studies will have only just begun. There is nothing better than working hands-on and practicing the many different aspects of layout in all of its complexity and diversity. The theory learned can be applied and a personal approach to layout or graphic design can be developed.

And that is the true goal of this book: to present the basics required to develop the skills that allow anyone to work independently and creatively in the area of their choice. There is still so much to discover in this young field, which is always open for new perspectives.

Have you ever noticed how design principles and their interactions play a central role in a graphic *composition*? A *headline* that isn't in the middle of the space allotted for it, an unusual *color* combination, a special material or texture, an unexpected *fold* – all of these things effect our perception, and highlight the importance of graphic design. In artistic design there are no rigid rules, but there are elements and principles that one needs to understand to develop an eye for designing.

The different design principles summarized in this *section*, such as symmetry, balance, *contrast*, *rhythm*, etc., are not intended to be a complete list. Instead, they explain rules and illuminate the multitude of possibilities for bending or breaking them in the pursuit of a coherent *composition*. These principles affect all areas of design. One encounters them not only in design but also in music, dance, and architecture.

The observation, recognition and analysis of these principles and their appropriateness in relationship to the context and the topic is an important first step. It can serve to sharpen one's perception and to enhance one's practical and planning skills.

Part

01

Headline

Foundations of visual form

Contents

*"The final harmony would be attained if one approached things from the one tiny place they share, the center. Then, when they met there, a kind of peace would arise that one can equate to complete inertia.
A harmony that [...] is dead, an inactive harmony.
What we need is an active harmony. This requires deviation. We can deviate in different ways, by keeping the central point fixed in our imagination, but deviating from it in practice. One can attain active harmony through variations. [...] Well-composed paintings produce a wholly harmonious effect.
But the layman is mistaken when he assumes that to create this complete harmony, one has to produce each section harmoniously. The result would be weak. Once the first part is brought into harmony with the second part, no third part is needed. Only if there is tension between the first and second part is there need for a third to transform the tension into harmony. This new three-part harmony is much more effective. Now, one must proceed responsibly in order to produce humanistic harmony; then, the harmony will be powerful. In our search for harmony or pictorial totality we are dealing not only with a problem of form and color; the problem of mental wholeness also remains to be solved."* – Paul Klee

Paul Klee said this to the Bauhaus students (1921–1922) about harmonious-organic design

"Composition is the art of finding and representing the variety within the unity." – Plato

Foundations of visual form
Introduction

Composition
In *layout*, *composition* means the choosing and placing of elements required by the project on a *surface*. The artistry involves connecting the required elements in a coherent manner. The elements in the *composition* – or the components – are artistic in nature (shape, *light*, *color*, material) and influence the contents.

Visible language
Visual design is a language that combines many areas:
- The area of morphology covers the characteristics of shapes, how their arrangement effects each other, and their effect on the *composition* as a whole.
- The area of *light* and *color* covers the characteristics of lightness and/or *color*, their interaction, and their arrangement in a *composition*.
- The area of materials covers the physical qualities of the elements, their arrangement and their application.

A close examination of the visual language exposes the "density" of a *composition* and its complexity of meaning to us. A structure appropriate to the theme needs to be developed for placing the visual design elements within a *composition*. The goal is to place the elements in the given space in a way that underscores the intended meaning in a harmonious manner (or not).

Harmony
We call a *composition* harmonious when it strives for an optical balance within the area to be designed. Artists and art critics have developed countless theories on this subject. We are guided by the understanding of *harmony* developed in the Renaissance and at the Bauhaus. Étienne Souriau, professor for aesthetics at the Sorbonne and director of the Revue d'esthétique, defines *harmony* in his Vocabulaire d'esthétique as follows: "*Harmony* is the relationship that brings different parts of a complex whole into sync [...], and in such a way that this connection forms a coherent, successful, pleasant whole for the spirit and the senses." In the arts the creative human being arranges all the parts so that their mutual relationships lead to a unified whole. The proportions of the whole are also essential for the work to be a success. The Greek philosopher Plato summed up the foundation of a harmonious *composition* as: "*Composition* is the art of finding and representing the variety within the unity." Paul Klee developed this idea further with his students at the Bauhaus.

Principles of visual form
A *composition*'s contents need to be sufficiently varied to capture attention. Yet, this variety needs to be integrated into a coherent, ordered whole to avoid confusion and chaos. However, some topics provoke disorder. Then one has to find the right balance between the concept and visual means to achieve a harmonious result. Chaos is always a relative term. The graphic designer always asks himself the following questions: How can I arrange the diverse images and texts elegantly? How can I create a coherent *composition* from a random collection of diverse informational elements? If you are proficient in the operative principles of visual *layout* then you are able to deal with complexity and diversity in design.

Instinct, intuition and chance
"Beware of principles" – Jean Baptiste Greuze (French painter, 1725–1805)

Applying geometric rules produces a well constructed but occasionally dull *composition*. The unexpected personal contribution is often a large part of a *composition*'s impact. Sometimes one has to take a chance, or take a risk, or let one's creative instinct decide when to follow the rules, when to bend them, and when to break them.

Cézanne said: *"As soon as I begin to think about it, all is lost."*

Ideas and movements
There are many possible solutions for arranging forms. We love change, follow fashions and aesthetic trends.

Traditions, beliefs and taste play an important role in the evolution of new ideas and forms over time. These are even more important than the abstract aspects mentioned here. For example, a medieval formal geometry develops further in the Renaissance and strives for greater simplicity as well as greater flexibility and agility.
We can compare the preferred *composition* methods to the schools of thought and sociological tendencies of a given time period. The pyramid-like, well-ordered and hierarchical *compositions* common in the Middle Ages correspond to the school of thought of this period. The appeal of geometry remains, but when applied in design it is often simplified or its rules ignored.

Today we have very different and more complex *compositions*. These *compositions* are made up of independent zones touching, overlapping, reflecting like cell structures. Texts that were once regarded as subordinate are sometimes as important as the main text. (The series Découvertes by Gallimard is an example of this.)

A dialogue
A *composition* or a *layout* is always presented to the viewer, who may or may not begin a "conversation" with the piece. What does this dialogue look like? Does the *layout* leave room for the viewer (white space, resting spaces, quiet places, reading flow or free flow)? Is it open and easily understood? Does it overwhelm or make one unsure? Does it allow a slow approach – as the rules of politeness dictate? Does it offer an introduction, the appropriate distance, time for perusal, preparation for the encounter before one gets down to business? The first *pages* of a *book* are a fine example of this (see pages 180, 188f.).
These ideas are an integral part in the arts of *layout* and *composition*.

Format
In terms of designable *surfaces* the simple, yet compelling form of the rectangle has triumphed over time and fashion. The form itself divides the contents in the sense of a discrete hint or a rigid structure. Due to the fixed framing and edges that give the content a form, a *composition* achieves – even before it is thought through – unity. Hence, the *format* strongly influences a *composition* (see pages 38–43).

The fundamental orientation
The French dyslexia expert Patrick Quercia maintains that a child can give the impression that he lacks intelligence, simply because he lacks basic orientation skills.
These orientation skills, which come from the eyes and feet, define the vertical and are the first step towards abstraction, which in turn is the basis of complex thought. So when we talk about structure, good division of space, frames, support, *grids*, "backbone" but forget the fundamental orientation, we ignore intelligence, transcendence, sense. Might one say that a *composition* has both a physical and a metaphysical meaning?

The creative act
One may be an experienced designer who has mastered the principles of *composition* and juggles these skillfully, but he might still be unable to make something that is of semantic, visual or true artistic value. The designer must invest something of himself, if he wants to create something excellent and refine his expression. He must find a way to elicit the emotions or feelings that the project released in his mind.

Symmetry
Harmony and balance

We refer to a symmetric *composition* when all the design elements are arranged on either side of a central axis or around a central point, so that both or all sides match. The principle of symmetry is often used in *compositions*, because it is visually strong and offers the eye greater clarity. A symmetrical *composition* gets noticed, it attracts attention. The symmetrical axes create true *"lines of force"* that are more apparent if the axes are augmented visually.

In the Western culture symmetry represents ideas such as order, power, authority, stability or grandeur. Symmetry is clearly visible in the human body and in nature. The rectangular *format* most common in *layout* lends itself to symmetrical *compositions*.

1. *Kahil El'Zabar's Ritual Quartet*, poster
   Niklaus Troxler
2. *Was ihr wollt*, poster
   Bayerische Staatsoper
   Pierre Mendel design studio, Pierre Mendel
3. *Kitty-cuts*, record album sticker
   kitty-yo int.
   Angela Lorenz

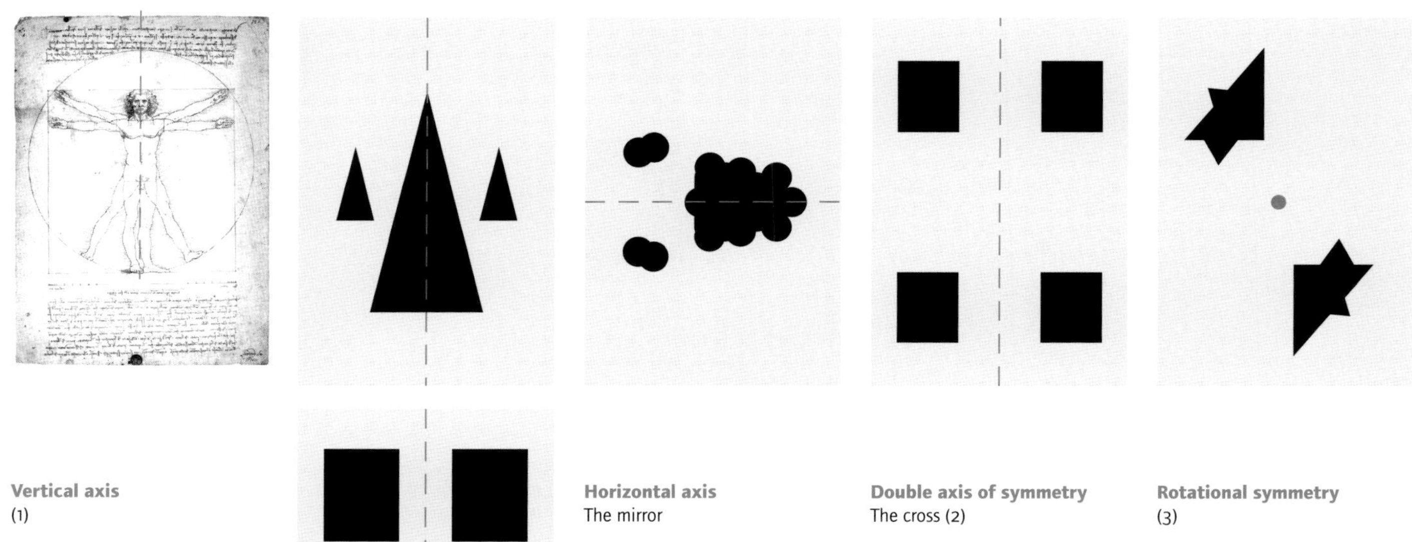

Vertical axis
(1)

Horizontal axis
The mirror

Double axis of symmetry
The cross (2)

Rotational symmetry
(3)

1

2

3

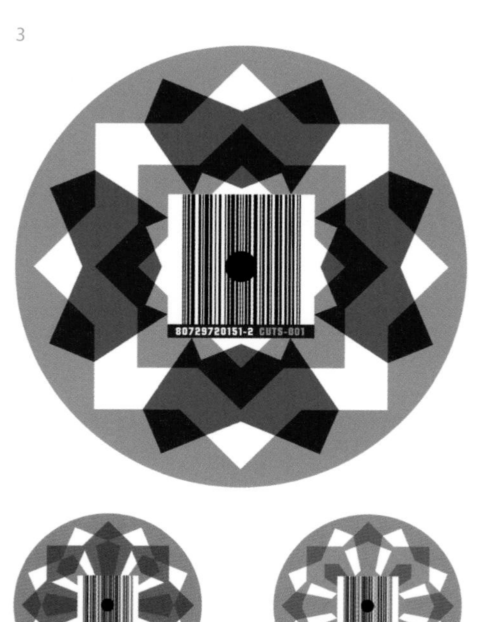

Offset symmetry, asymmetry
Unity and variety

Since too much symmetry can be monotonous it is wise to apply this principle loosely. For example, nuances can be reached through larger or smaller deviations from the geometric rule. These deviations can be applied to any of the visual levels (shape, *color*, *light*, texture, etc.) and can lead to Plato's variety in the unity (see page 10).

One rarely works with "absolute" symmetry in graphic design, because it requires the mirroring of all parts which makes structuring the information into hierarchies difficult. The symmetry in the examples 1, 2 and 3 works due to the fact that there are only a few different elements in play. Deviations from symmetry have a surprising effect, and become eye-catchers. The structuring power of symmetry creates different but related spaces that allow a connection between various elements.

Depending on the amount of deviation from perfect symmetry can express ideas more or less clearly. If the placement of the elements is seemly without principle, and the *composition* is asymmetrical or is divided by multiple axes of symmetry, then the *composition* tends to express independence, movement – even imbalance, chaos or anarchy.
In example 5 one sees how the principle of symmetry can create a strong clear image that will certainly prove visible in an environment likely filled with visual competition. The symmetry used here undoubtedly creates unity and is capable of structuring the diversity and differences in the information.

4. *F4 Trickraum*, poster
Museum für Gestaltung, Zurich
Martin Woodtli
5. *La dame de pique*, poster
Opéra de Lyon
Hartland Villa
6. *Door to door*, poster
Stadtgalerie, Bern
Martin Woodtli

Difference in arrangement, form, scale
(4)

Difference in light

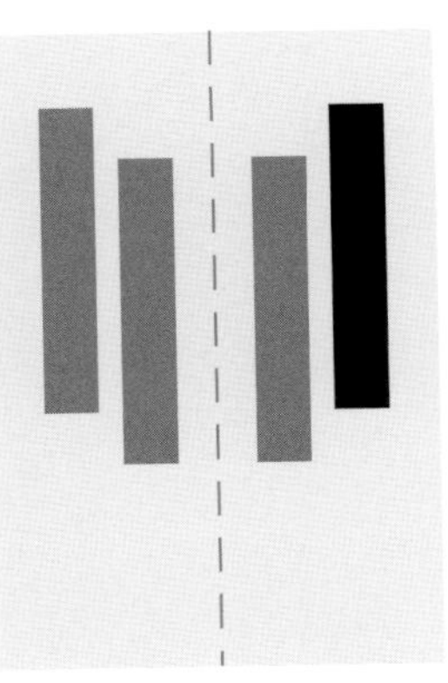

Difference in color
(5)

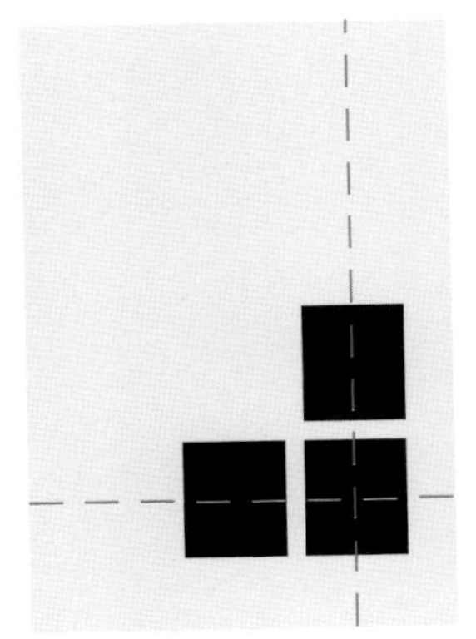

Off-center axis

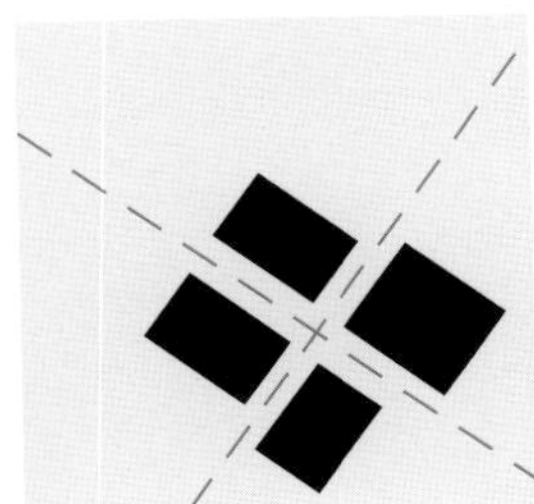

Tilted axis
(6)

4

5

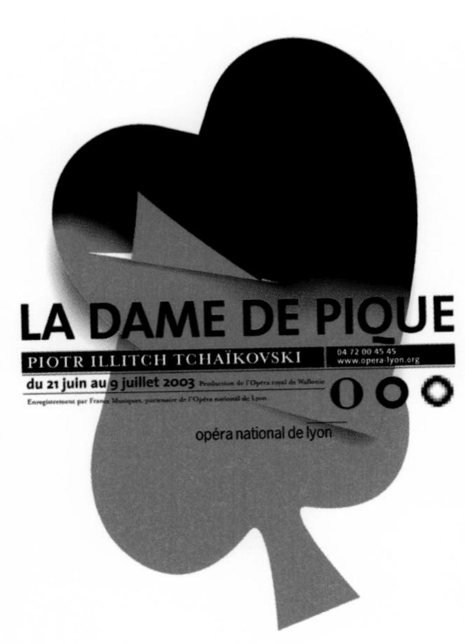

6

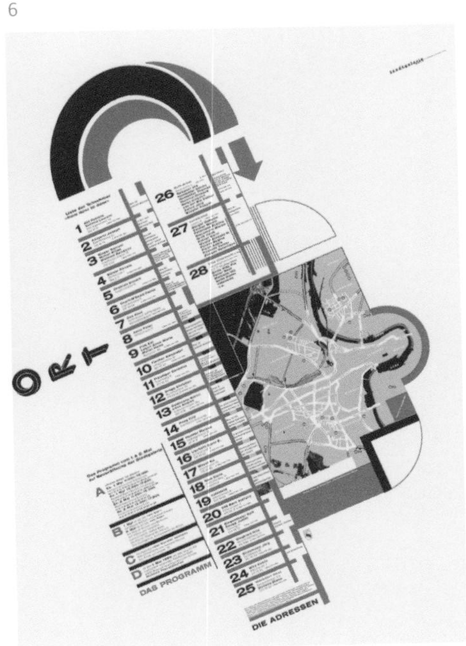

Asymmetry
Balance, compensating mass

Symmetry is not the only means that leads to unity and *equilibrium* in a *composition*.
"The sense of vertical is active in us, so we won't fall [...]. In special cases we extend the horizontal, like a tightrope artist with a balancing pole." – Paul Klee

The same as the human body, which has to change the position of limbs at every movement in order to remain balanced, a *composition* too depends on the right distribution of elements. This leads to unity and stability and even enables true variety. A chaotic distribution of *mass* exhausts our gaze as it jumps here and there, because the viewer is unsure of where to look.

We understand *mass* to be the visual weight of the design elements. The value of *mass* is determined by factors such as size, shape, brightness, or *color* intensity. This value can be modified by changing its proximity to other elements, or its relationship to the page, and its relationship to the remaining white space.

Points of reference
We are all bound by the laws of gravity. They dictate our movements, our orientation, and this physical experience has effects on our visual perception and our imagination. A dark *surface* or *mass* in the upper part of a *composition* looks as if it would "fall", or slip down the page. This gives it a certain amount of dynamism. On the other hand a *mass* in the lower part of the *composition* seems heavier and more stable.

Balancing mass(es)
1. *Masses* with difference values. A dark *mass* is "heavier" than a *light* one.
2. *Masses* with different size (*contrast* between near and far).
A large *mass* is "heavier" than a small one, although one must consider the effect of perspective that suggests near and far. A *mass* in the foreground seems closer than one which is in the background.
3–5. Progressively increasing *mass* imbalance.

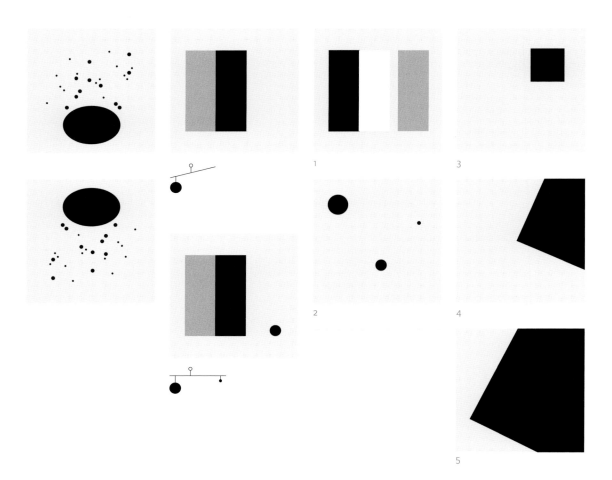

1

3

2

4

5

Asymmetry
Balance, imbalance, movement

6. This series of typographic *compositions* plays with the basic design principles of weight, depth, *contrast*, *balance*, movement ...

7. Abstract *compositions* with four black stripes of equal length in a white square. It is astounding how much the *compositions* differ in their effect, even though the basic elements are the same. The proportions and distance between the black and white *surfaces*, as well as their arrangement in the square *format* create balance, imbalance or movement.

8. These typographic compositions work with the basic design principles of weight, depth, contrast, balance, movement, etc.

6 Musée Nicéphore Niépce, exhibition graphics
Le Petit Didier
8. Compositions created during workshops at the École régionale des beaux-arts in Valence and the École Intuit Lab

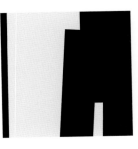

6

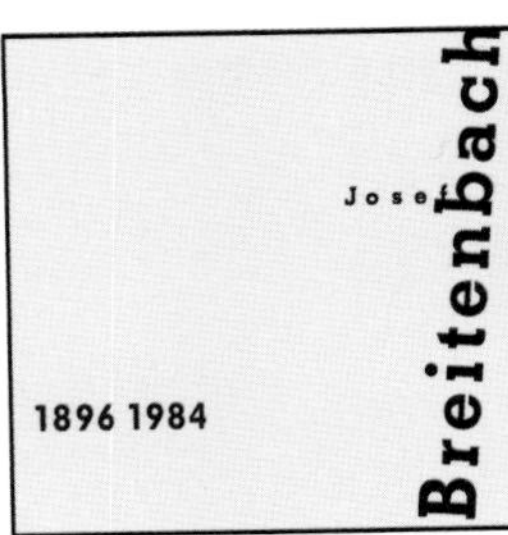

7

8

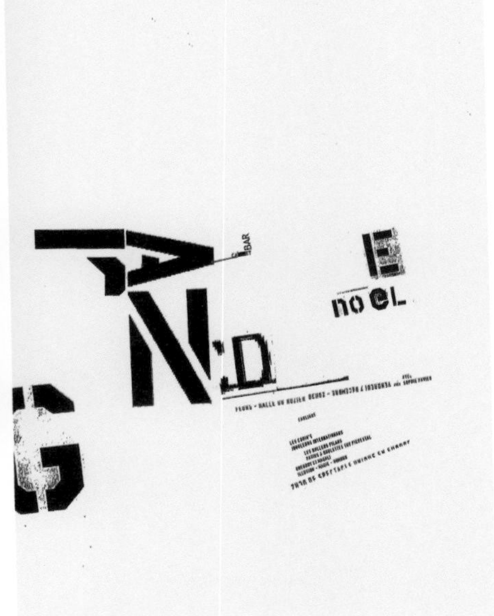

Golden section
The search for an aesthetic ideal

Golden ratio

The so-called *golden section* corresponds a mathematic ratio that is used to divide lines and *surfaces* harmoniously.
It is the result of a search for the ideal proportions found in nature. Ancient architects, medieval and Renaissance artists – dedicated to expressing the perceived *harmony* in nature rationally – all worked with the *golden section*.
Thinkers and artists of the antiquity discovered that certain structures in the universe recur and are perceived to be beautiful. They therefore concluded that certain measures that are also found in nature form a harmonious relationship between the parts and the whole. The *golden ratio* or *golden mean*, which has been so named since the Renaissance, was understood to be God-given.

The Roman architect Vitruvius defined the aesthetic rule as follows: "If a space which is divided into uneven parts should be pleasing and beautiful, then the ratio between the smallest and the largest part should be the same ratio as between the largest and the whole."

The *golden ratio* defines a particular relationship between two segments of different length, and is derived from what Pythagoras called perfect geometric forms: the square and the circle. This ratio is equivalent to the number 1.6180339887. To calculate it, one needs to complete the following geometric construction:
1. Start with the square ABCD and draw the midpoint M along the segment AB. Then draw a line MC. Using a compass transfer the length of MC to MC', extending the straight line from A and B. The ratio between the segments AB and BC' is approximately 1.618.

Golden sections (2) and golden points (3) can be defined using the *golden ratio*. The golden point is a natural resting place for our gaze.
These golden points or sections are strategic points in a *composition*. The rule applies to this day even if it is often simplified (one-third rule, related proportions 8/5 and 5/3) or applied intuitively.

Modulor

The Modulor, a system based on the *golden ratio* and the human body, is the work of the architect Le Corbusier, who applied it to architectural space.
2. *Golden section*
3. Golden point
4. Proportions derived from the Fibonacci numbers
5. Perfect spiral
6. Drawing of the Modulor

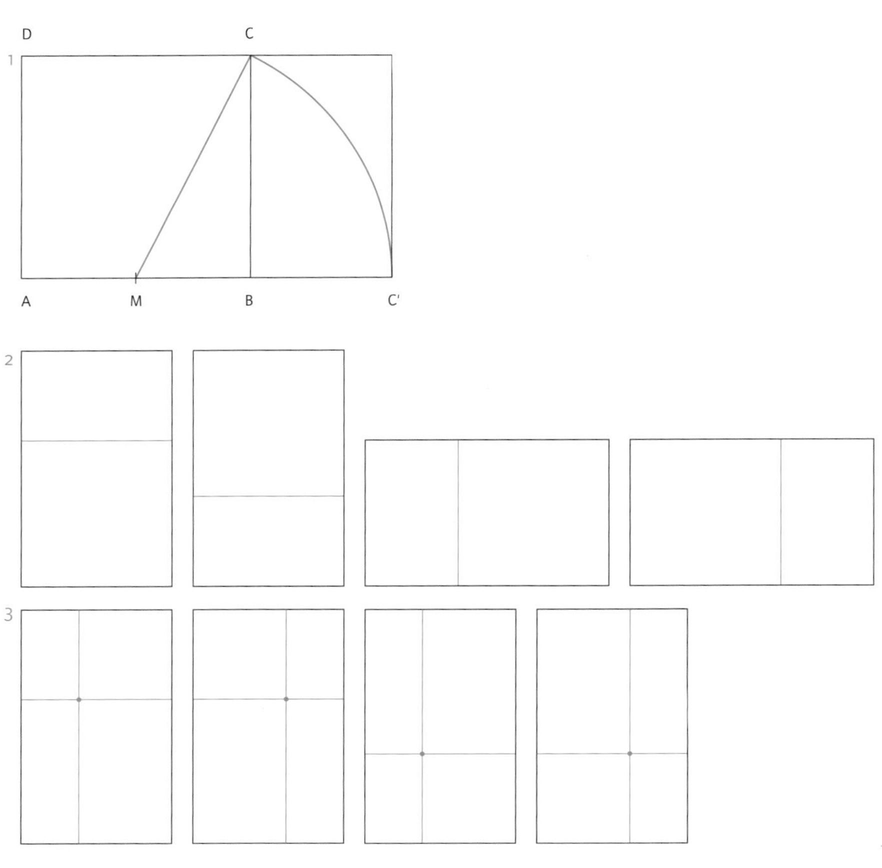

$$\text{Goldene Zahl} = \frac{1+\sqrt{5}}{2} = 1{,}618 \approx \frac{8}{5} \approx \frac{5}{3}$$

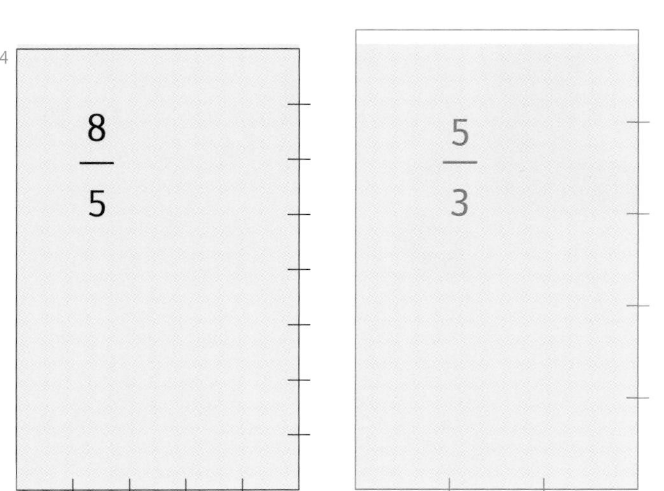

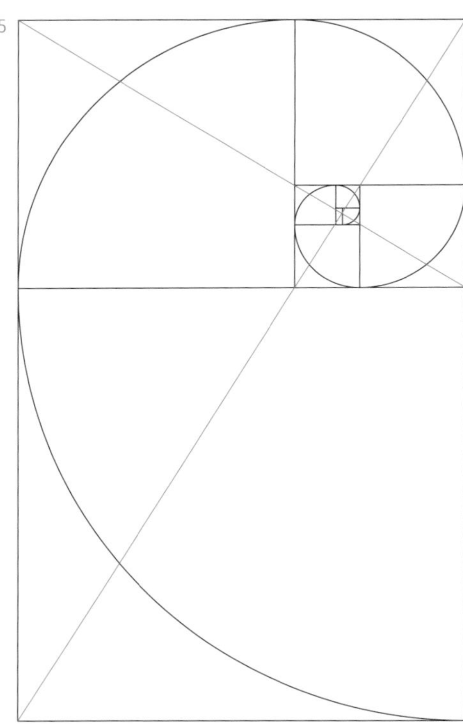

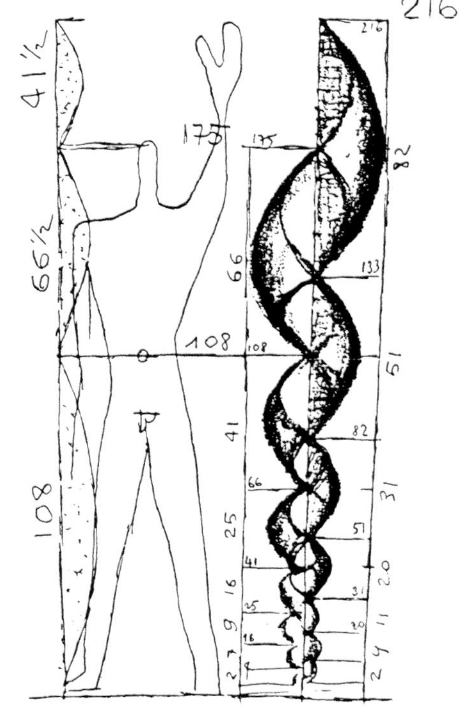

7. The elements are arranged around a point determined with the *golden mean*. The *composition* is undeniably balanced.
8. This graphic designer, who is able to create such complex yet so well-balanced *compositions*, certainly knows about the *golden section*.

The series of numbers 1, 1, 2, 3, 5, 8, 13, 21, 34 … gives us proportions such as 1:2, 2:3, 3:5, 5:8 that step by step bring us closer to the golden number (4).

6. *Le Modulor*, 1945
Le Corbusier
7. *Victory 1945–1995. Death wins every war.* (50th anniversary of the end of the Second World War), poster
LiniaGraphica! Moscow
Uwe Loesch
8. *Chiasso Cultura*, poster
Bruno Monguzzi

7

8

Rhythm
Order and uniformity, movement and harmony

Paul Klee wrote: *"We can perceive* rhythm *with senses at the same time. First, we hear it, second, we see it and third, we can feel it in our muscles."*

In music, *rhythm* is the division of a measure of time into a series of segments that are connected to each other by a related frequency. *Rhythm* is a principle in life, and nature offers us many examples: seasons, tides, breathing, sexuality, etc. In design it is responsible for a vibrant connection of all elements in a *composition*. It is also a principle of order, a principle of variety, unity and of *harmony*.

Rhythm is unavoidable

It enables the division of space and time. It consists of units of time or points of reference that are perceived either consciously or unconsciously, depending on how strong (or weak) they are. *Rhythm* makes reading easier, because it structures our access to a *composition*. It dictates a specific measure of time. In *layout* one finds equivalents to music, such as the feeling of duration or intensity: strong or gentle (fortissimo, pianissimo), slow or fast, loud or quiet.
A rhythmic effect can be created by the distribution of: lighter and darker patches, *colors*, formal elements or material properties. *Rhythm* is all the more attractive if allowed to develop freely and give a *composition* a touch of the infinite. It is therefore a basic principle.

Conscious or intuitive

The *layout grid* can be seen as a rhythmic structure, a scaffold that can either be barely or clearly visible depending on the goal (see part 3).
Rhythm can be applied both consciously or intuitively. It is fascinating to see that every artist, every culture and every century establishes its own *rhythm*. Every designer has his or her own methods and sensitivity when working with *rhythm*.

1. *Mme Said*, program poster
La bonne merveille
2. *Full swing (edits)*, album cover
Orthlorng Musork
Angela Lorenz
3. *Laub: unter anderen bedingungen als liebe*, album cover
kitty-yo int.
Angela Lorenz
Photograph: Magnus Winter

1

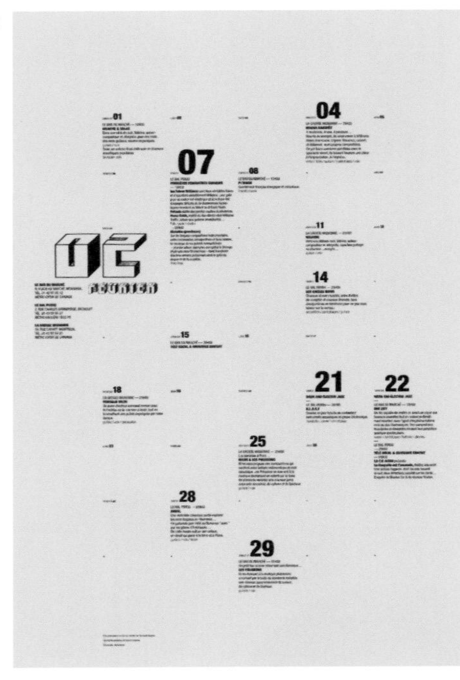

2

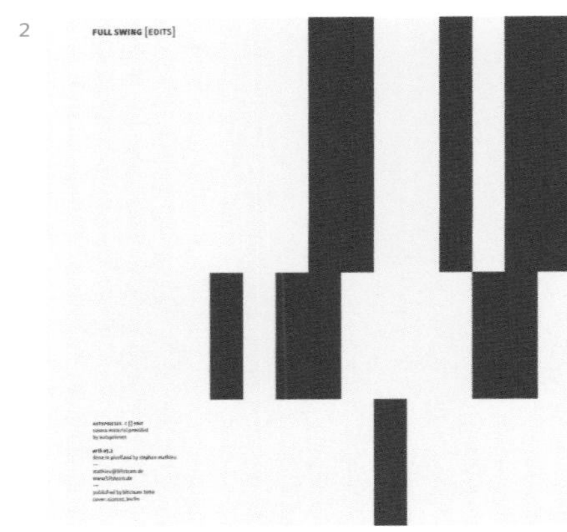

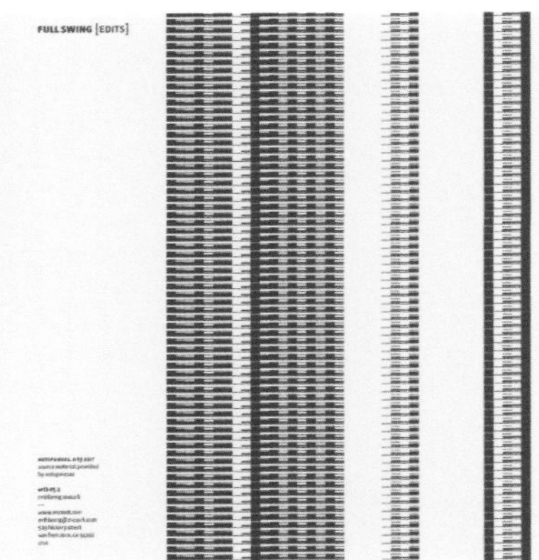

4. *Arte africana. Han Coray*, posters
Museo cantonale d'arte, Lugano
Bruno Monguzzi

3

4

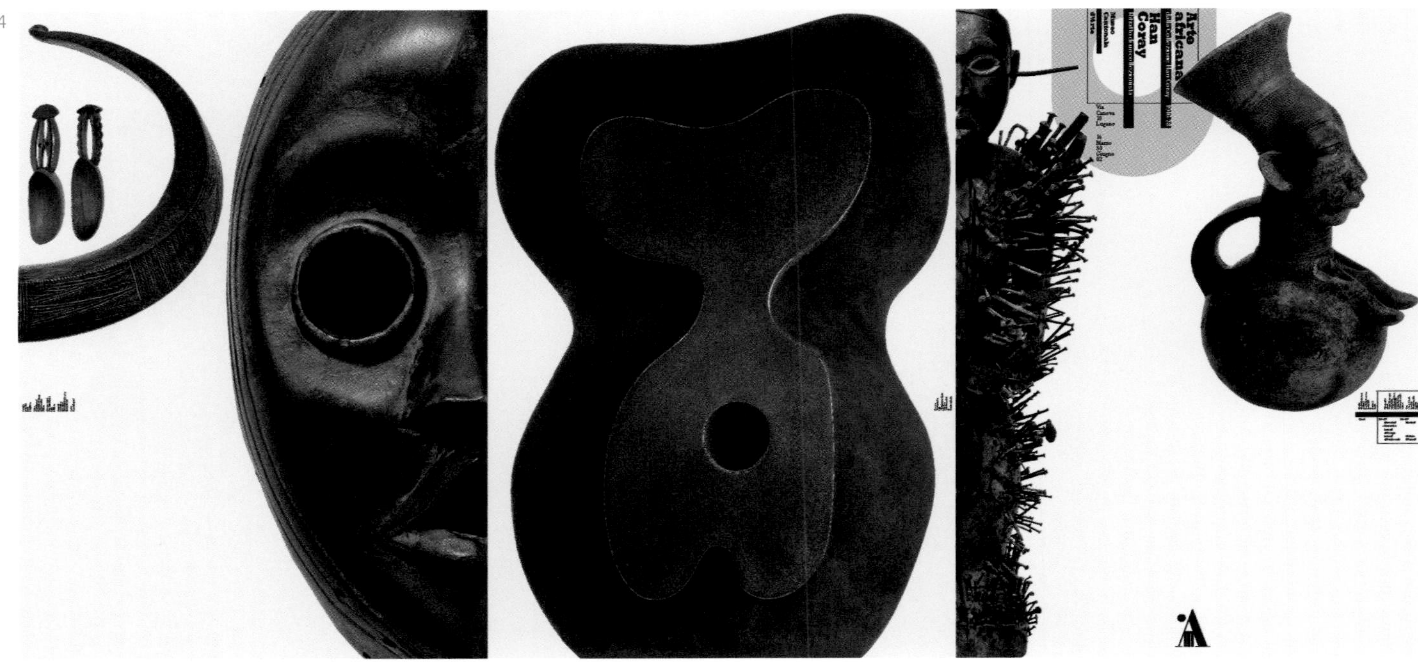

5. Jürgen Schadeberg, invitation
Musée Nicéphore Niépce
Le Petit Didier

Musical divisions: scores and melodies
The Italian Renaissance architect and humanist Alberti explained that the pleasing musical intervals octave, fifth and fourth are equivalent to third or quarter of the string of an instrument. These proportions named diapason, diapente, diatessaron are also fundamental to the fine arts and architecture. Even though they are rarely used, because they are considered scholarly, these proportions beautifully demonstrate the concept of *rhythm* in *composition* during the Renaissance. Two representative works of the Florentine Renaissance – Allegory of Spring and The Birth of Venus by Botticelli – are based on these musical divisions. The first is built according to a double diapente 4/6/9, and the second built according a double diatessaron 9/12/16.

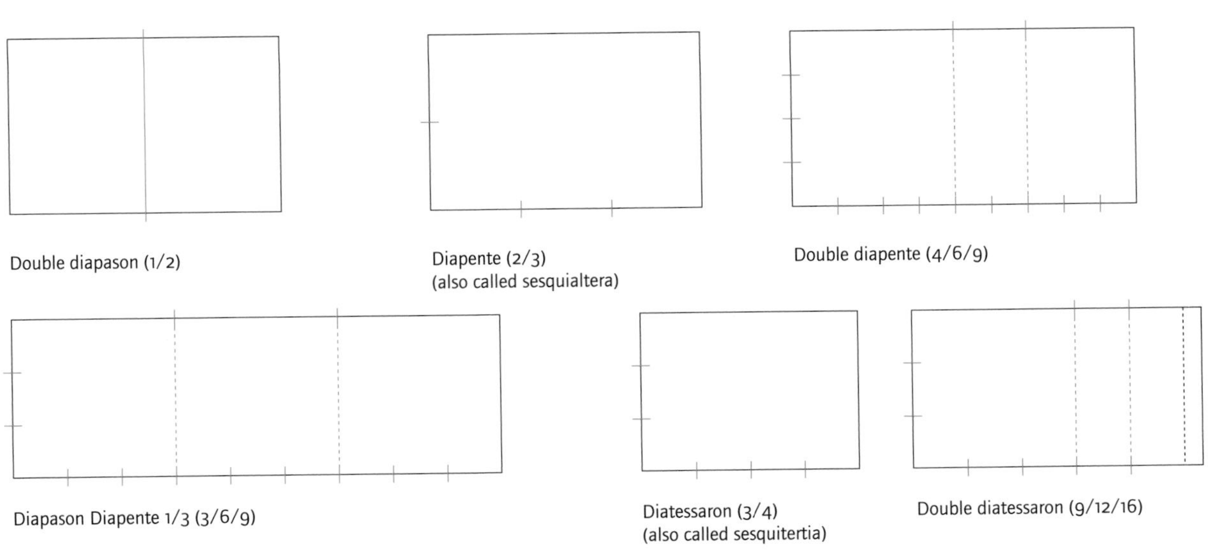

5

Contrasts
Unity and variety

The law of contrast
Contrast means a difference that can extend to the complete opposite. It allows connections and separations. One can refer to unity and coherence with perfectly balanced, and precisely calculated differences, the same as a pair of opposites. Two opposing elements in a design can form a unit. This is true for pairs such as: black and white, red and green, circle and square ...
Contrasts help us reveal and emphasize the unique qualities of individual *compositions*. One can use *contrasts* to: create order, increase the visual effect, draw attention, make a *composition* more expressive.

In design the term *contrast* can be applied to: shape (their gestalt or their weight), the orientation (horizontal, vertical, oblique), *colors* (complementary, warm and cool, *light* and dark, etc.) and *surfaces* (rough or smooth, matte or glossy, etc.). The law of *contrast* can enable a transition, an exchange between the different effects within the *composition* as well as the relationships to the *format* as a whole.

The composition's surface: a shape in the design
The edges of a *composition*, defined by the *format*, form a *surface* with its own formal importance that needs to be considered. In the following examples the presence of the rectangle is particularly visible. The commonly used rectangular format participates in the *composition* as a whole. It is either at odds with (2, 5, 6) or in *harmony* with (1, 3, 4) the rest of the *composition*.

1. *Aida*, poster
Bayerische Staatsoper
Pierre Mendel design studio, Pierre Mendel
2. Exhibition of Pierre Bernard's work in Osaka and Tokyo, poster
Galerie ddd & ggg
Pierre Bernard
3. *Trois sœurs*, poster
Hartland Villa

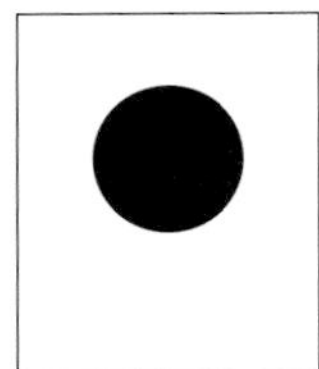

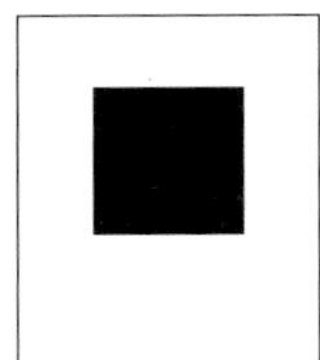

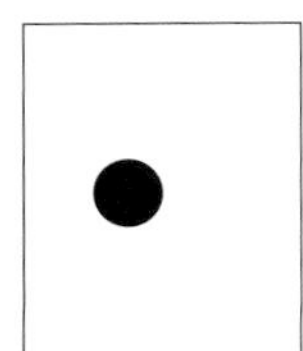

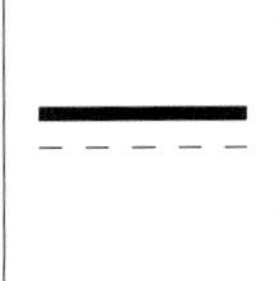

Contrast in geometric forms
Geometric forms are favored in design, because they are easily identified, logical and structured. Their geometric nature guarantees unity, even if there is *contrast* between round and angular forms (1). The rectangle, the right triangle, the unilateral triangle, and the ellipse form the basis of traditional artistic *composition*. Furthermore, one finds combinations that are similar to typographic forms (L, J, S, Z, C, Y).

Contrast between different types of forms
The simultaneous use of different types of forms creates a very strong *contrast*. One differentiates between geometric forms, forms from the material world (including organic forms) and those created by our imagination. The first are perfect and mathematical. The second correspond to things we have seen, or are analogous to reality. The third are unexpected (2). The *contrast* is particularly high if forms of different origin (photography, drawing, type) are combined with each other.

Contrast in functions
Forms differ in a *composition* due to their design function. Kandinsky speaks of a form grammar in the use of point, line and plane.
- All things that resemble a point structure or accentuate a *composition*. They can be used as a signal, pivot, or marking.
- The line structures, connects or separates, guides and underscores. It is direction, path, border or conclusion.
- The plane corresponds to a *surface*, an extension, a field. It can consist of a *mass*, a shape or a mesh of points and lines (3).

1

2

3

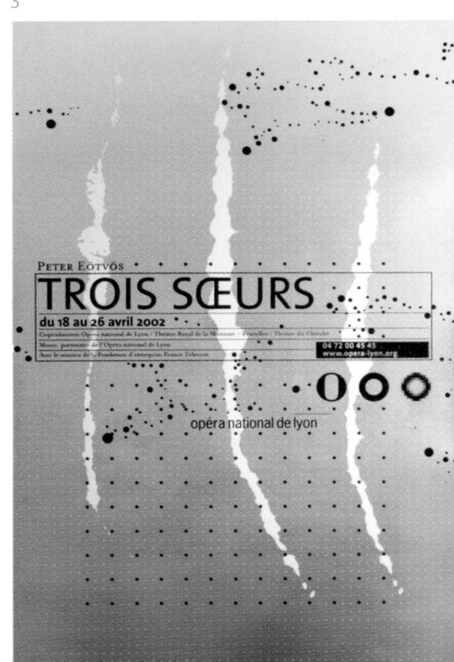

4. *Aki Takase – Silke Eberhard*, poster
Niklaus Troxler
5. *L'immagine... ritrovata*, poster
Museo cantonale d'arte, Lugano
Bruno Monguzzi
6. *Atmo. Brtschitsch: Rockstar* and *White hole: Holy Ghost*, album cover
Silke Maurer
Angela Lorenz

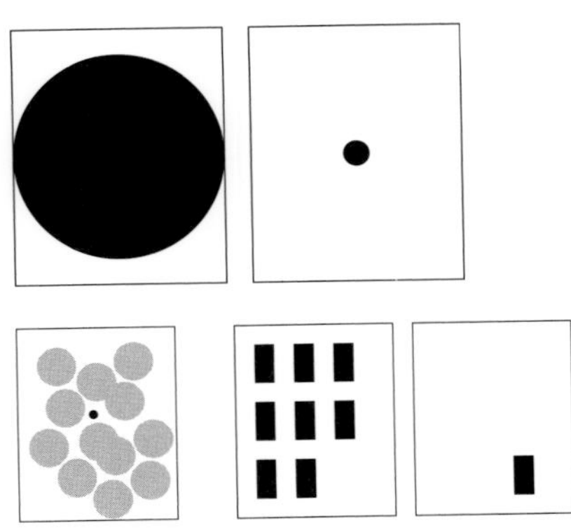

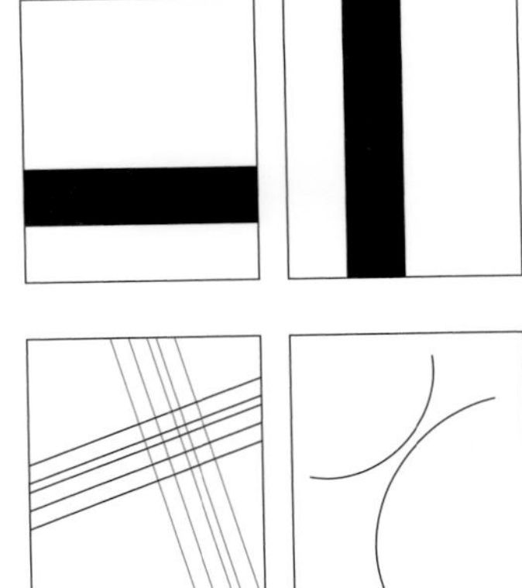

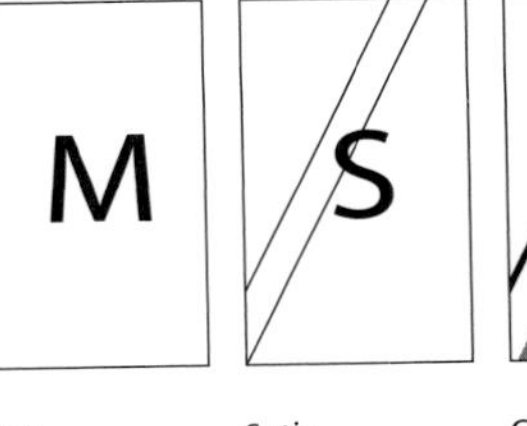

Mat Satin Glossy

Contrast in size, in quantity or in "force"
Contrast can be visible in a balance of power between dominant and dominated. A difference between two elements in scale (large/small), in thickness (*bold/hairline*), or in quantity (many/few) can affect this balance (4).

Contrast in movement or direction
Horizontal/vertical, linear/circular movement, ascending/descending angles, concave/convex curves are all *contrasts* used in *compositions*. Due to our experience and reading habits we decode them as follows:

- We inevitably associate the vertical with a man standing, balance, life ...
- The horizontal represents distance, stability, death and passivity ...
- A slope is motion between the horizontal and the vertical, between balance and passivity. It is positive when it slopes upwards, and negative when it slopes downwards (if one reads left to right) (5).

Contrast in material or texture
This *contrast* can either be real or suggested. *Grids* or images can suggest diverse material qualities. Two kinds of paper with different *surfaces* (rough, smooth) with matte, satin or glossy varnish, letterpress or *debossing* (*embossing*) are all ways of creating texture *contrasts* (6).

Contrast in light and color
See pages 24–27

4

5

6

Equivalents
Unity and harmony

The principle of equivalence is a principle of unity and *harmony*. It connects many different elements with each other and with the design space. One can find semantic equivalents if elements share a meaning or concept. If there are similarities between different elements one also refers to visual equivalence. Equivalents can be created in all areas of design, in shape, in *light*, in *color* or in texture. Multiple equivalents can be combined in the same *composition*. One finds this principle also in a rhythmic *composition*.

Equivalence between "seeing" and "reading"
When reading one misses the spirit of form, because one concentrates on the meaning. Nonetheless, reading and seeing are on the same level when the mind looks for connections between the abstraction of "reading" and the visually direct of "seeing".
In the examples 3 and 6 the *graphic elements* obscure the text and encourage us to read. In example 4 the *headline* crosses the man's gaze. Seeing and reading come together in the literal sense of the words. In example 5 the text meanders through the different image layers.

1. *Sempacher Bundesfeier 2001*, poster
   Erich Brechbühl (Mixer)
2. *Collecting flowers – Spring*, program poster
   Oslo Architects Association
   Grandpeople
3. *Die Räuber*, poster
   Hessisches Staatstheater, Wiesbaden
   Gunter Rambow

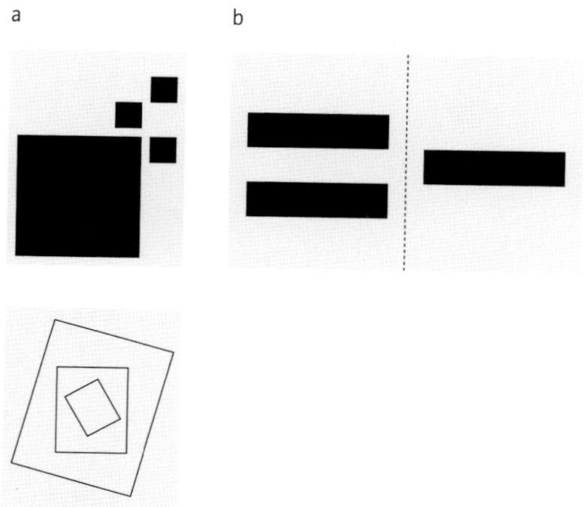

Equivalence of shape
The unity of a *composition* can be supported by:
- the dominance and repetition of a shape
- the arrangement of shapes
- the relationship of the shapes to the design space

In design the negative (empty) shapes are equally important to the positive (solid) shapes (a, b, c) (1, 2).

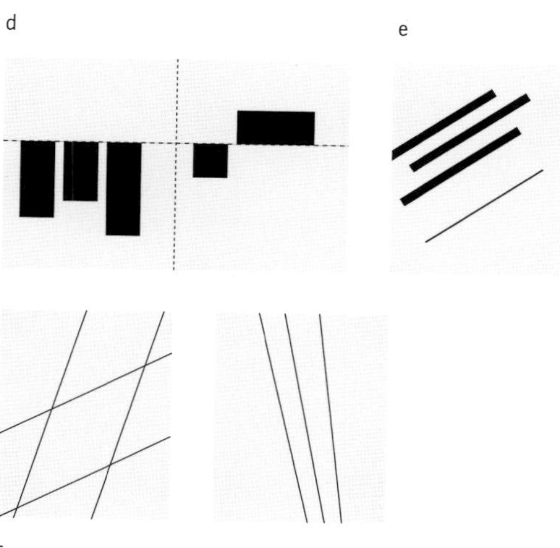

Equivalence in lines or direction
The guidelines used to organize a *composition* play a major role. One has to pay special attention to them. Equivalents are found between the elements if they are arranged along one or more guidelines (d, e, f, g) (3).

1

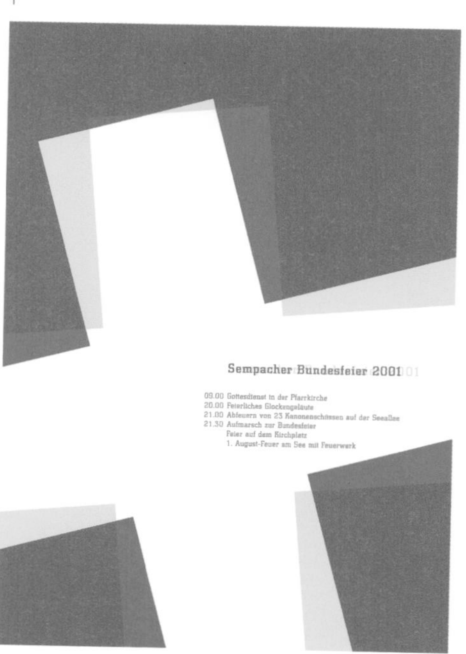

2

3

4. *Miniatures de l'émoi*, poster
Théâtre d'Angoulême
Annette Lenz
5. *La tête dans les nuages*, poster
Théâtre d'Angoulême
Annette Lenz
6. *Die 100 besten Plakate 06 Deutschland Österreich Schweiz*, poster
Erich Brechbühl (Mixer)

Equivalence in color
The *colors* in a *composition* are said to be in *harmony* if the *colors* are all close to one another on the *color* wheel (see page 24f.). A yellow and an orange-brown can create *harmony* in a *composition*. Shades of a *color* also give a *composition* a chromatic unity. A two-*color* image (also called a duotone) is a common *monochrome* principle. Multiple documents can be unified by using the same *color* palette (4).

Equivalence in value
One can also achieve *harmony* in the *color* value by adjusting the *colors* in a *composition* to have the same intensity, or if the elements in a *composition* have the same brightness –optically the same *gray value* (5).

Equivalence in texture
One can create equivalence between multiple elements by treating their *surface* in the same way, by giving them the same texture (line screen, pattern or by using spot varnish, etc.) (6).

4

5

6

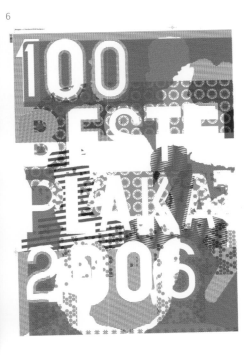

Color
Design principles: harmony and contrast

Why color?
Color plays a primary role in a *composition* for many reasons. First of all it determines the visual balance or imbalance in a *composition*. On the other hand it draws attention to itself (or not), it arouses the viewer's interest, stirs up feelings and moods and helps us understand perspective and space. *Color* can emphasize an idea, symbol or custom.

Color can tell a story, trigger memories, inspire imagination. It offers unlimited possibilities! Choosing *colors* is therefore a critical phase in the design process – critical for successful design. The *colors* are what a viewer usually sees first. It is imperative for those who want to express their ideas visually to have a good sense of *color* and a good theoretical knowledge of *color*. How *color* "works" was the subject of Newton's, Goethe's and Chevreul's research.

Harmony and contrast
When choosing appropriate *colors* the principle of *harmony* and the principle of *contrast* are reliable tools.

The interaction of color
Colors should never be considered in isolation, but always in the context of the neighboring *colors*. "It is all a question of rapport", said Cézanne. *Colors* and their effects are influenced by the surrounding *colors*.
A *color* seems darker on a white background and lighter on a black background. The balance of every *composition* is affected by any *color* added.

Color wheel (3)
A simplified representation of the *color* spectrum as a diagram illustrates some of the fundamental aspects of *color* theory. With the circular diagram's help we can better understand the terms *primary color, secondary color*, or the principle of *complementary colors* and their harmonious combinations.

1

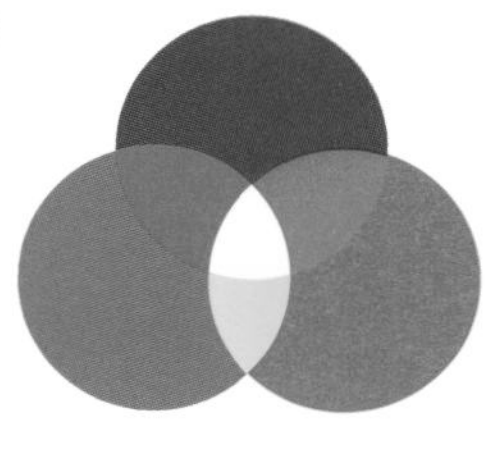

Additive color and subtractive color
The two systems of *color*: additive *color* (1) (the adding of different waves of *light* to one another as used by screens in the RGB *color* system) and subtractive *color* (2) (the mixing of pigments – that absorb *light* and are seen as *colors* – as used in printing by the CMYK system) should not be confused with each other.

2

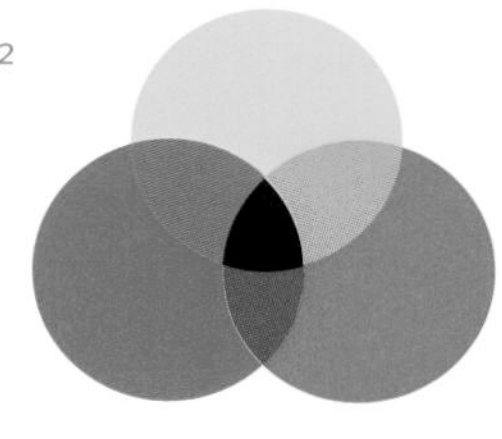

3

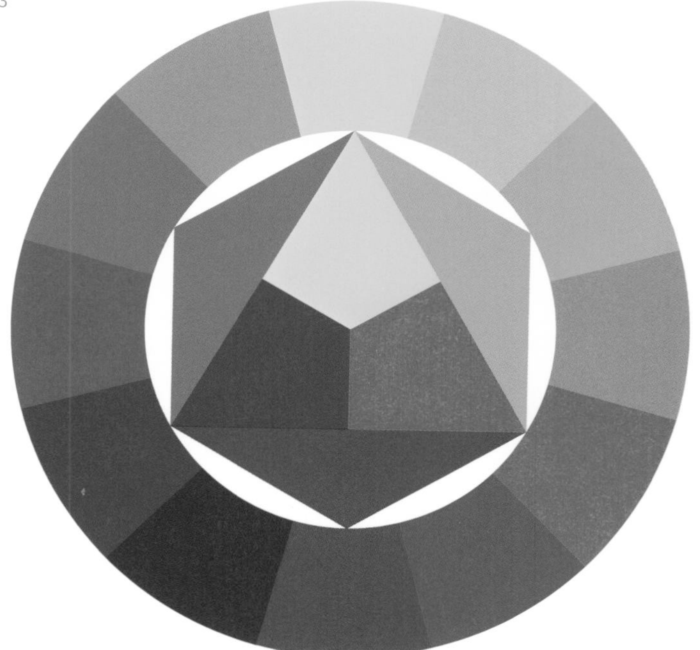

Primary colors *Secondary colors* *Tertiary colors*

Flat color
A uniform *color hue* without shading or variation.

Primary colors
Red, blue and yellow are primary or pure *colors*. They cannot be mixed from other *colors*.

Secondary colors
A secondary *color* can be mixed with two *primary colors*. Orange, green and violet are *secondary colors*. The resulting *color* depends on the two *primary colors* (red, yellow or blue) chosen.

Tertiary colors
A tertiary *color* is made by mixing a *primary color* in equal parts with a neighboring *secondary color* on the *color* wheel: red-orange, yellow-orange, yellow-green, blue-green, blue-violet and red-violet.

Hue
Another word for *color*.
One could refer to a reddish *hue* or to the *color* red.

Monochrome
All *color* shades that are derived from a single *color* or based on *colors* that are close to each other on the *color* wheel.

Transparency and opacity
The degree of transparency is equivalent to the amount of *light* a *color* allows to pass through to (and be reflected by) the underlying *color*. Transparency gives depth to a flat *surface*.
The opposite of transparency is *opacity*. One also refers to the coverage of a *color*.

Subdued color
A pure *color* that has been mixed with another *color* hence reducing its intensity and purity.

Muted color
A darker *color*, achieved by adding black or a darker *hue*.

Brighter color
A lighter *color* achieved by adding white or a lighter *hue*.

5

5. *Kn6ox !*, poster
Celebrating Niklaus Troxler's 6oth birthday
GGGrafik / Götz Gramlich

Spatial qualities of color
Color has spatial qualities. It influences how we perceive the depth of an image. A yellowish *hue* on a black background appears to "advance", whereas a violet *hue* seems to "recede". The same *colors* have the opposite effect on a white background.

On color and tastes
We know that *color* choice is very subjective. One may like a *color* palette, see it as harmonious, and someone else may perceive exactly the opposite. In any case, one should be familiar with the fundamental relationships between *colors*, and the effect of certain *color* combinations on our psychology and their meaning in an image (see page 28f.).

Objective color harmony
Itten maintains that an objective *color harmony* exists based on the principle of visual unity or balance. The eye looks for *color* combinations where the *colors* balance each other out. The visual combination produces a neutral gray tone.

Reduced color range
According to Van Gogh's observations, many *compositions* contain a reduced *color* palette. One dominant *color* ensures a unified impression and conciseness, and one or two additional *colors* accentuate the *composition*.

On flat color
Flat color is commonly used to emphasize the plane or reading *surface*. At the same time it suggests a definite space, an imaginary space. A *flat color* distances us from reality, where *colors* occur in many nuances. It creates an abstraction. *Flat color* simplifies, unifies and assures visual emphasis.

6. *Trovesi-Coscia*, poster
   Niklaus Troxler
7. New Year's greetings from the Bösch screen printers,
   poster
   Niklaus Troxler
8. Poster exhibition by Annette Lenz,
   poster
   Niklaus Troxler

4

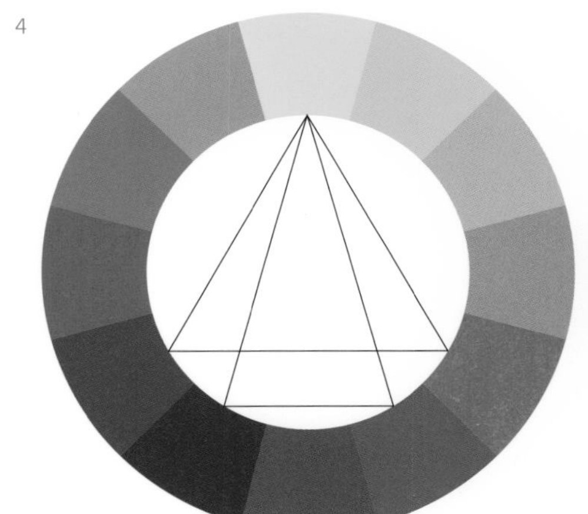

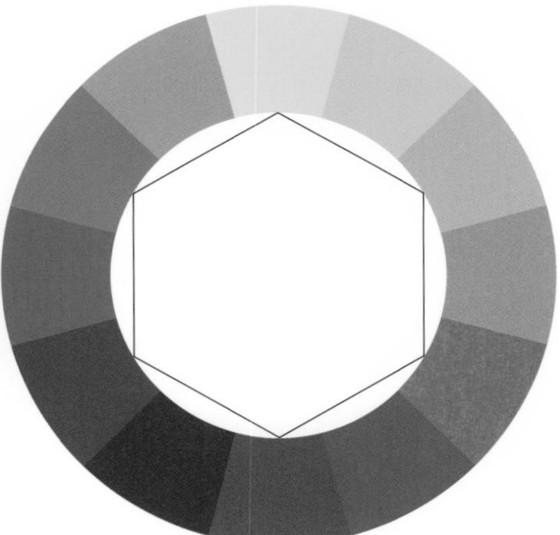

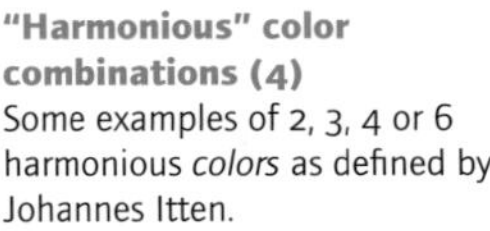

"Harmonious" color combinations (4)
Some examples of 2, 3, 4 or 6 harmonious *colors* as defined by Johannes Itten.

These are derived by drawing different geometric forms in the *color* wheel:
- diagonal lines on the wheel define two *complementary colors*
- equilateral and isosceles triangles define three *colors*
- a square or rectangle defines four *colors*
- a hexagon defines six *colors*

When selecting a *color* palette, all of these geometric constructions prove useful as a base. However, they do not cover all aspects of *color* and of artistic or semantic *composition*.

"The number of colors *and shapes is infinite. Why not also their combinations and their effects? This material is inexhaustible."*
Wassily Kandinsky

6

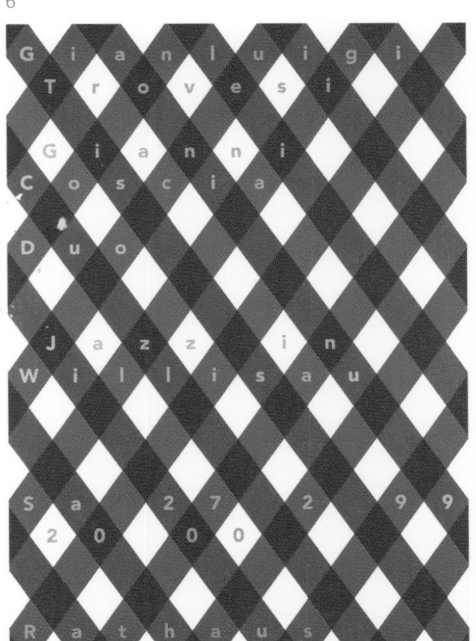

7

Ein rundum gutes Neues Jahr wünscht Bösch Siebdruck, 6371 Stans. boeschdruck@datacomm.ch

8

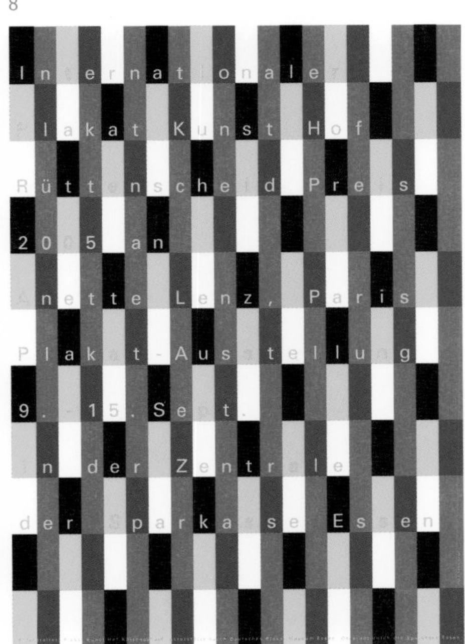

Color contrasts

Color contrasts say a great deal. They emphasize the relationships between elements in a *composition*. They attract attention, establish a *hierarchy* of the elements and can carry meaning. The visibility and readability of a *composition* depend on *contrast*.
The principle of *contrast* aids our *color* perception. The seven *color contrasts* were defined by the Bauhaus teacher Johannes Itten. These are: *contrast* of *hue*, *light*–dark, cold–warm, complementary *contrast*, *contrast* of extension, *contrast* of saturation, and simultaneous *contrast* (based on the physiological principle that the human eye spontaneously creates the complementary *color* of the *color* observed).

Visibility/readability

The visibility of a *color* depends on its intensity (pure *colors* have the highest intensity), their *surface* (a *flat color* is more visible than a gradient) and the *contrast* to the neighboring *colors* (in the *composition* or in the context around it). If something is more or less readable depends above all on the *contrast* in luminosity (*light*/dark).
Since the greatest *contrast* exists between black and white, this relationship creates the best readability – especially when a black shape is on a white background.
Complementary *color* combinations are high in *contrast*, but they also create vibrations that make reading difficult. The most problematic is the pair red and green since both *colors* have a similar level of brightness.

Contrast of hue

This *contrast* results when three bright and pure *colors* meet. The three *primary colors* create the strongest *contrast* of *hue*. It is always a strong colorful presence (1).
The *contrast* gets weaker and less expressive the greater distance the *colors* have to the *primary colors*.

Complementary contrast

Complementary colors are opposites on the *color* wheel. One refers to the interplay between pairs of complements. Red and green, orange and blue are pairs of complements. If *complementary colors* are placed next to each other they magnify each other's intensity. If they are mixed they diminish or neutralize this intensity.

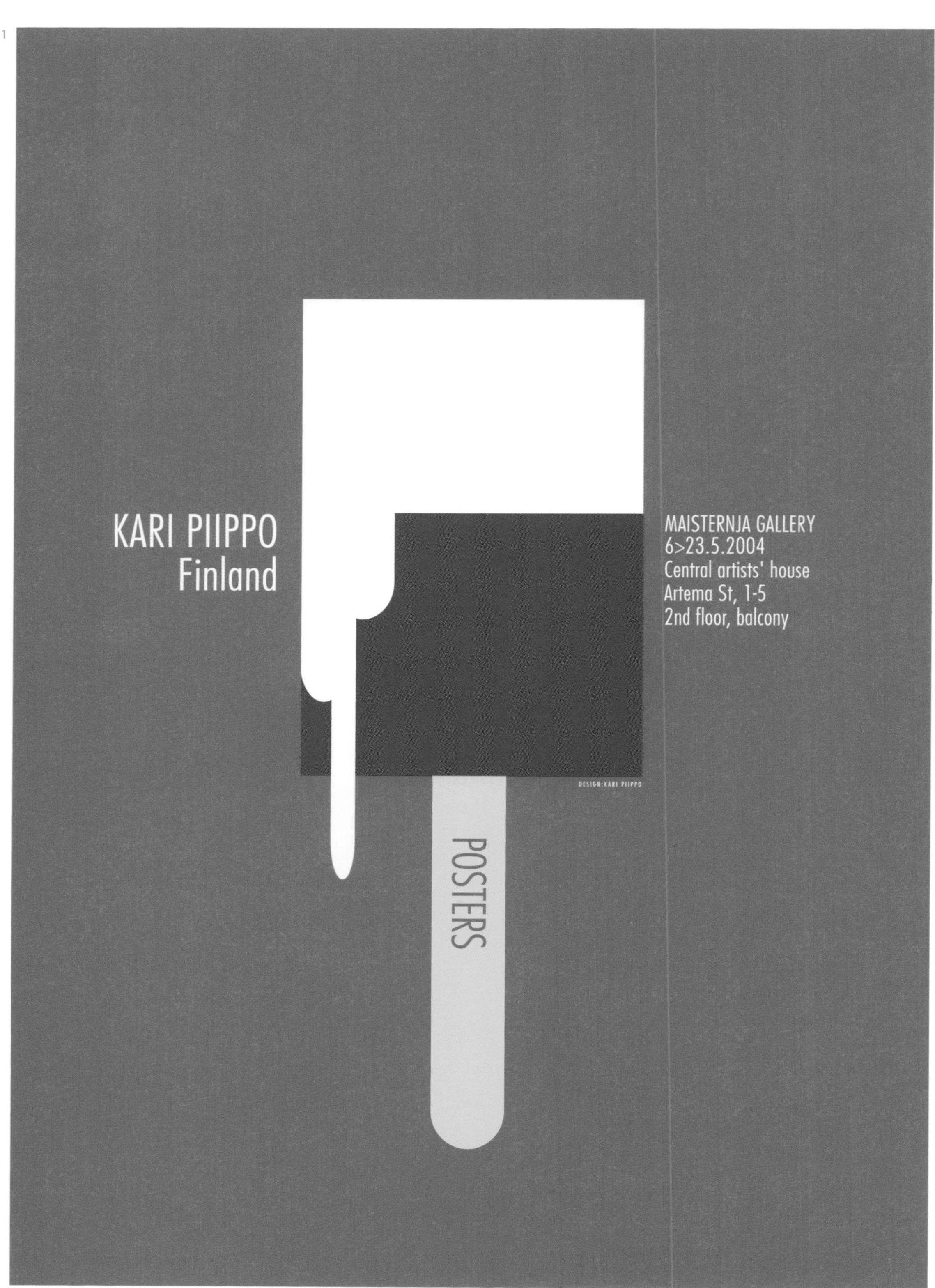

1. *Kari Piippo*, poster
Maisternja Gallery, Ukraine
Kari Piippo

Cold-warm contrast

Colors are considered to be warm or cool. The *color* wheel has a warm side (reds, oranges, and yellows) and a cool side (greens, blues and violets). However, this definition is relative. Cadmium yellow is warmer than lemon yellow. Visually speaking, *warm colors* seem to advance, whereas *cool colors* seem to recede. This phenomenon allows a sense of depth to be created.

Light-dark contrast

Shade: This term refers to a *color* that has been darkened by mixing it with black, a darker *color* or a second complementary *color*. The resulting *color* is muddier or less intense. The term "value" or "tone" describes the lightness or darkness of a *color*. It should not be confused with the term "intensity".

Contrast of saturation

Saturation: This term defines the relative purity of *color hue*. One also refers to intensity. All pure *colors* – red, blue, yellow – are saturated *colors*. The *contrast* between a saturated and a muddier or less intense *color* allows possibilities for expression while preserving the unity thanks to a shared base *color*.

Contrast of extension

The *contrast* of extension is connected to the relative *surface* areas of two or more *colors*. If the proportions are very different, then the major *color* provides unity, and the minor *color(s)* provide(s) variety.

2. *Nicéphore days*, program
   Musée Nicéphore Niépce
   Le Petit Didier
3. x^e *festival de théâtre intime*, card
   Théâtre du Jarnisy
   Le Petit Didier
4. *Boogiecup 2007*, poster
   GGGrafik / Götz Gramlich

The quantity ratios of the complementary pairs shown establish a balance between the two colors. In this case one refers to a harmonious relationship between complementary colors.

The relationship between warm and cool colors can create a particularly expressive contrast. Conversely, a dominant warm or cool color can unify a composition.

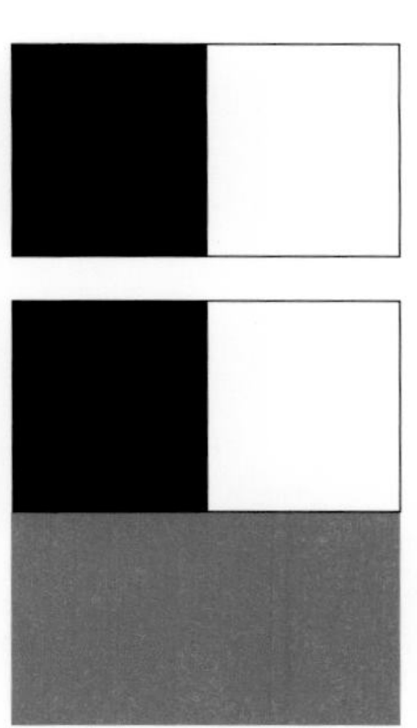

The strongest light-dark contrast is created by black and white. There are many possible variations between these two extremes. Black and white are often combined with a bright color to create a strong impact

One way to achieve color harmony is to choose colors that are close to one another on the color wheel which are referred to as analogous colors.

2

3

4

Color
Semantic principles

Color and culture

"Colors have a turbulent history that expresses the evolution of our mentality. They carry taboos and prejudices that we unknowingly obey. They have hidden meanings that influence our environment, our behavior, our language, our imagination. All this is governed by an unwritten code, and the colors know the secret." – Michel Pastoureau

The language of *colors* is complex, but not universal, even if certain interpretations seem widespread. Every culture assigns *colors* meanings and roles that evolve with the culture's fashions and history. For a long time man has perceived more or less chaotically the power of *color*'s messages and associated concepts with them. *Color* has established a code by consensus. It has attained a symbol's rank.

Beyond a *color*'s meaning by analogy with reality (for example, the *color* red refers to blood, to a ripe fruit, to a blossoming flower (1), to melting material, etc.), the interpretation of *color* varies according to its context of use, the culture and the identity of the sender and receiver.

Color and context

"Color looses its meaning when it is in disharmony with its subject and when it fails to stimulate the imagination of the viewer." – Eugène Delacroix

Color codes vary depending on the context of their application. *Colors* in a religious or heraldic context have a very different meaning than those used in traffic signs, in the food or the cultural sector. However, their meanings can overlap.

Color, shape and material

Shape, gesture and texture combined with *color* influence its interpretation. Thus, red in the shape of a drop or a heart each carries a different meaning. Red splatters are perceived differently from a flat red *surface*.

Color and receiver

Depending on their culture, age, sex, personal experience a viewer sees and interprets *color* differently. Child or adult, man or woman, orient or occident, sculptor, sociologist or physicist – all perceive the same *color* differently.

1

2

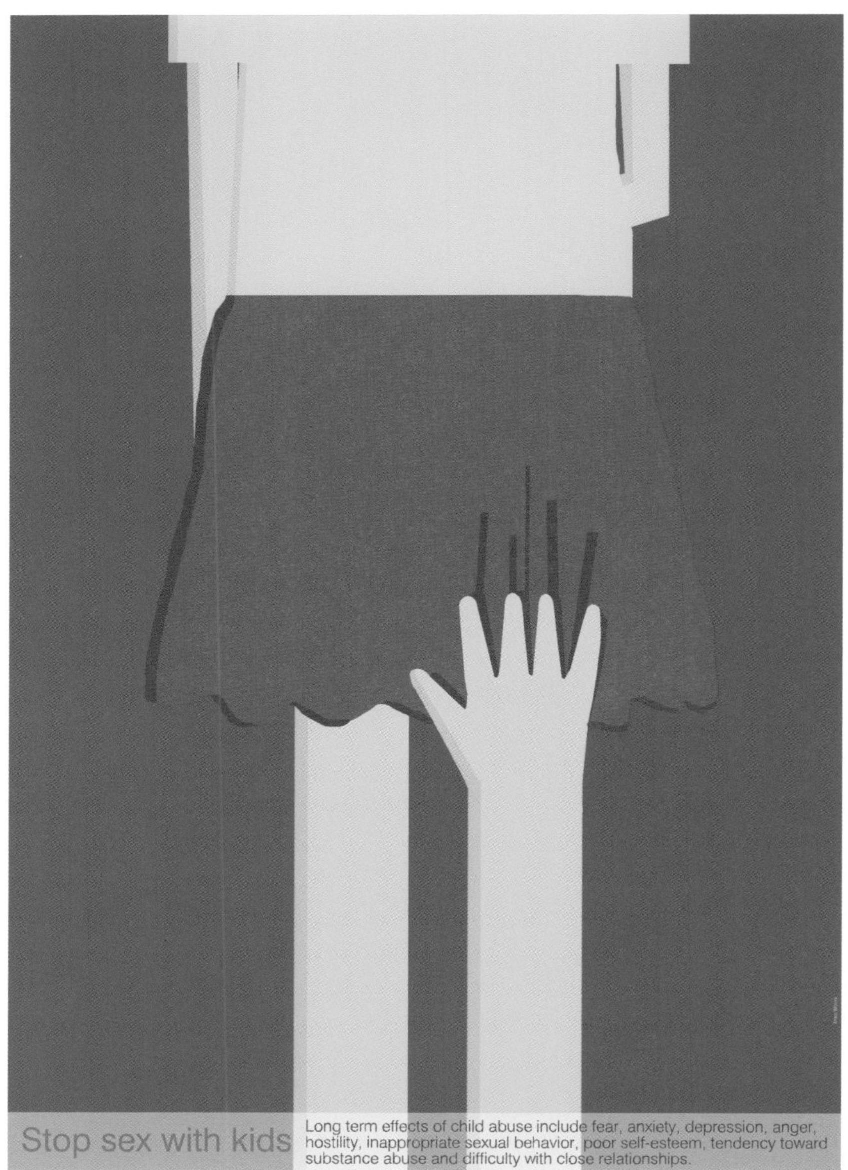

Stop sex with kids
Long term effects of child abuse include fear, anxiety, depression, anger, hostility, inappropriate sexual behavior, poor self-esteem, tendency toward substance abuse and difficulty with close relationships.

In the Western European context the dominant connotations of red are: power, enthusiasm, virility. The *color* of blood and fire, symbol of virtue and sin. Red can have different meanings depending on the context: violence, warlike or revolutionary pride (5, 7), anger (7), passion (3, 8), dangerous or forbidden (2).

Light red: energy, victory, joy.
Dark red: more serious, more sensual.
Purple red: dignity, wealth.
Symbol of established power (4, 6).

1. *Maximilian Hecker: Daylight*, CD cover
kitty-yo int.
Angela Lorenz
Photograph: Alexander Obst
2. *Stop sex with kids*, poster
Maja Wolna

Color as an addition to words

Color delivers information either in highly concentrated form or in all its complexity. It supplements or complements what words communicate. For example, *color* plays a major part in the *poster* Stop sex with kids (2). On the one hand the *poster* is visually striking (strong *contrast* of *hue*); on the other hand it communicates a childish universe (pure *colors*) and also an urgent message (*primary colors* underscore the fundamental message). The red of the skirt allows a number of interpretations. Does it describe how the victim feels? Does it represent red-faced anger or shame? Is it a warning such as "danger, forbidden territory"? It is evident that the *color* should mean something that can't be spoken or written. A change in the *color* palette would have obvious consequences for the perception and interpretation of the message.

Intuition and reasoning

Color in a *composition* can be approached in an intuitive or opportunistic manner. However, one must push aside his own preconceptions and reflect on his own relationship to *color* carefully. It is important to ask oneself questions now and again.
What does the *composition* need? What are the communication goals and who is the intended audience? What emotions should the *color* arouse, knowing full well that it can soothe, stimulate or irritate? Which fashion or culture is referred to, etc.? An outsider's view helps us check our *color* choices.

3. *The rape of Lucretia*, poster
   Bayerische Staatsoper
   Pierre Mendel design studio,
   Pierre Mendel with Annette Kröger
4. *Don Carlo*, poster
   Bayerische Staatsoper
   Pierre Mendel design studio, Pierre Mendel
5. *Schlachthof 5*, poster
   Bayerische Staatsoper
   Pierre Mendel design studio,
   Annette Kröger and Pierre Mendel
6. *Boris Goudounov*, poster
   Opéra de Lyon
   Hartland Villa
7. *Fucking A*, poster
   The public theater
   Paula Scher, Pentagram
8. *Romeo et Juliette*, poster
   Opéra national du Rhin
   Hartland Villa
   Photograph: Jean-Luc Tanghe

3

4

5

6

7

8

Hierarchy, eye movement and point of convergence
A visual and intellectual journey

Leading the eyes
The *composition* should not distract from the subject, and should not let the gaze wander aimlessly. It should also prevent one from looking away too quickly. The subject is presented best by *leading* the viewer's eyes through the *composition*.

Visual attention span
One looks at the point of convergence (where the attention should focus) immediately or after a visual journey. The time it takes to absorb and understand an image depends on the *composition*. Depending on the medium, subject and context, the length of this visual attention span can either be an advantage or disadvantage.

Hierarchy
Designing implies choosing a few clear paths and accents that catch the eye and structure the *composition*. All elements in the *composition* may be treated equally if the subject, context and time allow or demand it. The lack of reference points can be seen in these *compositions*. The *hierarchy* here is more discreet, occasionally disappearing in favor of a more complex whole. One should note that beyond all design considerations the subject itself will guide the eyes. A person is, for example, a fascinating subject. Nothing interests people more than other people.

A human body in a *composition* has a strong impact and is a powerful eye-catcher. A body is appealing in any state. A pair of eyes for example speaks directly to the reader.

A metaphor for reading
"Posters *can almost be seen as metaphors for reading.*"
– Anne-Catherine Céard

1. Reading as random scanning, where one reaches an unformed meaning
2. Reading like a caress
3. Reading like a boat crossing
4. Reading like a journey
5. Reading like an ascent
6. Reading like a manifesto

1

2

3

1. *Uwe Loesch ... fly by*, poster
PAN kunstforum niederrhein, Emmerich
Uwe Loesch
2. *Design Renaissance*, poster
International conference, organized by Icograda
Atelier de création graphique
3. *Il ritorno di Ulisse in patria*, poster
Bayerische Staatsoper
Pierre Mendel design studio,
Pierre Mendel with Annette Kröger

Scale

The scale relationships between the design elements are important in establishing a *hierarchy* for the project as a whole. All elements should form mutually related groups. As each element adapts to its group, it distances itself from its original context. This is an important part of the graphic designer's work: to separate, to fragment, to divert, to filter, to disguise, to superimpose, to insert, to inlay ... These interventions ensure the *hierarchy* and unity of the *composition*.

In example 2, the scale of the earth adapts to the scale of the hand, which is scaled to the size of the *poster*. Simultaneously, the black background shadow connects with the black shapes and the type, giving the *composition rhythm*.

Specifically, we are confronted with several scales that are connected with different *levels of reading*. One can distinguish the scale of reading from the scale of the imaginary space one sees. The designer's challenge is to negotiate between what can be seen from far away to what is read up close – all in one *composition*.

One also has to remember the scale of the viewer. The designer has to imagine – or test – how the viewer will encounter the *composition* in the physical world. For example, things placed at eye level will be most readily seen.

4. *Tulp 02*, poster
Richard Niessen

5. *L'autre côté*, poster
Opéra national du Rhin
Hartland Villa

6. *The diva is dismissed*, poster
The public theater
Paula Scher, Pentagram

4

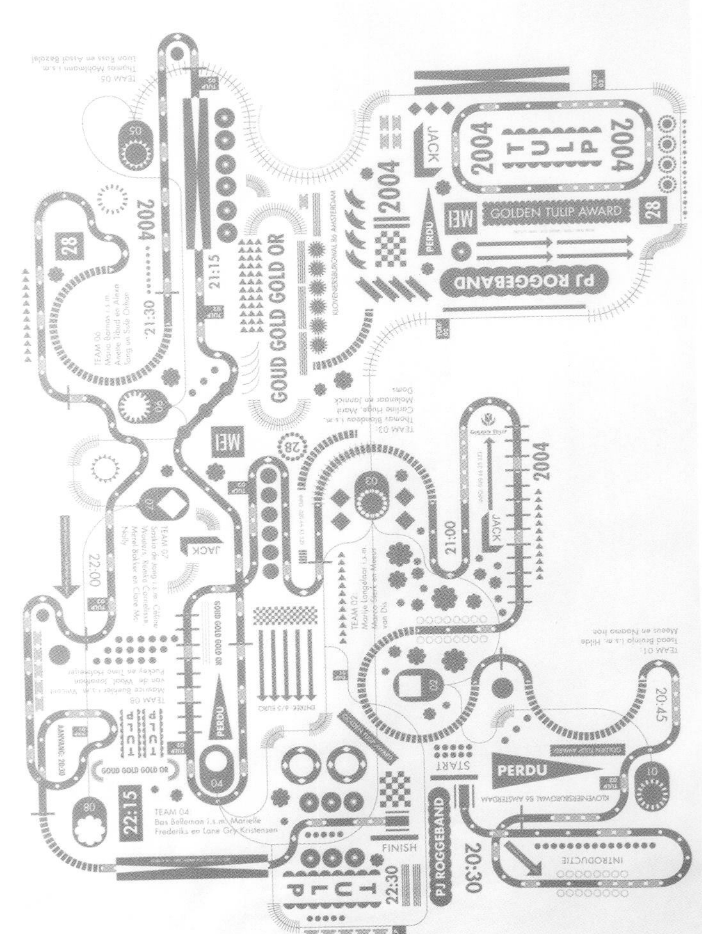

5

6

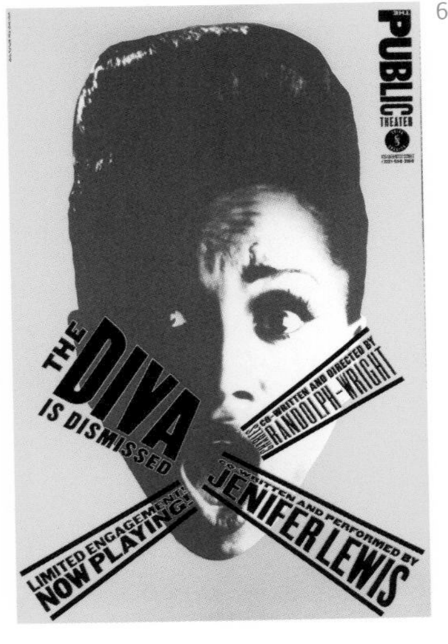

Figure and ground, full and empty
A balance of power

The figure-ground relationship

According to the art historian Norman Bryson, the white ground represents the empty space where an image appears. This empty space, Bryson says, "is present in our perception but is absent in the *composition*". The ground can be seen as a silent *surface*, something undefined where the figure appears. It offers things a potential place. Furthermore, the figure is only fully defined against the (back)ground. This figure-ground relationship is the foundation of "Gestalt Theory".
The greater the *contrast* between figure and ground, the more the two separate and emphasize each other. In a *composition* the "empty" or "almost empty" parts are just as important as the "full" parts.

The "white" ground offers a vital space around the figure – a calm space, like a moment of rest in music – an abstract space full of possibilities.

Relationships to be examined

The relationships between figure and ground, between full and empty sections are constantly being questioned, either consciously or unconsciously by the designer. He can play with this idea and create ambiguity among the different elements. The white space can assume different roles in one *composition*: as figure or ground (2), as flat *surface* that is sometimes foreground, sometimes background (1), as a three-dimensional space or as a mysterious abyss (3, 4, 6). The white space can be seen to be imposing (7) or subtle. It can also be seen as absence (1) or an *omission* (in example 5 one has the impression that the writing is cut into the black), or as an overlay (8).

These examples demonstrate how rewarding – both semantically and artistically – exploring these figure-ground relationships can be. Sometimes they can be essential in making a *composition* a success.

If the relationships are well chosen then they can: be surprising (6), encourage reading (7), dictate a *rhythm* (1–7), create a relief (4, 5), create a sense of depth or confront the viewer with a *surface* (6). They can create unity and variety and help a *composition*, or hurt it if they are poorly or unclearly placed.

1. *Typo Plakate, Exhibition*, poster Niklaus Troxler
2. *Plakate, Schwarz-Weiß*, poster Niklaus Troxler
3. *The Modern Jazz Quartet*, poster Niklaus Troxler

1

2

3

4. *Un forum pour l'après bac*, poster
   Superscript2
5. *Joe McPhee Trio X*, poster
   Niklaus Troxler
6. *Es werd ned andersch*, poster
   Jugendtheater Willisau
   Paula Troxler
7. *Mer läbid of em Land*, poster
   Jugendtheater Willisau
   Paula Troxler
8. *Marty Ehrlich Quartet*, poster
   Niklaus Troxler

4

5

6

7

8

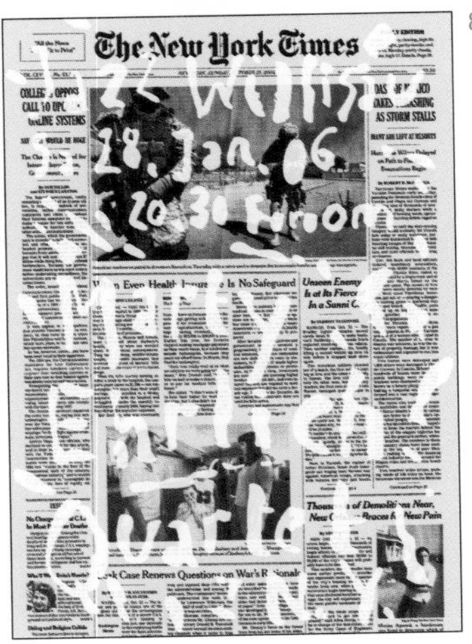

Edges and crossing them
Challenging the edges

A *composition* has edges, a frame, sometimes borders that represent real or virtual edges.
It is exciting to see the elements in a design question the edges in many ways, and establish a strategic dialogue with them, all in the service of the *composition*. The idea of the edge raises questions in all fields of application; it is intimately linked to our idea of freedom and creativity.
It can be seen as a restriction or as an opportunity.

Typically, the design elements are contained by the edges and respect these. However, they can sometimes be "cheeky" when they get close to the edges, challenge them, or even threaten to cross them or cross them altogether.

Inside and outside of the frame

The frame is defined by the real or virtual edges of the *composition*. It can be the result of the *cropping* of the paper, the edge of the material, or a more or less visible edge in a space. The frame(s) can be single or multiple, independent or related, visible, discrete or unspoken, constructive, constraining or liberating.

In photography one chooses a certain view at the moment of exposure, and defines the edges of the image.
Every change in how the image is cropped changes the *composition* and creates a new perception. The laws of perspective developed in the Renaissance laid the ground work for the camera obscura and the "window on the world", and the idea that the picture frame is only a piece of a larger whole was established. Today this window metaphor is being debated.

All current aesthetic trends question the term "frame" (e.g. the support/surface movement, American expressionism). The dominant shape of the frame is an upright rectangle, imposed due to technical considerations, and contrary to physiological perception. Undeniably, it is also man's mark on nature.

Inside and outside the design space

The design space designates the space defined by the frame. However, the *composition* can give the impression that it exceeds the frame. For instance, when the real space goes beyond the photographic frame, or a window in architecture. We imagine the continuation virtually.
The part evokes the whole.

1. *Opus BmWB*, poster
Théâtre du Jarnisy
Le Petit Didier

1

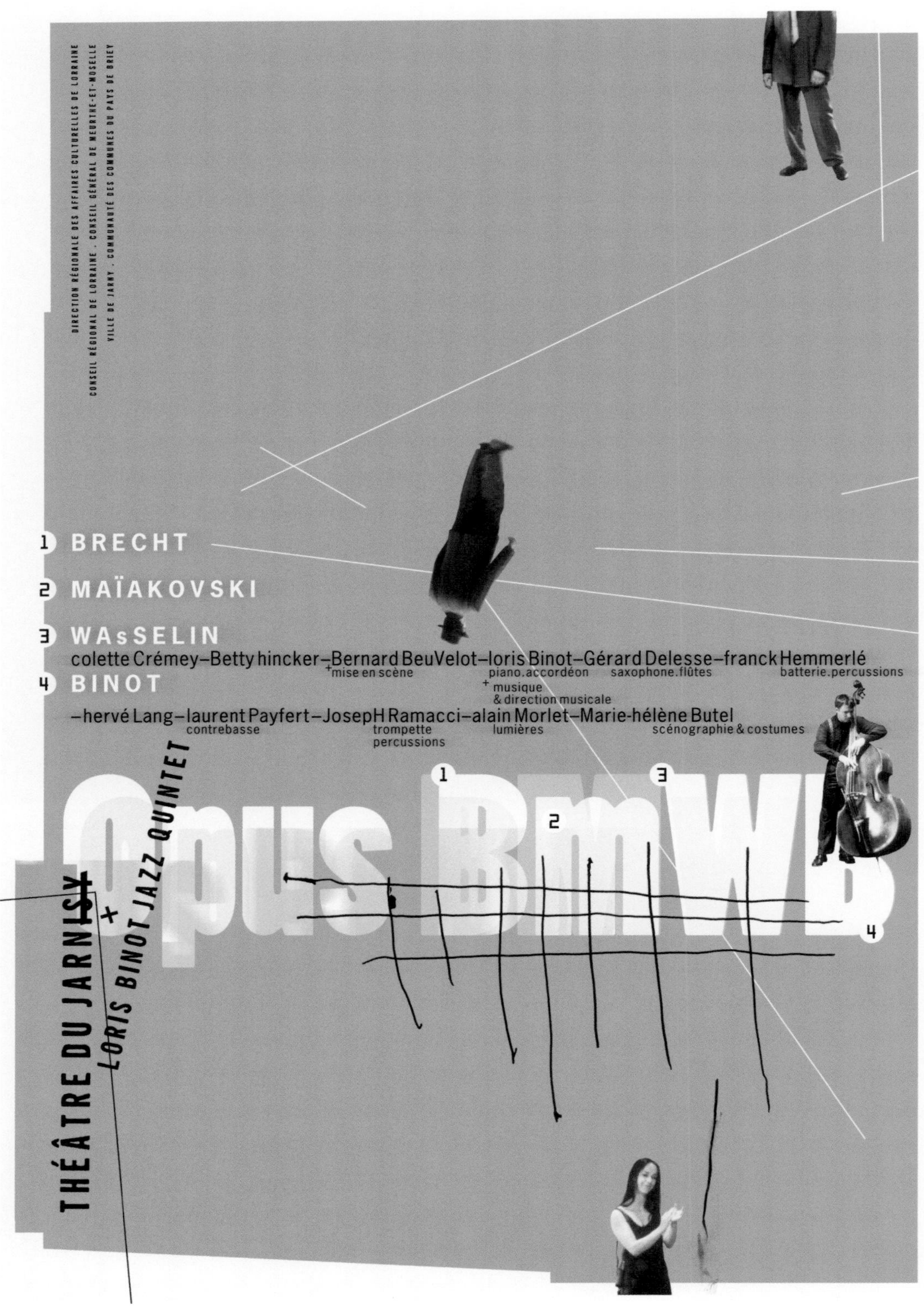

The frame defines a design space and consequently an area beyond the design space. Even though not part of the *composition*, it is potentially present. It opens the design space or constrains it. What is there and can't be seen creates energy. Tension (attraction/rejection) exists between the design space and what is beyond, between what is inside and what is outside of the frame – and thus outside of the image. How one imagines the area beyond doesn't only depend on what the image shows, but also on the individual (imagination, cultural references, personal experience, knowledge of representational codes).
The design space becomes a transit area, a meeting place for many even contradictory forces. The area beyond the design space can be implied in a variety of ways: through the extension of a line – extended in our mind, through a partly visible element – that we complete, through movement in an image that we follow beyond the frame.

All of these things reinforce the space beyond the design space. It is invisible, but can be felt. It is unknown and stirs our curiosity. It is a hidden source of surprises.

Margins

The *margins* are commonly used in editorial design to create an ideal transition to the adjacent frame. They allow the designer to emphasize, isolate, protect or enhance the design space. The *margins* create a rest area for the eyes, and provide a space for handling the *book*. They can also be disrupted and form a dynamic and surprising space. They may even form a strategic part of the *composition* (see page 48/49).

2. *Fragile*, poster
Museo cantonale d'arte, Lugano
Bruno Monguzzi

2

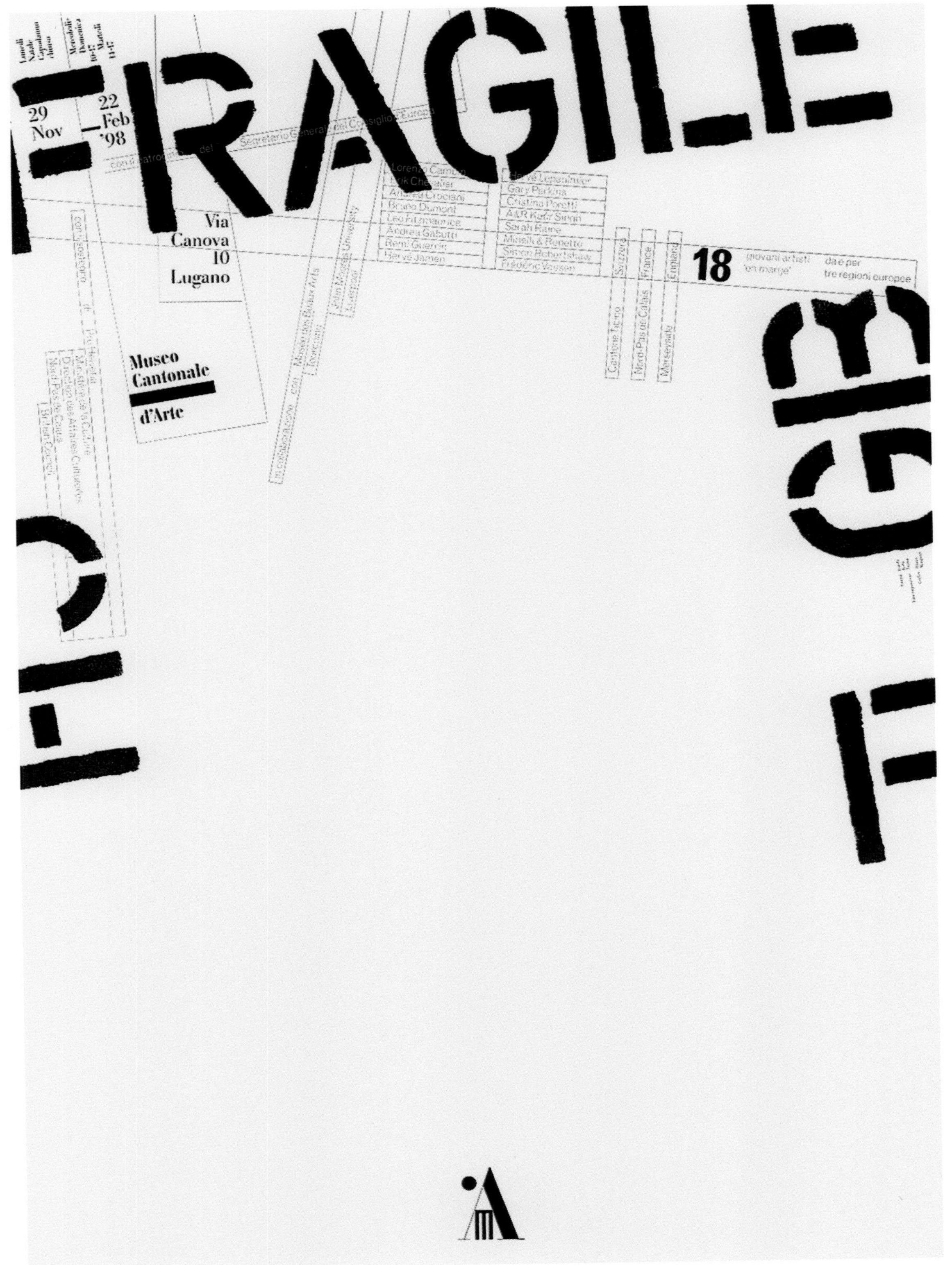

In the second part of this *book* we introduce the fundamental design parameters. These parameters can be modified by the designer to give a *composition* more or less depth. It would be foolish to pretend that one has mastered the art of design, and ignore these fundamentals, their importance and how they interact.

The *format*, which determines the designer's workspace, whether given or chosen, influences the spirit of the *composition*. The *margins* determine the useable space, and their arrangement on the *page* sets up the first important decisions. Of course the *typography* the choice of one or more *typefaces* and *type sizes*, and their arrangement influence the character of the *composition*. This character is occasionally reinforced by the use of *graphic elements* such as: lines, patterns, frames, boxes, etc. The images, whether provided or chosen due to their subject, their construction, and their character, play a decisive role in the perception of a *composition*. Their relationship to the text and to each other must also be carefully considered.

Part

02

Headline

Basic elements

Contents

Surface, formats
From historic formats to the screen

The *surface* is where a graphic designer works. Regardless of its size – whether working on a postage stamp, a *book*, a *newspaper page* or a *poster* – the proportions, or the ratio of width to height, have a direct effect on the *composition*. Over the centuries the practice of *page* design developed a number of common *formats*, which have prevailed because of their inherent *harmony*. They are called historical *formats*. Geometric *formats* are also used: the square and double square (horizontal or vertical). Other *formats* are derived from geometric constructions. The *formats* derived from the *golden section* are undoubtedly the most famous (see *page* 16).

Standard formats?
Standardization arises from the printing presses. Deviating from the standard can result in higher costs. The *ISO*-DIN *formats* are standard in most countries today. Using standard *formats* can be very useful, if one is working on an international project, where the design is done in one country and the printing in another.
However, with *books*, the *format* is not only chosen for financial or technical reasons. The type of *book*, its contents, how it will be used (hand-held, on a table, publicly or privately read, etc.) and its durability all play a role. One can't plan a *pocket edition book* that can't be held in one hand, or an art *book* with minuscule images.

With *posters*, standardized billboards and display systems dictate the *formats* so that non-standard *formats* are often difficult. Smaller *posters* (roughly 40 × 60 cm) are an exception. *Poster formats* differ from country to country, so it is imperative to research these requirements before one begins the design.
Newspaper formats also correspond to the printing presses (rotary offset or *sheet*-fed offset). One needs to know the printing parameters when choosing a *format*.

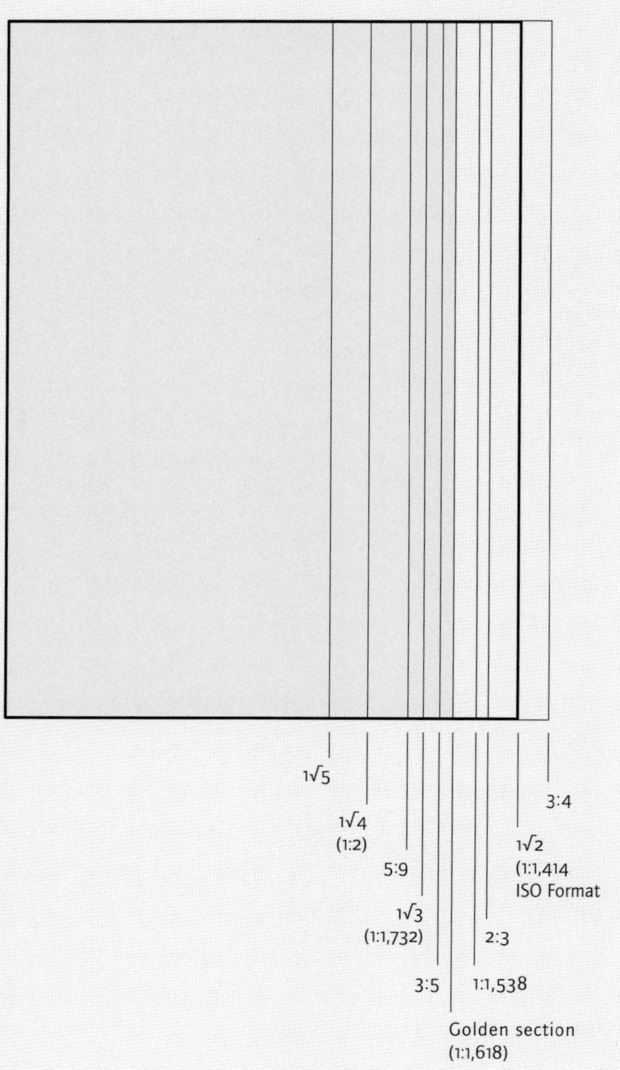

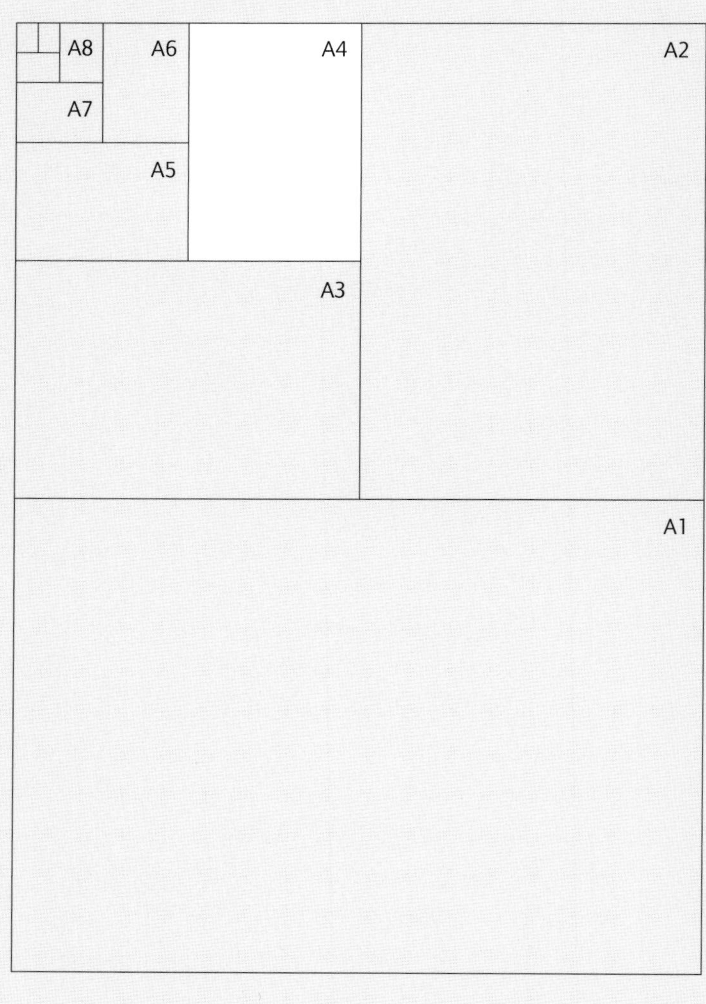

Historic formats
The most common *formats* have the following proportions:
5:9, 3:5, 21:34, (1:1,681 – *golden section*), 2:3, 1:1,414 (1:√2), 3:4

ISO formats
To further standardization internationally the *ISO* (International Organization for Standardization) defined a series of *formats* based on each other (at the time of the French Revolution).

The smaller *format* is calculated by dividing the larger *format* into two equal parts. The ratio of height to width is 1:√2.
The starting A0 *format* has an area of one square meter.

A0 = 841 × 1 189 mm
A1 = 594 × 841 mm
A2 = 420 × 594 mm
A3 = 297 × 420 mm
A4 = 210 × 297 mm
A5 = 148 × 210 mm
A6 = 105 × 148 mm
A7 = 74 × 105 mm
A8 = 52 × 74 mm
A9 = 37 × 52 mm
A10 = 26 × 37 mm

Technical formats
Some documents use special *formats* that are defined by the reproduction machines or the type of product (see page 40/41).

Some countries use their own formats, for example the USA:
Statement (140 × 216 mm)
Executive (190 × 254 mm)
Letter (216 × 280 mm)
Legal (216 × 356 mm)
Tabloïd (280 × 432 mm)
Ledger (432 × 280 mm)

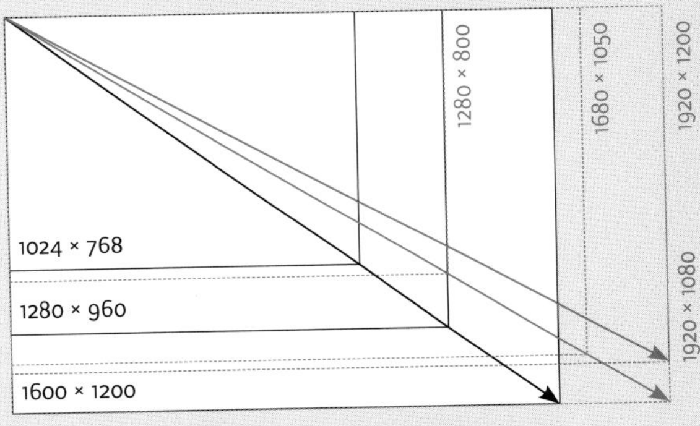

4:3 screens 16:9-Bildschirme screens

A4

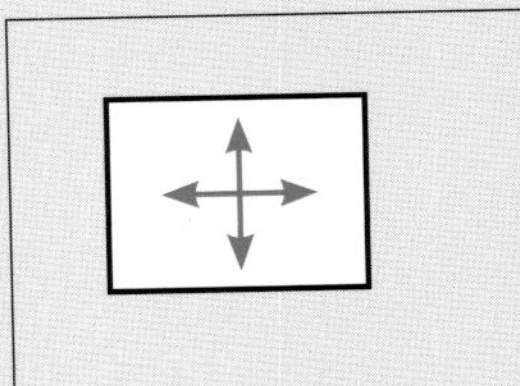

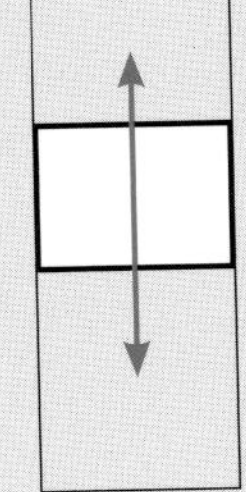

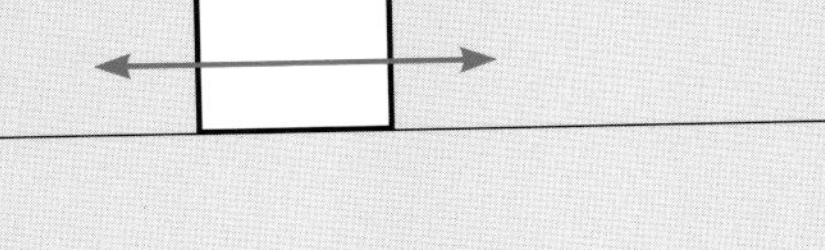

Screen formats
The screen *format* or aspect ratio is no longer the key dimension for digital devices. The "multimedia" have introduced a new concept connected to the virtual nature of the page: the infinite *format* where one can scroll (similar to the ancient *format* of the scroll which was unrolled to be read piece by piece).

The *page* is no longer limited to the visible *surface*, but can be scrolled (vertically and horizontally) using the scroll bars on the edge of the screen.

A design *grid* (see part 3) therefore has to repeat endlessly in any direction.

Screens (or displays) are measured in inches, with the diagonal dimension given. Today there are numerous *formats* and the standard *format* of 4:3 is no longer the rule.
Wide screen *formats* are on the rise and are either 16:9 or 16:10 in ratio.

The most common screen sizes (in pixels)

4:3

800 × 600	SVGA	15/17 "
1024 × 768	XGA	15/17 "
1280 × 1024	SXGA	17/19 "
1400 × 1050	SXGA+	19/20/21 "
1600 × 1200	UXGA	17/20/21 "

The screen diagonal inch measurements are only approximations. For example, the diagonal of a 17 inch display is between 41 and 43 centimeters.

16:9

964 × 544	WSVGA	17 "
1280 × 720	WXGA – H	15/17 "
1366 × 768	WXGA	12/15/17 "
1920 × 1080	WUXGA	17/20/21 "

16:10

1280 × 800		15/17 "
1440 × 900	WXGA+	17 "
1680 × 1050	WSXGA+	20/21/22 "
1920 × 1200	WUXGA+	17/20/21 "

25:16

1600 × 1024	WSXGA	20/21 "

Surface, formats
Common formats

Common DIN formats
1a = 55 × 85 mm (business card)
1b = 105 × 148 mm (postcard)
1c = 99 × 210 mm (one third of A4 – also called DIN long)
1d = 148 × 210 mm (A5)
1e = 210 × 297 mm (A4)
1f = 297 × 420 mm (A3)

Simple geometric formats
2a = 150 × 150 mm (square)
2b = 105 × 210 mm (double square)
2c = 200 × 200 mm (square)
2d = 300 × 300 mm (square)

Proportional formats
3:4 ratio
3a = 150 × 200 mm
3b = 180 × 240 mm
3c = 210 × 280 mm

2:3 ratio
4a = 120 × 180 mm
4b = 180 × 270 mm
4c = 240 × 360 mm

4:5 ratio
5a = 200 × 250 mm
5b = 240 × 300 mm
5c = 320 × 400 mm

Pocket formats
6a = 105 × 165 mm (pocket)
6b = 100 × 180 mm (10:18, folio)
6c = 110 × 180 mm (pléiade)

Video/hi-fi formats
7a = 125 × 120 mm (CD cover)
7b = 130 × 185 mm (DVD cover)
7c = 125 × 200 mm (VHS cover)
7d = 185 × 185 mm (single cover)
7e = 315 × 315 mm (album cover)

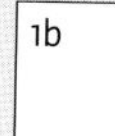

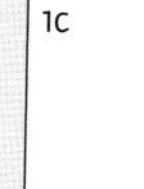

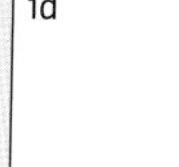

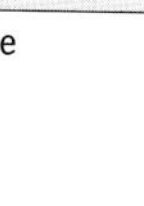

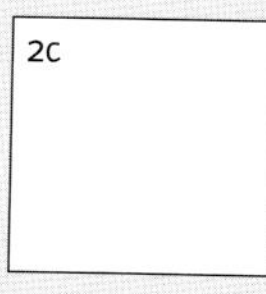

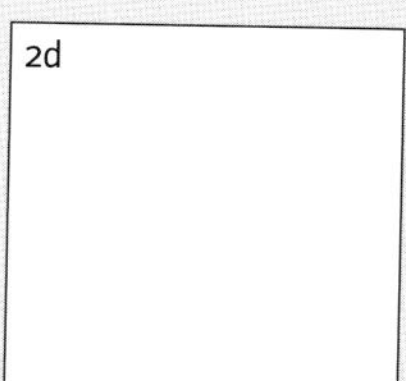
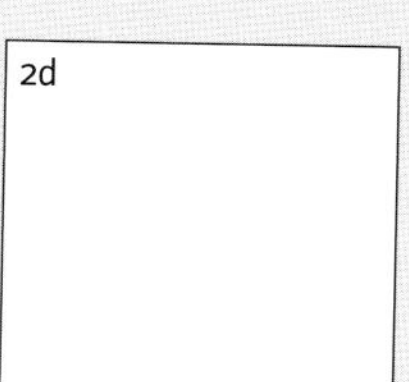
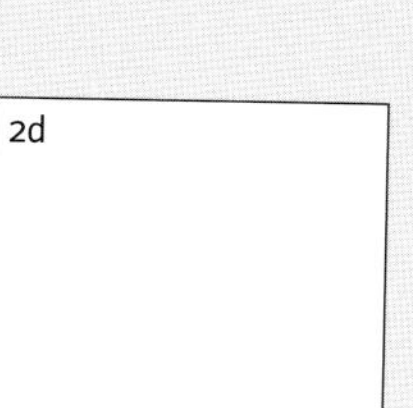
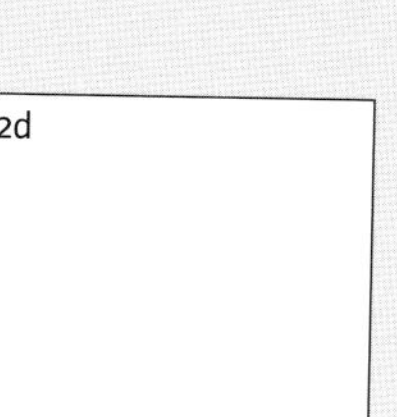

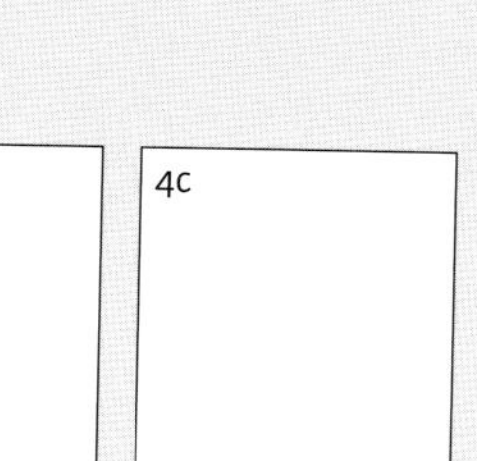
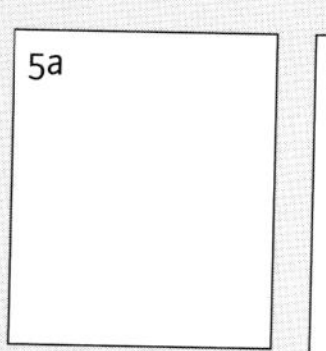

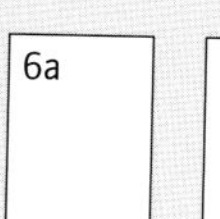

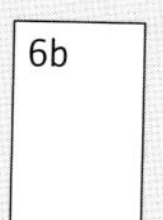

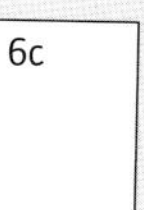

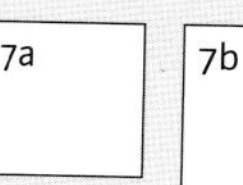

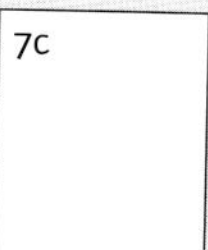

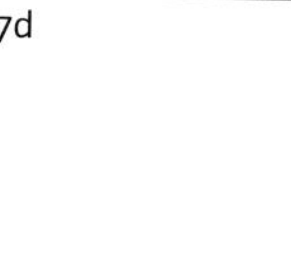

Glossary of names and terms used with formats

The final (folded) size depends on the original size of the *sheet* of paper. However, there are common *book* sizes:

Plano
Very large *format*; unfolded *sheet* or two *pages*.

Folio
Atlas *format*, a *sheet* folded once, resulting in four *pages*.

Quarto
Large *book* size, the original *sheet* is folded twice, resulting in four leaves of the same size, or eight *pages*.

Octavo
Small schoolbook size, the original *sheet* is folded three times, resulting in eight leaves of the same size, or 16 *pages*.

Duodecimo, sextodecimo, octodecimo
Pocket edition format, with 16 leaves of the same size. The original *sheet* is folded four times or divided into sections of 6/6, 8/4, 14/14, 12/6.

Vigesimo-quart, trigesimo-segundo
Very small *formats*.

All smaller *formats* are referred to as *miniature formats*. Their size is always indicated in centimeters, even if they are one of the classically named *formats* (e.g. sexagesimo-quarto).

Newspaper formats

Up until the beginning of the 19th century *newspapers* were mainly set in quarto *format*. The first French *newspaper* to be produced in folio *format* was Le Moniteur Universel. Today, the so-called popular press uses the *tabloid format* more and more often. This *format* is also called "the *format* for people in transit" which is smaller and more convenient. Nonetheless, *formats* vary from *newspaper* to another and depend on the width of the rotary press used.

8a = Broadsheet (large *format*): 410 × 578 mm
8b = Rheinish *format*: 350 × 510 or 360 × 530 mm
8c = Berliner or midi *format*: 320 × 470 mm
8d = Tabloïd (A3): 410 x 290 mm (or: 374 × 289 mm)
8e = Half tabloïd (A4): 290 × 210 mm

French poster formats

9a = 40 × 60 cm (small *posters*)
9b = 120 × 176 cm
9c = 320 × 240 cm
9d = 300 × 400 cm (4 × 3)

9a
9b
9c
9d

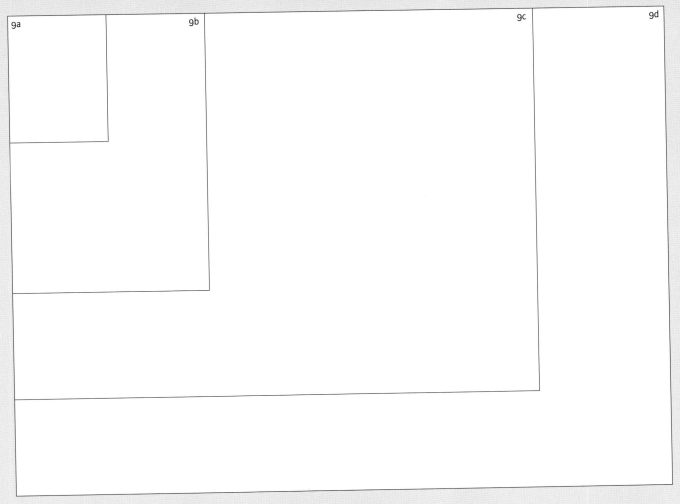

Surface, formats
The format as a unifying feature

A particular *format* and matching proportions in the diverse printed matter can be a characteristic element of a corporate design (visual appearance of a company or institution), the same as the choice of *typeface* or *color* are.

1. All printed information used by the Musée Nicéphore Niépce (France) are based on a square *format*. The *posters* are clearly recognizable and differentiate themselves from others due to their *format*. These *posters* are 40 × 40 cm in size and can't be used in the standard display areas. Despite the diversity in size and *folding* the printed communication forms a "family".
This principle of similarity gives the designer more freedom in the graphic language without the risk of loosing the audience.

1. Musée Nicéphore Niépce, posters, cards, leaflets, stamps
Le Petit Didier

1

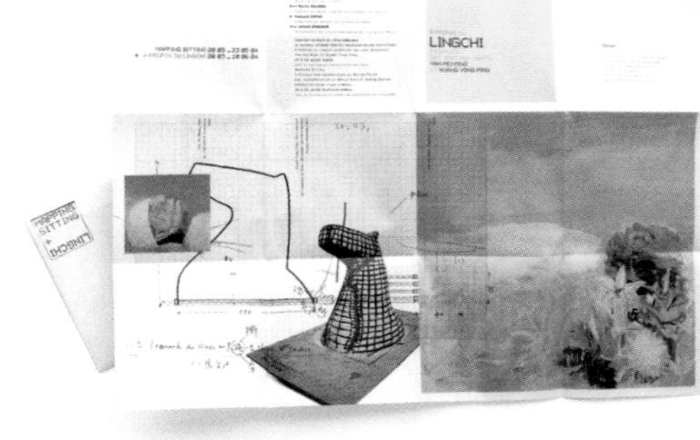

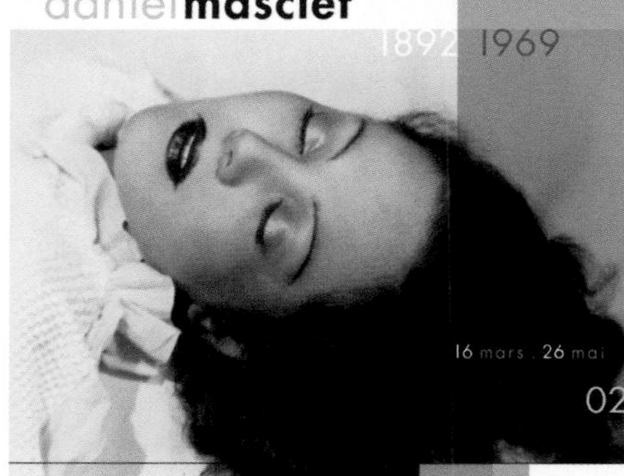

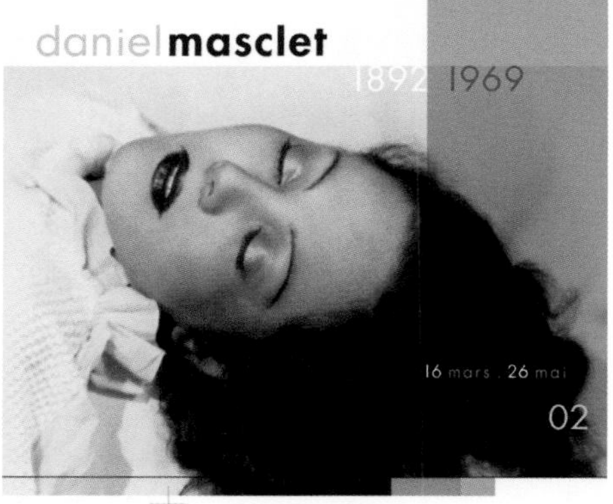

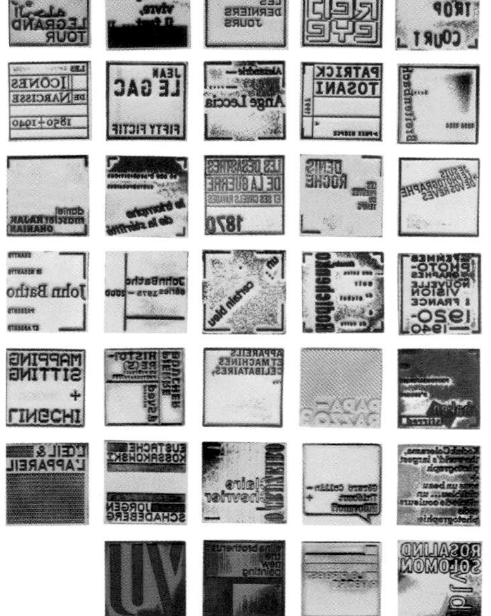

2. In order to create an overall sense of coherence all documents (except those with pre-defined *formats*) use a *format* with a ratio of 1:1.25 between height and width. The printed communications can be both landscape as well as portrait *format*. Despite their difference in size, the consistent proportions contribute to the brand identity (corporate identity).

a. catalogue
b. *flyer*
c. product labels

2

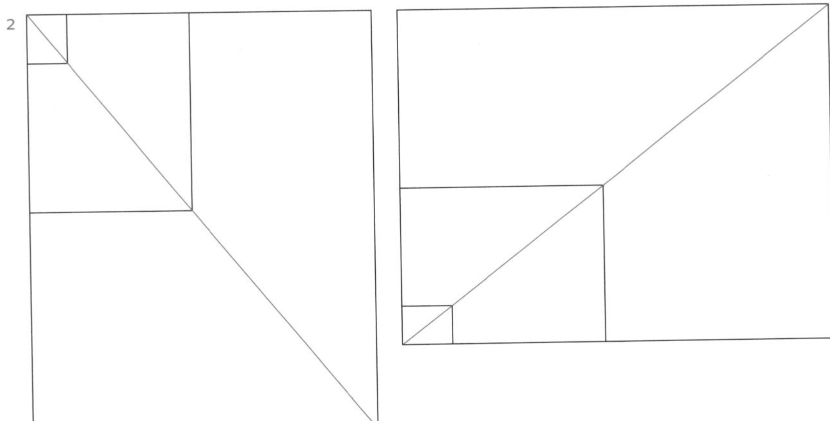

a b c

Margins
The harmony of composition

Not only the *page format* is important. The proportional relationship between the printed area (*type area*) and the *page format* (which defines the *margins*), as well as the proportional relationship between the *margins*, are parameters in determining a *composition*'s balance.
An experienced eye recognizes this *harmony* intuitively, and several typographers have sought the rules that define these parameters precisely. The most famous of these are *Rosarivo*, *van de Graaf* and *Tschichold*. They studied the most beautiful manuscripts to discover the aesthetic rules that govern them. Each in their own way, all of them found rules that we use to this day.

1. *Jan Tschichold** discovered that the most beautiful manuscripts are based on a *canon*, where the height of the *type area* is equal to the width of the page, and the *type area* and *page* have the same proportions.

2. *Raúl Rosarivo** proved that the *canon* discovered by *Tschichold* in 1953 was the one used by the first printers, including Gutenberg. *Rosarivo's* construction is based on nine divisions of the height and width of the *page* which has the proportions of 2:3.

3. *Van de Graaf* needed only a few lines to determine the proportions and position of the *type area* on a *page* with proportions of 2:3.

Many authors have shown that the position of the *type area* and the relationship of the *margins* to each other are linked to a long tradition. This is why many designers – unconsciously – use the principle of rotating *margins*: the smallest is the inside margin, then increases progressively from the *header* to the *outer margin* and finishing with the *lower margin* (*footer*). The idea of visual weight also affects the relationship between the upper and *lower margins*. If both are the same the *footer* appears smaller and needs to be larger to keep the *page* balanced.

1

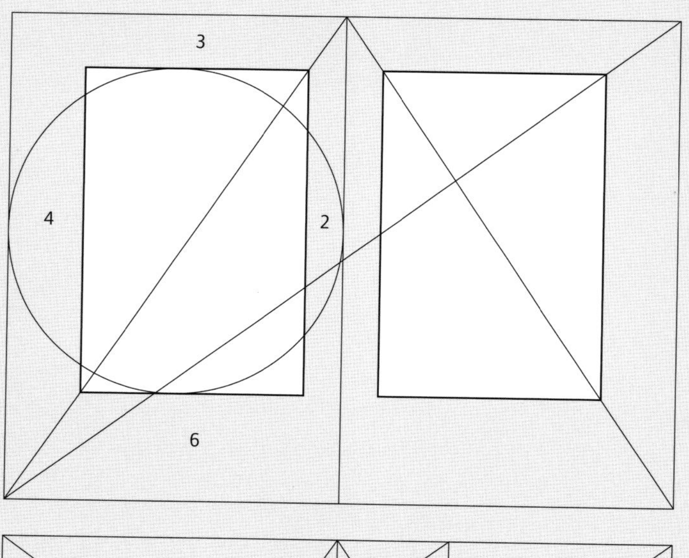

2

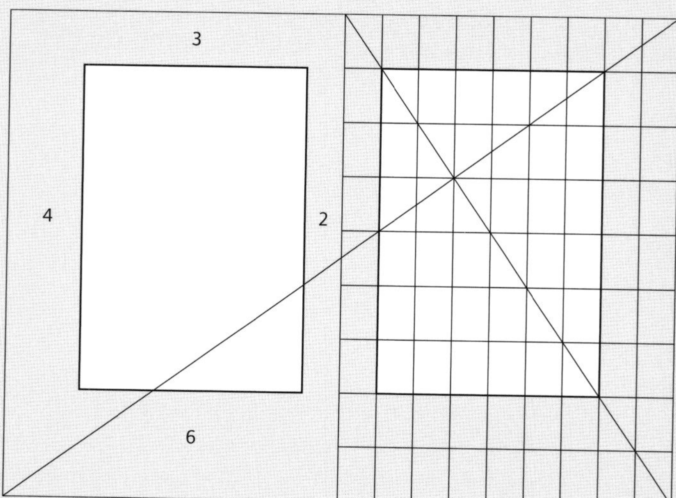

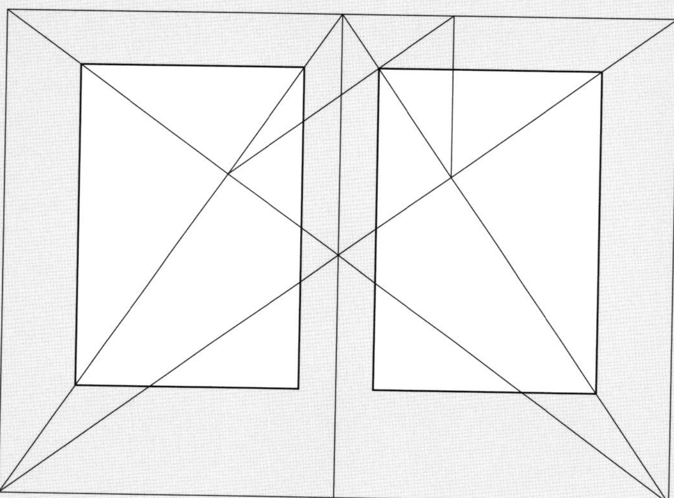

3

***Jan Tschichold** (1902–1974)
Typographer, calligrapher, teacher, author. He was one of the passionate advocates of the *New Typography*, but later returned to the classical rules of *layout*.
He spent many years studying ancient manuscripts to unlock the secrets of their beauty.

***Raúl Rosarivo** (1903–1966)
Draftsman, painter, typographer, teacher. In 1940 he began his research on the proportions of works printed by Gutenberg and his contemporaries.
In his *book* Divina Proporcion Tipográfica Ternaria published in 1948, he showed that the ratio of 2:3 is the most logical for *typography*.

In most cases the left and right *pages* are symmetrically *centered* on the *binding*.

A = *inner margin*
B = *upper margin* (*header*)
C = *outer margin*
D = *lower margin* (*footer*)

Experiments at first connected with the *New Typography* in Germany, then by the Swiss design schools developed new approaches to *page layout*. Among others the principle of asymmetrical *pages*, by shifting the left *page margins* to the right page, was introduced and broke with the symmetrical arrangement. The dimensions of the right hand page's inner *margin* and *outer margin* are inverted in regard to the left hand page.
Graphic designers from these schools that preferred geometric *formats* (e.g. the square) started calculating the *margins* and their relationships rationally. Challenging the established principles, they also unified or inverted *margins* (for example by making the *header* larger than the *footer*).

Remark
Defining the *margins* is not just a theoretical process. One also has to consider the practical handling of the printed piece in the reader's hands, its weight, and how it will be used. Where does one hold the printed piece, when will it rest on a lectern or a table? One has to consider what relationship the reader will have to the piece.

Naturally, one doesn't hold a *newspaper* the same way one holds a *magazine*. Nor does one hold a *pocket edition* the same way one holds a coffee-table *book*. The designer has to consider the type of *book* when defining the *margins*. Different bookbindings determine how far a *book* can be opened. If the inner *margin* is too narrow, the text tends to "slide" into the *binding*.

1. A double-*page* spread based on *Tschichold*'s rediscovered *canon*. The principle of symmetry and of rotating *margins* is clearly visible. Broad outer and *lower margins* make the *book* easy to hold – the thumbs won't cover the text. The broad *footer* is the preferred place for the *page number* that is traditionally set *centered* below the *type area*.

2-3. *Header* and *footer* are equal, the *type area* occupies more space, the *page layout* is more economical. Nonetheless, the *outer margins* are generous. The *page number* (also called *folio*) is set either in the *footer* (2) or in the *outer margin* (3).

1

Précis de typographie

Un texte est, cela est évident, une succession de lettres groupées en mots. Comment donc la typographie, composant unique, ne pourrait-elle pas avoir une incidence sur la perception d'un texte ? Pourquoi d'ailleurs existerait-il autant de caractères différents, si leurs formes n'avaient aucune importance ? Pourtant, beaucoup pensent que la typographie ne peut avoir un rôle significatif. Il est vrai que la structure quasi immuable des lettres de l'alphabet semble laisser bien peu de possibilités d'interprétation au dessinateur de caractères. De toute manière, comment les spécificités d'une typographie, aussi remarquables soient-elles, pourraient-elles être perceptibles sur quelques millimètres de hauteur, et changer l'appréciation d'un texte, alors que le lecteur n'y accorde, a priori, aucune importance ?

Ces arguments semblent irréfutables. Pourtant des études ont montré que les lecteurs remarquent, et apprécient bel et bien, une correspondance de style entre un caractère et un texte ; un caractère leur semble mieux convenir pour une utilisation qu'un autre.

Les caractères ont donc un style, soit, mais est-il alors possible de le déterminer avec précision, ou cela se limite-t-il à une vague impression au moment de la lecture ? Comme l'écriture manuscrite peut faire l'objet d'études graphologiques et aboutir à des conclusions claires, la typographie peut être analysée selon des critères précis.

Pourtant des études ont montré que les lecteurs remarquent, et apprécient bel et bien, une correspondance de style entre un caractère et un texte ; un caractère leur semble mieux convenir pour une utilisation qu'un autre. Les caractères ont donc un style, soit, mais est-il alors possible de le déterminer avec précision, ou cela se limite-t-il à une vague impression au moment de la lecture ? Comme l'écriture manuscrite peut faire l'objet d'études graphologiques et aboutir à des conclusions claires, la typographie peut être analysée selon des critères précis : les proportions des lettres, l'univers des formes utilisées – étroites ou larges, rondes ou anguleuses –, l'épaisseur des traits – pleins et déliés –, l'axe du caractère – vertical ou oblique –, la largeur des lettres – constante ou variable –, etc.

Le style d'un caractère ne peut d'autre part être dissocié du contexte dans lequel il a été créé. En effet un rapprochement peut souvent être fait entre ces deux paramètres. Les nouvelles technologies, l'informatique entre autres, influencent directement la création contemporaine de caractères. L'informatique est devenue un outil de création dont les spécificités « guident » la main du dessinateur. Nombre d'expérimentations ont par exemple utilisé le pixel ou le vecteur comme base de création.

Il en est ainsi depuis l'apparition de l'imprimerie. La gravure sur bois a très longtemps limité la précision des formes des caractères, l'apparition de la gravure sur métal a permis d'affiner les déliés, de préciser les empattements. Par leur contraste exacerbé entre pleins et déliés, les caractères Didot rappellent le contexte historique mouvementé de l'époque. Les caractères robustes, parfaitement stables sur des empattements lourds, créés à l'époque de la révolution industrielle, font directement référence aux premières constructions industrielles et montrent la confiance en cette ère de progrès. Bien sûr, le dessinateur lui-même déterminera en partie le style du caractère qu'il crée. Il détermine la forme des lettres selon deux paramètres : l'utilisation

– 22 –

Introduction

envisagée du caractère et son goût personnel. Il peut en effet dessiner un caractère pour une utilisation précise, et les contraintes spécifiques ont une incidence directe sur la forme des lettres. Le Times doit ses formes aux limites de l'impression.

Chaque caractère est conçu pour une utilisation « idéale », définie par de très nombreuses variables. Corps, espacement des lettres, justification, interlignage sont quelques-uns des paramètres que le dessinateur prend en considération au cours de son travail. Le maquettiste averti peut alors utiliser cette « expressivité » des caractères pour servir son travail. Il lui suffit déjà de choisir le caractère adapté, de régler les paramètres typographiques de manière judicieuse, pour que le texte typographié prenne une autre dimension. Il peut en effet agir sur chaque paramètre pour accentuer un aspect du caractère, ou au contraire en atténuer un autre, de manière à correspondre parfaitement à l'utilisation qu'il en fait. Malheureusement, il faut bien remarquer que ce souci de précision, pourtant garant de qualité, est souvent ignoré. Les outils informatiques ont accentué ce fait en rendant la typographie accessible à tous.
Malgré toute l'importance que peuvent avoir la typographie, et la manière de l'utiliser pour présenter un texte, il ne faut pas oublier le paramètre qui se trouve au début du processus de lecture et qui, par conséquent, décide de l'ensemble : le lecteur lui-même. Nous savons qu'il peut revêtir des visages très différents, avoir des centres d'intérêt opposés… Nous savons aussi qu'il sera bien souvent peu motivé à entreprendre la lecture et qu'il faudra d'abord le séduire. Même un lecteur passionné peut ne pas être bien disposé au moment où le texte est sous ses yeux. Il peut aussi, même s'il est intéressé, abandonner la lecture si la présentation n'est pas soignée. Inversement, une présentation agréable peut décider un lecteur réticent à prendre connaissance d'un document. Même s'ils s'en défendent, les lecteurs jugent d'abord un texte par sa présentation, ensuite, seulement, ils jugeront de la qualité de son contenu : la présentation est le premier obstacle que le lecteur rencontre.

Un texte est, cela est évident, une succession de lettres groupées en mots. Comment donc la typographie, composant unique, ne pourrait-elle pas avoir une incidence sur la perception d'un texte ? Pourquoi d'ailleurs existerait-il autant de caractères différents, si leurs formes n'avaient aucune importance ? Pourtant, beaucoup pensent que la typographie ne peut avoir un rôle significatif. Il est vrai que la structure quasi immuable des lettres de l'alphabet semble laisser bien peu de possibilités d'interprétation au dessinateur de caractères. De toute manière, comment les spécificités d'une typographie, aussi remarquables soient-elles, pourraient-elles être perceptibles sur quelques millimètres de hauteur, et changer l'appréciation d'un texte, alors que le lecteur n'y accorde, a priori, aucune importance ?

Ces arguments semblent irréfutables. Pourtant des études ont montré que les lecteurs remarquent, et apprécient bel et bien, une correspondance de style entre un caractère et un texte ; un caractère leur semble mieux convenir pour une utilisation qu'un autre.

Les caractères ont donc un style, soit, mais est-il alors possible de le déterminer avec précision, ou cela se limite-t-il à une vague impression au moment de la lecture ? Comme l'écriture manuscrite peut faire l'objet d'études graphologiques et aboutir à

– 23 –

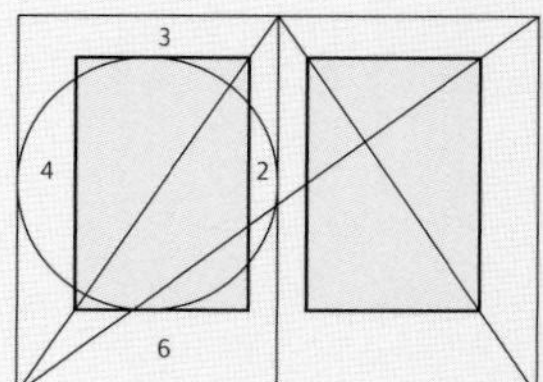

2

3

If one is familiar with the historic rules for defining the *margins* and position of the *type area*, then one can also break these rules in order to provoke a surprising effect.

4. The double-*page* spread is composed according to the principle of asymmetrical *pages* (left and right *pages* are identical). The *margins* do not match each other and increase in size as they progress counterclockwise. The *page number* is set in the wider side margin. This *composition* is a compromise between traditional and modern.

5. The double-*page* spread is composed according to the principle of asymmetrical *pages*. Although the *margins* respect the historic proportions, the *page layout* seems modern due to the arrangement of the *margins*. The broad *lower margin* gives the *page* personality. The *page number* further emphasizes the *lower margin*.

6. The double-*page* spread is composed according to the principle of asymmetrical *pages*, yet the proportions of the upper and lower *pages* are reversed. The *page number* is set at the top of the page. This type of design has a distinctly contemporary feel.

4

22 Un texte est, cela est évident, une succession de lettres groupées en mots. Comment donc la typographie, composant unique, ne pourrait-elle pas avoir une incidence sur la perception d'un texte ? Pourquoi d'ailleurs existerait-il autant de caractères différents, si leurs formes n'avaient aucune importance ? Pourtant, beaucoup pensent que la typographie ne peut avoir un rôle significatif. Il est vrai que la structure quasi immuable des lettres de l'alphabet semble laisser bien peu de possibilités d'interprétation au dessinateur de caractères. De toute manière, comment les spécificités d'une typographie, aussi remarquables soient-elles, pourraient-elles être perceptibles sur quelques millimètres de hauteur, et changer l'appréciation d'un texte, alors que le lecteur n'y accorde, a priori, aucune importance ?

Ces arguments semblent irréfutables. Pourtant des études ont montré que les lecteurs remarquent, et apprécient bel et bien, une correspondance de style entre un caractère et un texte ; un caractère leur semble mieux convenir pour une utilisation qu'un autre.

Les caractères ont donc un style, soit, mais est-il alors possible de le déterminer avec précision, ou cela se limite-t-il à une vague impression au moment de la lecture ? Comme l'écriture manuscrite peut faire l'objet d'études graphologiques et aboutir à des conclusions claires, la typographie peut être analysée selon des critères précis.

Pourtant des études ont montré que les lecteurs remarquent, et apprécient bel et bien, une correspondance de style entre un caractère et un texte ; un caractère leur semble mieux convenir pour une utilisation qu'un autre. Les caractères ont donc un style, soit, mais est-il alors possible de le déterminer avec précision, ou cela se limite-t-il à une vague impression au moment de la lecture ? Comme l'écriture manuscrite peut faire l'objet d'études graphologiques et aboutir à des conclusions claires, la typographie peut être analysée selon des critères précis : les proportions des lettres, l'univers des formes utilisées – étroites ou larges, rondes ou anguleuses –, l'épaisseur des traits – pleins et déliés –, l'axe du caractère – vertical ou oblique –, la largeur des lettres – constante ou variable –, etc.

Le style d'un caractère ne peut d'autre part être dissocié du contexte dans lequel il a été créé. En effet un rapprochement peut souvent être fait entre ces deux paramètres. Les nouvelles technologies, l'informatique entre autres, influencent directement la création contemporaine de caractères. L'informatique est devenue un outil de création dont les spécificités « guident » la main du dessinateur. Nombre d'expérimentations ont par exemple utilisé le pixel ou le vecteur comme base de création.

Il en est ainsi depuis l'apparition de l'imprimerie. La gravure sur bois a très longtemps limité la précision des formes des caractères, l'apparition de la gravure sur métal a permis d'affiner les déliés, de préciser les empattements. Par leur contraste exacerbé entre pleins et déliés, les caractères Didot rappellent le contexte historique mouvementé de l'époque. Les caractères robustes, parfaitement stables sur des empattements lourds, créés à l'époque de la révolution industrielle, font directement référence aux premières constructions industrielles et montrent la confiance en cette ère de progrès. Bien sûr, le dessinateur lui-même déterminera en partie le style du caractère qu'il crée. Il détermine la forme des lettres selon deux paramètres : l'utilisation envisagée du caractère et son goût personnel. Il peut en effet dessiner un caractère pour une utilisation précise, et les contraintes spécifiques ont une incidence directe sur la forme des lettres. Le Times doit ses formes aux limites de l'impression.

Chaque caractère est conçu pour une utilisation « idéale », définie par de très nombreuses variables. Corps, espacement des lettres, justification, interlignage sont quelques-uns des paramètres que le dessinateur prend en considération au cours de son travail. Le maquettiste averti peut alors utiliser cette « expressivité » des caractères

Précis de typographie

23 pour servir son travail. Il lui suffit déjà de choisir le caractère adapté, de régler les paramètres typographiques de manière judicieuse, pour que le texte typographié prenne une autre dimension. Il peut en effet agir sur chaque paramètre pour accentuer un aspect du caractère, ou au contraire en atténuer un autre, de manière à correspondre parfaitement à l'utilisation qu'il en fait. Malheureusement, il faut bien remarquer que ce souci de précision, pourtant garant de qualité, est souvent ignoré. Les outils informatiques ont accentué ce fait en rendant la typographie accessible à tous.
Malgré toute l'importance que peuvent avoir la typographie, et la manière de l'utiliser pour présenter un texte, il ne faut pas oublier le paramètre qui se trouve au début du processus de lecture et qui, par conséquent, décide de l'ensemble : le lecteur lui-même. Nous savons qu'il peut revêtir des visages très différents, avoir des centres d'intérêt opposés… Nous savons aussi qu'il sera bien souvent peu motivé à entreprendre la lecture et qu'il faudra d'abord le séduire. Même un lecteur passionné peut ne pas être bien disposé au moment où le texte est sous ses yeux. Il peut aussi, même s'il est intéressé, abandonner la lecture si la présentation n'est pas soignée. Inversement, une présentation agréable peut décider un lecteur réticent à prendre connaissance d'un document. Même s'ils s'en défendent, les lecteurs jugent d'abord un texte par sa présentation, ensuite, seulement, ils jugeront de la qualité de son contenu : la présentation est le premier obstacle que le lecteur rencontre.

Un texte est, cela est évident, une succession de lettres groupées en mots. Comment donc la typographie, composant unique, ne pourrait-elle pas avoir une incidence sur la perception d'un texte ? Pourquoi d'ailleurs existerait-il autant de caractères différents, si leurs formes n'avaient aucune importance ? Pourtant, beaucoup pensent que la typographie ne peut avoir un rôle significatif. Il est vrai que la structure quasi immuable des lettres de l'alphabet semble laisser bien peu de possibilités d'interprétation au dessinateur de caractères. De toute manière, comment les spécificités d'une typographie, aussi remarquables soient-elles, pourraient-elles être perceptibles sur quelques millimètres de hauteur, et changer l'appréciation d'un texte, alors que le lecteur n'y accorde, a priori, aucune importance ?

Ces arguments semblent irréfutables. Pourtant des études ont montré que les lecteurs remarquent, et apprécient bel et bien, une correspondance de style entre un caractère et un texte ; un caractère leur semble mieux convenir pour une utilisation qu'un autre.

Les caractères ont donc un style, soit, mais est-il alors possible de le déterminer avec précision, ou cela se limite-t-il à une vague impression au moment de la lecture ? Comme l'écriture manuscrite peut faire l'objet d'études graphologiques et aboutir à des conclusions claires, la typographie peut être analysée selon des critères précis.

Pourtant des études ont montré que les lecteurs remarquent, et apprécient bel et bien, une correspondance de style entre un caractère et un texte ; un caractère leur semble mieux convenir pour une utilisation qu'un autre. Les caractères ont donc un style, soit, mais est-il alors possible de le déterminer avec précision, ou cela se limite-t-il à une vague impression au moment de la lecture ? Comme l'écriture manuscrite peut faire l'objet d'études graphologiques et aboutir à des conclusions claires, la typographie peut être analysée selon des critères précis : les proportions des lettres, l'univers des formes utilisées – étroites ou larges, rondes ou anguleuses –, l'épaisseur des traits – pleins et déliés –, l'axe du caractère – vertical ou oblique –, la largeur des lettres – constante ou variable –, etc.

Le style d'un caractère ne peut d'autre part être dissocié du contexte dans lequel il a été créé. En effet un rapprochement peut souvent être fait entre ces deux paramètres. Les nouvelles technologies, l'informatique entre autres, influencent directement

Introduction

5

Précis de typographie
22

Introduction
23

6

Précis de typographie

Introduction

Margins
The margins as a graphic principle

The definition of the *margins* can in itself be a graphic principle in the design. For example by strictly following the traditional codes to present a contemporary subject, or by questioning these rules (inverting the values of the upper and *lower margins*, or inverting the inner and *outer margins*).

1. The absence of rotating *margins* and the strong use of an image allows the side *margins* to connect one double-*page* spread to the next.

2. This *book*'s design principle is based among other things on a generous inner margin, where the artists' names and *captions* are prominently placed.

1. *Scènes de ménages, Petits accrochages entre amis*, book
   Frac Lorraine
   Le Petit Didier
2. *100 chefs-d'oeuvre de Lorraine*, book
   Éditions Serpenoise
   Le Petit Didier

1

2

3. The success of this *composition* is in the choice of the image and placement of *typography* and peripheral elements (blocks of *color* and fragments of images).

3. *Eustache Kossakowski*, invitation card
Espace EDF Electra
Le Petit Didier

3

Typography

The importance of choosing a typeface and its use

A text is obviously a series of letters grouped into words. Why does *typography*, the central component, have an impact on the perception of the text? Furthermore, why would there be so many different *typefaces* if their shape is irrelevant? Nonetheless, many people think that *typography* is unimportant. At first glance the inflexible structure of letters of the alphabet seems to leave the type designer little room for interpretation. How can the characteristics of a *typeface* – as unusual as they might be – change the interpretation of a text and be noticed, when they are only a few millimeters tall, and most people don't see these details?

This seems to be an irrefutable argument. However, studies have shown that readers notice and prefer a stylistic connection between *typeface* and content. A given *typeface* seems to be better suited to some tasks rather than to others. *Typefaces*, therefore, have their own style, but how can we pinpoint this style precisely? Or is it just a vague impression one has while reading?
In the same way that one can analyze handwriting with graphology and draw clear conclusions, *typefaces* can be analyzed according to precise criteria: the proportions of the letters; the universe of shapes used – narrow or wide, round or angular; the thickness of the stroke – thin or thick; the inclined stress – vertical or tilted; the character width – constant or variable; and so on. These parameters help us understand why the perception of a text changes when the *typeface* used changes. A subjective aspect of this perception is undeniable. Every reader perceives through individual cultural and emotional filters. A reader's mood and personality can also influence his judgement of a given typeface.

A typeface's style cannot be separated from the context of its creation; there is usually a connection between the two. New technologies, computer science for example, have a direct impact on how typefaces are currently made. Computers and software have become a creative tool, that "guides" the hand of the type designer. Many experimental typefaces are based on pixels or vectors.

Typefaces and how they are made have been connected with one another since the advent of printing. Engraving letters in wood limited the accuracy of shapes. With the invention of metal engraving *hairlines* became thinner, *serifs* more defined. The *typeface Didot* with its extreme *contrast* between thick and thin strokes reminds us of the spirit of that time. At the end of the century of the Enlightenment, one observed the dawn of Neo-Classicism and a search for stability and rationalism. The solid letterforms with their *slab serifs*, developed during the Industrial Revolution, remind us of the first industrial buildings and demonstrate unlimited confidence in the era of progress.
Of course, the type designer influences the style of the typeface. His designs are based on two parameters: the intended use of the *typeface* and personal taste. If the *typeface* is designed for a specific use, the associated constraints have a direct impact on the letterforms. The *typeface* Times was shaped in part by limits in the printing technology at the time. *Typefaces* optimized for reading on screen need revision as the technology evolves. Obviously, the personality of the type designer also influences his work. Every *typeface* is designed for an ideal purpose, based on many variables. Size, *letterspacing*, alignment and *leading* are some of the parameters considered by the draftsman during his work.
The experienced designer uses the typeface's "expressiveness" to serve the project. He only needs to choose the appropriate typeface, and set it skillfully and carefully and the text will reach a new level. He can adjust each typographic parameter to emphasize a specific aspect of the typeface, or soften another so that the type fits perfectly to its intended use.
Unfortunately, this concern for precision – so often a guarantee of quality – is often ignored. Computers and software have accentuated this trend by making *typography* accessible to all. The unwitting user considers type as a neutral material, which the software can shape in any way he likes.

Raising your awareness of the richness, finesse and subtlety of *typography* will enable you to better understand how to handle it with care and sensitivity.

Why classify typefaces?
Faced with the multitude of available *typefaces* and seeking to better understand *typography*, two typographers have developed classifications that categorize *typefaces*; these are the *Thibaudeau* classification and the *Vox*-ATypI classification.

Francis Thibaudeau proposed a classification of *typefaces* based on the shape of their *serifs* in 1921. He originally divided the *typefaces* into four families. His simple system is easy to understand, but conveys an overly simplistic idea of *typography*, and doesn't represent the diversity of *typefaces*.
In 1952 Maximilien *Vox* presented a classification of eleven groups based on a number of criteria that were typical of an era (stroke *weight*, inclined stress, shape of *serifs*, etc.). This classification system was adopted by the Association Typographique Internationale (ATypI = International Typographic Association) in 1962.

Both classification systems define – with greater or lesser precision – archetypes of *typefaces*. In some cases a *typeface* can carry characteristics of two archetypes. The fascination with these systems is due to the fact that they provide the novice with a comprehensive overview of a complex subject. They also show how *typefaces* evolved over the centuries and their intimate relationship with the historical context in which they were developed.

How does one choose a typeface?
One doesn't choose a *typeface* based on scientific criteria, nor is the choice based only on formal aspects or their connotations. One needs to test a *typeface* in different sizes, judge its *rhythm* and its *color*. Does it correspond to the spirit of the *composition* and to its content? It is difficult to be certain, but careful observation of different *typefaces* gives one a feeling for accurate choices.

The *typefaces* presented in this *book* were chosen for their history, their popularity, their quirks, and their tone. Type catalogues offer many more choices. Discover them yourself!

Historical reference	Thibaudeau classification	Vox-ATypI classification		Notes
Mid-15th century	Elzévirs	Humanist Mape	Historic: eM Contemporary: eM	– handcrafted look – primarily thick *serifs* – *axis* strongly inclined to the left – often slanted "e" crossbar
16th century 17th century		Geralde Mape	– more slender *serifs* – strong thick-thin *contrast* in stroke – horizontal "e" crossbar	
18th century Encyclopaedic era: Rationalism and realism		Transitional Mape	– more rational letters – clean precise shapes – more delicate *serifs* – near vertical *axis* – strong thick-thin *contrast* in stroke	
End of the 18th century Empire and restauration	Didots	Didone Mape	– strict, intellectual style – vertical *axis* – very thick *stems*, extremely thin *hairline* strokes	
Mid-19th century Triumph of the machine Industrial upswing	Égyptiennes	Mechanistic Mape	Historic: eM Transitional: eM Modern: eM	– more robust functional *typefaces* – thick rectangular *serifs*
End of the 19th century and the first half of the 20th century	Antiques 	Lineal Mape	Grotesk: eM Constructed: eM Geometric: eM Humanistic: eM	– typefaces invented for posters (bolder, compacter, etc.) – architectural letterforms, mechanical in design, very studied curves with emphasis on the horizontal and vertical – uniform stroke and clear structure lends itself to multiple *weights*
Second half of the 20th century		Glyphic Mape	– inspired by letters carved in stone – emphasized triangular *serifs* – thicker *stem* strokes	
		Script* Mape	– imitation of script styles – originals drawn with diverse tools: quill, marker, brush – often calligraphic	
		Graphic* Mape	– strong influence of handwriting, however, without the intention of making a typeface	
		Blackletter* Mape	– groups the *blackletter typefaces* (widely used in Germany)	
		Non-latin* Μαρε	– groups all non-Latin *typefaces*	
		Experimental typefaces* Mape	– *typefaces* with very diverse characteristics, often the result of technical experiments	
		Typeface superfamilies MapeMapeMapeMape		A large family of *typefaces* that were drawn based on the same fundamental shape, but which can be assigned to different typeface classifications.

*These classes group *typefaces* from a longer time period. The exact date of origin for these *typefaces* often cannot be determined.

Typography
On criteria for choosing a typeface

1. Morphology
The relationship between *main stroke* and *hairline* stroke, or, in other words, between the thickest and thinnest parts of a letter and their orientation or *axis* of stress, are important for the text *rhythm* and the *gray value* of a typeface.

2. Serifs
The spirit or feeling of a text changes depending on if it has *serifs* or not. *Serifs* emphasize the line of text, but it would be hasty to assume that a *serif typeface* is more readable than one without, since readability also depends on many other factors.

3. Gray value
The thickness of a typeface, the *weight* of the letterforms, influences the *gray value* of the text and its impact (see page 64).

1

O O O

Main stroke and hairline
Main stroke and hairline
Main stroke and hairline

2

sans serif

Un texte est, cela est évident, une succession de lettres groupées en mots. Comment donc la typographie, composant unique, ne pourrait-elle pas avoir une incidence sur la perception d'un texte ? Pourquoi d'ailleurs existerait-il autant de caractères différents, si leurs formes n'avaient aucune importance ? Pourtant, beaucoup pensent que la typographie ne peut avoir un rôle significatif. Il est vrai que la structure quasi immuable des lettres de l'alphabet semble laisser bien peu de possibilités d'interprétation au dessinateur de caractères. De toute manière, comment les spécificités d'une typographie, aussi remarquables soient-elles, pourraient-elles être perceptibles sur quelques millimètres de hauteur, et changer l'appréciation d'un texte, alors que le lecteur n'y accorde, a priori, aucune importance ?

hybrid

Un texte est, cela est évident, une succession de lettres groupées en mots. Comment donc la typographie, composant unique, ne pourrait-elle pas avoir une incidence sur la perception d'un texte ? Pourquoi d'ailleurs existerait-il autant de caractères différents, si leurs formes n'avaient aucune importance ? Pourtant, beaucoup pensent que la typographie ne peut avoir un rôle significatif. Il est vrai que la structure quasi immuable des lettres de l'alphabet semble laisser bien peu de possibilités d'interprétation au dessinateur de caractères. De toute manière, comment les spécificités d'une typographie, aussi remarquables soient-elles, pourraient-elles être perceptibles sur quelques millimètres de hauteur, et changer l'appréciation d'un texte, alors que le lecteur n'y accorde, a priori, aucune importance ?

serif

Un texte est, cela est évident, une succession de lettres groupées en mots. Comment donc la typographie, composant unique, ne pourrait-elle pas avoir une incidence sur la perception d'un texte ? Pourquoi d'ailleurs existerait-il autant de caractères différents, si leurs formes n'avaient aucune importance ? Pourtant, beaucoup pensent que la typographie ne peut avoir un rôle significatif. Il est vrai que la structure quasi immuable des lettres de l'alphabet semble laisser bien peu de possibilités d'interprétation au dessinateur de caractères. De toute manière, comment les spécificités d'une typographie, aussi remarquables soient-elles, pourraient-elles être perceptibles sur quelques millimètres de hauteur, et changer l'appréciation d'un texte, alors que le lecteur n'y accorde, *a priori*, aucune importance ?

3

color color **color** **color**

4. Proportions
The width of the letterforms (*body width*) affects the type density and *reading* rhythm. Narrow *typefaces* are well suited to *headlines*, however, one must be careful when using them at small sizes.
Condensed *typefaces* are more difficult to read due to their proportions. On the one hand the letters are too similar, and on the other because they have smaller *counters*. The more condensed a *typeface* is, the smaller the *counters*, the more narrow the *body width* and corresponding *tracking*.

Some *typefaces* are available in different *body widths* and are ideal for various uses. For example, the *type family* Univers was drawn by Adrian Frutiger with the goal of creating the "ideal" typeface. Univers encompasses 21 styles and four different *body widths* (5).

4

U

Ultra Condensed

Un texte est, c'est une évidence, une succession
de lettres groupées en mots.
Comment donc la typographie, composant unique,
ne pourrait-elle pas avoir une incidence sur la perception
d'un texte ? Pourquoi d'ailleurs existerait-il
autant de caractères différents, si leurs formes
n'avaient aucune importance ?

Condensed

Un texte est, c'est une évidence, une succession
de lettres groupées en mots.
Comment donc la typographie, composant unique,
ne pourrait-elle pas avoir une incidence sur la perception
d'un texte ? Pourquoi d'ailleurs existerait-il
autant de caractères différents, si leurs formes
n'avaient aucune importance ?

5

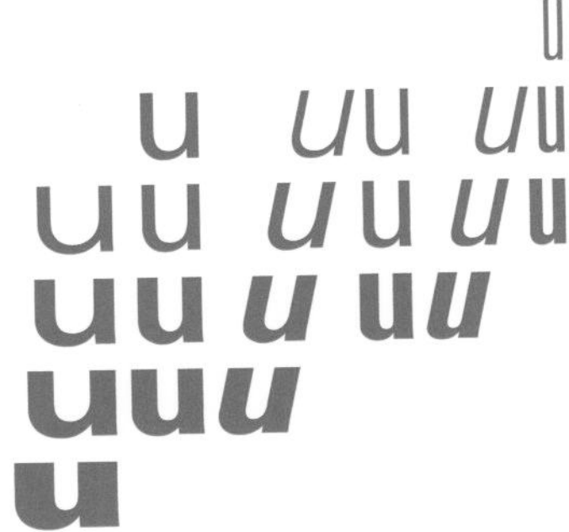

U

Normal

Un texte est, c'est une évidence, une succession
de lettres groupées en mots.
Comment donc la typographie, composant unique,
ne pourrait-elle pas avoir une incidence sur la perception
d'un texte ? Pourquoi d'ailleurs existerait-il
autant de caractères différents, si leurs formes
n'avaient aucune importance ?

Extended

Un texte est, c'est une évidence, une succession
de lettres groupées en mots.
Comment donc la typographie, composant unique,
ne pourrait-elle pas avoir une incidence sur la perception
d'un texte ? Pourquoi d'ailleurs existerait-il
autant de caractères différents, si leurs formes
n'avaient aucune importance ?

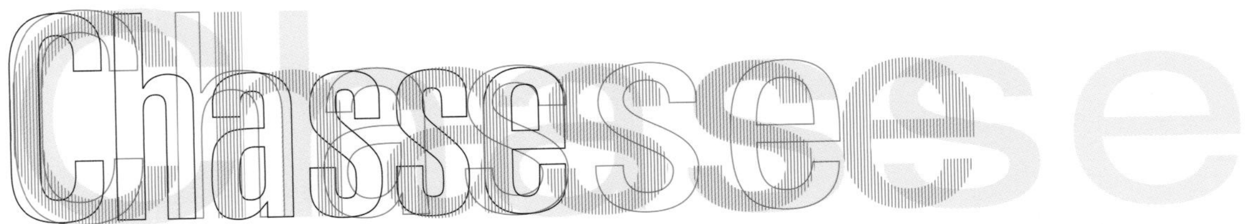

Ultra Condensed Condensed *Normal* Extended

Typography
The analysis of typefaces

Which parameters should be considered when choosing a typeface? Why does one *font* seem more appropriate for one job than another? Why does one *typeface* appear larger than another, even though they have the same point size? Why does the text look different when the *typeface* used to set it changes? These are all questions that need to be answered when choosing a typeface. Studying a few of these parameters helps to explain how they work.

1. Typefaces with the same body size
Although all four *typefaces* shown have the same body size, differences in their *ascenders* and *descenders* means that the total height – between the horizontal lines – and corresponding white space is distributed differently.

From left to right: Garamond, Bodoni, Univers, Rotis SemiSans.

The face of the typeface
The ratio of *x-height* to *ascenders* and *descenders* varies significantly from *typeface* to typeface. The larger the *x-height*, the larger the *typeface* appears, even at the same point size. One might refer to a small, middle or large face.

The relationship between thick and thin
The *contrast* (or visual balance) between the thick and thin strokes, and the thickness of the *stems* gives each *typeface* their own characteristic appearance.

1
Proportions, contrasts

140 Pica points

alp alp

Adobe Garamond

Bodoni

Rhythm

2

acehnopu acehnopu

3

acehnopu acehnopu

4
Specimen
Text set in 9 pt with 11 pt *leading*

Comment la typographie, composant unique, ne pourrait-elle pas avoir une incidence sur la perception d'un texte? Pourquoi d'ailleurs existerait-il autant de caractères différents, si leurs formes n'avaient aucune importance? Pourtant, beaucoup pensent que la typographie ne peut avoir un rôle significatif. Il est vrai que la structure quasi immuable des lettres de l'alphabet semble laisser bien peu de possibilités d'interprétation au dessinateur de caractères. De toute manière, comment les spécificités d'un caractère, aussi remarquables soient-elles, pourraient-elles être perceptibles sur quelques millimètres de hauteur, et changer l'appréciation d'un texte, alors que le lecteur n'y accorde, *a priori*, aucune importance? Ces arguments semblent irréfutables. Pourtant des études ont montré que les lecteurs remarquent, et apprécient bel et bien, une correspondance de style entre un caractère et un texte; un caractère leur semble mieux convenir pour une utilisation qu'un autre.

Comment la typographie, composant unique, ne pourrait-elle pas avoir une incidence sur la perception d'un texte? Pourquoi d'ailleurs existerait-il autant de caractères différents, si leurs formes n'avaient aucune importance? Pourtant, beaucoup pensent que la typographie ne peut avoir un rôle significatif. Il est vrai que la structure quasi immuable des lettres de l'alphabet semble laisser bien peu de possibilités d'interprétation au dessinateur de caractères. De toute manière, comment les spécificités d'un caractre, aussi remarquables soient-elles, pourraient-elles être perceptibles sur quelques millimètres de hauteur, et changer l'appréciation d'un texte, alors que le lecteur n'y accorde, *a priori*, aucune importance? Ces arguments semblent irréfutables. Pourtant des études ont montré que les lecteurs remarquent, et apprécient bel et bien, une correspondance de style entre un caractère et un texte; un caractère leur semble mieux convenir pour une utilisation qu'un autre.

2. Inclined stress
The (more or less marked) inclination of the *axis* gives each *typeface* a specific dynamic. Axes and their inclination originate from how the types were originally drawn. One refers to the inclined stress of a typeface.

3. Character width
The variation or consistency of the letters' width affects the *reading rhythm*. *Typefaces* with different character widths have proportional spacing, and *typefaces* with a constant character width are called monospaced. *Typefaces* based on the original handwritten forms and letterforms with different widths are easier to read since they are more easily recognizable. The text has *rhythm*.

Gray value of type
Every text (4) has a certain *color* or *gray value* that is either dense or open (see example 4 where all four texts are set at the same size and with the same *leading*). This can be seen as proof of how important the characteristics of type are: *color*, *rhythm*, *axis*, etc.

Influence of language
The language used in the text also affects its appearance. The frequency of different letters, or the use of *capitals* and special characters (accents for example) all play a role.

Defining the leading
Specific characteristics of the *typeface* are used to define the *leading* (see pages 68–69) and the *tracking* (see page 65).

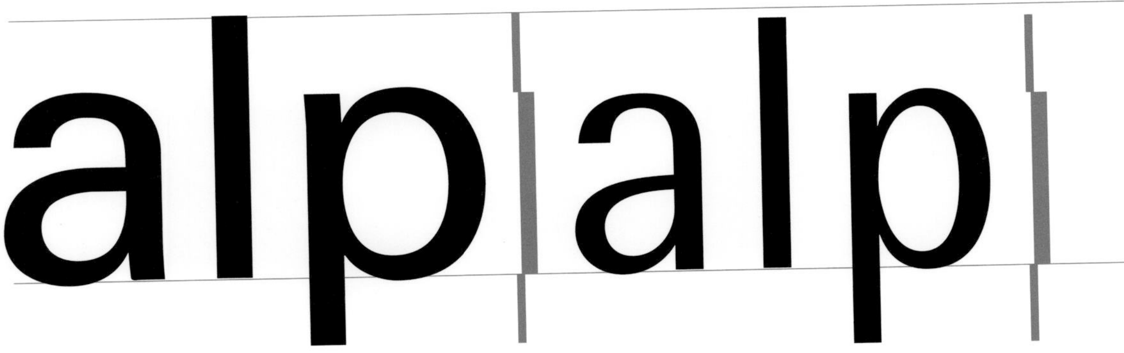

Univers 55 Rotis SemiSans

acehnopu acehnopu

acehnopu acehnopu

Comment la typographie, composant unique, ne pourrait-elle pas avoir une incidence sur la perception d'un texte? Pourquoi d'ailleurs existerait-il autant de caractères différents, si leurs formes n'avaient aucune importance? Pourtant, beaucoup pensent que la typographie ne peut avoir un rôle significatif. Il est vrai que la structure quasi immuable des lettres de l'alphabet semble laisser bien peu de possibilités d'interprétation au dessinateur de caractères. De toute manière, comment les spécificités d'un caractère, aussi remarquables soient-elles, pourraient-elles être perceptibles sur quelques millimètres de hauteur, et changer l'appréciation d'un texte, alors que le lecteur n'y accorde, a priori, aucune importance? Ces arguments semblent irréfutables. Pourtant des études ont montré que les lecteurs remarquent, et apprécient bel et bien, une correspondance de style entre un caractère et un texte; un caractère leur semble mieux convenir pour une utilisation qu'un autre.

Comment la typographie, composant unique, ne pourrait-elle pas avoir une incidence sur la perception d'un texte? Pourquoi d'ailleurs existerait-il autant de caractères différents, si leurs formes n'avaient aucune importance? Pourtant, beaucoup pensent que la typographie ne peut avoir un rôle significatif. Il est vrai que la structure quasi immuable des lettres de l'alphabet semble laisser bien peu de possibilités d'interprétation au dessinateur de caractères. De toute manière, comment les spécificités d'un caractère, aussi remarquables soient-elles, pourraient-elles être perceptibles sur quelques millimètres de hauteur, et changer l'appréciation d'un texte, alors que le lecteur n'y accorde, a priori, aucune importance? Ces arguments semblent irréfutables. Pourtant des études ont montré que les lecteurs remarquent, et apprécient bel et bien, une correspondance de style entre un caractère et un texte; un caractère leur semble mieux convenir pour une utilisation qu'un autre.

The three *typefaces* on this *page* are representative of the *Humanist* classification. The first (Jenson Adobe) is the original form, the second (Mendoza ITC) is a recent interpretation, while the third (Fairplex) is unusual and seems inspired by the first – *Humanist* – printed types.

1. Adobe Jenson, 1996
Robert Slimbach – www.adobe.com
This *roman typeface* is based on a Venetian *type cut* by Nicolas Jenson in 1470, however, the *italics* are inspired by a *typeface* by Ludovico Vicentino degli Arrighi. It has a small *x-height* and distinctly formed letters that make it particularly readable. Some details such as the shape of the *serifs* remind one of calligraphy.

2. ITC Mendoza Roman, 1991
José Mendoza y Almeida – www.itcfonts.com
Undoubtedly a contemporary *typeface* that best represents the *Humanist* group: heavy *serifs*, low *contrast* between thick and thin strokes, high *x-height*. Despite its classic appearance this *typeface* has personality and can be used today. The spirit of the *typeface* dictates a dense *gray value* and hence tighter *leading*.

3. Fairplex, 2002
Zuzana Licko – www.emigre.com
During her type experiments based on Garamond No. 3 Zuzana Licko developed a *serif typeface* with low *contrast* (between thick and thin strokes). In her opinion higher *contrast* in a *typeface* leads to poorer readability, especially at smaller sizes.
Fairplex is divided into two distinct families: Narrow and Wide. Although the first impression is historic, multiple subtle details reveal its contemporary nature.

1

Authentic *Authentic*
AUTHENTIC
Authentic

abcdefghijklmnopqrstuvwxyz
ABCDEFGHIJKLMNOPQRSTUVWXYZ

Un texte est, évidemment, une succession de lettres groupées en mots. Comment donc la typographie, composant unique, ne pourrait-elle pas avoir une incidence sur la perception d'un texte ? Pourquoi d'ailleurs existerait-il autant de caractères différents, si leurs formes n'avaient aucune importance ? Pourtant, beaucoup pensent que la typographie ne peut avoir un rôle significatif.

7/9 pt

Il est vrai que la structure quasi immuable des lettres de l'alphabet semble laisser bien peu de possibilités d'interprétation au dessinateur de caractères. De toute manière, comment les spécificités d'une typographie, aussi remarquables soient-elles, pourraient-elles être perceptibles sur quelques millimètres de hauteur, et changer l'appréciation d'un texte, alors que le lecteur n'y accorde, a priori, aucune importance ?

9/12 pt

2

Rustic *Rustic*
Rustic *Rustic*
Rustic *Rustic*

abcdefghijklmnopqrstuvwxyz
ABCDEFGHIJKLMNOPQRSTUVWXYZ

Un texte est, évidemment, une succession de lettres groupées en mots. Comment donc la typographie, composant unique, ne pourrait-elle pas avoir une incidence sur la perception d'un texte ? Pourquoi d'ailleurs existerait -il autant de caractères différents, si leurs formes n'avaient aucune importance ? Pourtant, beaucoup pensent que la typographie ne peut avoir un rôle significatif.

7/9 pt

Il est vrai que la structure quasi immuable des lettres de l'alphabet semble laisser bien peu de possibilités d'interprétation au dessinateur de caractères. De toute manière, comment les spécificités d'une typographie, aussi remarquables soient-elles, pourraient-elles être perceptibles sur quelques millimètres de hauteur, et changer l'appréciation d'un texte, alors que le lecteur n'y accorde, *a priori*, aucune importance ?

9/12 pt

3

ai

Atypical *Atypical*
Atypical *Atypical*
Atypical *Atypical*
Atypical *Atypical*

abcdefghijklmnopqrstuvwxyz
ABCDEFGHIJKLMNOPQRSTUVWXYZ

Un texte est, évidemment, une succession de lettres groupées en mots. Comment donc la typographie, composant unique, ne pourrait-elle pas avoir une incidence sur la perception d'un texte ? Pourquoi d'ailleurs existerait-il autant de caractères différents, si leurs formes n'avaient aucune importance ?

Fairplex Narrow book 7/9 pt

Il est vrai que la structure quasi immuable des lettres de l'alphabet semble laisser bien peu de possibilités d'interprétation au dessinateur de caractères. De toute manière, comment les spécificités d'une typographie, aussi remarquables soient-elles, pourraient-elles être perceptibles sur quelques millimètres de hauteur, et changer l'appréciation d'un texte, alors que le lecteur n'y accorde, *a priori*, aucune importance ?

Fairplex Narrow book 9/12 pt

These three *typefaces* belong to the *Geralde* classification group.

4. Adobe Garamond, 1989
Robert Slimbach – www.adobe.com
One of the most accurate new interpretations of the original Garamond cut by Claude Garamond in 1532.
It is emblematic of the *Geralde* group of *typefaces*. Its low *x-height*, proportions and inclined stress give it an elegant *gray value* and particularly readable texts.

5. Sabon, 1967
Jan Tschichold – www.linotype.com
A group of German printers hired *Jan Tschichold* to develop a *typeface* based on Garamond that could easily be used in *typesetting* of any kind. Constrained by the Linotype and Monotype *typesetting* equipment, he designed an *italic* (and *bold*) style with the same *body width* as the *roman* and that was inspired by the *typeface* Granjon. *Jan Tschichold*, the "father" of the *New Typography*, later defender of typographic tradition, drew this *typeface* based on Stanley Morison's (Monotype Inc.'s typographic advisor) principles, where a successful type is unremarkable.
He removed the typical details of the original typeface, making Sabon a modern type. It is more narrow than Garamond and has a larger *x-height*. Sabon combines elegance and the classicism of Garamond with the sobriety of a *Lineal* typeface.
Perfectly readable and not necessarily historic in feel, Sabon is often used in *book* design.

6. Plantin, 1913
Frank Hinman – www.linotype.com
The robust look of this *typeface* that among other things is due to its low *contrast* between thick and thin strokes and the heavy *serifs*, makes it particularly readable at small sizes. The triangularly shaped *serifs* emphasize the basic feel of this type. The short *ascenders* and *descenders*, a characteristic of Plantin, make it possible to set texts compactly and economically. In 1931 Stanley Morison based his *typeface* Times New Roman on Plantin's *silhouette*.

4

ai

Elegance *Elegance*
Elegance Elegance
Elegance *Elegance*
ELEGANCE
ELEGANCE

abcdefghijklmnopqrstuvwxyz
ABCDEFGHIJKLMNOPQRSTUVWXYZ

Un texte est, évidemment, une succession de lettres groupées en mots. Comment donc la typographie, composant unique, ne pourrait-elle pas avoir une incidence sur la perception d'un texte? Pourquoi d'ailleurs existerait-il autant de caractères différents, si leurs formes n'avaient aucune importance? Pourtant, beaucoup pensent que la typographie ne peut avoir un rôle significatif.

7/9 pt

Il est vrai que la structure quasi immuable des lettres de l'alphabet semble laisser bien peu de possibilités d'interprétation au dessinateur de caractères. De toute manière, comment les spécificités d'une typographie, aussi remarquables soient-elles, pourraient-elles être perceptibles sur quelques millimètres de hauteur, et changer l'appréciation d'un texte, alors que le lecteur n'y accorde, *a priori*, aucune importance?

9/12 pt

5

Sobriety *Sobriety*
Sobriety *Sobriety*

abcdefghijklmnopqrstuvwxyz
ABCDEFGHIJKLMNOPQRSTUVWXYZ

Un texte est, évidemment, une succession de lettres groupées en mots. Comment donc la typographie, composant unique, ne pourrait-elle pas avoir une incidence sur la perception d'un texte? Pourquoi d'ailleurs existerait-il autant de caractères différents, si leurs formes n'avaient aucune importance? Pourtant, beaucoup pensent que la typographie ne peut avoir un rôle significatif.

7/9 pt

Il est vrai que la structure quasi immuable des lettres de l'alphabet semble laisser bien peu de possibilités d'interprétation au dessinateur de caractères. De toute manière, comment les spécificités d'une typographie, aussi remarquables soient-elles, pourraient-elles être perceptibles sur quelques millimètres de hauteur, et changer l'appréciation d'un texte, alors que le lecteur n'y accorde, *a priori*, aucune importance?

9/12 pt

6

ai

Robustness *Robustness*
Robustness *Robustness*
Robustness *Robustness*
Robustness *Robustness*

abcdefghijklmnopqrstuvwxyz
ABCDEFGHIJKLMNOPQRSTUVWXYZ

Un texte est, évidemment, une succession de lettres groupées en mots. Comment donc la typographie, composant unique, ne pourrait-elle pas avoir une incidence sur la perception d'un texte? Pourquoi d'ailleurs existerait-il autant de caractères différents, si leurs formes n'avaient aucune importance?

7/9 pt

Il est vrai que la structure quasi immuable des lettres de l'alphabet semble laisser bien peu de possibilités d'interprétation au dessinateur de caractères. De toute manière, comment les spécificités d'une typographie, aussi remarquables soient-elles, pourraient-elles être perceptibles sur quelques millimètres de hauteur, et changer l'appréciation d'un texte, alors que le lecteur n'y accorde, *a priori*, aucune importance?

9/11 pt

The three *typefaces* on this *page* are representative of the *Transitional* classification. The first (Baskerville Berthold) is an authentic representative of this group, the second (New Baskerville ITC) is a typical reinterpretation of the ITC (International *Typeface* Corp.), which designed high *contrast typefaces* to meet the tastes of the advertising scene. The third (Mrs Eaves) is a recent *typeface* that, following the designer's wish, revives the original characteristics of the *typeface* by John Baskerville.

1. Baskerville Berthold, 1980
Günter Gerhard Lange – www.bertholdtypes.com
Baskerville takes its name from the printer John Baskerville (1706–1775), who perfected the techniques of his time and invented a process for producing *coated paper*. He had a thinner, more delicate *typeface* drawn and cut. His types influenced Didot and Bodoni.
The variant of the 1772 type Great Primer by John Baskerville shown here is more robust and less showy than the New Baskerville.

2. New Baskerville, 1978
Matthew Carter, John Quaranta – www.itcfonts.com
One notices that the New Baskerville ITC is inspired more by the metal type in the *typeface* Great Primer (used by John Baskerville in 1772) than by its printed impression. *Typefaces* appear heavier when printed because the ink soaks into the paper (compare this type with the *typefaces* Baskerville by Berthold and Mrs Eaves). Due to its fine *hairline* strokes its use at smaller sizes is limited. It is better suited for printing on *coated paper*.

3. Mrs Eaves, 1996
Zuzana Licko – www.emigre.com
While designing this *typeface* Zuzana Licko sought to obtain the original *gray value* that the *typeface* Baskerville designed by John Baskerville in 1772 had when set and printed. Although the forms are reminiscent of the New Baskerville by ITC, it has an entirely different *gray value* (compare with New Baskerville by ITC).
Zuzana Licko distilled many contemporary details into a *typeface* that is fundamentally classical. The numerous (formerly common) *ligatures* that occasionally seem strange (some are brand new) connect past and present, and are one of the strengths of this typeface.

1

Reliable *Reliable*
Reliable *Reliable*
Reliable ***Reliable***
Reliable

abcdefghijklmnopqrstuvwxyz
ABCDEFGHIJKLMNOPQRSTUVWXYZ

Un texte est, évidemment, une succession de lettres groupées en mots. Comment donc la typographie, composant unique, ne pourrait-elle pas avoir une incidence sur la perception d'un texte ? Pourquoi d'ailleurs existerait-il autant de caractères différents, si leurs formes n'avaient aucune importance ? Pourtant, beaucoup pensent que la typographie ne peut avoir un rôle significatif.

7/9 pt

Il est vrai que la structure quasi immuable des lettres de l'alphabet semble laisser bien peu de possibilités d'interprétation au dessinateur de caractères. De toute manière, comment les spécificités d'une typographie, aussi remarquables soient-elles, pourraient-elles être perceptibles sur quelques millimètres de hauteur, et changer l'appréciation d'un texte, alors que le lecteur n'y accorde, *a priori*, aucune importance ?

9/12 pt

2

Elegant *Elegant*
Elegant ***Elegant***

abcdefghijklmnopqrstuvwxyz
ABCDEFGHIJKLMNOPQRSTUVWXYZ

Un texte est, évidemment, une succession de lettres groupées en mots. Comment donc la typographie, composant unique, ne pourrait-elle pas avoir une incidence sur la perception d'un texte ? Pourquoi d'ailleurs existerait-il autant de caractères différents, si leurs formes n'avaient aucune importance ? Pourtant, beaucoup pensent que la typographie ne peut avoir un rôle significatif.

7/9 pt

Il est vrai que la structure quasi immuable des lettres de l'alphabet semble laisser bien peu de possibilités d'interprétation au dessinateur de caractères. De toute manière, comment les spécificités d'une typographie, aussi remarquables soient-elles, pourraient-elles être perceptibles sur quelques millimètres de hauteur, et changer l'appréciation d'un texte, alors que le lecteur n'y accorde, *a priori*, aucune importance ?

9/12 pt

3

ai

Æsthetic *Æsthetic*
Æsthetic
ÆSTHETIC
ÆSTHETIC

abcdefghijklmnopqrstuvwxyz
ct ee fh fj fr ft gg gi ip it ky oe sp st tt tty tw
ABCDEFGHIJKLMNOPQRSTUVWXYZ
AV AA MB OC MD ME FF OG HE FI UB NK FL LA NT OO MP
TE RU DT TU PV AT WH ET WH EU LT YU LT YU R

Un texte est, évidemment, une succession de lettres groupées en mots. Comment donc la typographie, composant unique, ne pourrait-elle pas avoir une incidence sur la perception d'un texte ? Pourquoi d'ailleurs existerait-il autant de caractères différents, si leurs formes n'avaient aucune importance ? Pourtant, beaucoup pensent que la typographie ne peut avoir un rôle significatif.

7/8,5 pt

Il est vrai que la structure quasi immuable des lettres de l'alphabet semble laisser bien peu de possibilités d'interprétation au dessinateur de caractères. De toute manière, comment les spécificités d'une typographie, aussi remarquables soient-elles, pourraient-elles être perceptibles sur quelques millimètres de hauteur, et changer l'appréciation d'un texte, alors que le lecteur n'y accorde, *a priori*, aucune importance ?

9/11 pt

These three *typefaces* presented on this *page* are members of the *Didone* classification.

4. Bodoni, 1909–1939
Morris Fuller Benton
The original *typeface* was drawn in 1790 by Giambattista Bodoni. Like all *Didone typefaces*, the letterforms have a high *contrast* between thick and thin strokes. This means it is suitable for relatively short texts, since the reader tires when reading longer texts.

5. Walbaum (env. 1800)
Justus Erich Walbaum – www.linotype.com
This *typeface* is characteristic of German types of the time. It is elegant and distinguished. Its overall shape is not as round as Bodoni and makes it appear austere. Its larger *x-height* makes it more readable.

6. Linotype Didot, 1991
Adrian Frutiger – www.linotype.com
Due to its delicate *hairlines*, this *typeface* is appropriate as a *display typeface* rather than a *bread-and-butter typeface*. The thin strokes tend to disappear at smaller sizes making reading more difficult. *Didot*'s delicate shapes and sophisticated proportions make it a truly elegant typeface.

4

ai

Autorithy *Autorithy*
Autorithy *Autorithy*
Autorithy *Autorithy*
Autorithy *Autorithy*

abcdefghijklmnopqrstuvwxyz
ABCDEFGHIJKLMNOPQRSTUVWXYZ

Un texte est, évidemment, une succession de lettres groupées en mots. Comment donc la typographie, composant unique, ne pourrait-elle pas avoir une incidence sur la perception d'un texte? Pourquoi d'ailleurs existerait-il autant de caractères différents, si leurs formes n'avaient aucune importance? Pourtant, beaucoup pensent que la typographie ne peut avoir un rôle significatif.

7/9 pt

Il est vrai que la structure quasi immuable des lettres de l'alphabet semble laisser bien peu de possibilités d'interpré-tation au dessinateur de caractères. De toute manière, comment les spécificités d'une typographie, aussi remarquables soient-elles, pourraient-elles être perceptibles sur quelques millimètres de hauteur, et changer l'appréciation d'un texte, alors que le lecteur n'y accorde, *a priori*, aucune importance?

9/12 pt

5

ai

Distinction *Distinction*
Distinction *Distinction*
Distinction *Distinction*

abcdefghijklmnopqrstuvwxyz
ABCDEFGHIJKLMNOPQRSTUVWXYZ

Un texte est, évidemment, une succession de lettres groupées en mots. Comment donc la typographie, composant unique, ne pourrait-elle pas avoir une incidence sur la perception d'un texte? Pourquoi d'ailleurs existerait-il autant de caractères différents, si leurs formes n'avaient aucune importance? Pourtant, beaucoup pensent que la typographie ne peut avoir un rôle significatif.

7/9 pt

Il est vrai que la structure quasi immuable des lettres de l'alphabet semble laisser bien peu de possibilités d'interprétation au dessinateur de caractères. De toute manière, comment les spécificités d'une typographie, aussi remarquables soient-elles, pourraient-elles être perceptibles sur quelques millimètres de hauteur, et changer l'appréciation d'un texte, alors que le lecteur n'y accorde, *a priori*, aucune importance?

9/12 pt

6

ai

Sophistication

abcdefghijklmnopqrstuvwxyz
ABCDEFGHIJKLMNOPQRSTUVWXYZ

Un texte est, évidemment, une succession de lettres groupées en mots. Comment donc la typographie, composant unique, ne pourrait-elle pas avoir une incidence sur la perception d'un texte? Pourquoi d'ailleurs existerait-il autant de caractères différents, si leurs formes n'avaient aucune importance? Pourtant, beaucoup pensent que la typographie ne peut avoir un rôle significatif.

7/9 pt

Il est vrai que la structure quasi immuable des lettres de l'alphabet semble laisser bien peu de possibilités d'interpré-tation au dessinateur de caractères. De toute manière, comment les spécificités d'une typographie, aussi remar-quables soient-elles, pourraient-elles être perceptibles sur quelques millimètres de hauteur, et changer l'apprécia-tion d'un texte, alors que le lecteur n'y accorde, a priori, aucune importance?

9/12 pt

The *typefaces* on this *page* illustrate the richness of the *Mechanistic* classification (also called slab *serifs*). They hark back to earlier types (Century Schoolbook), are robust and typical for the Industrial Revolution (Clarendon) or purely geometric (ITC Lubalin Graph).

1. Century Schoolbook, 1918–1921
Morris Fuller Benton – www.linotype.com
This *typeface* represents a transitional *Mechanistic* type, or types that have characteristics of earlier *serif typefaces*, yet have details that offer a taste of more robust *slab serif typefaces* like Clarendon. Due to its solid form and low *contrast* in strokes, this type is suitable for setting longer texts. It was long used as a *typeface* in *newspapers*.

2. Clarendon, 1953
Hermann Eidenbenz – www.linotype.com
www.elsner-flake.com
This *typeface* with its *slab serifs* and low *contrast* represents the industrial era of the mid-19th century perfectly.
The original type was drawn in 1845 by Benjamin Fox.
Its robustness makes it an expressive *headline typeface*.
Clarendon Light is more appropriate for use at small sizes.

3. ITC Lubalin Graph, 1974
Herb Lubalin, Helga Jörgenson – www.itcfonts.com
The main characteristics of this *typeface* are the *x-height* and its fundamental geometric shape. Herb Lubalin based this *typeface* on its predecessor Avant Garde.
It is hard to read because of the tight *kerning* and similarities in letterforms. Using it as a *bread-and-butter typeface* is rather risky.

1

Intermediary
Intermediary
Intermediary
Intermediary

abcdefghijklmnopqrstuvwxyz
ABCDEFGHIJKLMNOPQRSTUVWXYZ

Un texte est, évidemment, une succession de lettres groupées en mots. Comment donc la typographie, composant unique, ne pourrait-elle pas avoir une incidence sur la perception d'un texte ? Pourquoi d'ailleurs existerait-il autant de caractères différents, si leurs formes n'avaient aucune importance ?

7/9 pt

Il est vrai que la structure quasi immuable des lettres de l'alphabet semble laisser bien peu de possibilités d'interprétation au dessinateur de caractères. De toute manière, comment les spécificités d'une typographie, aussi remarquables soient-elles, pourraient-elles être perceptibles sur quelques millimètres de hauteur, et changer l'appréciation d'un texte, alors que le lecteur n'y accorde, *a priori*, aucune importance ?

9/12 pt

2

Industrial
Industrial
Industrial

abcdefghijklmnopqrstuvwxyz
ABCDEFGHIJKLMNOPQRSTUVWXYZ

Un texte est, évidemment, une succession de lettres groupées en mots. Comment donc la typographie, composant unique, ne pourrait-elle pas avoir une incidence sur la perception d'un texte ? Pourquoi d'ailleurs existerait-il autant de caractères différents, si leurs formes n'avaient aucune importance ?

7/9 pt

Il est vrai que la structure quasi immuable des lettres de l'alphabet semble laisser bien peu de possibilités d'interprétation au dessinateur de caractères. De toute manière, comment les spécificités d'une typographie, aussi remarquables soient-elles, pourraient-elles être perceptibles sur quelques millimètres de hauteur, et changer l'appréciation d'un texte, alors que le lecteur n'y accorde, a priori, aucune importance ?

9/12 pt

3

ai

Geometric
Geometric
Geometric
Geometric

abcdefghijklmnopqrstuvwxyz
ABCDEFGHIJKLMNOPQRSTUVWXYZ

Un texte est, évidemment, une succession de lettres groupées en mots. Comment donc la typographie, composant unique, ne pourrait-elle pas avoir une incidence sur la perception d'un texte ? Pourquoi d'ailleurs existerait-il autant de caractères différents, si leurs formes n'avaient aucune importance ?

7/9,5 pt

Il est vrai que la structure quasi immuable des lettres de l'alphabet semble laisser bien peu de possibilités d'interprétation au dessinateur de caractères. De toute manière, comment les spécificités d'une typographie, aussi remarquables soient-elles, pourraient-elles être perceptibles sur quelques millimètres de hauteur, et changer l'appréciation d'un texte, alors que le lecteur n'y accorde, *a priori*, aucune importance ?

8,5/12 pt

All three *typefaces* shown on this *page* are based on typewriter types. Some are monospace (that means all characters, like the i and the m, have the same width), others are proportional in width.

4. Pica 10 Pitch, 1980
IBM – www.bitstream.com/fonts
This *typeface* is based on the IBM ball typewriter, where one could easily change the typeface. It is a monospaced *typeface* with a single stroke *weight* that is appreciated for its particularly light gray *color* and "low-tech" look.

5. American Typewriter, 1974
Joel Kaden, Tony Stan – www.itcfonts.com
Despite the proportional or varied width of the letterforms, this *typeface* reminds one of mechanical typewriting. Its unique personality comes from the rounded letters and *serifs* that sometimes make it harder to set. It is a typical product of the 1970s and was originally designed as a *headline typeface*.

6. Courier, 1955
Howard Kettler – www.linotype.com
www.adobe.com/type
Courier is a monospaced *typeface* designed for IBM. Its shapes are more severe than Pica 10 Pitch (compare for example the a and c). The *gray value* that this *typeface* creates is very unique and not suitable for longer texts. It is not usable at smaller sizes since it is so delicate.

4

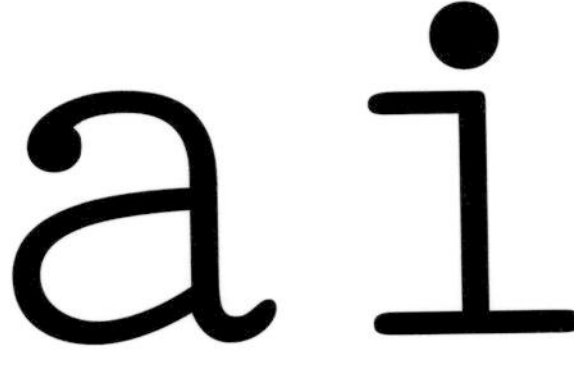

Authentic

abcdefghijklmnopqrstuvwxyz
ABCDEFGHIJKLMNOPQRSTUVWXYZ

Un texte est, évidemment, une succession de lettres groupées en mots. Comment donc la typographie, composant unique, ne pourrait-elle pas avoir une incidence sur la perception d'un texte? Pourquoi d'ailleurs existerait-il autant de caractères différents, si leurs formes n'avaient aucune importance?

7/9 pt

Il est vrai que la structure quasi immuable des lettres de l'alphabet semble laisser bien peu de possibilités d'interprétation au dessinateur de caractères. De toute manière, comment les spécificités d'une typographie, aussi remarquables soient-elles, pourraient-elles être perceptibles sur quelques millimètres de hauteur, et changer l'appréciation d'un texte, alors que le lecteur n'y accorde, a priori, aucune importance?

8,5/12 pt

5

Fancy
Fancy
Fancy

abcdefghijklmnopqrstuvwxyz
ABCDEFGHIJKLMNOPQRSTUVWXYZ

Un texte est, évidemment, une succession de lettres groupées en mots. Comment donc la typographie, composant unique, ne pourrait-elle pas avoir une incidence sur la perception d'un texte? Pourquoi d'ailleurs existerait-il autant de caractères différents, si leurs formes n'avaient aucune importance?

7/9 pt

Il est vrai que la structure quasi immuable des lettres de l'alphabet semble laisser bien peu de possibilités d'interprétation au dessinateur de caractères. De toute manière, comment les spécificités d'une typographie, aussi remarquables soient-elles, pourraient-elles être perceptibles sur quelques millimètres de hauteur, et changer l'appréciation d'un texte, alors que le lecteur n'y accorde, a priori, aucune importance?

9/12 pt

6

Modern *Modern*
Modern

abcdefghijklmnopqrstuvwxyz
ABCDEFGHIJKLMNOPQRSTUVWXYZ

Un texte est, évidemment, une succession de lettres groupées en mots. Comment donc la typographie, composant unique, ne pourrait-elle pas avoir une incidence sur la perception d'un texte?

7/9 pt

Il est vrai que la structure quasi immuable des lettres de l'alphabet semble laisser bien peu de possibilités d'interprétation au dessinateur de caractères. De toute manière, comment les spécificités d'une typographie, aussi remarquables soient-elles, pourraient-elles être perceptibles sur quelques millimètres de hauteur, et changer l'appréciation…

9/12 pt

The *typefaces* presented on this double-page spread belong to the *Lineal* classification and illustrate its wide range. They originated at the end of the 19th century (so-called grotesques) and formed the basis for numerous typographic experiments (*New Typography*, Swiss and French *typography* of the 50s and 60s, etc.)

1. Futura, 1926
Paul Renner – www.adobe.com/type, www.linotype.com
Although their creator was not a member of the Bauhaus, Futura is the archetype of the geometric types based on the Bauhaus theory and *typefaces* of *the New Typography* by *Jan Tschichold* (functionalism, combination of basic forms). The minor differentiation between letterforms limits its readability especially at smaller sizes.

The accentuated *ascenders* and *descenders* weaken the resulting *gray value*'s density. This is, however, what sets it apart from many other *Lineals*.

2. Grotesque MT, 1926
Morris Fuller Benton – www.fonts.com
This *typeface* is inspired by the "grotesque" *typefaces* developed at the end of the 19th century. It has their robustness, the careful design and large *x-height*. The Monotype Grotesque is one of the first *sans serif typefaces* designed for the Monotype – a *typesetting* machine where the letters are cast one by one in lead directly from a matrix (negative form). This *typeface* works well for setting longer texts and especially the bolder and condensed styles work well for *headlines*.

3. Gill Sans, 1929
Eric Gill – www.adobe.com/type, www.linotype.com
Directly inspired by the London Railway *typeface* by Edward Johnston, the *typeface* Gill was commissioned by Monotype's typographic consultant Stanley Morison. This member of the *Lineal* classification is more closely related to the *Humanist* group than the *sans serif typefaces* drawn at the end of the 19th century – Gill is often chosen to represent the Humanist subgroup when detailing the *Lineals*. It is completely different from Futura which was designed at the same time.
Gill takes its shape from the designer's observations of historical *typefaces* and how their legibility works. The result is a *font* with a small *x-height*, strongly differentiated letterforms and *uppercase* letters that are very similar to the *roman capitals*.

1

ai

Geometric
Geometric
Geometric
Geometric
Geometric

abcdefghijklmnopqrstuvwxyz
ABCDEFGHIJKLMNOPQRSTUVWXYZ

Un texte est, évidemment, une succession de lettres groupées en mots. Comment donc la typographie, composant unique, ne pourrait-elle pas avoir une incidence sur la perception d'un texte ? Pourquoi d'ailleurs existerait-il autant de caractères différents, si leurs formes n'avaient aucune importance ?

7/9 pt

Il est vrai que la structure quasi immuable des lettres de l'alphabet semble laisser bien peu de possibilités d'interprétation au dessinateur de caractères. De toute manière, comment les spécificités d'une typographie, aussi remarquables soient-elles, pourraient-elles être perceptibles sur quelques millimètres de hauteur, et changer l'appréciation d'un texte, alors que le lecteur n'y accorde, *a priori*, aucune importance ?

9/12 pt

2

Grotesk *Grotesk*
Grotesk
Grotesk

abcdefghijklmnopqrstuvwxyz
ABCDEFGHIJKLMNOPQRSTUVWXYZ

Un texte est, évidemment, une succession de lettres groupées en mots. Comment donc la typographie, composant unique, ne pourrait-elle pas avoir une incidence sur la perception d'un texte ? Pourquoi d'ailleurs existerait-il autant de caractères différents, si leurs formes n'avaient aucune importance ?

7/9 pt

Il est vrai que la structure quasi immuable des lettres de l'alphabet semble laisser bien peu de possibilités d'interprétation au dessinateur de caractères. De toute manière, comment les spécificités d'une typographie, aussi remarquables soient-elles, pourraient-elles être perceptibles sur quelques millimètres de hauteur, et changer l'appréciation d'un texte, alors que le lecteur n'y accorde, a priori, aucune importance ?

9/12 pt

3

ai

Humanist *Humanist*
Humanist *Humanist*
Humanist
Humanist
Humanist

abcdefghijklmnopqrstuvwxyz
ABCDEFGHIJKLMNOPQRSTUVWXYZ

Un texte est, évidemment, une succession de lettres groupées en mots. Comment donc la typographie, composant unique, ne pourrait-elle pas avoir une incidence sur la perception d'un texte ? Pourquoi d'ailleurs existerait-il autant de caractères différents, si leurs formes n'avaient aucune importance ?

7/9 pt

Il est vrai que la structure quasi immuable des lettres de l'alphabet semble laisser bien peu de possibilités d'interprétation au dessinateur de caractères. De toute manière, comment les spécificités d'une typographie, aussi remarquables soient-elles, pourraient-elles être perceptibles sur quelques millimètres de hauteur, et changer l'appréciation d'un texte, alors que le lecteur n'y accorde, *a priori*, aucune importance ?

9/11 pt

4. Helvetica, 1957
Max Miedinger – www.linotype.com
Max Miedinger, type designer at the Haas type foundry, modernized the Haas Grotesk typeface, and the New Haas Grotesk was born. But it wasn't until 1961, when the Stempel type foundry released the *typeface* under the name Helvetica, that it reached the success that it enjoys to this day.
Helvetica's neutrality corresponds perfectly to the Swiss style of the 50s and 60s: functional, clear, international. It is often used, which makes this *typeface* sometimes appear commonplace. However, its frequent use shows us how readable it is. Many *weights* and styles were added in the years that followed.

5. Antique Olive, 1963
Roger Excofon – www.adobe.com/type
This *typeface* is the "French" answer to the Swiss *typeface* Helvetica which was enormously popular at the time. It is based on the nine letters in the Air France logotype designed by Roger Excoffon. It is recognized by the large *x-height*, very short *ascenders* and *descenders*, as well as the "swelling" at the top of the *lowercase letters*. The unusual letterforms, the proportions and the pronounced *counters* all give texts set in this *typeface* a unique flavor.

6. Vista Sans and Vista Sans Alternate, 2004
Xavier Dupré – www.emigre.com
This recently designed *typeface* proves that the creative force in *typography* persists despite a multitude of *fonts*. Some of the details remind one of the attention Eric Gill paid to the differentiation of the letterforms for better legibility. This did not prevent the designer from creating an "alternate" version (compare the differences in the *capital* letters). This *typeface* also exists in a slanted style (classic version) and as a true cursive ("alternate" version).

4

Neutrality *Neutrality*
Neutrality *Neutrality*

abcdefghijklmnopqrstuvwxyz
ABCDEFGHIJKLMNOPQRSTUVWXYZ

Un texte est, évidemment, une succession de lettres groupées en mots. Comment donc la typographie, composant unique, ne pourrait-elle pas avoir une incidence sur la perception d'un texte? Pourquoi d'ailleurs existerait-il autant de caractères différents, si leurs formes n'avaient aucune importance?

7/9 pt

Il est vrai que la structure quasi immuable des lettres de l'alphabet semble laisser bien peu de possibilités d'interprétation au dessinateur de caractères. De toute manière, comment les spécificités d'une typographie, aussi remarquables soient-elles, pourraient-elles être perceptibles sur quelques millimètres de hauteur, et changer l'appréciation d'un texte, alors que le lecteur n'y accorde, *a priori*, aucune importance?

9/12 pt

5

ai

Srange *Strange*
Strange
Strange

abcdefghijklmnopqrstuvwxyz
ABCDEFGHIJKLMNOPQRSTUVWXYZ

Un texte est, évidemment, une succession de lettres groupées en mots. Comment donc la typographie, composant unique, ne pourrait-elle pas avoir une incidence sur la perception d'un texte?
Pourquoi d'ailleurs existerait-il autant de caractères différents, si leurs formes n'avaient aucune importance?

6,5/9,5 pt

Il est vrai que la structure quasi immuable des lettres de l'alphabet semble laisser bien peu de possibilités d'interprétation au dessinateur de caractères. De toute manière, comment les spécificités d'une typographie, aussi remarquables soient-elles, pourraient-elles être perceptibles sur quelques millimètres de hauteur, et changer l'appréciation d'un texte, alors que le lecteur n'y accorde, *a priori*, aucune importance?

8,5/12 pt

6

ai

Inspiration *Inspiration*
Inspiration *Inspiration*
Inspiration *Inspiration*
Inspiration *Inspiration*

Vista Sans

abcdefghijklmnopqrstuvwxyz
ABCDEFGHIJKLMNOPQRSTUVWXYZ

Vista Sans Alternate

abcdefghijklmnopqrstuvwxyz
ABCDEFGHIJKLMNOPQRSTUVWXYZ

Un texte est, évidemment, une succession de lettres groupées en mots. Comment donc la typographie, composant unique, ne pourrait-elle pas avoir une incidence sur la perception d'un texte? Pourquoi d'ailleurs existerait-il autant de caractères différents, si leurs formes n'avaient aucune importance?

6,5/9 pt

Il est vrai que la structure quasi immuable des lettres de l'alphabet semble laisser bien peu de possibilités d'interprétation au dessinateur de caractères. De toute manière, comment les spécificités d'une typographie, aussi remarquables soient-elles, pourraient-elles être perceptibles sur quelques millimètres de hauteur, et changer l'appréciation d'un texte, alors que le lecteur n'y accorde, *a priori*, aucune importance?

8,5/11 pt

A *typeface* is available in different styles that range from *hairline* to ultra *bold*, not to mention the *italics*.
The differences in *rhythm* and *color* that these styles create can enrich a text or a page. Bear in mind that the styles should make reading easier rather than harder!

Italic

The use of *italics* allows one to emphasize a word or an idea – through a slight change in *rhythm* – within a text set in *roman*. One should note that the letters will often have different shapes (for example the letter "a"). In the case of an inclined *roman* typeface, the *italics* are often more slanted.

Bold

The "blacker" letters in the *bold type style* contrast with the *regular weight*. Larger or smaller differences in stroke thickness can be used to emphasize a word in a text or one text as compared to a second neighboring one. The higher the *contrast*, the higher the emphasis.

Typographic rules

While the use and juxtaposition of different type *weights* is up to everyone's own judgement, the use of *italics* is governed by typographic rules.

Nuances
Nuances

Contrasts
Contrasts
Contrasts

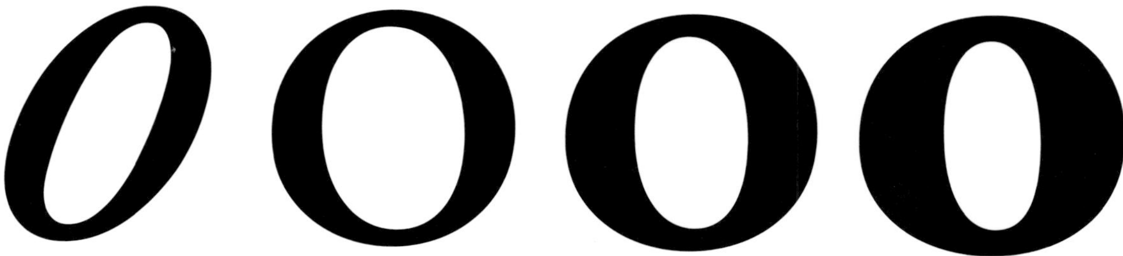

Adobe Garamond *italic* Adobe Garamond *roman* Adobe Garamond semibold Adobe Garamond *bold*

Chaque caractère est conçu pour une utilisation «idéale», définie par de très nombreuses variables. Corps, espacement des lettres, justification, interlignage sont quelques-uns des paramètres que le dessinateur prend en considération au cours de son travail. Le maquettiste averti peut alors utiliser cette «expressivité» des caractères pour servir son travail. Il lui suffit déjà de choisir le caractère adapté, de régler les paramètres typographiques de manière judicieuse, pour que le texte typographié prenne une autre dimension. Il peut en effet agir sur chaque paramètre pour accentuer un aspect du caractère, ou au contraire en atténuer un autre, de manière à correspondre parfaitement à l'utilisation qu'il en fait.

Un texte est, cela est évident, une succession de *lettres* groupées en *mots*. Comment donc la *typographie*, composant unique, ne pourrait-elle pas avoir une incidence sur la perception d'un texte? Pourquoi d'ailleurs existerait-il autant de *caractères* différents, si leurs formes n'avaient aucune importance? Pourtant, **beaucoup pensent que la typographie ne peut avoir un rôle significatif.** Il est vrai que la structure quasi immuable des lettres de l'*alphabet* semble laisser bien peu de possibilités d'interprétation au dessinateur de caractères. De toute manière, comment les spécificités d'une typographie, aussi remarquables soient-elles, pourraient-elles être perceptibles sur quelques millimètres de hauteur, et changer l'appréciation d'un texte, alors que le lecteur n'y accorde, *a priori*, aucune importance?

*Ces arguments semblent irréfutables.
Pourtant des études ont montré
que les lecteurs remarquent, et apprécient
bel et bien, une correspondance de style
entre un caractère et un texte;
un caractère leur semble mieux convenir
pour une utilisation qu'un autre.*
Les caractères *ont donc un style, soit,
mais est-il alors possible de le déterminer
avec précision, ou cela se limite-t-il
à une vague impression au moment
de la lecture? Comme l'écriture
manuscrite peut faire l'objet d'études
graphologiques et aboutir
à des conclusions claires,* la typographie
*peut être analysée selon des critères
précis.*

Typography
Column width

The number of characters (character count) per line determines the readability and *reading rhythm*:

1. Narrow columns
Only possible with short texts set *flush left* ragged right. The *column width* is based on the longest words, and the line breaks are left to chance.

2. 30 characters per line
The "jerky" *rhythm* favors quick reading. Justified *columns* below this measure are difficult to set without multiple *hyphenations* and *rivers* of white.

3. 55 to 65 characters per line
This *column width* allows relaxed reading. The lines are neither too long nor too short.

4. 80 to 90 characters per line
The eye works harder to read. This *line length* is unsuitable for longer texts. Generous *leading* can increase readability (see page 69).

Several parameters must be considered when defining the *column width*:

The text
With a *flush left* ragged right setting the line breaks can be chosen according to the text's syntax.

The typeface
The *body width* of the *typeface* influences the *column width*.
5. Univers 55, *type size* 9 pt, *column width* 92 mm.
6. Rotis SansSerif, *type size* 10 pt, *column width* 85 mm.

The leading
Adjusting the *leading* depending on the *typeface* and *column width* can greatly affect the *reading rhythm* (see pages 68–69).

1 La présentation des documents est primordiale pour donner envie de lire. Elle peut éviter que certains y trouvent une raison de ne pas s'y intéresser,

2 La présentation des documents est primordiale pour donner envie de lire. Elle peut éviter que certains y trouvent une raison de ne pas s'y intéresser, peut-être même arrivera-t-elle à leur donner le sentiment que la lecture n'est pas aussi pénible qu'ils l'imaginaient. Pour d'autres, les passionnés, elle confirme que la lecture est un plaisir. Comment en effet encourager celui qui n'« aime pas » lire à le faire si, visiblement, aucun effort n'a été fait pour lui rendre un texte plus agréable ? Si le texte lui semble clair, s'il lui est facile de saisir rapidement sa structure et son contenu, en repérant les différents niveaux de lecture, il aura nécessairement moins de peine à y rentrer.

2 La présentation des documents est primordiale pour donner envie de lire. Elle peut éviter que certains y trouvent une raison de ne pas s'y intéresser, peut-être même arrivera-t-elle à leur donner le sentiment que la lecture n'est pas aussi pénible qu'ils l'imaginaient. Pour d'autres, les passionnés, elle confirme que la lecture est un plaisir. Comment en effet encourager celui qui n'« aime pas » lire à le faire si, visiblement, aucun effort n'a été fait pour lui rendre un texte plus agréable ? Si le texte lui paraît clair, s'il lui est facile de prendre rapidement connaissance de sa structure et de son contenu, en repérant les différents niveaux de lecture, il aura nécessairement moins de peine à y rentrer. Les passionnés, eux aussi, aiment à voir que l'on a pris soin de rendre

3 La présentation des documents est primordiale pour donner envie de lire. Elle peut éviter que certains y trouvent une raison de ne pas s'y intéresser, peut-être même arrivera-t-elle à leur donner le sentiment que la lecture n'est pas aussi pénible qu'ils l'imaginaient. Pour d'autres, les passionnés, elle confirme que la lecture est un plaisir. Comment en effet encourager celui qui n'« aime pas » lire à le faire si, visiblement, aucun effort n'a été fait pour lui rendre un texte plus agréable ? Si le texte lui paraît clair, s'il lui est facile de prendre rapidement connaissance de sa structure et de son contenu,

4 La présentation des documents est primordiale pour donner envie de lire. Elle peut éviter que certains y trouvent une raison de ne pas s'y intéresser, peut-être même arrivera-t-elle à leur donner le sentiment que la lecture n'est pas aussi pénible qu'ils l'imaginaient. Pour d'autres, les passionnés, elle confirme que la lecture est un plaisir. Comment en effet encourager celui qui n'« aime pas » lire à le faire si, visiblement, aucun effort n'a été fait pour lui rendre un texte plus agréable ? Si le texte lui paraît clair, s'il lui est facile de prendre rapidement connaissance de sa structure et de son contenu, en repérant les différents niveaux de lecture, il aura nécessairement moins de peine à y rentrer. Les passionnés, eux aussi, aiment voir que l'on a pris soin de rendre agréable un texte, surtout s'il s'agit d'un ouvrage qu'ils apprécient particulièrement.

5 La présentation des documents est primordiale pour donner envie de lire. Elle peut éviter que certains y trouvent une raison de ne pas s'y intéresser, peut-être même arrivera-t-elle à leur donner le sentiment que la lecture n'est pas aussi pénible qu'ils l'imaginaient.
Pour d'autres, les passionnés, elle confirme que la lecture est un plaisir. Comment en effet encourager celui qui n'« aime pas » lire à le faire si, visiblement, aucun effort n'a été fait pour lui rendre un texte plus agréable ?
Si le texte lui paraît clair, s'il lui est facile de prendre rapidement connaissance de sa structure et de son contenu, en repérant les différents niveaux de lecture, il aura nécessairement moins de peine à y rentrer. Les passionnés, eux aussi, aiment voir que l'on a pris soin de rendre agréable un texte, surtout s'il s'agit d'un ouvrage qu'ils apprécient particulièrement.

6 La présentation des documents est primordiale pour donner envie de lire. Elle peut éviter que certains y trouvent une raison de ne pas s'y intéresser, peut-être même arrivera-t-elle à leur donner le sentiment que la lecture n'est pas aussi pénible qu'ils l'imaginaient.
Pour d'autres, les passionnés, elle confirme que la lecture est un plaisir. Comment en effet encourager celui qui n'« aime pas » lire à le faire si, visiblement, aucun effort n'a été fait pour lui rendre un texte plus agréable ?
Si le texte lui paraît clair, s'il lui est facile de prendre rapidement connaissance de sa structure et de son contenu, en repérant les différents niveaux de lecture, il aura nécessairement moins de peine à y rentrer. Les passionnés, eux aussi, aiment à voir que l'on a pris soin de rendre agréable un texte, surtout s'il s'agit d'un ouvrage qu'ils apprécient particulièrement.

Typography
Ragged settings

The white space of the *page* emphasizes the shape of the text. This shape is one of many *graphic elements* that give the reader a first impression before they begin to read. A poorly set text can be discouraging. There are several types of text alignment, and one should know the advantages and disadvantages of each in order to use them appropriately.

Ragged, unjustified type

1. Text set flush left
Reading is easy because the eyes, when they jump to the next line, orient themselves along the left vertical axis.
2. Centered text
The uneven left edge of the text makes reading more difficult.
3. Text set flush right
Reading is slowed down, because with each new line the eye has to find the starting point anew.

Text silhouette
If one wants to have balanced line breaks, then manual interventions are needed in a longer text. This is the *hand-corrected setting*. In theory a *ragged setting* – with its uneven *line length* – requires no *hyphenations*. *Hyphenations* give a *text silhouette* an anonymous feel. Yet with a narrow *column* no *hyphenations* lead to a very uneven right edge, which disturbs the reader with longer texts. The *text silhouette* changes depending on how "ragged" the edge is:
a. moderate *silhouette*
b. accentuated *silhouette*
A text is more understandable if prepositions, pronouns, etc. are at the beginning of a line. In other words, by not separating parts of a sentence that are connected by syntax.

1 Malgré toute l'importance que peuvent avoir la typographie
et la manière de l'utiliser pour présenter un texte, il ne faut
pas oublier le paramètre qui se trouve au début du processus
de lecture et qui, par conséquent, décide de l'ensemble :
le lecteur lui-même. Nous savons qu'il peut revêtir des visages
différents, avoir des centres d'intérêt opposés… Nous savons
aussi qu'il sera bien souvent peu motivé à entreprendre
la lecture et qu'il faudra d'abord le séduire. Même un lecteur
passionné peut ne pas être bien disposé au moment où
le texte est sous ses yeux. La typographie ne peut conduire
le lecteur à faire ce qu'il n'a pas envie. Heureusement, il garde
l'autonomie de décider ce qu'il lira !

2 Malgré toute l'importance que peuvent avoir la typographie
et la manière de l'utiliser pour présenter un texte,
il ne faut pas oublier le paramètre qui se trouve au début
du processus de lecture et qui, par conséquent, décide
de l'ensemble : le lecteur lui-même. Nous savons
qu'il peut revêtir des visages différents, avoir des centres
d'intérêt opposés… Nous savons aussi qu'il sera bien souvent
peu motivé à entreprendre la lecture et qu'il faudra d'abord
le séduire. Même un lecteur passionné peut ne pas
être bien disposé au moment où le texte est sous ses yeux.
La typographie ne peut conduire le lecteur à faire ce qu'il
n'a pas envie. Heureusement, il garde l'autonomie
de décider ce qu'il lira !

3 Malgré toute l'importance que peuvent avoir la typographie
et la manière de l'utiliser pour présenter un texte, il ne faut
pas oublier le paramètre qui se trouve au début du processus
de lecture et qui, par conséquent, décide de l'ensemble : le
lecteur lui-même. Nous savons qu'il peut revêtir des visages
différents, avoir des centres d'intérêt opposés… Nous savons
aussi qu'il sera bien souvent peu motivé à entreprendre
la lecture et qu'il faudra d'abord le séduire. Même un lecteur
passionné peut ne pas être bien disposé au moment où
le texte est sous ses yeux. La typographie ne peut conduire
le lecteur à faire ce qu'il n'a pas envie. Heureusement, il garde
l'autonomie de décider ce qu'il lira !

a. *Hand-corrected setting*,
without *hyphenations*, moderate *silhouette*.

Malgré toute l'importance que peuvent avoir la typographie
et la manière de l'utiliser pour présenter un texte,
il ne faut surtout pas oublier le paramètre qui se trouve
au début du processus de lecture et qui, par conséquent,
décide de l'ensemble : le lecteur lui-même.
Nous savons qu'il peut revêtir des visages différents,
avoir des centres d'intérêt opposés…
Nous savons aussi qu'il sera bien souvent peu motivé
à entreprendre la lecture et qu'il faudra d'abord le séduire.
Même un lecteur passionné peut ne pas être bien disposé
au moment où le texte est sous ses yeux.
La typographie ne peut conduire le lecteur à faire
ce qu'il n'a pas envie. Heureusement, il garde l'autonomie
de décider ce qu'il lira !

Malgré toute l'importance que peuvent avoir la typographie
et la manière de l'utiliser pour présenter un texte,
il ne faut surtout pas oublier le paramètre qui se trouve
au début du processus de lecture et qui, par conséquent,
décide de l'ensemble : le lecteur lui-même.
Nous savons qu'il peut revêtir des visages différents,
avoir des centres d'intérêt opposés…
Nous savons aussi qu'il sera bien souvent peu motivé
à entreprendre la lecture et qu'il faudra d'abord le séduire.
Même un lecteur passionné peut ne pas être bien disposé
au moment où le texte est sous ses yeux.
La typographie ne peut conduire le lecteur à faire
ce qu'il n'a pas envie. Heureusement, il garde l'autonomie
de décider ce qu'il lira !

Malgré toute l'importance que peuvent avoir la typographie
et la manière de l'utiliser pour présenter un texte,
il ne faut surtout pas oublier le paramètre qui se trouve
au début du processus de lecture et qui, par conséquent,
décide de l'ensemble : le lecteur lui-même.
Nous savons qu'il peut revêtir des visages différents,
avoir des centres d'intérêt opposés…
Nous savons aussi qu'il sera bien souvent peu motivé
à entreprendre la lecture et qu'il faudra d'abord le séduire.
Même un lecteur passionné peut ne pas être bien disposé
au moment où le texte est sous ses yeux.
La typographie ne peut conduire le lecteur à faire
ce qu'il n'a pas envie. Heureusement, il garde l'autonomie
de décider ce qu'il lira !

b. *Ragged setting* (hard rag),
without *hyphenations*, accentuated *silhouette*.

Typography
Justified type

Although it is simple to set a justified text the result is often disappointing. The space between letters is sometimes so different that the eyes have trouble following the lines. *Letterspacing* and *word spacing* should not be too large if the lines are to remain coherent. A uniform *gray value* in *justified type* depends on the following factors:

Hyphenations
These ensure evenly spaced lines of text.

Letterspacing and word spacing
The justification of the lines of text is achieved by modifying the *letterspacing* and *word spacing*. Both must be considered in unison. The correct relationship between the two ensures a regular *rhythm* and hence an optimal readability.

A few points to remember:
4–5. Increasing the *letterspacing* should not be noticed by the reader, and change the *rhythm* of the lines.
6–7. Word spaces can be reduced up to 75 percent without effecting readability.

Hyphenation and justification
When *justifying* a line of text, one adjusts the parameters of *hyphenation* and justification. It is preferable not to make the *letterspacing* too tight, and to loosen it only slightly. The *word spacing* can be set between a range of 75 percent and 125 percent of the original value.

Case for case
All of these methods are not systematic, instead, they have to be adapted to each specific case (*line length*, typeface, *type size*, etc.).
Changing the *word spacing* doesn't affect the line density as strongly as changing the *letterspacing*, which quickly makes a line too dark or too light.

Column width and type size
The *column width* depends on the *type size* and number of characters per line.

La présentation de ce texte convient-elle ? Correspond-elle à ce que le lecteur attend ? Le lecteur est habitué à une certaine présentation pour chaque type de document ; il souhaite (cela semble logique) qu'un journal ressemble à un journal, une revue à une revue ou un prospectus à un prospectus ! Chaque fois qu'il prend connaissance d'un document, il le « juge » et cherche à retrouver les schémas qui lui sont familiers. Cette analyse est souvent inconsciente : le lecteur ressent seulement un sentiment – positif ou négatif – à l'égard du document ; il n'aura que rarement un avis clair. Mais l'existence de ces modèles dans la mémoire du lecteur fait qu'il a de la peine à cautionner une tentative qui remet en cause ses habitudes et constitue une véritable barrière que le maquettiste connaît et cherche toujours à surmonter.

4 ris clair. Mais l'existenc

5 ont qu'il a de la peine

6 ses habitudes et consti

7 onnaît et cherche touj

Leading in a text is an effective way to change how it looks. One can create a typographic *gray value* that is lighter or darker, and either create a linear impression or one of a *surface*.

Balance
A text is readable when our gaze wanders freely and naturally from one line to the next, or when the lines of text and the *line spacing* are in balance.

Leading
Leading is the distance between the *baseline* of one line and the *baseline* of the next line of text (see the blue lines). It should not be confused with the space between the *descenders* of one line and the *ascenders* of the next (*line spacing*). The examples on this *page* illustrate how typographic parameters like typeface, *type size* and *line length* effect choices in *leading*.

1. The typeface's importance
There is no exact relationship between *type size* and *leading* that is applicable to all *typefaces*. A typeface's proportions – *x-height*, *ascenders* and *descenders*, width, *rhythm*, etc. – all directly effect how a text appears (see pages 54–55)

- At the same *leading* a *typeface* with a larger *x-height* seems more compact than one with a smaller *x-height*.
- The length of the *ascenders* and *descenders* effect a text's appearance, because they occupy the white space that the eye uses to find its way back to the beginning of the next line. If they get too close reading slows down.
- Width, stroke width and the *counter's* size all define the *contrast* between the line of type and the white space between the lines, and thus effecting choices in *leading*.

Type size 10 pt, *leading* 12 pt

La présentation des documents est primordiale pour donner envie de lire. Elle peut éviter que certains y trouvent une raison de ne pas s'y intéresser, peut-être même arrivera-t-elle à leur donner le sentiment que la lecture n'est pas aussi pénible qu'ils l'imaginaient. Comment en effet décider celui qui n'« aime pas » lire à le faire si, visiblement, aucun effort n'a été fait pour lui rendre le texte qui est sous ses yeux plus agréable ? Si le texte lui apparaît clair, c'est-à-dire s'il lui est facile de prendre très rapidement connaissance de sa structure et de son contenu, en repérant les différents niveaux de lecture, il aura nécessairement moins de peine à y rentrer et à le lire.

fet décide
re si visib
pour lui re

Type size 10 pt, *leading* 16 pt

La présentation des documents est primordiale pour donner envie de lire. Elle peut éviter que certains y trouvent une raison de ne pas s'y intéresser, peut-être même arrivera-t-elle à leur donner le sentiment que la lecture n'est pas aussi pénible qu'ils l'imaginaient. Comment en effet décider celui qui n'« aime pas » lire à le faire si, visiblement, aucun effort n'a été fait pour lui rendre le texte qui est sous ses yeux plus agréable ? Si le texte lui apparaît clair, c'est-à-dire s'il lui est facile de prendre très rapidement connaissance de sa structure et de son contenu, en repérant les différents niveaux de lecture, il aura nécessairement moins de peine à y rentrer et à le lire.

fet décide
re si visib
pour lui re

Type size 10 pt, *leading* 20 pt

La présentation des documents est primordiale pour donner envie de lire. Elle peut éviter que certains y trouvent une raison de ne pas s'y intéresser, peut-être même arrivera-t-elle à leur donner le sentiment que la lecture n'est pas aussi pénible qu'ils l'imaginaient. Comment en effet décider celui qui n'« aime pas » lire à le faire si, visiblement, aucun effort n'a été fait pour lui rendre le texte qui est sous ses yeux plus agréable ? Si le texte lui apparaît clair, c'est-à-dire s'il lui est facile de prendre très rapidement connaissance de sa structure et de son contenu, en repérant les différents niveaux de lecture, il aura nécessairement moins de peine à y rentrer et à le lire.

fet décide
re si visib

2. The relationship between column width and leading
The longer a line is the more difficult it is to follow it with our eyes, and sometimes our gaze "slips" into the line below. One improves readability by increasing the *leading* in texts with a long *line length*.

3. Effects on the text silhouette
The irregular *line length* of a *ragged typesetting* creates a dynamic *rhythm*, but can be tiresome with a longer text. By increasing the *leading* one softens this effect, because the white space between the lines lets them "breathe" better.

Adobe Garamond *type size* 9 pt, *leading* 11 pt

1 La présentation des documents est primordiale pour donner envie de lire. Elle peut éviter que certains y trouvent une raison de ne pas s'y intéresser, peut-être même arrivera-t-elle à leur donner le sentiment que la lecture n'est pas aussi pénible qu'ils l'imaginaient. Pour d'autres, les passionnés, elle confirme que la lecture est un plaisir. Comment en effet encourager celui qui n'« aime pas » lire à le faire si, visiblement, aucun effort n'a été fait pour lui rendre un texte plus agréable ?

Univers 55, *type size* 9 pt, *leading* 12.5 pt

La présentation des documents est primordiale pour donner envie de lire. Elle peut éviter que certains y trouvent une raison de ne pas s'y intéresser, peut-être même arrivera-t-elle à leur donner le sentiment que la lecture n'est pas aussi pénible qu'ils l'imaginaient. Pour d'autres, les passionnés, elle confirme que la lecture est un plaisir. Comment en effet encourager celui qui n'« aime pas » lire à le faire si, visiblement, aucun effort n'a été fait pour lui rendre un texte plus agréable ?

Gill Sans, *type size* 9 pt, *leading* 12 pt

La présentation des documents est primordiale pour donner envie de lire. Elle peut éviter que certains y trouvent une raison de ne pas s'y intéresser, peut-être même arrivera-t-elle à leur donner le sentiment que la lecture n'est pas aussi pénible qu'ils l'imaginaient. Pour d'autres, les passionnés, elle confirme que la lecture est un plaisir. Comment en effet encourager celui qui n'« aime pas » lire à le faire si, visiblement, aucun effort n'a été fait pour lui rendre un texte plus agréable ?

Adobe Garamond *type size* 9 pt, *leading* 11 pt

2 La présentation des documents est primordiale pour donner envie de lire. Elle peut éviter que certains y trouvent une raison de ne pas s'y intéresser, peut-être même arrivera-t-elle à leur donner le sentiment que la lecture n'est pas aussi pénible qu'ils l'imaginaient. Pour d'autres, les passionnés, elle confirme que la lecture est un plaisir. Comment en effet encourager celui qui n'« aime pas » lire à le faire si, visiblement, aucun effort n'a été fait pour lui rendre un texte plus agréable ? Si le texte lui paraît clair, s'il lui est facile de prendre rapidement connaissance de sa structure et de son contenu, en repérant les différents niveaux de lecture, il aura nécessairement moins de peine à y rentrer.

Adobe Garamond *type size* 9 pt, *leading* 13 pt

La présentation des documents est primordiale pour donner envie de lire. Elle peut éviter que certains y trouvent une raison de ne pas s'y intéresser, peut-être même arrivera-t-elle à leur donner le sentiment que la lecture n'est pas aussi pénible qu'ils l'imaginaient. Pour d'autres, les passionnés, elle confirme que la lecture est un plaisir. Comment en effet encourager celui qui n'« aime pas » lire à le faire si, visiblement, aucun effort n'a été fait pour lui rendre un texte plus agréable ? Si le texte lui paraît clair, s'il lui est facile de prendre rapidement connaissance de sa structure et de son contenu, en repérant les différents niveaux de lecture, il aura nécessairement moins de peine à y rentrer. Les passionnés, eux aussi, aiment à voir que l'on a pris soin de rendre agréable un texte, surtout s'il s'agit d'un ouvrage qu'ils apprécient particulièrement. Pour ce qui est des autres documents, même s'ils sont de moindre importance, un souci de présentation évitera qu'ils pensent que ce qui leur est proposé n'est vraiment pas intéressant à lire. Les lecteurs n'analysent pas un document, mais ils s'en font pourtant rapidement une idée sur sa présentation, avant même d'en avoir lu une seule ligne.

Adobe Garamond *type size* 9 pt, *leading* 12,5 pt

3 La présentation des documents est primordiale pour donner envie de lire. Elle peut éviter que certains y trouvent une raison de ne pas s'y intéresser, peut-être même arrivera-t-elle à leur donner le sentiment que la lecture n'est pas aussi pénible qu'ils l'imaginaient. Pour d'autres, les passionnés, elle confirme que la lecture est un plaisir. Comment en effet encourager celui qui n'« aime pas » lire à le faire si, visiblement, aucun effort n'a été fait pour lui rendre un texte plus agréable ? Si le texte lui paraît clair, s'il lui est facile de prendre rapidement connaissance de sa structure et de son contenu, en repérant les différents niveaux de lecture, il aura nécessairement moins de peine à y rentrer.

Typography
Typography as a unifying element

Typography can be a key feature. It can create a connection between multiple documents and become a "brand" for a firm or an organization that always uses the same typeface.

1. Type is the only design element used in these *posters*. Even though only one almost commonplace *typeface* was used, the *poster* series is still unique.

1. *Under construction*, posters
ETH Studio Basel / Kunsthalle Basel
The Remingtons, Ludovic Balland
and Jonas Voegeli

Typeface: Stanley-Reader
© Ludovic Balland

1

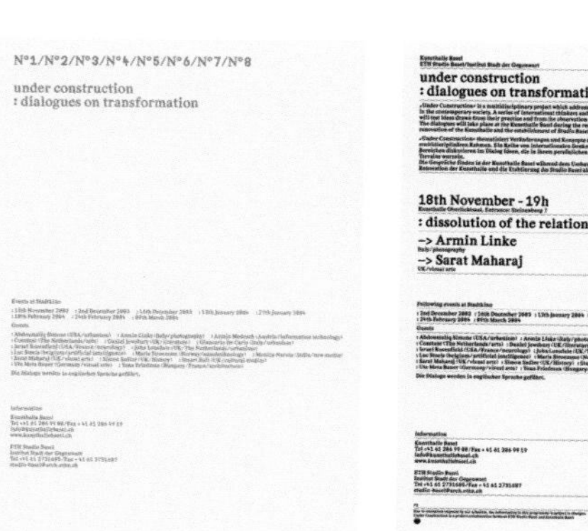

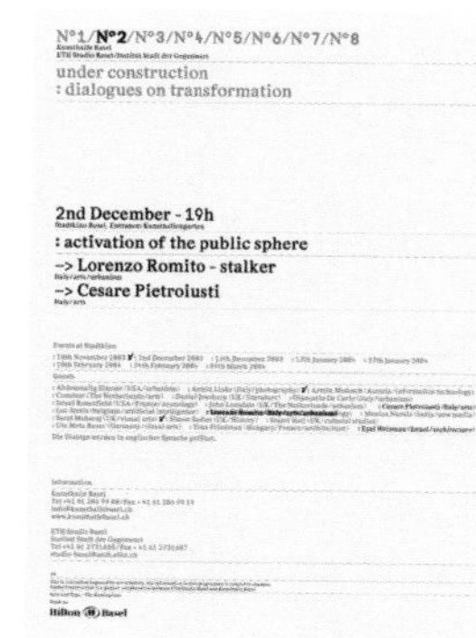

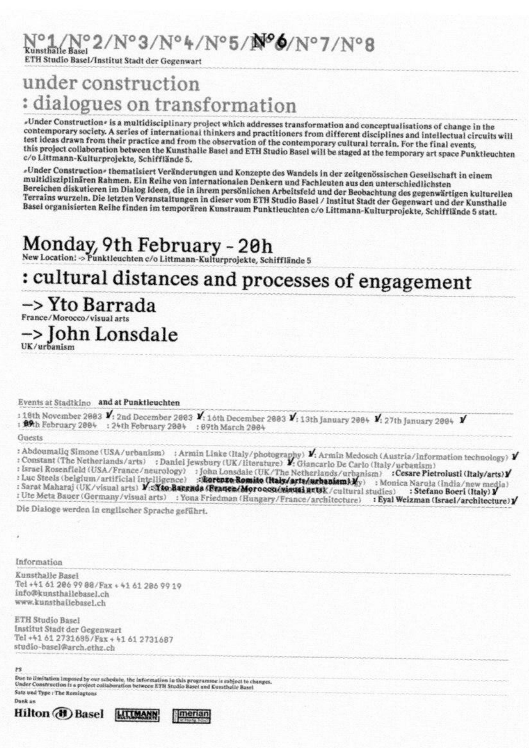

N°1/N°2/**N°3**/N°4/N°5/N°6/N°7/N°8
Kunsthalle Basel
ETH Studio Basel/Institut Stadt der Gegenwart

under construction
: dialogues on transformation

16th December - 19h
Stadtkino Basel, Entrance: Kunsthallengarten

: contemporary urban warfare and political architecture

-> Eyal Weizman
Israel/architecture

-> Daniel Jewsbury
Northern Ireland/literature

Events at Stadtkino
: 18th November 2003 : 2nd December 2003 : 16th December 2003 : 13th January 2004 : 27th January 2004
: 10th February 2004 : 24th February 2004 : 09th March 2004

Guests
: Abdoumaliq Simone (USA/urbanism) : Armin Linke (Italy/photography) : Armin Medosch (Austria/information technology)
: Constant (The Netherlands/arts) : Daniel Jewsbury (UK/literature) : Giancarlo De Carlo (Italy/urbanism)
: Israel Rosenfield (USA/France/neurology) : John Lonsdale (UK/The Netherlands/urbanism) : Cesare Pietroiusti (Italy/arts)
: Luc Steels (belgium/artificial intelligence) : Lorenzo Romito (Italy/arts/urbanism) ... : Monica Narula (India/new media)
: Sarat Maharaj (UK/visual arts) : Simon Sadler (UK/History) : Stuart Hall (UK/cultural studies)
: Ute Meta Bauer (Germany/visual arts) : Yona Friedman (Hungary/France/architecture) : Eyal Weizman (Israel/architecture)

Die Dialoge werden in englischer Sprache geführt.

Information
Kunsthalle Basel
Tel +41 61 206 99 00/Fax + 41 61 206 99 19
info@kunsthallebasel.ch
www.kunsthallebasel.ch

ETH Studio Basel
Institut Stadt der Gegenwart
Tel +41 61 2731685/Fax + 41 61 2731687
studio-basel@arch.ethz.ch

PS
Due to limitation imposed by our schedule, the information in this programme is subject to changes.
Under Construction is a project collaboration between ETH Studio Basel and Kunsthalle Basel
Satz und Type : The Remingtons
Dank an
Hilton Basel

N°1/N°2/N°3/N°4/N°5/N°6/**N°7**/N°8
Kunsthalle Basel, Architekturmuseum Basel
ETH Studio Basel/Institut Stadt der Gegenwart

under construction
: dialogues on transformation

9th March - 19h
New Location! -> Punktleuchten c/o Littmann-Kulturprojekte, Schifflände 5

: self-organisation and complex systems
Perception of the self & non-hierachical communities

-> Yona Friedman with an introduction by Ulrike Jehle
Hungary/France/architecture
-> Israel Rosenfield
France/USA/neurology
-> Luc Steels
Belgium/artificial intelligence
-> Monica Narula
India/visual arts

Events at Stadtkino and at Punktleuchten

Guests

Die Dialoge werden in englischer Sprache geführt.
Simultanübersetzung ins Deutsche steht zu Verfügung.

Information
Kunsthalle Basel
Tel +41 61 206 99 00/Fax + 41 61 206 99 19
info@kunsthallebasel.ch
www.kunsthallebasel.ch

Architekturmuseum Basel
Tel +41 61 261 14 13/Fax +41 61 261 14 28
am@architekturmuseum.ch
www.architekturmuseum.ch

ETH Studio Basel
Institut Stadt der Gegenwart
Tel +41 61 2731685/Fax + 41 61 2731687
studio-basel@arch.ethz.ch

PS
Dank an
Hilton Basel

When designing a *book* the choice of *typeface* is particularly important. The choice of *typeface* defines the *gray value* for both the eyes of the expert as well as the eyes of the novice. Its form and special characteristics establish a certain stance and relationship to the subject. The designer considers *typefaces* right from the start while working on a project.

2. The *book* shown below illustrates how carefully the graphic designer used *typography*. His choice of *typeface* is very subtle.
3. The slightest change in *weight* of a few letters differentiate the *typeface* from the "classic" typeface. The typographic *gray value* (*type size* and *leading*) fits perfectly to the simple *grid* (three *columns*). The *centered headlines* (*running head*, subtitle and *paragraph* heading) and the *page numbers* emphasize the classic nature of the *layout*, yet several details and typographic choices stand out and show that the designer wanted to design a thoroughly modern *book*.
3–4. The notes integrated into the main text, the thick and thin lines (red *footnotes*, vertical lines), the occasional use of *italics* and a second *typeface* give the design elegance and sophistication.

Additionally, the designer paid close attention to the quality of paper and the *binding*, both of which make this *book* a true "*book* object" (see page 204).

2. *Altitude*, book
Die Gestalten Verlag
Onlab/Nicolas Bourquin
3. ibid.
4. ibid.

2

– Deutsche Texte –

— Going Public —

— Design ist Orientierung —

— Making Things Public —

— Come Together —

– 222 –

– Deutsche Texte –

— Kollaboratives Design —

— Zwischen Grafikdesign und Kunst —

— Swiss Made —

– 223 –

3

sie zu Kommunikation und Handlung führt, eben zu visueller Massenkommunikation. Insofern ist Design hoch politisch, und es könnte zu einer Leitdisziplin der Informationsgesellschaft werden".[5] Obwohl der Begriff der Informationsgesellschaft nicht unumstritten ist, wird diese These auch von wissenschaftlicher Seite gestützt. Demzufolge lägen gegenwärtig die Probleme nicht unbedingt auf der Ebene der Bereitstellung von Informationen, sondern vielmehr in deren Transformation in Wissen. Dieses sei im Unterschied zur Information stets bedeutungs-, handlungs- und kontextbezogen.[6] Diese Feststellung bekräftigt, dass Grafikdesign über eine visuelle Orientierungshilfe hinaus, einen hilfreichen Beitrag zur Kontextualisierung und Vermittlung von Wissen in öffentlichen Diskursen leisten kann.

Die Tendenz eines gesellschaftlichen Bewusstseins im Design ist nicht neu. Dennoch wird sie auch gegen-

5 Schneider, Beat: Design als demokratische Orientierungshilfe, in: du, Nr. 4, Mai 2006, S. 58 f

6 Bonß, Wolfgang: Riskantes Wissen? Zur Rolle der Wissenschaft in der Risikogesellschaft, in: Heinrich-Böll-Stiftung (Hg.): Gut zu Wissen – Links zur Wissensgesellschaft, Verlag Westfälisches Dampfboot, 2002

Publikation oder da
so wird verschieder
phärischen Bedingu
tationen, Mediatio
Netzwerken und Pl
öffentlich gemacht w

8 Latour, Bruno; Weibel, Peter, ZKM (Hg.): Making Things Public. Atmospheres of Democracy, Cambridge, 2005. Zit. aus: http://makingthingspublic.zkm.de/fa/dings/politik_publications_de.htm

Intimen an Bedeutu
stellt sich die Frage,
tung bei der Differe
ten und öffentliche

8 Schneider, Beat: Design als demokratische Orientierungshilfe, in: du Nr. 4, Mai 2006, S. 59

4

1 - 3 FULGURO. **Les Urbaines** (Lausanne, CH, 2004) -> pages: 24, 55 | Festival featuring artistic creations. The work includes all the printed matters as well as the visual communication and signposting in the 10 places showing the young creations.
4 - 6 **Les Urbaines** (Lausanne, CH, 2005) -> page: 24 | Festival featuring artistic creations. The work includes all the printed matters as well as the visual communication and signposting in the 11 places showing the young creations.
7 SÉBASTIEN VIGNE, JULIEN NOTTER **Science et Cité** "Stups & Fiction" exhibition design.

1. Avant Garde, with its characteristically unusual *ligatures*, is the unifying element in all print materials distributed by the École nationale supérieure d'architecture de Lyon.

1. École nationale supérieure d'architecture de Lyon, calendar, brochures, booklet
Damien Gautier

1

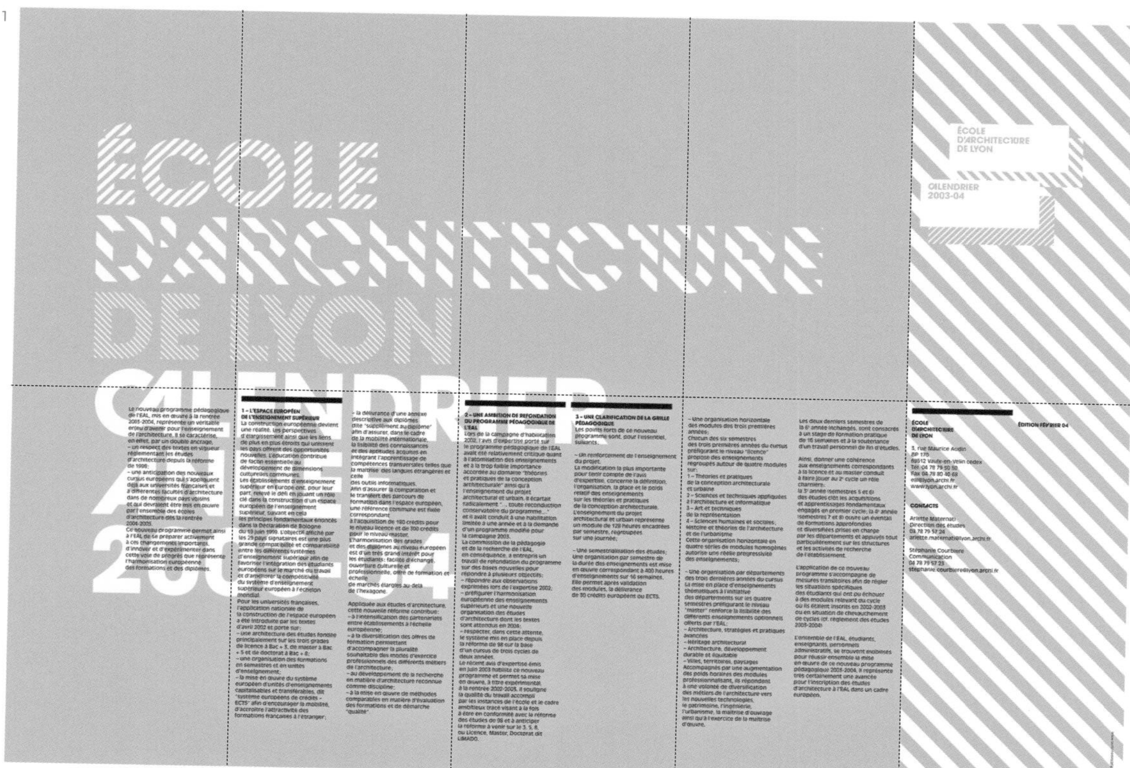

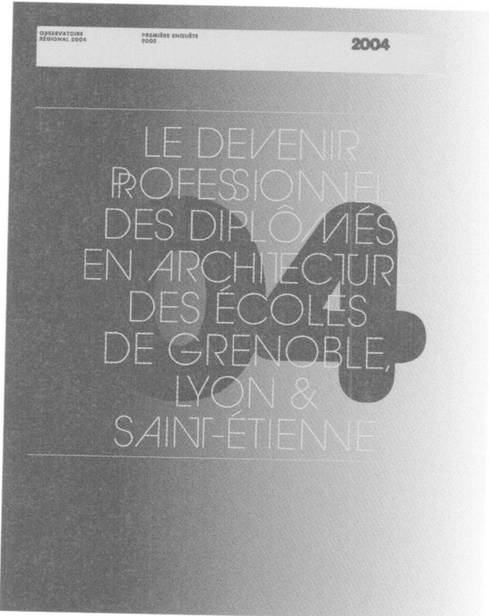

COLLECTION MÉMOIRE DE PROJETS /
ÉCOLE D'ARCHITECTURE DE LYON
DÉMARCHE
PROJETS URBAINS
LE GRAND PROJET
DE VILLE DE
VAULX-EN-VELIN

2. The *typeface* is a clearly recognizable feature in this *poster* series. Using only one *typeface* accentuates the idea of series. The juxtaposition of different *type styles* (width, *weight*) – a characteristic of the *typeface* Knockout (by Hoefler and Frere-Jones) – and the design of the titles (*type size*, overlapping) allow the *posters* text-image combinations or purely typographic *composition*.

2. *Les châteaux de la Drôme,* posters and cards
Le Petit Didier

2

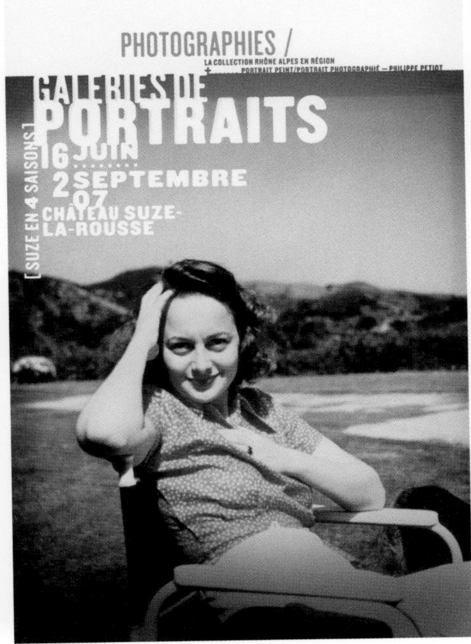

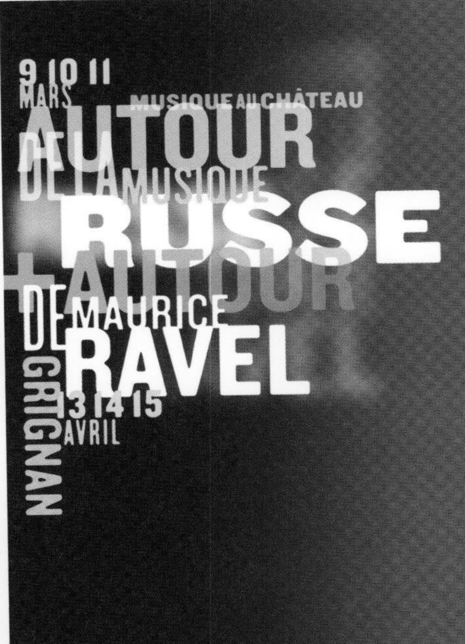

Graphic elements
Lines, patterns, frames, boxes, etc.

Graphic elements such as lines, boxes or *flat colors* can improve a *composition*. They can emphasize the *hierarchy* between the different elements in the *composition*. They define spaces, distinguish elements from each other, create connections between multiple elements, etc.

1. The horizontal lines whose length is defined by the *column width* that they highlight determine the *rhythm* and personality in the design of this newsletter. The line thickness varies and creates a visual *hierarchy*.

2. The principle of repeating boxes, and the use of colored boxes on *color* backgrounds is used to structure and separate the contents. The *layout* principle is based on the boxes that are aligned to the hang line in the upper third of the page. The images are placed above this line. Texts are connected to the corresponding image by a thin hand-drawn line. The unusual and original typographic choices round out the *composition*. The use of many different *typefaces* with extremely varied styles creates an attractive ensemble.

1. *Lyon Vision Mode*, newsletter
   Damien Gautier
2. *Gogo*, magazine
   Labomatic

1

2

3. Horizontal and vertical lines and blocks of *color* structure the *pages* and define specific spaces for each type of information.

4. The horizontal and vertical lines not only structure the *page* and its contents, they also serve as decorative elements and give the *composition* its personality.

3. Musée de l'Imprimerie de Lyon, newsletter
Damien Gautier
4. Villa Gillet, brochure
Cédric Gatillon

3

L'imprimerie, miroir de son temps
Du 21 avril au 29 juillet 2007, du mercredi au dimanche inclus.
Tarif d'entrée de l'exposition : 4 €, ouvrant également aux collections permanentes du Musée.
Un catalogue de la manifestation L'esprit d'un siècle accompagne l'exposition.

Commissaire de l'exposition
Dominique Varry, professeur d'histoire du livre à l'Enssib, avec la collaboration de François Robert, chercheur au Larhra et de Laurent Gonon, maître-imprimeur.

Conférence
L'imprimerie à Lyon au XIXe siècle, une histoire à écrire, par Dominique Varry, 3 mai à 18 h 15, aux Archives municipales, 18 rue Dugas Montbel Lyon 2e (entrée libre).

Visites guidées et démonstrations tous publics, visites et ateliers scolaires
Informations et inscriptions au 04 78 37 65 98, du mercredi au dimanche inclus.

¶ L'imprimerie Histoire et techniques

Tout ce que vous avez toujours voulu savoir sur l'imprimerie

¶ Si l'on trouve d'abondantes publications sur l'histoire du livre et de l'édition, il n'existait aucun ouvrage consacré à l'évolution des techniques d'imprimerie depuis Gutenberg et jusqu'au XXe siècle. Lacune désormais comblée grâce à l'étonnant petit livre de Michael Twyman, L'imprimerie, histoire et techniques, édité par ENS Éditions, l'Institut d'histoire du livre et l'Association des Amis du Musée de l'imprimerie, avec le mécénat de Fot imprimeurs, le fabricant de papier Sappi et la société Adéquat. L'ouvrage est une traduction du British Library guide to printing que l'auteur a adapté au contexte français, en s'appuyant notamment sur les collections du Musée de l'imprimerie. ¶ En 118 pages abondamment illustrées, M. Twyman, professeur émérite au Département de typographie et de communication graphique de l'Université de Reading (Royaume-Uni), fidèle partenaire du Musée, retrace la chronologie des techniques graphiques et décrit leur évolution avec brio et clarté, faisant d'un sujet habituellement peu accessible une histoire passionnante, qui se lit comme l'aventure du texte et de l'image.
En vente sur place ou par correspondance à la librairie du Musée ou chez votre libraire, au prix de 20 €.

Les collections voyagent

Le Musée a participé par des prêts à plusieurs grandes expositions françaises.

Du 10 nov. 2006 au 10 mars 2007 : la presse typographique dite de Gutenberg a rejoint Temple Neuf à Metz pour « Huguenots, de la Moselle à Berlin, les chemins de l'exil ».

Du 13 nov. au 15 déc. 2006, le fonds consacré à l'architecte Fernand Pouillon, a enrichi l'exposition marquant les cinquante ans de la Bibliothèque universitaire de droit et d'économie de l'université Paul Cézanne (Aix-Marseille III), dont F. Pouillon fut l'architecte.

La donation de ce fonds au Musée, par Catherine Sayen, sera prochainement présentée à l'aval de la commission scientifique de la Direction des musées de France et de la Drac.

Du 2 nov. au 30 déc. 2006, la Médiathèque de l'Agglomération troyenne a reçu la presse de cabinet du XVIIIe siècle pour « Je suis né auteur pour ainsi dire », exposition consacrée à Nicolas-Edme Restif de la Bretonne.

Du 9 au 27 octobre, lors de l'hommage rendu à Louis Moyroud, co-inventeur de la photocomposition avec René Higonnet, la commune de Moirans a emprunté la Lumitype-Photon du Musée ainsi que plusieurs incunables de la photocomposition.

À l'occasion de cette vibrante célébration de l'enfant du pays, Alan Marshall, directeur du Musée, historien de la photocomposition et interlocuteur de longue date de Louis Moyroud, a pu converser par visioconférence avec l'inventeur, âgé de 92 ans, qui se trouvait en Floride où il réside.

Rappelons qu'Alan Marshall a publié récemment un ouvrage consacré à la photocomposition et à ses inventeurs, « Du plomb à la lumière » (Maison des sciences de l'homme, 2005).

Ils nous ont quittés

¶ Ladislas Mandel, le 20 octobre 2006. Créateur d'alphabets pour Deberny et Peignot et Photon Inc., auteur de deux ouvrages remarquables sur l'histoire de l'écriture et de la typographie, il était aussi un ami et un fidèle conseiller du Musée, auquel il avait également donné un riche fonds documentaire.

¶ Henri-Jean Martin, le 13 janvier 2007. Il était regardé comme le fondateur de la « nouvelle histoire » du livre. Son rôle à Lyon est immense : conservateur en chef à la bibliothèque municipale de Lyon de 1958 à 1970, il contribuera, avec Maurice Audin, à la création du Musée de l'imprimerie (1964), auquel il a porté un regard attentif tout au long de sa carrière à l'École des chartes et à L'École pratique des hautes études.

France-Culture sur la trace des imprimeurs lyonnais

¶ En janvier dernier, France-Culture conviait Dominique Varry, professeur d'histoire du livre à l'Enssib, Yves-Jocteur Montrozier, responsable du fonds ancien à la Bibliothèque de la Part-Dieu et Alan Marshall, directeur du Musée pour une promenade à travers les rues de Lyon, sur les traces des grands imprimeurs lyonnais du XVe au XIXe siècle et de leurs officines. De Saint Nizier à la rue Mercière, ils ont revisité toute l'histoire des industries graphiques lyonnaises, évoquant pour les auditeurs les principales figures de notre cité, autrefois l'une des capitales européennes du livre.

Travaux : où en est-on ?

¶ Après la réfection de la toiture, le troisième étage (futures réserves), a gagné une charpente rénovée et une isolation thermique accrue ; la peinture des murs est en cours. La création de la future salle de l'image repose sur le percement d'un mur au deuxième étage, qui devrait permettre de gagner quelque quarante mètres carrés pour évoquer l'illustration par les procédés photomécaniques et électroniques.
¶ L'aménagement des anciens bureaux, en cours, permettra d'étendre de façon significative la surface des salles d'expositions temporaires et des locaux dédiés aux jeunes participants des ateliers, scolaires ou individuels.

URDLA : ça roule !

¶ Le Musée a inauguré un partenariat très prometteur avec l'URDLA, Centre international estampes & livres (Villeurbanne, président : Max Schoendorff). Vincent Brunet, graveur taille-doucier, réalisera des impressions sur la presse Stanhope (début du XIXe siècle), dans le cadre des visites du dimanche nouvelle formule (visites guidées accompagnées de démonstrations).

Machines : deux nouvelles recrues

¶ Alan May, professeur de typographie à l'université de Reading (Royaume-Uni), a installé au Musée, en décembre dernier, la presse typographique qu'il a construite de ses mains, fac-similé d'une presse du XVIIIe siècle conservée à la Smithsonian Institution à Washington. En parfait état de marche, elle est actionnée lors des visites commentées. Au deuxième étage, une presse Stanhope de marque Gaveaux a repris du service grâce à Erik Desmyter, collectionneur de Stanhope et consultant pour les musées belges.
¶ Après une révision exhaustive du mécanisme et la fabrication d'une nouvelle frisquette, la Gaveaux a retrouvé une nouvelle jeunesse et sera particulièrement à l'honneur les dimanches 6 mai, 3 juin, 1er juillet, 8 juillet de 14 h 30 à 17 h 30, lors des démonstrations proposées par Vincent Brunet (URDLA).

La bibliothèque Ponot s'organise

¶ Le Musée a reçu en don la bibliothèque de René Ponot, docteur en sémiologie de la typographie, décédé en 2004. L'inventaire de cette bibliothèque technique a été réalisé sur 2005 et 2006 ; hébergée par la Bibliothèque de la Part-Dieu, elle s'apprête à regagner le Musée dans de nouveaux espaces de réserves. Le Musée a en projet l'informatisation des fiches manuelles, elles seraient alors exploitables par les chercheurs, mais le coût s'avère assez élevé : à bon entendeur mécène…

4

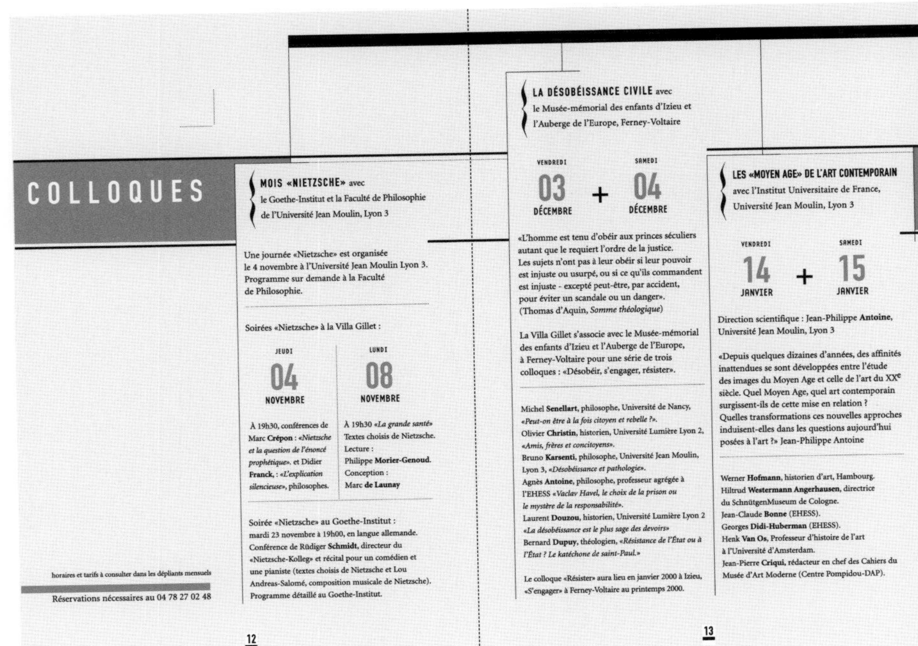

COLLOQUES

MOIS «NIETZSCHE» avec le Goethe-Institut et la Faculté de Philosophie de l'Université Jean Moulin, Lyon 3

Une journée «Nietzsche» est organisée le 4 novembre à l'Université Jean Moulin Lyon 3. Programme sur demande à la Faculté de Philosophie.

Soirées «Nietzsche» à la Villa Gillet :

JEUDI 04 NOVEMBRE

À 19h30, conférences de Marc **Crépon** : *«Nietzsche et la question de l'énoncé prophétique»*. et Didier **Franck**, : *«L'explication silencieuse»*, philosophes.

LUNDI 08 NOVEMBRE

À 19h30 *«La grande santé»* Textes choisis de Nietzsche. Lecture : Philippe **Morier-Genoud**. Conception : Marc **de Launay**

Soirée «Nietzsche» au Goethe-Institut : mardi 23 novembre à 19h00, en langue allemande. Conférence de Rüdiger **Schmidt**, directeur du «Nietzsche-Kolleg» et récital pour un comédien et une pianiste (textes choisis de Nietzsche et Lou Andreas-Salomé, composition musicale de Nietzsche). Programme détaillé au Goethe-Institut.

horaires et tarifs à consulter dans les dépliants mensuels

Réservations nécessaires au 04 78 27 02 48

12

LA DÉSOBÉISSANCE CIVILE avec le Musée-mémorial des enfants d'Izieu et l'Auberge de l'Europe, Ferney-Voltaire

VENDREDI 03 DÉCEMBRE + SAMEDI 04 DÉCEMBRE

«L'homme est tenu d'obéir aux princes séculiers autant que le requiert l'ordre de la justice. Les sujets n'ont pas à leur obéir si leur pouvoir est injuste ou usurpé, ou si ce qu'ils commandent est injuste - excepté peut-être, par accident, pour éviter un scandale ou un danger». (Thomas d'Aquin, *Somme théologique*)

La Villa Gillet s'associe avec le Musée-mémorial des enfants d'Izieu et l'Auberge de l'Europe, à Ferney-Voltaire pour une série de trois colloques : «Désobéir, s'engager, résister».

Michel **Senellart**, philosophe, Université de Nancy, *«Peut-on être à la fois citoyen et rebelle ?»*.
Olivier **Christin**, historien, Université Lumière Lyon 2, *«Amis, frères et concitoyens»*.
Bruno **Karsenti**, philosophe, Université Jean Moulin, Lyon 3, *«Désobéissance et pathologie»*.
Agnès **Antoine**, philosophe, professeur agrégée à l'EHESS *«Vaclav Havel, le choix de la prison ou le mystère de la responsabilité»*.
Laurent **Douzou**, historien, Université Lumière Lyon 2 *«La désobéissance est le plus sage des devoirs»*
Bernard **Dupuy**, théologien, *«Résistance de l'État ou à l'État ? Le katéchone de saint-Paul.»*

Le colloque «Résister» aura lieu en janvier 2000 à Izieu, «S'engager» à Ferney-Voltaire au printemps 2000.

LES «MOYEN AGE» DE L'ART CONTEMPORAIN avec l'Institut Universitaire de France, Université Jean Moulin, Lyon 3

VENDREDI 14 JANVIER + SAMEDI 15 JANVIER

Direction scientifique : Jean-Philippe **Antoine**, Université Jean Moulin, Lyon 3

«Depuis quelques dizaines d'années, des affinités inattendues se sont développées entre l'étude des images du Moyen Age et celle de l'art du XXe siècle. Quel Moyen Age, quel art contemporain surgissent-ils de cette mise en relation ? Quelles transformations ces nouvelles approches induisent-elles dans les questions aujourd'hui posées à l'art ?» Jean-Philippe Antoine

Werner **Hofmann**, historien d'art, Hambourg.
Hiltrud **Westermann Angerhausen**, directrice du SchnütgenMuseum de Cologne.
Jean-Claude **Bonne** (EHESS).
Georges **Didi-Huberman** (EHESS).
Henk **Van Os**, Professeur d'histoire de l'art à l'Université d'Amsterdam.
Jean-Pierre **Criqui**, rédacteur en chef des Cahiers du Musée d'Art Moderne (Centre Pompidou-DAP).

13

Images
Fundamental principles

The same as text, photographic images are an important part of the "raw materials" in a *composition*. First of all, one has to take a stance on the material being used: respect, when dealing with a work of art, appropriation and misappropriation with anonymous visuals or material suitable for manipulation. The *cropping*, *color* and texture may or may not be changed, depending on the usage rights. Works of art must be presented as well as possible. When placing multiple images, (see pages 100–105) relationships to adjacent texts are unavoidable (see pages 88–89). As a result one often has to alter either text or image. In order to avoid mistakes during this alteration, one has to appreciate the fundamental principles of an image. One must be able to see an image, understand its nature and respect this essence when using it.

Frame

The rectangular shape of the image doesn't reflect the (elliptical) way people see. It is a product of Western culture and technical considerations. The frame was long considered the window on the world, because it defines a unique and static viewpoint. The choice of image *cropping* defines the place where the actions are. The frame is the space where the image is composed and affects its balance (see page 79).

Field of view and beyond

The frame defines the field of view, or a space, and consequently a space outside the field of view. It is natural for someone who looks at an image to think that it describes a landscape, an action, a fact that "spills" out of the field of view. The landscape extends left and right, the action takes place in a larger space, the photographed subject falls within a specific context. Hence, an image is always read in the context of what is not seen. What is imagined is based on the clues, signs and information in the image and is determined by the person who "decodes" it. Although not present in the image, the space outside the field of view potentially exists. The things not seen are still perceived (see pages 34–35). This missing presence helps put the viewer in a particular frame of mind. Things outside the field of view can disturb, provoke our curiosity, or surprise. It also allows the mind to see the image over time. When reading left to right, the mind sees a before and after. Perspective also gives one the chance to read the image temporally: What is far away or emerges from the frame seems to be in the past or the future. The foreground is the present.

The photographer decided to focus on the shooter's face. Our attention centers on this area of the image because of the shallow depth of field. To understand the image the viewer will probably examine the shooter's eyes, masked by the reflections in his glasses, to unlock the meaning. Who is he?

The image *composition* raises the question in our minds: What or who is the target? Every clue is subject to interpretation, such as the earmuffs or the location. Some will look for the answers to their questions in the reflections in his glasses or in the background.

– Julien Guinand
Untitled
(series *Les tireurs*), 2006
113 × 90 cm
Color photograph
Courtesy Galerie Le Réverbère

Depth of field
This is the area in focus. It is centering on the point where the photographer focused and the space in front and behind. By choosing an area to focus on the photographer establishes a reading of the image. The eye is drawn to the sharper areas, and the blurry less defined areas are open to interpretation. The depth of field orders an image, creates *hierarchy*. It also accentuates the temporal aspect.

Formats
1. Panorama *format*. Close to the 16:9 *format*.
2. Landscape *format*. Static, horizontal *format*.
3. Portrait *format*. Dynamic, vertical *format*.
4. Square *format*. Balanced stable *format*.

A *format* seems more dynamic or static depending on the ratio between height and width. The *format* underscores an image's meaning.

Shots
The type of *shot* defines which elements (landscape, people, objects, etc.) are in the field of view and how they are shown. Beginning with the extreme long *shot*, where the viewer is at a great distance, to the extreme *close-up*, changing the type of *shot* changes how an object is framed in the image. *Composition* depends on framing and how dynamic an image is depends on the *composition*.
Each *shot* delivers its own set of information (A, B), actions (C, D), emotion (E, F, G).

Therefore, it is important to study an image carefully before *cropping* it (if this is possible). When taking a picture, one needs to consider all the image options beforehand in order to get as close as possible to the desired result.

Julien Guinand
Untitled
2004
76 × 95 cm
Color photograph
Courtesy Galerie Le Réverbère

1

2

3

4

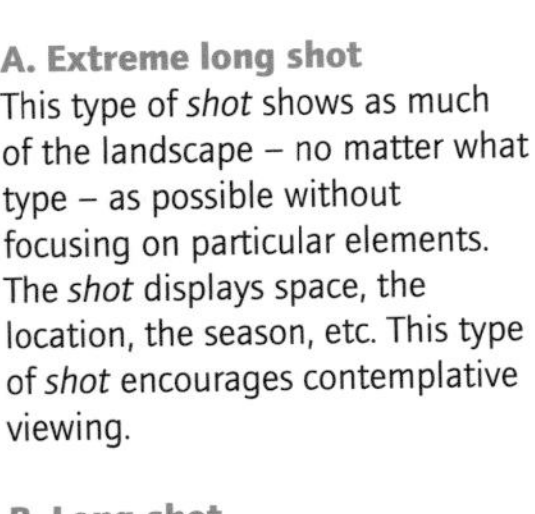

A. Extreme long shot
This type of *shot* shows as much of the landscape – no matter what type – as possible without focusing on particular elements. The *shot* displays space, the location, the season, etc. This type of *shot* encourages contemplative viewing.

B. Long shot
The *shot* focuses on a central point of interest, an action, a group. People shown are not cropped.

C. Full shot
The main subject is more tightly framed and not cropped.

D. Cowboy shot
The main subject is cropped at the knees. The term cowboy *shot* comes from the film era where tall actors weren't completely shown in the image. This *shot* was common to westerns in order to show the cowboy's face and revolver simultaneously.

E. Medium shot
The main subject is shown from head to the middle of the chest.

F. Close-up
If the subject is a person, then the *close-up* shows only the head or the face. If an object is shown, then this fills the entire frame.

G. Italian shot (extreme close-up)
If the subject is a person, then the Italian *shot* shows only a part of the face. If an object is shown, then it shows a detail.

A

B

C

D

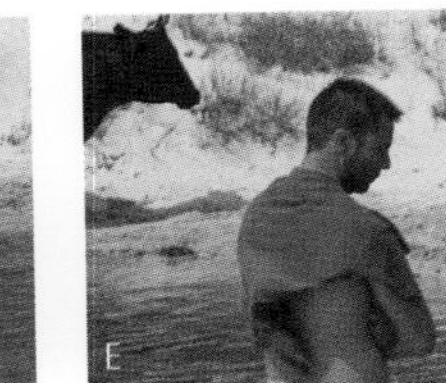
E

F

G

Perspective
The human eye is built to perceive reality in three different ways:
1. From eye level. This is equivalent to a person standing across from a scene. An image *shot* in this way presents an objective point of view. It has the status of an eyewitness account, it is informative.
2. From *bird's-eye view*. This is the viewpoint of a towering giant or bird in flight. This point of view gives the viewer a sense of security, and the feeling that he could own the object shown.
3. From the *worm's-eye view*. It is the opposite of the *bird's-eye view*, of someone dwarfed by the surroundings. This point of view gives the feeling of uncertainty, inaccessibility and powerlessness.

All three points of view can be emphasized or de-emphasized depending on where it is placed on the page. An image taken from a *bird's-eye view* that is placed at the top of the *page* has a stronger effect. An image taken from *worm's-eye view* is exactly the opposite, and an image from eye level is strongest when placed near the center of the page.

Light and color
We need *light* to see. *Light* helps us perceive shapes, *colors* and space. Conventionally daylight (sunlight) is shown coming from above and from the left to the right. A photographer who breaks this convention surprises, provokes, questions and offers an unexpected perspective on reality.

Lighting helps the photographer set a specific atmosphere that is just as important to the image as the subject or the *cropping*:
4. *Light* from the side: realistic situation
5. *Light* from above: a spiritual atmosphere
6. Diffuse lighting: creates a special atmosphere, depending on the *light* source (warm *light*, cold *light*, brightness, etc.)
7. Back lighting: The subject is in front of the *light* source and is consequently transformed into a *silhouette* that is more or less in focus. The sense of depth and details are lost in favor of a more graphic image.

Depending on the type of *light*, the *colors* in an image can seem brilliant, muted or modified.

1

2

3

4

5

6

7

Point of view

The photographer's art involves showing what he sees (physically or intellectually). By choosing a point of view he suggests a particular reading of the image. He defines foreground and background (see depth of field, page 77), chooses a wide or *close-up shot* (13, 14), decides where the horizon line is (15) and uses the effects of different views, like the *bird's-eye view* or the *worm's-eye view* (16). He approaches the image from a realistic point of view or reinforces the imaginary linked to the image content.

Composition

The academic image *composition* emphasizes the optical center of the image (approximately at the intersection of the diagonals) where the main subject is located. A landscape is shown as seen by the human eye, that means the land occupies one third, and the sky the upper two thirds. The *composition* is *centered*, symmetrical, static (8–10).

Art photography was faithful to this concept for a long time. The Bauhaus developed a new idea of image *composition*, where the equilibrium of the forces in the image was less important. Instead, the idea of harnessing the tension between the various elements in the image was important. The emphasis shifted to movement, balance (on the edge of imbalance) (11, 12).
The visual construction of each image (proportions, horizon line, vanishing point, etc.) creates lines of emphasis that allow the designer to arrange multiple images, and create a dialogue between them. These lines should also be seen in relation to the text blocks and the *lines of force* on the page.

– Photographs:
Siegfried Marque

8

9

10

11

12

13

14

15

16

Images
Is photography a reproduction of reality?

Have you ever asked yourself if what is shown by a photograph is actually real? Can we trust what is shown, whether it is an object, a person, an event? Leaving editing and retouching aside, does a photograph prove that what it captured exists?
A photograph is in fact never an exact reproduction of the real, contrary to what people usually think, even if the photographer truly tries to capture it faithfully. The process of photography alone has so many parameters that "transform" reality.

Whether it is while taking pictures (film sensitivity, choice of lens, point of view, depth of field, etc.) or while developing the film and printing, the photographer makes many choices that affect the final result.

While the invention of photography in 1826 gave the illusion of putting the world in a box, the photographer has since been freed of this obligation to recreate reality. During its development photography has slowly achieved its current status as an independent art form. Even in news photography or in documentary photography – which is supposed to inform us about events – the photographer's influence is undeniable.

A new generation of photojournalists care less about describing the world and more about using their sensitivity, emotions, and choices to translate what they feel into the world they "seize". The photographer's personality and sensitivity are assets today.

1. Julien Guinand
Untitled
2004
80 × 65 cm
Color photograph
Courtesy Galerie Le Réverbère
2. Julien Guinand
Untitled
2004
95 × 76 cm
Color photograph
Courtesy Galerie Le Réverbère

1

2

1. It is obvious that *light* plays a major role in this image. It gives the image depth. The rays of sun lead our eyes to the cabin with the open door, where one expects to see what it was that inspired the photographer to take this picture.

2. The bare stony environment, the man's posture in the center of the image, the *color harmony*, every detail gives this photo an aesthetic and sculptural dimension that make it a work of art.

3. The people seem precisely posed, their gestures orchestrated, as if to compose a painting.

4. Even though it is only a series of photographs of greyhounds, it is undeniable that the images have a painterly quality to them that lifts them above simple documentary images.

3. Julien Guinand
Groundwork
2004
95 × 76 cm
Color photograph
Courtesy Galerie Le Réverbère

4. Julien Guinand
Untitled
2005
95 × 76 cm
Color photographs
Courtesy Galerie Le Réverbère

3

4

When mastering the use of an image and the role it plays in a communication process, it is important to understand the viewer's process of perception – whether consciously or unconsciously. Your perception of an image is not necessarily the same as the person who finally sees it.
So what are the mechanisms that play a role in this process?
The "decoding" of an image is specific to the individual and involves a complex mental process in which his history, his culture, his achievements, his education, and his society, etc. all play a role. Since we only perceive what we know, our process of perception is anything but universal and not inborn. The context and the sender also influence the way an image is read.

Sender/receiver

An image is made by an individual for himself or for another person or organization. He wants to communicate a message to a known or unknown receiver. The sender inevitably influences the design of the image.
His personality, his convictions, his intentions, his ideas appear in the choices (conceptual, aesthetic, technical) that he makes.
If the receiver is known, the image is designed to be as monosemic (having a single meaning) as possible to reach his objective.
But the receiver is not always the only audience.
The image may also be viewed in a different environment or a different context than intended by the maker. Aren't we constantly confronted with images not intended for us? Consciously or unconsciously, carefully or fleetingly, we interpret them all.

Context

The situation where we see an image can effect its interpretation considerably. In which environment is the image seen? The same image can be a *poster* in the subway, in an art gallery, on the door of the refrigerator. It may be published in a journal, a *newspaper* or a *book*. What is the status of the medium, and why was the image published?
An image will be read differently if shown as an illustration, as evidence, or as documentation. What are its immediate surroundings on the page? Is it alone or surrounded by other images? Is it accompanied by text? What kind of text? What is the overall context? What is the political, social, economic context? What is the receiver's state of mind?

1

2

3

4

1. Anne-Catherine Céard
Bords, series
2. ibid.
3. ibid.
4. ibid.

Denotation/connotation
There are both denotations and connotations in the same image. The denotation comes directly from the image, what is seen and recognized is named. But an image is never limited to this reading alone. It also contains indirect meanings of the elements shown (objects, people, etc.) and how the artist chose to make it (framing, *composition*, *light*, etc.).

Filters
Reading an image is automatically altered through general and individual filters. Every symbol or sign, posture or gesture, details in clothing or environment is coded according to a shared ideology. These filter systems govern our customs, our beliefs, our feelings, our morals, and no image escapes their interpretation.

From image to message
Depending on how well the sender knows the image codes, he sends a more or less complex and more or less hidden message with the image. The receiver perceives this message –consciously or unconsciously – if he has the codes to decipher it. Everything "means" something, like an advertisement where each element is orchestrated to encourage the receiver to buy.

Text-image-ratio
In the communication process an image is rarely without an associated text: its source (title, author, date, etc.), a *caption* (descriptive or additional), and/or a text that it illustrates literally or allegorically. One needs to consider the nature of both elements and design their mutual relationship with both content and form in mind (see pages 88–99).

Placing several images next to each other requires additional thought (see pages 100–105).

5. Delphine Balley
Ursulla et ses filles, series 11,
Henrietta street
Dublin 2007
Courtesy Galerie Le Réverbère

5

1–4. The following elements recur in each of these four images:
· the square *format* (emphasizes the *composition*'s feeling)
· *light* (seen as twilight by some, as threatening by others)
· clothing (which might seem carelessly abandoned, some see them as remains of an accident)

Obviously, the photographer is not trying to give her images a universal clarity. She plays with the ambivalence of place, of *light*, of the scene to stimulate the viewer's imagination. This has a different effect depending on their current state of mind (emotions, situation) and their personality (who or what he is, etc.).

5. The photographer seems to be playing with the image's meaning. She seems conscious of its perplexing effect on the viewer.

The image is loaded with elements that visibly confront the viewer with their meaning (the classical painting, the threadbare sofa, the veiled woman, the pale children in white, an injured baby elephant, the carpets ... everything in a luxurious but decaying environment).

Images
Silhouette and outline

If our brain is under pressure, then it analyzes images step by step, without us noticing this process. First, it takes in the basic shape of the image. If it is familiar or it recognizes it, then it assumes things and shortens the perception process. On the other hand unknown forms draw attention. The brain turns to an image's contents only after successfully completing the first phase.

1. First, the eye decodes an image based on its *silhouette*, which directly addresses the visual memory. A *silhouette*'s impact is due to the fact that it reduces an image to its most basic form. Without details and in a single *color* that often accentuates the shape's clarity.

2. One image can contain another. Here, one sees a young woman's face whose hair forms the borders of Switzerland.

2. *La belle voisine*, poster
Trafik

1

2

3. *La tête dans les nuages*, poster
Théâtre d'Angoulême
Annette Lenz

4. *Rossignol*, multimedia animation
Trafik

3. This *poster*'s image seems to reassemble the "debris" of two images. Its rough *silhouette* is certainly what captures attention, before the mind begins to analyze its content and meaning.

4. A honeycomb *grid* of lines overlays the images and destroys the original rectangular *format*. The honeycomb *grid* unifies the different photographs, gives them motion and *rhythm*, and permits the playful integration of type.

3

4

Images
Treatment, manipulation and appropriation

The image itself can be manipulated, changed and dismantled. It might adopt a texture (1) or a visible *grid* (2), it can be the result of a photomontage (3) or reveal a hidden meaning (4). These manipulations allow the designer to create distance from reality that, once appropriated by the image, can be integrated into their visual universe. The image can be combined with other manipulated images, and project the viewer into a visual fantasy world.
The designer's modifications play with the "readability" of an image. The effect of these modifications depends on the degree of change and the viewer's distance to the image. For example, an image pixelated at small size is more enigmatic at large size especially when seen from a short distance.

1. The image is a simple assemblage of colored pixels. The faint pattern that one sees at second glance is the description of the four process *color* values of each pixel.

2. The image is composed of blue and black pixels. The image remains readable despite the extreme simplification. The technical dimension is strongly emphasized here.

1. *Robin Hood*, folded poster
Trafik
2. *Mix Film Fest*, poster
Erich Brechbühl (Mixer)

1

2

C: 86 M: 68 J: 48 N: 2	C: 70 M: 45 J: 23 N: 1	C: 62 M: 41 J: 20 N: 1	C: 79 M: 63 J: 43 N: 1	C: 89 M: 81 J: 59 N: 2
C: 78 M: 67 J: 46 N: 2	C: 64 M: 49 J: 27 N: 1	C: 61 M: 51 J: 30 N: 1	C: 81 M: 75 J: 62 N: 2	C: 90 M: 84 J: 65 N: 2
C: 78 M: 75 J: 70 N: 2	C: 85 M: 71 J: 52 N: 2	C: 78 M: 65 J: 44 N: 1	C: 88 M: 71 J: 54 N: 2	C: 73 M: 55 J: 34 N: 1
C: 81 M: 80 J: 82 N: 2	C: 87 M: 75 J: 57 N: 2	C: 78 M: 54 J: 30 N: 1	C: 77 M: 43 J: 21 N: 1	C: 30 M: 15 J: 4 N: 0
C: 83 M: 83 J: 75 N: 2	C: 78 M: 64 J: 40 N: 1	C: 54 M: 38 J: 17 N: 1	C: 56 M: 38 J: 18 N: 1	C: 25 M: 17 J: 6 N: 0

3. A coarse, clearly visible dot matrix disturbs the reading of the images. The strict use of black and white gives the *composition* a touch of nostalgia.

4. The image is composed of many *miniatures* with different *gray values*. At first the image is difficult to understand, yet the attentive observer will soon discover a wealth of meaningful clues for a second reading. Here, the graphic designer plays with the viewing distance and/or the image's reproduction size.

3. *Polar & the old school*, posters
Restaurant Parterre
Erich Brechbühl (Mixer)
4. *Niklaus Troxler*, poster
Erich Brechbühl (Mixer)

3

4

Text-image-relationship
Principles

Text and image often appear together in the same piece. They refer to each other, they oppose each other or complement each other. But how are they organized, and which principles guide their use?

A *composition*, and how it is read, changes according to the text-image ratio. The text, a series of words organized to argue, to inform, to speculate, to voice opinion, inspires reflection and is close to rational thought. The image appeals above all to our senses, even if that is the result of a thought process. The text-image *composition* defines the relationship between reflection and sensitivity.

The first glance at a *page* allows the reader to "gauge" this relationship, and either he wants to keep reading or stop:

- The text dominates the image, the intellect dominates sensitivity.
- Text and image are equals, reflection and sensitivity are stimulated equally.
- The image dominates the text, feelings are followed by reflection.

It is a question of making choices based on the importance of each element and the desired reading style.

1. Text and image are placed on separate *pages* and refer to each other across the fold.
2. Based on the same principle, the *headline*'s impact balances the image's importance.
3. The image occupies the left-hand page. On the right-hand *page* the text, small image and *caption* respond to the other page.
4. Text and image blend on these *pages*. The *page* on the left holds the *headline* and body copy. On the right *page* images are connected to the text and the *captions* are placed opposite near the inner *margin*.

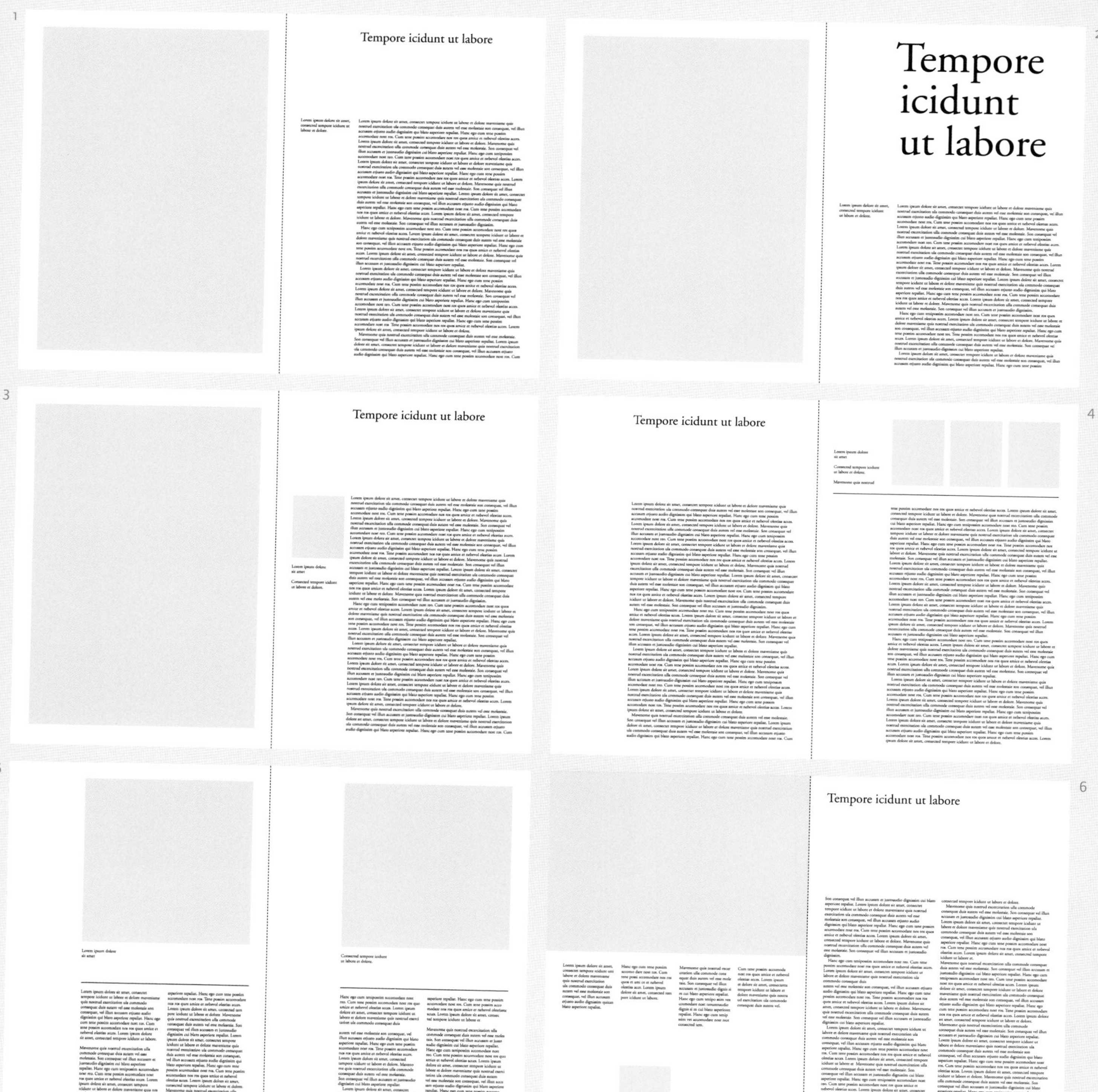

5. Text and image are equally distributed on each of the two *pages*. Images are placed above, the texts below and the *captions* connect the two elements.
6. The left-hand *page* uses the large image to draw attention, and the right *page* carries the main text. The large image is offset by the small image at the bottom of the same page. The white space at the top of the right-hand *page* corresponds to the space at the bottom of the left-hand page.

When working on an editorial project, it is also important to consider how the elements will be placed over a longer sequence of *pages*. This placement is key in creating an attractive *rhythm* for the reader. To accomplish this the designer must study the visual materials, consider their proportions, the *cropping* options, the number of images per *page* and the type and length of text, *reading levels* and so on.
7. The images are integrated into the text and refer to it directly.
8. Text and images are arranged on a *modular grid* (see pages 138–159).
9. The arrangement establishes a clear relationship between the largest image and the smaller ones.

10. Text and image are directly related.
11. The images offer an opportunity to arrange them in a playful *composition*.
12. The text overlaps the image. The text presents the opportunity to hide part of the image.

The possible relationships between text and image are numerous and are constantly reinvented.

Text-image-relationship
Examples

90 There are many examples that show a chosen relationship between text and images. A single principle might be selected for all *pages* in a publication, or it might be a relationship specific to the content of each *page* or section. Sometimes a real game develops between the two elements in a *poster* (see pages 94–95 and 170–171).

1. The images are above, the text below. The *headline* and *deck* link the two.

2. On this double-*page* spread a text-image pair is dedicated to each theme. Their different sizes and shapes give the *composition rhythm*.

1. *Chill*, magazine
Ill studio/L. Vernhet, N. Malinowsky, T. Audurand
2. *Beaux-Arts magazine*
Nicolas Hofman

1

242·SKATEBOARD

Connaissez vous 242 ? Ceux qui ont eu la chance de mettre la main sur la Bill Gates vidéo savent de quoi je parle... Jason et Basile ont créé leur shop, ils gèrent parallèlement leur marque, et apportent un vent de fraîcheur dans l'univers skateboardistique et graphique suisseuropéen. Tout cela bien sûr, quand ils ne sont pas en train de performer de nouveaux tricks sur les curbs d'Ouchy avec le team...

Vous ne connaissez sûrement pas **Guy Meldem**... sachez qu'il est suisse et skateboarder, qu'il aime beaucoup dessiner des animaux du premier coup, ou sinon attacher un chaton à un bébé lapin pour voir ce que ça donne... Guy collabore depuis quelques temps avec 242, pour le plus grand plaisir de nos yeux d'enfants...

2

1900–1909

1910–1919

1920–1929

3. Texts and images intermingle and create a loose *composition*, where the outline and the image relationships play a major role.

4. Texts and images seem intimately connected. The cleverly arranged images on the right respond to the *captions* placed on a full bleed image on the left-hand page.

3. *Beaux-Arts magazine*
Nicolas Hofman

4. *Cneai*, catalogue raisonné 1997–2004
Christophe Jacquet, called Tofe

3

4

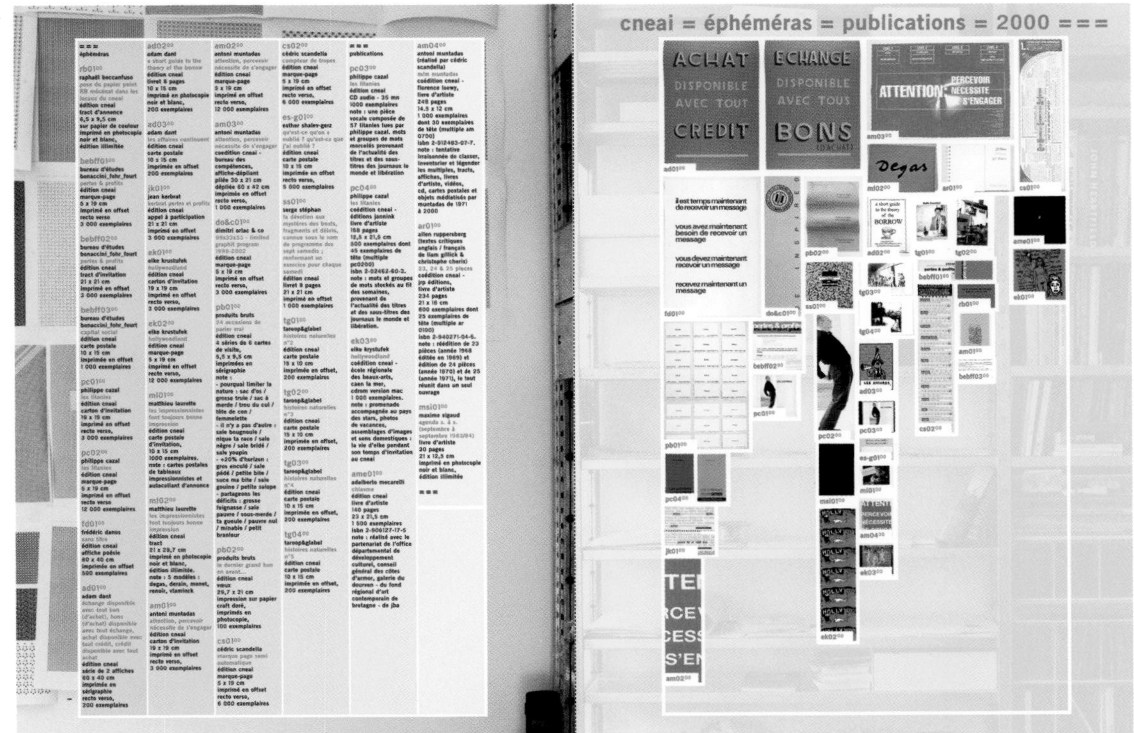

The *text-image-relationship* not only greatly effects our perception of a *composition*, it also can be used to define strong graphic principles. These principles can be used to unify a *composition* or as a visual identity for a *poster* or *book*, etc.

The relationship between several images may also be the foundation for a *composition* that is based on their dissimilarity or dialogue.

1. The main design principle in this exhibition catalogue is based on an unexpected *text-image-relationship*. The text is in the center, "surrounded" by images that refer to it. Even though this principle is used throughout the catalogue, each *page* has its own identity due to the specific content and reinvented *composition*.

1. *L'art du tampon*, catalogue
Musée de la Poste
Annette Lenz

1

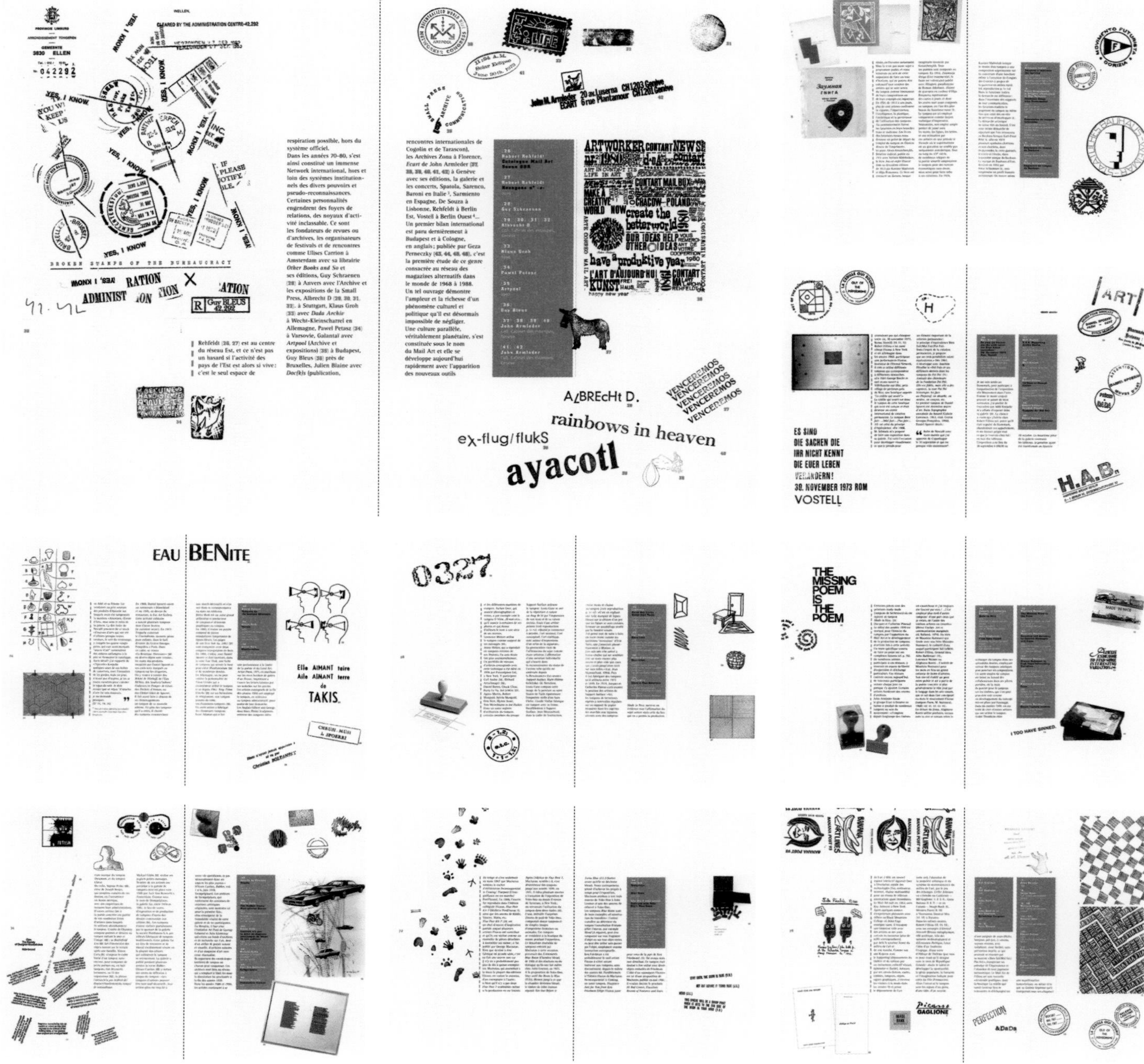

2. Text and images clash and overlap. The mostly covered *headline* is the pretext for the *composition*.

3. Overlaying the text on the image, thus completely covering the people's faces, creates the unifying principle of the *magazine* and makes it instantly recognizable.

2. *Crac – Centre de recherche et d'action artistique*, program poster
Trafik
3. *BEople*, magazine
Base design

2

3

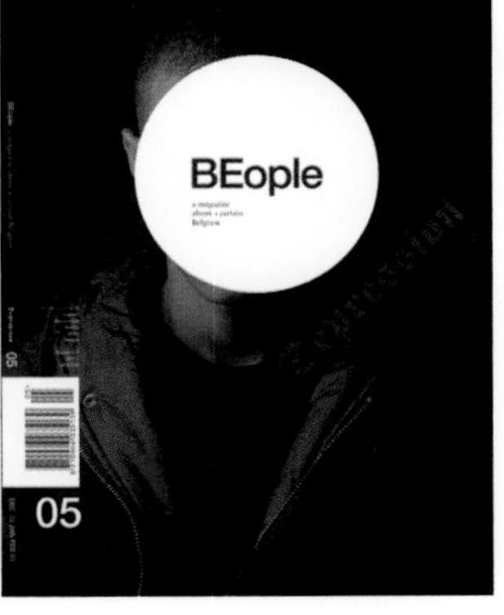

Posters are a special place where text and image battle each other intensely. The text sits at the heart of the image and plays with it.

1. Texts and images collide. The written information dominates the image which is half covered. What is the text hiding? Maybe just what it reveals?

2. The text is an integral part of the *composition*. It completes and extends the image. Its placement gives it meaning.

1. Théâtre Nanterre-Amandiers 2004-2005, posters Labomatic Photographies trouvées Grore Images
2. Théâtre National de la Colline, posters Michal Batory

1

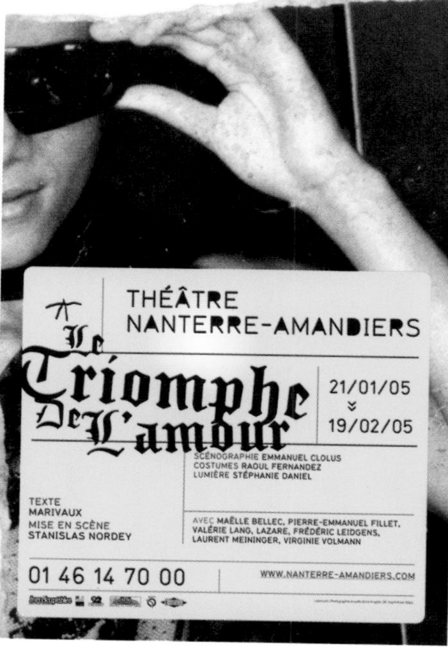

2

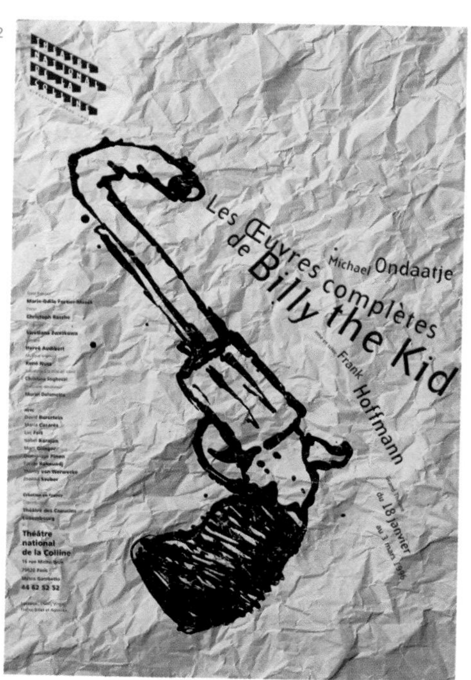

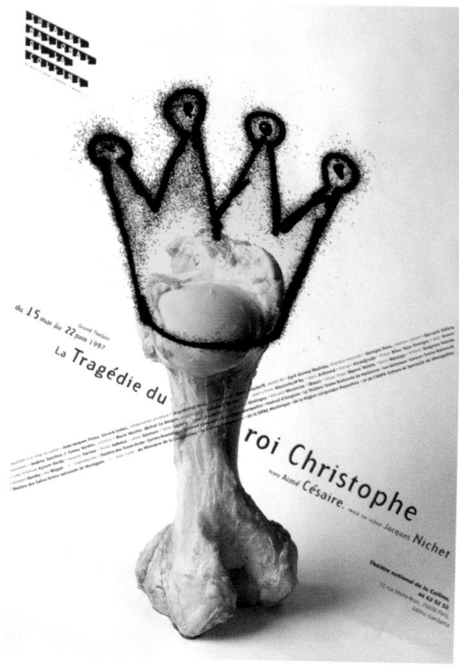

3. The random *letterspacing* transforms the text into a visual element that interacts with the image.

4. At first glance the text set on the image appears to be a *caption*. Upon a closer look, one realizes that it transforms the image's meaning by referring to the atomic bomb dropped on Japan.

5. Text and image are treated equally. Their systematic arrangement makes the *poster* memorable.

6. *Headline* and image are decoded simultaneously by the viewer, since the letters and images are arranged like building blocks.

7. Text and image are one. One can't exist without the other.

3. *Gefühlsecht. Grafikdesign der 90er Jahre*, poster
Museum für Kunst und Gewerbe Hamburg
Uwe Loesch
4. *"Little boy"*
(50th anniversary of the destruction of Hiroshima by the "Little boy" atomic bomb), poster
Le Mouvement de la Paix, Paris
Uwe Loesch
5. *Images au centre*, poster
MAJi, Maroussia Jannelle
6. *Die arabische Nacht*, poster
Erich Brechbühl (Mixer)
7. *DeValence*, poster
Superscript² & Popular Standard

3

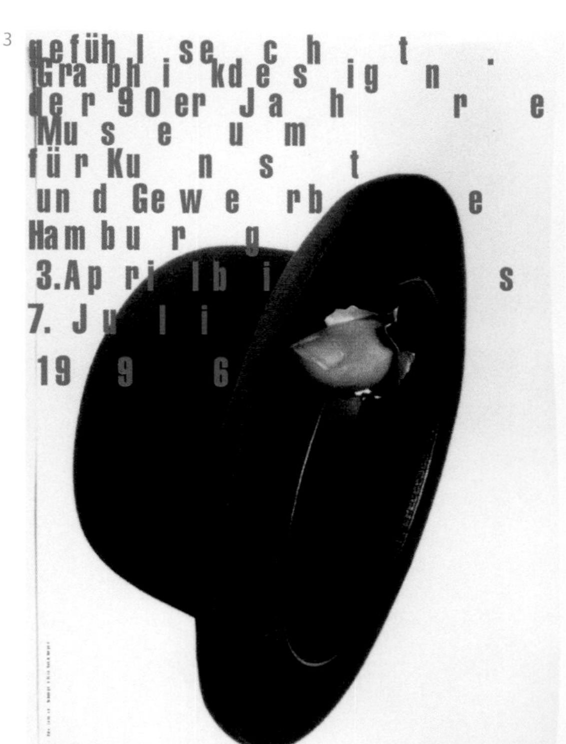

4

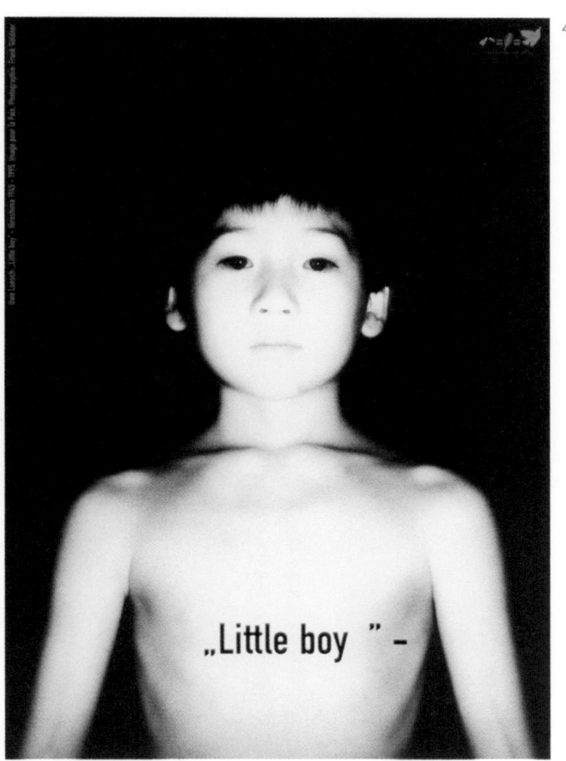

5

6

7

1. The *type area* leaves the *outer margin* ample space for notes and smaller images. The main images are placed at the bottom of the *page* below the text, and a small image is inserted into the text. Each element (*headline*, text, images, notes) seems to have a fixed place, but one can clearly see that the designer plays with their relationship to balance the *composition*.

2. The small silhouetted figure on the left offsets the full bleed image on the right. The text and generous white space highlighting the figure secure the design's balance.

1. *Beaux-Arts magazine* Nicolas Hofman
2. ibid.

1

62 VOYAGE

VENISE

WEEK-END SÉRÉNISSIME

par Laurence Castany

À l'occasion de la biennale de Venise, promenade dans les dédales de la capitale internationale de l'art à la rencontre de ses innombrables créateurs de prestige et de ses trésors.

63

2

86 MODE

QUE PENSER DE L'EXPOSITION ?

L'HOMME EST UNE FEMME COMME LES AUTRES

3. Text and image interact without interfering with each other. Balance is maintained due to the respective "weights" of the text and image. Note the link between the *light* in the image and the white created by the arrangement of the text.

4. The designer skillfully combines the text and image to pace the *pages* of the article and hold the reader's interest. By trying to find the balance between repetition and disruption, he must consider the design elements of each page.

3

42 LIEU

LA CHAPELLE RODIN
LUMIÈRE NOUVELLE

Après sept ans de fermeture, la chapelle du musée Rodin, à Paris, s'ouvre aux expositions temporaires. Un espace d'exception qui rend grâce à la modernité du sculpteur.

par
VÉRONIQUE BOURUET-AUBERTOT

Fermée depuis 1998, la chapelle Rodin rouvre ses portes. Un événement pour l'un des musées les plus fréquentés de la capitale puisque cette rénovation par l'architecte Pierre-Louis Faloci apporte des espaces d'expositions temporaires de 400 m² et tout un équipement qui manquait cruellement au musée. Pour fêter cette nouvelle infrastructure qui fait office de poumon, une exposition particulièrement subtile met en lumière sous un jour inhabituel la modernité du grand Rodin. Cette fois, ce n'est ni sa technique de taille ni son réemploi et recyclage constant d'éléments et de figures qui sont mis en avant pour plaider le rôle révolutionnaire du sculpteur, mais son approche et sa conception de l'espace. Loin d'être fastidieuse, la démonstration est passionnante comme une enquête lumineuse avec de jolis va-et-vient vers des auteurs qui lui succéderont tels Brancusi, Giacometti et, plus proches de nous, Louise Bourgeois, Didier Vermeiren ou Richard Wentworth.
Expérimentateur, tête chercheuse, Rodin concevait la sculpture comme un objet dans l'espace avec une implication aiguë. En 1909, au faîte de sa célébrité, il n'hésite pas à faire déplacer de son atelier de Meudon aux jardins du Palais Royal le plâtre de son monument à Victor Hugo pour une série d'essais sur l'axe idéal et sur l'inscription dans le site. La réflexion qu'il mène autour de ses illustres *Bourgeois de Calais* s'étire dans le temps. Alors qu'il suggère à la ville de placer le groupe soit au ras du sol pour se mêler à la foule, soit en net surplomb pour la dominer puissamment, Rodin, en 1895, n'est pas entendu : les *Bourgeois* prennent place à la hauteur banale, habituelle de tout monument, ni trop haut ni trop bas. Vaincu, il trouvera meilleure oreille dix ans plus tard chez les Anglais. Lorsqu'il se penche sur l'installation du même monument aux jardins de Westminster à Londres, il bâtit un échafaudage dans son jardin de Meudon, étudie de nouveau la hauteur idéale du socle. Ses instructions sont cette fois respectées et l'effet – rendu de manière frappante dans l'exposition – diffère radicalement puisque les figures accablées et courbées nous fixent et nous dominent. Dans son pavillon de 1900 au pont de l'Alma, Rodin, artiste et maître d'œuvre de l'exposition, choisit ses socles : des gaines antiques ou des colonnes qu'il multiplie via le moulage. Rodin joue des hauteurs, des axes, des décentrages. La colonne sert parfois de support au modelage. À chaque fois, le socle l'oriente, l'interprète, jusqu'à littéralement prendre corps avec l'œuvre à l'image de la délicate tête assoupie de Madame Fenaille, perchée sur un long fût telle une étonnante femme cygne. ⊠

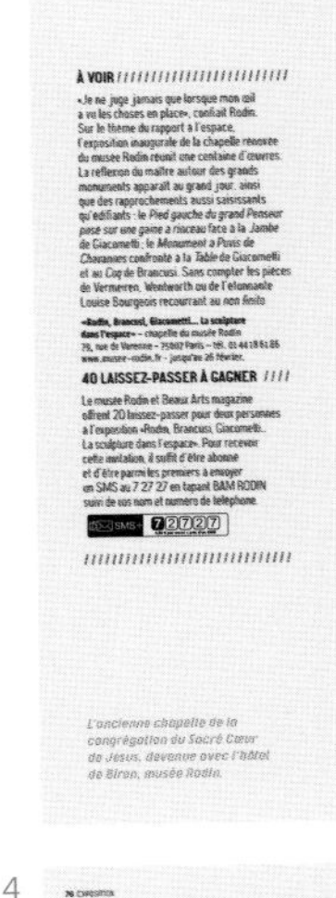

À VOIR

«Je ne juge jamais que lorsque mon œil a vu les choses en place», confiait Rodin. Sur le thème du rapport à l'espace, l'exposition inaugurale de la chapelle rénovée du musée Rodin réunit une centaine d'œuvres. La réflexion du maître autour des grands monuments apparaît au grand jour, ainsi que des rapprochements aussi saisissants qu'édifiants : le *Pied gauche du grand Penseur posé sur une gaine à rinceau* face à la *Jambe* de Giacometti ; le *Monument à Puvis de Chavannes* confronté à la *Table* de Giacometti et au *Coq* de Brancusi. Sans compter les pièces de Vermeiren, Wentworth ou de l'étonnante Louise Bourgeois recourant au non finito.

«Rodin, Brancusi, Giacometti... La sculpture dans l'espace» – chapelle du musée Rodin 79, rue de Varenne – 75007 Paris – tél. 01 44 18 61 86 www.musee-rodin.fr – jusqu'au 26 février.

40 LAISSEZ-PASSER À GAGNER

Le musée Rodin et Beaux Arts magazine offrent 20 laissez-passer pour deux personnes à l'exposition «Rodin, Brancusi, Giacometti... La sculpture dans l'espace». Pour recevoir cette invitation, il suffit d'être abonné et d'être parmi les premiers à envoyer un SMS au 7 27 27 en tapant BAM RODIN suivi de vos nom et numéro de téléphone.

SMS+ 7 2 7 2 7

L'ancienne chapelle de la congrégation du Sacré Cœur de Jésus, devenue avec l'hôtel de Biron, musée Rodin.

4

CARAVAGE REMBRANDT
COMMUNION SECRÈTE

Caravage n'a jamais côtoyé Rembrandt. Le parallèle établi à Amsterdam entre les deux maîtres du clair-obscur et des sujets humbles et mystiques s'impose pourtant avec évidence.

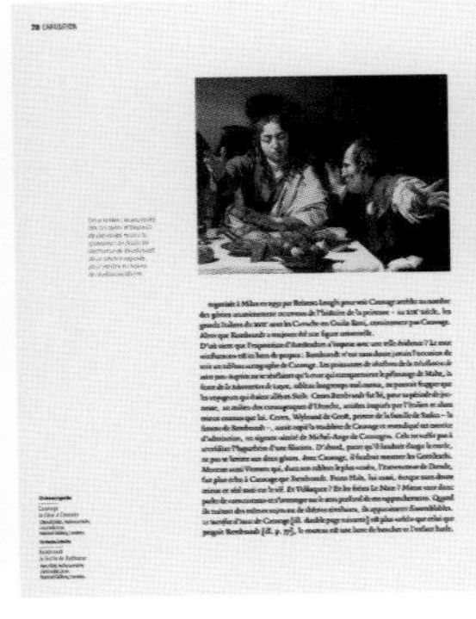

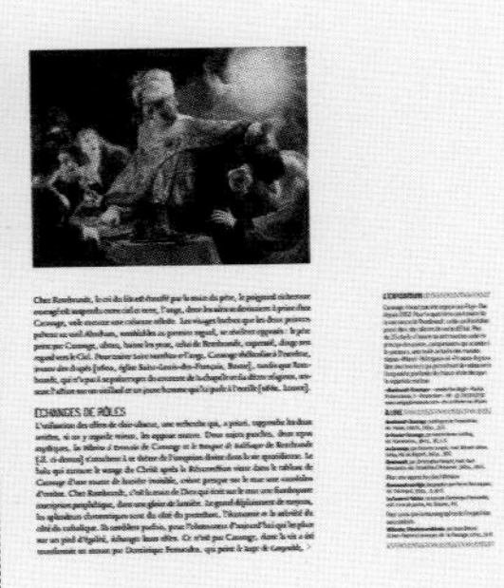

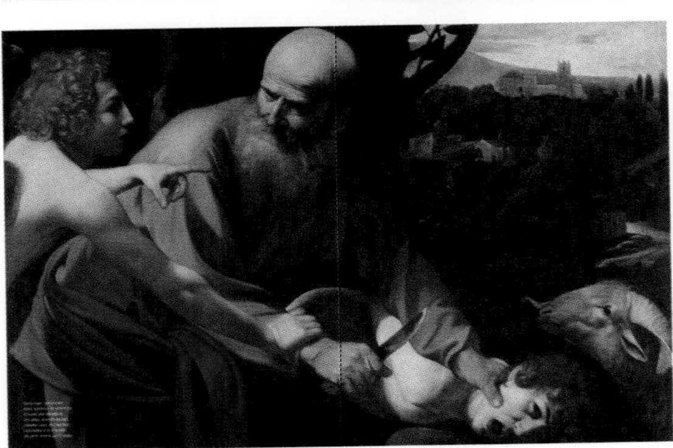

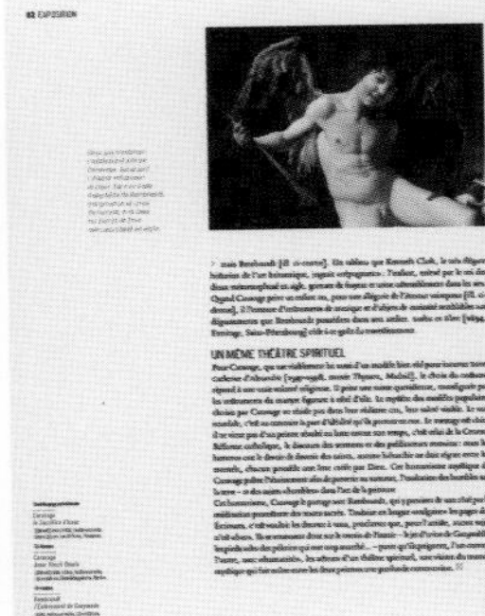

Beyond their roles in the *composition*, text and image should complement one another's contents. The images should not just illustrate the text, but should contribute their own information. The *caption* should not only describe the image, but also complete it by providing additional information. It can also echo the main ideas in the text.

Designing a *page* with texts and images often involves placing multiple images. Managing many images means considering what affects their arrangement causes. Do they struggle for dominance, or balance well? Are there semantic or formal relationships, etc.? Fundamentally, one must analyze their form (the way each image is composed), their strength (*color* and *contrast*) and their content (see pages 76–87).

By taking these parameters into account, the *composition* will be reinforced by the meaning it conveys.

1. Each article begins with a striking image that spans two text *columns*. The small images, placed to balance the *composition*, form a visual counterweight and provide additional information. The image arrangement follows the series principle (a series of objects) and the sequence (to describe a movement, an action).

1. *Azimuts – 26*, magazine
École Régionale des beaux-arts de Saint-Étienne
Graphic concept directed by Denis Coueignoux

1

Bloomberg

The Emperor's New Clothes

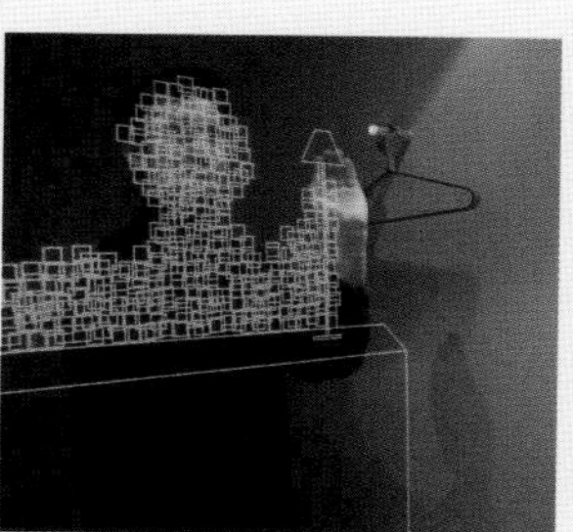

19 REPÈRE BRAUN

2. *Azimuts – 26*, magazine
École Régionale des beaux-arts
de Saint-Étienne

2. Even though this is the same *magazine* as in example 1, you will notice that this image sequence is composed of both photographs and scientific illustrations and diagrams. Each image type provides its share of the information:

- A diagram informs quickly and comprehensively about a process, an action, etc.
- A scientific or educational illustration is ideal for communicating information.
- A photograph, even if it appears purely descriptive, is always partly subjective. It is evocative and appeals directly to the reader's feelings.

In this sequence, the designer has chosen to vary the framing and deliver different information. The overviews show context and atmosphere, and the *close-ups* show details. The photographer undeniably valued the image quality, even with the small more "technical" images.

2

Image-image-relationship
Principles

The designer often has to decide on the relationship between multiple images on a single *page* or double-*page* spread. In a *book* he must consider each *page* as the sequel to the preceding page, and the introduction to the following page. He must deal with the *pages' rhythm*.

1. Equal size.

2. Images of equal size introduce narrative through their arrangement. Their order cannot be left to chance.

3. Small images combine forces in order to compete with the large one above. Their diversity may capture the reader's interest.

4. The small image has less visual weight than the large one, but the white space around it emphasizes it. The two images communicate with each other.

5. The smaller images and the large image are organized into a *composition*.

6. Dominant relationship: The smaller images at the bottom are overwhelmed by the large image above.

7. The images are nested. The relationship between the two images depends on their content and type.

8. Although the same size as the other images, the lowest image, which is placed by itself, is emphasized by this *composition*.

The arrangement of several images in a space must take the *contrast* relationships based on their qualities into account (see pages 76–79).

Arranging multiple images while considering their construction, their *colors*, their key features and their content is a designer's daily bread. He can use a specific image-to-image relationship on all *pages*, or alternatively he can vary the relationship on each *page* and constantly renew a reader's attention. His design space encompasses all *pages*, which are either considered separately or as a whole.

Image-image-relationship
Examples

1. The principle of vertical divisions and the interplay of the images evoke the feeling of a film sequence with cuts and flashbacks. The small images are embedded in the full bleed images.

2. In the second *composition* the vertical bands play with the image by repeating details.

1. Oxbow, brochure
   Damien Gautier
2. ibid.

1

2

Images are often combined in different ways within the same piece. For example in a *magazine*, the *rhythm* across the *pages* is created – among other things – by varying the relationships between the images from *page* to page. A few *pages* of a *magazine* demonstrate this here.

3. On the contents *page* of this *magazine*, images illustrating different articles come together. The designer pays close attention in his choices to their nature, quality and construction (*colors*, *contrast*, weighting, *lines of force*, etc.) to make the *composition* work.

4. The images are arranged like a contact sheet. The images are next to each other and dissect the movement so that an interested reader can reconstruct the action, the details, and even reproduce the movement.

5. The juxtaposition of several images repeats a similar motif, but plays with different angles, scales and points of view.

6. The two images placed face to face accent their complementarity; *close-up* versus overview, earth and flowers versus tree tops and sky, warm versus *cool colors* (see pages 24–27).

7. The relationship between the two images lives through *contrast*. The difference in size, and the difference in content: The first shows the action on the ground, the second is almost motionless and turned skywards.

3. *Chill*, magazine
Ill studio/L. Vernhet, N. Malinowsky, T. Audurand
4. ibid.
5. ibid.
6. ibid.
7. ibid.

3

4

5

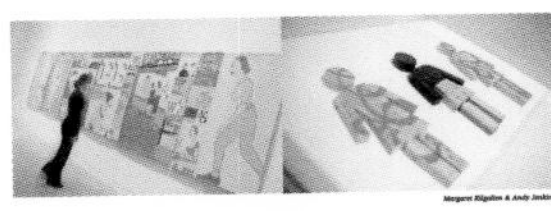

6

7

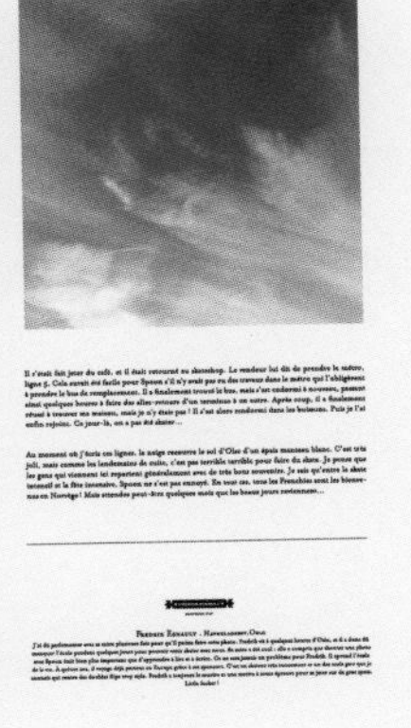

1. This *book* illustrates *page* after *page* how images can be combined in multiple and skilled ways, and which criteria play a role in this process:
· differences in scale
· relationship between *colors*
· dominance relationships
· *color* and black-white relationships
· focus relationships
· etc.

1. *Die Rückkehr der Physiognomie*, magazine etc. publications
A collaboration with Biel/Bienne Festival of Photography, Switzerland
onlab/Nicolas Bourquin
assisted by Cathy Larqué,
Ursina Völlm, Ayelet Yanai

1

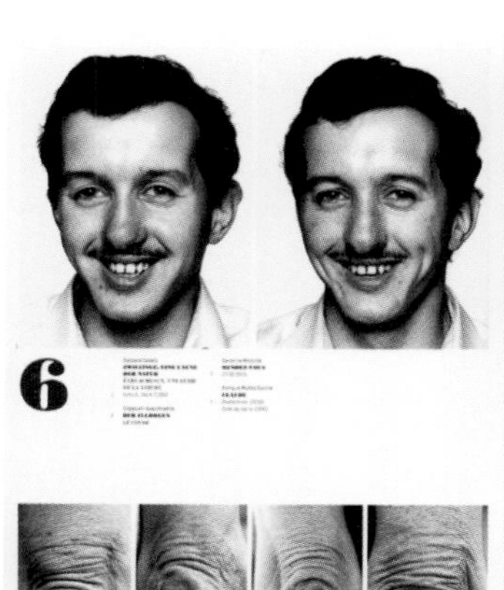

2. An original *image-image-relationship* is presented in this artist's catalogue. The series of images always completely fills the available space of the double-*page* spread. The series continues from spread to spread, and the first image on the new *page* is always the same size as the last image on the preceding page. The images get smaller in size from *page* to page. The first *page* shows two images and the last *page* shows 32 images in total.

2. *6 mètres avant Paris*
in: *Eustache Kossakowski*,
exhibition catalogue
Espace EDF Electra
Le Petit Didier

The need for visual and editorial organization, efficiency and rigor – essential for the design of certain documents – spawned the more or less complex structural principles for the designer.
Swiss designers, driven by the necessity to deal with bilingual or trilingual content (French, German, English), developed the principle of the multi-*column grid*.
Extending the Bauhaus theory, the *Swiss School* (of design) also developed the principle of the *modular grid* to organize the elements on a *page* (texts and images) based on unshakeable logic and rigor.

The challenge is to know these design rules without being their prisoner: to control them rather than suffer from them, to render them invisible, to play with them masterfully. One should know these principles well enough to bend them. Mastery can be demonstrated by introducing irritations, disruptions and surprises.

Part

03

Title

Grid principles

Contents

Grid principles
Introduction

No matter what the project may be – from the *poster*, *book*, *newspaper* to the *leaflet* – the designer tries to place the elements harmoniously. Over the centuries, many have tried to find the "golden rules" for this art of *composition*.

Why is one *page* harmonious and the other obviously not? Are there fundamental principles that define the *harmony* and balance for a page, even the success of a *composition*?

Rules of thumb
The analysis and comparison of other art forms such as painting and architecture using geometry and mathematics showed that the *page* is governed by the same "rules" as a painting or a cathedral's facade. A number of principles for *composition* were deduced that regulate the relationship between the *format*, the *margins* and the *type area*.
These principles were developed mainly by *Villard de Honnecourt*, *Raúl Rosarivo* and *Jan Tschichold*...

The Swiss School
Between 1945 and 1960 the so-called *Swiss School* (of design) developed the principle of the *grid*, which proved applicable to all types of graphic design projects. A *grid* gives all elements a place that ensures the overall *harmony* of the page. The pioneers and masters of this principle were Josef Müller-Brockmann, Emil Ruder and others.
They developed the idea of absolute coherence of all *pages* in a *book*, where the modular principles allow the elements to be placed on a *grid*. In this way the cover, *spine* and inside *pages* all work in unison. This principle creates unity and identity in a collection of *books* or in a *poster* series.

Form and function
The *grid* also meets functional criteria. It is designed with ease of use and legibility in mind. Form and function are therefore closely related.
The efficiency and applicability of the *grid* depend on its "pragmatism". The idea is to create *harmony* while taking advantage of the given constraints; otherwise the *grid* can't be applied to several *pages* or a series of documents.
A *grid* that seems too complicated and too difficult to use is undoubtedly badly designed. We suggest those with doubts take a closer look at the principles discussed.

Submission
To truly see and appreciate the benefits of the *grid*, the designer has to submit himself to it. If he tries to get around it, for the sake of greater freedom, he will only see the disadvantages and the results won't have the same *harmony* that a *grid* can provide. With this negative attitude the designer should instead work without a *grid*. If he does so, however, his work on a *book*, a *magazine* or printed series will be more complicated.

Freedom
The lack of mastery or rigor in the application of a *layout grid* leads to visible "errors" (misplaced or illogically placed elements, conflicts in the graphic decisions made by the *grid*, text-image distribution contradicts the *grid*, etc.).
Understanding a *grid* and the principles it implies allows the designer at a later stage to "play" with it, and to find principles that go beyond it without questioning its foundations. The resulting "accidents" free one from blindly following the *grid*.

A *grid* helps define the proportions of the elements on the *page* and unify the design of multiple *pages*. It also assures coherence in a series of documents or in the *pages* of a *book* even if these are different kinds of *pages*.
An efficient *grid* can also incorporate "parasitic" (not *grid*-conform) elements without risking the continuity of the *pages*, rather make the *pages* more dynamic. Furthermore, a *grid* is not exclusive. It allows the designer to work on all manner of projects and to cater to his own preferences.
He can adapt the *composition* to fit the elements at hand, while still respecting the *grid*.

The *grid* is often seen as a synonym for "monotony". This is either because it is really too strict for its chosen use, or because the designer hasn't completely embraced its application. It should not be forgotten that a *grid* is a framework and not a closed, authoritarian, simplistic system. The designer still has to apply the basic principles of *composition* (*contrast*, balance, weight relationships, etc.). A *book* is only successful if each *page* or double-*page* spread has received the same attention, the desire to make it a "piece" in itself, while integrating it into the logic of the *page* sequence. You will notice that this is not a matter of the number of *colors*, paper quality, the *binding* or *finishing*, but simply an intellectual challenge. Numerous effects and tricks can mask mediocre graphic design, but they will reveal the desire for showiness mixed with a lack of prior thinking.

In other words, a *grid* must be used with both rigor and flexibility!

How does one define a grid?
Defining an optimal *grid* for a project, one has to study the elements to be used on the *page* carefully:
· Image(s)
 – type (photographs, illustrations, graphics)
 – quantity (per page)
 – specifics (*cropping*, miniature size, *silhouette*, etc.)
· Text(s)
 – quantity (characters per page)
 – nature (*reading levels*)
 – *hierarchy*, organization (introduction, main text, notes, *captions*, etc.)
· All other elements (*running head*, *page number*, etc.)

Don't forget that the *grid* needs to allow variations in these parameters depending on whether it is for the *pages* of a *book*, a *magazine* or a *newspaper*.

Multi-column grid
Basic principles

The principle of the multi-*column grid* consists of dividing the width of the *format* within the *margins* into several *columns* separated by *gutters*. A harmonious division results from well proportioned side *margins*, *columns* and *gutters*. *Columns* with widths in whole numbers and that are multiples of the *gutter* width are easier to use.

1. *Format* width: 285 mm: *gutter* 5 mm, division of the *page* in three *columns* of 85 mm and side *margins* of 10 mm each. If the *columns* are divided in half, they measure 40 mm. If divided in thirds, they are 25 mm wide. Whatever the division, the *column width* remains a whole number.

1

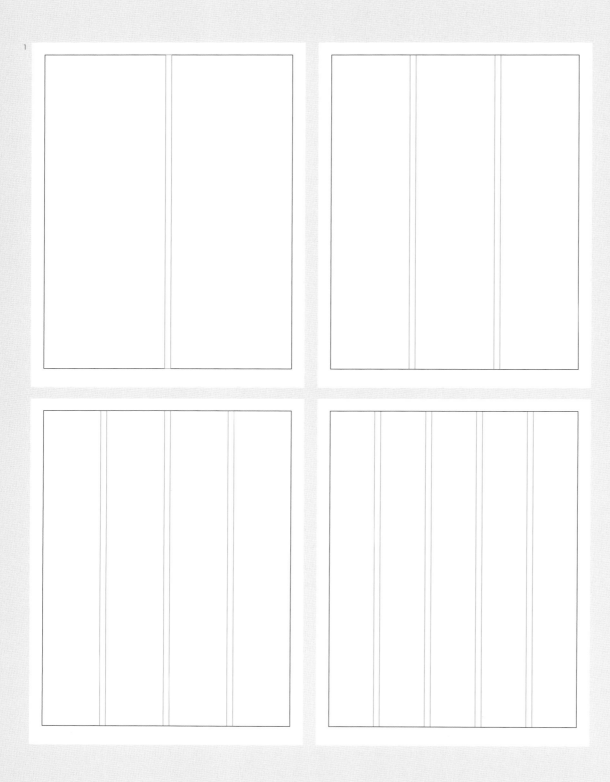

A multi-*column grid* makes many different combinations possible by applying the *composition* areas to one, two or three *columns*. Each area is hence constantly in *harmony* with the others.
Because the *column widths* are multiples of each other, they always have a harmonious relationship to each other and the alignments are obvious.

Multi-column grid
Examples

In editorial design, the multi-*column grid* makes the alignment of elements simple and help unify the *pages*.

1. The document's *format* of 245 × 340 mm (*format* when open) is divided into seven equal *columns*. The *margins* are 14 mm and the *gutters* are 3.5 mm. The resulting *column width* is 28 mm.
Texts and images can be aligned according to the *composition*'s requirements. *Headlines* and texts are set one, two or three *columns* wide depending on their importance and their characteristics.

Note that the odd number of *columns* creates an inherently dynamic system, where asymmetric *compositions* can be explored.

1. *Archinova*, exhibition catalogue
Alliade
Damien Gautier

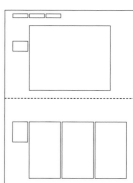

1

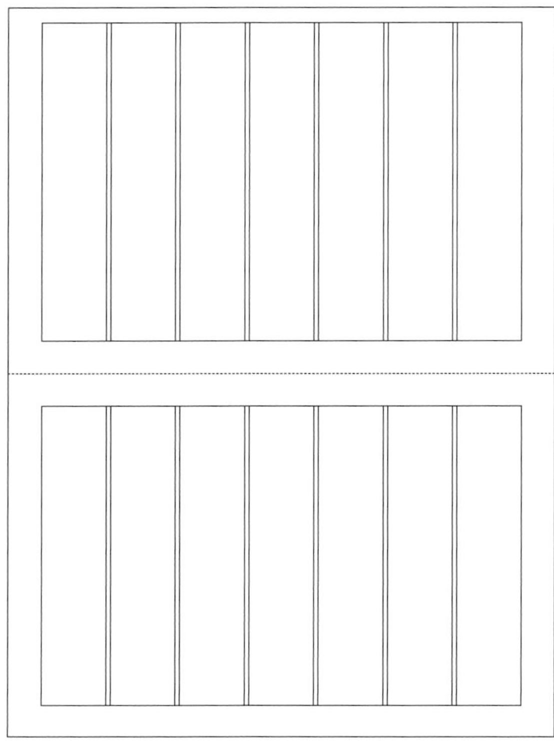

Archi'nova
Alliade

2/3

Sommaire

10 projets / 10 équipes

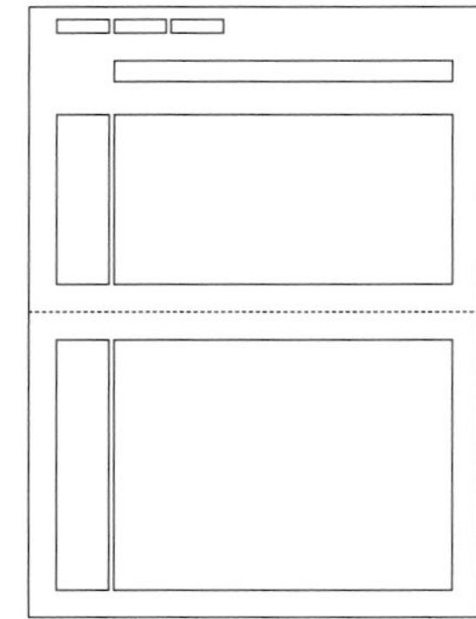

Archi'nova
Alliade

8/9

Alliade lance le concours Archi'nova sur Lyon-La Duchère

Archi'nova, concours d'idées ouvert à de jeunes équipes d'architectes, porte sur la conception et la construction d'un ensemble de cinquante logements dans le quartier des Bleuets, à La Duchère. Inscrit dans le Grand Projet de Ville (GPV) de Lyon, il est organisé par Alliade, groupe généraliste de l'habitat.

Un concours original pour améliorer la vie des quartiers
Convaincu que la transformation de sites comme Lyon-La Duchère mérite une approche architecturale créative et enthousiaste, Alliade lance en avril 2004 à l'intention des jeunes architectes le concours d'idées Archi'nova.
En soutenant ces nouveaux talents, le Groupe s'engage aux côtés des collectivités à participer au renouvellement de l'agglomération lyonnaise.

Enfin, c'est une façon de contribuer activement à une réflexion qui lui est chère : comment concilier nouveaux modes de vie, mixité des publics et cohabitation harmonieuse ?
Ce concours organisé par Alliade et par les trois écoles d'architecture de la région (Grenoble, Lyon et Saint-Étienne) s'adresse à de jeunes architectes âgés de moins de 40 ans.

Les professionnels appelés à concourir ont dû intégrer dans leur équipe des étudiants en cinquième ou sixième année d'architecture. Fait rare dans les concours d'idées habituellement mis en place, les dix équipes sélectionnées ici perçoivent chacune une indemnité de 10 000 euros. Enfin, l'équipe retenue au terme de ce concours suivra la réalisation de son projet, puisque la construction des cinquante logements est inscrite au Grand Projet de Ville (GPV) de Lyon.

Archi'nova
Alliade

6/7

Hervé Laurent
Président
du groupe Alliade

"2004 a marqué à la fois le 50e anniversaire de la CILL, notre organisme collecteur du 1 % logement et la création du Groupe Alliade qui a réuni, sous une marque commune, les différentes structures nous composant. Cette démarche fédératrice et cet anniversaire nous ont semblé des événements importants que nous devions accompagner d'une action marquant notre volonté d'apparaître comme un opérateur régional majeur dans le logement dans toutes ses composantes.
Ainsi est née cette idée d'un concours d'architectes, ouvert aux jeunes professionnels, associant qualité, créativité et enthousiasme.
Nous avons voulu, avec ce concours, montrer à nos partenaires et clients notre implication dans la recherche de solutions innovantes et adaptées pour répondre aux nouvelles donnes générées par le renouvellement urbain et l'évolution de l'habitat dans des quartiers en pleine mutation.
Ce concours s'inscrit vraiment dans une réflexion transversale que mène Alliade, dont les différentes structures et compétences ont pour objectif premier de proposer des solutions de cohabitations mixtes, équilibrées et harmonieuses pour le mieux vivre de tous."

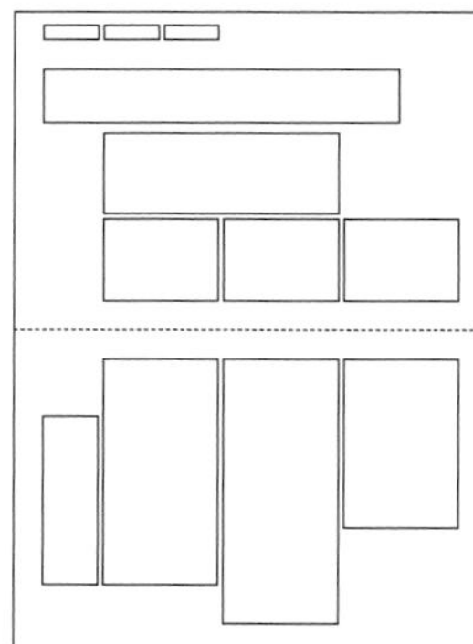

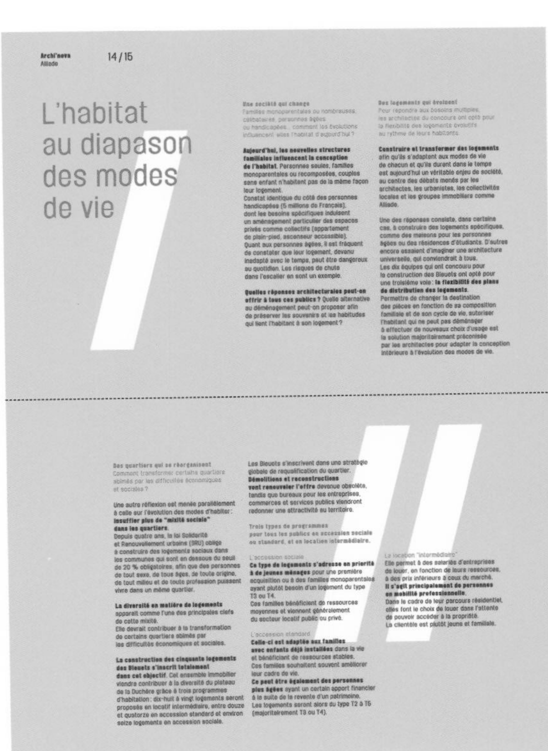
Archi'nova
Alliade
14/15
L'habitat
au diapason
des modes
de vie

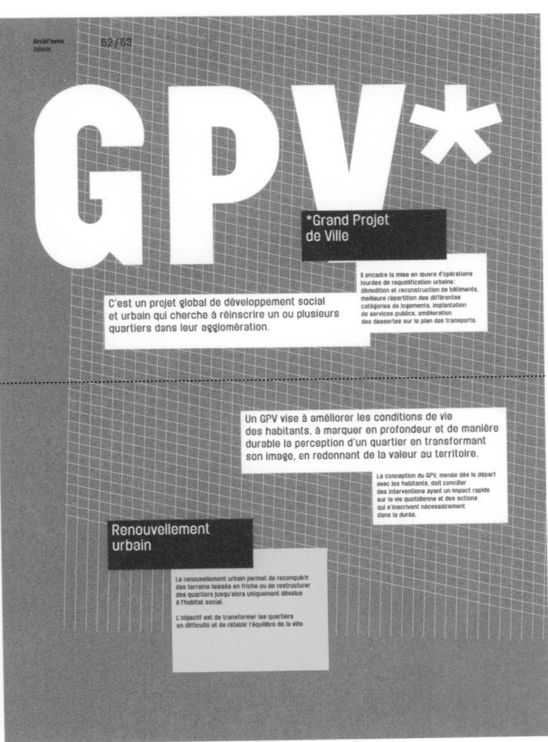
GPV*
*Grand Projet
de Ville
C'est un projet global de développement social et urbain qui cherche à réinscrire un ou plusieurs quartiers dans leur agglomération.
Un GPV vise à améliorer les conditions de vie des habitants, à marquer en profondeur et de manière durable la perception d'un quartier en transformant son image, en redonnant de la valeur au territoire.
Renouvellement
urbain

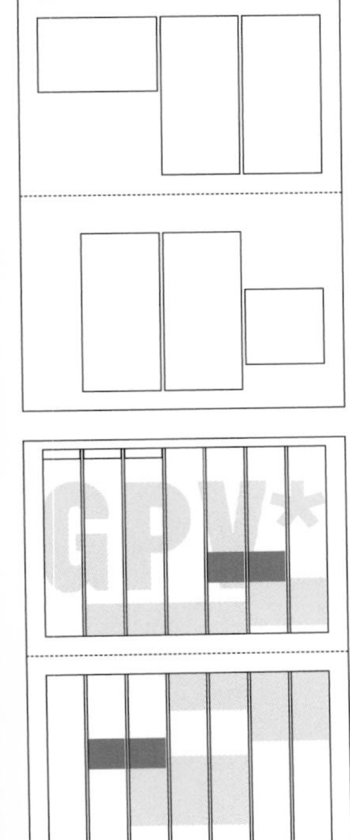

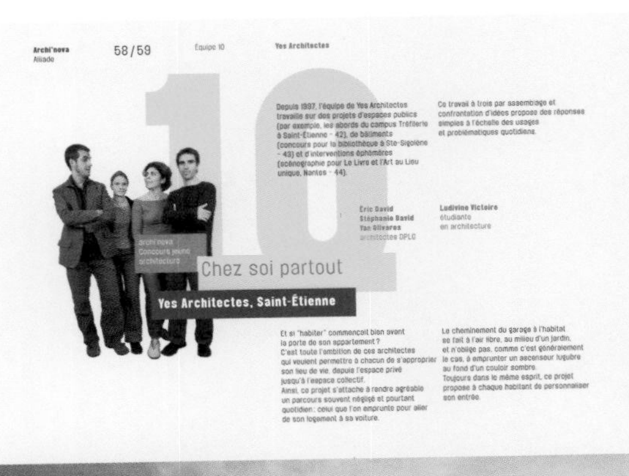
Archi'nova
Alliade
58/59
Équipe 10
Yes Architectes
Chez soi partout
Yes Architectes, Saint-Étienne

"Le logement, comme le vêtement, caractérise la personne"

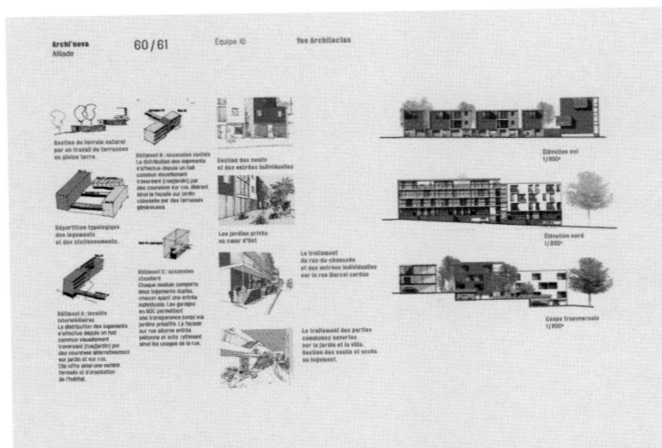
Archi'nova
Alliade
60/61
Équipe 10
Yes Architectes

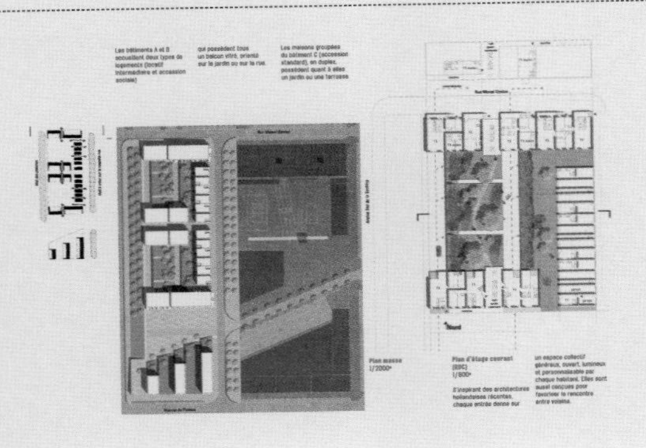

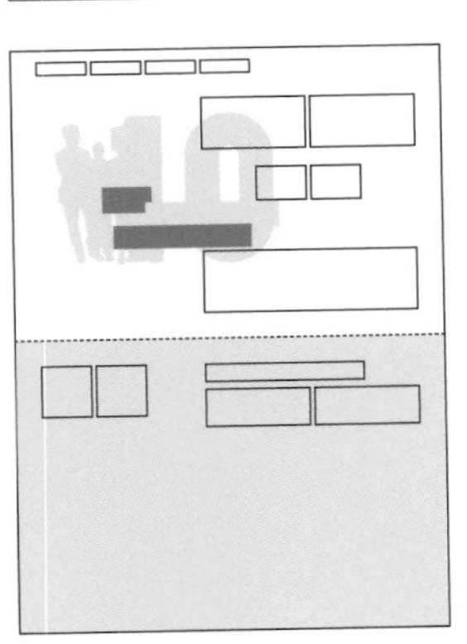

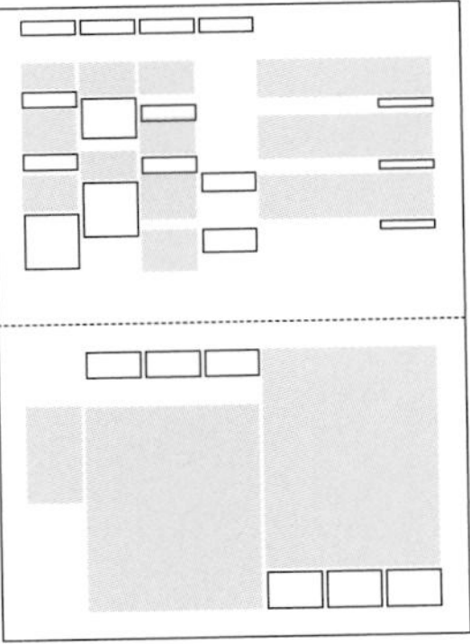

A multi-*column grid* gives a document structure, but isn't necessarily limiting. The *grid* should be used "in the background" of a *composition*, defining the alignments and offering stability, but not intended to be seen right away.

1. Behind this, at a first glance unstructured, *composition* is a 12-*column grid* that guides the positioning of the various *text boxes*. The *gutters* are also used to position the drop shadows.

1. École nationale supérieure d'architecture de Lyon, study calendar Damien Gautier

1

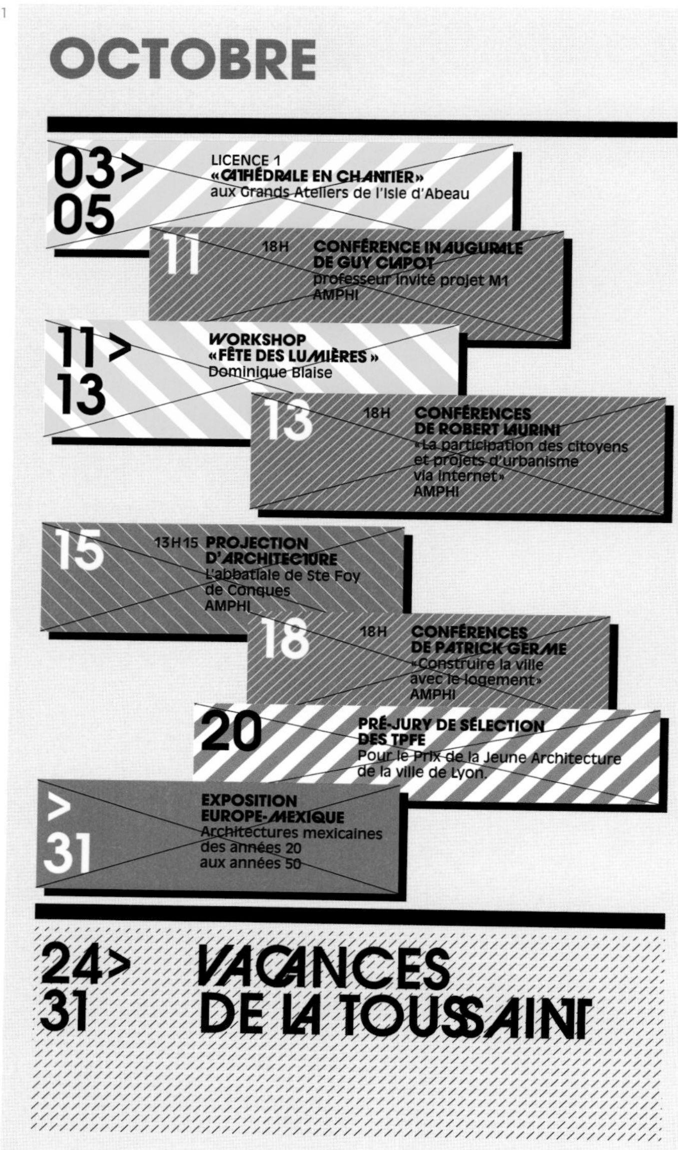

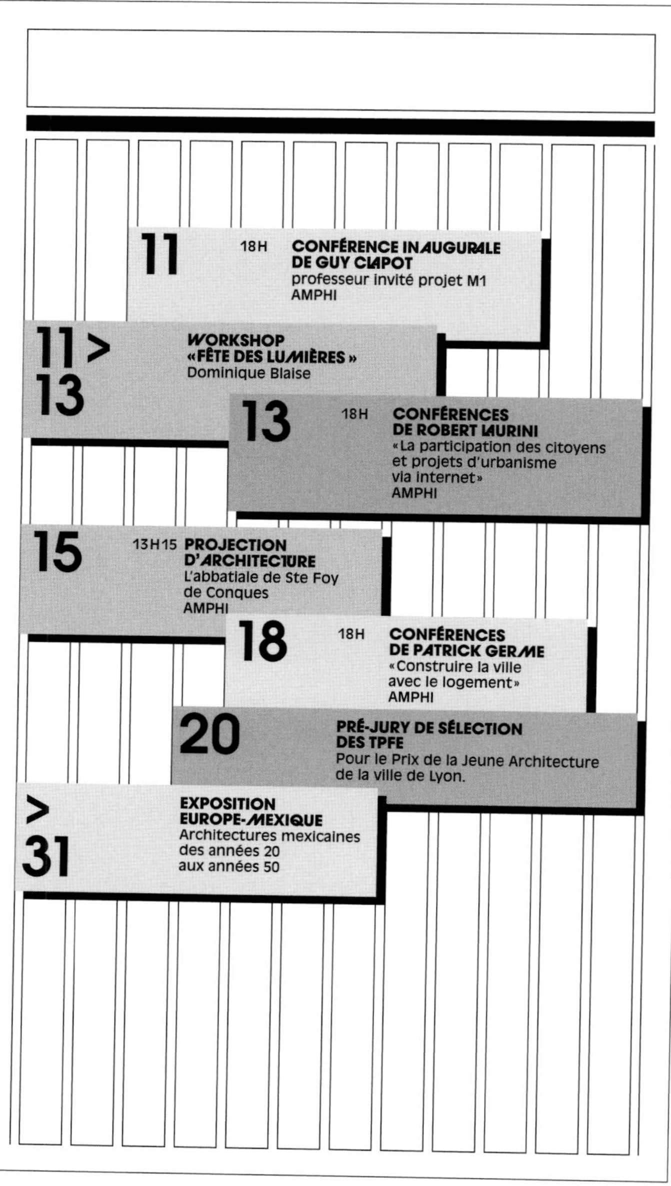

2. As opposed to the typical *newspapers*, this example is designed on the basis of a fine underlying *grid* of 11 *columns*. The *line length* of the body copy equals two *columns*, some *captions* and other short texts are only a single *column* wide.
This principle lets the *page* "breathe" and the different text widths vary the *reading rhythm*. This "breathing" and the diverse *gray values* differentiate the different articles on the double-*page* spread.

A newspaper like this stands out from the rest of the traditional press. The main article is read horizontally, and the short pieces are read from top to bottom. Similarly alternating from justified text (main article) and the *ragged setting* of the short pieces adds to the overall *contrast*. The *newspaper*'s vertical *masthead* also follows the *grid* and occupies two *columns*' width on the *front page*.

2. *La République du Centre,* newspaper layout project Rose-Marie Le Corre

2 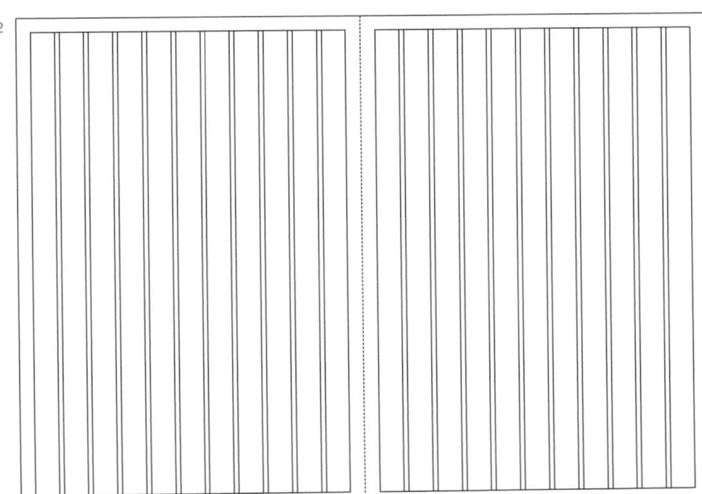

LOIRET

HIER APRÈS-MIDI, EN PÉRIODE DE SOLDE, UNE TORNADE DE MANIFESTANTS A DÉFERLÉ SUR LE CENTRE VILLE.

LES EXPLOITANTS ONT DÉVERSÉS PUIS BRÛLÉS LEURS TROP PLEIN DE TOMATE ET DE MELONS DEVANT LA PREFECTURE.

LES PRODUCTEURS DÉCLARENT LA GUERRE

Des manifestations surprises continuent à gêner les usagers

Contestation d'une formation financée par l'ANPE

A 11 heures, tous sur les rails

Ecoliers et lycéens rejoignent les manifestants

OUI

La République DU CENTRE

TRISTE RÉCOLTE

Le ras-le-bol des nounous !

Flash-Back sur l'incendie criminel

La poudre aux yeux des lessiviers

une semaine loin du petit écran

Les terroristes visent le président

Le cri du peuple s'est fait piégé

TISSUS - MODE - DÉCO - VOILAGES

-50 %

MONTIGNY PRÊT-À-PORTER SOLDES

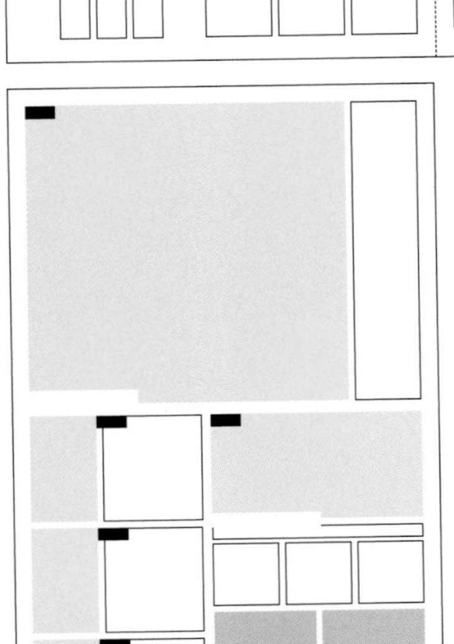

1. The five-*column grid* is used on all *pages* to place the elements (texts, *color* blocks, images, frames) and it is even juxtaposed with some of the images.

1. École nationale supérieure d'architecture de Lyon, brochure Élodie Michée

1

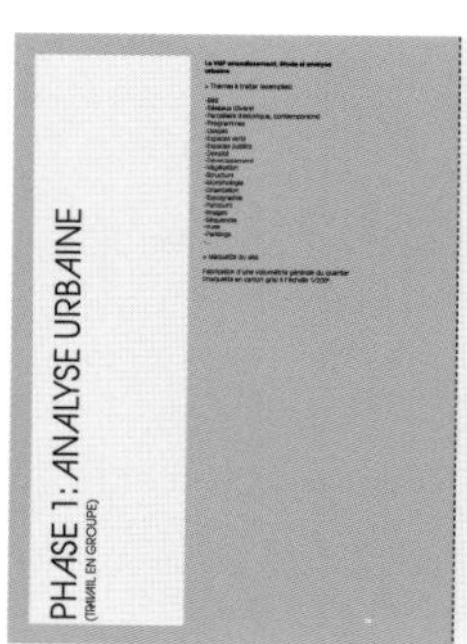

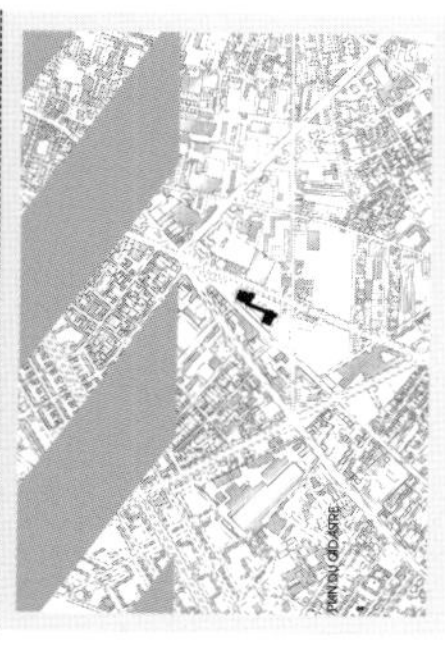

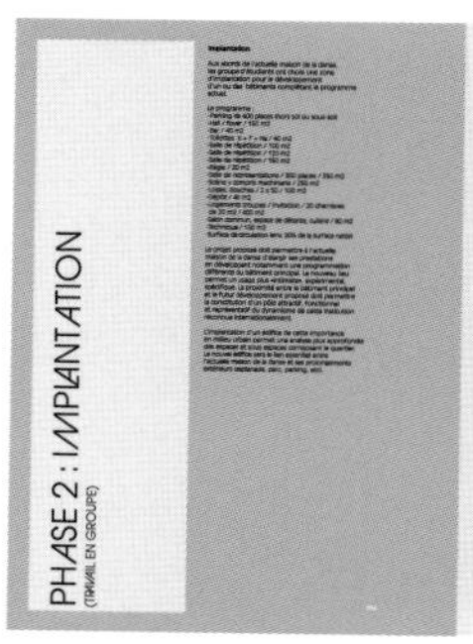

The multi-*column grid* principle can also be applied to digital and online media and serve their *compositions*. The designer has the option of varying the *column width* in proportion to the width of the window.

2. four-*column grid*
3. three-*column grid*
4. four-*column grid*

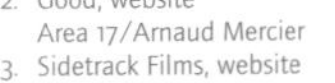

2. Good, website
Area 17/Arnaud Mercier
3. Sidetrack Films, website
Area 17/Arnaud Mercier
4. Giant Step, website
Area 17/Arnaud Mercier

2

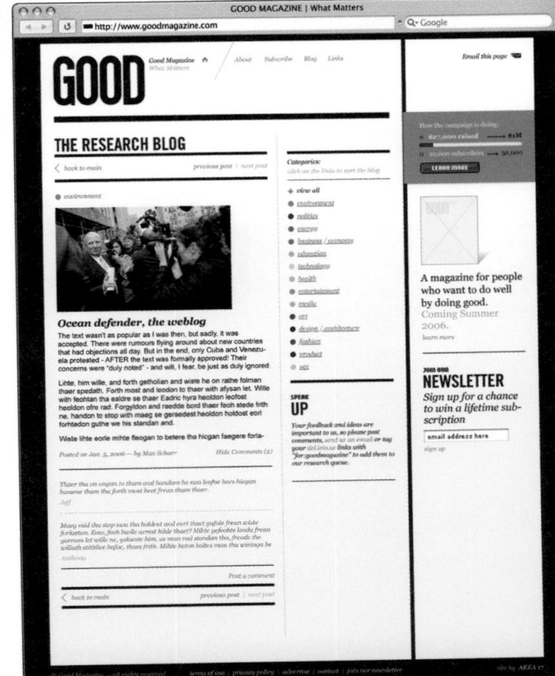

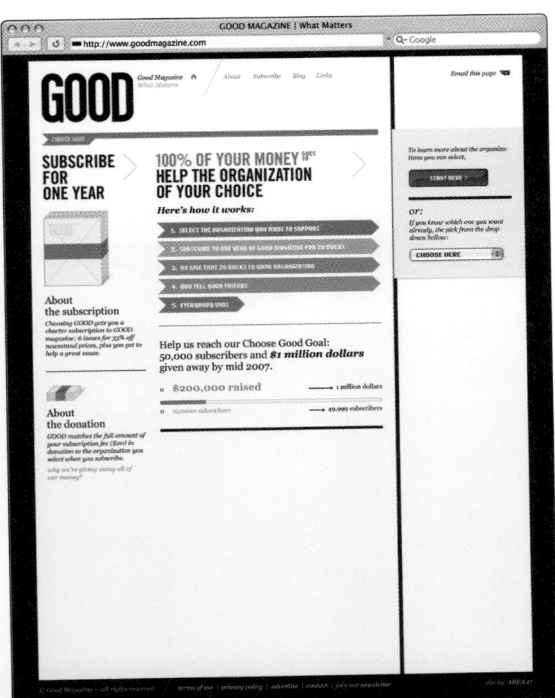

3

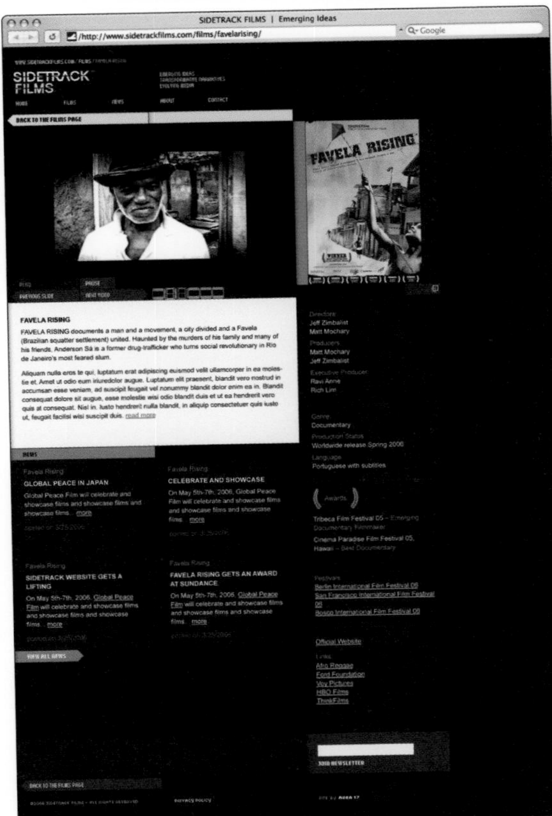

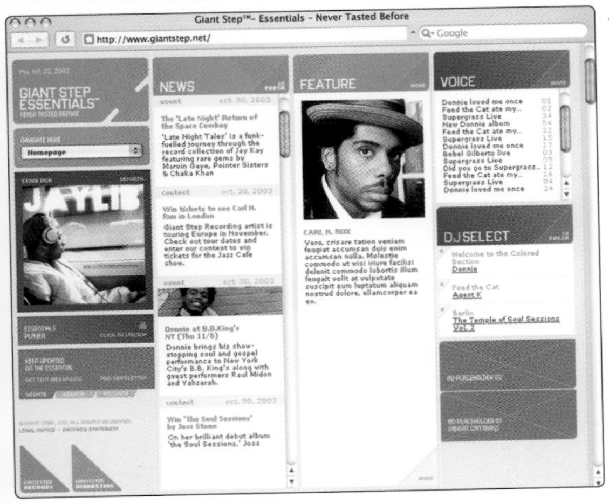

4

Multi-column grid
Overlapping grids

Two distinct multi-*column grids* with the same *margins* can be superimposed on the same page. These can be used together to arrange the elements according to a precise logic (type of elements: *headline*, text, image; type of texts: long texts, short texts, *captions*, etc.)

1. The two overlapping *grids* (four and three *columns*) allow *rhythm* in the *composition* by playing with images of different sizes.

1. *b.dule*
Trafik

1

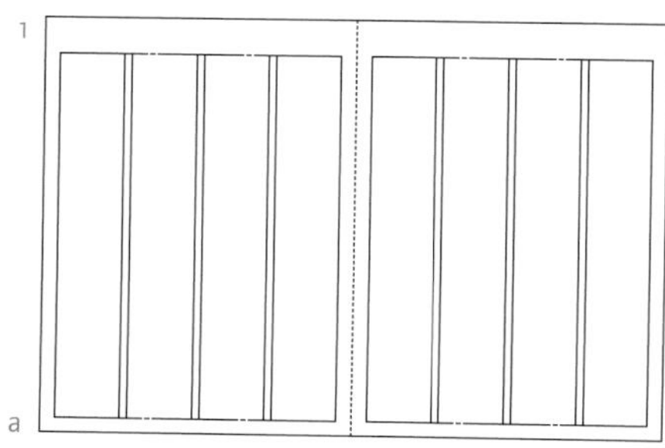

a

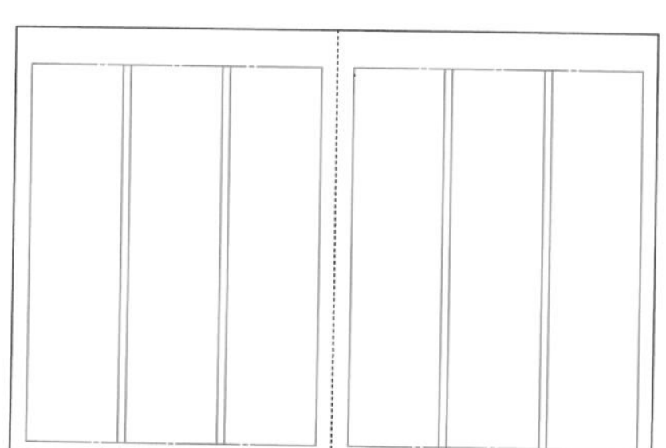

b

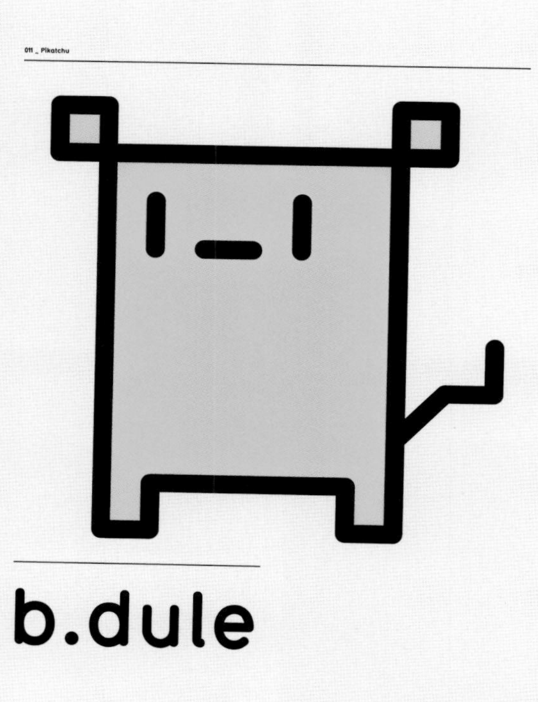

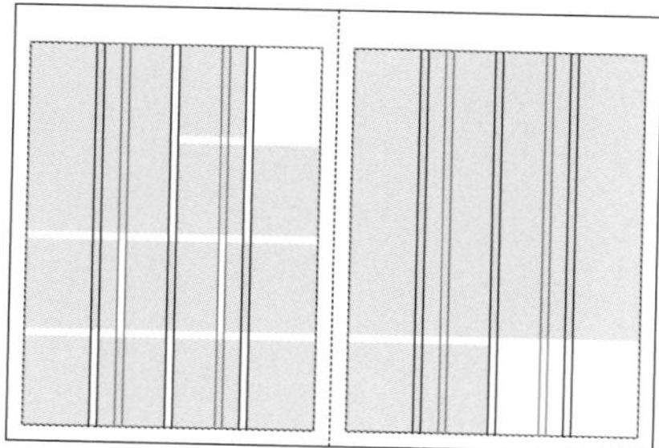

a+b

The partial overlapping of two *grids* can produce more complex *compositions* by playing with text blocks in different widths and interlaced *columns*.

2. A four-*column grid* (b) is superimposed on five *columns* of the first six-*column grid* (a).

2

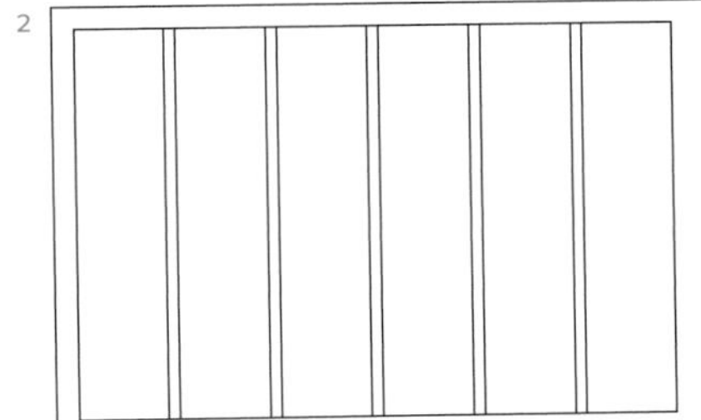

a

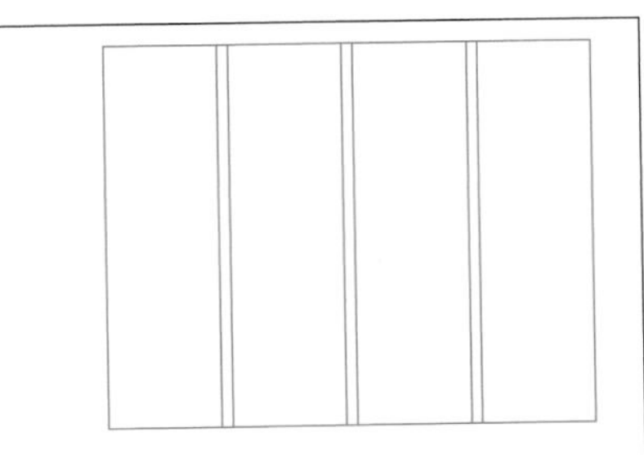

b

Histoires de caractères
D'où nous viennent ces caractères et que signifient-ils?

Une police de caractères standard contient 256 caractères. Mais beaucoup d'entre eux sont énigmatiques. Voici sur cette page la signification, l'origine et l'utilisation de la plupart de ces signes étranges ou étrangers. Parmi ces signes, des lettres capitales et minuscules, des chiffres – alignés ou elzéviriens – qui ont une véritable histoire au cours des siècles et des civilisations. La forme des caractères italiques découle directement de leur origine, et leur usage a évolué depuis leur apparition au XVIe siècle.

Tous ces *signes* sont présents dans une *police de caractères* standard et sont par conséquent au clavier (parfois en ayant recours à des raccourcis clavier compliqués): Accents étrangers (brève, "caron", double accent aigu, "macron", "ogonek", "overdot", "ring", tilde), æ et œ (Æ et Œ), Alinéa, section, Apostrophe, Astérisque, Arobas, Barre, "pipe", Barre oblique et barre oblique inversée ("slash" et "backslash"), Cédille, Copyright, Croix et double croix, Degré, Esperluette (ou perluette), Eszett, Fraction, Guillemets «français», Guillemets "anglais", Ligatures «f», Minute, Monnaies, Négation logique, o supérieur, Paragraphe, Puce et point centré, Points d'exclamation et d'interrogation inversés, "Registered", Seconde, Signes mathématiques, "Swung dash", "Thorn", "Trademark".

Les mots entre guillemets sont les termes anglo-saxons dont il ne m'a pas été possible de trouver une traduction fiable.

Capitales
Le terme «capitale» vient du latin «capitalis monumentalis», nom donné à la première écriture latine romaine. Ce sont les capitales gravées sur la colonne dédiée à l'empereur Trajan qui deviennent le modèle de l'écriture latine. La forme de ces *capitales* est le fruit d'une évolution de plusieurs siècles: de l'écriture cunéiforme découlent les *capitales* grecques (1100 av. J.-C.) qui évoluent ensuite pour donner naissance aux *capitales* étrusques (700 av. J.-C.) et aboutir enfin aux *capitales* romaines (400 av. J.-C.).

Au cours des siècles, les lettres *capitales* continuent à évoluer sous la main des copistes. Plus rapides à calligraphier, elles donnent naissance à la Quadrata et à l'Onciale. Dans les premiers textes composés en *italique*, les *capitales* étaient droites (n'existant pas en *italique*) mais elles s'inclineront bientôt pour suivre le rythme… Les *petites capitales* voient le jour vers 1550.

Minuscules
Les lettres *minuscules* sont issues de cette évolution de l'écriture qui se poursuivit encore. Les lettres minuscules découlent de la cursive romaine suivie de la semi onciale. Pour asseoir son empire, Charlemagne imposa la *minuscule* caroline dont s'inspirèrent les typographes de la Renaissance pour créer les premiers *caractères* typographiques.

Italique
L'*italique* a été créé par Alde Manuce en 1501 sur la base de la cancelleresca (écriture de chancellerie courante à cette poque) pour une collection de livres dits de poche (format in-8°). Ce *caractère* était en effet plus étroit que les *caractères romains* alors utilisés et correspondait donc particulièrement à un livre de petit format.

Son origine calligraphique explique le dessin cursif de l'*italique*, même si avec l'évolution des *caractères* au cours des siècles, elle s'est stabilisée pour parfois ne devenir qu'un *romain* penché. Alors que les *caractères italiques* sont à l'origine plus étroits que les *caractères romains*, les *caractères penchés* ayant pour modèle

les *caractères romains* sont de même *chasse*, voire plus encombrants. L'informatique a de plus donné la possibilité d'incliner les *caractères* en les déformant pour se substituer (bien médiocrement) aux *caractères italiques*. Ce n'est qu'au milieu du XVIe siècle que *romain* et *italique* ont été composés ensemble.

Auparavant, un livre pouvait être composé entièrement en *italique* alors qu'il est aujourd'hui tenu pour moins lisible que les *caractères romains*. Aujourd'hui, l'*italique* est simplement un complément du *romain*. Seuls des textes courts sont composés entièrement en *italique* (la préface d'un livre par exemple).

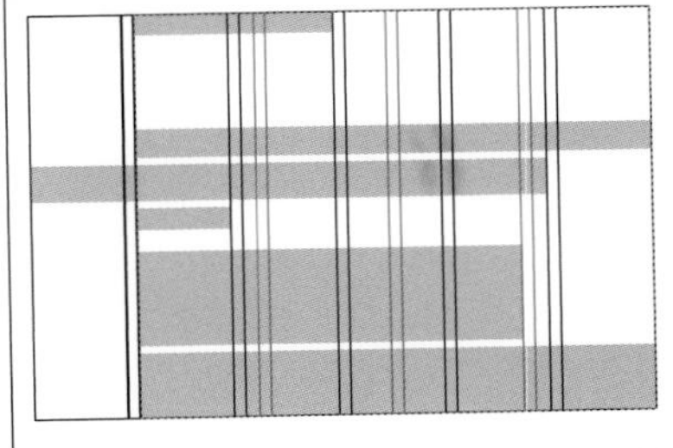

a+b

Un texte est souvent perturbé par de nombreux signes qui viennent s'y insérer: sigles, mots en capitales, chiffres, fractions, appels de note…: Les grandes capitales et les chiffres alignés utilisés au sein d'un texte en minuscules créent des taches qui nuisent au rythme typographique et ralentissent la lecture.

Certaines lettres juxtaposées entrent en collision et créent des «nœuds» qui compliquent la reconnaissance des mots. Quels que soient les réglages des logiciels concernant la taille de l'exposant et de l'indice, les fractions sont peu soignées.

Les chiffres ou lettres réduits sont toujours trop maigres et la barre oblique ("slash") se substitue trop souvent à la véritable barre de fraction.

Alors que les solutions proposées par les logiciels ne sont souvent qu'approximatives, certains caractères possèdent des séries de caractères additionnels étudiées pour apporter de véritables réponses: Les petites capitales sont dessinées pour apparaître de la même hauteur et de la même graisse que les minuscules.

Les chiffres elzéviriens sont spécialement dessinés pour s'intégrer dans un texte sans rompre son rythme. L'utilisation des ligatures (couples de lettres spécialement déssinés) permet d'éviter les collisions qui peuvent s'avérer gênantes en petit corps. Fractions, lettres et chiffres supérieurs sont dessinés pour apparaître de la même graisse que les minuscules.

Caractères additionnels
Quelles différences avec les *caractères* standard?

3 Grande *capitale* — Petite *capitale* agrandie à la hauteur d'une grande *capitale*

R R

2

influence
différence
difficile
influence
différence
difficile

4

A 1234567890

5

8 ½ 16 mo 12 12

1 et 2. Caractères ligaturés.

3. Comparaison entre petite et grande capitales.

4. Chiffres elzéviriens

5. Véritables fractions, lettres et chiffres supérieurs.

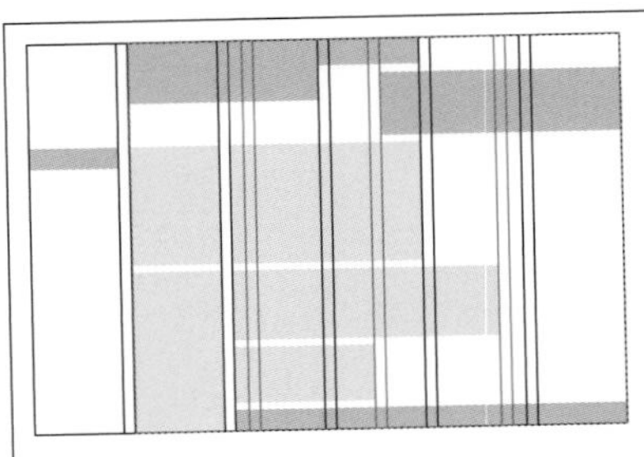

a+b

1. For the *layout* of this *newspaper*, the two overlapping multi-*column grids* create different *reading rhythms* depending on the *headlines* and articles. The five-*column grid* (a) is reserved for short articles and the four-*column grid* (b) is for longer articles. The reading speed is slowed due to the longer *line length*.
The superimposition of the two *grids* also allows some "air" (vertical space) into a *page* that is usually tightly packed. The shifts break the normal stiffness of a *newspaper layout*.

1. *Réforme*, newspaper
Damien Gautier

1

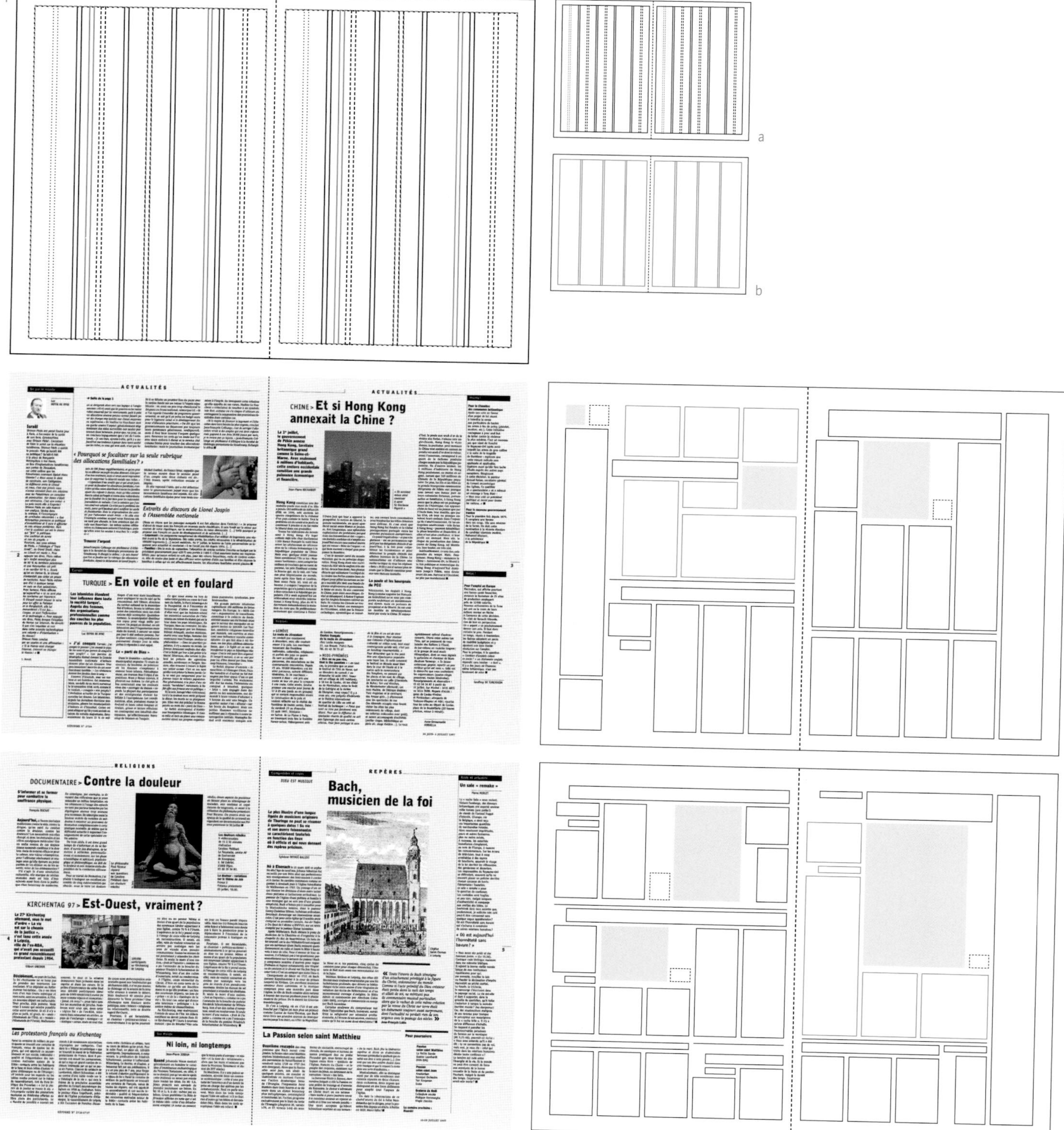

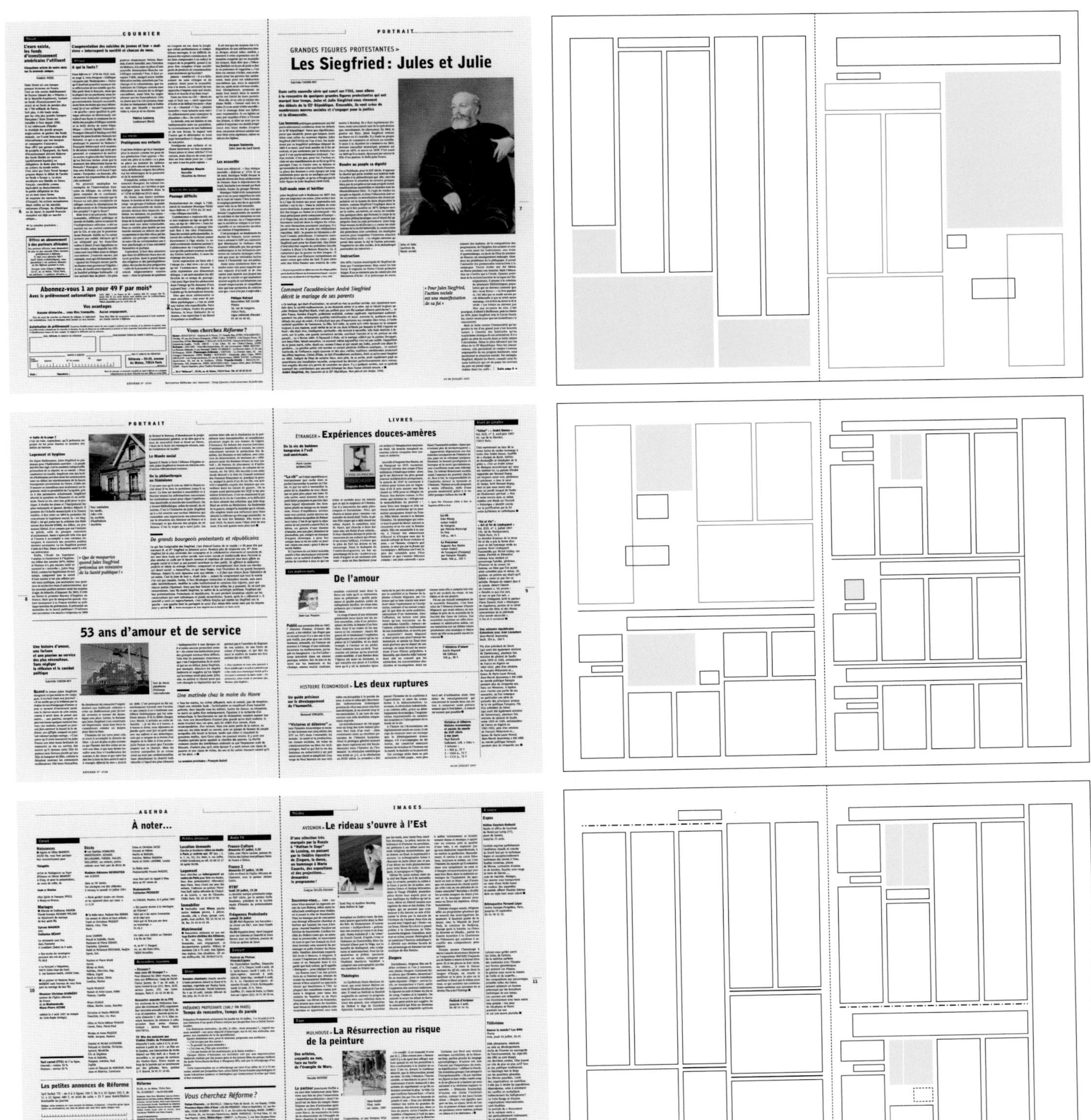

1. The multi-*column* is used here as a structure for the vertically placed *headline*. The *gutters* are used to place the vertical black lines interspersed with the texts. On the back side a second *grid* partially overlaps the first, and the resulting discrepancies add *rhythm* to the composition.

1. *Alain Savouret et les élèves du CNR*, folded poster
Grame
Trafik

1

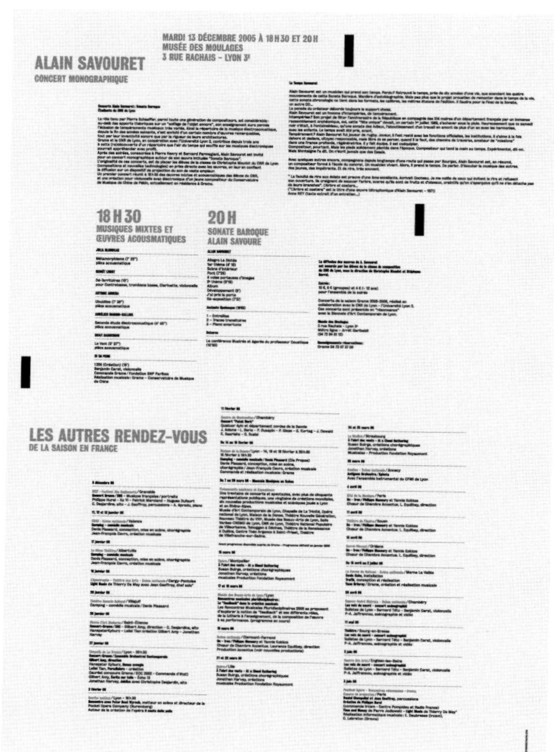

Each *grid* can also be applied to a part of the page. The two *grids* don't overlap, instead, we refer to a combination of *grids*.

2. three-*column* and four-*column grids*
3. two-*column* and five-*column grids*
4. left hand page: three, four and six-*column grids*
right hand page: two and four-*column grids*

2. *Chill*, magazine
Ill studio / L. Vernhet, N. Malinowsky, T. Audurand
3. ibid.
4. ibid.

2

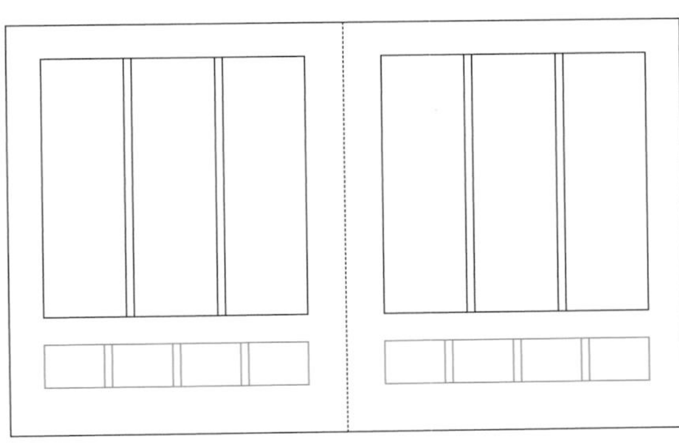

3

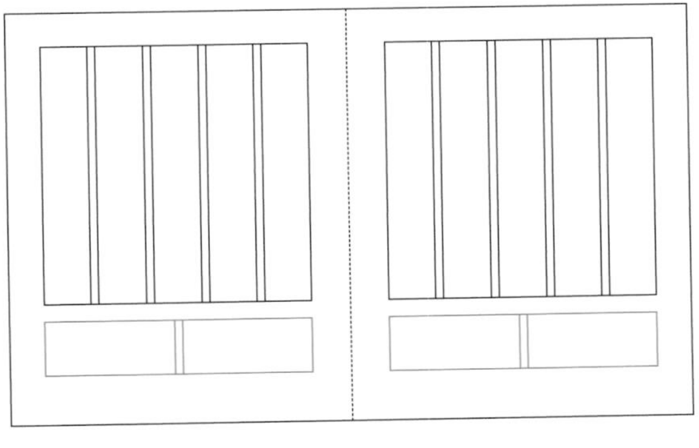

4

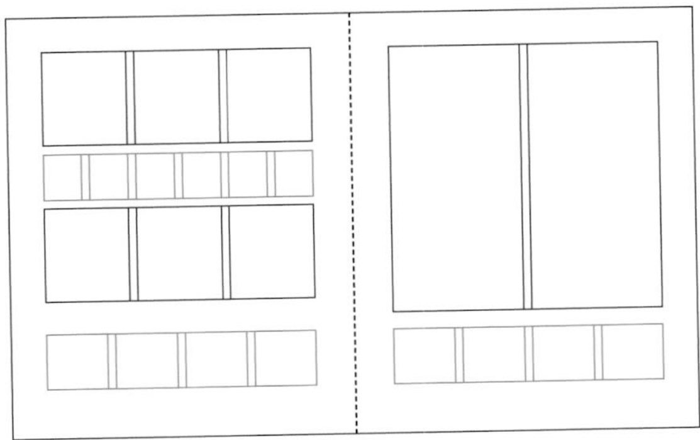

Lines of force
Basic principles and examples

By defining one or more "*lines of force*", where elements in the *composition* are placed along axes, one creates a *composition* principle that visually structures the space and information. This same principle can be used to create a strong connection between several *pages* in a *book*.

Proportional divisions
The lines of force may divide the page height into equal parts: division by two, three, four or more. The resulting lines are used as reference points for placing all or some of the elements on the page.

Examples of designs with a central line of force

1. The *composition* is arranged on each side of the central line. Text and images communicate between the upper part and the lower part.

1. Galerie nationale du Jeu de Paume, posters
Gérard Plénacoste – Visuel design

1

2. The center line is visible as an axis that organizes the texts and images without producing a strictly symmetrical *composition*.

3. Here, too, the texts and images are positioned along the central *line of force*.

2. *Le café du xx e siècle*, double-page spread
Damien Gautier
3. *Chill*, magazine
Ill studio/L. Vernhet, N. Malinowsky, T. Audurand

2

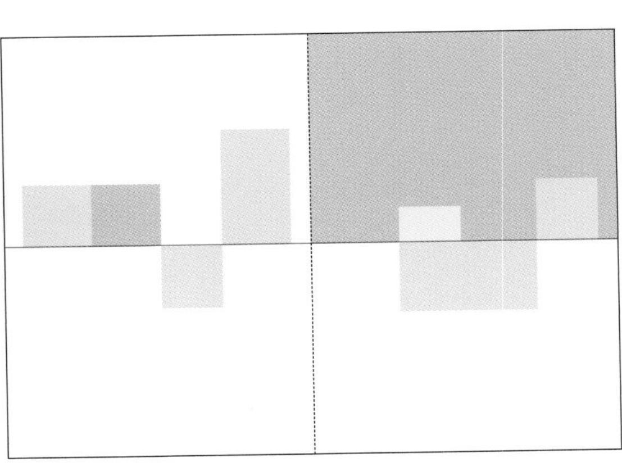

3

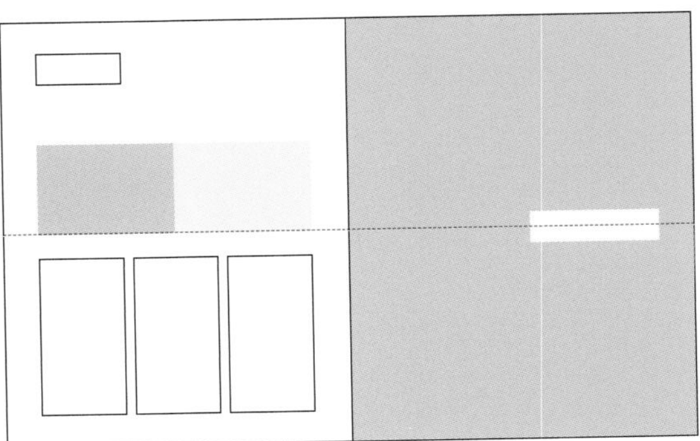

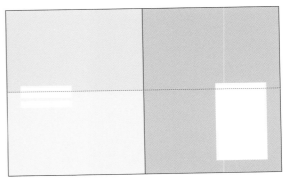

Composition based on a central line of force

1. Although the elements (*headlines*, texts and images, etc.) are placed freely along the central *line of force*, this line still forms the commonality between the individual *compositions*.
On the *front page* the *text box* indicates the *line of force* by resting on it. In the first double-*page* spread the line is marked by the image above and the text which hangs from it in the lower half.
The second, less systematic *composition*, however, clearly displays the central *line of force*.

1. *Le journal des laboratoires n° 1*
November 2003
Les laboratoires d'Aubervilliers
deValence

1

info@leslaboratoires.org www.leslaboratoires.org
NOVEMBRE 2003 LE JOURNAL
NUMÉRO UN 32 PAGES DES LABORATOIRES
Scoli Acosta/Sandy Amerio/Marco Berrettini/Xavier Boussiron/Yvane Chapuis
Maud Desseignes/Thomas Hirschhorn/Christophe Kihm/Maurizio Lazzarato
Sabine Macher/François Piron/Marcus Steinweg/Loïc Touzé

1 Une inauguration modifiée

Sommaire

22
Entretien
Xavier Boussiron/
François Piron
octobre 2003

Entretien
Marco Berrettini/
Loïc Touzé
mai 2003

26

Composition based on lines of force derived by the proportional division of the page height

2. Two *lines of force* placed at one sixth and one third of the *page* height are used to place texts and images. The *composition*'s structure is emphasized by thick lines which mark the *lines of force*.

2

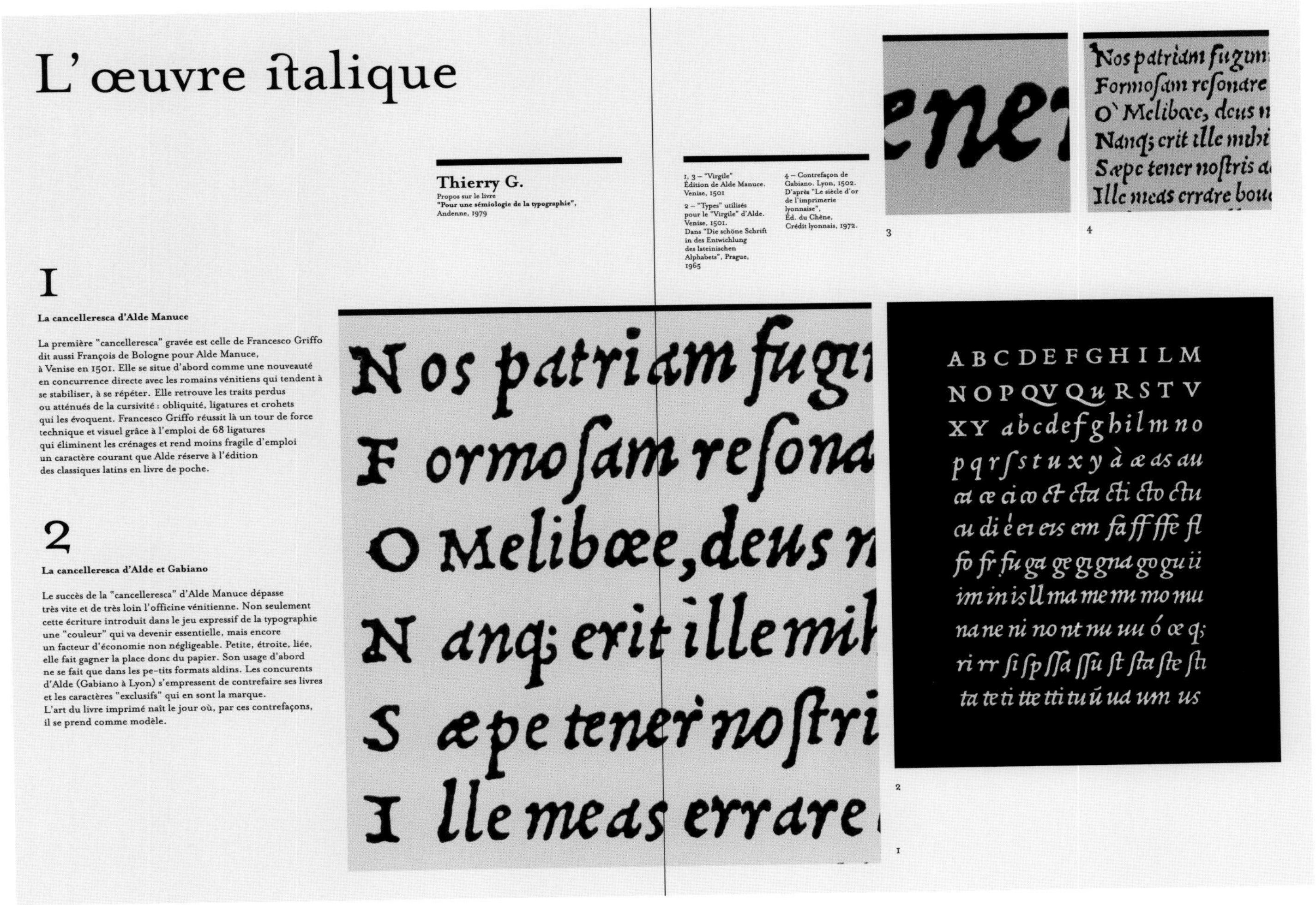

L'œuvre italique

Thierry G.
Propos sur le livre
"Pour une sémiologie de la typographie",
Andenne, 1979

1, 3 – "Virgile" Édition de Alde Manuce. Venise, 1501

2 – "Types" utilisés pour le "Virgile" d'Alde. Venise, 1501. Dans "Die schöne Schrift in des Entwichlung des lateinischen Alphabets", Prague, 1965

4 – Contrefaçon de Gabiano. Lyon, 1502. D'après "Le siècle d'or de l'imprimerie lyonnaise", Éd. du Chêne, Crédit lyonnais, 1972.

3

4

I

La cancelleresca d'Alde Manuce

La première "cancelleresca" gravée est celle de Francesco Griffo dit aussi François de Bologne pour Alde Manuce, à Venise en 1501. Elle se situe d'abord comme une nouveauté en concurrence directe avec les romains vénitiens qui tendent à se stabiliser, à se répéter. Elle retrouve les traits perdus ou atténués de la cursivité : obliquité, ligatures et crohets qui les évoquent. Francesco Griffo réussit là un tour de force technique et visuel grâce à l'emploi de 68 ligatures qui éliminent les crénages et rend moins fragile d'emploi un caractère courant que Alde réserve à l'édition des classiques latins en livre de poche.

2

La cancelleresca d'Alde et Gabiano

Le succès de la "cancelleresca" d'Alde Manuce dépasse très vite et de très loin l'officine vénitienne. Non seulement cette écriture introduit dans le jeu expressif de la typographie une "couleur" qui va devenir essentielle, mais encore un facteur d'économie non négligeable. Petite, étroite, liée, elle fait gagner la place donc du papier. Son usage d'abord ne se fait que dans les pe-tits formats aldins. Les concurents d'Alde (Gabiano à Lyon) s'empressent de contrefaire ses livres et les caractères "exclusifs" qui en sont la marque. L'art du livre imprimé naît le jour où, par ces contrefaçons, il se prend comme modèle.

2

1

1/6

1/3

1/3

1/3

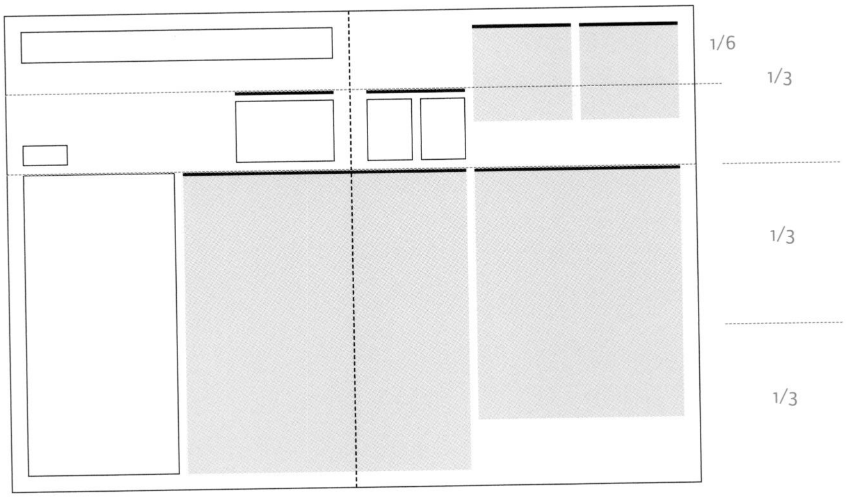

Composition based on lines of force derived by the proportional division of the page height

The design principle can be more complex and juxtapose two different divisions (for example, dividing the *page* height by three and four). Each of these divisions can be used to define *lines of force* which can be used to "hang" specific elements.

1. The *page* height has been divided by three and four. The division by three is used to place the main text, and the division by four is used to place illustrations and additional elements such as *captions*.

1. *Des yeux pour l'Himalaya*, brochure
Photographs: © Didier Syre
Damien Gautier

1

1/4
1/3
1/4
1/3
1/4
1/3
1/4

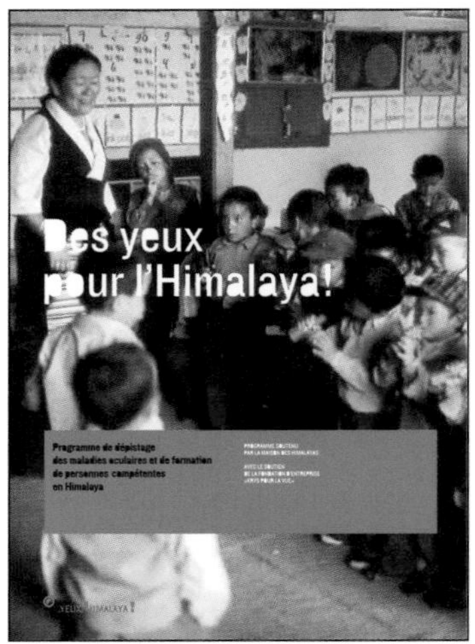

Programme de dépistage
des maladies oculaires et de formation
de personnes compétentes
en Himalaya

**Des yeux
pour l'Himalaya!**

Introduction

On estime aujourd'hui à 180 millions le nombre de personnes qui souffrent de déficiences visuelles graves dans le monde.

État des lieux

Les vices de réfraction et la baisse de vision ont aussi été recensées comme priorités immédiates dans le cadre du programme 2020 de l'OMS.

Besoins

L'un des problèmes principaux à résoudre pour éliminer la cécité évitable, à l'avenir, sera de pouvoir disposer d'un personnel qualifié et convenablement formé. Il sera également nécessaire de maîtriser les coûts dans les pays en voie de développement grâce au transfert de nouvelles technologies et à l'adaptation des techniques existantes.

L'Inde est l'un des pays les plus touchés.

Une situation critique agravée par le climat et les difficultés d'accès

Dans l'Himalaya indien, zone géographique sur laquelle nous voulons porter notre action, les soins oculaires sont encore plus difficiles à mettre en œuvre en raison de l'isolement important des villages et des conditions climatiques rigoureuses.

La période hivernale, au Ladakh ou au Zanskar, s'étend sur plus de six mois et rend la circulation des hommes ainsi que des marchandises très aléatoire. De ce fait, la situation y est certainement encore plus critique qu'ailleurs.

Programme d'action

1

Dans un premier temps, nous nous limiterons à des opérations simples, d'efficacité prouvée, rapides à mettre en œuvre et permettant de sensibiliser le public :

2

Cela nous permettra ensuite d'initier des actions de plus grande envergure, en complément des précédentes qui seront maintenues et soutenues :

3

Une autre facette de notre action sur place portera sur les ressources humaines par :

À terme, nous souhaitons continuer à fournir des matières premières, neuves et usagées, aux techniciens, issus des populations locales, lesquels procéderont eux-mêmes aux dépistages et évaluations, puis réaliseront et distribueront les équipements adéquates.

Sources Coordonnées

YEUX HIMALAYA !

Composition based on lines of force derived by the proportional division of the page height

1. This brochure's design is based on a *grid* of four *columns*:
- the introductory text fills three *columns*
- presentation text fills two *columns*
- descriptions, calendar fill one *column*

This grid is complemented by three *lines of force*, calculated by dividing the *page* height into four equal parts. Most of the elements on the *page* are aligned to these lines. Some of the elements, however, deviate from this rule in order to add *rhythm* to the *pages*.

1. Orchestre national de Lyon, brochure
Damien Gautier

1

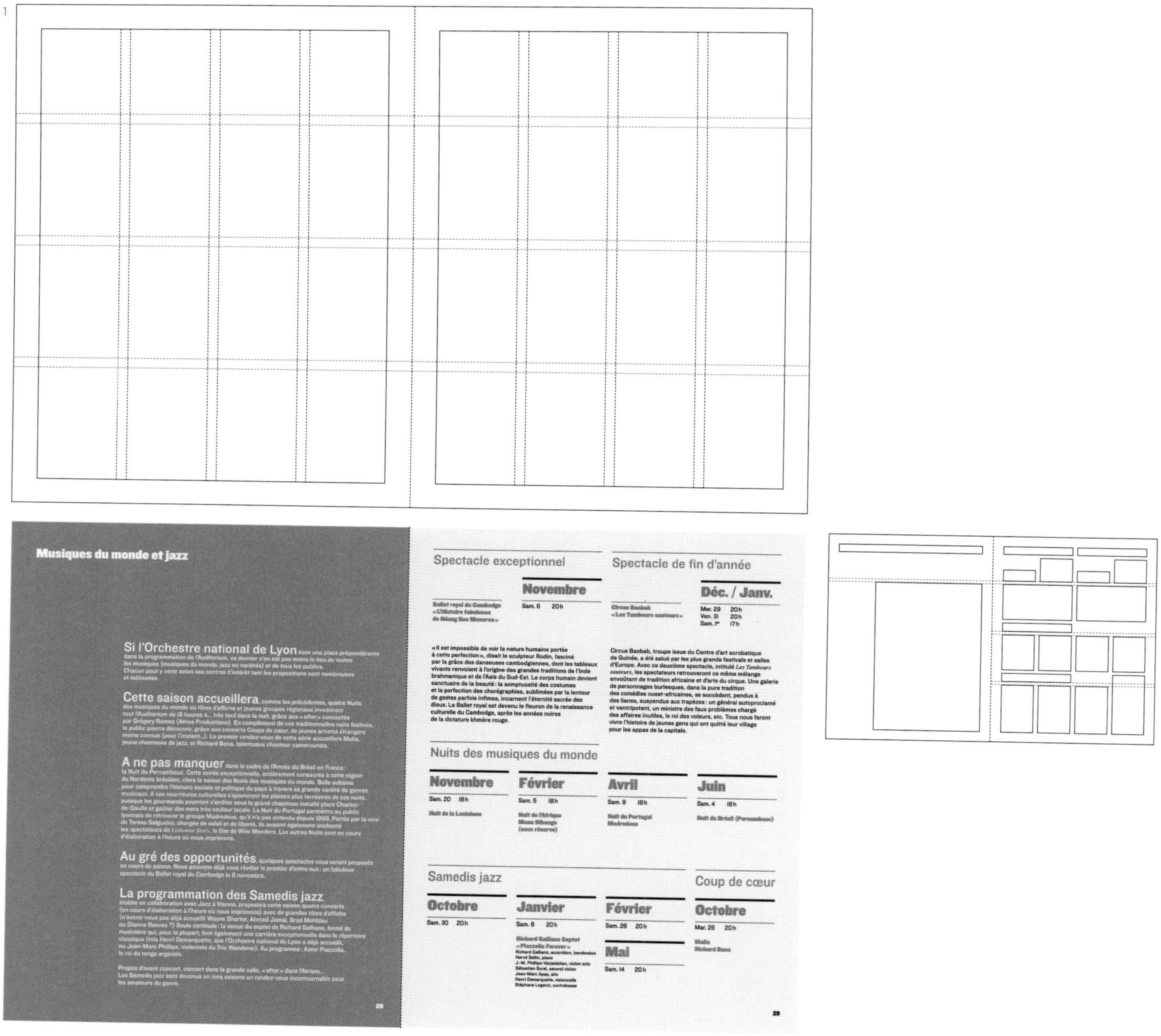

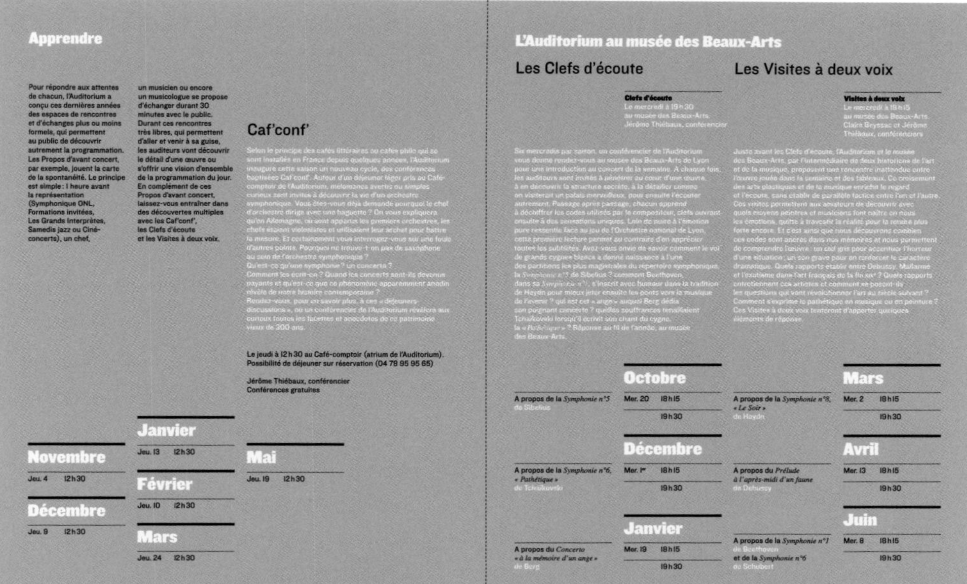

Apprendre

Pour répondre aux attentes de chacun, l'Auditorium a conçu ces dernières années des espaces de rencontres et d'échanges plus ou moins formels, qui permettent au public de découvrir autrement la programmation. Les Propos d'avant concert, par exemple, jouent la carte de la spontanéité. Le principe est simple : 1 heure avant la représentation (Symphonique ONL, Formations invitées, Les Grands Interprètes, Samedis jazz ou Ciné-concerts), un chef, un musicien ou encore un musicologue se propose d'échanger durant 30 minutes avec le public. Durant ces rencontres très libres, qui permettent d'aller et venir à sa guise, les auditeurs vont découvrir le détail d'une œuvre ou s'offrir une vision d'ensemble de la programmation du jour. En complément de ces Propos d'avant concert, laissez-vous entraîner dans des découvertes multiples avec les Caf'conf', les Clefs d'écoute et les Visites à deux voix.

Caf'conf'

Le jeudi à 12 h 30 au Café-comptoir (atrium de l'Auditorium). Possibilité de déjeuner sur réservation (04 78 95 95 65)

Jérôme Thiébaux, conférencier
Conférences gratuites

Novembre
Jeu. 4 12 h 30

Décembre
Jeu. 9 12 h 30

Janvier
Jeu. 13 12 h 30

Février
Jeu. 10 12 h 30

Mars
Jeu. 24 12 h 30

Mai
Jeu. 19 12 h 30

40

L'Auditorium au musée des Beaux-Arts

Les Clefs d'écoute

Clefs d'écoute

Octobre
A propos de la *Symphonie n°5* — Mer. 20 18 h 15 / 19 h 30

Décembre
A propos de la *Symphonie n°6, « Pathétique »* — Mer. 1er 18 h 15 / 19 h 30

Janvier
A propos du *Concerto « à la mémoire d'un ange »* — Mer. 19 18 h 15 / 19 h 30

Les Visites à deux voix

Visites à deux voix

Mars
A propos de la *Symphonie n°8, « Le Soir »* — Mer. 2 18 h 15 / 19 h 30

Avril
A propos du *Prélude à l'après-midi d'un faune* — Mer. 13 18 h 15 / 19 h 30

Juin
A propos de la *Symphonie n°1* et de la *Symphonie n°6* — Mer. 8 18 h 15 / 19 h 30

41

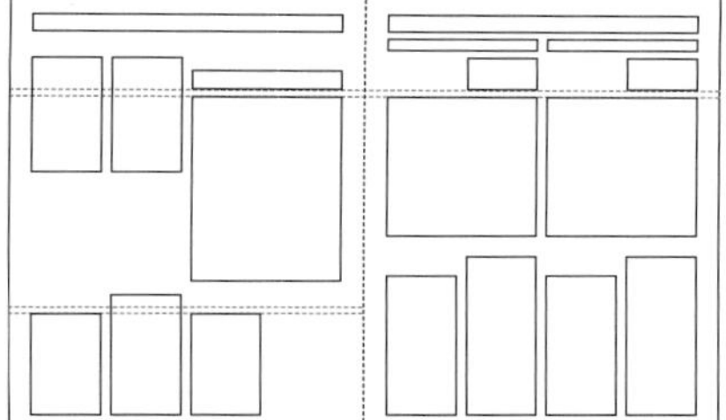

Novembre

Fauré
Pelléas et Mélisande (suite d'orchestre)

Saint-Saëns
Concerto pour piano et orchestre n°5, en fa majeur, op. 103

Schumann
Symphonie n°3, en mi bémol majeur, op. 97, « Rhénane »

Ven. 26 20 h 30

Orchestre national de Lyon
Roberto Minczuk, direction
Jean-Yves Thibaudet, piano

Fauré, St-Saëns, Schumann

Le Lyonnais Jean-Yves Thibaudet s'est fait reconnaître comme l'ambassadeur privilégié de la musique française, et le concerto de Saint-Saëns en est un fleuron, malgré quelques inflexions orientales (il fut composé en partie à Louqsor). Le *Pelléas* de Fauré, musique de scène pour la création anglaise de la pièce de Maeterlinck (1898), attira fort injustement les quolibets de Debussy, peu sensible à sa grâce et à son mystère – il parla même d'une « Fileuse pour casinos de stations balnéaires ». Rien de languide en tout cas dans la « *Rhénane* » de Schumann (1850), évocation éclatante du « fleuve sacré », comme le compositeur le décrivait dix ans plus tôt dans un lied des *Amours du poète*.

Décembre

Rachmaninov
Concerto pour piano n°2, en ut mineur, op. 18

Tchaïkovski
Symphonie n°6, en si mineur, op. 74, « Pathétique »

Retrouvez nos Concerts de Noël p. 16

Jeu. 2 20 h 30
Sam. 4 18 h

Orchestre national de Lyon
Manfred Honeck, direction
Lang Lang, piano

Rachmaninov, Tchaïkovski

Emblématiques du romantisme russe, ces deux œuvres fiévreuses jusqu'à la violence sont filles de la douleur. Rachmaninov composa son *Deuxième Concerto* au terme d'un long mutisme créateur, duquel le sauvèrent des séances d'hypnose ; il faut un Lang Lang, nouvelle coqueluche des salles de concert internationales, pour venir à bout d'un tel marathon pianistique. Chant du cygne de Tchaïkovski, la « *Pathétique* » précède de quelques semaines son suicide, qu'elle semble pressentir. Elle est à la mesure du talent de Manfred Honeck, chef autrichien invité par les plus grands orchestres et curieusement méconnu en France.

Janvier

Haydn
Symphonie n°88, en sol majeur, Hob I:88

Jolivet
Concerto pour trompette et orchestre n°2

Berio
Sequenza X, pour trompette

Wagner
Le Crépuscule des dieux : Prélude – Aube et Lever du jour – Adieux de Siegfried et Voyage de Siegfried sur le Rhin – Marche funèbre

Ven. 14 20 h 30
Sam. 15 18 h

Orchestre national de Lyon
Hugh Wolff, direction
David Guerrier, trompette

Haydn, Jolivet, Berio, Wagner

Né il y a vingt ans à Pierrelatte, dans la Drôme, David Guerrier porte déjà très haut les couleurs de l'école de vents française. Il collectionne les engagements et les récompenses, jusqu'à une Victoire de la musique en 2004, au titre du « meilleur soliste instrumental ». En cette année où l'on célèbre le centenaire de la naissance d'André Jolivet, l'un des musiciens les plus originaux du xxe siècle français, il nous présente ce concerto insolite de 1954, où la trompette dialogue avec un orchestre de vents, piano et percussions. Dans cette œuvre comme dans la *Sequenza* de Berio, ce cuivre auquel les compositeurs classiques ont peu donné la vedette révèle une palette digne de la clarinette ou du violon.

12

Janvier

Berg
Concerto pour violon et orchestre « à la mémoire d'un ange »

R. Strauss
Mort et Transfiguration, poème symphonique op. 24

R. Strauss
Till l'Espiègle, poème symphonique op. 28

Jeu. 20 20 h 30
Sam. 22 18 h

Orchestre national de Lyon
Marc Albrecht, direction
Viviane Hagner, violon

Berg, Strauss

A Vienne, au début du xxe siècle, coexistaient des talents aussi divers que Richard Strauss, le dernier romantique, et Alban Berg, qui fut avec Schoenberg et Webern l'artisan d'une mutation radicale. Ces trois œuvres partagent toutefois de mettre à nu les émotions humaines les plus fondamentales, notamment l'angoisse de la mort : avec humour (*Till*), emphase (*Mort et Transfiguration*) ou douleur (Berg).
Le *Concerto « à la mémoire d'un ange »* fut composé sous le choc du décès de Manon Gropius, fille en secondes noces d'Alma Mahler. Berg ne l'entendit jamais, étant mort trois mois avant sa création. Le requiem pour Manon était devenu son propre requiem.

Mahler
Symphonie n°7, en si mineur, « Chant de la nuit »

Jeu. 27 20 h 30
Sam. 29 18 h

Orchestre national de Lyon
Alan Gilbert, direction

Mahler

Composée en 1904-1905, la *Septième Symphonie* de Mahler fut dès sa création, à Prague, l'une des plus controversées. Purement romantique dans l'inspiration, elle révèle en certains passages une modernité harmonique inhabituelle chez le compositeur, et cette dualité heurta plus d'un commentateur. Mais cette convergence de moyens n'est pas de trop pour peindre la diversité de la nuit mahlérienne, de la marche funèbre peuplée de fantômes à la sérénade amoureuse (avec guitare et mandoline). L'ONL s'en remet pour la traverser à un guide très sûr, dont il a déjà pu apprécier la maîtrise : Alan Gilbert, le jeune chef de l'Orchestre philharmonique de Stockholm.

Février

Zender
Bardo, concerto pour violoncelle et orchestre

Bruckner
Symphonie n°3, en ré mineur, « Wagner-Symphonie »

Jeu. 10 20 h 30
Sam. 12 18 h

Orchestre national de Lyon
Hans Zender, direction
Gustav Rivinius, violoncelle

Zender, Bruckner

Comme avant lui Mendelssohn, Schumann ou Mahler, Hans Zender appartient à la grande tradition des Kapellmeister germaniques, chez qui les métiers de chef d'orchestre et de compositeur sont intimement liés. A la monumentale *Troisième Symphonie* que Bruckner dédia à Wagner, partition empreinte de mystère, il adjoint son propre *Bardo* (2000), inspiré par le Livre des morts tibétain (le terme désigne cet état intermédiaire entre la mort et la renaissance). L'œuvre est interprétée par son créateur, Gustav Rivinius, violoncelliste au jeu particulièrement intelligent et chaleureux, qui fut l'élève de Heinrich Schiff et le premier Allemand à remporter, en 1990, le Concours Tchaïkovski de Moscou.

13

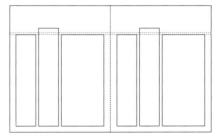

The *line of force* principle can consist of cutting a page's height into equal "slices". The resulting *lines of force* can be used to align all of the elements.

1. The *page* height has been divided into 14 equal parts. The *lines of force* are sometimes shown on the page. Some are used to emphasize the *headlines*. Others are used to align the *color* backgrounds, *text boxes* and information graphics.

1. *Observatoire des débouchés*, brochure
École nationales supérieures d'architecture de Lyon, Grenoble and Saint-Étienne
Damien Gautier

1

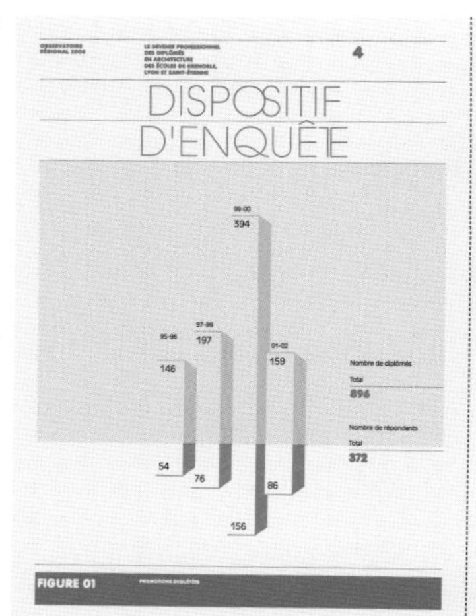

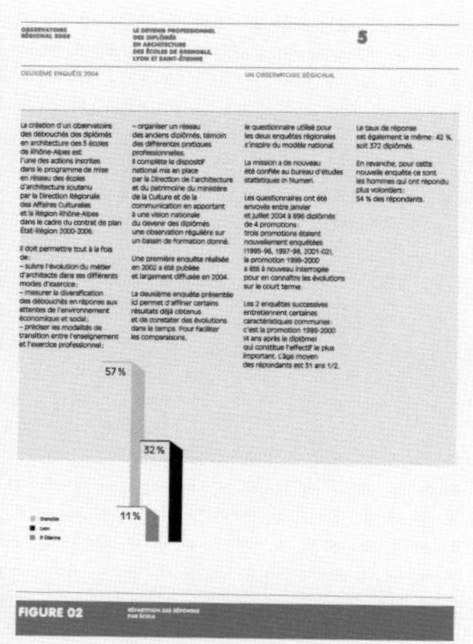

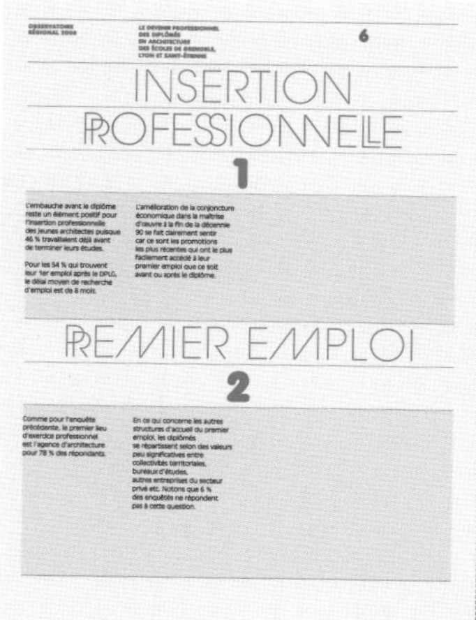

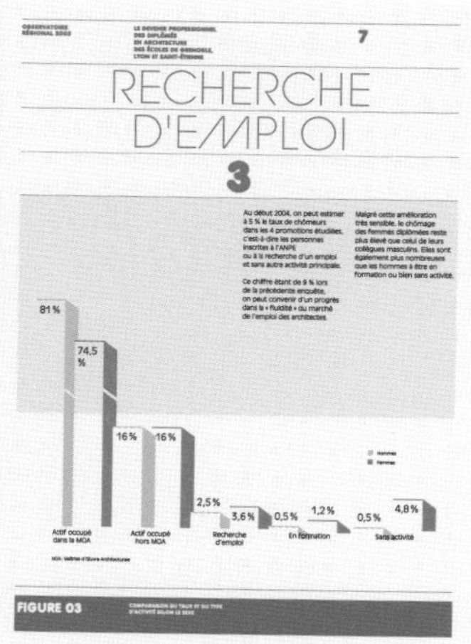

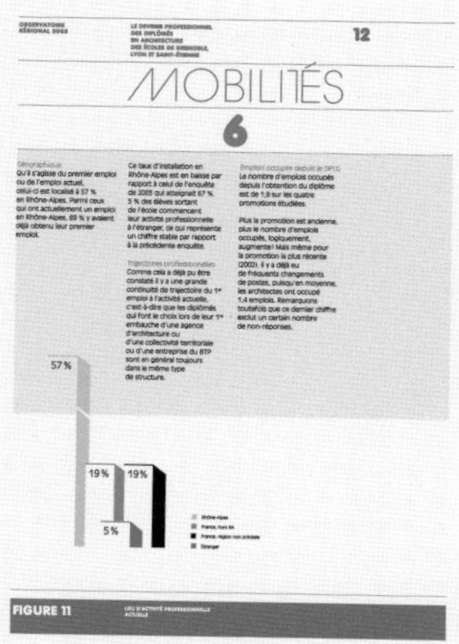

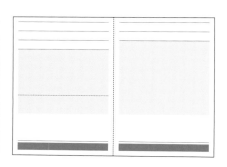

2. The *format*'s height is divided by twelve creating eleven *lines of force*, which are used to "attach" the design elements: lines, *color* fields, texts. The *silhouettes* disregard this alignment scheme and add *contrast* to the strict structure.

2. *Pantiero 2003*, poster
Trafik

2

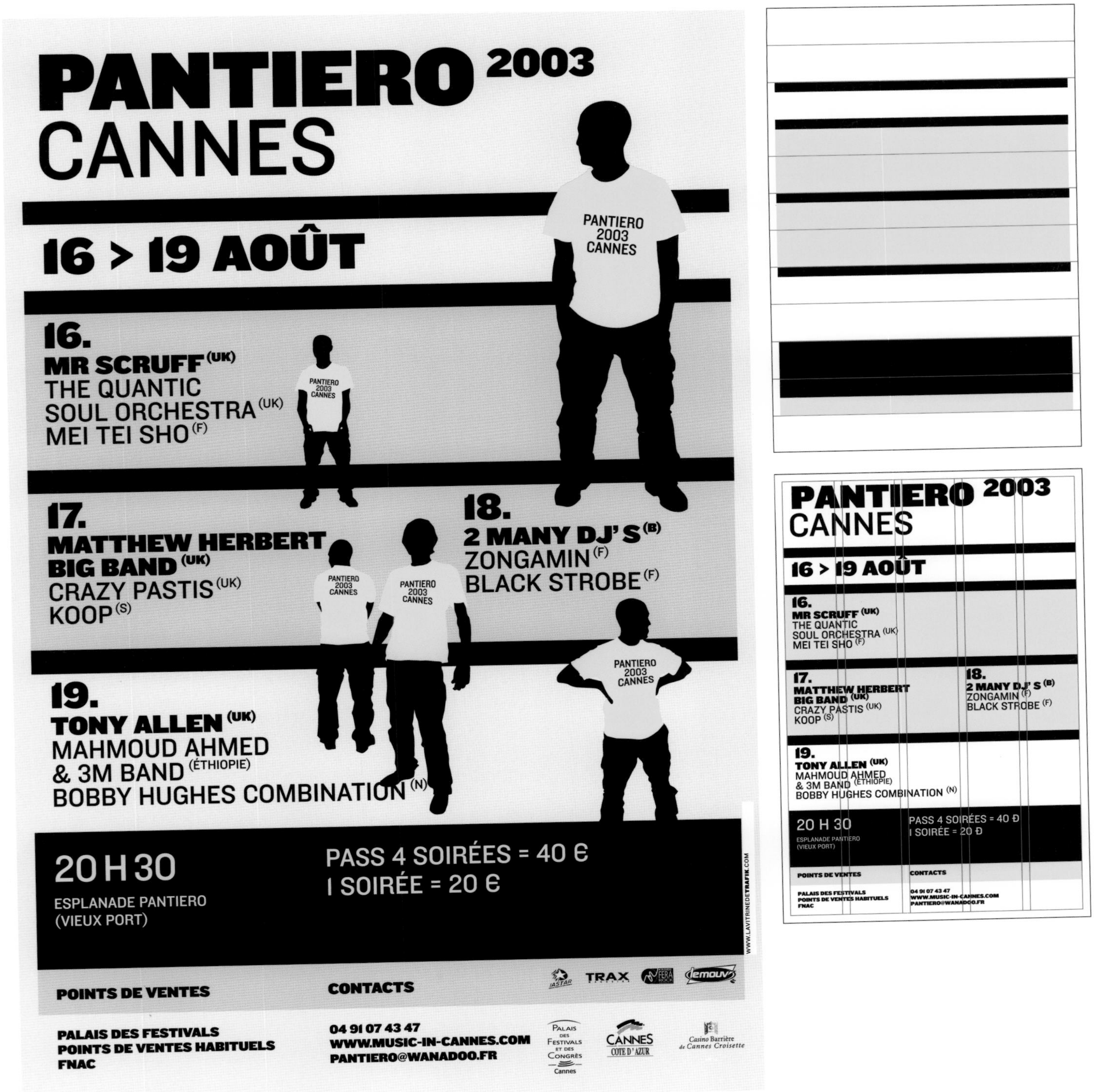

PANTIERO 2003
CANNES

16 > 19 AOÛT

16.
MR SCRUFF (UK)
THE QUANTIC
SOUL ORCHESTRA (UK)
MEI TEI SHO (F)

17.
MATTHEW HERBERT
BIG BAND (UK)
CRAZY PASTIS (UK)
KOOP (S)

18.
2 MANY DJ'S (B)
ZONGAMIN (F)
BLACK STROBE (F)

19.
TONY ALLEN (UK)
MAHMOUD AHMED
& 3M BAND (ÉTHIOPIE)
BOBBY HUGHES COMBINATION (N)

PANTIERO 2003 CANNES

20 H 30
ESPLANADE PANTIERO
(VIEUX PORT)

PASS 4 SOIRÉES = 40 €
1 SOIRÉE = 20 €

WWW.LAVITRINEDETRAFIK.COM

POINTS DE VENTES
PALAIS DES FESTIVALS
POINTS DE VENTES HABITUELS
FNAC

CONTACTS
04 91 07 43 47
WWW.MUSIC-IN-CANNES.COM
PANTIERO@WANADOO.FR

TRAX
lemouv'
Palais des Festivals et des Congrès Cannes
CANNES CÔTE D'AZUR
Casino Barrière de Cannes Croisette

PANTIERO 2003
CANNES
16 > 19 AOÛT
16.
MR SCRUFF (UK)
THE QUANTIC
SOUL ORCHESTRA (UK)
MEI TEI SHO (F)
17.
MATTHEW HERBERT
BIG BAND (UK)
CRAZY PASTIS (UK)
KOOP (S)
18.
2 MANY DJ'S (B)
ZONGAMIN (F)
BLACK STROBE (F)
19.
TONY ALLEN (UK)
MAHMOUD AHMED
& 3M BAND (ÉTHIOPIE)
BOBBY HUGHES COMBINATION (N)
20 H 30
ESPLANADE PANTIERO
(VIEUX PORT)
PASS 4 SOIRÉES = 40 €
1 SOIRÉE = 20 €
POINTS DE VENTES
PALAIS DES FESTIVALS
POINTS DE VENTES HABITUELS
FNAC
CONTACTS
04 91 07 43 47
WWW.MUSIC-IN-CANNES.COM
PANTIERO@WANADOO.FR

Lines of force may also run vertically, allowing the elements to be attached to a kind of "backbone".

1. In a five-*column grid* the *gutter* between the second and third *column* serves as a *line of force* to arrange the images, sometimes on the left, sometimes on the right. Even though the main image and the text are positioned according to the *grid* and use all five *columns*, the *leaflet's* "backbone" remains visible and structures the *composition*.

The *line of force* principle can also apply to interactive media. Here, the design can also position the elements based on one or more *lines of force*.

2. The design of this website is based on a 14-*column grid*. Four *lines of force* are used to position the following elements: *lede*, numbers, *headlines*, texts, *captions*, links and images.

1. *LeVoxx*
   Damien Gautier
   Photographs: © Siegfried Marque
2. École nationale supérieure d'architecture de Lyon, website
   Damien Gautier

1

2

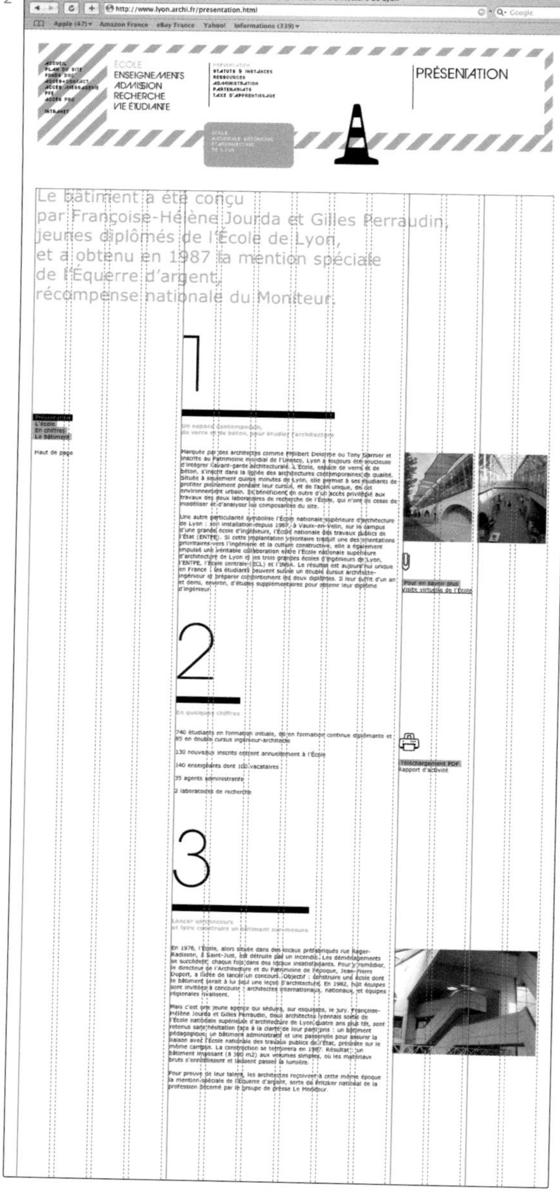

3. The alignment of the main (black) text shows the line of force in the *composition*. This *line of force* structures the *page* even though the remaining texts are aligned to the left-hand margin.

3. *Thomas Hirschhorn Musée Précaire Albinet*, catalogue
Les laboratoires d'Aubervilliers / Éditions Barral, 2005
deValence

3

Connaissant votre intérêt pour cette ville et le travail que vous lui consacrez, j'ai pensé que vous étiez sans doute l'une des personnes les plus à même de répondre. C'est la raison pour laquelle je me permets de vous écrire aujourd'hui.

Je serai très heureuse de pouvoir vous entendre sur ce sujet et espère que cette demande ne vous importunera pas. Vous pouvez me joindre aux Laboratoires au 01 53 56 15 90.

Très cordialement,
Yvane Chapuis

Deux ans et demi après notre première rencontre, nous nous mettrons donc au travail. Entre-temps, Thomas avait installé son atelier à Aubervilliers dans le quartier du Landy. Le projet des Laboratoires quant à lui avait été restructuré et était désormais entièrement dévolu à la production artistique. Nous agirons en tant que commanditaires et producteurs délégués du projet. Nous nous engagerons ainsi à réunir les fonds nécessaires à sa réalisation et à accompagner l'artiste dans sa mise en œuvre. Thomas n'affectionne pas particulièrement ce terme de commanditaire, lui préférant celui d'invitation, sans doute parce qu'il a quelque chose d'autoritaire. Néanmoins, dans nos premières discussions, je lui signifierai mon intérêt pour un projet associant les habitants. Il sortait de l'expérience de Kassel et n'était pas sûr de trouver l'énergie nécessaire pour un tel projet. Il m'expliquera que du temps était indispensable pour se ressourcer, pour digérer et tirer les « leçons » de ce genre d'expérience. Si j'avais imaginé qu'Aubervilliers serait l'occasion de réaliser un quatrième monument, je devais me préparer à une tout autre forme de proposition. Ce que recouvre la notion de commanditaire risquait de se poser très concrètement. Quelle argumentation devais-je être en mesure de développer dans l'éventualité d'une proposition telle que ses petits autels, comme il l'avait évoqué au cours d'une discussion ? L'envergure d'un projet artistique est-elle nécessairement déterminée par la valeur symbolique des cadres qui le produisent ? Un projet discret, qui prend le risque d'être ignoré, avait-il du sens dans le cadre d'un programme dont la philosophie consiste à conduire l'art à exister là où il est totalement marginalisé ? Ces questions n'auront pas à être formulées, le projet qu'il allait proposé les intégrera d'emblée.

—

14 novembre 2002

Document : e-mail
Émetteur : Guillaume Désanges, secrétaire général des Laboratoires d'Aubervilliers
Destinataire : Thomas Hirschhorn
Objet : Premier point

Cher Thomas,

Suite à notre rendez-vous aux Laboratoires, un premier petit point.

Nous avons fait un tour avec Yvane dans le quartier du Landy pour repérer les structures existantes.

Il y a donc bien un « Café Rosa », actuellement fermé (et vraisemblablement pour un certain temps encore), géré par l'OMJA. Dans la même rue Albinet, au numéro 8, l'OMJA gère également la « Maison des jeunes Rosa Luxembourg », leurs activités : atelier d'accompagnement scolaire, projets autour de la santé et de l'hygiène, organisation de moments festifs, participation aux rencontres annuelles de Cecina (Italie) contre le racisme, participation à des chantiers et des actions de solidarité internationale (Mali, Mauritanie, Palestine…). Si tu le souhaites, nous pouvons prendre RV avec son responsable, M. Skiker.

Concernant la bibliothèque jeunesse, nous avons pris le rendez-vous le mardi 26 novembre à 15 h avec sa responsable, Mme Emmanuelle Foudhaili. Peux-tu nous confirmer ta disponibilité ? (autre possibilité : le lendemain à 11 h).

Nous avons également contacté la coordinatrice de quartier (Véronique Yarza) pour un RV, elle doit nous rappeler. Elle gère le Centre Roser (rue Gaëtan-Lamy), c'est un centre de loisirs qui accueille des associations, organise des animations pour les enfants, les retraités et propose diverses actions sociales.

Nous continuons nos investigations, et particulièrement sur les autres associations du quartier et les monuments de la Ville.

Restant à ta disposition pour tout renseignement complémentaire.

Cordialement,
Guillaume

Entre novembre et janvier, nous regarderons la ville, avec une attention particulière pour cinq cités : La Frette (308 logements), Jules Vallès (544 logements), La Villette (700 logements), le 112, rue Cochenec (248 logements) et la barre Albinet (111 logements). Nous rencontrerons des éducateurs de rue, des animateurs, des coordinatrices de quartier, des bibliothécaires et des associations. Nous les écouterons sur ce qu'ils savaient du quartier, de sa population, du logement, sur leur action. Thomas les interrogera sur les manques, sur d'éventuelles expériences artistiques menées sur place, en précisant chaque fois que nous étions actuellement dans une phase de repérage. L'idée qu'un projet puisse se réaliser semblait les intéresser. Thomas hésitera quelque temps entre la cité de La Frette et la cité Albinet. Le premier site l'attirait pour des raisons topographiques. Le second, pour sa proximité avec son atelier. C'est en janvier, après un rendez-vous avec l'association La part de l'art qui anime des ateliers de pratique artistique dans la barre HLM du 112, rue Cochenec, dont Thomas avait repéré le travail grâce à des tableaux d'enfants fixés à l'entrée de chaque montée d'escalier de l'immeuble, et qu'il décidera par la suite d'associer au *Musée Précaire*, qu'il nous fera part de son projet. Nous avions eu avec les deux femmes de cette association une discussion au sujet de leur projet initial (sa visée transgénérationnelle) et de sa transformation (une participation exclusive des enfants). Avaient été évoquées les questions de l'adaptation au terrain, de la place de l'art dans ces quartiers, du rêve de l'art (possibilité d'autres valeurs), de l'intérêt de Thomas pour la rue (visibilité 24 h/24, accessibilité, intransigeance de la réception du public) et de sa méthode (partir de son idée et demander de l'aide pour la réaliser).
Au café, il nous dévoilera donc son projet. Il voulait amener des chefs-d'œuvre de l'histoire de l'art dans une cité. Il prit pour exemples l'urinoir de Duchamp et le *Carré noir sur fond blanc* de Malevitch. J'étais gênée par l'aspect héroïque d'une telle idée. Ma première lecture se heurtait à la « volonté de puissance » qui semblait l'animer. Comment envisageait-il pouvoir conduire les trésors de la culture occidentale à quitter leurs temples pour un quartier pauvre ? L'artiste avait déjà à plusieurs reprises manifesté son intérêt pour la pensée de Nietzsche (que l'on pense à *Critical Laboratory*, 1999, *Jumbo Spoons*, 2000, ou encore *Nietzsche-Map*, 2003), j'allais découvrir que cette référence dépassait la simple citation. Elle le nourrissait et l'encourageait dans la formulation même d'une idée. En observant la manière dont il allait défendre celle du *Musée Précaire Albinet*, je comprendrai que si sa proposition était effectivement en prise avec la démesure, l'excès, ceux-ci ne concernaient pas tant la figure de l'artiste que l'art lui-même. Tout le projet du *Musée Précaire Albinet* est ainsi construit sur l'affirmation que l'art est doté d'une force transformatrice, qu'il est actif, et la méthode de Thomas consiste à œuvrer pour y croire. C'est une conviction intime d'ordre quasi religieux qui l'anime. Ce n'est pas un hasard si les formes que prend la dévotion vernaculaire l'intéresse particulièrement. Que l'on pense au motif de l'autel qui revient dans nombre de ses œuvres (*Sculpture Direct*, 1999, *Deleuze Monument*, 2000, et Altars destinés à Piet Mondrian, 1997, Otto Freundlich, 1998, Ingeborg Bachmann, 1999, et Raymond Carver, 1998), à la figure du supporter (*Artists' Scarves*, 1996) ou à celle du fan (« I love Foucault » par exemple, inscrit sur un ensemble de produits dérivés – jeans, cendriers, briquets, etc. – figurant dans « la boutique » de l'installation qu'il dédie au philosophe).
De manière plus concrète (moins symbolique), c'est sur ce principe de force active de l'art que Thomas a d'abord imaginé puis défendu l'idée que des œuvres majeures de l'histoire de l'art du XXe siècle puissent sortir de leur état patrimonial et emprunter d'autres réseaux que ceux qui transitent par les réserves et les salles d'exposition des plus grands musées occidentaux. De ce point de vue, le *Musée Précaire Albinet* est une alternative aux institutions muséales. Une alternative avant tout géographique qui interroge les politiques qui président à l'aménagement du territoire.

—

18 novembre 2002

Document : e-mail
Émetteur : Thomas Hirschhorn
Destinataire : Yvane Chapuis, codirectrice des Laboratoires d'Aubervilliers
Objet : Les monuments de la ville d'Aubervilliers

Chère Yvane,

merci pour ton mail.
Je veux bien rencontrer le monsieur des « monuments ».
Ce qui m'intéresse ce sont les monuments d'Aubervilliers, peut-être on peut le voir ensemble (je ne suis pas à Paris du 9/12 au 15/12).

À bientôt, best,
Thomas

—

15 janvier 2003

Document : lettre
Émetteur : Yvane Chapuis, codirectrice des Laboratoires d'Aubervilliers
Destinataire : Alfred Pacquement, directeur du musée national d'Art moderne
Objet : Première demande de rencontre

Cher Alfred Pacquement,

Les Laboratoires d'Aubervilliers, espace de recherche et de production artistique, ont invité Thomas Hirschhorn à réaliser un projet dans l'espace public à Aubervilliers. Sa visibilité est prévue à l'automne prochain, aux mois d'octobre et de novembre 2003.

La mise en œuvre de ce projet, qui a débuté en novembre dernier, est actuellement dans sa première phase. Celle-ci consiste en une prise de contact avec le territoire à travers un ensemble de rencontres avec des acteurs du terrain (travailleurs sociaux pour la plupart). À partir de ce travail, l'artiste déterminera la localisation précise ainsi que la thématique de son intervention. L'une des directions qui se dessine aujourd'hui concerne plus particulièrement l'engagement à l'égard de l'accessibilité de l'art au plus grand nombre, dont tout l'œuvre de Thomas Hirschhorn témoigne. Son objectif serait d'exposer des œuvres clés de l'histoire de l'art du XXe siècle au cœur d'un quartier de cette ville de banlieue.

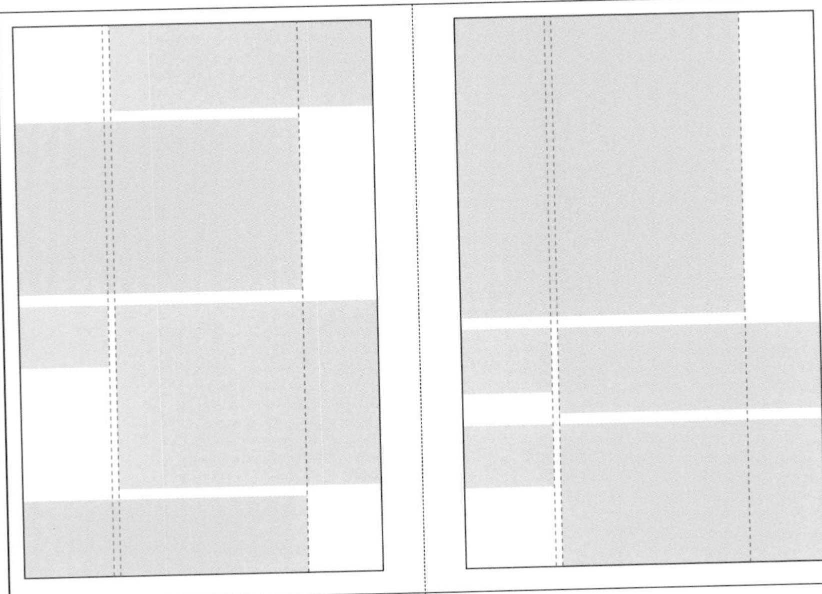

Points of force
Basic principles and examples

The so-called points of force – the intersection of two *lines of force*, one horizontal and one vertical – work similarly to the *lines of force*. Elements are anchored to these points. This principle ensures rigor without constraints, and conveys the impression of freedom.

1. The images are anchored with their lower left corner to a point of force. Images on the same horizontal line are bottom-aligned, and those stacked vertically left-aligned. The width and height of each image can be chosen freely. *Captions* are placed below the images and left-aligned to their left side.

1. *Les clubs du livre. Une aventure*, poster
Damien Gautier

1

2. Images and texts are placed according to points of force located at their lower left corner. The lower edges of the images are aligned and their heights vary. The *captions* are anchored on their upper left corner to the points of force, and are aligned to the left side of the corresponding image.

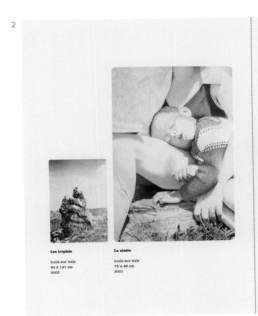

2

Les trophés

huile sur toile
94 x 141 cm
2003

La sieste

huile sur toile
72 x 48 cm
2001

La baignade

huile sur toile
141 x 94 cm
2002

Sept tableaux aux bords arrondis. Trois formats.
Un titre : Les Diapos de mon père.
Soit une série de peintures réalisée par Philippe Jacquin-Ravot
en 2003 à partir de diapositives extraites d'archives familiales.
Aux dires du peintre ces œuvres ne témoignent d'aucune forme d'affect.
Quand on l'interroge sur son éventuelle signification, sur la part
de sentiments qui aurait dû logiquement innerver cette série, l'artiste
prend ses précautions, pèse ses mots et se met à l'abri de tout
débordement discursif qui pourrait dévoiler un soupçon d'intimité
ou provoquer un épanchement inopportun.
À l'en croire, seules semblent l'intéresser la virtuosité et la fidélité
inhérentes au processus de transposition picturale qu'il a eu à cœur
de mener à bien.
À première vue, Jacquin-Ravot nous donne l'impression de vouloir
s'inscrire dans une filiation parfaitement balisée.
Celle de l'hyperréalisme et de sa dette complexe envers le modernisme.
Celle de l'évacuation des émotions. D'une peinture repliée sur
ses propres fondements et dont le sujet ne serait, pour reprendre
la formule de Malcolm Morley, qu'« un sous-produit de la surface ».
Les Diapos de mon père ne sauraient dès lors, si l'on veut bien souscrire
aux assertions de l'artiste, échapper à cette apologie des propriétés
d'une image "transportée" et pour ainsi dire "décollée" de sa réalité tant
photographiée que photographique.

pjr

Sept. Trois. Un.
Les diapos de mon père,
une inquiétante
familiarité.

Éric Verhagen

Modular grid
Basic principles

The basic principle of the *modular grid* consists of dividing the design space into *modules* separated by *gutters*.

Principle

The principle of the *modular grid* is optimized when *modules*, *margins* and *gutters* are related to the page's *format*. The *type size* and *leading* for the different *reading levels* are calculated to be multiples of (or a division of) the *module*'s height and the *gutter*'s height. Then the *module*, the *gutter* and the *baseline grid* (see pages 142 and 154) all fit. The images are cropped so that their dimensions correspond to one or more *modules*.

The *composition* then involves arranging the elements on the *modules* and "playing" with different principles of *composition* (see part 01).

1. The square *page* is divided into 16 square *modules*. *Margins* and *gutters* have the same width. Each *module* contains ten lines of text. The unit of the *baseline grid* equals the distance between two *modules*.

In order to have the text fit the *grid*, simply set units of the standard *baseline grid* defined by the *layout* software to match the distance between the *modular grid* lines and then "attach" the text to the *baseline grid*.

1

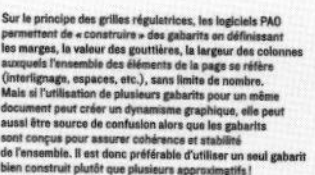

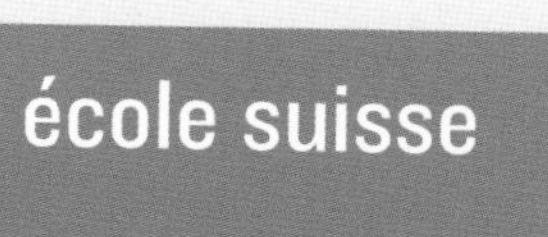

intro
Dans une surface donnée, le graphiste assemble
des éléments de natures différentes : textes, images, signes
en fonction de leurs valeurs.
Tel un peintre, le graphiste utilise les différents éléments
de la mise en page en fonction de leurs valeurs respectives
afin de composer une page. Il recherche un rapport
dynamique entre eux, privilégiant l'équilibre et l'harmonie
ou plutôt une impression de déséquilibre et d'opposition.
L'école suisse, par la main de quelques
graphistes, a développé les grilles
régulatrices basées sur les éléments
typographiques (justification, corps,
interlignage).
La page est divisée en plusieurs modules
identiques sur lesquels les éléments
de la page s'appuient.

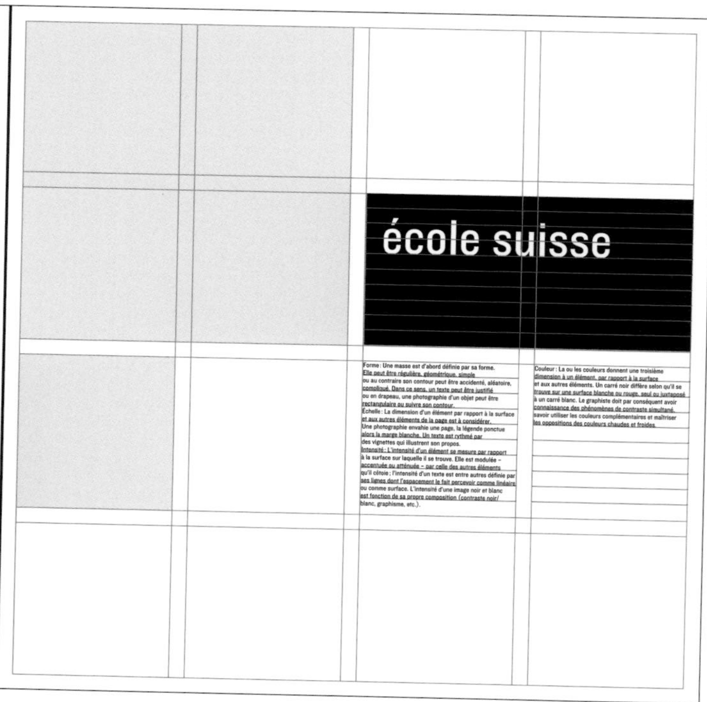

There are numerous possibilities for distributing texts and images.

Examples of grids with the same page format
The examples shown cover only a small number of the possible combinations.

Nine divisions (3 × 3)
The design area is divided into a *grid* of nine *modules*, all identically spaced.

Note that *books* or *magazines* can use several related *grids* in order to create *rhythm* in the *composition* and to respond to the specific requirements of each page.

16 divisions (4 × 4)
The design area is divided into a *grid* of 16 *modules*, all identically spaced.

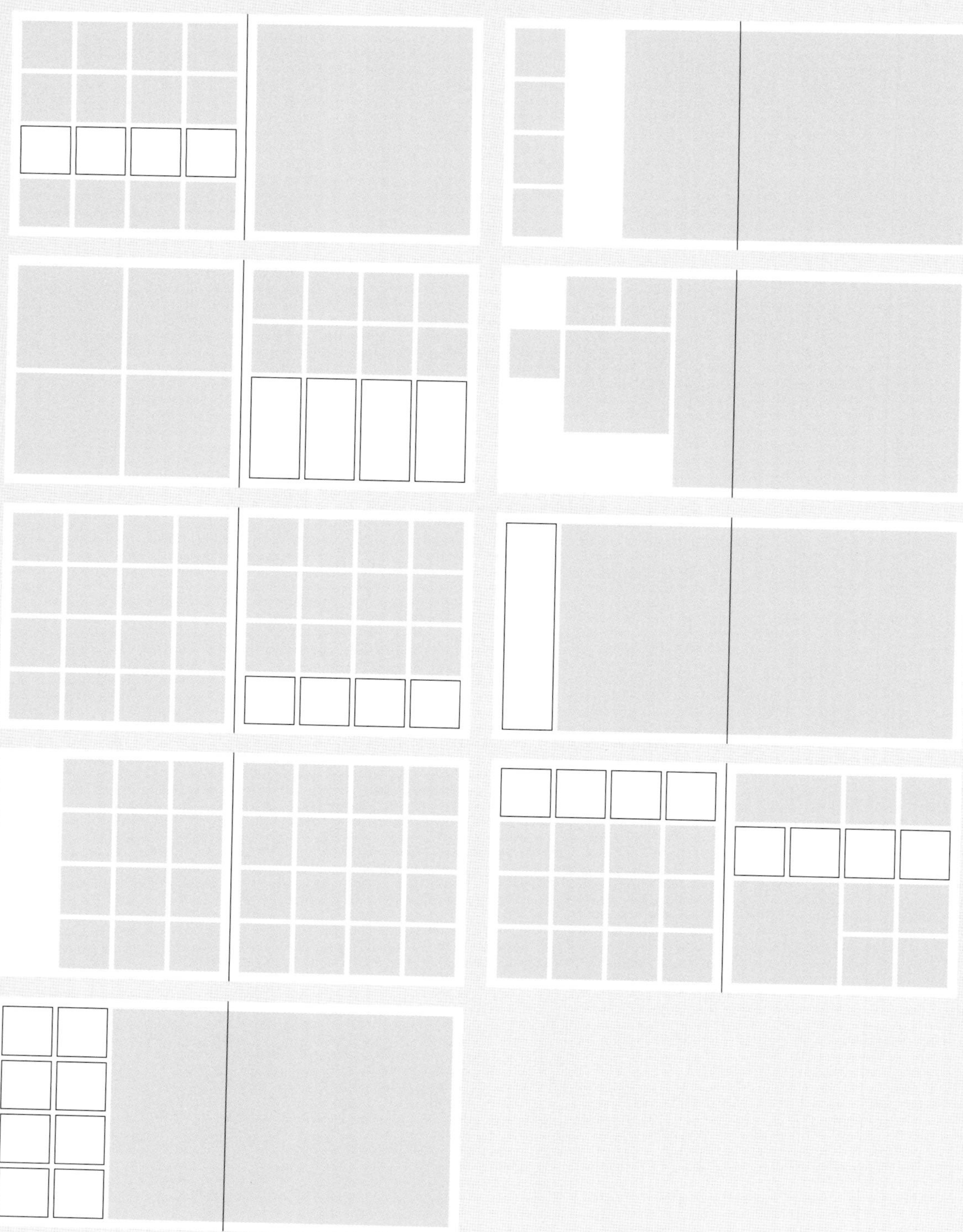

25 divisions (5 × 5)
The design area is divided into a *grid* of 25 *modules*, all identically spaced.

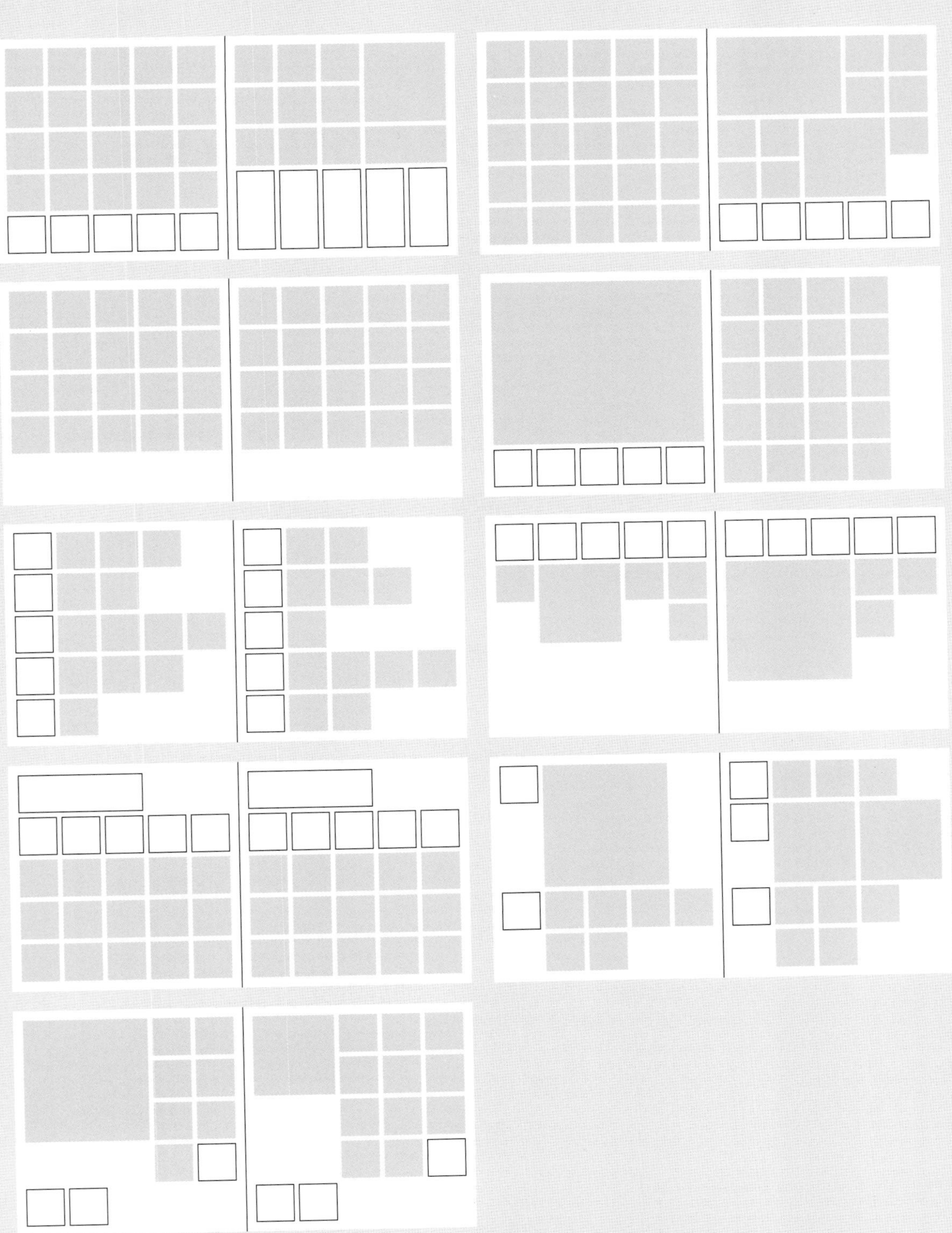

Modular grid
Text and grid

A *modular grid* cannot be conceived without considering the text that it will structure.
The height of the *modules* must be a multiple of the lines of text, and the space between the *modules* should be equal to one or more lines of text. All text elements then align to the resulting *baseline grid*. Depending on the *type size*, the *leading* is a multiple of the *baseline grid unit*. Images, lines and other *graphic elements* also align to this *grid*, preferably aligned to the *ascenders* of the neighboring lines of text.

Les enjeux de la présentation

Un lecteur, même s'il est intéressé, peut abandonner la lecture si la présentation n'est pas soignée. Inversement, une présentation agréable peut décider un lecteur réticent à prendre connaissance d'un document.
Car les lecteurs, même s'ils s'en défendent, jugent tout d'abord un texte par sa présentation, ensuite, seulement, ils jugeront de la qualité de son contenu.
La présentation est le premier obstacle que le lecteur rencontre.
Le franchira-t-il ? C'est ici que se situent l'enjeu de la présentation et le rôle du maquettiste qui doit connaître le public qu'il vise pour lui faire correspondre son travail.
Mais il ne peut savoir comment sera disposé le lecteur au moment où il aura le document sous les yeux. Sera-t-il disponible, pressé, énervé… ?
Une présentation peut plaire un jour et déplaire un autre jour, suivant l'état d'esprit du lecteur ! Il peut tout juste imaginer que certains documents intéresseront, a priori plus que d'autres, le public qu'il souhaite atteindre. Il sait aussi d'avance si le document apparaîtra seul – bien que cela soit de plus en plus rare avec la multiplication des imprimés de tous genres – ou noyé au milieu d'autres qui lui ressemblent. Dans le premier cas, il peut se limiter à rendre le texte agréable, lisible, en cherchant à trouver la présentation qui lui parait être la mieux adaptée. Dans le second cas, il doit intégrer un paramètre qui a alors une très grande importance :
attirer l'attention pour que le lecteur choisisse son document plutôt qu'un autre.

Upper optical alignment

aa

Lower alignment to the *grid*

Il faut aujourd'hui remarquer que la plupart des documents sont régis par ce facteur et s'y limitent trop souvent. Les couleurs, la taille des titres, la multiplication des "astuces", pour étonner ou se différencier, tout va dans ce sens. Mais souvent cette démarche nuit ensuite au document lorsque le lecteur est enfin décidé à le lire. Ce qui a d'abord servi à attirer son attention risque de le lasser rapidement, car il souhaite maintenant que la lecture lui soit facilitée.
Le maquettiste doit toujours avoir ces deux étapes à l'esprit lorsqu'il conçoit un document : convaincre le lecteur de s'y intéresser, et lui donner ensuite envie de le lire, et jusqu'au bout ! Sinon le lecteur risque bien, après avoir été séduit par la présentation, de se laisser attirer par un autre document qui aura utilisé les mêmes artifices. Le maquettiste sait également que la présentation ne peut pas tout. Si elle peut rendre attrayant un texte ennuyeux, elle ne peut en effet le rendre intéressant s'il ne l'est pas, et ne peut, par conséquent, convaincre le lecteur de poursuivre s'il n'a plus d'intérêt.

Ce qui a d'abord servi à attirer son attention risque de le lasser rapidement

Une belle présentation peut appuyer la qualité d'un texte par le choix judicieux des paramètres typographiques qui sauront le mettre en valeur, mais elle peut aussi rendre la médiocrité du contenu encore plus flagrante. Les lecteurs sont d'ailleurs aujourd'hui avertis, et se méfient de ce qui leur paraît trop "voyant", en sachant que cela est souvent fait pour attirer leur attention sur ce qui n'a que peu d'intérêt.

.2 Autonomie des lecteurs

Malgré toute l'importance que peut avoir la typographie, et la manière de l'utiliser pour présenter un texte, il ne faut pas oublier le paramètre qui se trouve au début du processus de lecture et qui, par conséquent, décide de l'ensemble : le lecteur lui-même. Nous savons qu'il peut revêtir des visages très différents, avoir des centres d'intérêt opposés… Nous savons aussi qu'il sera bien souvent peu motivé à entreprendre la lecture et qu'il faudra d'abord le séduire. Même un lecteur passionné peut ne pas être bien disposé au moment où le texte est sous ses yeux.

Les habitudes des lecteurs
La présentation de ce texte convient-elle ? Correspond-elle à ce que le lecteur attend ? Le lecteur est habitué à une certaine présentation pour chaque type de document ; il souhaite – cela semble logique – qu'un journal ressemble à un journal, une revue à une revue, ou un prospectus à un prospectus !
Chaque fois qu'il prend connaissance d'un document, il le « juge » et cherche à retrouver les schémas qui lui sont familiers. Cette analyse est souvent inconsciente : le lecteur ressent seulement un sentiment – positif ou négatif – à l'égard du document ; il n'aura que rarement un avis tranché.
Mais l'existence de ces « modèles » dans la mémoire du lecteur fait qu'il a de la peine à cautionner une tentative qui remet en cause ses habitudes et constitue une véritable barrière que le maquettiste connaît et doit toujours chercher à surmonter.

Upper optical alignment

; ;

Lower alignment to the *grid*

Un texte est, cela est évident, une succession de lettres groupées en mots.

Comment donc la typographie, composant unique, ne pourrait-elle pas avoir une incidence sur la perception d'un texte ? Pourquoi d'ailleurs existerait-il tellement de caractères différents, si leurs formes n'avaient aucune importance ?

Pourtant, beaucoup pensent que la typographie ne peut avoir un rôle significatif. Il est vrai que la structure quasi-immuable des lettres de l'alphabet semble laisser bien peu de possibilités au dessinateur de caractères.

De toute manière, comment les spécificités d'une typographie, pourraient-elles être perceptibles sur quelques millimètres de hauteur, et changer l'appréciation d'un texte, alors que le lecteur n'y accorde, a priori, aucune importance ?

Modular grid
Examples

The principle of the *modular grid* can be applied to a range of media and *formats*. Obviously, the project requirements and contents are used to define the *grid*.

1. For this record album cover the *modular grid* defines a structural framework where the elements (images, *headlines*, texts, logos, etc.) are arranged according to the principles of balance, tension, *mass* relationships, etc. (see part 01).
Because the *typeface* used here has many different *weights*, each line of text could be made to fit the *module* height and the *line length* equals a multiple of the *module*'s width.

1. *Just Rock'n Roll*, record album cover
Damien Gautier

1

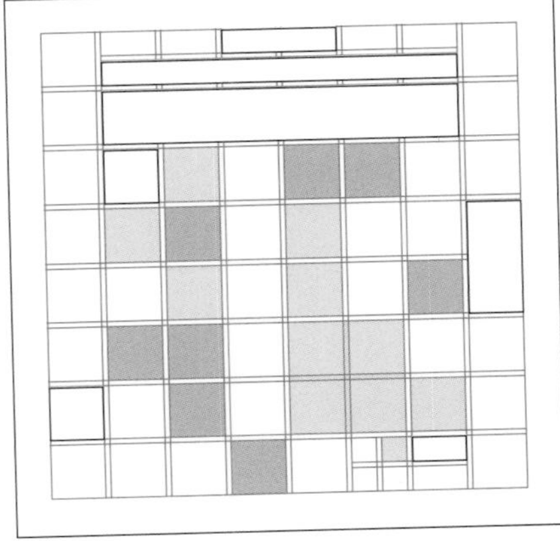

1. In this example the A4 landscape *format* is divided into *modules* of 20 × 20 mm, surrounded by a *margin* of 10 mm. A row of half *modules* let the *grid* fit within the A4 *format*'s width and height. The remaining 7 mm in the width are used for the *binding*:
height = 10 mm + (9,5 × 20 mm) + 10 mm = 210 mm
width = 7 mm + 10 mm + (13,5 × 20 mm) + 10 mm = 297 mm

The text blocks and images are assembled like a simple puzzle, with each *page* having a different distribution. Even the *page number* is integrated into the *composition*. Note the absence of *gutters* in this *grid*. The text was simply inset 1 mm from the left edge of the *text box*.

1. *Le cinéma expérimental*, student project
Geoffray Culty

1

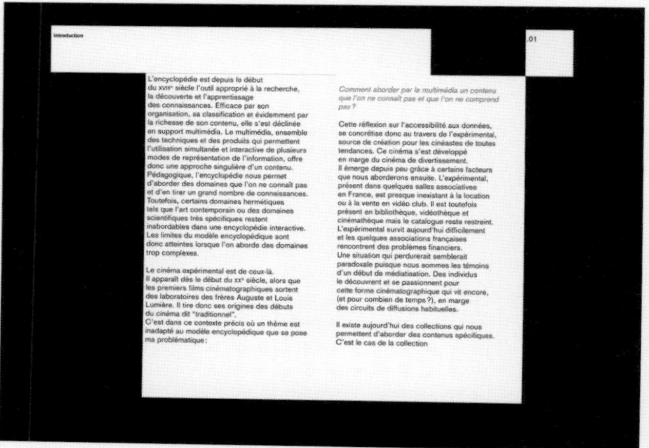

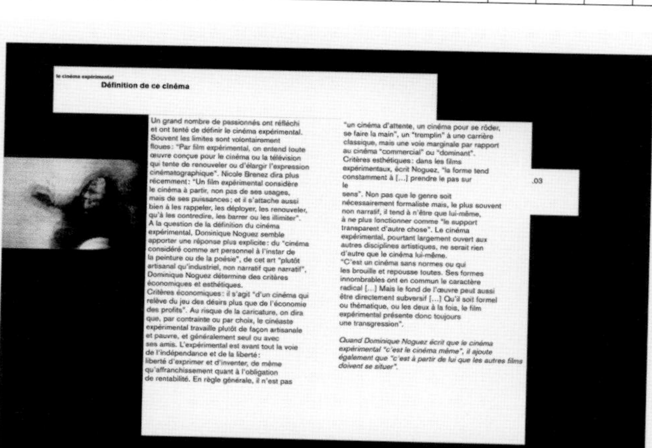

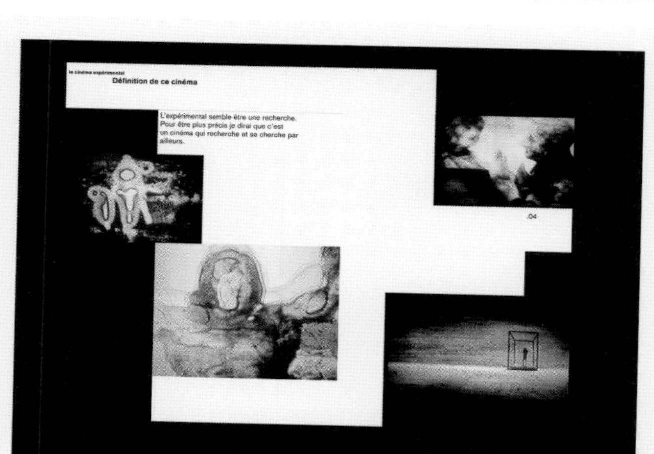

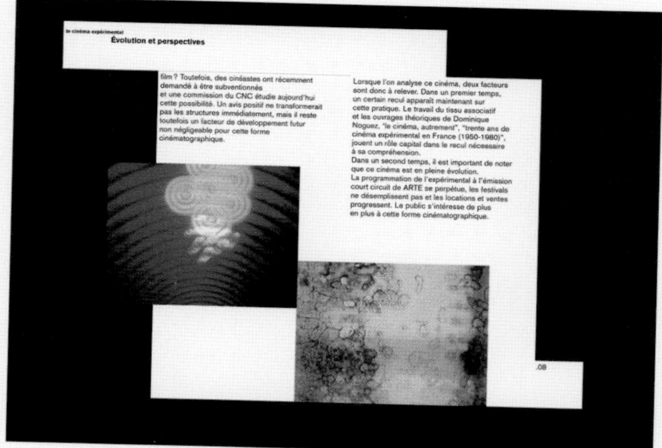

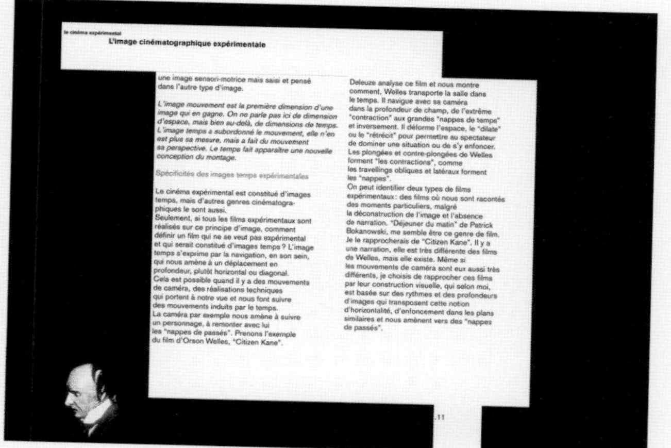

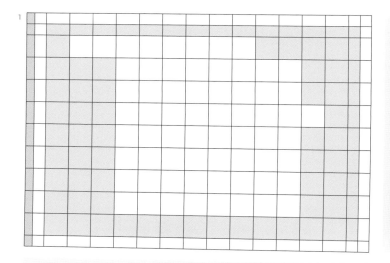

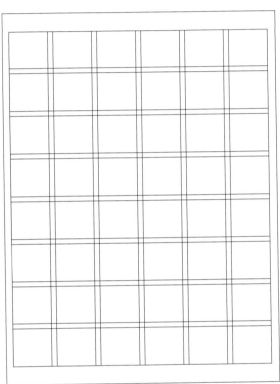

2. Independent of the document's *format* the *modular grid* can serve as a basic structure for any type of *composition* with different elements (texts, images, etc.).

2. École nationale supérieure d'architecture de Lyon, leaflet Élodie Michée

2

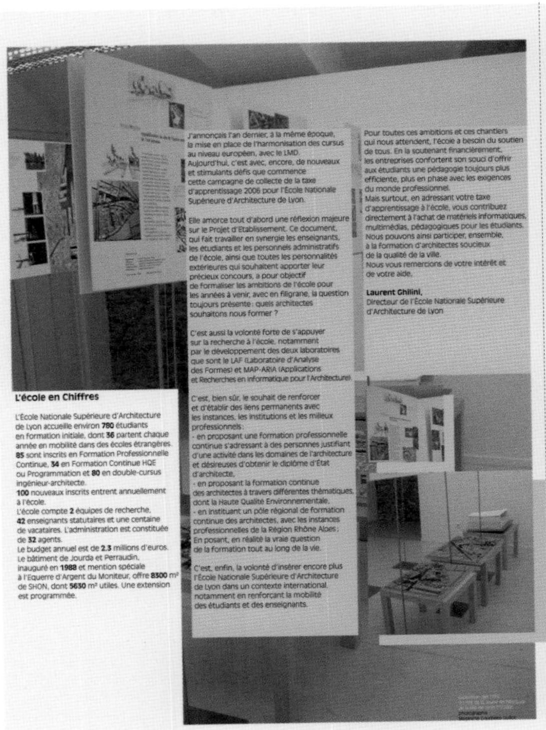

The *modular grid* principle can also be applied to interactive media. The special characteristics of these media combined with the *grid* can inspire new ideas and be a useful tool in arranging the content.
Let us remember that it is not a question of applying a *grid* without thinking – that would make it a hindrance – but to define a specific structure to the design.

1. Here the *grid* plays with the fact that the *format* of the internet *page* changes depending on the user (see page 39). The *modular grid* adapts dynamically to the window's *format*, redistributing the design elements. Hence, resizing the window allows the user to reconstruct an image that was originally abstract.

2. The *grid* principle creates a link between the different communication media.

1. Yes architectes, website
Damien Gautier
2. Yes architectes, folding poster
Damien Gautier

1

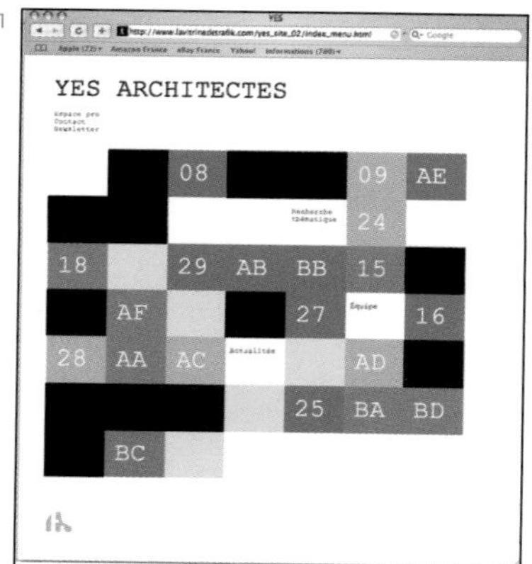

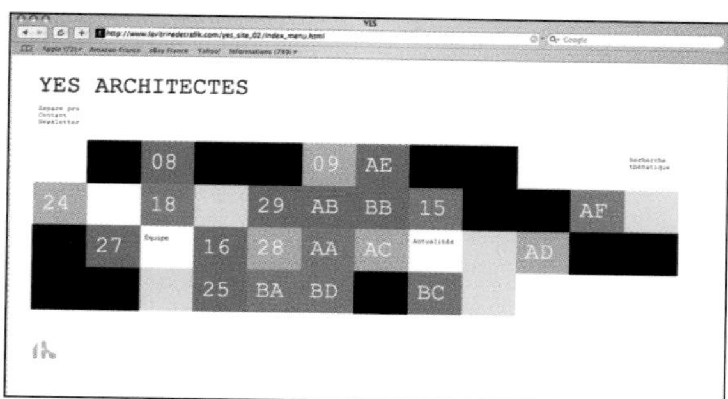

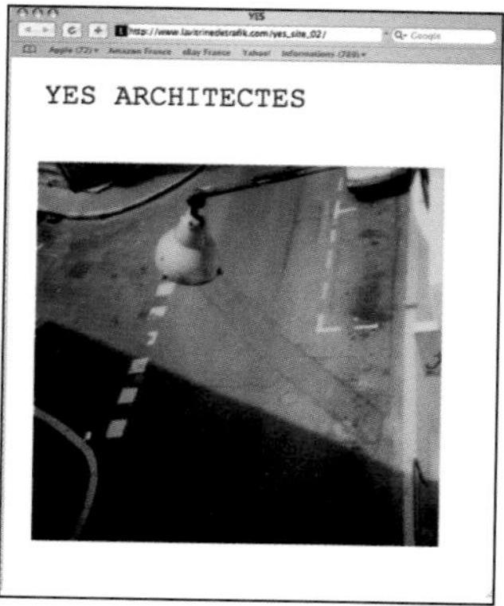

2

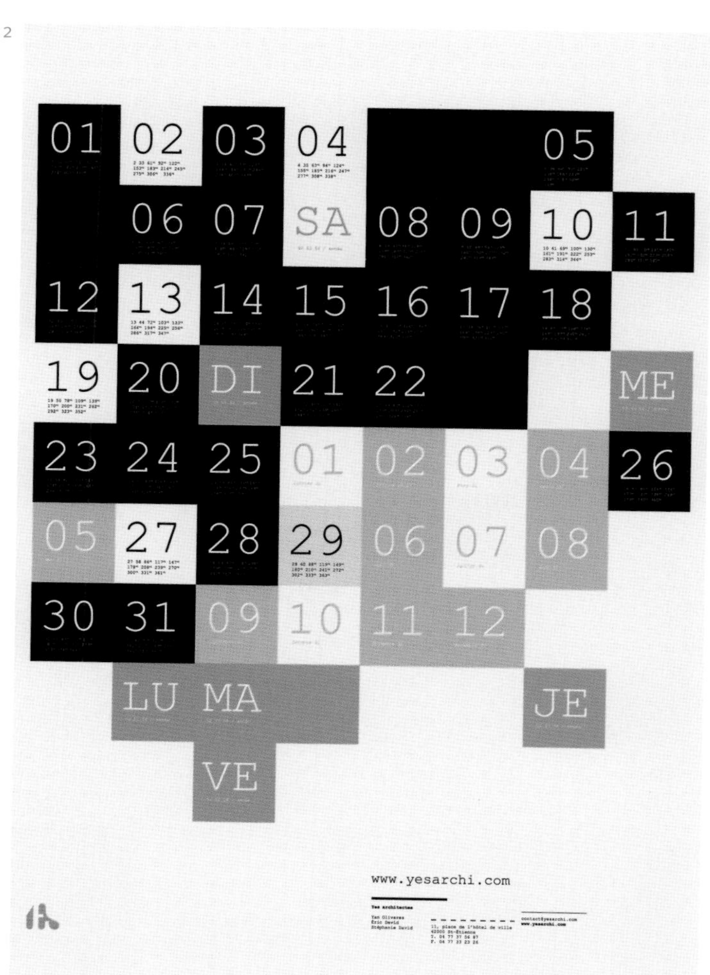

3. Based on a simple *modular grid*, the design is made up of text blocks and images. The *line length* varies according to the number of *modules*, while images push into the blocks of text. It is a subtle game of typographic grays and *masses*. The way the text is read changes from *page* to page.
The use of this particular *grid* was driven by the desire to present several articles on a double page. At first the reader doesn't know which text matches which image. Some texts begin at the top of the *page* and continue at the bottom of the next page. The reading is really guided by the different *type sizes* which distinguish the texts from one another.

The skewed *headlines* and off-center images are added to the game of typographic grays (also see pages 172–177).

3. *Le journal des laboratoires n° 3*
December 2004
Les Laboratoires d'Aubervilliers
deValence

3

TOUTE PERSONNE MORTE OU VIVANTE
NOTES POUR UN PROJET A NUREMBERG

«PREUVES» DE CINEMA
LA TRIBU DE STEPHANE BERARD JOUE *A FAIRE COMME SI*

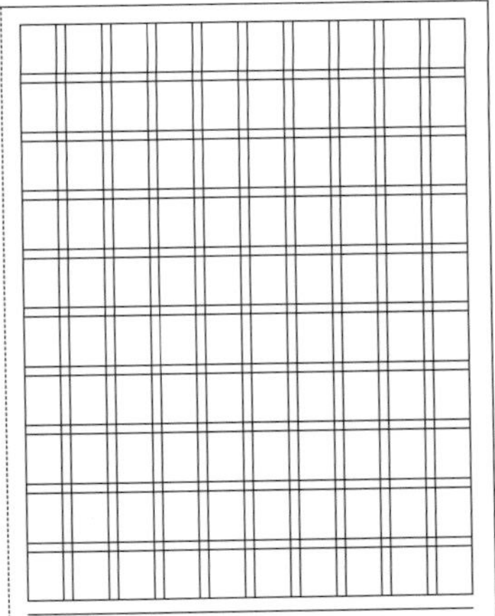

UN SUJET FLAMBANT NEUF —ANDY WARHOL

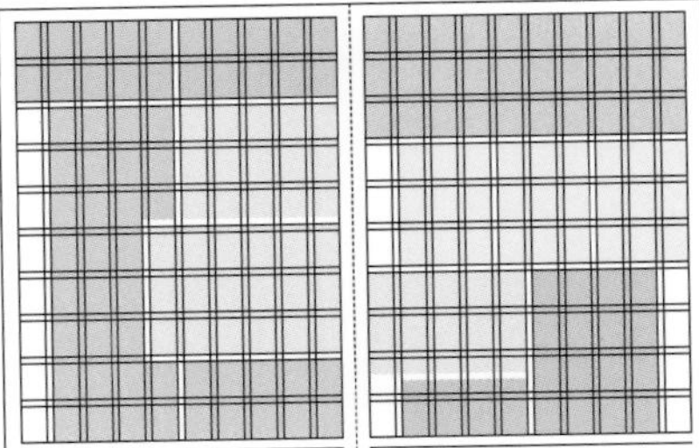

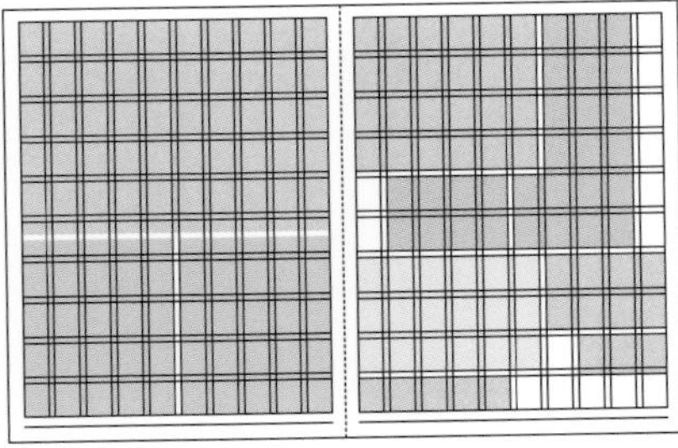

SOUVENIR BREF
DU MUSÉE PRÉCAIRE ALBINET, PLUS UN COMMENTAIRE

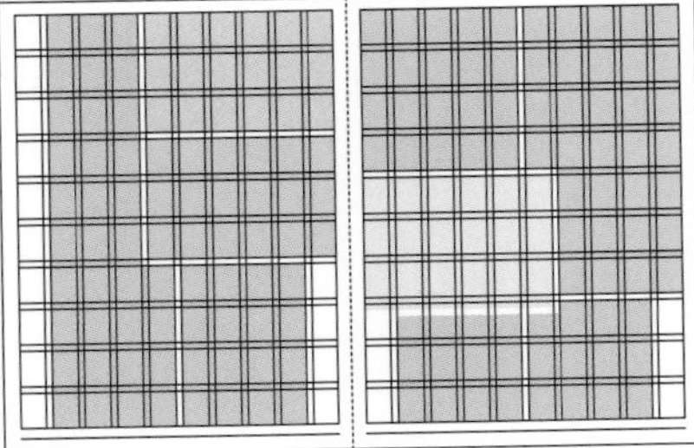

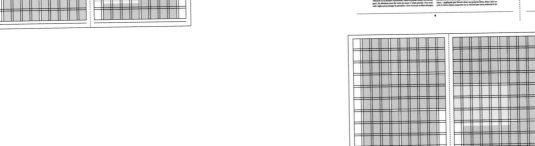

1. These program *poster* designs are based on a *grid* of six *modules* which are used to distinguish and place each information group. A single *printed sheet* is used to create a *poster* and *flyers*. *Flyers* are made by cutting the *posters* along the *grid* into six single *sheets*.

1. *Kurs musik*, poster/flyer
VHS Saarbrücken
Angela Lorenz

1

2. Images are placed according to a *modular grid* on every *page* of this brochure. The unique aspect of this *grid* is the use of rounded corners. These contribute to the originality of each page.

2. *La Ferme du Buisson*, program
MAJi, Maroussia Jannelle
and Benjamin Gomez

2

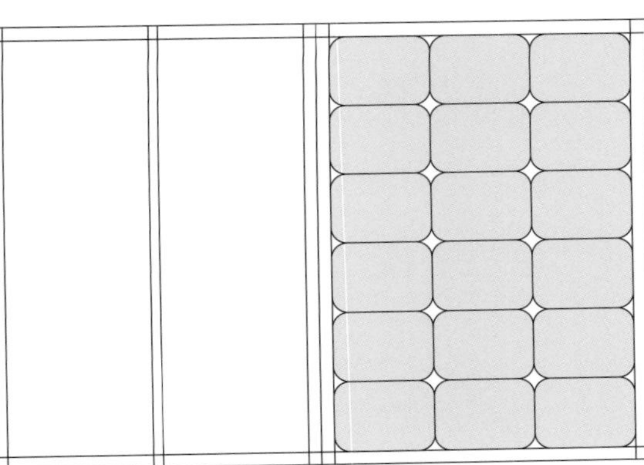

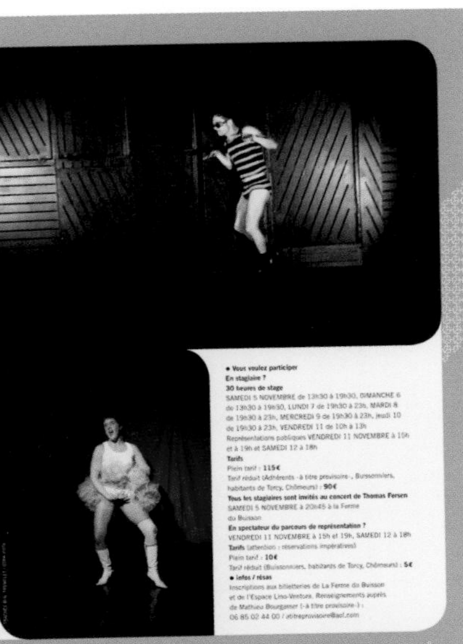

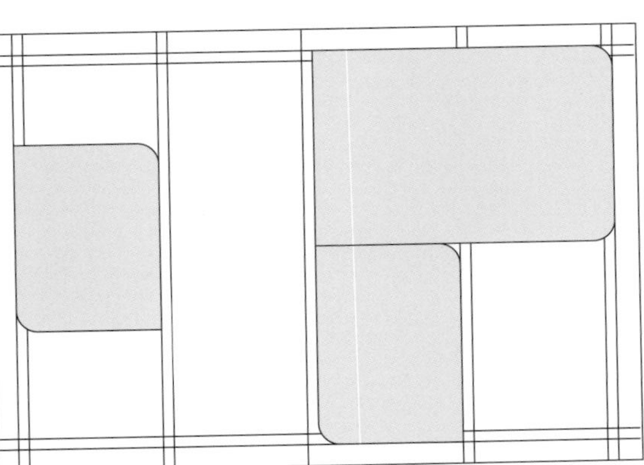

Modular grid
The principle of unity

Using the same *grid* for several documents makes it possible to create a link between them. It can also save a significant amount of time on a large project.

1. Regardless of the document's *format*, the *grid*'s *module* remains the same. Thus, the A4 *format* is divided into 48 *modules* (6 × 8), while the compliment card has only 12 *modules* (6 × 2), and the business card has only four. The website is also based on the same *modular grid* (6 × 8 *modules*).

a. letterhead with letter
b. project folder (letterhead rotated 90°)
c. compliment card
d. business card
e. website

The *grid* is designed so that the A4 *format* can be used both as portrait (vertically, 1) and landscape (horizontally, 2). Since the letterhead and other documents were designed by the architect personally, the *modular grid* allows him to quickly find his bearings and not to question elements' placement each time.

You will notice that only the logotype changes its position on the *grid* and breaks up the strictness of the design. Even though the images have no background *color*, the eye still perceives the *grid*'s structure.

1. Architekturbüro AS+R, stationery, project folder, website
Damien Gautier

1

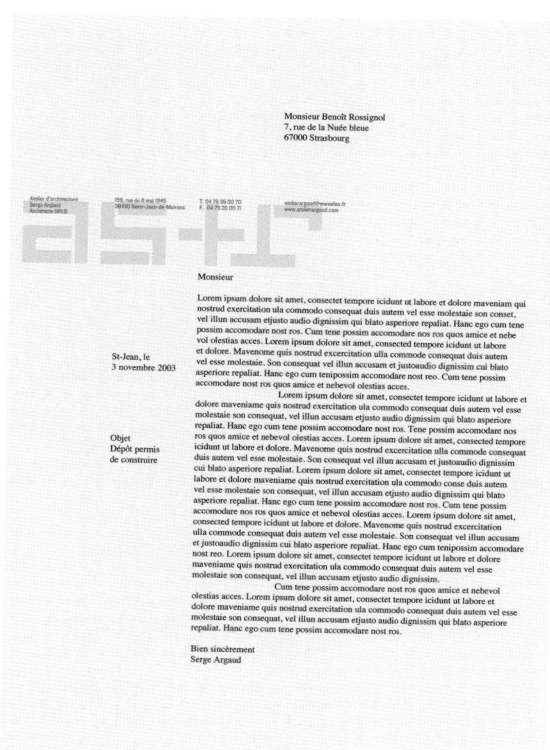

Monsieur Benoît Rossignol
7, rue de la Nuée bleue
67000 Strasbourg

Atelier d'architecture
Serge Argaud
Architecte DPLG

159, rue du 8 mai 1945
38430 Saint-Jean-de-Moirans

T. 04 76 35 00 70
F. 04 76 35 00 71

atelierargaud@wanadoo.fr
www.atelierargaud.com

St-Jean, le
3 novembre 2003

Objet
Dépôt permis
de construire

Monsieur

Lorem ipsum dolore sit amet, consectet tempore icidunt ut labore et dolore maveniam qui nostrud exercitation ula commodo consequat duis autem vel esse molestaie son conset, vel illun accusam etjusto audio dignissim qui blato asperiore repaliat. Hanc ego cum tene possim accomodare nost ros. Cum tene possim accomodare nos ros quos amice et nebe vol olestias acces. Lorem ipsum dolore sit amet, consected tempore icidunt ut labore et dolore. Mavenome quis nostrud excercitation ulla commode consequat duis autem vel esse molestaie. Son consequat vel illun accusam et justoaudio dignissim cui blato asperiore repaliat. Hanc ego cum tenipossim accomodare nost reo. Cum tene possim accomodare nost ros quos amice et nebevol olestias acces.

Lorem ipsum dolore sit amet, consectet tempore icidunt ut labore et dolore maveniame quis nostrud exercitation ula commodo consequat duis autem vel esse molestaie son consequat, vel illun accusam etjusto audio dignissim qui blato asperiore repaliat. Hanc ego cum tene possim accomodare nost ros. Tene possim accomodare nos ros quos amice et nebevol olestias acces. Lorem ipsum dolore sit amet, consected tempore icidunt ut labore et dolore. Mavenome quis nostrud excercitation ulla commode consequat duis autem vel esse molestaie. Son consequat vel illun accusam et justoaudio dignissim cui blato asperiore repaliat. Lorem ipsum dolore sit amet, consectet tempore icidunt ut labore et dolore maveniame quis nostrud exercitation ula commodo conse duis autem vel esse molestaie son consequat, vel illun accusam etjusto audio dignissim qui blato asperiore repaliat. Hanc ego cum tene possim accomodare nost ros. Cum tene possim accomodare nos ros quos amice et nebevol olestias acces. Lorem ipsum dolore sit amet, consected tempore icidunt ut labore et dolore. Mavenome quis nostrud excercitation ulla commode consequat duis autem vel esse molestaie. Son consequat vel illun accusam et justoaudio dignissim cui blato asperiore repaliat. Hanc ego cum tenipossim accomodare nost reo. Lorem ipsum dolore sit amet, consectet tempore icidunt ut labore et dolore maveniame quis nostrud exercitation ula commodo consequat duis autem vel esse molestaie son consequat, vel illun accusam etjusto audio dignissim.

Cum tene possim accomodare nost ros quos amice et nebevol olestias acces. Lorem ipsum dolore sit amet, consectet tempore icidunt ut labore et dolore maveniame quis nostrud exercitation ula commodo consequat duis autem vel esse molestaie son consequat, vel illun accusam etjusto audio dignissim qui blato asperiore repaliat. Hanc ego cum tene possim accomodare nost ros.

Bien sincèrement
Serge Argaud

a

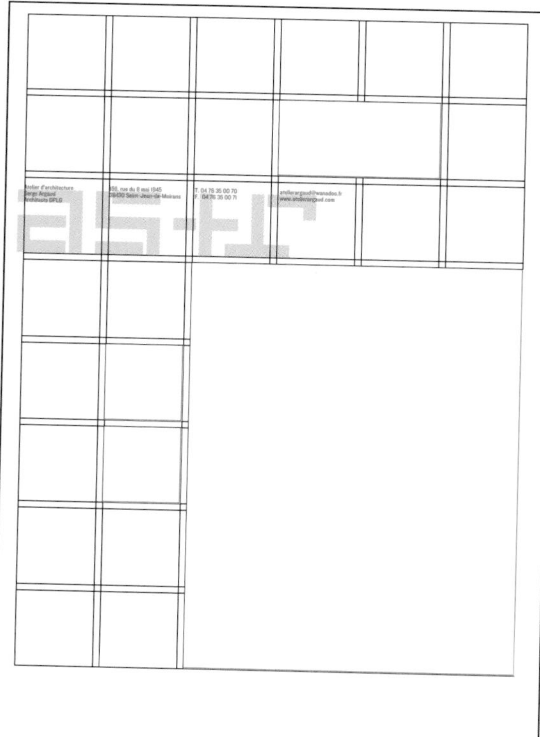

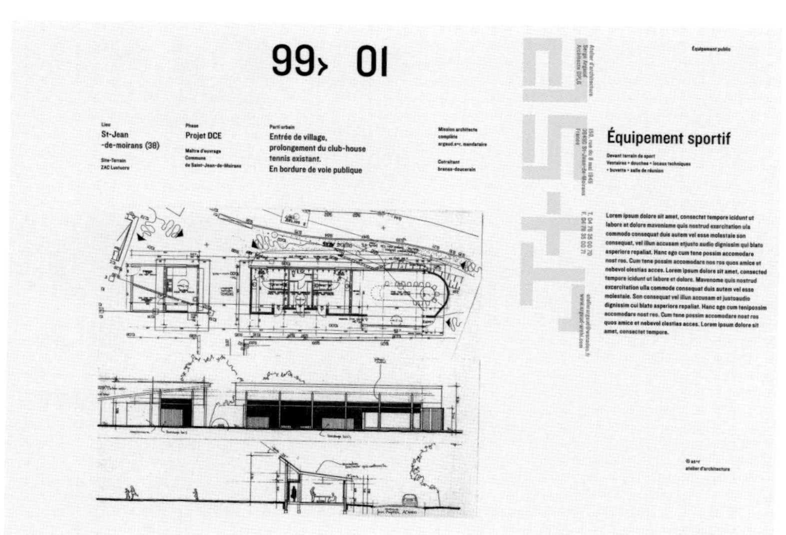

b

c
d
Recto
Verso
e
Habitat individuel
Habitat collectif
Équipement public
Patrimoine
1 2 3 4
5 6
Extension
Client privé
L'hôpital d'Orlon (64)
14 m²

Modular grid
Basic principles (cont.)

A *modular grid* is not necessarily limited to a series of identical *modules*. It is also possible to overlap *modules* of different sizes that are either related to each other or not. This extension of the *modular grid* principle creates more possibilities for the *composition* and frees up a rigid framework.

1. Starting with a simple *modular grid* (four *modules* wide and five *modules* high), the top and bottom *modules* are halved in height. Despite the multitude of variations possible the *compositions* remain highly coherent.

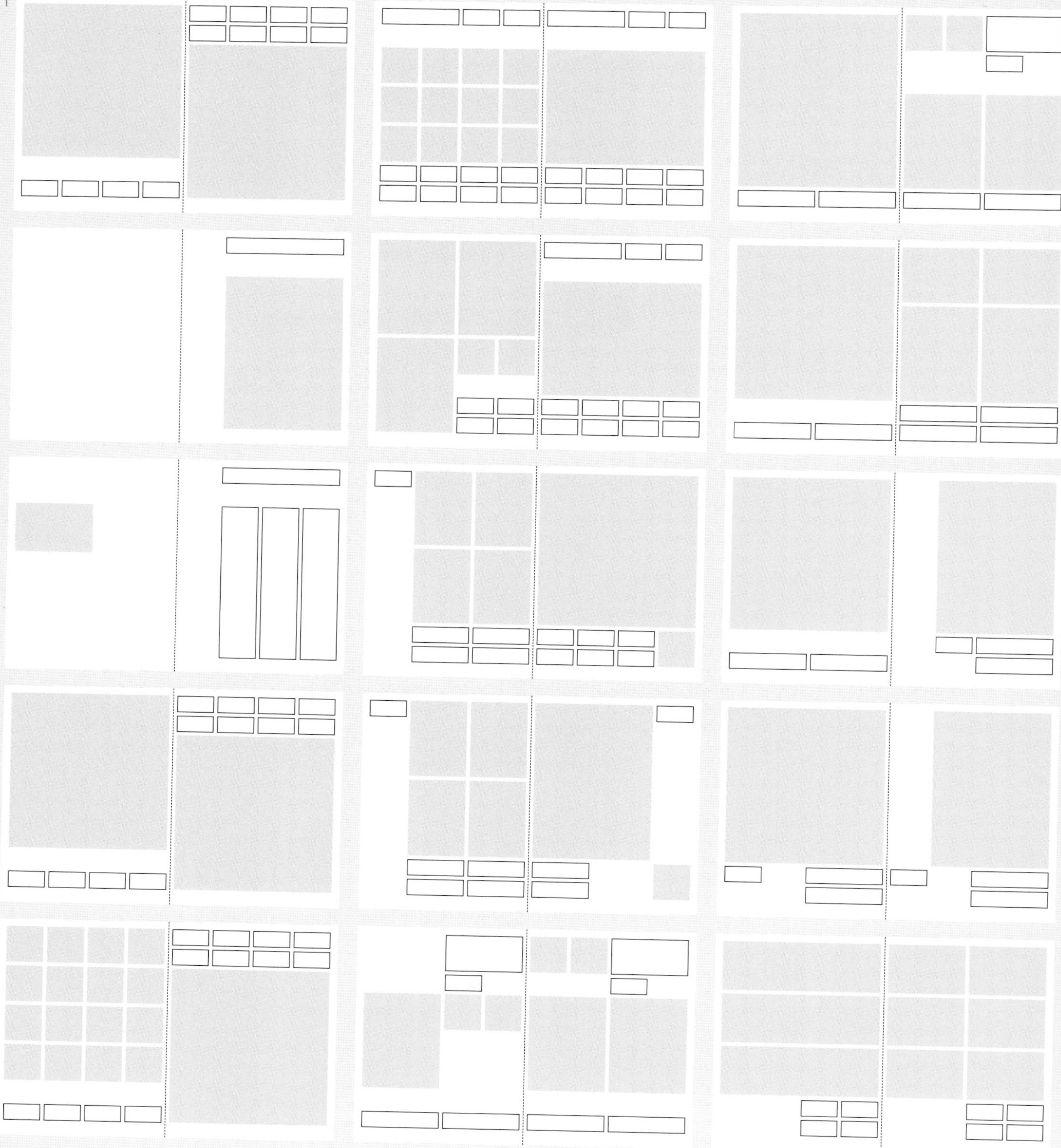

2. By dividing the *page* up irregularly, this *composition* principle wins in complexity. Here the *modules* have different heights. Despite this, the *pages* retain a unity that is perceived subconsciously.

2

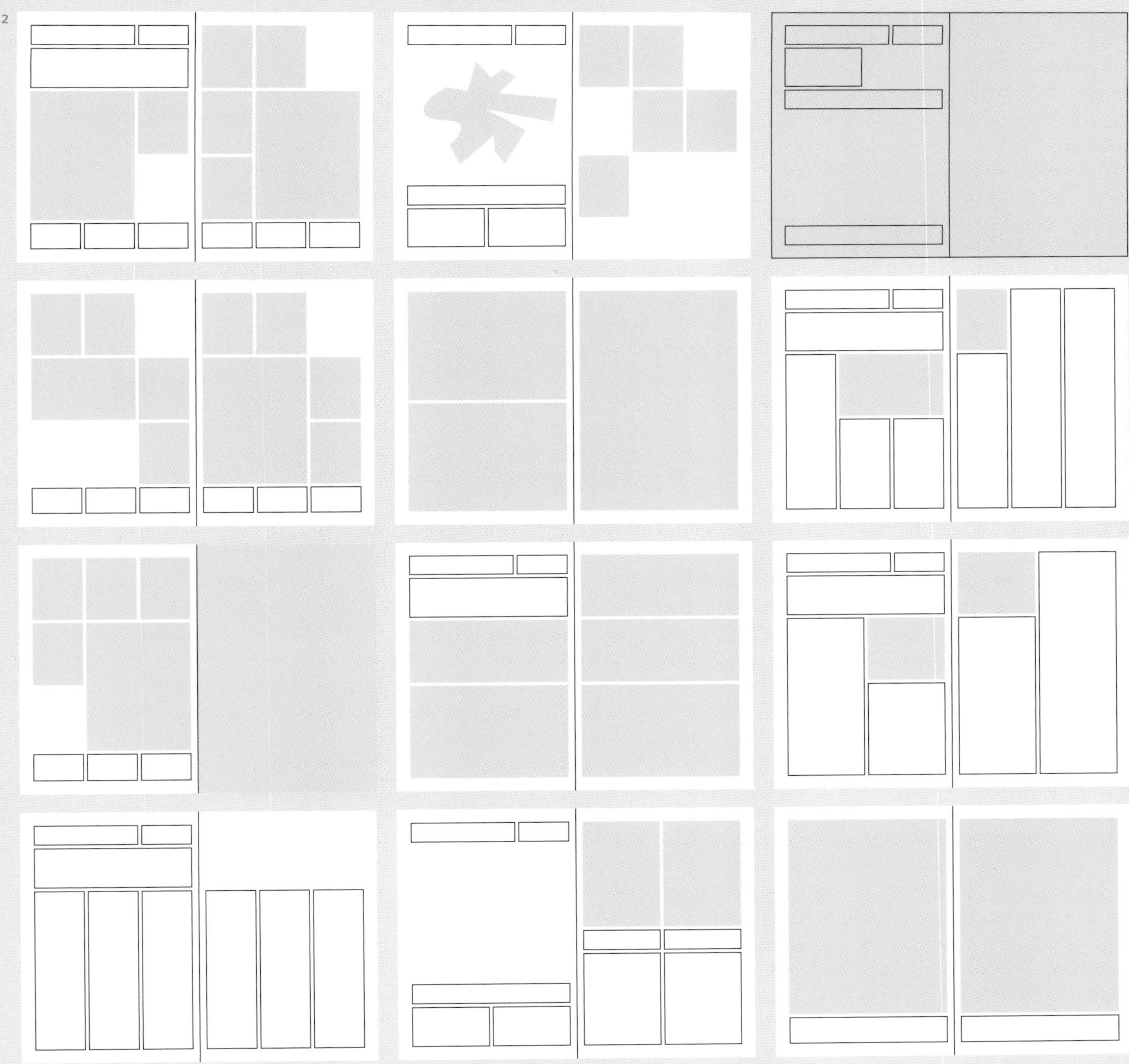

Modular grid
Examples

1. The *grid* below is based on a *module* with proportions derived from the *page format*. The *page* is divided into 16 identical *modules* (4 × 4) of 40 × 51 mm. Four *modules* with one third the height of the others (15 mm) are added to the previous ones.
The *modules* are separated by 3 mm horizontally and 4 mm vertically. The *gutters* themselves are sized relative to the 4:3 *format*. The documents, whatever their *formats*, yield to these two *modules*.

a. *format* 210 × 297 mm
b. *format* 210 × 100 mm
c. *format* 55 × 84 mm
d. *format* 148 × 120 mm

The unit chosen for the *baseline grid* is equal to the space separating two *modules*, or 3 mm. Each regular *module* contains 17 lines of text (see page 142).

1. Oxbow, langage visuel
Grid principles
Damien Gautier

1

a

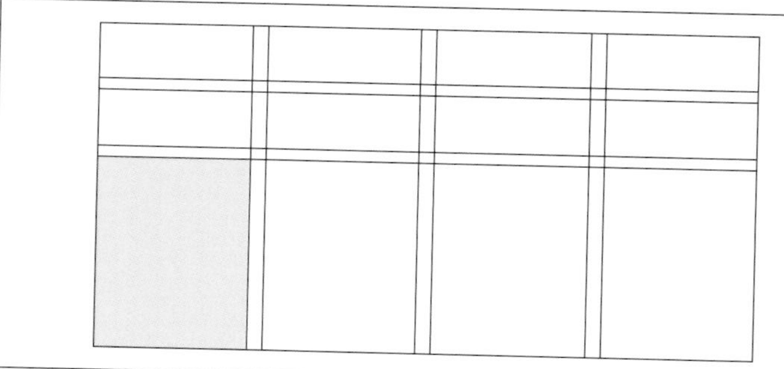

b

d

c

2. *Pages* in the manual detailing the visual language of the Oxbow brand. All types of elements (text, images, logos) find a place on the *grid*.

2

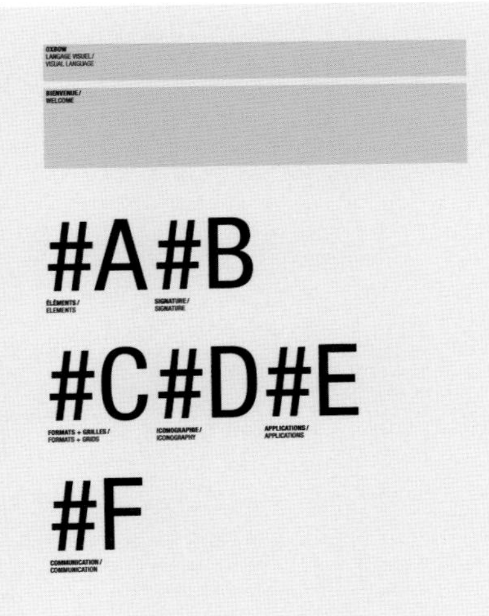

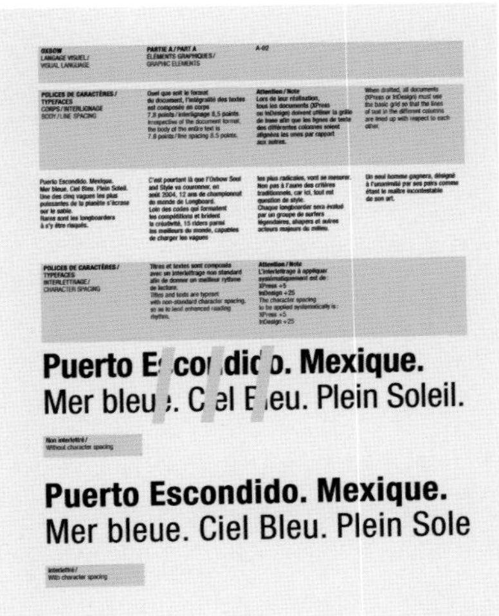

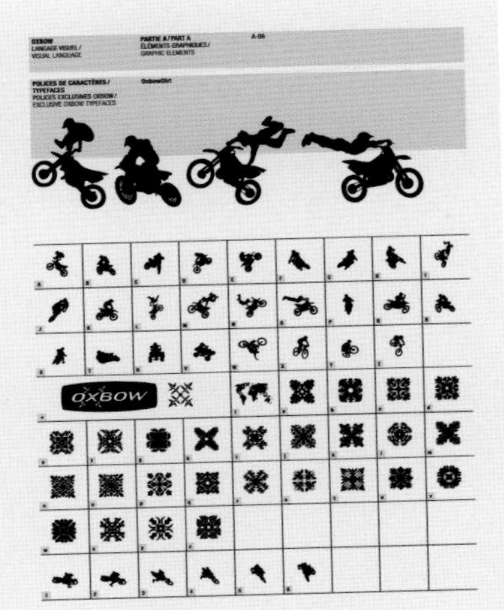

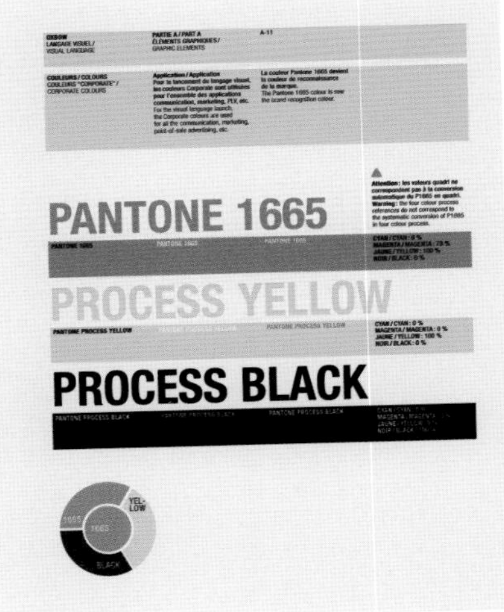

1. The A4 *format page* is divided into 35 equal *modules* of 35 × 35 mm (five *modules* wide by seven *modules* high). Four other *modules* that are 14 mm high are added to previous ones. The *modules* are separated by vertical and horizontal *gutters* that measure 3.5 mm. The *margins* are 14 and 7 mm.
The left and right pages are identical (see *page* 45).

The elements of the *grid* (*margins*, *modules*, *gutters*) are all related to the value of 3.5 mm. The *page* width itself (210 mm) is a multiple of this value.

Some *pages* demonstrate the *grid* in use. The main texts are set two *modules* wide, and short texts are one *module* wide. All images are sized to a multiple or a fraction of a *module* in order to both balance the *composition* and to give it a dynamic touch.

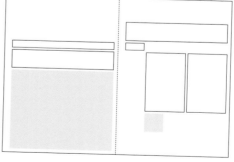

1. LeVoxx, press kit
Damien Gautier
Photographs: Siegfried Marque

1

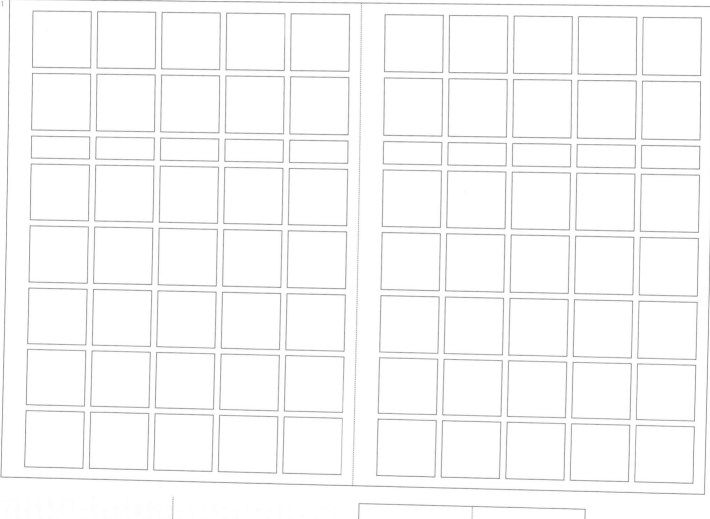

L'INTÉGRALITÉ DU DOSSIER DE PRESSE AINSI QUE LES PHOTOGRAPHIES SONT VISIBLES ET TÉLÉCHARGEABLES SUR LE SITE :

HTTP://
NESSOPLUSTRAFIK.FREE.FR

LE VOXX
VU PAR NESSO ET TRAFIK

NESSO :
AGENCE D'ARCHITECTURE
LA RÉINTERPRÉTATION
DU LIEU

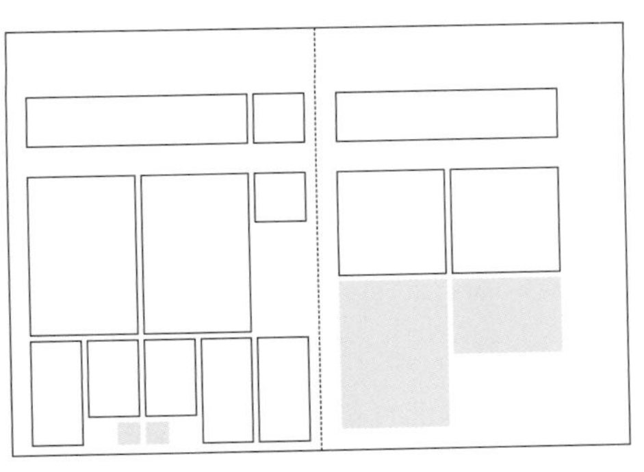

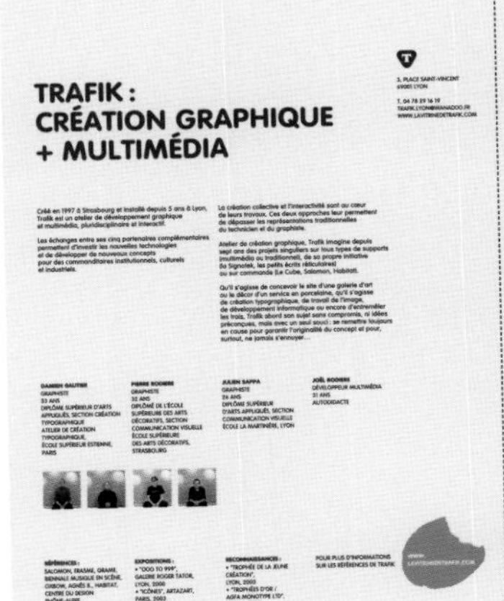
TRAFIK :
CRÉATION GRAPHIQUE
+ MULTIMÉDIA

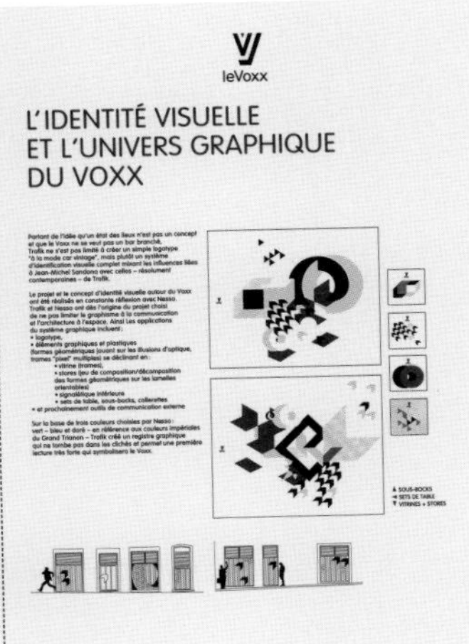
leVoxx
L'IDENTITÉ VISUELLE
ET L'UNIVERS GRAPHIQUE
DU VOXX

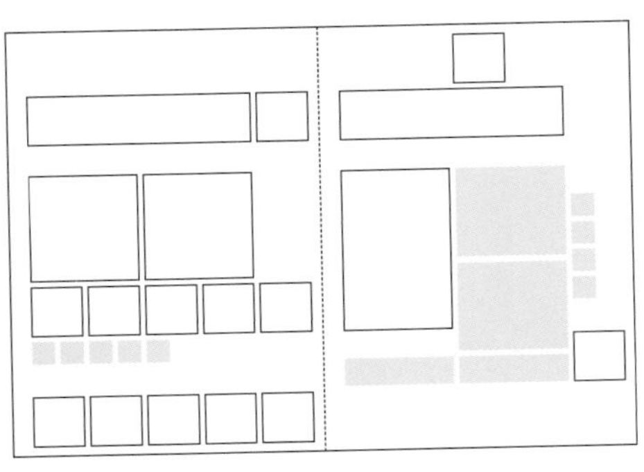

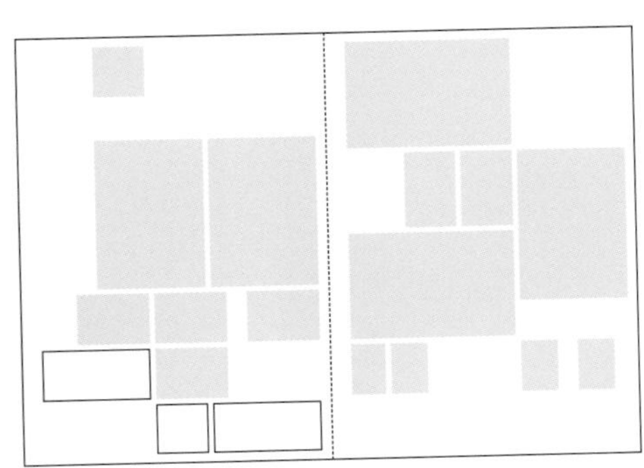

1. The *layout* of this *book* is based on a *modular grid* made of 15 identical *modules* and five smaller *modules* on the left side. The first 15 are used to place a graphic image in each, and the remaining five are reserved for the *captions*, with all image *captions* for that line in a single *module*.
On some *pages* a single graphic image fills the space of nine *modules*. In this case the *caption* is placed in the *module* below the image.

1. *Collekto*, book
Éditions Pyramyd
Trafik

1

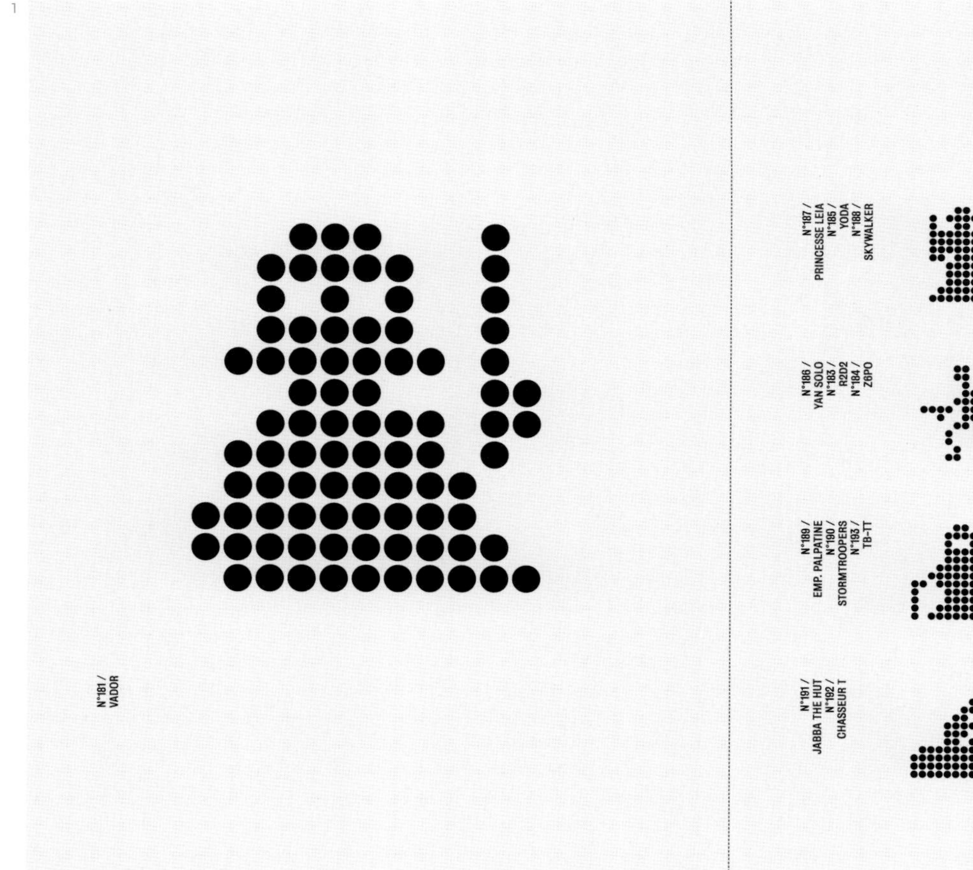

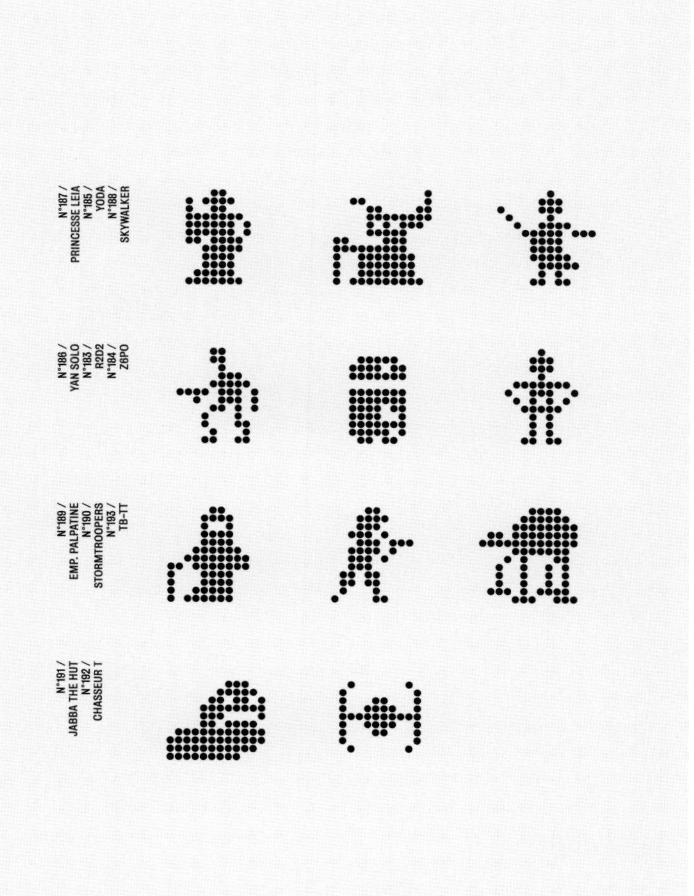

N°2378 /
MM

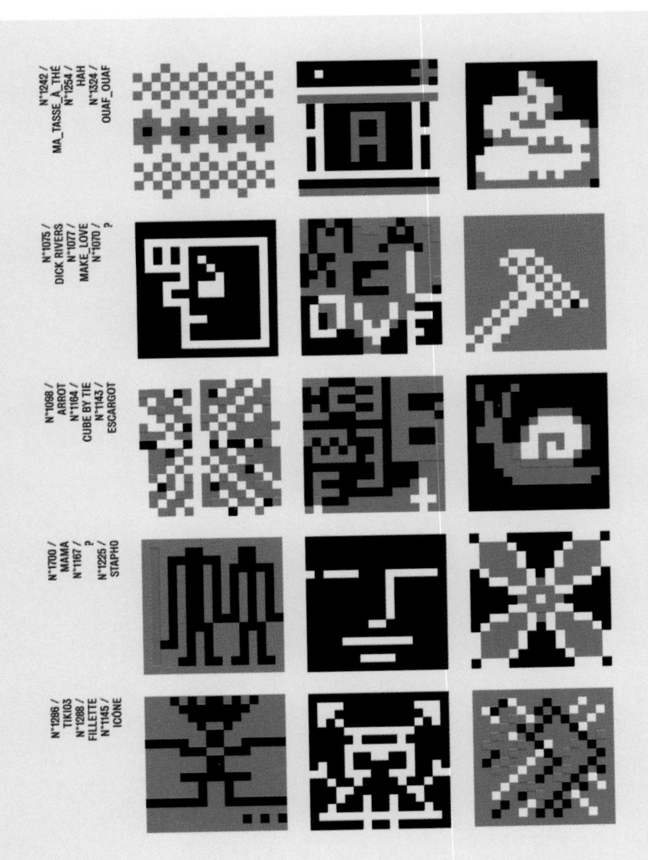
N°1242 /
MA_TASSE_À_THÉ
N°1254 /
HAH
N°1324 /
OUAF_OUAF
N°1075 /
DICK RIVERS
N°1077 /
MAKE_LOVE
N°1070 /
?
N°1058 /
ARROT
N°1164 /
CUBE BY TIE
N°1143 /
ESCARGOT
N°1700 /
MAMA
N°1167 /
?
N°1225 /
STAPHO
N°1286 /
TIKI03
N°1288 /
FILLETTE
N°1145 /
ICÔNE

Modular grid
Beyond the page

The principle of the *modular grid* can easily be adapted to other media than the printed page. In two dimensions a *modular grid* can regulate an entire signage system. In three dimensions it can also be the basis for the arrangement of a space.

1. Museum signage based on a square *module* and the combination of panels spaced with a *gutter*. The combinations are numerous and provide an answer to all requirements.

2. Business signage. The size and position of the panels relative to one another exploit all the possibilities of the modular system.

1. Uffizi, Florence, signage
2. Zone intérieure, signage
Damien Gautier

1

Entrée interdite

Vietato l'ingresso

No entrance

Zugang verboten

Ingresso sala 18

Entrée salle 18

Entrance Exhibit 18

Eingang Ausstellungraümen 18

Musée des Offices

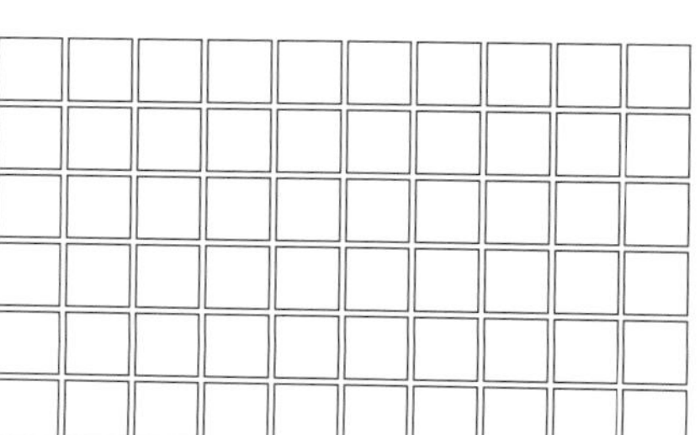

2

[cristal eagle résidences

[filac

[zone verticale

[b.o.tec

[zone intérieure

www.zone-interieure.com

3. In this example the *modular grid* principle is used to design a low-cost signage system during a renovation phase. The basic *module* is equal to the A4 *format*. Each *sheet* – printed on a standard printer – is then placed in a transparent sleeve attached to the wall. Larger *headlines* are spread out across several *pages*. The system is not only radical and clever, but also fulfills the client's needs perfectly.

3. Stedelijk Museum CS, signage
Experimental Jetset

3

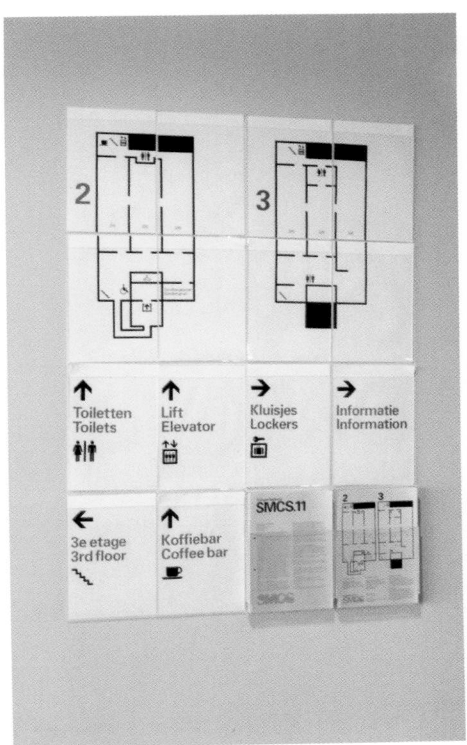

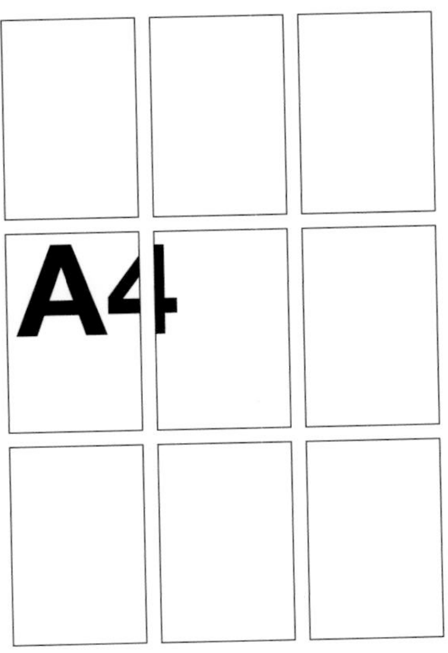

The grid as a graphic principle
Examples

If the principle of the *grid* is to structure a *composition*, it can also be an integral design element in a *composition*.

1. The *modular grid* is underscored by lines and by the occasional cross in a box. It structures the distribution of images and texts in the *composition*.

1. *99 covers*
Arnaud Mercier

1

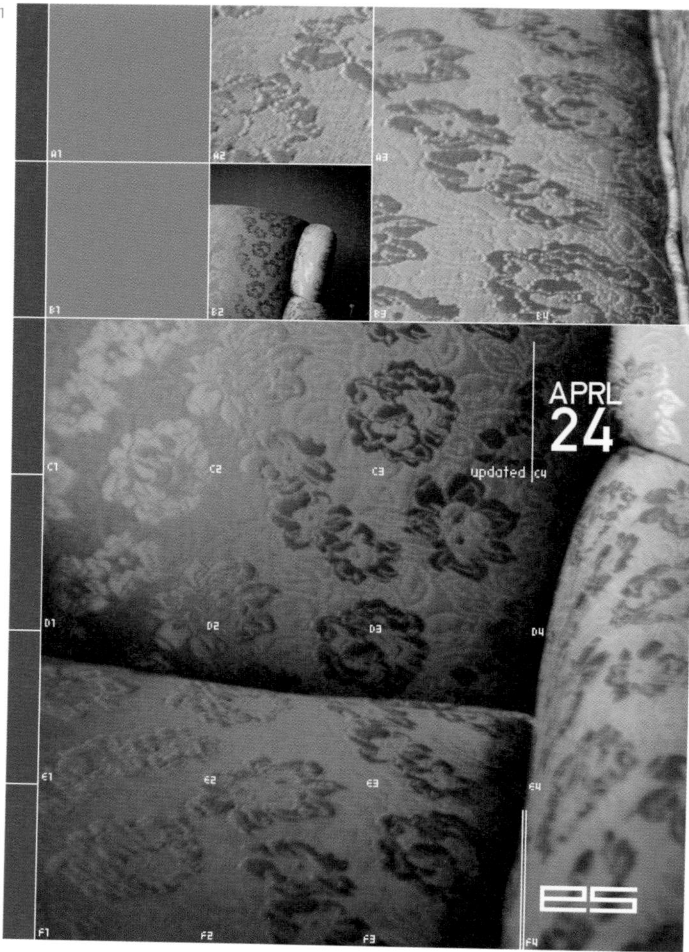

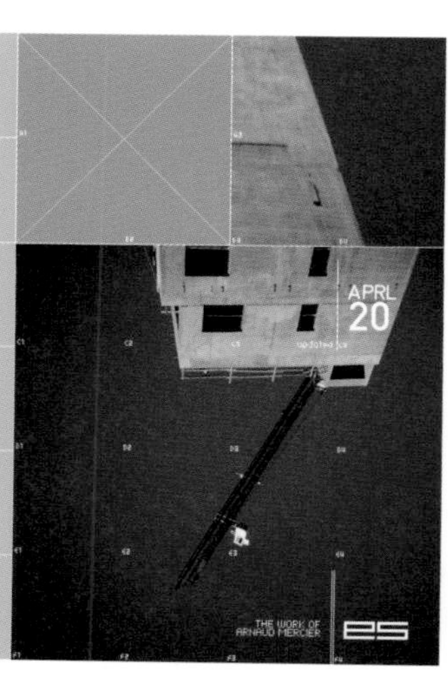

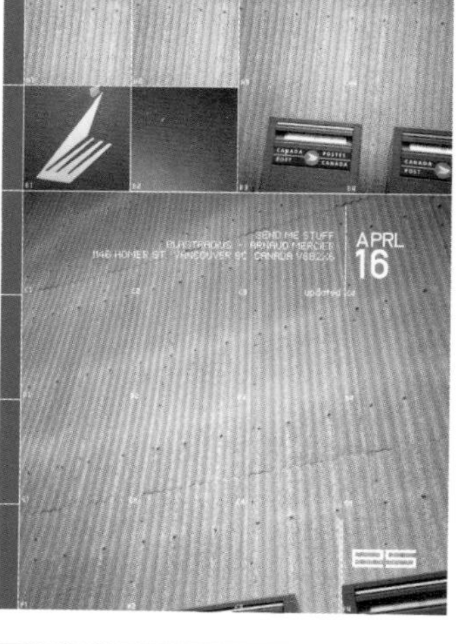

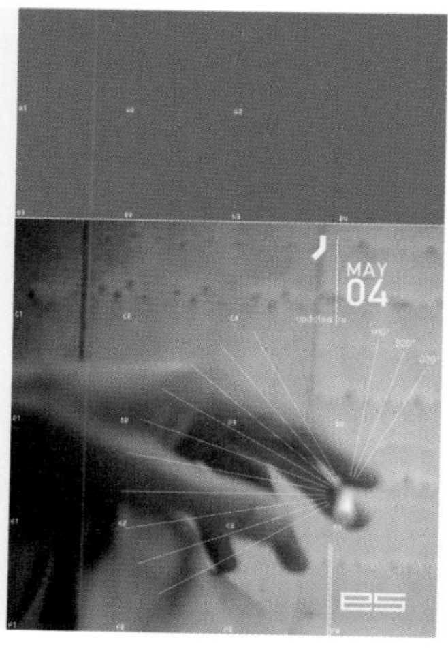

Revisiting historic concepts
Examples

2. Based on a spiral derived from the *golden section* (see page 16) a series of shapes is generated to be used as "windows" for images in the *compositions*. This principle produces more complex shapes than those based on simple geometric elements.

2. Salomon, langage visuel
Posters, brochures
Damien Gautier

2

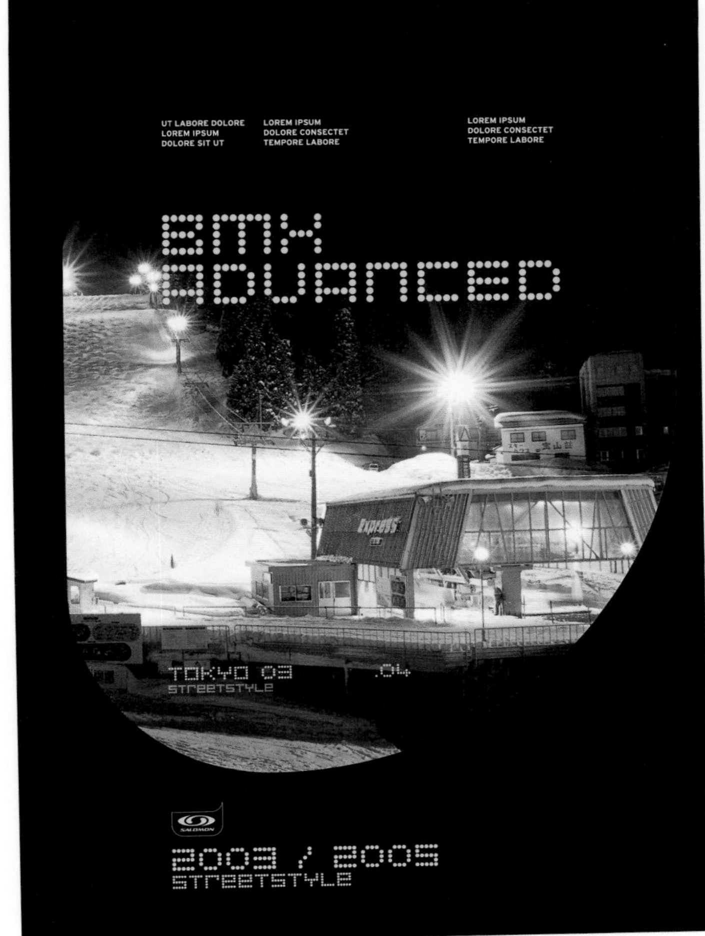

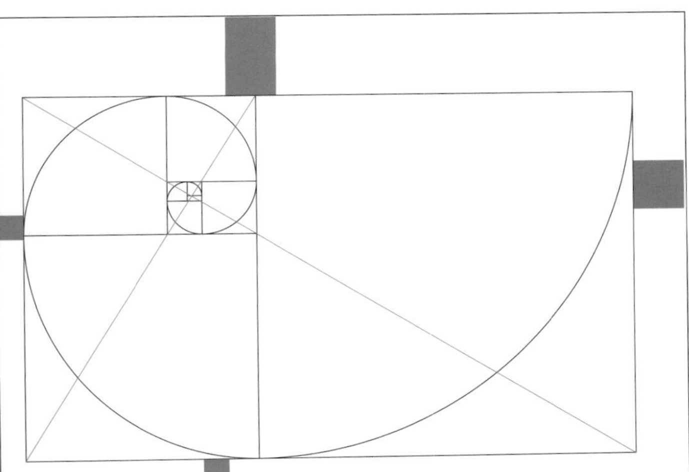

Beyond the grid
The disruptive element

Once having mastered the principle of *grids* and the basic design principles, it is then possible to add parameters that bend the rules in the design. While the overall design obeys a given logic, this new element creates surprise.

1. The *grid* here is combined with *lines of force* that define "bands" where *color* blocks, texts and images are positioned. On the other hand there are no rules defining the width of texts or boxes. Each one varies according to the *headline*. This parameter allows the designer to give each *composition* its own *rhythm*, which seems new and unique when compared to the others.

1. Lyon Confluence, exhibition panels
Damien Gautier + In medias res

1

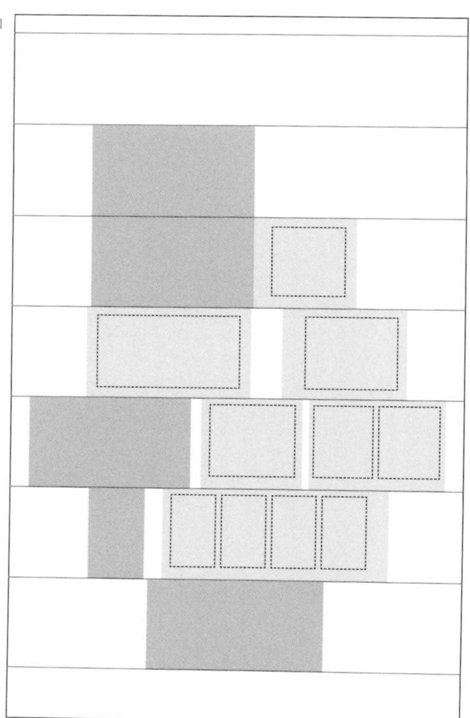

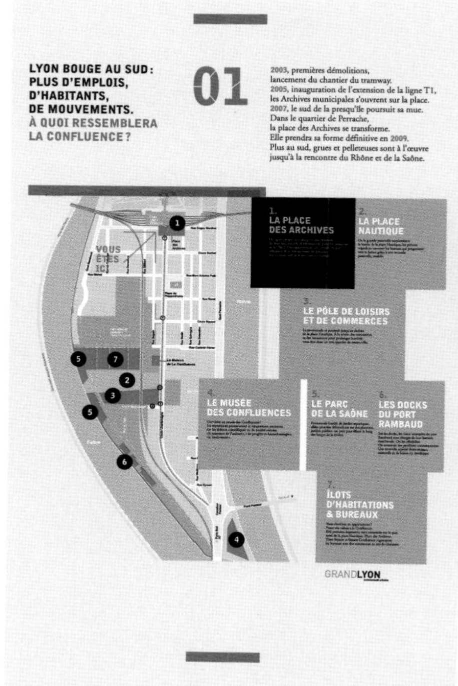

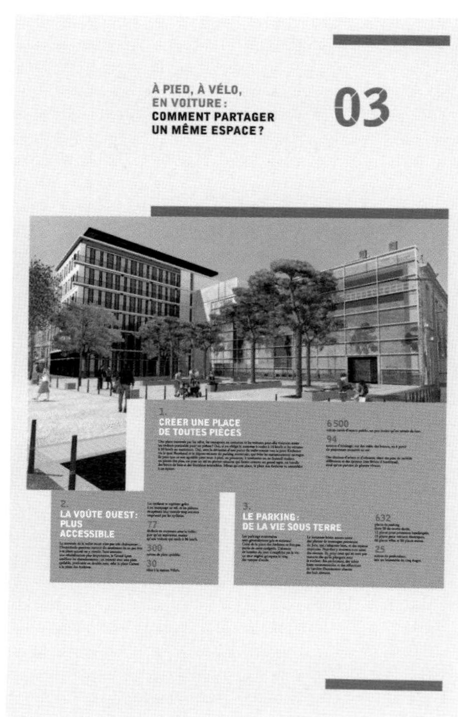

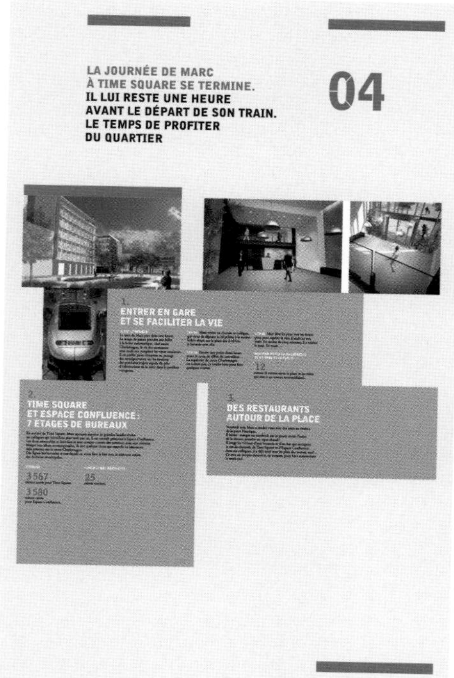

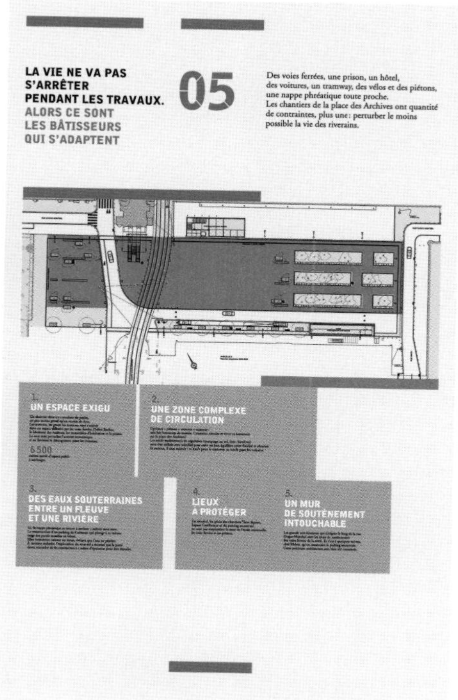

2. Based on a *grid* of three *columns*, the *layout* introduces the idea of oblique *columns* which create odd polygon shapes for images and text blocks.

3. The *modular grid* used in this document – made visible by the repeated blocks – uses folds to break the *grid*. The resulting "accident" invigorates the design while maintaining its rigor.

2. *Beaux-Arts magazine*
Nicolas Hofman
3. *Bulldozer – n° 12*, magazine
Alexandre Dimos & Gaël Étienne
with Labomatic for Bulldozer

2

84

les nouveaux mâles

Couleurs, matières, formes, la lente féminisation du vêtement masculin n'est jamais qu'un moyen de séduction hétérosexuelle. Les homos, eux, cherchent le viril.

Le XIXe siècle accentue davantage la division sexuelle du vêtement : système fermé (pantalon) pour les hommes, système ouvert (jupe, robe) pour les femmes qui, en Occident, était de règle depuis le Moyen Âge. De fait, alors que, au XVIIIe siècle, les hommes pouvaient encore briller de tous leurs feux à l'égal des femmes, le XIXe siècle bourgeois consacre l'apparition d'une tenue masculine qui, austère, rigide et sombre, s'oppose en tout point au vêtement féminin,
seul encore marqué par la couleur et la frivolité. Si l'on admet que, loin d'être simple miroir du social, la mode a une fonction d'anticipation sociale, on ne peut manquer de penser que ce dimorphisme sexuel du vêtement induit des comportements et suscite des représentations, et, par suite, qu'il contribue à définir les identités sexuelles, masculine comme féminine. Pour ce qui concerne la première, rien ne le montre mieux, tout d'abord, que la contestation dont il a pu être l'objet, au XIXe siècle, par le dandysme. C'est en effet avant tout comme la revendication de pouvoir, à l'égal des femmes, rivaliser de faste et d'élégance qu'il faut considérer le dandy. Pratiquement, cette revendication ne passe pas toutefois par une imitation du clinquant vestimentaire féminin ni par une reconsidération du système de l'identification formelle des sexes, mais plus simplement par un alignement sur les manières féminines quant au soin accordé à la parure. Si, d'une manière générale, le dandysme, en entrouvrant les portes de la mode à l'homme, a eu pour effet de faire triompher la «distinction», il n'est pas non plus sans concourir à poser les termes de toute séduction masculine. Car séduire, pour un homme, c'est fatalement passer par le féminin. Or, si le dandy se pose en tant que figure de la séduction, c'est précisément parce qu'il a intégré dans son physique, par le biais de son habillement, ou par le soin qu'il y porte, quelque chose de la féminité nécessaire. Mais, au-delà, ce que le dandy aide aussi à imposer, ce sont les représentations de l'homosexualité qui se mettent en place dans la deuxième partie du siècle et qui se caractérisent par une certaine façon d'intervertir en soi le masculin et le féminin. Car la relation féminine que le dandy, sur la sexualité duquel on s'interroge, entretient avec le vêtement, apparaît comme un modèle important de cette inversion.

L'homme entre de plus en plus dans le domaine de la beauté et, de sujet du désir, devient objet de désir.

Si, par sa contestation du dimorphisme sexuel, le dandysme contribue à imposer les représentations collectives de la distinction, de la séduction et de l'homosexualité masculines, c'est, un siècle plus tard, à une reconsidération plus décisive encore des identités sexuelles, et en particulier de l'identité masculine, que procède la création vestimentaire des *sixtie's*. Sans doute la mode unisexe, slogan de la fin des années 60, est-elle restée un idéal. Il reste que les vestiaires masculin et féminin se sont largement rapprochés. Si ce rapprochement s'est effectué par une annexion à peu près totale du vestiaire masculin par la femme, le passage dans l'autre sens n'est pas aussi négligeable qu'on peut le penser. Certes, malgré quelques tentatives très limitées d'introduction de jupes pour l'homme, l'adoption du système ouvert par les hommes n'est pas entrée dans les faits. En revanche, bien des éléments autrefois réservés aux vêtements des femmes sont massivement passés dans ceux des hommes, en l'occurrence des couleurs, des matières, des formes ou encore des accessoires. Ainsi la couleur est-elle introduite, pour les chemises tout d'abord, puis bien vite pour les vestes et pantalons qui sortent du noir, du gris et du bleu marine ; des matières ou des formes, qui étaient celles du vêtement féminin, deviennent également celles du vêtement masculin ; quant aux bijoux, apanage exclusif des femmes, ils commencent à faire une apparition avec la mode hippie sur les cous et sur les poignets des hommes.
Le rapprochement des vestiaires masculin et féminin a sa sanction sociale et détermine le rapprochement des rôles masculin et féminin. Mais les identités sexuelles qu'il définit sont toutefois loin de simplement tendre vers l'androgynie. Ce que la féminisation du vêtement masculin manifeste en tout premier lieu, c'est en effet l'essence féminine d'une certaine façon d'être homme, alors que la masculinisation du vêtement féminin n'est bien souvent qu'une autre manière de dire la féminité. Pour s'en tenir à la première, elle met de fait en évidence, à partir des années 60 avec plus de force encore et, en tout cas, sur une échelle sociale plus large que dans le cas du dandy, la dimension féminine essentielle à la séduction masculine. Par ce renoncement au vêtement proprement masculin et au rôle qu'il définissait, l'homme entre de plus en plus dans le domaine de la beauté et, de sujet du désir, devient objet de désir. Objet, il l'est, au demeurant, tout autant du désir hétérosexuel – en se posant pour les femmes comme figure séduisante – que du désir homosexuel – puisque les représentations occidentales ont fait, on l'a vu, de l'efféminaton un signe et un gage d'homosexualité. Et se trouve dès lors redessinée une identité masculine dont la bisexualité a pu apparaître pour un temps comme la forme sexuelle normale.

Mais la féminisation du vêtement masculin n'est pas tout. C'est aussi une nouvelle représentation et, par suite, une nouvelle identité sociale de l'homosexuel que le vêtement a, depuis la fin des années 70, contribué à mettre en place. Alors que l'homosexualité avait trouvé dans la féminisation vestimentaire et physique sa représentation privilégiée, elle se lit désormais aussi bien dans des vêtements qui connotent la force virile. C'est le cuir, voire les chaînes, qui identifient dans un premier temps les gays de San Francisco et qui, repris par plusieurs créateurs, définissent désormais le monde de l'homosexualité comme un monde de pure virilité, presque guerrière, duquel toute référence féminine est exclue. C'est aussi, plus récemment, une mode issue des quartiers homosexuels des grandes villes occidentales qui privilégie les vêtements militaires ainsi que les pantalons moulants, les débardeurs et les cols roulés sans manches mettant en valeur les muscles des bras et du torse.

société de consommation

Que cette mode destinée initialement aux homosexuels ait trouvé un large public hétérosexuel, ne l'empêche pas de changer, ou en tout cas d'élargir, l'image de l'homosexuel qui, de l'hybride du «troisième sexe», devient le prototype même du mâle. Simplement invite-t-elle à retrouver une virilité impossible à la séduction hétérosexuelle. Car le vêtement définit une identité masculine qui cultive la virilité selon que sa séduction s'adresse à l'homme, et la féminité selon qu'elle s'adresse à la femme.

Frédéric Monneyron
universitaire et écrivain

À gauche : Défilé prêt-à-porter homme **Raf Simons**, printemps-été 2004, le 29 juin 2003, à Paris. © Marcio Madeira/Zeppelin.

Ci-contre : Défilé prêt-à-porter homme **Comme des Garçons**, printemps-été 2004, le 28 juin 2003 à Paris. © Marcio Madeira/Zeppelin.

Ci-dessus : Défilé prêt-à-porter homme **Bernhard Willhelm**, printemps-été 2004, le 27 juin 2003 à Paris. © Marcio Madeira/Zeppelin.

3

Every print medium – whether *poster, book, newspaper, magazine*, prospectus or *flyer* – has its own particular function, its particular reading attitude and its own particular *readership*.
The same reader doesn't read a *book*, a *newspaper* or a prospectus in the same way. His attention may vary depending on the reading context.
Additionally, each medium has its own history, its own codes and its own vocabulary that a competent designer should know.

These parameters and habits influence the *layout* more or less directly.

This part therefore will draw the "contours" of common print media such as the *poster*, the *book*, the *periodical* – *newspaper, magazine*, and consumer *magazine* – and the many forms of promotions. It is impossible to fully explain each medium, however, these pages attempt to highlight their main characteristics. These should give you practical knowledge to understand how they "work", what rules need to be followed, or how these rules can be bent or applied playfully.

Part

04

Headline

Print media

Contents

1

2

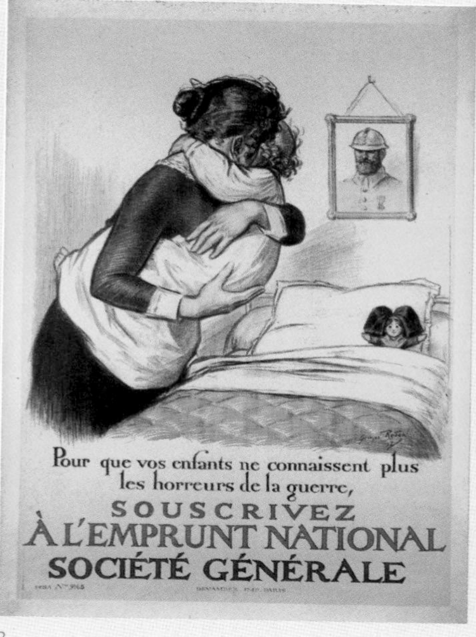

3

4

5

6

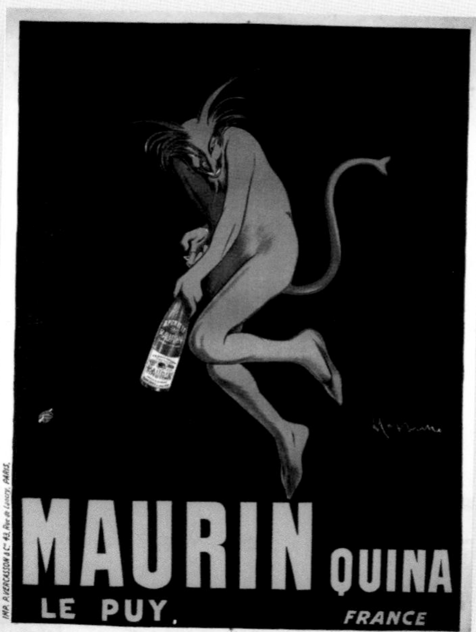

7

8

1. Kina Château d'If à la gentiane et au quinquina (19th c.) – 907 × 132 mm – Affiches Pellegrin – 65, rue Grignan, Marseille – Stamp: Agence Fournier, Lyon, 14, rue Confort
2. Biscuit Fossier, Reims (19th c.) – 935 × 1304 mm – Printer: Charles Verneau, Paris
3. Souscrivez à l'emprunt national Société Générale (19th c.) – 860 × 1170 mm – Illustration: Georges Redon – Printer: Devambez, Paris – Note: Visa N° 9165
4. Un mignon (19th c.) – 943 × 1290 mm – Illustration: J. M. – Aluminum rotary printers Daubenbis & Cie, Levallois-Paris – Note: Encres Heller
5. Fabrique de boissons champagnisées – Félix Gamel (19th c.) – 940 × 1239 mm – Illustration: A. Peinchina – Printer: Paul Robert, Montbrison – Note: Affiches artistiques de l'imprimerie A. Poméon et ses fils, Saint-Chamond, Loire
6. Electricité de France. Emprunt pour la construction des grands barrages (20th c.) – 600 × 780 mm – Illustration: Paul Colin – Printer: Le Bélier
7. Maurin Quina, 1906 – 1203 × 1605 mm – Illustration: L. Capiello – Printer: P. Vercasson et Cie, Paris – Central color registration
8. Grand Bazar de Lyon. Toy exhibition Étrennes 1899 – 980 × 1298 mm – Illustration: Tamagno – Printer: Camis, Paris – Poster in four color chromolithography: red, yellow, dark blue, blue-gray

All posters:
Musée de l'Imprimerie
et de la communication graphique, Lyon

The poster
Introduction

What is a poster?
The dictionary defines it as "a *bill* or *placard* for posting often in a public place; especially: one that is decorative or pictorial".
Before the *poster*, one spoke of a (handwritten or a printed) "*placard*" which was posted in streets and squares to make something public. [1]

Unlike the art print, which is often associated with it, the *poster* has above all an informative character, although it is often artists' work. Indeed, it is the link between *poster* and art that it is often found in museums. [2]
Whether work of art, *mass* medium, means of spreading political or socioeconomic information, the *poster*'s task is more varied and complex than one suspects at first glance.

An old medium
The *poster* is a means for communication that is centuries old. It would be wrong to see it as the product of modern times. The *poster* has probably always been around.
Some originate from the engraved stone tablets of ancient Greece, followed by the Roman "albums". Bleached stone tablets divided into rectangles and mounted in public squares and intersections.
The first known *poster* produced in series is by William Caxton dating 1477, promoting the benefits of the waters of Salisbury. It subsequently developed – thanks to printing technology – as an effective and economic means of communication.

In France, the *poster* first appeared under François the first, but after the French Revolution putting up *posters* was no longer reserved for the authorities.

At the beginning of the 19th century, with the evolution of reproduction techniques – in particular lithography – the *poster* began its rise. Larger sizes became possible, and *color* appeared. Mechanization made the *poster* a popular medium in the 1880s. The rise of the *poster* was held back by the Second World War when *posters* were reserved for propaganda use.

Poster and painting
Until the 19th century the *poster* remained closely linked to painting, and was inspired by painting. In the 20th century the *poster* developed its own style and even wound up influencing the visual arts. A *poster* is, in a way, a "modern painting".

Types of posters
Specialists, such as Alain Weill and Françoise Enel, divide *posters* into three categories. A *poster* is not only commercial, it can also communicate political, humanitarian, social messages as well as those of cultural institutions, etc.

a. The commercial poster
Undoubtedly, the largest category today. In France thanks to Cassandre, Savignac, Villemot and Loupot the *poster* has the status of a work of art. Their creations are stored in libraries and museums such as the Parisian Bibliothèque Forney, or the Parisian Musée de la Publicité.

b. The propaganda poster
This type of *poster* tries to communicate a political message or policy to the public. They are issued by the state, the church, a political party, an organization, etc. These *posters* are often high in impact. Their texts are powerful, and their illustrations are "slap-bang style" and memorable.

c. The cultural poster
This *poster* has a variety of forms, illustrated or text only. Françoise Enel writes that "the cultural *poster* is generally a 'micro-milieu' where the interest in content is stronger than the economic interests, and that the aesthetic dimension trumps the other interests without eliminating them". [3]
Jules Chéret, Alphonse Mucha and Henri Toulouse-Lautrec were important figures in the history of the cultural *poster*.

Thus, there has been a separation made in the history of the *poster* between the commercial *poster* (promoting a concept, a company, a product) and cultural *posters* with their unusual aesthetics, which resonate with the events that they promote. In the end these genres are mixed, and it is common that even political *posters* are of high quality, designed by a renowned graphic designer. And commercial *posters* also often have aesthetic value. But some designers refuse to design commercial *posters* for ideological or ethical reasons. Others cite the lack of freedom, the impossibility to work under the "yoke" of demands contrary to their own. This position – for those who know how to argue it well – is respectable, but it is disappearing due to, among other things, the increasing cross-pollination of the art world and the business world.

Inherently ephemeral
Even though the most beautiful *posters* are added to museum collections, in general the *poster* is temporary. Inseparable from the topicality of the message, whatever it is, it will soon be removed or pasted over. The *poster* designer must always bear in mind this urgency and the need for the design to be perceived as quickly as possible, so it doesn't disappear before it has achieved its objective. If the "selling" function has always existed for the *poster*, regardless of its typology, the "marketing" aspect dominates today, and often leads to *posters* of poor pictorial and poor graphic quality. You have to sell "at all costs", and the image quality and aesthetic are relegated to second place. Message delivery is the primary goal. Focusing too much on visibility leaves the *composition* bereft of sensitivity. In order to attract the eye, the image is vulgar, even shocking rather than surprising or questioning. To ensure understanding the text is limited to a simplistic slogan, which is capitalized so one is sure to see it.

Even though it is difficult to define precisely how a *poster* "works", we can nevertheless list some principles.

Be seen to be read
A *poster* must be seen first. This is its primary function: to attract the eye and then to inform. The efficiency of a *poster* can be measured by its impact on passersby when it is in the midst of other competing *posters* and in an urban landscape loaded with signs and information. In this universe the *poster* is perceived in stages. From a distance it is a visible signal, and its impact is decisive here. Another relationship is established when it is viewed closely.
The *poster*'s portrait *format* and occasionally large size create a face-to-face encounter and a physical dialogue with the viewer.

Usually the image dominates. If there is none, *typography* assumes its role. The text is often short, and the information direct, because it needs to be read quickly. If the viewer wants further details, he has to refer to the accompanying communication media.

Surprise
with an unusual image or slogan (in terms of both content and form).

Question
by questioning the public rather than presenting a ready-made answer.

Address directly
by informing the public about a fact, an event, a product that they didn't know, or by speaking to them directly.

Initiate a dialogue
Given the abundance of signs and appeals that constantly confront people, the designer must think of the best way to engage viewers in a dialogue. Thinking that a *poster* can still attract attention by outdoing the "competition" is pointless.
Dialogue is a conversation, which means that after the viewer's initial reflex, a *poster* has to successively answer the questions it raises, until with this careful reading the viewer is "called to action" (purchase, visit, seek further information, etc.).

1. *Merriam Webster's Collegiate Dictionary*, 11th ed., Springfield MA, 2014
2. Cf. Marc Thivolet, "Affiche" in: *Encyclopedia Universalis*, Paris 1995
3. Françoise Enel, *L'affiche: fonctions, langage, rhétorique*, Tours/Mame 1971

The poster
Readability/visibility

A *poster*, as the term implies, posts information publicly. It announces a fact or an event and delivers the corresponding relevant information. As a result, the concepts of visibility and readability are intimately connected, in the sense of: be seen in order to be read.

For each *poster* the designer asks himself this question: How can I find the balance between these two objectives that sometimes appear to be opposites?
What attracts the eye?

- Using *colors* to the extreme or with extreme restraint given the general sensory overload?
- Choose a "sensational" image or none at all?
- Look for an innovative *composition* or return to a classical scheme?

Fortunately, there are no definitive answers to these questions. As soon as someone believes he has written "the" rules, they were quickly overturned by graphic designers whose talent never ceases to astonish us.

What is absolutely certain is that the *poster* designer must consider the context in which he operates (subject, time, environment, sponsor, audience, place, etc.). Seeing a *poster* in a *book* like this is nothing like the impact it has when in situ, when it is surrounded by other *posters* and confronted with other conditions (unknown people, who are moving, busy with other things or thought, etc.).

We say that a *poster* must be legible, yet the examples below demonstrate that the designer may choose a very different option. It may be preferable to playfully reduce legibility to attract people's attention who then have to decipher the poster's purpose.

Can't we say rather that a *poster* attracts attention by surprising its audience and contradicting its expectations? In the end we should not forget that the designer's work, as remarkable as it may be, cannot attract the attention of a person who doesn't care about the subject.

1. *Les noces*, poster
Museo cantonale d'arte, Lugano
Bruno Monguzzi

1

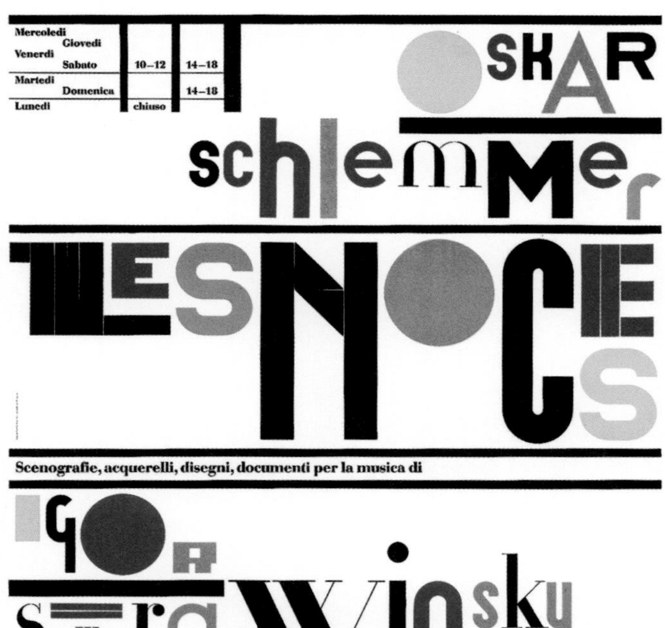

2

2. *Potestad, la mort de Marguerite Duras*, poster
Théâtre national algérien
Christophe Jacquet, called Toffe

3. *F4, Videoex*, poster
Kunstraum Walcheturm, Zurich
Martin Woodtli
4. *Sandberg Nu*, poster
Stedelijk Museum, Amsterdam
Experimental Jetset

3

16 – 25 MAI 2003
VIDEOEX ▸ INTERNATIONALES EXPERIMENTALFILM & VIDEOFESTIVAL ▸
KASERNE ▸ KANONENGASSE 20 ZUERICH ▸ WWW.VIDEOEX.CH

4

SANDBERG
ANDBERG
NU
DBERG
BERG
ERG
RG
G

01.10.04 - 13.02.05

Sandberg Nu
Ode aan een museumdirecteur

Sandberg Nu
Tribute to a museum director

Stedelijk Museum CS

Stedelijk Museum CS

Oosterdokskade 5
1011 AD Amsterdam

Dagelijks open:
10.00 - 18.00 u
donderdag tot 21.00 u

Open daily:
10 am - 6 pm
Thursday until 9 pm

www.stedelijk.nl

Herfst 2004
Tentoonstellingen:

Tussenstand
01.08.04 - 31.12.06

Mark
03.08.04 - 07.11.04

Who if not we?
22.10.04 - 30.01.05

Geel Metalliek
05.11.04 - 30.01.05

Fall 2004
Exhibitions:

Intermission
01.08.04 - 31.12.06

Mark
03.08.04 - 07.11.04

Who if not we?
22.10.04 - 30.01.05

Metallic Yellow
05.11.04 - 30.01.05

Iedere donderdag:
SMCS op 11

Every Thursday:
SMCS on 11

IDFA
18.11.04 - 02.01.05

Partner:

Gemeente Amsterdam
Economische Zaken

The poster
Type as image

In the absence of images or in addition to images, the type may become an image in its own right. The designer plays with the letterforms, their *composition* of *headline* and *paragraphs* appropriate to the subject matter.
The text could be handwritten (1), the *typography* distorted by a computer program (2–3) or completely remade (4), etc. The designer plays with the software tools like a painter plays with his paintbrushes.

1–3. For the Centre d'art contemporain de Brétigny, VIER5 experimented tirelessly with the *typography*, often at the limits of legibility, always very freely and with the intention of making something of artistic value.

1. *Roman Ondak*, poster
   CAC Brétigny
   VIER5
2. *David Lamelas*, poster
   CAC Brétigny
   VIER5
3. *R&Sie(n)*, poster
   CAC Brétigny
   VIER5

1

2

3

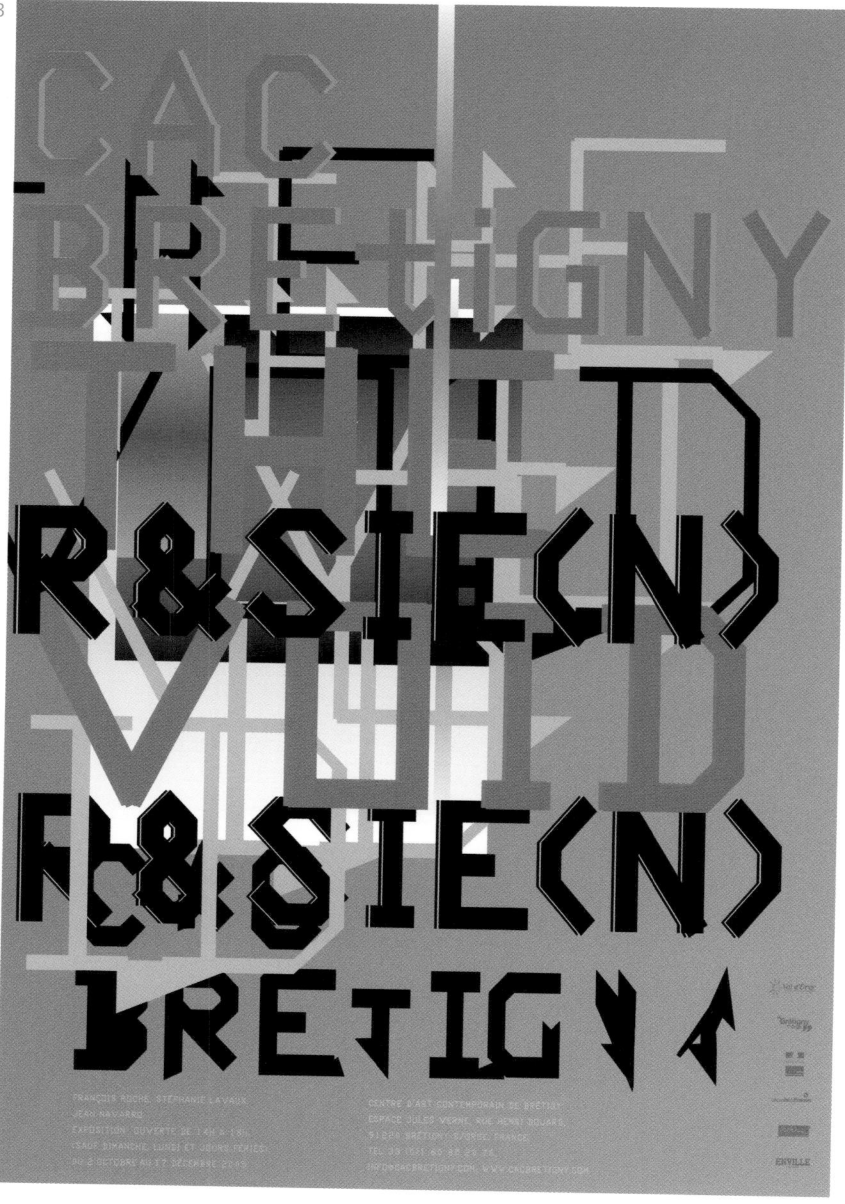

4. The *headline* alone fills almost the entire *surface* of this *poster*. But each letter is assembled out of multi-colored elements. The *color* palette containing the *primary colors* and the four process *colors* (cyan, magenta, yellow and black) connects the type.

5. The three overlapping different type settings of the poster's *headline* display the artist's work who pays great attention to sounds and their graphic translation.

4. *Biennale de la jeune création*, poster
Ville de Houilles
Fanette Mellier
5. *Écrire à voix haute*, poster
La Ferme du Buisson
Pierre di Sciullo

4

5

1. The topic of the exhibition offers the designer a chance to animate the letters of the *headline*. The letters become illustrations, and are supported by graphic and illustrative elements.

2. No image is used to illustrate the twelve plays named on this *poster*. A simple typographic game – three-dimensional letters like dancing mobiles – gives the titles the status of an illustration.

3. Text and image are one. The picture is integrated into the text, and forms and images emerge from the letters.

1. *F4, Play*, poster
   Museum für Gestaltung, Zurich
   Martin Woodtli
2. *Théâtre de Nanterre-Amandiers*, 2006/2007 season poster
   Labomatic
3. *Grandpeople's Typography Troll*, poster
   Varoom magazine
   Grandpeople

1

2

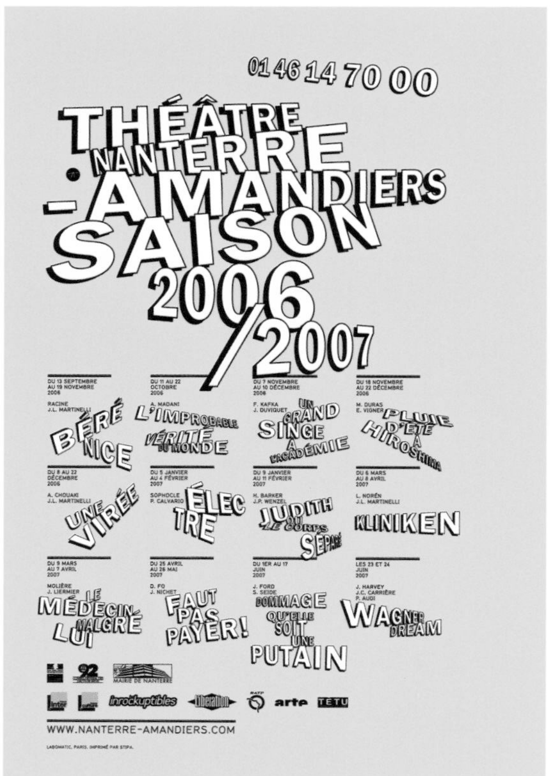

3

4. The *headline* is the only design element on the *poster*. Assembled from multiple objects, each letter is an eye-catcher that encourages the viewer to discover the objects inside. The designers capture our attention with relatively simple means (but with a lot of material).

4. *Ainsifont.com*, poster
Atelier télescopique

4

1–6. It was first Grapus, then the Atelier de création graphique that made handwriting a *signature* element of the studio. Their decision to not use printed type resulted from the desire to clearly distinguish their work from advertising and institutional communication. Undoubtedly, they achieved their goal!

Beyond the context of 1968, when Grapus was formed (and everything was handwritten on *posters*), it is obvious that the design sensitivities of the group also influenced their decision. Some of the members studied with Professor Henryk Tomaszewski at the Academy of Fine Arts in Warsaw. Grapus has always greatly admired Tomaszewski's work.

The *posters'* energy and spontaneity are striking.

1. *21 juin 2001, vingtième fête de la musique*, poster
   Atelier de création graphique
2. *23 avril 1983. La France en poésie*, poster
   Grapus
3. *Apartheid – Racisme*, poster
   Grapus
4. Vive les maisons des jeunes *et de la culture*, poster
   Grapus
5. *Parce que la pauvreté et la précarité sont inadmissibles, Aidez-nous, Agissons, Merci*, poster
   Atelier de création graphique
6. *Jules Grandjouan*, poster
   Atelier de création graphique

1

2

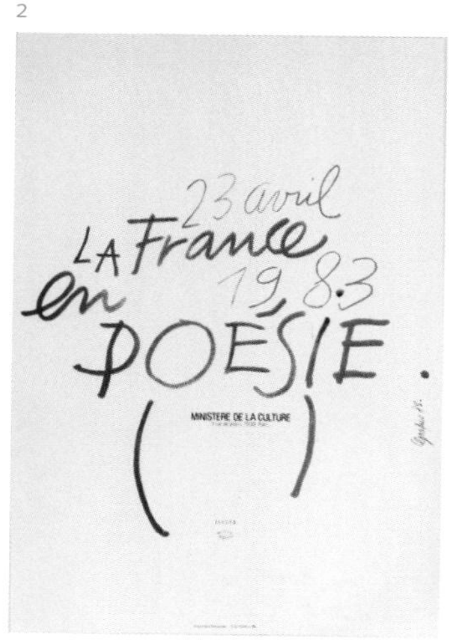

3

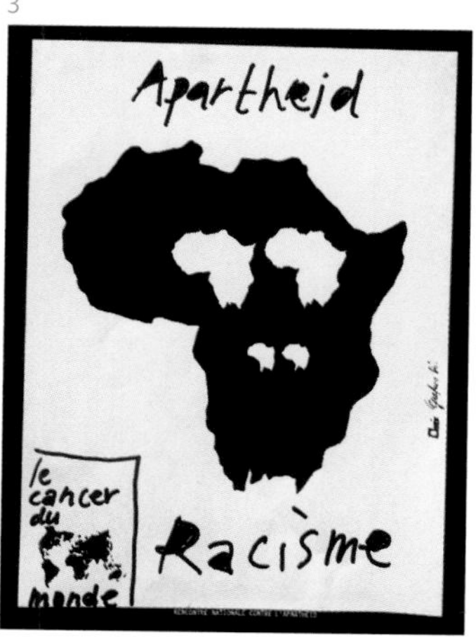

4

5

6

7–10. Despite the diversity of *typefaces* and very free *compositions*, *typography*, the dominant element in The Public Theater *posters*, forms the link between them all. The occasional image on the *posters* can't break this unity.

7. *The Public Theater*, posters
Paula Scher, Pentagram
8. ibid.
9. ibid.
10. ibid.

7

8

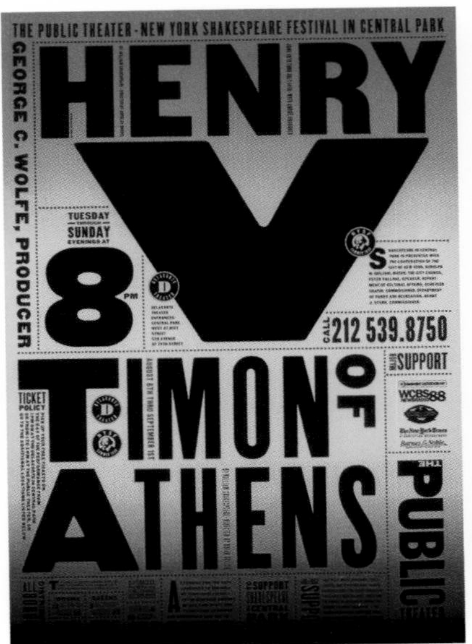

9

10

The poster

Cultural poster versus commercial poster?

It is not unusual to hear that a graphic designer who creates cultural or social *posters* is a *poster* artist, while the designer who is dedicated to commercial *posters* is an ad man. What exactly is the difference?
The former prefers public *poster* walls and museums, and the latter knows the standardized display networks in urban areas (see page 41) by heart. The former claim they prefer to present works of art or to defend ideas and ideals, while the latter are forced to promote products, services, the know-how of a brand or the image of a company.

Although *poster* artists and ad men intrinsically have the same mission (to promote), it must be admitted that when these two large families of *posters* are compared, they are in fact relatively different. Cultural, social and political *posters* are more artistic, more daring, and sometimes at the limits of understanding. Commercial *posters*, on the other hand, are often limited to a basic graphic language and are mostly limited to a very simple advertising language.
Yet greats like Loupot, Cassandre or Savignac knew how to combine aesthetics and commercial requirements. They always kept the effect of the image in mind. The choice of image material (illustrations, photography, etc.) and type, its arrangement and relationship to the image, was well considered, and produced masterfully.

But we should admit that after the "dark age" there are companies who invest in high quality advertising.
Famous graphic designers like Neville Brody or David Carson have upset the brand worlds of Nike and Quicksilver with their revolutionary *posters*. Some agencies retain the services of a graphic artist or recognized artist for certain projects. Thus, Piaget engaged the artists Pierre and Gilles, and the retail chain Galeries Lafayette hired Jean-Paul Goude. Calvin Klein worked with M/M.

1. Oxbow, magazine advertisement
   Damien Gautier
2. Foot Locker, postcards

1

2

Even though the trench between the two families visually is narrowing, conceptually it will remain significant. Some companies work with the established codes of the cultural and political *posters* in order to give their products a cultural aura. The corporate image is kept tidy and relatively innovative graphic principles are applied. The brand is sometimes even relegated to the background. Some *posters* imitate paintings, the product that they present should attain the status of a sacred object. Fashion brand Marithé + François Girbaud mimicked Leonardo da Vinci's painting of the Last Supper of Christ and his apostles.

The objective is always to improve the image of the company and its products. Benetton is a prime example of this approach. The images of photographer Oliviero Toscani have religious, social and even political dimensions.

3. Wassingue, posters
Atelier télescopique
4. Heschung, advertising campaign
Base design

3

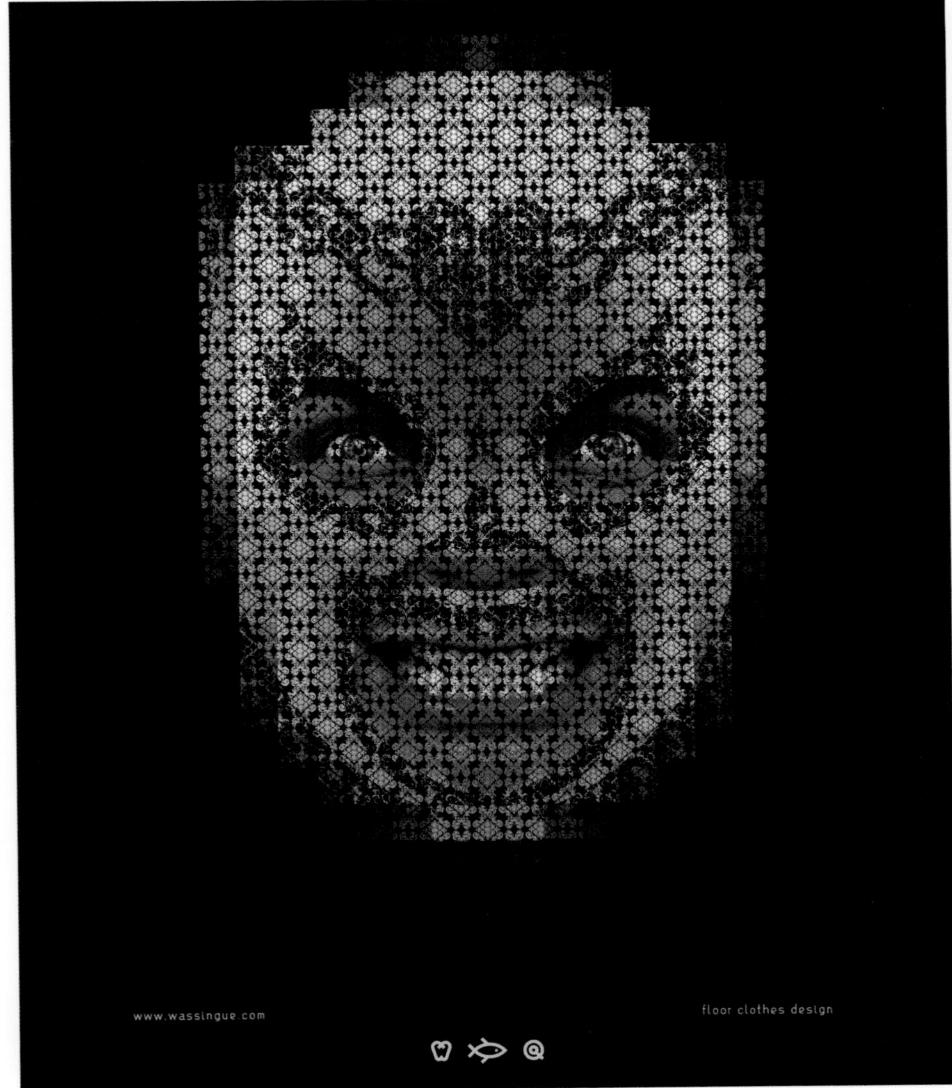

4

JEAN DE LA VILLE DE MIRMONT
LES DIMANCHES DE JEAN DÉZERT
ÉDITIONS CENT PAGES
JEAN
DE LA VILLE
DE MIRMONT
LES
DIMANCHES
DE JEAN
DÉZERT
ÉDITIONS
CENT PAGES
2007
DÉZERT AVEC UN Z.
IV
Après tout
I
II
IV
Ce livre est fabriqué
par les Éditions cent pages
et dessiné sauf le dimanche
par ɸMillot, Paris.
Dans son livre Twentieth
Century Type Designers,
Sebastian Carter
cite Matthew Carter:
Le dessin d'alphabets
n'est plus l'apanage
de quelques industriels
importants, il est
maintenant le fait
d'un millier de fonderies,
pas plus grandes
qu'une table de cuizine.

The book
Introduction

Le petit Bossu
Roberto Arlt
Éditions Cent pages
Book design by spmillot

The book: an object
Like many other media the *book* is first and foremost an object. It has an undeniable material dimension: its weight, its *format*, the way it is held in the hand.

A first impression...
Every reader, whether he is a bookworm or not, has a relationship with *books* and a first glance at a *book* creates a first impression. A larger *format* suggests a beautiful *book*, a smaller *format* implies a *pocket edition*. The type of cover, hard or soft, and the *binding* are all aspects that contribute to the first impression, and whether it is a high quality edition or a low-budget version. The number of *pages* impacts the weight directly, and demonstrates the importance of the subject.

The cover's visual "show" – via illustration, type and *layout* – all play a decisive role, especially for the undecided reader who is perusing the shelves in a bookstore or a library. The cover assumes the role of a *poster*, it must attract the eye, be "read" in an instant, seduce the viewer. The attention publishers pay to their *covers* confirms this. However, this care can still lead to disappointing results. The graphic quality of the cover is sacrificed in favor of a more "sellable" design. This leads some publishers to trust someone "capable" of making a striking cover whereas the interior is designed by someone who has a "feel" for *typography*.

... is confirmed in the first pages
However, a beautiful edition cannot be created where the cover and interior *pages* are not designed in *harmony*. The *book* is a whole and the cover is the point of departure. The first impression given by the *book*'s exterior must be confirmed by each detail inside. Not only the material properties such as paper quality (touch, thickness and *color*), but also the first visible typographic elements. The spare *typography* on the half-title *page* sets the tone and shows the *page* design to come.

These *preliminary pages* (half-*title page*, *title page*, preface, foreword, contents, dedication, etc.) whet the reader's appetite and encourage him to turn the *pages*, while the end matter concludes the *book* beautifully. What a disappointment to hold a *book* and to discover that only the "facade" of the *book* was designed with care!

The layout
In some print media a lack of coherence and lack of defined and methodically applied *composition* principles – depending on the ingenuity of the designer – may not be noticed immediately, because people are distracted by any number of things. The *book*, however, is unthinkable without a well-considered *layout* (*format*, *margins*, *typography*, *leading*, *page numbering*, chapter headings). Here, the reader's attention is quite different and centered on the text. Reading is mostly done continuously *page* after page. And if someone just flips through the *pages*, the differences between the *pages* are even more obvious due to small number of elements used.

Once again, every detail counts. Beyond the purely functional aspects (*margin* width for handling, the choice of *typeface* for readability, etc.) every decision determines a parameter that has to be followed.
Whatever the chosen typeface, remember that it has its own history and echoes a certain time period. Its *weight*, even at small sizes, gives clues to the given printed content. The *margins* and their proportions give the *book* a certain feel: classic, contemporary, economic, etc. Even the position of the *page number* and *running title* or the design of the notes impact the reader's impression of the *book*.

A world of books
There are many types of *books*, from special edition *books* to *paperbacks* and *pocket editions*. There are the so-called deluxe editions, there are *book* objects and the *artists' books*, which are true works of art. Then there are novels, photography *books*, schoolbooks or textbooks. They all have their own families with their own codes and their own *readership*.
Even though we won't be able to cover each type thoroughly, we will try to define broad principles for some of them.

Give a taste, stimulate reading desire
Readers also have their own preferences. They will react differently depending on the *book* and how they plan to use it. Sometimes the financial aspects play a role in a reader's decision to buy a *book*. The publisher has to integrate this factor into the design when choosing paper, *binding*, etc.
Conversely, some readers look for special editions without worrying about the price. All of this requires planning the structure and production of the *book* with great care.

The series
Most readers think about the series that a *book* is part of when loaning or buying a *book* simply because the series unifies the best of a genre, is accompanied by clever commentaries, or because of its practical *format* or a charming design ...

The principle of the *book series* is important in the publishing world for various reasons. A series allows the publisher to structure his offer and to make it understandable. Series are often synonymous with saving (in design and production) and they are very often designed to distinguish themselves from the competition. Besides their recognizability, series also echo the publisher's philosophy.
It is no coincidence that some of the best graphic designers have worked for the largest publishers (*Jan Tschichold* for Penguin Books, Massin for Gallimard, etc.). Which Frenchman doesn't recognize the series Folio, 10/18, Série noire immediately?
The principle of the *book series* therefore presents the designer with a particular task: to know his *readership*, and find an effective identity-building concept. Again, all the relevant factors in *book* design must be handled with know-how, ingenuity or audacity.

Even if the *book* has a rich history of several centuries and obeys established codes, nothing prevents the designer and editor from breaking with tradition, to find a design that is inspired by the historical *canon* but offers something new. Why choose between tradition and innovation?

Anatomy of the book

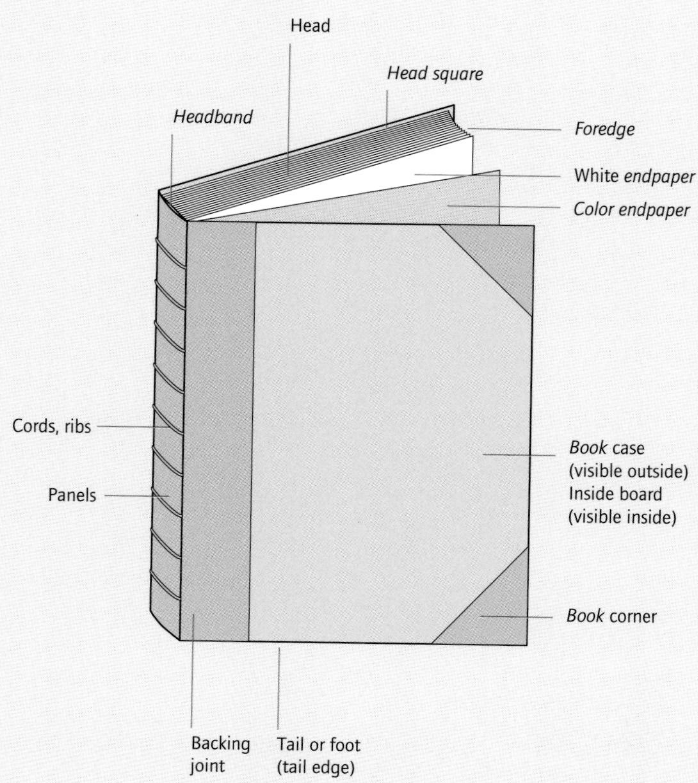

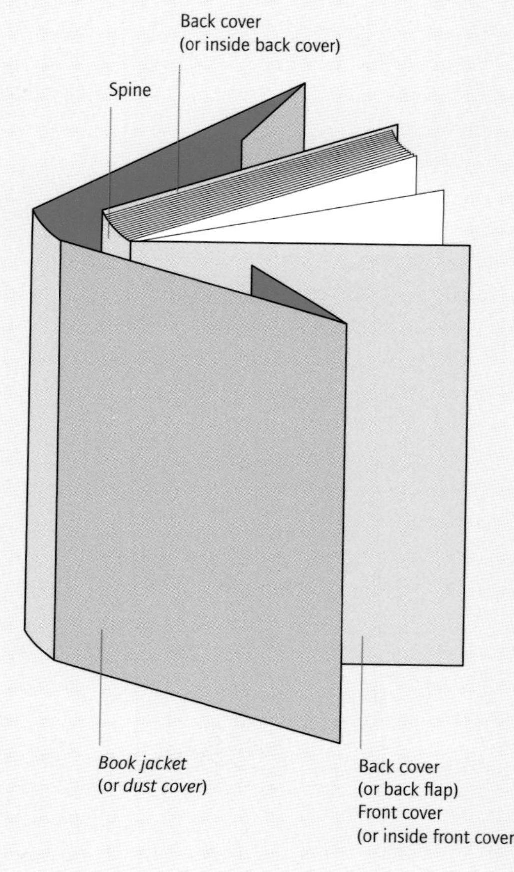

Book cover board
The (card)board that forms the cover of a *book*. It can be covered with leather, linen or (marbled) paper, etc. The reverse side of the *book cover board* is the inside front cover.

Book jacket (or dust cover)
The removable paper cover or jacket that is wrapped around and tucked inside the front and back cover of a bound *book*. The *book jacket* is also important in selling the *book*.

Copyright
A reference to the intellectual property rights of a work of art, literature or music. The *copyright* indicates the owner and the year the relevant work was published.

Endpapers (end sheets)
White or colored paper *sheets* that mark the end of the *book block* and form the connection to the (hard)cover. Luxury *bindings* sometimes use marbled paper.

Fly sheets
The unprinted *sheets* at the beginning or end of a *book*.

Single sheet (of a book)
Has two sides: front side and *back side*. Called an interleaf if it is not bound into the *book*.

Groove
The hinge between the two *covers* and *spine* of a hardbound *book*.

Headband
The narrow woven beaded cloth ribbon glued to the head and tail of the *book block* for stability. It fills the gap between the *book block* and the *spine*.

Headcap
The slightly thicker end of the *spine* at the head (and tail) of a (hardbound) *book*.

Head square (or foredge square, tail square)
In a case-bound *book* the narrow protective flange of the cover (see diagram) that extends past the *book block* on top (*head square*), front (*foredge square*) and bottom (*tail square*).

ISBN
International Standard *Book* Number.
This number is a unique permanent identity number for *books*. It is intended to help *book* dealers, libraries, sales departments, etc. organize and manage *books* digitally.

Offprint
A special printing of a *magazine* article or *book* contribution.

Page
One of the two sides of a *sheet*.

Page number (also folio)
The page *number* of the *book* (see pages 192–193).

Preliminary pages (front matter)
The first *pages* of a *book*, located before the actual contents (see pages 188–191).

Recto
Because the reader sees the right-hand (uneven) *pages* first when browsing through a *book*, chapters should begin on an odd-numbered *page* in a well designed *book*.

Reprint
The new printing of an old or out-of-print publication as a facsimile.

Ribbon marker
The narrow cloth band attached to the head of the *book block*'s *spine* which is used to mark one's place in a *book* where the reading stopped.

Running head (also running title)
The *headline* that is usually set in the upper or *lower margin* of each *page* of the *book* or brochure (see pages 192–193).

Sheet (also leaf)
The *sheet* contains two *pages*: a *front* and a *back page*.

Anatomy of the page

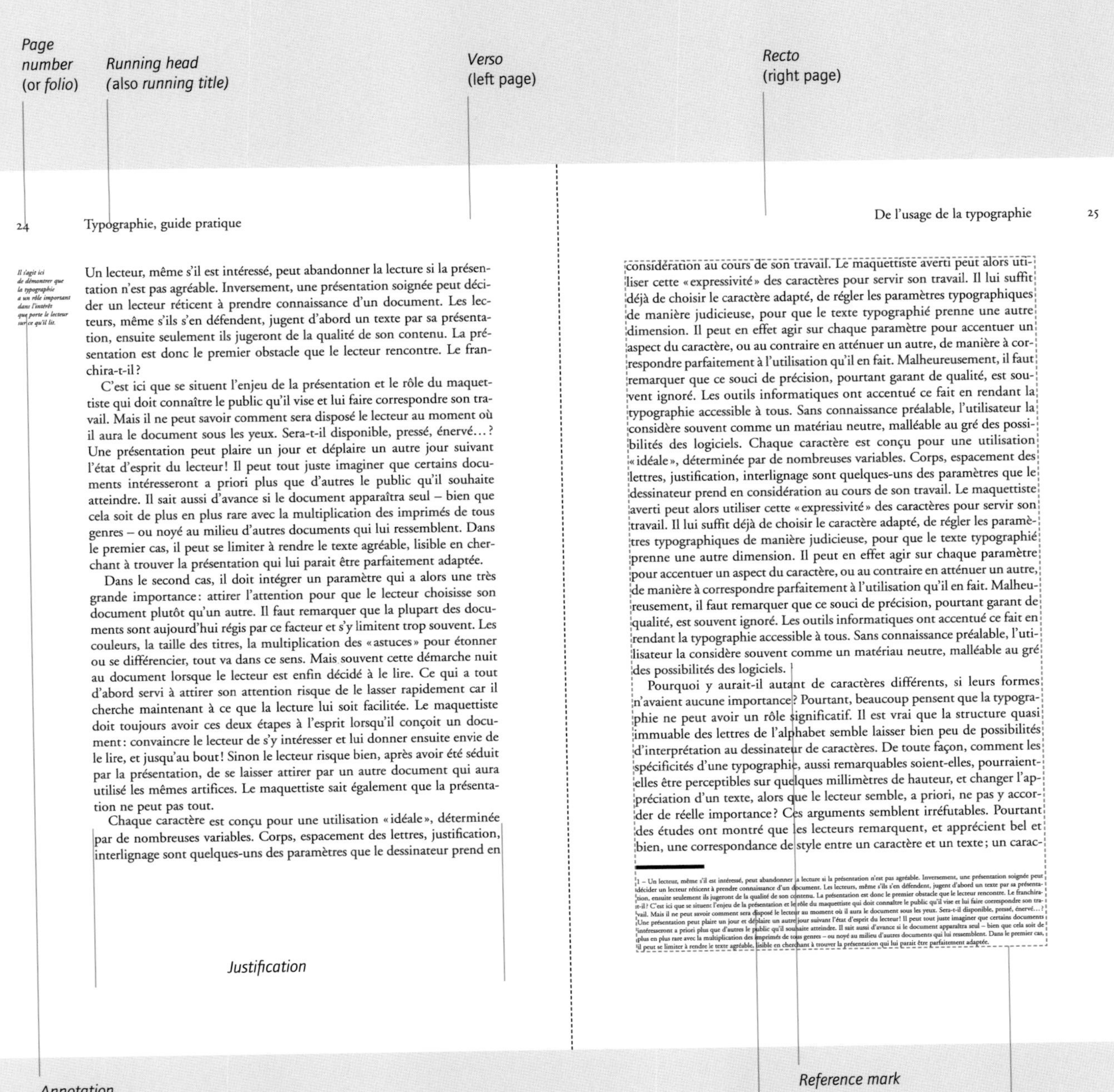

24 Typographie, guide pratique

Il s'agit ici de démontrer que la typographie a un rôle important dans l'intérêt que porte le lecteur sur ce qu'il lit.

Un lecteur, même s'il est intéressé, peut abandonner la lecture si la présentation n'est pas agréable. Inversement, une présentation soignée peut décider un lecteur réticent à prendre connaissance d'un document. Les lecteurs, même s'ils s'en défendent, jugent d'abord un texte par sa présentation, ensuite seulement ils jugeront de la qualité de son contenu. La présentation est donc le premier obstacle que le lecteur rencontre. Le franchira-t-il ?

C'est ici que se situent l'enjeu de la présentation et le rôle du maquettiste qui doit connaître le public qu'il vise et lui faire correspondre son travail. Mais il ne peut savoir comment sera disposé le lecteur au moment où il aura le document sous les yeux. Sera-t-il disponible, pressé, énervé… ? Une présentation peut plaire un jour et déplaire un autre jour suivant l'état d'esprit du lecteur ! Il peut tout juste imaginer que certains documents intéresseront a priori plus que d'autres le public qu'il souhaite atteindre. Il sait aussi d'avance si le document apparaîtra seul – bien que cela soit de plus en plus rare avec la multiplication des imprimés de tous genres – ou noyé au milieu d'autres documents qui lui ressemblent. Dans le premier cas, il peut se limiter à rendre le texte agréable, lisible en cherchant à trouver la présentation qui lui parait être parfaitement adaptée.

Dans le second cas, il doit intégrer un paramètre qui a alors une très grande importance : attirer l'attention pour que le lecteur choisisse son document plutôt qu'un autre. Il faut remarquer que la plupart des documents sont aujourd'hui régis par ce facteur et s'y limitent trop souvent. Les couleurs, la taille des titres, la multiplication des « astuces » pour étonner ou se différencier, tout va dans ce sens. Mais souvent cette démarche nuit au document lorsque le lecteur est enfin décidé à le lire. Ce qui a tout d'abord servi à attirer son attention risque de le lasser rapidement car il cherche maintenant à ce que la lecture lui soit facilitée. Le maquettiste doit toujours avoir ces deux étapes à l'esprit lorsqu'il conçoit un document : convaincre le lecteur de s'y intéresser et lui donner ensuite envie de le lire, et jusqu'au bout ! Sinon le lecteur risque bien, après avoir été séduit par la présentation, de se laisser attirer par un autre document qui aura utilisé les mêmes artifices. Le maquettiste sait également que la présentation ne peut pas tout.

Chaque caractère est conçu pour une utilisation « idéale », déterminée par de nombreuses variables. Corps, espacement des lettres, justification, interlignage sont quelques-uns des paramètres que le dessinateur prend en

De l'usage de la typographie 25

considération au cours de son travail. Le maquettiste averti peut alors utiliser cette « expressivité » des caractères pour servir son travail. Il lui suffit déjà de choisir le caractère adapté, de régler les paramètres typographiques de manière judicieuse, pour que le texte typographié prenne une autre dimension. Il peut en effet agir sur chaque paramètre pour accentuer un aspect du caractère, ou au contraire en atténuer un autre, de manière à correspondre parfaitement à l'utilisation qu'il en fait. Malheureusement, il faut remarquer que ce souci de précision, pourtant garant de qualité, est souvent ignoré. Les outils informatiques ont accentué ce fait en rendant la typographie accessible à tous. Sans connaissance préalable, l'utilisateur la considère souvent comme un matériau neutre, malléable au gré des possibilités des logiciels. Chaque caractère est conçu pour une utilisation « idéale », déterminée par de nombreuses variables. Corps, espacement des lettres, justification, interlignage sont quelques-uns des paramètres que le dessinateur prend en considération au cours de son travail. Le maquettiste averti peut alors utiliser cette « expressivité » des caractères pour servir son travail. Il lui suffit déjà de choisir le caractère adapté, de régler les paramètres typographiques de manière judicieuse, pour que le texte typographié prenne une autre dimension. Il peut en effet agir sur chaque paramètre pour accentuer un aspect du caractère, ou au contraire en atténuer un autre, de manière à correspondre parfaitement à l'utilisation qu'il en fait. Malheureusement, il faut remarquer que ce souci de précision, pourtant garant de qualité, est souvent ignoré. Les outils informatiques ont accentué ce fait en rendant la typographie accessible à tous. Sans connaissance préalable, l'utilisateur la considère souvent comme un matériau neutre, malléable au gré des possibilités des logiciels.

Pourquoi y aurait-il autant de caractères différents, si leurs formes n'avaient aucune importance ? Pourtant, beaucoup pensent que la typographie ne peut avoir un rôle significatif. Il est vrai que la structure quasi immuable des lettres de l'alphabet semble laisser bien peu de possibilités d'interprétation au dessinateur de caractères. De toute façon, comment les spécificités d'une typographie, aussi remarquables soient-elles, pourraient-elles être perceptibles sur quelques millimètres de hauteur, et changer l'appréciation d'un texte, alors que le lecteur semble, a priori, ne pas y accorder de réelle importance ? Ces arguments semblent irréfutables. Pourtant des études ont montré que les lecteurs remarquent, et apprécient bel et bien, une correspondance de style entre un caractère et un texte ; un carac-

1 – Un lecteur, même s'il est intéressé, peut abandonner la lecture si la présentation n'est pas agréable. Inversement, une présentation soignée peut décider un lecteur réticent à prendre connaissance d'un document. Les lecteurs, même s'ils s'en défendent, jugent d'abord un texte par sa présentation, ensuite seulement ils jugeront de la qualité de son contenu. La présentation est donc le premier obstacle que le lecteur rencontre. Le franchira-t-il ? C'est ici que se situent l'enjeu de la présentation et le rôle du maquettiste qui doit connaître le public qu'il vise et lui faire correspondre son travail. Mais il ne peut savoir comment sera disposé le lecteur au moment où il aura le document sous les yeux. Sera-t-il disponible, pressé, énervé… ? Une présentation peut plaire un jour et déplaire un autre jour suivant l'état d'esprit du lecteur ! Il peut tout juste imaginer que certains documents intéresseront a priori plus que d'autres le public qu'il souhaite atteindre. Il sait aussi d'avance si le document apparaîtra seul – bien que cela soit de plus en plus rare avec la multiplication des imprimés de tous genres – ou noyé au milieu d'autres documents qui lui ressemblent. Dans le premier cas, il peut se limiter à rendre le texte agréable, lisible en cherchant à trouver la présentation qui lui parait être parfaitement adaptée.

The book
Front cover, spine and back cover

The cover is the *book*'s "salesman". While special or luxury editions prefer a high quality *binding* and *book jacket* (which is often discarded after the purchase), cheaper editions use the hardcover directly to promote the *book*.

Except for the *format*, the *book cover* resembles a *poster*. It must attract and capture attention, surprise, create interest, promote the contents in a way that the potential buyer or reader picks up the *book*.
The cover choice and the production of the cover is therefore of great importance. The connection to the text should guarantee visibility and readability, as it needs to be both seen and read.

The *spine* and text on the back cover should not be neglected. On shelves in bookstores and libraries, the *spine* is visible first. Reading the text on the back cover should give the reader a clear idea of the *book*'s content (abstract, excerpt, reviews). These three parts of a *book* are rarely viewed as a unit although they are physically closely connected.

Typically, the designer connects these parts by using the same *margins* and the same *typefaces*. In special cases he creates a true connection between the cover illustration or even with the title itself.

1. The illustration extends across both *covers* and the *spine*, and invites the reader to turn the *book* over.

2. Both *covers* are treated identically. The *spine* forms a border between the two.

3. The back *cover* here seems to form a counterweight to the front *cover*.

4. Here, the graphic designer has played with the complementarity of the two *covers*. Turning the brochure over reveals a new reading of the title.

1. *Was machen Sie dort am Schloss?*, book
Katya Bonnenfant

1

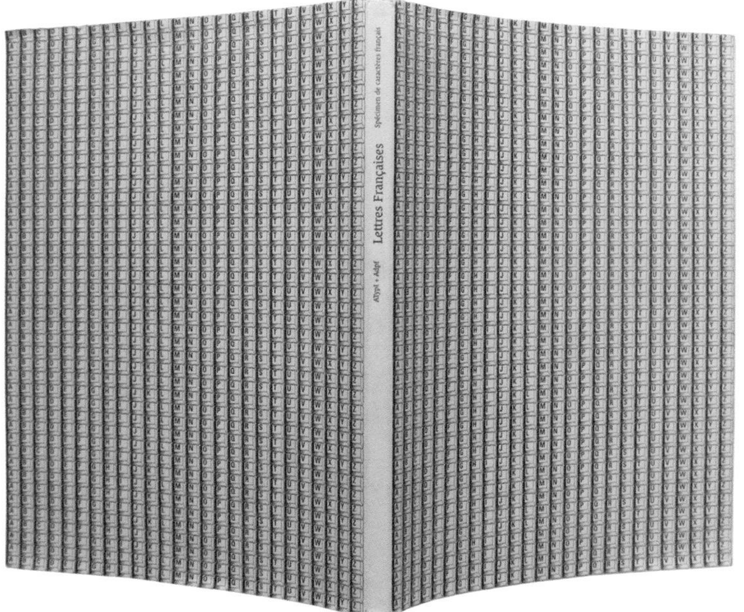

2

3

4

2. *Lettres françaises, specimen de caractères français*, book
Philippe Millot
3. *Histoire de l'art*, book
E. H. Gombrich
Éditions Phaïdon
4. *DTL Paradox*, brochure
Gerard Unger

5. Mandatory logos give any graphic designer a headache who cares about the integrity of their design. In this case they are inspiration for a playful game between the parts of the cover.
The superimposed boxes on the front cover are connected with delicate lines that cross the *spine* and lead to the appropriate logo on the back cover.

6. The illustration ignores the limits of the front cover, and spreads across the *spine* onto the back cover.

7. The name of the design group is split down the middle from *spine* to back cover, and this offset is echoed on the front cover.

5. *Les partenariats des bibliothèques*, book
   Association pour la difusion de la pensée française
   Damien Gautier
6. *La formation à la maîtrise de l'information à l'heure européenne: problèmes et perspectives*, book
   Éditions de l'enssib
   Damien Gautier
7. *Simply droog*, book
   Droog design
   Thonik

5

6

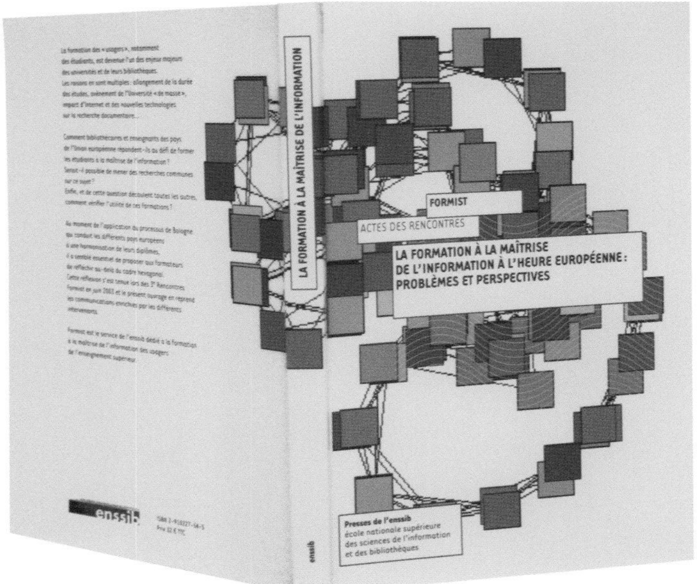

7

The book

The relationship between cover and inside pages

Logically, the cover is the *book*'s showcase, both in terms of form and content. For this reason, there should be a close association between the cover design and the design of the interior (*margins*, *typography*, *lines of force*, etc.) Imagine the reader's disappointment when they discover that care given to cover's design was only a pretext to sell the *book*. All too often *books* suffer from a mismatch between inside *pages* and cover.

1. Cover and inside *pages* are linked via the same typographic and *color* principles. The definition of the *type area* of the interior *pages* allows the coherent positioning of different elements on the cover (author, title, publisher). The *margins* used on the cover are the same as those used inside.

2. The *book jacket* and the *endpapers* are the same *color*. The design principle used on the cover (black block, *typeface* and title *type size*) is repeated for the chapter headings on the inside *pages*.

1. *Le bonheur des dames*, book
   Cover and inside pages layout principles
   Damien Gautier
2. *Histoire de l'art*, book
   E. H. Gombrich
   Éditions Phaïdon
   Sonya Dyakova

1

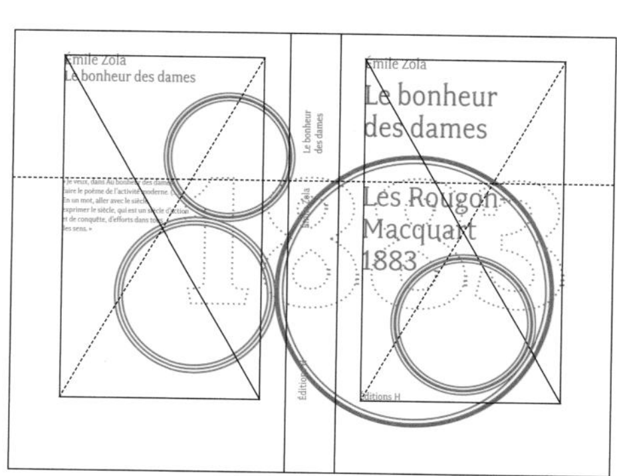

rant les boutiques. Devant la porte, deux commis, montés sur une échelle double, finissaient de pendre des lainages, tandis que, dans une vitrine de la rue Neuve-Saint-Augustin, un autre commis, agenouillé et le dos tourné, plissait délicatement une pièce de soie bleue. Le magasin, vide encore de clientes, et où le personnel arrivait à peine, bourdonnait à l'intérieur comme une ruche qui s'éveille.
— Fichtre ! dit Jean. Ça enfonce Valognes... Le tien n'était pas si beau.

Denise hocha la tête. Elle avait passé deux ans là-bas, chez Cornaille, le premier marchand de nouveautés de la ville ; et ce magasin, rencontré brusquement, cette maison énorme pour elle, lui gonflait le coeur, la retenait, émue, intéressée, oublieuse du reste. Dans le pan coupé donnant sur la place Gaillon, la haute porte, tout en glace, montait jusqu'à l'entresol, au milieu d'une complication d'ornements, chargés de dorures. Deux figures allégoriques, deux femmes riantes, la gorge nue et renversée, déroulaient l'enseigne : Au Bonheur des dames. Puis, les vitrines s'enfonçaient, longeaient la rue de la Michodière et la rue Neuve-Saint-Augustin, où elles occupaient, outre la maison d'angle, quatre autres maisons, deux à gauche, deux à droite, achetées et aménagées récemment. C'était un développement qui lui semblait sans fin, dans la fuite de la perspective, avec les étalages du rez-de-chaussée et les glaces sans tain de l'entresol, derrière lesquelles on voyait toute la vie intérieure des comptoirs. En haut, une demoiselle, habillée de soie, taillait un crayon, pendant que, près d'elle, deux autres dépliaient des manteaux de velours.
— Au Bonheur des dames, lut Jean avec son rire tendre de bel adolescent, qui avait eu déjà une histoire de femme à Valognes. Hein ? c'est gentil, c'est ça qui doit faire courir le monde !

Mais Denise demeurait absorbée, devant l'étalage de la porte centrale. Il y avait là, au plein air de la rue, sur le trottoir même, un éboulement de marchandises à bon marché, la tentation de la porte, les occasions qui arrêtaient les clientes au passage. Cela partait de haut, des pièces de lainage et de draperie, mérinos, cheviottes, molletons, tombaient de l'entresol, flottantes comme des drapeaux, et dont les tons neutres, gris ardoise, bleu marine, vert olive, étaient coupés par les pancartes blanches des étiquettes. À côté, encadrant le seuil, pendaient également des lanières de fourrure, des bandes

18 19

CHAPITRE

1

Denise était venue à pied de la gare Saint-Lazare, où un train de Cherbourg l'avait débarquée avec ses deux frères, après une nuit passée sur la dure banquette d'un wagon de troisième classe. Elle tenait par la main Pépé, et Jean la suivait, tous les trois brisés du voyage, effarés et perdus au milieu du vaste Paris, le nez levé sur les maisons, demandant à chaque carrefour la rue de la Michodière, dans laquelle leur oncle Baudu demeurait. Mais, comme elle débouchait enfin sur la place Gaillon, la jeune fille s'arrêta net de surprise.
— Oh ! dit-elle, regarde un peu, Jean !

Et ils restèrent plantés, serrés les uns contre les autres, tout en noir, achevant les vieux vêtements du deuil de leur père. Elle, chétive pour ses vingt ans, l'air pauvre, portait un léger paquet ; tandis que, de l'autre côté, le petit frère, âgé de cinq ans, se pendait à son bras, et que, derrière son épaule, le grand frère, dont les seize ans superbes florissaient, était debout, les mains ballantes.
— Ah bien ! reprit-elle après un silence, en voilà un magasin !

C'était, à l'encoignure de la rue de la Michodière et de la rue Neuve-Saint-Augustin, un magasin de nouveautés dont les étalages éclataient en notes vives, dans la douce et pâle journée d'octobre. Huit heures sonnaient à Saint-Roch, il n'y avait sur les trottoirs que le Paris matinal, les employés filant à leurs bureaux et les ménagères cou-

17

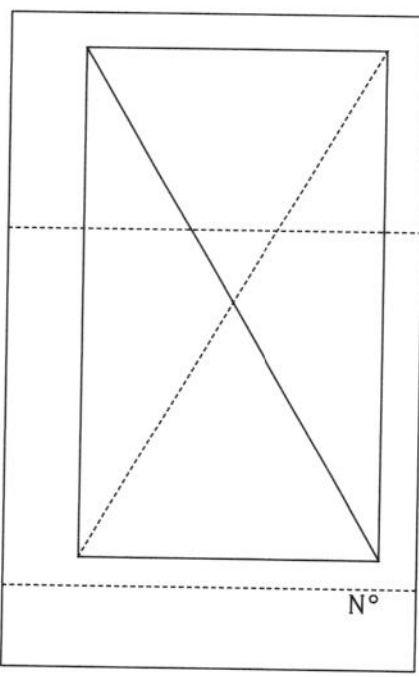

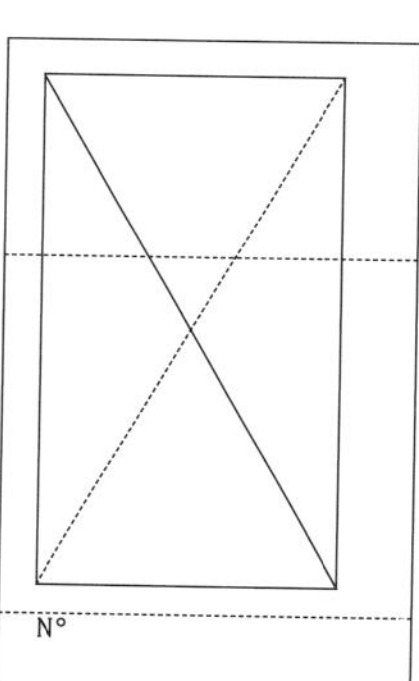

Histoire de l'art
E.H. Gombrich
PHAIDON

Histoire de l'art

Histoire de l'art
E.H. Gombrich

1
Mystérieux débuts

Sommaire

The book
The first pages

The first *pages* of the *book*, beginning with the *endpapers*, are too often ignored. But these *pages* set the stage for reading the *book*'s main content.
The arrangement and design of these *pages* lead the reader into the *book* and simultaneously inform him or her about: title, author, publisher, people who produced the *book*, illustrator, translator, etc.
These *pages* – also called the *front matter* – are a discrete introduction to the design of the object that he holds in his hands: *margins*, *page layout*, typographic choices.

This is one example of the *preliminary pages* of a *book*.

1

2

3

Au bonheur des dames

4

Du même auteur

5

Émile ZOLA

Au bonheur des dames

Les Rougon-Macquart
1883

Éditions H
Lyon – 2007

Préface

Introduction

CHAPITRE

1

17

6

ISBN : 0-7454-0324-7

Avant-Propos

« Je veux, dans Au bonheur des dames, *faire le poème de l'activité moderne. (...) En un mot, aller avec le siècle, exprimer le siècle, qui est un siècle d'action et de conquête, d'efforts dans tous les sens. »*

Après une crise de pessimisme qu'il traverse en 1880-1881, Zola décide d'écrire un roman optimiste touné vers la puissance et la gaieté. Après Pot-Bouille, Au bonheur des dames, le onzième des vingt volumes des Rougon-Macquart, marque un tournant dans son oeuvre. L'auteur ne se contente plus de rejeter la société du second Empire, il glorifie les formes qui peuvent, selon lui, conduire à un monde meilleur : progrès, travail, amour de la vie, goût du défi et de la domination. Mélange du Bon Marché et du Louvre, Au bonheur des dames incarne, sur fond de révolution industrielle, le commerce moderne et l'essor du capitalisme. Monstre dévorant, le grand magasin occupe la première place dans ce roman, symbole du siècle nouveau et de la vie triomphante.

rant les boutiques. Devant la porte, deux commis, montés sur une échelle double, finissaient de pendre des lainages, tandis que, dans une vitrine de la rue Neuve-Saint-Augustin, un autre commis, agenouillé et le dos tourné, plissait délicatement une pièce de soie bleue. Le magasin, vide encore de clientes, et où le personnel arrivait à peine, bourdonnait à l'intérieur comme une ruche qui s'éveille.
— Fichtre ! dit Jean. Ça enfonce Valognes... Le tien n'était pas si beau.

Denise hocha la tête. Elle avait passé deux ans là-bas, chez Cornaille, le premier marchand de nouveautés de la ville ; et ce magasin, rencontré brusquement, cette maison énorme pour elle, lui gonflait le coeur, la retenait, émue, intéressée, oublieuse du reste. Dans le pan coupé donnant sur la place Gaillon, la haute porte, tout en glace, montait jusqu'à l'entresol, au milieu d'une complication d'ornements, chargés de dorures. Deux figures allégoriques, deux femmes riantes, la gorge nue et renversée, déroulaient l'enseigne : Au Bonheur des dames. Puis, les vitrines s'enfonçaient, longeaient la rue de la Michodière et la rue Neuve-Saint-Augustin, où elles occupaient, outre la maison d'angle, quatre autres maisons, deux à gauche, deux à droite, achetées et aménagées récemment. C'était un développement qui lui semblait sans fin, dans la fuite de la perspective, avec les étalages du rez-de-chaussée et les glaces sans tain de l'entresol, derrière lesquelles on voyait toute la vie intérieure des comptoirs. En haut, une demoiselle, habillée de soie, taillait un crayon, pendant que, près d'elle, deux autres dépliaient des manteaux de velours.
— Au Bonheur des dames, lut Jean avec son rire tendre de bel adolescent, qui avait eu déjà une histoire de femme à Valognes. Hein ? c'est gentil, c'est ça qui doit faire courir le monde !

Mais Denise demeurait absorbée, devant l'étalage de la porte centrale. Il y avait là, au plein air de la rue, sur le trottoir même, un éboulement de marchandises à bon marché, la tentation de la porte, les occasions qui arrêtaient les clientes au passage. Cela partait de haut, des pièces de lainage et de draperie, mérinos, cheviottes, molletons, tombaient de l'entresol, flottantes comme des drapeaux, et dont les tons neutres, gris ardoise, bleu marine, vert olive, étaient coupés par les pancartes blanches des étiquettes. À côté, encadrant le seuil, pendaient également des lanières de fourrure, des bandes

18

étroites pour garnitures de robe, la cendre fine des dos de petit-gris, la neige pure des ventres de cygne, les poils de lapin de la fausse hermine et de la fausse martre. Puis, en bas, dans des casiers, sur des tables, au milieu d'un empilement de coupons, débordaient des articles de bonneterie vendus pour rien, gants et fichus de laine tricotés, capelines, gilets, tout un étalage d'hiver aux couleurs bariolées, chinées, rayées, avec des taches saignantes de rouge.

Denise vit une tartanelle à quarante-cinq centimes, des bandes de vison d'Amérique à un franc, et des mitaines à cinq sous. C'était un déballage géant de foire, le magasin semblait crever et jeter son trop-plein à la rue. L'oncle Baudu était oublié. Pépé lui-même, qui ne lâchait pas la main de sa soeur, ouvrait des yeux énormes. Une voiture les força tous trois à quitter le milieu de la place ; et, machinalement, ils prirent la rue Neuve-Saint-Augustin, ils suivirent les vitrines, s'arrêtant de nouveau devant chaque étalage.

D'abord, ils furent séduits par un arrangement compliqué : en haut, des parapluies, posés obliquement, semblaient mettre un toit de cabane rustique ; dessous, des bas de soie, pendus à des tringles, montraient des profils arrondis de mollets, les uns semés de bouquets de roses, les autres de toutes nuances, les noirs à jour, les rouges à coins brodés, les chair dont le grain satiné avait la douceur d'une peau de blonde ; enfin, sur le drap de l'étagère, des gants étaient jetés symétriquement, avec leurs doigts allongés, leur paume étroite de vierge byzantine, cette grâce raidie et comme adolescente des chiffons de femme qui n'ont pas été portés. Mais la dernière vitrine surtout les retint. Une exposition de soies, de satins et de velours, y épanouissait, dans une gamme souple et vibrante, les tons les plus délicats des fleurs : au sommet, les velours, d'un noir profond, d'un blanc de lait caillé ; plus bas, les satins, les roses, les bleus, aux cassures vives, se décolorant en pâleurs d'une tendresse infinie ; plus bas encore, les soies, toute l'écharpe de l'arc-en-ciel, des pièces retroussées en coques, plissées comme autour d'une taille qui se cambre, devenues vivantes sous les doigts savants des commis ; et, entre chaque motif, entre chaque phrase colorée de l'étalage, courait un accompagnement discret, un léger cordon bouillonné de foulard crème. C'était là, aux deux bouts, que se trouvaient, en piles colossales, les

19

Endpapers
Pages 1 and 2
These are normally unprinted *pages*, commonly two, but in special editions four *pages* are used. These are the first discovered, and they inform the reader about the *format* of the *book* and the paper *format*. They should start the *book* with a "clean slate", and prepare the reader mentally. They also protect the first printed page.

Half-title page
Page 3
The *book*'s title is the only thing printed here, and usually in the upper third where the reader's gaze naturally alights. Since it is the first printed page, the design and typographic decisions should be subtle and restrained.

Title verso
Page 4
This *page* is sometimes used for an illustration or *frontispiece* (this was common in bibliophile *books* from the 16th to the 18th centuries), or it may be used for a list of the author's *books*. In many cases this *page* remains blank.

Title page
Page 5
The following appear in order: author's name, *book* title, publisher's name, publisher's location (city), year of publication. If necessary add the names of: illustrators, translator, authors of the preface, etc.

The *title page* is obviously more elaborate than the half-*title page*. The position of the *book*'s title is the same as on the half-*title page*, and forms a *line of force*. The first element (author's name) and last element (year of publication) define upper and *lower margins* (head and *foot*). The white space between the elements should create a logical connection between the author's name and *book*'s title.

The logical *hierarchy* of elements on this *page* is: *book* title/author/city/date of issue. If there is an illustration placed opposite, it should not weaken the *title page*, but rather strengthen it. In graphic terms a suitable progression from *page* to *page* is logical.

Imprint page (title verso)
Page 6
The *copyright* notice is located on the back of the *title page*, and placed at the bottom of the page. The print run (number of printed copies) and other publisher and production details may be included.

Dedication *(optional page)*
The dedication is traditionally set starting at the middle of the page, in *italics*. This *page* can also have a more contemporary design.

These first *pages* usually have no *page numbers*.

Table of contents
Uneven page
The table of contents or contents *page* contains a more or less detailed list of the chapter titles (and *sections*). The tradition is to place the table of contents at the beginning of the *book*.

Credits for illustrations, pictures, tables, abbreviations, etc.
(optional page)
Uneven page
A *book* must have as many credits as it has categories, such as illustrations, tables, etc. (Some *books* place this information at the end of the *book*.)

Preface *(optional page)*
Uneven page
The preface always starts on a right-hand *page* and runs as many *pages* as required. The preface *pages* are usually numbered with roman numerals. This introductory text is usually written by a relevant person who focuses on the *book*'s content.

Foreword
Uneven page
In this text, the author briefly presents the origins of the *book*, his research on the subject, his intentions and methods, etc. The author may also thank specific people, if there is no separate *page* for acknowledgements.

Acknowledgments
Uneven page
Material on this *page* thanks people and organizations who assisted the author in his work on the *book*.

Chronology
Even or uneven page
A chronology is useful in biographies.

Introduction
Uneven page
This text is often essential in understanding a *book*, because it outlines the main issue and the contents of the various *sections*. Depending on the scope of the *book*, the introduction is sometimes its first chapter. The *page numbering* with Arabic numerals begins here.

Chapter opener
Uneven page
Following the *preliminary pages* this is the "real" first *page* of the *book*, and is traditionally a right-hand page.

1. Even though this is only a “simple” guide, the *preliminary pages* fulfill an important function of a step-by-step introduction. The classical design principles were abandoned in favor of an asymmetrical *layout* (see pages 44–45).
Nevertheless, the *page* order follows the logic of *book* design:

· Half-*title page*
· *Title page*
· Dedication
· Chapter heading
· Chapter opening
· Main text

1

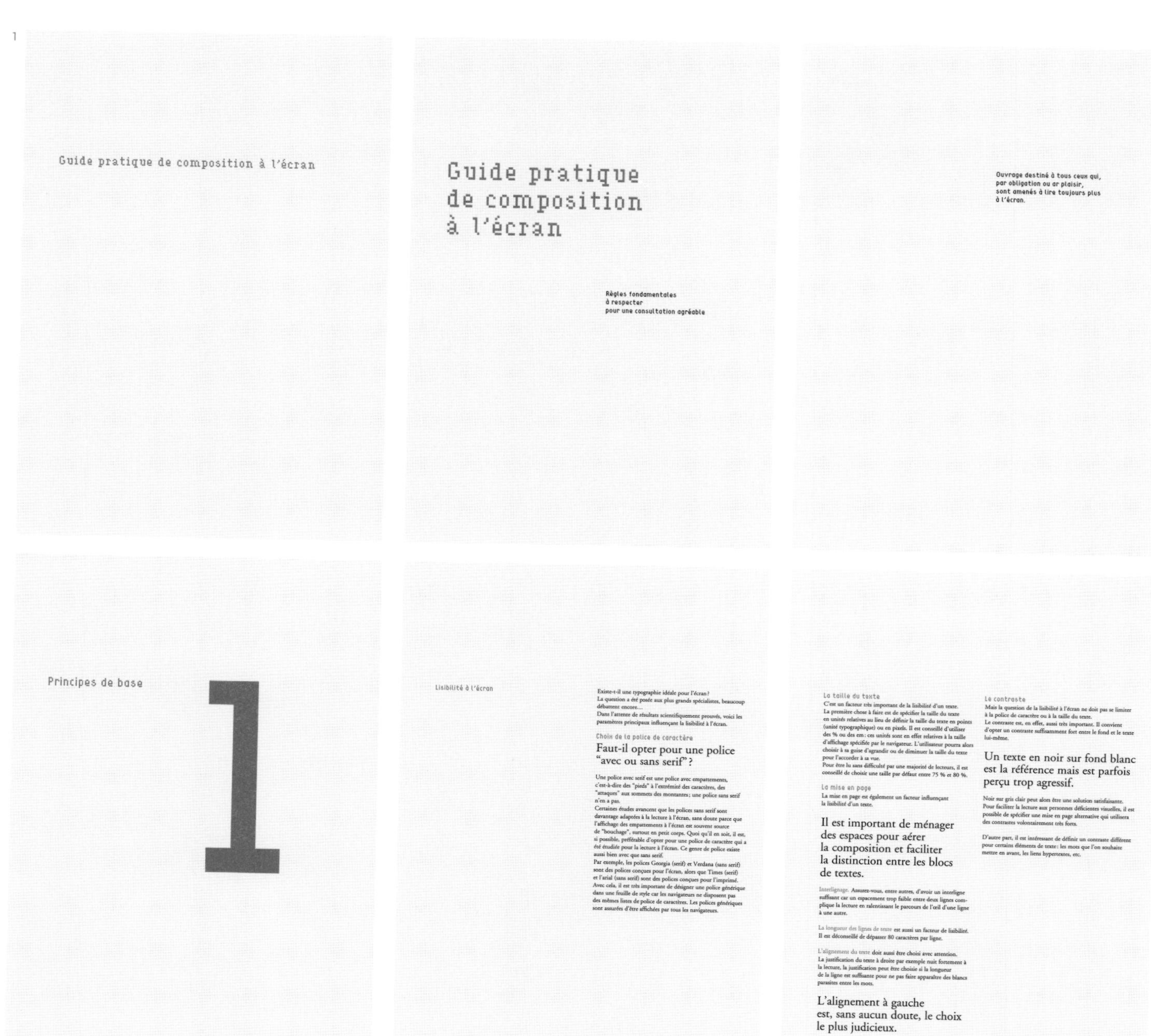
Guide pratique de composition à l’écran

Guide pratique
de composition
à l’écran

Règles fondamentales
à respecter
pour une consultation agréable

Ouvrage destiné à tous ceux qui,
par obligation ou ar plaisir,
sont amenés à lire toujours plus
à l’écran.

Principes de base

1

Lisibilité à l’écran

Existe-t-il une typographie idéale pour l’écran?
La question a été posée aux plus grands spécialistes, beaucoup débattent encore…
Dans l’attente de résultats scientifiquement prouvés, voici les paramètres principaux influençant la lisibilité à l’écran.

Choix de la police de caractère

Faut-il opter pour une police “avec ou sans serif”?

Une police avec serif est une police avec empattements, c’est-à-dire des “pieds” à l’extrémité des caractères, des “attaques” aux sommets des montantes; une police sans serif n’en a pas.
Certaines études avancent que les polices sans serif sont davantage adaptées à la lecture à l’écran, sans doute parce que l’affichage des empattements à l’écran est souvent source de “bouchage”, surtout en petit corps. Quoi qu’il en soit, il est, si possible, préférable d’opter pour une police de caractère qui a été étudiée pour la lecture à l’écran. Ce genre de police existe aussi bien avec que sans serif.
Par exemple, les polices Georgia (serif) et Verdana (sans serif) sont des polices conçues pour l’écran, alors que Times (serif) et l’arial (sans serif) sont des polices conçues pour l’imprimé. Avec cela, il est très important de désigner une police générique dans une feuille de style car les navigateurs ne disposent pas des mêmes listes de police de caractères. Les polices génériques sont assurées d’être affichées par tous les navigateurs.

La taille du texte

C’est un facteur très important de la lisibilité d’un texte.
La première chose à faire est de spécifier la taille du texte en unités relatives au lieu de définir la taille du texte en points (unité typographique) ou en pixels. Il est conseillé d’utiliser des % ou des em: ces unités sont en effet relatives à la taille d’affichage spécifiée par le navigateur. L’utilisateur pourra alors choisir à sa guise d’agrandir ou de diminuer la taille du texte pour l’accorder à sa vue.
Pour être lu sans difficulté par une majorité de lecteurs, il est conseillé de choisir une taille par défaut entre 75 % et 80 %.

La mise en page

La mise en page est également un facteur influençant la lisibilité d’un texte.

Il est important de ménager des espaces pour aérer la composition et faciliter la distinction entre les blocs de textes.

Interlignage. Assurez-vous, entre autres, d’avoir un interligne suffisant car un espacement trop faible entre deux lignes complique la lecture en ralentissant le parcours de l’œil d’une ligne à une autre.

La longueur des lignes de texte est aussi un facteur de lisibilité. Il est déconseillé de dépasser 80 caractères par ligne.

L’alignement du texte doit aussi être choisi avec attention. La justification du texte à droite par exemple nuit fortement à la lecture, la justification peut être choisie si la longueur de la ligne est suffisante pour ne pas faire apparaître des blancs parasites entre les mots.

L’alignement à gauche est, sans aucun doute, le choix le plus judicieux.

Le contraste

Mais la question de la lisibilité à l’écran ne doit pas se limiter à la police de caractère ou à la taille du texte.
Le contraste est, en effet, aussi très important. Il convient d’opter un contraste suffisamment fort entre le fond et le texte lui-même.

Un texte en noir sur fond blanc est la référence mais est parfois perçu trop agressif.

Noir sur gris clair peut alors être une solution satisfaisante. Pour faciliter la lecture aux personnes déficientes visuelles, il est possible de spécifier une mise en page alternative qui utilisera des contrastes volontairement très forts.

D’autre part, il est intéressant de définir un contraste différent pour certains éléments de texte: les mots que l’on souhaite mettre en avant, les liens hypertextes, etc.

2. The graphic design's work begins here with the design of the *endpapers* that create a playful pattern (*recto* and *verso*). In spite of the unusual design of the *preliminary pages*, we find them in a revised form of their traditional order:

- *Endpapers*
- Half-*title page*
- *Title page*
- Foreword
- Table of contents

2

The book

Page numbers and running head

These details are usually very restrained and noticed by very few readers. Yet their presence is important in order to navigate a large number of *pages*, or to go directly to a *page* that you are looking for, or to find a particular *page* from the table of contents.

Page number (*folio*) and *running head* (*running title*) are active members of a *page layout*, since they are positioned relative to the *type area*. Depending on their position, they emphasize either the upper or *lower margins* outside the *type area*, highlight the axis of symmetry (1) or underscore the transmission of the left *page* to the right *page* (2).

The *running head*, as the name suggests, runs through the whole *book*. Generally, the *book* title is placed on the left-hand *page* and the title current chapter is placed on the right-hand page.
Beyond their strictly practical function these elements can actively participate in the *composition* due to their unusual size, *typeface* or striking *color*.

Running head
Page number

1

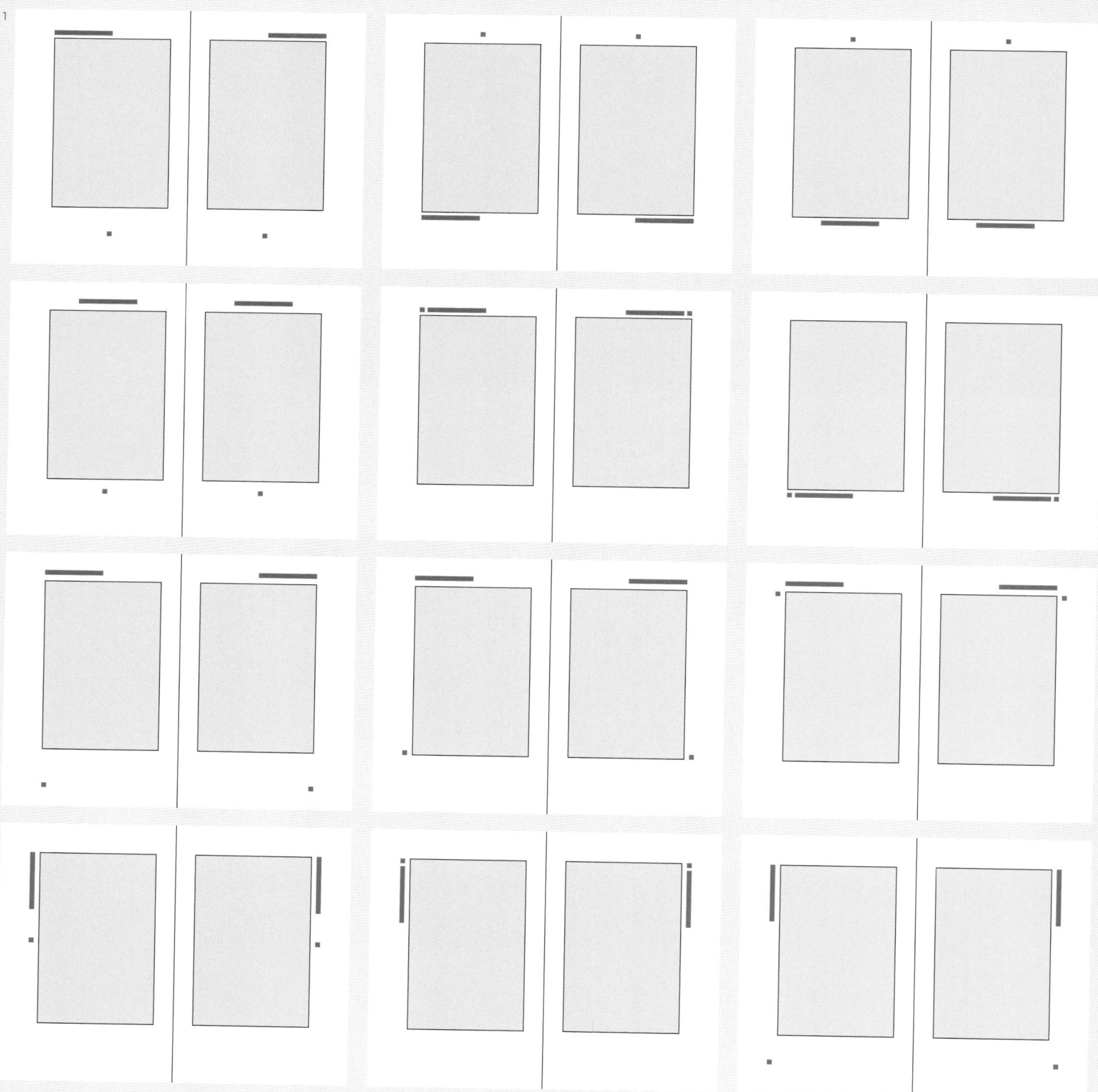

2

194 The principle of notes is common for textbooks and reference *books*. Notes are indicated to in the main text using a *reference mark* (number, letter, asterisk, etc.):

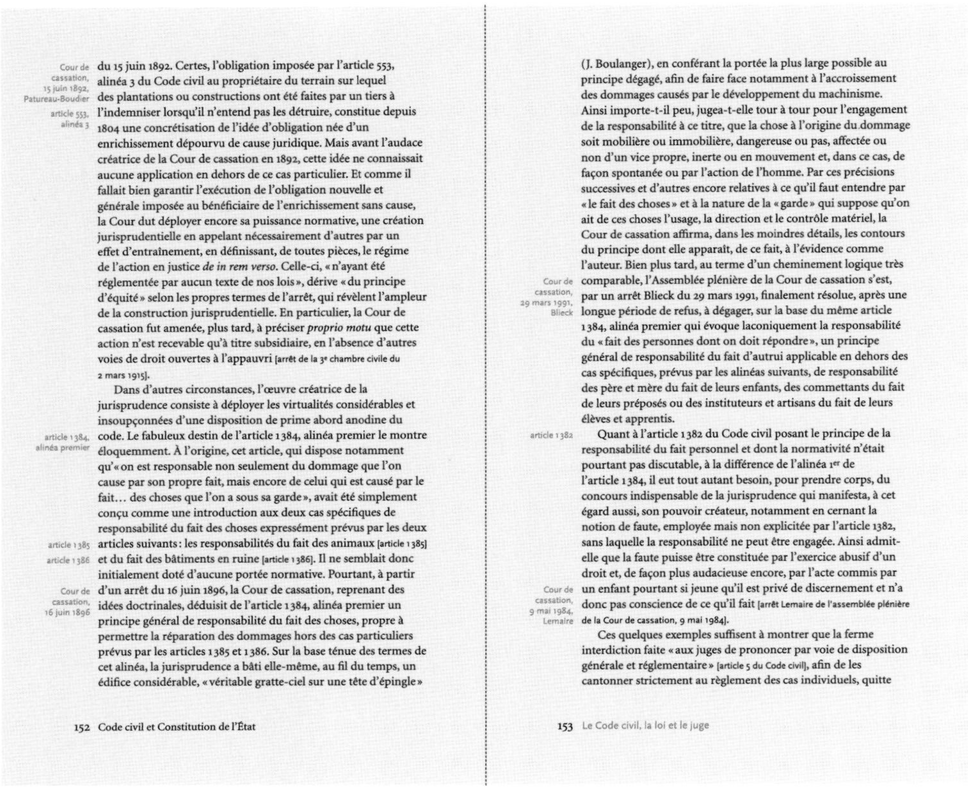

- * ** *** (rare)
- * † ‡ (in older *books*)
- 1 2 3 4 (common today)
- a b c d (relatively common today)

Notes are usually set somewhat (at least one point) smaller than the main text.

Notes are either placed in the *margin* (for example, they are placed in the side *margins*, at the height of the appropriate *reference mark*) (1,3) or as *footnotes* (for example, at the bottom or *foot* of the page) (2).

1. This *book* is inspired by ancient *books*, where the marginal notes and their *reference marks* were often set in another *color*, red in particular. The annotations supplement, inform or differentiate the main message. They are also called comments.

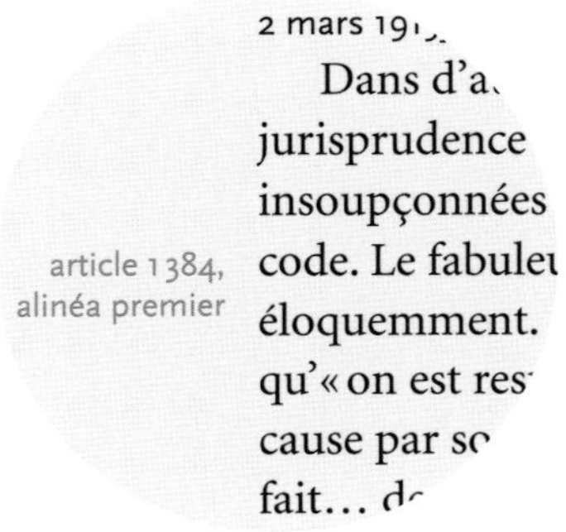

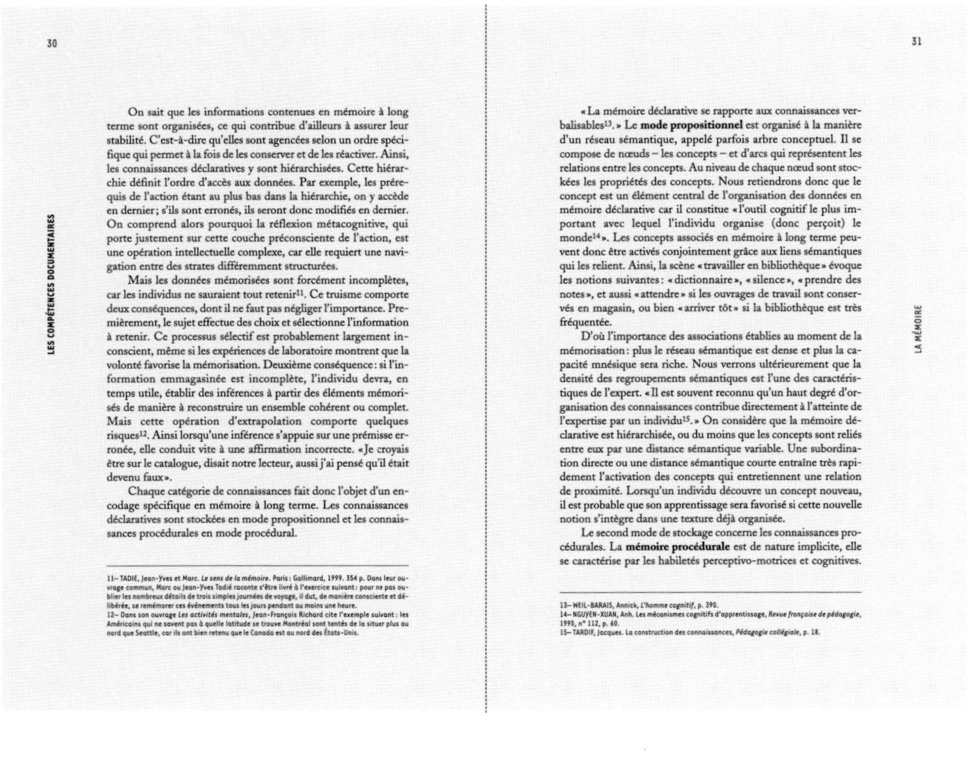

2. *Footnotes* are mostly set in black, and are often separated from the main text by a line spanning the entire *line length* (or less).

Some *books* use both kinds of notes (marginal notes and *footnotes*) in order to distinguish two types of information.

1. *200 ans de code civil*, book
   Éditions adpf
   ÉricandMarie
2. *Les compétences documentaires : des processus mentaux à l'utilisation de l'information*, book
   Éditions enssib
   Damien Gautier

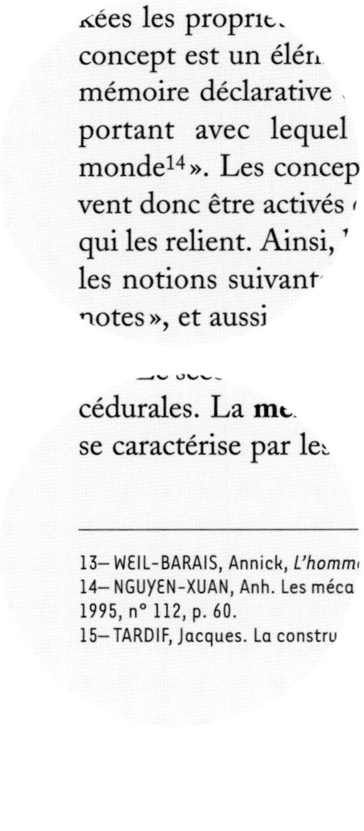

3. *R/B, Roland Barthes*, exhibition catalogue
Centre Georges Pompidou
David Poullard and Philippe Lakits

3. The design principle of this manifesto demonstrates the importance of the notes. The *lower margins* are aligned with the numerous lengthy notes that "dress up" each page.

Notes can also be placed according to other principles:

- Notes can be set in the *footer* in two *columns* as wide as the main text.
- The notes from two facing *pages* can be *gathered* at the bottom of the right-hand page, and with sequential numbering from both *pages*.
- Marginal notes can also be placed in the *footer*.
- All notes from a chapter (numbered sequentially throughout the chapter) can be grouped at the end of each chapter.
- The notes from the entire *book* can be *gathered* at the end of the *book*.

In the last two cases, the reader is often obliged to flip through the *pages* in order to refer to the notes in the text. This makes reading more difficult.

3

56 R/B

SAVEUR DE BARTHES

/ NICOLAS CASTIN

TEXTES / NICOLAS CASTIN 57

116 R/B

LA RÉSISTANCE AU CINÉMA

/ DOMINIQUE PAÏNI

TEXTES / DOMINIQUE PAÏNI 117

The Book
The principle of the book series

196 In order to make their *books* more memorable (for reasons of recognition), publishers have long grouped their *books* into series. These series are organized around a common element (theme, *format*, *layout*, *typographic* features, *cover*, price, etc.). Each series has its own *readership* and its own unique identifying features.

The series La Pléiade from the french publisher Gallimard for example is famous for its bible paper and its unmistakeable *cover*. The series Série noire from the same publisher – which is popular with mystery readers – is easily recognized because of its black and yellow cover. The french *non-fiction series* Que sais-je? is a must for anyone who wants information on a specific theme at a low price.

In a high-class *book series* one pays more attention to the production process (*paper*, *cover*, hard cover, special printing, *embossing*, etc.). Cheaply produced *books* can also be offered at lower prices.

1–2. The *font* and the *type size* of the *book* title, the *text-image-ratio*, the white background and the type of image modification all make these *book covers* unusual.

3. The design principle in all of these *books* is based on overlapping lines. The *typeface* Tarzana was chosen for its "personality" (and because of the unique *"fi" ligature*). It is used as *headline font* inside as well.

1. *Inventeurs des formes* series
   Éditions Images modernes
   Change is good
2. ibid.
3. *Référence* series
   Éditions enssib
   Damien Gautier
4. Éditions Belem
   Romin Favre

1

MONTAGE
EISENSTEIN
JACQUES
AUMONT
IMAGES MODERNES CINÉMA

MATIÈRE
D'IMAGES JACQUES
AUMONT

IMAGES MODERNES CINÉMA

2

ÉCRITS
MICHELANGELO
ANTONIONI

LE CINÉMA DE
MICHELANGELO
ANTONIONI
ALAIN BONFAND

SCÉNARIOS
NON RÉALISÉS
MICHELANGELO
ANTONIONI

3

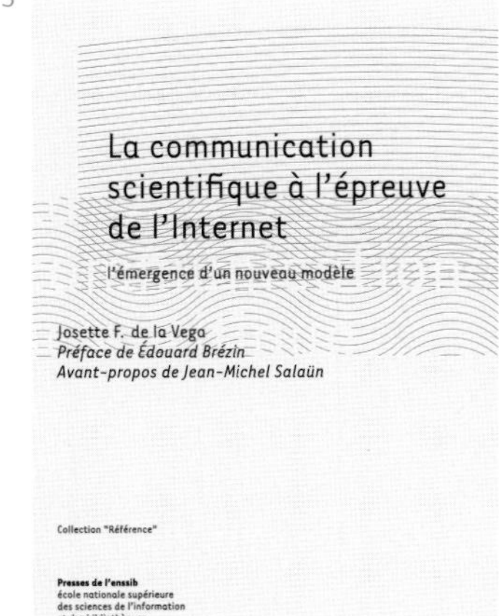

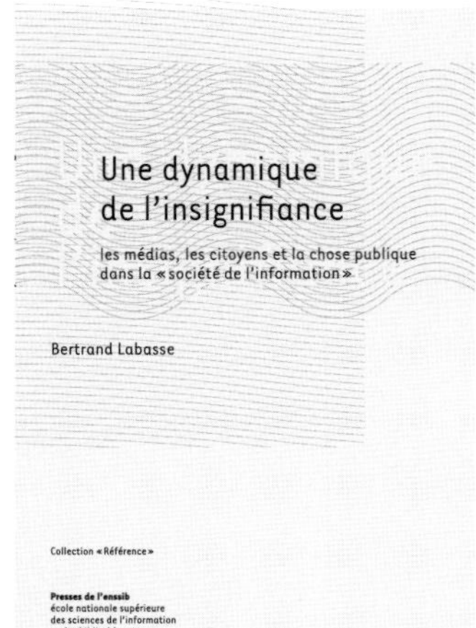

4

5. Éditions Zulma
David Pearson design
6. *Verdier poche* series
Éditions Verdier
Pierre di Sciullo
7. *Incult* series
Yann Legendre

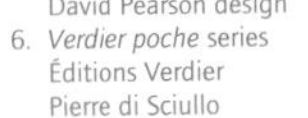

4. All *covers* use a *typeface* specifically designed by the graphic designer. Despite the differences the series is recognizable due to the following:
- the *format* (14 × 18 cm)
- the image elements and their role in the design
- the relationship between image and *headline*

5. The *books* in this series are easy to recognize. Both the *full bleed* pattern and the *headline* set in a triangle of the same size are simple, effective means. Despite the broad range of titles the series achieves a strong sense of *harmony*.

6–7. These *covers* also have a strong presence, undoubtedly due to their restraint and combination of severity with whimsy.

5

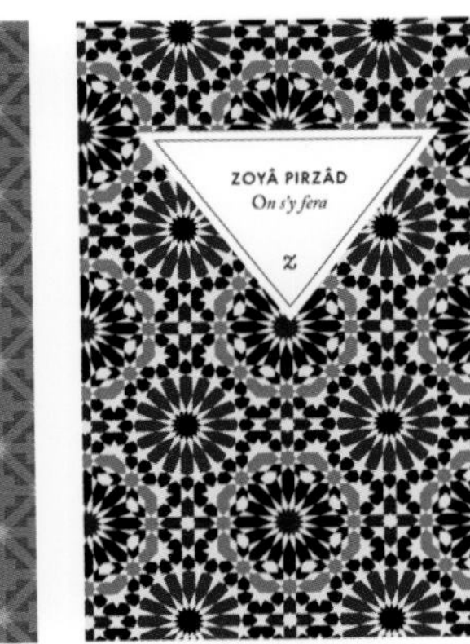

6

7

A publisher often creates more than one *book series* in parallel in order to cover different themes, or to address different audiences or to cater to special concepts. He needs to strengthen the publisher' s identity, find new readers that are drawn to his concepts, and keep the individual series distinct from each other so that the entire palette of *books* is understandable. Once again unity in the variety is essential.

The publisher of the famous Penguin Books has achieved this special mix since 1935, the same year that the first modern *paperbacks* were introduced. The original intention of producing unabridged classics and contemporary authors as hardback *pocket editions* for a reasonable price is still valid today. Design was always given to a prominent specialist. For exemple *Jan Tschichold* was their artistic director from 1947 until 1949.

1. At the end of 2004, the Penguin Publishers added the series *Great ideas* based on the same guiding principles. The goal was to present famous philosophical writings to a broader audience, not just students and academics. The series was started with 20 titles released at the same time, and 20 more in the following year.

In reference to the acclaimed Penguin *covers*, the designer chose to work only with type on the *covers* of the new series. Using the idea—that philosophy provokes thought on its own—as a point of departure, he wanted to avoid a predefined understanding that comes from illustrations. His *typographic* design is often witty, with a tendency for irritation, that leaves the design open to interpretation.

Each *cover* design displays a balance of classic and modern elements. David Pearson paid special attention to the production quality, and proposed offset paper without varnish but always *embossed* for the *jacket*. The *books* should invite one to pick them up to touch them, and that the *cover* will get dirty from being touched is perceived as an advantage. The first series was printed in the *colors* black and red (the traditional accent *color*), and the second series in blue.

1

The publisher's logo appears on none of the *covers*, however the series title and the pubisher's name are an integral part of the *composition*. Pearson answered the critics of his approach simply that it would be equally absurd under the pretext of their timelessness to rely on outdated interpretations

2. This simplicity is hard to beat, a *color* mostly likely chosen for its effect, title and name of the author typeset *centered* on the upper half of the page, and separated from each other by a line. This restraint is reminiscent of the original *covers*, since the *typeface* reminds one a little of the first editions.

3. This collection is memorable not only through graphic and *typographic* idiosyncrasies, but also due to the rounded corners that remind one of *handbooks* or *logbooks*. The *bold* design of the *spines* is also immediately visible on *book* shelves.

1. *Great ideas* series
   Penguin Books
   David Pearson design
2. *Popular classics* series
   Penguin Books
   David Pearson design
3. *Penguin reference* series
   Penguin Books
   David Pearson design

2

3

The book
The pocket edition

The idea of small *books* is very old. Editions of this type date back to the Middle Ages, think of the prayer *books* that were intended to always be carried by their owner. The development of transportation in the 19th century led to the idea of "reading while traveling", but the so-called *pocket editions* really took off between the two World Wars:

- Albatross (a German series), 1932
- Penguin Books, 1935
- Livre de poche, 1952
- J'ai lu, 1958
- 110/18, 1962
- Garnier-Flammarion, 1964
- Folio, 1972

...

The idea is to publish *books* for a wide audience at a lower price. Everything is defined according to this objective: *format*, paper, *layout*, printing, etc. The content is carefully chosen and varies depending on the publisher: classics, contemporary literature, novels, thrillers, mysteries, etc. – something for everyone.

The *composition* is designed to maximize the use of space while ensuring readability. This compromise doesn't always work out. Often the *margins* are very narrow and make the *book* hard to hold comfortably.

All publishers want their series to be different from the others. Sometimes they choose an unusual *format* (see page 40), *typography* and cover design can be strong elements of recognition. Publishers made no mistake when they hired great typographers (*Jan Tschichold*, Pierre Faucheux, Massin, etc.).

1. *Pocket edition* series Folio and Folio classique, 1972
Original *layout* by Massin
2. *Pocket edition* series Point
Original *layout* by Pierre Faucheux
3. *Pocket edition* series Poésie Gallimard
Original *layout* by Massin, 1966
4. *Pocket edition* series Folio Essais
Original *layout* by Massin, 1985

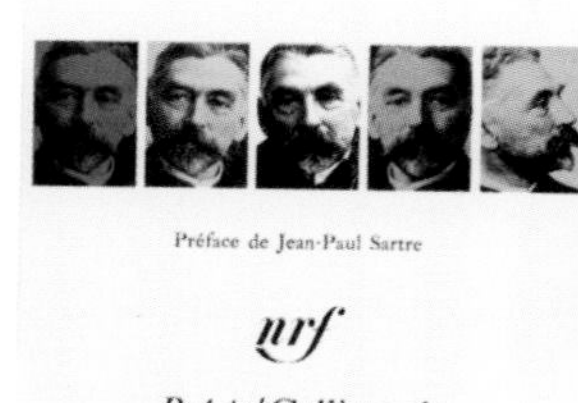

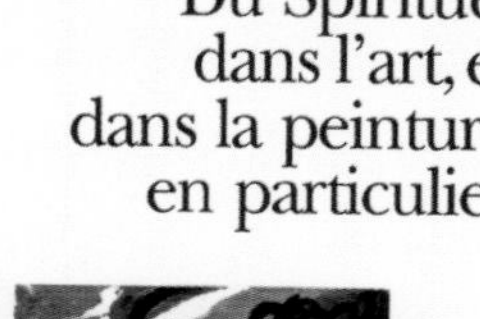

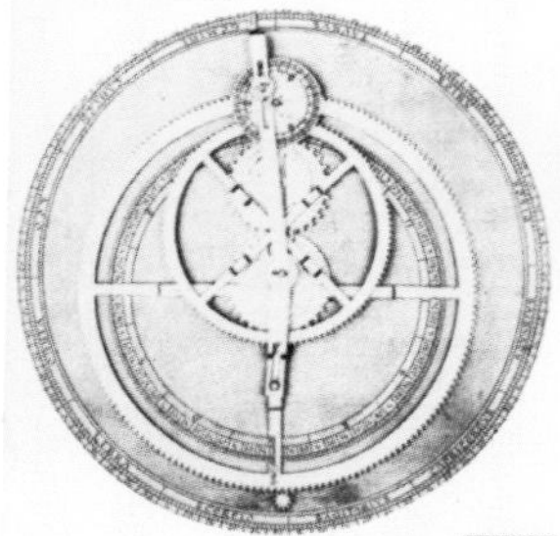

1 2 3 4

5. *Pocket edition series* Le livre de poche, 1953
From no.1 to no. 1800 (1967) Jean-Claude Forest designed most of the *covers*, later the *covers* were designed by Pierre Faucheux
6. *Pocket edition series* Série noire, 1945
Original *layout* by Germaine Duhamel
7. *Pocket edition series* Espionnage, Éditions Fleuve noir, 1950
8. *Pocket edition series* 10/18, 1962

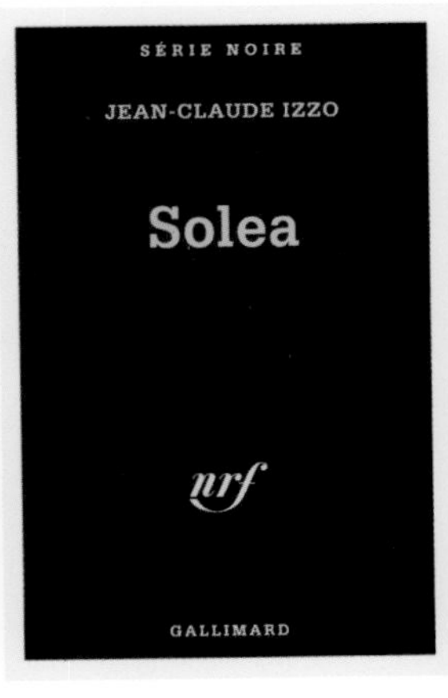

6

7

5

8

The book
The book club adventure

At the end of the Second World War many readers wanted to build their own libraries. During this period clubs were established based on the American model of the *book* club, and were used to compensate for a lack of sales infrastructure. The subscribers, for example the readers of the Club français du Livre (French *book* club), were mailed up to four *books* (classics or new releases) a month.
In terms of cover design the question remained: classic design or new designs? Publishers of the second editions retained the services of graphic designers such as Pierre Faucheux or Massin to express the *books* visually and amaze the readers. Who can be the most creative among the designers? Anything goes: unusual materials, eccentric *typefaces*, unexpected *compositions*, etc.

Pierre Faucheux designed no fewer than 255 *book covers* between 1948 and 1954 for the Club français du Livre, and 480 *covers* for the Club des libraires de France between 1954 and 1964. He worked for the *book series* Livre de poche thereafter.

The output of these *book* clubs was phenomenal both in terms of quality and quantity.

In less than ten years their numbers grew rapidly:
- Le Club français du Livre, 1946
- Le Club du meilleur livre, 1952
- Le Club de l'honnête homme
- Le Club des libraires de France, 1954
- Le Club des éditeurs
- Le Club des femmes

etc.

As early as 1960 the French *book* clubs began losing ground to the *pocket edition* series "Livre de poche", which was established in 1952, and due to the fact that many people had rebuilt their personal collections. The majority of these clubs have disappeared. France Loisirs is one of the few survivors of this rich past.

1. *Le salaire de la peur*, 1953
Le Club du meilleur livre
Original *layout* by Massin
Black linen cover with a facsimile of a US dollar bill glued to the front cover and front inside *endpaper*.

1

2

3

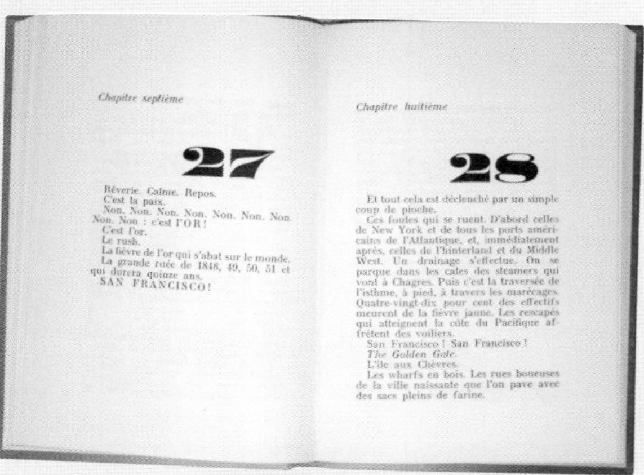

Chapitre septième

27

Rêverie. Calme. Repos.
C'est la paix.
Non. Non. Non. Non. Non. Non. Non. Non. Non : c'est l'OR!
C'est l'or.
Le rush.
La fièvre de l'or qui s'abat sur le monde.
La grande ruée de 1848, 49, 50, 51 et qui durera quinze ans.
SAN FRANCISCO!

Chapitre huitième

28

Et tout cela est déclenché par un simple coup de pioche.
Ces foules qui se ruent. D'abord celles de New York et de tous les ports américains de l'Atlantique, et, immédiatement après, celles de l'hinterland et du Middle West. Un drainage s'effectue. On se parque dans les cales des steamers qui vont à Chagres. Puis c'est la traversée de l'isthme, à pied, à travers les marécages. Quatre-vingt-dix pour cent des effectifs meurent de la fièvre jaune. Les rescapés qui atteignent la côte du Pacifique affrètent des voiliers.
San Francisco ! San Francisco !
The Golden Gate.
L'île aux Chèvres.
Les wharfs en bois. Les rues boueuses de la ville naissante que l'on pave avec des sacs pleins de farine.

4

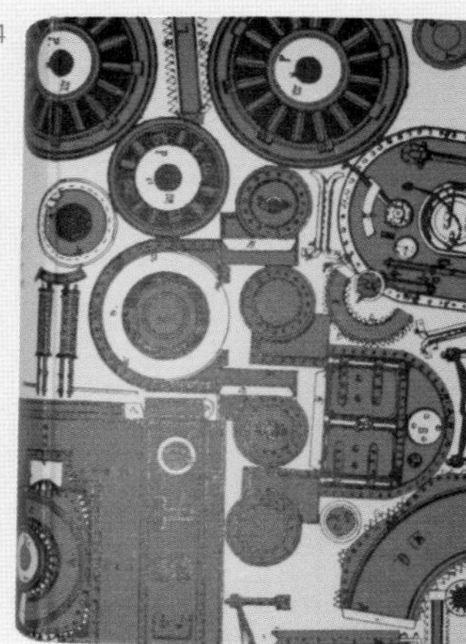

2. *Les copains*, 1953
Le Club du meilleur livre
Original *layout* by Massin
Black linen cover with eye labels on both front and back. Massin spread the half-*title page* over 18 *pages* in this *book*!

3. *L'or*, 1956
Le Club du meilleur livre
Original *layout* by Massin
White linen cover, four-*color* printing. The cover design runs across front, back and *spine*.

4. *Le bonheur des dames*, 1959
La Guilde du livre
Original *layout* by Pierre Faucheux
The *endpapers* are just as carefully designed as the cover.

5. *La prodigieuse vie d'Honoré de Balzac*, 1959
Club des libraires de France
Original *layout* by Henri Huchot
The cover is extremely sober, but this edition contains several facsimiles of type specimens from the printer De Berny, which Balzac had purchased.

6. *Le pont de la rivière Kwaï*, 1953
Le Club du meilleur livre
Original *layout* by Massin
The front and back *covers* are connected by the striking game with the *capital* letter. *Endpapers* and *preliminary pages* continue the graphic experiments started on the cover.

5

6

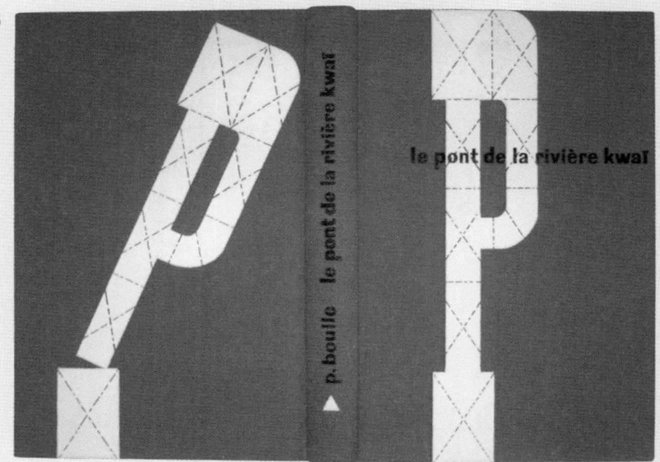

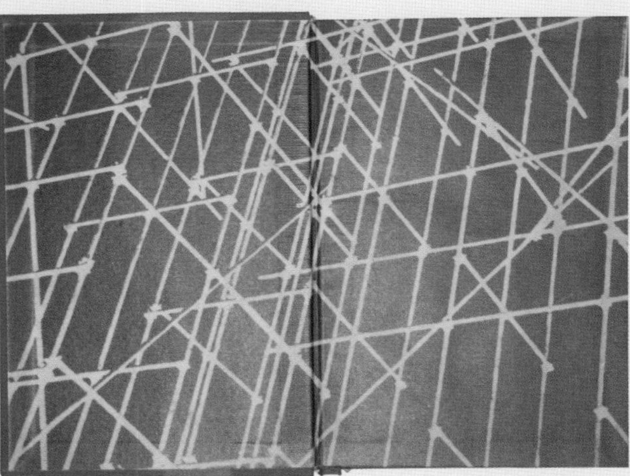

The book
The "beautiful book"

In the art *book*, coffee-table *book* or "beautiful *book*", the formal aspects (*layout*, iconography, paper, *binding*, etc.) are a major factor. These *books* are often larger and richly illustrated. The design often uses ample white space to accentuate the large images.
These *books* aren't always tied to a given graphic principle, but may be part of a larger themed series. The designer often has more freedom in his choices. The *layout* and *typography* are related directly to the *book* and its contents, or the artist's work, or the author's intent.

This type of *book* uses high quality paper (most often coated) to ensure the best reproduction of the images. The *binding* is also of high quality, most commonly *section* sewn with a square back, which guarantees the strength and quality that one expects from a high-priced *book*. The designer sometimes can use expensive *finishing* processes: *embossing*, a complicated trimming, hot foil stamping, unusual cover materials, etc.

With *books* intended for a wide audience, the cover design receives more attention. Unfortunately, publishers often focus on the external form of the "beautiful *book*" without adequate attention to the design of the inside *pages*. The design choices made for the *book*, for instance, are typographically sloppy, and the arrangement of the elements on the *page* is often careless.

1. Every detail is carefully considered: the *layout* and *typography*, the paper and *binding*, edges of the *book block*, *headband*, and *book jacket*.

2. This *book* is presented in a slipcase so one can see the exposed *spine binding*, which leaves the thread used to sew the *sections* together visible. The collating marks form a band of *color* across the *spine*. Once out of the slipcase, the *book* seems intentionally fragile. A hot foil stamp adorns the soft front cover.

1. *Vitamin D*, book
   Phaidon Press
   Julia Hasting
2. *Altitude*, book
   Die Gestalten Verlag
   onlab / Nicolas Bourquin

1

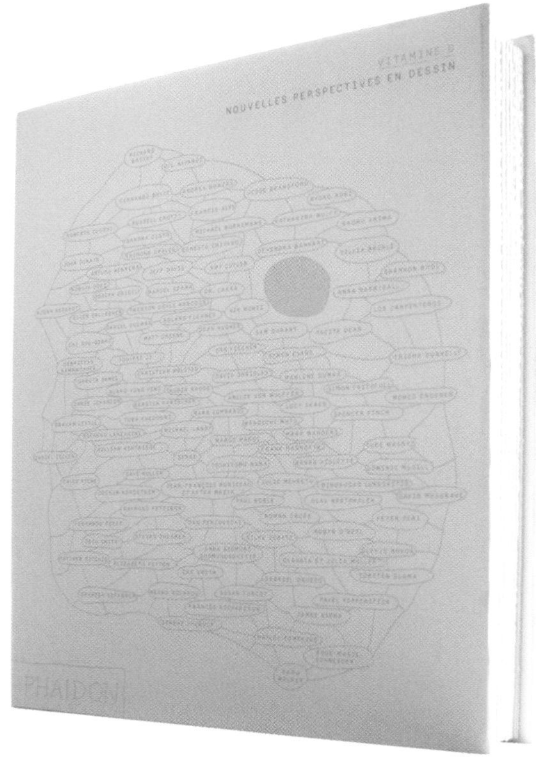

2

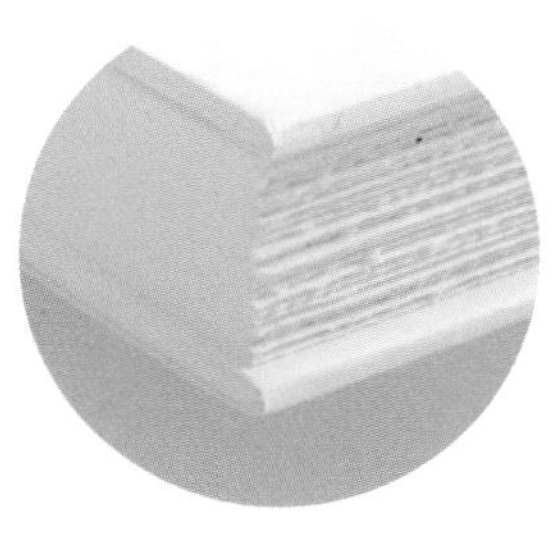

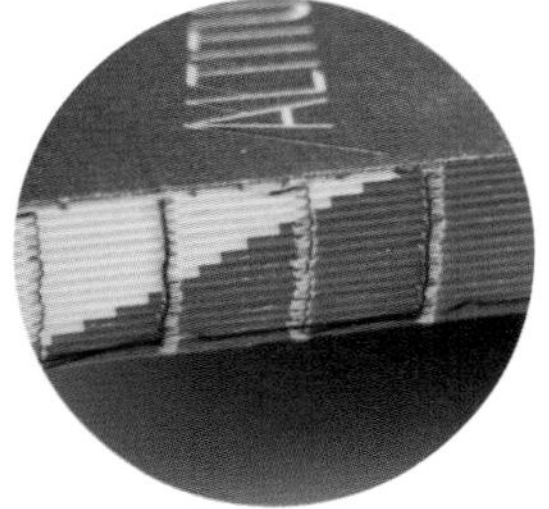

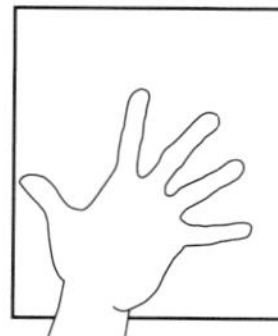

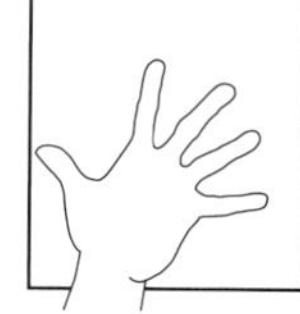

3. The cover is made of silk-screen printed thick plain cardboard. The die-cut letters let one see the blue *endpapers* and make the *book*'s title visible. The *spine* is covered with linen.

4. The cover is made of sealed plastic which is printed with silk screen. Despite the *book*'s weight it is surprisingly flexible.

5. A thick pictogram with the *book*'s title is glued to the flexible plastic cover. The cover's raised texture, as opposed to the smooth pictogram, encourages one to pick the *book* up and feel it.

6. A cover without printing. The *book* seems mute, until the *light* reveals the relief. The subtle play of shadows reveals the title on the totally white cover.

3. *Type one*, book
Die Gestalten Verlag
Mika Mischler, Nik Thoenen
4. *XXe / MNAM / Collections, une histoire matérielle*, book
Éditions du Centre Georges Pompidou
M/M Paris
5. *JPG*, book
Éditions Actar
Ramon Prat and Sandra Neumaier
6. *EndextenD*, book
Loris Gréaud
Éditions HYX

3

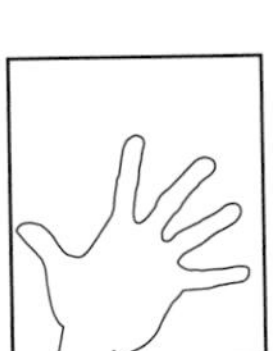

4

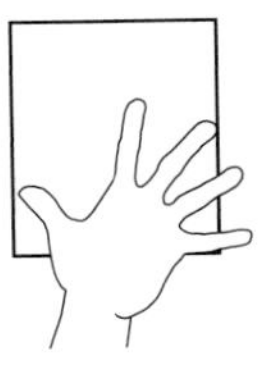

5

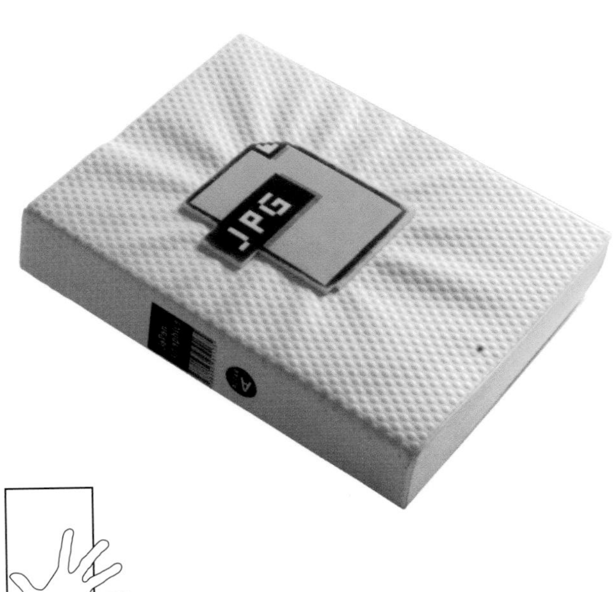

6

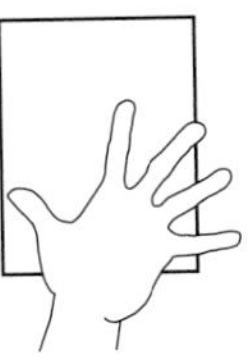

1–2. These *books* are surprising in size. Measuring over 40 centimeters in height and hundreds of *pages* they are simply too heavy to be read while on the go. They are meant to be consulted while on a table, like the tomes of the past.

The Taschen publishing house, once known for their cheap *books*, produces ostentatious *books* today.

1. *The world of ornament*, book
Taschen publishers

1

2. *Atlas of human anatomy and surgery*,
book
Taschen publishers

2

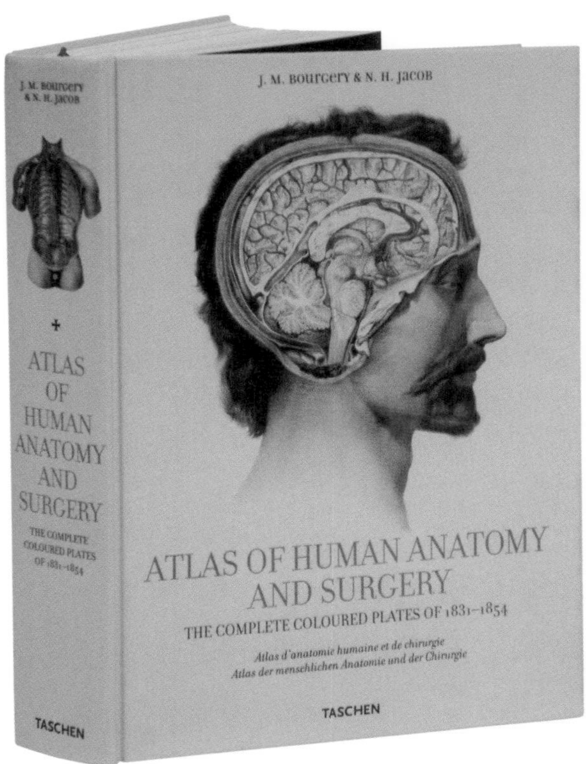

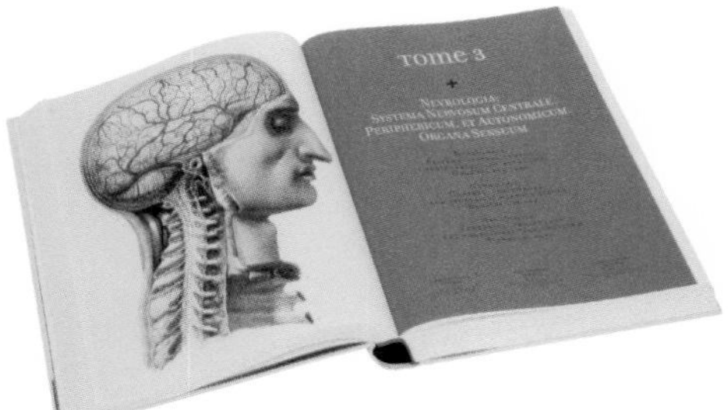

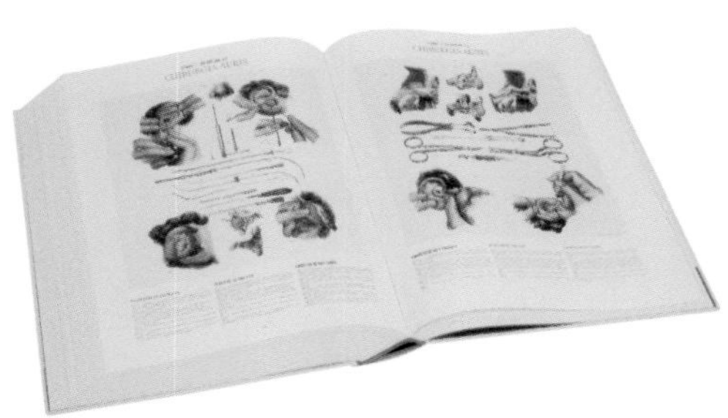

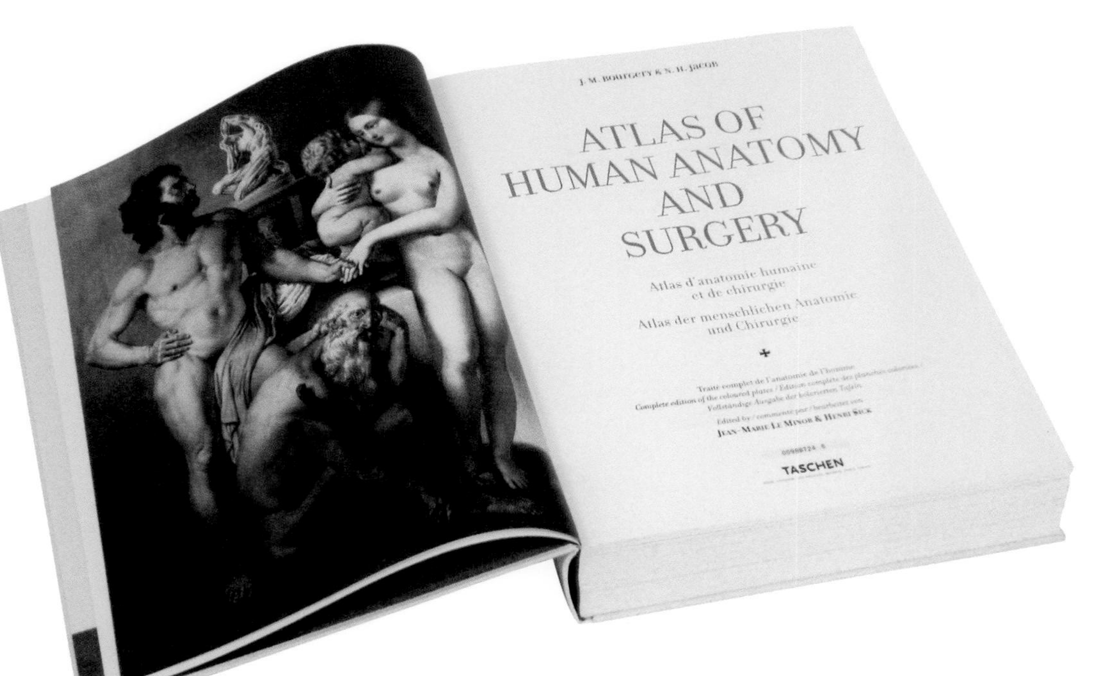

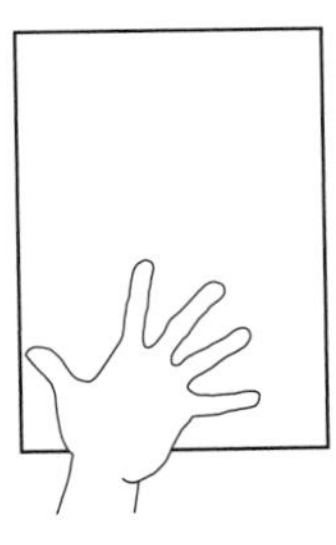

The book
The exhibition catalogue

An exhibition catalogue can have various forms and may be based on a *book*, *newspaper* or promotional brochure. The catalogue's scope is often linked to the exhibition's scope, and it is financed with the budget that is reserved for a written "record" of the event.
The art logically occupies a predominant place and is profusely described and commented on. The content is often organized in the same manner as the exhibition, and may serve as a guide during the exhibition and later as a memory.

However, size and a large number of *pages* are not always synonymous with quality. Some catalogues, despite their modest budget, are lovingly designed, and can compete with those accompanying major exhibitions.

1. In the spirit of the exhibition the Dada catalogue strives to be the complete summary of the subject with over a thousand *pages*. The use of *newspaper*, the *format* and *softcover* suggest the idea of mass media rather than a high-end art catalogue (high quality production, case *binding*, faithful reproductions, etc.).

2. The catalogue of the Starck exhibition on the other hand is tiny. Resembling a *book* of prayers, bound in pink imitation leather, it matches the exhibition's scenography, in which the designer proclaims his views like a religious message.

1. *Dada*, exhibition catalogue
Centre Georges Pompidou
deValence
2. *Starck, explications*, exhibition catalogue
Centre Georges Pompidou
Starck and Thibaut Mathieu

1

2

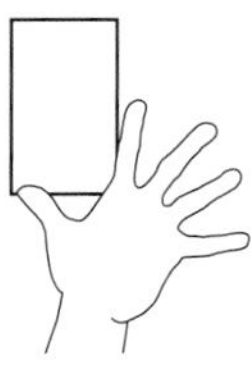

The book
The book as object

The *book* truly becomes an object when the designer experiments with the goal of giving it a unique form. Each parameter is a jumping-off point for experimentation: *folding*, *binding*, *format*, paper, special inks, etc. These *books* are designed to be touched and explored, and slowly reveal their characteristics to the perceptive eye.

Artists' books are the perfect chance for the designer to create a link between the *book* and its content. Rules are not helpful; rather, an intense dialogue with the artist and publisher, technical experiments and adaptations of production techniques are called for.

3. When the *book*'s cover is unfolded it provides an artificial field where the *book* can "nestle". On the other side of the cover, students seem to be floating across the page. *Format*: A5 folded; 630 × 880 mm open

4. The unusual shape of this *book* is simply the result of combining portrait *format* with landscape *format pages*.

3. Book for the Department of Architecture & Interiors at the Royal College of Art in London
ÉricandMarie
4. Portfolio
ÉricandMarie

3

4

Hollande-Royal : un couple en plein divorce fiscal

P. 2 et 3

Sacre de Sarko

Le document qui prouve le bidonnage des chiffres

P. 3

Sarkozy la joue "calme" et "serein" :

Le Canard enchaîné

Journal satirique paraissant le mercredi

c'est Mission impassible !

Après les cafouillages de Hollande sur les impôts

Le PS envisage une fiscalité moins bourde !

COUP DE FIL DE CHIRAC À SARKO

SCORE DE COMBAT

IL NE FAUT PAS S'IMPOSER !

La violence des stats

UNE VISION À LONG TERME

Huchon martyr du féminisme

La noix d'honneur

HOLLANDE ANNONCE DES HAUSSES D'IMPÔTS

LES INTERVIEWS (PRESQUE) IMAGINAIRES DU "CANARD"

François Hollande : "Je ne suis pas marié avec les classes moyennes !"

Pour Ségo, la justice c'est du chinois !

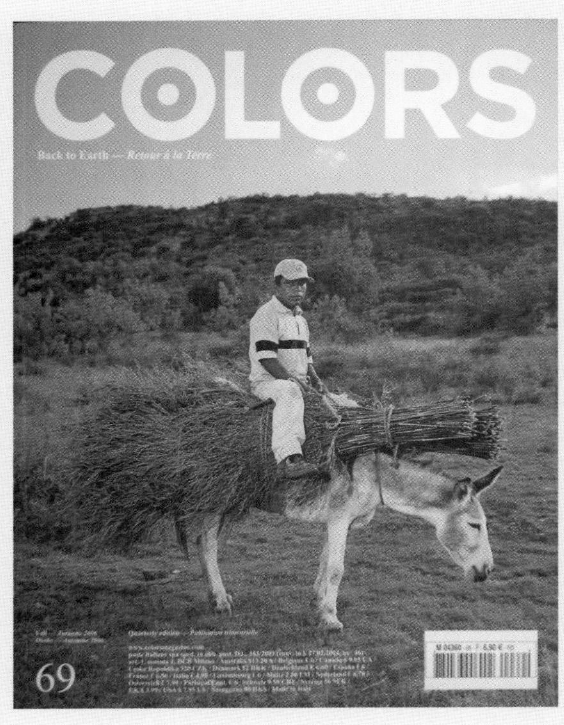

Periodicals
Introduction

We define *periodicals* here as all publications that are published regularly, regardless of the *rhythm* (annually, bi-annually, quarterly, every two months, monthly, weekly or daily), content, or audience.

The subject is consequently vast. Although we won't be able to cover all of it here, we will try to define some design principles and highlight specific characteristics of the different types of *periodicals*.

Newspaper/magazine

In almost all *magazines* the aesthetics of the *page* are more important than with *newspapers*, since the primary "obligation" of the latter is to provide the most information and current news. A *magazine* allows itself white space, whereas *newspapers* use every available space, except for *newspapers* that resemble the British *tabloids* (for example The Sun, The Daily Mirror) which use images to attract attention and as a buying incentive. It is interesting that free *newspapers* (20 minutes, Métro, etc.) resemble this second type of *newspaper*. Since they are distributed free of charge, one questions the amount of real information offered.

The relationship between form and content

The editorial rules determine the relationship between *headline*, text and image, the accessibility of the content (text legibility) and the desired tone. A more or less complex and original *layout* depends on the target audience.

The newspaper

From its obligation to deliver information the *newspaper* draws the principle of clarity and optimal legibility.
When planning a *newspaper* the designer has to honor this principle and still find an original aesthetic.
Every *newspaper* corresponds to a tone of voice that is often related to an ideology, social group or political view. This tone is felt when reading, but also visually in some ways, and it affects the design (*typography*, image choice, *text-image-relationship*, etc.) significantly.

Beyond the ordering of space on the page, *typography* is very important, both for *headlines* and for the body copy. It is becoming more common for a *newspaper* to commission a custom *typeface* for the following reasons:
1. The text is the primary information transmitter. The information needs to be transferred as legibly as possible.
2. Low-quality newsprint and *rotary printing* (high speed and liquid ink) make poor-quality printing (although it has much improved). A custom *typeface* can reduce the number of printing imperfections.
3. A body copy is set between 8 and 9 points in size, so the *typeface* can be optimized to seem large, but not take as much space. *Typefaces* for *newspapers* often have a higher *x-height*, shorter *ascenders* and *descenders* to keep the *leading* to a minimum.
4. One reads a *newspaper* rapidly. The desire for information outweighs the desire for in-depth reading. The reader sails across the page, reads "diagonally". In addition to speeding up reading, narrow text *columns** have become a graphic language specific to the *newspaper* (as opposed to the *column width* in *magazines*). Multiple *columns* create the impression of a large mass of information, which is exactly what the reader wants.

The magazine

Three categories can be defined: information *magazines* (also called news *magazines*) where the content (text and/or images) are of utmost importance, entertainment *magazines* (that primarily want to entertain and appeal to the audience), and finally sensational *magazines* (designed to captivate the reader)**.
Each of these three groups has their own range of nuances determined by the *readership* (female/male, age group, socio-professional category), the subject, the tone of voice, etc.

Apart from a few specialty *magazines* – where the graphic design is important or even of primary importance*** and where every *page* is a space for experimentation – *magazine layout* is developed in terms of graphic consistency, *typography* and arrangement (even if it is only done to save time). The designer tries to define recurring typographic choices, a *grid* that allows a logical *composition* of the texts and images throughout the *pages*.

Magazine printing methods (sheet-fed offset, rotogravure or photogravure printing) give the designer a large number of choices in terms of *format*, paper and number of *colors*. Additionally, the printing precision allows sophisticated graphics that are unthinkable in *newspaper* design.

The consumer magazine

Edited and published by a company brand to promote its image or its products, the consumer *magazine* is in fact a catalogue disguised as a *magazine* or a so-called "magalogue".
Layout, design area, content, everything is conceived like a real magazine. It is planned and designed down to the smallest detail by the respective company (brand). They know exactly how to address the target audience, and how to distribute it so that the readers feel like they have discovered it, and want to flip through the *pages*.
Some of these *magazines*, after many years and having established a strong following, have taken a step back from their brands. Nonetheless, their echo as initiators remains in the readers' mind.

* The column width of a magazine is often 50 to 60 characters per line, and a newspaper's column is usually 40 to 45 characters per line.

** The often thematically focused press oscillates between information and entertainment, and chooses mixed topics accordingly.

*** Ray Gun, Rolling Stone, Crash, Magic! and other magazines covering music, extreme sports and/or skateboarding are aimed at audiences who value aesthetics and the image associated with the magazine.

One needs to be familiar with the technical terms in order to be able to name the design elements and technical processes in *newspaper* design correctly. One should note that American and British terms for the same thing can be different.

ENQUÊTE EXCLUSIVE : COMBIEN GAGNE UN TYPOGRAPHE ? Pages 8-9

UN LIVRE DÉDIÉ À LA TYPO ! Page 12

ARCHE TYPE

LE G DE CLAUDE GARAMOND SERAIT UN FAUX… Page 14

1re année - n°0 – 3,50 $ – France métropolitaine — Lundi 28 novembre 2005

ÉDITORIAL

Chaque caractère est conçu pour une utilisation « idéale », déterminée par de nombreuses variables. Corps, espacement des lettres, justification, interlignage sont quelques-uns des paramètres que le dessinateur prend en considération au cours de son travail. Le maquettiste averti peut alors utiliser cette « expressivité » des caractères pour servir son travail. Il lui suffit déjà de choisir le caractère adapté, de régler les paramètres typographiques de manière judicieuse, pour que le texte typographié prenne une autre dimension. Il peut en effet agir sur chaque paramètre pour accentuer un aspect du caractère, ou au contraire en atténuer un autre, de manière à correspondre parfaitement à l'utilisation qu'il en fait. Malheureusement, il faut remarquer que ce souci de précision, pourtant garant de qualité, est souvent ignoré. Les outils informatiques ont accentué ce fait en rendant la typographie accessible à tous. Sans connaissance préalable, l'utilisateur la considère souvent comme un matériau neutre, malléable au gré des possibilités des logiciels. Chaque caractère est conçu pour une utilisation « idéale », déterminée par de nombreuses variables. Corps, espacement des lettres, justification, interlignage sont quelques-uns des paramètres que le dessinateur prend en considération au cours de son travail. Le maquettiste averti peut alors utiliser cette « expressivité » des caractères pour servir son travail. Il lui suffit déjà de choisir le caractère adapté, de régler les paramètres typographiques de manière judicieuse, pour que le texte typographié prenne une autre dimension. Il peut en effet agir sur chaque paramètre pour accentuer un aspect du caractère, ou au contraire en atténuer un autre, de manière à correspondre parfaitement à l'utilisation qu'il en fait. Malheureusement, il faut remarquer que ce souci de précision, pourtant garant de qualité, est souvent ignoré. Les outils informatiques ont accentué ce fait en rendant la typographie accessible à tous. Sans connaissance préalable, l'utilisateur la considère souvent comme un matériau neutre, malléable au gré des possibilités des logiciels.

DU BON USAGE DE LA TYPOGRAPHIE 03

POLICES, QUESTIONS À UN EXPERT 05

GARAMOND, HISTOIRE D'UN CARACTÈRE 14

TYPOGRAPHIE

Cela est évident, un texte est une simple succession de lettres composées en mots et en phrases.

Comment la perception d'un texte ne serait-elle pas alors influencée par la typographie ?

LECTEURS SOUS INFLUENCE

Pourquoi y aurait-il autant de caractères différents, si leurs formes n'avaient aucune importance ? Pourtant, beaucoup pensent que la typographie ne peut avoir un rôle significatif. Il est vrai que la structure quasi immuable des lettres de l'alphabet semble laisser bien peu de possibilités d'interprétation au dessinateur de caractères.

EST-CE VRAI ?
De toute façon, comment les spécificités d'une typographie, aussi remarquables soient-elles, pourraient-elles être perceptibles sur quelques millimètres de hauteur, et changer l'appréciation d'un texte, alors que le lecteur semble, a priori, ne pas y accorder de réelle importance ? Ces arguments semblent irréfutables. Pourtant des études ont montré que les lecteurs remarquent, et apprécient bel et bien, une correspondance de style entre un caractère et un texte ; un caractère leur semble mieux convenir pour une utilisation qu'un autre. Pourquoi y aurait-il autant de caractères différents, si leurs formes n'avaient aucune importance ? Pourtant, beaucoup pensent que la typographie ne peut avoir un rôle significatif. Il est vrai que la structure quasi immuable des lettres de l'alphabet semble laisser bien peu de possibilités d'interprétation au dessinateur de caractères.

ARGUMENTS
De toute façon, comment les spécificités d'une typographie, aussi remarquables soient-elles, pourraient-elles être perceptibles sur quelques millimètres de hauteur, et changer l'appréciation d'un texte, alors que le lecteur semble, a priori, ne pas y accorder de réelle importance ? Ces arguments semblent irréfutables. Pourtant des études ont montré que les lecteurs remarquent, et apprécient bel et bien, une correspondance de style entre un caractère et un texte ; un caractère leur semble mieux convenir pour une utilisation qu'un autre.

a a

Swift et Bell Centennial : les 2 caractères utilisés pour la maquette de ce journal.

TYPOGRAPHIE PRATIQUE

Une utilisation idéale ?

FAUT-IL CROIRE QU'UN CARACTÈRE EST DESTINÉ À UNE UTILISATION PRÉCISE ?

Si le créateur de caractère a une idée du caractère qu'il veut dessiner et à quel usage il le destine, doit-on pour autant respecter ses choix ou trouver de nouveaux usages ?

CHAQUE CARACTÈRE est conçu pour une utilisation « idéale », déterminée par de nombreuses variables. Corps, espacement des lettres, justification, interlignage sont quelques-uns des paramètres que le dessinateur prend en considération au cours de son travail. Le maquettiste averti peut alors utiliser cette « expressivité » des caractères pour servir son travail. Il lui suffit déjà de choisir le caractère adapté, de régler les paramètres typographiques de manière judicieuse, pour que le texte typographié prenne une autre dimension. Il peut en effet agir sur chaque paramètre pour accentuer un aspect du caractère, ou au contraire en atténuer un autre, de manière à correspondre parfaitement à l'utilisation qu'il en fait. Malheureusement, il faut remarquer que ce souci de précision, pourtant garant de qualité, est souvent ignoré. Les outils informatiques ont accentué ce fait en rendant la typographie accessible à tous. Sans connaissance préalable, l'utilisateur la considère souvent comme un matériau neutre, malléable au gré des possibilités des logiciels. Chaque caractère est conçu pour une utilisation « idéale », déterminée par de nombreuses variables. Corps, espacement des lettres, justification, interlignage sont quelques-uns des paramètres que le dessinateur prend en considération au cours de son travail. Le maquettiste averti peut alors utiliser cette « expressivité » des caractères pour servir son travail. Il lui suffit déjà de choisir le caractère adapté, de régler les paramètres typographiques de manière judicieuse, pour que le texte typographié prenne une autre dimension. Il peut en effet agir sur chaque paramètre pour accentuer un aspect du caractère, ou au contraire en atténuer un autre, de manière à correspondre parfaitement à l'utilisation qu'il en fait. Malheureusement, il faut remarquer que ce souci de précision, pourtant garant de qualité, est souvent ignoré. Les outils informatiques ont accentué ce fait en rendant la typographie accessible à tous. Sans connaissance préalable, l'utilisateur la considère souvent comme un matériau neutre, malléable au gré des possibilités des logiciels. (suite de l'article et commentaires > page 2)

Certainement, un caractère peut en cacher un autre. TG.

ARCHETYPE
3, place Saint-Vincent
69001 Lyon
Tél. 0478291619
Fax 0478276360
FONDATEUR Damien Gautier. **DIRECTEUR** Pierre Rodière. **RÉDACT. EN CHEF** Julien Sappa. **RÉDACTION** Lionel Michée. **SECRÉTARIAT DE RÉDAC.** Gaël. **MAQUETTE** Martine Gulli **ADMINISTRATION** Martine Bizzette (chef de service), Sylvie Borgaret. **PUBLICITÉ** Marie Raneult.
CONSEIL D'ADMINISTRATION PRÉSIDENT Yves Doutrafis. **VICE-PRÉSIDENT** David Raguid, **TRÉSORIER** Etienne Moliprode. **SEC. GÉNÉRAL** Philippe Gollier. **ADMINISTRATEURS** Michel Binet, Alain Balliet, Jean-Hugues Corban, Jean Vibres, Jean-Louis Pocquemord, Anne Solves, Loïc Vorrey, Jean-Paul Balloud.
CONCEPTION GRAPHIQUE DG. **IMPRIMEUR** Imprimerie ITC, 63-65, bd. Malsherbes, 75015 Paris. **PHOTOCOMPOSITION** ITC.

50 CARACTÈRES NOUVEAUX CHAQUE MOIS
Pourquoi y aurait-il autant de caractères différents, si leurs formes n'avaient pas importance ? Pourtant, beaucoup pensent que la typographie ne peut avoir un rôle significatif. Il est vrai que la structure quasi immuable des lettres de l'alphabet semble laisser bien peu de possibilités d'interprétation au dessinateur de caractères. De toute façon, comment les spécificités d'une typographie, aussi remarquables soient-elles, pourraient-elles être perceptibles sur quelques millimètres de hauteur, et changer l'appréciation d'un texte, alors que le lecteur semble, a priori, ne pas y accorder de réelle importance ?

OPENTYPE : UN FORMAT D'AVENIR
Le format OpenType met fin a plusieurs décennies de guerre ouverte entre les partisans du PostScript et ceux du TrueType. Aujourd'hui un seul format réunit les avantages des deux formats qui plus est compatible avec toutes les plateformes d'exploitation. Que demander de mieux ?

+ 12%
C'est la croissance des ventes de polices de caractères sur les six derniers mois. (Source Sûre)

Above the fold
The upper half of the *newspaper*'s *front page* that is visible when folded.

At the fold
The middle part of the *newspaper*. Some editors refer to the central part of the *front page* as "at the fold".

Below the fold
The lower part of a *newspaper*.

Caption
An image must be accompanied by a *caption* that explains the image content and names the source (photographer, illustrator, etc.). It is very important because of its position next to an image, *captions* are almost always read. It needs to contain elements that encourage the audience to read the article. A good *caption* also contains key terms that summarize the main message.

Content plan, flatplan
The *content plan* provides an overview of the order of the *pages* and the location of the contents (text, images, adverts) of a planned *magazine* or *newspaper* (see pages 230–231).

Cross-ref, lure
A short enticing text on the *front page* referring to an article inside the *newspaper*.

Cutline
See: *caption*

Dummy copy
A line (or more) with nonsensical words that symbolizes a missing text or copy line.

Dummy layout
A rough plan of the *layout* of the page, which indicates the position of the elements (texts and images) on the page.

Ears, skybox
The space to the left and right of the *newspaper*'s *nameplate* or *flag*. Often used for advertising or to promote key stories.

Feature headline
A reference to a specific topic published in multiple editions (for example "French Soccer Championships" or "Presidential elections 2008").

Full page ad
An advertisement occupying a complete page, often designed and written like a *poster*.

Gutter
The space between two *columns* of text.

Headings
Running head, *headline*, *subhead*, etc.

Headline
In just a few words *headline* informs the reader about an article's content. Its job is to attract the reader's attention as they scan the page.
While composing a *headline* the following rules are important:
– A *headline* gets straight to the point. It contains only one, preferably new information and grabs the reader's attention.
– A *headline* should be as short as possible.
– The verbs in a *headline* should be active. Passive, interrogative and conditional forms should be avoided.
– A *headline* uses only the most common acronyms to avoid problems in understanding.

There are several different types of *headlines* used in a *newspaper*.
– The banner *headline*:
It is on the *front page*, is short and is the main focus of attention on the page. It rarely has a subtitle, but may if needed.
– The informative *headline*:
This is the "classic" article *headline*, preferably written as a simple sentence, and lists place, date, people involved, and article's subject. It does not comment.
– The enticing *headline*:
This *headline* not only informs, but also aims to surprise and entice reading.
– The commentary *headline*:
A *headline* reserved for certain types of articles such as analysis, editorial or commentary. It allows the reader to quickly absorb the article's message and the author's view.

Imprint
Information (partly required by law) about production, publishers of the publication (editor, author, editorial staff, company address, printer's information, etc.).

Layout sketch
The first rough drawing for the *layout* (text and images) on the page.

Lede, intro or kicker
The *lede* (lead) or *standfirst* is the short summary or introduction between the *headline* and the article. It is intended to grab the reader's interest and suggests the article's point of view.
This can be used to introduce a set of articles.

Masthead, masterhead
The upper part of a *newspaper*'s *front page*. It usually contains the *nameplate*, the *flag* or logo, and the key information about the *newspaper* (date, logo/name, publisher, price, etc.).

Pull quote
Often placed in the middle of the article, it highlights a few words from the text to encourage the reader to read the whole article.

Rez-de-chaussée, "at street level"
A French term referring to a multi-*column* article at the bottom of the page.

Rivers
An unsightly gap in several lines of *justified type*, resembling a river of white word spaces.

Running head
The recurring information about the *newspaper* set in the upper or *lower margin* (publication title, *page number*, date, etc.).

Short, news in brief
Characterized by its conciseness, a short is a text that relates a single piece of information. It has a *headline*.

Subhead, standfirst
An addition to the article *headline*. It gives the reader more information about the article's content and may offer more information about the *headline*.

Tabloid
A smaller *newspaper format*, intended for readers who use public transport (see page 41).

Textbox
This element often compliments an article with additional information (a reaction, breaking news, key facts, etc.).

Turnover, spill
An article that begins on the (lower right section) *front page* of a *newspaper* and that continues on the second *page* is called a turnover or a spill.

Typesetting error
See: typo

Typo
A missing or falsely set letter or word is called a typo.

Periodicals

Front page and layout: perception and appropriation

Showcase

It is the *front page* or cover that is the first point of contact – sometimes involuntarily – between the reader and the publication. It represents the image of the *periodical*. It is a major part of the publication's unmistakable identity, and encourages you to pick it up and buy it.
Above all, the *layout* for both the cover and inside *pages* is designed for the *readership* of the *newspaper* or magazine. The designer's personal style may have an influence, but the *layout* primarily reflects the editorial concept.
The *front page* or cover is in some ways the *periodical*'s showcase. The designer's challenge is to find the balance between something innovative and something clearly true to the spirit of the publication.

The *masthead* at the top condenses the *periodical*'s identity and values. It is also the constant element on all *covers* and is important for recognition. The typeface, the *color(s)*, and *outline* of the *masthead* are considered carefully.
Its evocative force and major role in the – sometimes long – history of the *newspaper* are so powerful, that it survives multiple redesigns unchanged or only slightly changed, as not to break with the *periodical*'s *readership*.

The *front page* of a *newspaper* differs from a magazine's cover. The *newspaper*'s *front page* often provides a detailed summary of the content of the inside *pages*. News editors place what they consider the most important subjects on the *front page*. On the other hand, a *magazine* cover shows only a handful of the articles inside, usually on top of a full bleed image (see pages 216–217).

But we shouldn't establish strict rules, since the examples show that one medium can often borrow aspects of the other.

Impact

The *front page* must be legible at a distance of three meters! The strength of a *front page* or cover is in the message that it sends. Photography and *headlines* are therefore chosen carefully.

Perception

The reader explores the cover like any other *page* in the *periodical* like a painting: as a whole and in individual parts. The eye has already scanned the whole *page* before the reader makes a conscious effort. The eye finds the *page* structure, and recognizes familiar elements (verbal or visual).

1

1,50 € NUMÉRO OFFERT !
Découvrez le premier hebdo lyonnais
Sarkozy
Pour ou contre ?
LE JOURNAL DES ESPRITS LIBRES
LYON CAPITALE
N°600
L'esprit libre,
Les nuits russes de Courchevel
Sirha
Le gotha de la gastronomie mondiale à Lyon
Femme de lettres.
BEAUMONT & FINET

2

SORTEZ DU QUOTIDIEN
GRATUIT N°91 – JEUDI 18 JANVIER 2007
Directsoir
GASPARD ULLIEL
Il est Jacquou le croquant
ÉDUCATION
LA NOTATION EN QUESTION
ONU
MENACES SUR L'AIDE AU DARFOUR
TÉLÉ
LE POKER SUR DIRECT 8
SIMONE VEIL
EN MÉMOIRE DES JUSTES
EXCLUSIF
JACQUES PRADEL
(Journaliste)
«Le Journal de 20h met l'actualité en spectacle»
Dernière minute
AIX-EN-PROVENCE : 10H56
PARIS : 11H49
www.directsoir.net

3

Daily Mail
PRINTED IN EUROPE THURSDAY
Vodka, ecstasy, cocaine ... and a hell-raising new star
WILL WILD LILY BE QUEEN OF THE BRITS?
THE BIG ISSUE?
Prisons full... NHS in crisis... more soldiers dying... inflation and bank rates up. So what was obsessing our political leaders yesterday? The Big Brother 'racism' row
SEE PAGES 12–13

4

20 minutes
lyon
Les moines bouddhistes défient la junte militaire birmane
« Le grand stade est une affaire de com »
Albanel cultive la colère des artistes
Les Lyonnais marquent le pas
15°C le matin
23°C l'après-midi
Fatal canin
Assurance Auto résiliée ?
SOS Malus Vous assure !
01 40 73 74 48

Signs and signals
To capture the reader's attention and encourage him or her to read, editors work with signal words. These are words that are recognized by their outline alone (before being read) and because they are decoded instantly, they give the reader the impression that the following information is important and they are prompted to learn more. Short *headlines*, which are read effortlessly, also act as beckoning signals.

Independence, appropriation
Despite the *layout*'s incentives, the reader judges the content according to his own criteria and may even be upset by the scheme that the editor is trying to dictate. The *page* should therefore be designed to allow everyone his or her own reading style, to reach the widest audience possible.

Cost/benefit
The reader judges a *page* in terms of cost-benefit ratio, or what it costs him to access the information, and what benefit the information gives. The reader evaluates this cost, or the energy he has to use to read the text, which is the result of the character density, the feel of the text *masses* (differences between the information) and the individual accessibility of the content. The cost depends on the reader. The feel of the text *masses* depends on the typographic *contrast* between text blocks. Not enough *contrast* is perceived as monotonous and therefore boring. Too much text is discouraging, because the content seems confusing and excessive. *Headlines* are very important both graphically and editorially. *Headlines* that are too weak don't motivate, *headlines* that are too strong are obtrusive and their message is often crude.

Emotion/reason
The (abstract) word, a string of letters with a meaning, appeals directly to the intellect and reason. The image on the other hand addresses the senses and emotions. The relationship between text and image lets the reader decide immediately and intuitively where the *newspaper/magazine* stands between reason and emotion.

1–8. The different *front pages* of these eight *newspapers* demonstrate how they work: to attract attention, to challenge, to seduce, to inform, to excite, etc. Each one also reflects the editorial concept and target audience.

5

Les Echos

LE QUOTIDIEN DE L'ÉCONOMIE

Airbus tombe dans le rouge malgré des ventes record

Présidentielle : l'ISF des candidats en débat

Un léger coup de pouce sur les salaires accordé aux fonctionnaires

Résultats historiques en vue pour les banques américaines

Augmentation de capital

6

la Repubblica

Ora è scontro sull'Afghanistan

Dopo Vicenza nuova lite nel governo. Prodi: scelta irrevocabile

Padoa-Schioppa contestato a Torino

Terremoto Alitalia, salta il Cda

Voci su un'offerta Air France, si fa avanti anche Lufthansa

Di mamma, papà oppure misto arriva il cognome fai-da-te

LUCIA ANNUNZIATA

1977

7

EL PAIS

DIARIO INDEPENDIENTE DE LA MAÑANA

Todos los partidos se plantan contra el el nuevo debate sobre ETA que exige el PP

"Mi libertad es morir con dignidad"

La investigación destapa los negocios urbanísticos del alcalde de Andratx

Merkel advierte que sin Constitución europea no habrá más ampliaciones de la UE

"La guerrilla me dijo: 'Su esposa se fue'"

Terroristas de Londres bajo vigilancia

CEF.- Formación 2007

8

l'Humanité

GUERRE D'IRAK

«Pourquoi nous avons déserté»

Trois soldats américains, réfugiés au Canada où notre envoyée spéciale les a rencontrés, expliquent leurs raisons de ne pas faire cette sale guerre. PAGE 2

PRESIDENTIELLE

M.-G. BUFFET À LA GRANDE BORNE

EUROPE

S. Royal veut un nouveau référendum.

ASSEMBLÉE

Enquête refusée sur les LBO.

SANS-PAPIERS

Deux succès en Val-de-Marne.

LE RENDEZ-VOUS DES LIVRES

ENTRETIEN AVEC OLIVIER CADIOT

Un Juste témoigne

Le courage de Roger Belbéoch, résistant infiltré au cœur de la police pour sauver des juifs de la déportation. Hommage aujourd'hui au Panthéon. PAGE 9

«À tous les surhommes, il faut préférer ce spectacle rare entre tous: un homme juste et juste un homme.»
PAUL CLAUDEL

Periodicals
The cover's impact

Make them look first, then read
A *magazine* cover is designed like a *poster*. Its function is to attract the reader's attention, serve as a buying incentive to learn more. The choice of image(s) and every word in the *headlines* and *subheads* are of primary importance.
The cover also gives you a "preview" of the content, the tonality and target audience. Sometimes a single glance at the newsstand is enough to help the uncertain and overwhelmed buyer to decide on one *magazine* over another.

It is therefore a question of finding a way of making a *magazine* as recognizable as possible, and at the same time, to create some kind of surprise to arouse curiosity and buying desire.

The *headline* often placed near the *masthead* is very important:
- It proposes what the viewer should read first. Typeface, their *layout* and *color* are chosen precisely.
- They are responsible for the visibility of the *magazine* on the shelves of the kiosks and newsstands.

Beat the competition
The designer is always aware that the *periodical* will compete – if subtly – with many others before it is chosen and winds up alone on the buyer's table.
Depending on the magazine, its content, its readers, and its distribution channels, the means used to compete for the buyers' attention change.

A scientific journal is more restrained to preserve its credibility, while a sensationalist *tabloid* will do anything graphically and editorially to be noticed, sometimes exceeding the limits of good taste.

The importance of the images
A cover has to be instantly noticeable and readable to attract and capture the reader's attention, including a reader who may not always have the time or even the intention of buying a *magazine* or *newspaper*. The image(s) chosen for the cover should have an intrinsically rapid understandability. They should also appeal to the reader's imagination, to his memory and to his senses. They should be intriguing or moving. Emotion triumphs over reason in this case.

The reader also looks to identify the familiar, and is sensitive to faces, to the presence of personalities and stars he or she recognizes. The selected images, however, may have to be partly obscured by a *headline* without harming their legibility.

Exceptions

While *periodicals* that compete and are tied to current events do indeed, in spite of their distinct qualities (*readership*, content tone, etc.), share the same rules (image impact, the shocking and evocative power of words), this does not apply to specialized *periodicals* (related to professions, for example). These publications have a defined (and faithful) audience that they continuously try to reach better. With *periodicals* that are often sold by subscription, the cover has less of a promotional function, rather works as an encouragement to "turn the page" and start reading.

The trade press is above all a tool for work. The cover and inside *pages* are designed to ease access to information. While this category of publications increasingly resembles the popular press (in terms of budget, marketing, etc.), there is no doubt that *periodicals* with low circulation (due to lack of budget and skills) often neglect their cover and *layout*.

A clever mix

The cover's design is not left to chance. The placement of the *headlines* and their relationship to others is carefully studied. Some *covers* are intentionally designed to give the effect of total chaos.
The position and *contrast* between the *headlines* (abrupt changes in typeface, many *colors*) demonstrates a specific attitude and captures the undecided reader's attention.

Other trade or specialized journals that have their own loyal readers have to show their competence by reporting clearly on current topics. These *periodicals* therefore prefer to limit the number of cover lines to two or three.

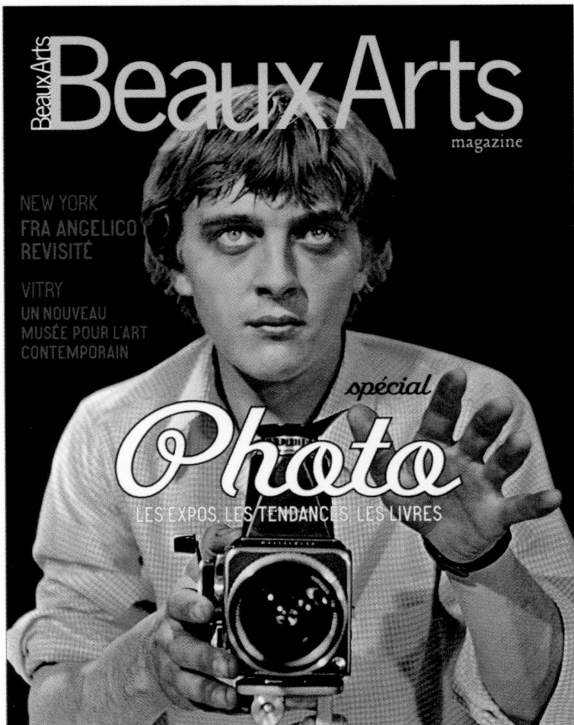

Periodicals
Consumer magazines

A consumer *magazine* is a publication connected to a brand or an organization. It is either designed and managed by the organization or the design can be delegated to others. This type of *magazine* is wide spread and there are few brands that don't have this type of promotional material today. Promotion is always primary even if the *magazine* also informs.

Dressing a consumer publication like a *magazine* (*format, layout*, structuring the content into *sections*, editorial style, etc.), the editorial team presents content that "serves" the brand in question. Product presentations, advice, commentaries or longer articles that fit the brand's spirit.

While reading the articles, the reader learns more or less directly about the brand values and is encouraged to consume the products and services presented on the *pages* that follow. Some consumer *magazines* are truly informative and are simply part of the brand's service. Who, for example, doesn't have a look at the SNCF *magazine* while traveling on the TGV (French high-speed train)?
With a print production of nearly 285,000 copies, the TGV *magazine* mainly contains cultural information (exhibitions, cinema, arts, literature, etc.), society *sections* (fashion, tourism, gastronomy, etc.), and *sections* that explain developments in the French train system, especially the TGV, project presentations, interviews, and so on.

The magazine's goal is to promote the French high-speed train as a link to these cultural events. It is also an excellent advertisement in the hands of a captive audience.

1. *Go sport*, éponyme brand magazine
2. *Rugged*, Carhartt brand magazine
3. *TGV mag*, SNCF magazine, distributed in all TGVs, published by Textuel

1

2

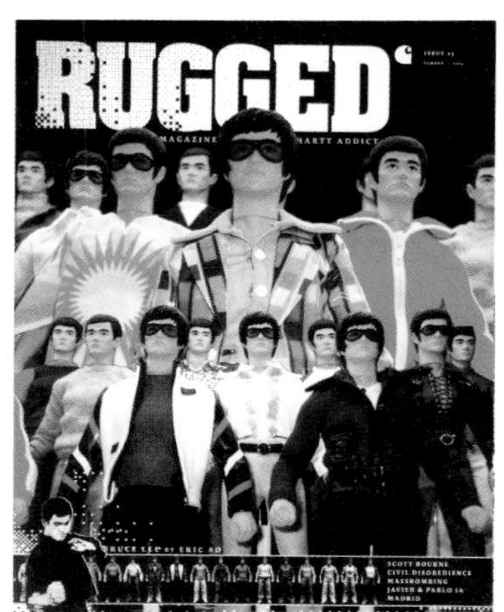

3

CE MAGAZINE VOUS EST OFFERT

TGV magazine

95

JUIN 2007

Diane Kruger, un envol en douceur

Psychotropes : la France, drôle de cas ?

White Stripes, blues furibard

+

CAHIER CENTRAL "NOUVEAUX HORIZONS" LE GUIDE DE LA MOBILITÉ AVEC TGV

TGV Prenez le temps d'aller vite

DE MOBILITE

TOUJOURS CONNECTÉ

ESCAPADES À GRANDE VITESSE

SUR UN AIR D'OPÉRA AVEC TGV.COM

OFFRIR LE MORBIHAN

SHOPPING TGV

Chics et mobiles

Des objets utiles, ludiques et élégants... La nouvelle panoplie griffée TGV accompagne tous les voyageurs dans leurs déplacements. À découvrir, avec toute la gamme TGV, sur www.tgv.com/boutique

CITY BREAK

Strasbourg au-delà des clichés

Capitale carte postale de l'Alsace, Strasbourg développe peu à peu une autre identité grâce à des réalisations culturelles, architecturales, urbanistiques, qui en font une sorte de modèle que l'arrivée du TGV va sans aucun doute renforcer.

Y aller avec TGV

DANS LES RÈGLES DE L'ART

"CHUT..."

L'ARTICHAUT

LA CASSEROLE

VOLTE/FACE

César

Michel Dubois

L'INTERVIEW

DIANE KRUGER

"QUAND J'ÉTAIS MANNEQUIN, JE N'AVAIS PAS DE VIE"

Agenda bien rempli. Diane Kruger enchaîne tournages américains, avec grosse caravane à la clé, production française avec réalisateur québécois (*L'Âge des ténèbres*, de Denys Arcand, sortie en septembre) et rôle de maîtresse de cérémonie au *Festival de Cannes*. Mais, sur son passeport, la nationalité reste allemande.

Periodicals
Examples

1. The *layout* of this trade *magazine* aims to differentiate it from the typical aesthetic of the scientific world. It delivers the required clarity and legibility for this type of journal, yet does so with an original graphic language:

- The articles are instantly visible thanks to the vivid *flat colors*.
- The *typography* is restrained and sober (*justified type* set in three *columns*) and expressive (the length of the *headers*).
- Text and image arrangement is obvious (images and graphics in the upper part of the page, separated from the main text by *captions*).
- The cover of each issue has an abstract full bleed image, which is partially covered by a *color* field and by a content summary.

The *typefaces* were carefully chosen:

- Thanks to its narrow *body width*, the *typeface* Solex (by Zuzana Licko) is especially fitting for *headlines* and *captions*. Her original design (especially the "r" and the "e") adds to the originality of the design.
- The *typeface* Proforma (by Petr van Blokland) was chosen as the *bread-and-butter typeface* because of its classic appearance and reading-friendly typographic *rhythm*.

1. *La revue d'optométrie*
Damien Gautier

1

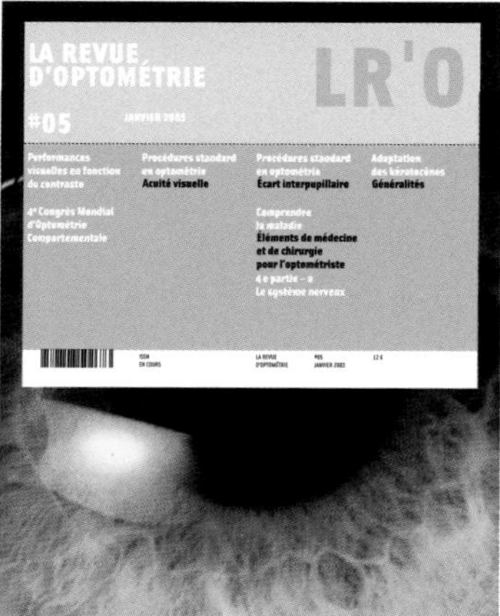

LR'O°09 OPTOMÉTRIE 10

La méthode en trois points de Parks
Application clinique

Danielle de Guise
OD, MSc
Professeure adjointe,
École d'optométrie,
Université de Montréal

Dominique Lesage
OD
Étudiante 2e cycle, École d'optométrie,
Université de Montréal
Chargée de clinique

La parésie d'un muscle oculaire extrinsèque entraîne une déviation incomitante, c'est-à-dire dont l'angle varie selon la direction de regard. Une déviation incomitante peut être mise en évidence lors du test des versions (cf. dossier pratique n°6 dans LR'O n°7), éventuellement lors du test du masquage alterné (cf. dossier pratique n°5 dans LR'O n°6), et doit être envisagée en cas de port de tête anormal ou symptôme de diplopie occasionnelle. Il est relativement aisé d'identifier le muscle parétique en cas de déviation incomitante horizontale. Mais quand la déviation est verticale ou comprend une composante verticale, l'identification du muscle atteint peut être difficile, spécialement quand le problème est ancien à cause des modifications musculaires pouvant s'établir avec le temps. Dans les cas de déviation verticale ou à composante verticale (tropie ou phorie), la méthode en trois points de Parks est une procédure objective et rapide qui permet d'identifier le muscle parétique dans la majorité des cas, même quand le problème est ancien.

Note de la rédaction

La rédaction de La revue d'Optométrie est heureuse de présenter à ses lecteurs cet article décrivant la méthode en trois points de Parks, son interprétation et les précautions nécessaires à sa bonne mise en œuvre.

L'histoire du test d'inclinaison de la tête de Bielschowsky, telle que décrite par Romano, Koch et von Noorden montre que dès 1871, Nagel expliquait le principe de l'intorsion et de l'extorsion qui permet le maintien de la position de l'œil quel que soit le degré d'inclinaison de la tête. Une trentaine d'années plus tard, Hofmann et Bielschowsky établissaient un lien entre le soula-gement de la diplopie et la position anormale de la tête présente dans certaines paralysies oculomotrices.

En 1935, Bielschowsky, utilisant cette constatation, décrivait un test qui permettait de diagnostiquer la paralysie d'un muscle oblique. Depuis lors, la contribution des muscles droits verticaux aux anomalies d'inclinaison de la tête a été établie, et à la fin des années cinquante, Parks systématisait une procédure en trois étapes successives, dont la dernière est le test d'inclinaison de la tête de Bielschowsky.

D. DE GUISE, D. LESAGE — LA MÉTHODE EN TROIS POINTS DE PARKS — APPLICATION CLINIQUE — **LR'O°09** OPTOMÉTRIE 11

Schéma récapitulatif des actions musculaires en position primaire. La longueur des flèches est proportionnelle à l'importance de l'action de chaque muscle (schéma de Baillart-Marquez d'après Hugonnier)

Figure 01

Champ d'action des muscles oculomoteurs. Position de regard pour laquelle l'action du muscle pointé par les flèches est maximale

Figure 02

Hyperdéviation droite en position primaire visible après interruption de la fusion avec un écran translucide (figure 3B)

Figure 03

Introduction

La première étape du test permet de restreindre de huit à quatre le nombre de muscles qui peuvent être touchés. La deuxième, de quatre à deux muscles, et la troisième permettent finalement d'identifier le muscle parésié. Le test est mieux connu sous le nom de Parks Three-Step Test ou parfois de Forced Head Tilt Difference, mais selon Romano, le test complet devrait porter le nom de Bielschowsky Head Tilt Test. Il s'agit d'une procédure apide, qui demande peu d'équipement et de manipulation. Elle est indiquée lorsque l'étude des mouvements oculaires ou le masquage révèle une déviation verticale. Lorsque celle-ci est suffisamment marquée, le test peut s'effectuer par la simple observation des yeux du sujet. Cependant quand la déviation est moins importante, l'utilisation de la tige de Maddox ou d'un masquage peut s'avérer nécessaire.

Méthode

L'interprétation adéquate de la méthode en trois points de Parks nécessite la connaissance des actions horizontales, verticales et en torsion de chacun des muscles oculomoteurs lorsque l'œil est en position primaire. Ces différentes actions sont illustrées à la figure 01. Ainsi, le petit oblique (PO) est élévateur, abducteur et extorteur; le grand oblique (GO) est abaisseur, abducteur et intorteur, le droit supérieur (DS) est élévateur, adducteur et intorteur alors que le droit inférieur (Dinf ou DI) est abaisseur, adducteur et extorteur. Les droit interne (Dint) et droit externe (DE) ont une action purement horizontale, respectivement d'adduction et d'abduction et ne sont pas concernés par la méthode de Parks (figure 01).

Les actions musculaires changent lorsque l'œil change de position. L'action du droit supérieur par exemple, n'est plus la même lorsque l'œil est en abduction, il devient alors purement élévateur. La position de regard pour laquelle l'action du droit supérieur est maximale, son champ d'action, est donc en haut et à l'extérieur. Il en est ainsi pour les autres muscles oculomoteurs. Les champs d'action des différents muscles sont représentés à la figure 02.

1re étape

La première étape consiste à identifier quel œil, gauche ou droit, est en hyperdéviation

Résumé
En 1935, Bielschowsky décrivait une technique pour mettre en évidence la paralysie d'un muscle à action cycloverticale par une simple inclinaison de la tête. Plusieurs années plus tard, Parks systématisait une procédure en trois étapes qui s'achevait par l'identification du muscle parésié ; le Parks Three-step Test. Il s'agit d'une procédure rapide qui demande peu d'équipement et de manipulation. Une illustration clinique des trois étapes du test est présentée de même que la méthode graphique décrite par Koch pour permettre d'identifier rapidement le muscle atteint. Toutefois, le test peut parfois conduire à un diagnostic erroné. Les différentes causes de faux diagnostics ainsi que la façon de les reconnaître sont également discutées.

Mots-clés
Méthode en trois points de Parks, test d'inclinaison de la tête de Bielschowsky paralysie oculomotrice, diplopie, diagnostic, déviation cycloverticale

Abstract
In 1935, Bielschowsky observed that isolated cyclovertical muscle palsy can be revealed by a simple head tilt. Many years later, Parks described a procedure in three stages that leads to the diagnosis of the paretic muscle ; the Three-Steps Test. The test is a rapid and easy technique that doesn't require specific equipment. A clinical illustration of each of the three stages of the test is presented, as well as a diagram proposed by Koch for rapid identification of the affected muscle. The Three-Steps Test may occasionally lead to an erroneous diagnosis. The misdiagnosis, their causes and the ways to recognize them are discussed.

Key words
Parks Three-Steps Test, Bielschowsky Head Tilt Test, vertical strabismus, cyclovertical muscle palsy, diplopia, diagnosis

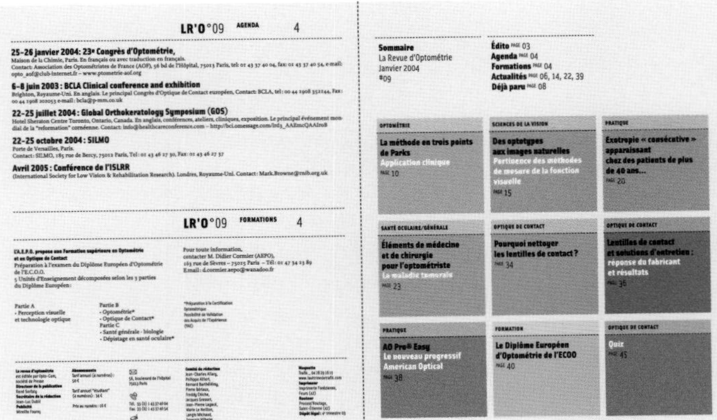

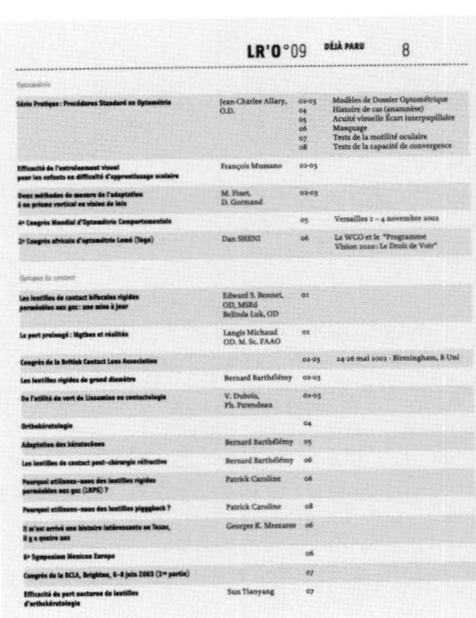

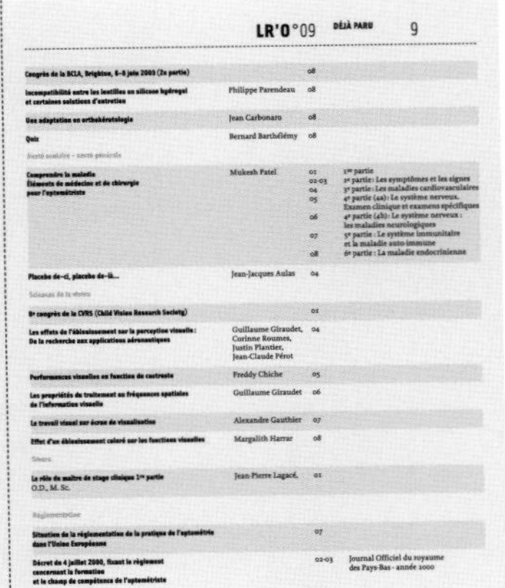

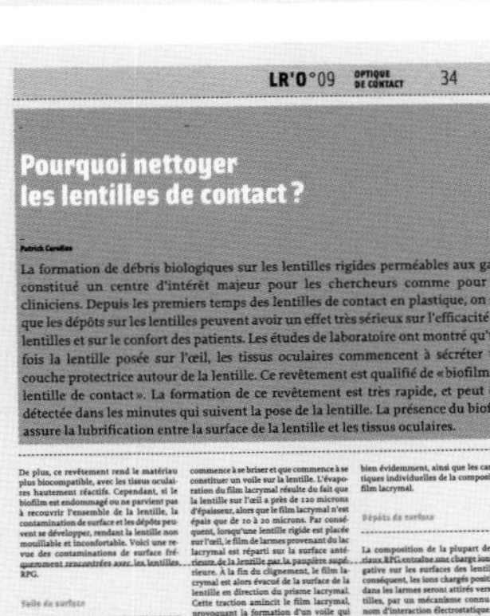

Pourquoi nettoyer les lentilles de contact ?

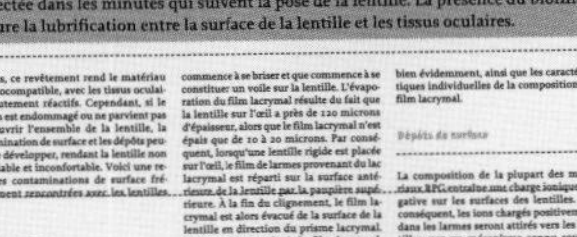

AO Pro® Easy Le nouveau progressif American Optical

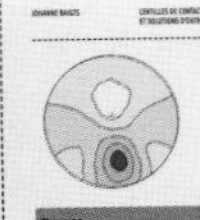

Le Diplôme Européen d'Optométrie de l'ECOO

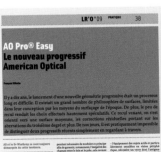

1. The briefing sent to the studio hired to design this *magazine* was as follows:

- The *covers* should be attractive and link to the inside *pages* strengthened.
- Recurring elements need to be more recognizable and the article-specific elements need more variation in images and *headlines*. The two types of elements also need to be more distinct from each other.

Each cover is designed with subtlety and finesse. The use of special printing techniques (UV inks, thermal inks, spot varnishes, etc.) make them especially attractive.

For the inside *pages*, the main text was set in only one *typeface* (and in a single *weight*). The very expressive *headline typefaces* are original designs by young typographers. The *magazine* is therefore a true platform for new *typefaces* and their designers to become well known.

The *layout* cleverly combines rigor and variety, simplicity and abundance.

1. *Items*
BIS Publishers
Studio Dumbar

1

Wolkenlucht
bij Universal Studio's – waar het altijd onbewolkt is. Foto: John Körmeling

Een Körmeling voor Zuid -Holland
Plan: John Körmeling. Tekst: Cornel Bierens. Ontwerp: space3, Eindhoven. Uitgave van Kunstgebouw, Stichting Kunst en Cultuur Zuid-Holland, Rijswijk, 2004

Kunstenaar en 'problem solver' John Körmeling vindt als Nederlander de Belgische ruimtelijke ordening – of het gebrek eraan – dik oké. En dat is goed voor heel wat commotie binnen het Vlaams-Belgische professionele establishment, dat van een snelle rechtzetting van de scheefgegroeide situatie een absolute prioriteit heeft gemaakt.

INTRIGERENDE KADERS VOOR EEN GEZONDE CHAOS

Landschapsplanning van John Körmeling

Caroline Goossens

John Körmeling (1951) houdt van België. Dat doen wel meer Nederlanders, maar de kunstenaar uit Eindhoven dweept vooral met dingen waar de Belgen zelf zich doorgaans alleen maar voor schamen. Als Körmeling het voor het zeggen had, zag heel Europa – nee, de hele wereld – eruit als België. Hij kickt op de megalomane vierbaanswegen in het land, niet alleen vanwege hun zelfregulerende efficiëntie - snel en doorgaand verkeer centraal, langzaam en lokaal verkeer aan de kant, fietsers en voetgangers toegestaan - maar ook vanwege de bebouwing langs de verbindingsassen. "Wat je daar allemaal ziet, dat hou je niet voor mogelijk. De meest diverse situaties, naadloos naast elkaar. Verlaten dancings op kale betonvlakken naast villa's in waanzinnige bouwstijlen. Restaurants naast tapijtcenters, overwoekerde braakliggende velden naast tankstations. Industriële ruïnes, lichtreclames, kapelletjes, apothekers, een doorzicht naar een achterliggend natuurgebied. Dat vind je nergens anders."

50 items 3|2005

items 3|2005 51

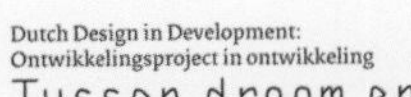

Dutch Design in Development:
Ontwikkelingsproject in ontwikkeling

Tussen droom en daad

Chris Reinewald

De effectiviteit van met veel tamtam gelanceerde idealistische samenwerkingsprojecten van ontwerpers met niet-westerse producenten valt moeilijk te meten. Dat is niet verwonderlijk. Iedere ontwikkelingswerker weet dat het samenwerken met buitenlandse partners veel geduld, inlevingsvermogen en dus de nodige tijd vergt. Het duurt daarom meestal vele jaren voor een project gestalte en daadwerkelijk een duurzaam karakter krijgt. Het is nu, na pakweg een half jaar, erg vroeg om te oordelen wat er terecht gaat komen van het Dutch Design in Development-project (DDiD).

Plompverloren zitbanken, tasjes en kragen van gerecycled materiaal zullen een verwende etnoshopper niet tot kopen verleiden

Back to the future met maïs

Wat hebben maïs en design met elkaar gemeen? Mexico. Maïs, de plant van het volk, zorgt voor verbondenheid, duurzaamheid, economische vooruitgang en culturele identiteit. Hoe? De in Nederland gevestigde Latin American Design Foundation herontwikkelt en benut een bijna uitgestorven techniek om een bijzonder materiaal te maken, en ondersteunt daarmee de economische zelfstandigheid van vrouwen in Mexicaanse lokale gemeenschappen.

Ineke Hans (38) en Maarten Baas (26)

"Schop onder je kont en niet zeuren"

Aanstormend ontmoet Arrivé

Ook vormgevers die al enige tijd terug naam maakten, studeerden ooit af, sprongen daarna in het diepe van de beroepspraktijk of besloten om verder te studeren in het buitenland. Misschien gingen ze wel kopje onder in zakelijke beslommeringen en media-aandacht. Ze werden wijs, soms door schade en schande. Wat kunnen deze ervaren ...

Lolita heeft vele gezichten

Lolita van Vladimir Nabokov is een klassiek geworden bestseller. Toch waren de Amerikaanse uitgevers er aanvankelijk huiverig voor het boek onder hun hoede te nemen, uit angst voor problemen met de overheid. Helemaal verwonderlijk is dat niet. Het wrange verhaal over een man van in de veertig, die een fatale liefde opvat voor de heel jonge Lolita en via haar aanvankelijk niets vermoedende moeder het meisje voor korte tijd in zijn macht krijgt, kan nog steeds schokken.

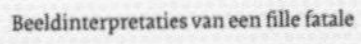

Beeldinterpretaties van een fille fatale

De allereerste uitgave van Lolita was zeer gedegen vormgegeven, waarschijnlijk om de schijn van ondeugd te vermijden

"We willen de wereld leuker maken"

Tjepkema Studio maakt sterk uiteenlopend werk: van een tiara voor Máxima tot een nestje van schuimrubberen takken als sofa. De projecten bewegen zich veelal op het vlak van merkbeleving en combineren sterk conceptuele uitgangspunten met styling en functie. Overgoten met een lagje onorthodoxe vrolijkheid. Onlangs is Tjepkema Studio genomineerd voor de Nederlandse Design Prijzen in de categorieën mode en interieur.

The objective of the *magazine* Fantastic Man is to reinvent the fashion *magazine* for men, and especially mature men. The *magazine* treats fashion as something very personal, preferring articles that highlight personalities from the world of fashion (fantastic guys wearing beautiful clothes) rather than publish images of models dressed in the latest fashions.
Consequently, the *magazine* reaffirms the importance of individuality and personality, in a time that seems to prefer a holistic homogenous approach that appeals to as many as possible.

Every issue takes a fresh approach precisely focused on style, taste and masculinity. It presents extensive detailed profiles of individuals, whose style is influenced by their character and personality. What is their story? What are they doing? What clothes do they wear? These interviews bring out the unique aspects of their style.

The *magazine* is primarily aimed at readers between 28 and 48 (80 percent male) who are mature, educated, and cosmopolitan. Its readers love an elegant lifestyle and love new things, although they are faithful to the things they love. They are convinced that style is a means of expression.

The written tone of the articles is challenging, and famous photographers collaborate with the magazine. The *layout*, designed by the award-winning graphic designer Jop van Bennekom, is a perfect example of style. The *magazine* is designed as an object, and is made of different papers and reveals a mastery of *typography*. *Typefaces* are set at large sizes and all *caps* for *headlines*, different line weights as separators, the *centered* alignment, are all an expression of elegance but with a constant sense of audacity and innovation.

1. *Fantastic Man*, magazine
Jop van Bennekom

1

FANTASTIC MAN

MISTER JOE

CASELY-HAYFORD

— LONDON, ENGLAND

UTTERLY CHARMING FASHION DESIGNER HOPES TO TAKE THE ART OF TAILORING INTO THE 21st CENTURY...

PHOTOGRAPHY—JASON EVANS • STYLIST—SIMON FOXTON
TEXT—MURRAY HEALY

– 50 –

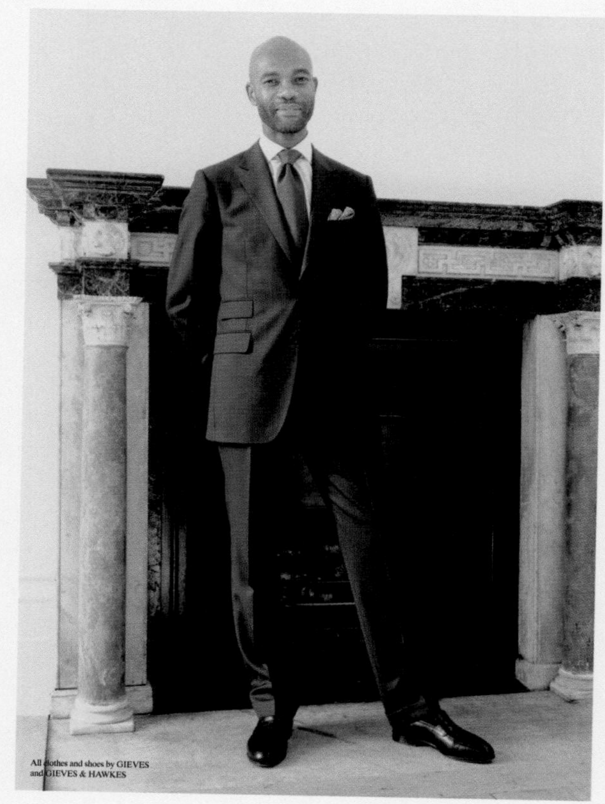

– 51 –

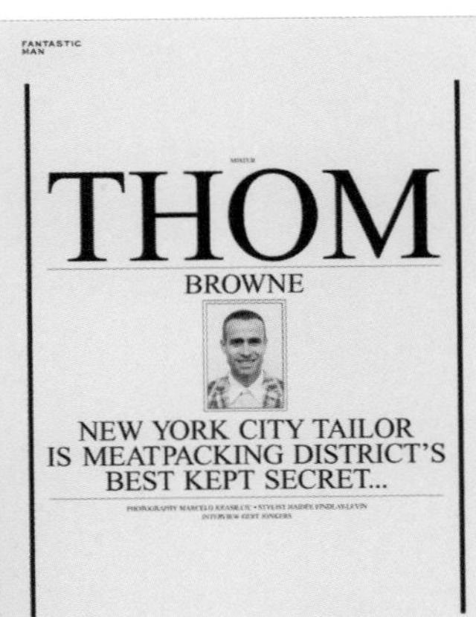
FANTASTIC MAN

THOM

BROWNE

NEW YORK CITY TAILOR IS MEATPACKING DISTRICT'S BEST KEPT SECRET...

THE PHOTOGRAPHER

THE CITY SET

TODAY'S MAN DEMANDS ELEGANCE AND STYLE

THE TRAVEL SET

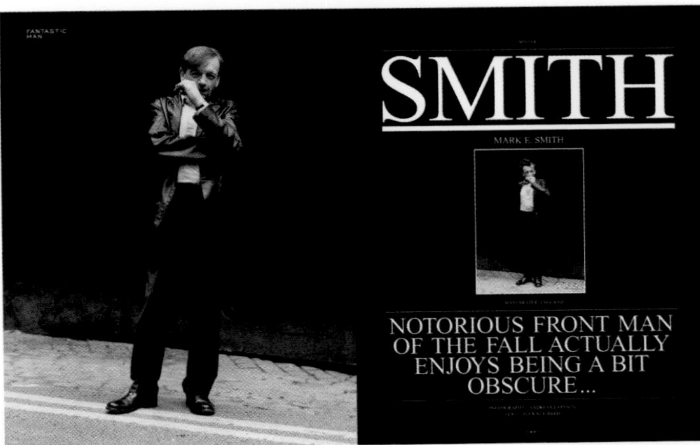
FANTASTIC MAN

SMITH

MARK E. SMITH

NOTORIOUS FRONT MAN OF THE FALL ACTUALLY ENJOYS BEING A BIT OBSCURE...

FANTASTIC MAN

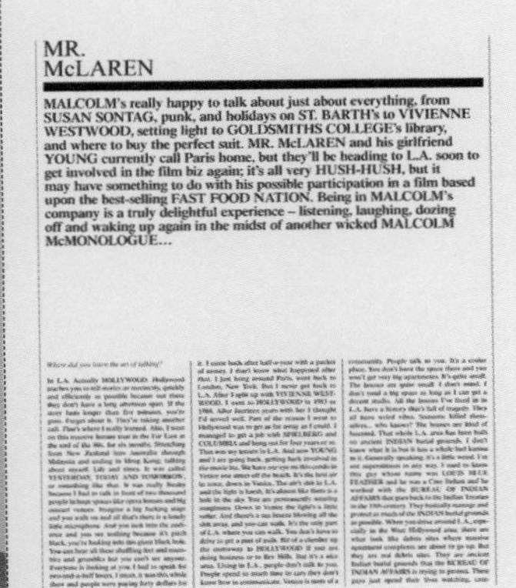
MR. McLAREN

MALCOLM's really happy to talk about just about everything, from SUSAN SONTAG, punk, and holidays on ST. BARTH's to VIVIENNE WESTWOOD, setting light to GOLDSMITHS COLLEGE's library, and where to buy the perfect suit. MR. McLAREN and his girlfriend YOUNG currently call Paris home, but they'll be heading to L.A. soon to get involved in the film biz again; it's all very HUSH-HUSH, but it may have something to do with his possible participation in a film based upon the best-selling FAST FOOD NATION. Being in MALCOLM's company is a truly delightful experience – listening, laughing, dozing off and waking up again in the midst of another wicked MALCOLM McMONOLOGUE...

FANTASTIC MAN

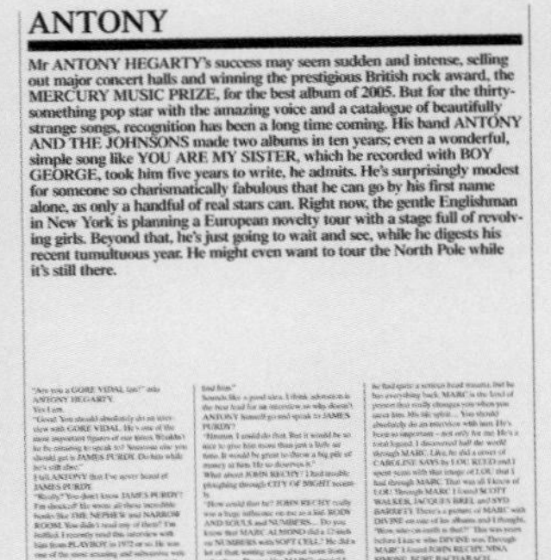
ANTONY

Mr ANTONY HEGARTY's success may seem sudden and intense, selling out major concert halls and winning the prestigious British rock award, the MERCURY MUSIC PRIZE, for the best album of 2005. But for the thirty-something pop star with the amazing voice and a catalogue of beautifully strange songs, recognition has been a long time coming. His band ANTONY AND THE JOHNSONS made two albums in ten years; even a wonderful, simple song like YOU ARE MY SISTER, which he recorded with BOY GEORGE, took him five years to write, he admits. He's surprisingly modest for someone so charismatically fabulous that he can go by his first name alone, as only a handful of real stars can. Right now, the gentle Englishman in New York is planning a European novelty tour with a stage full of revolving girls. Beyond that, he's just going to wait and see, while he digests his recent tumultuous year. He might even want to tour the North Pole while it's still there.

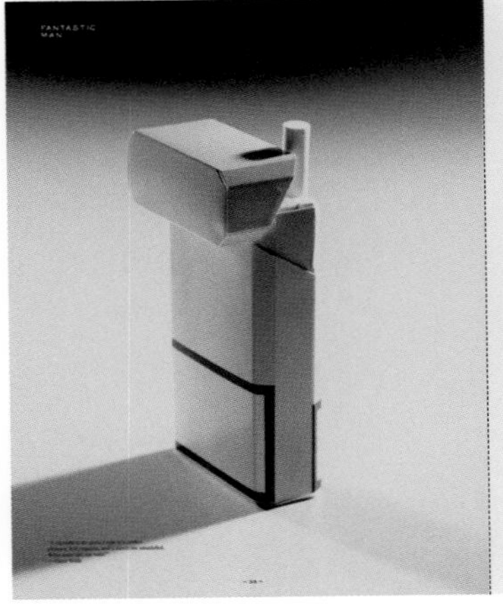
FANTASTIC MAN

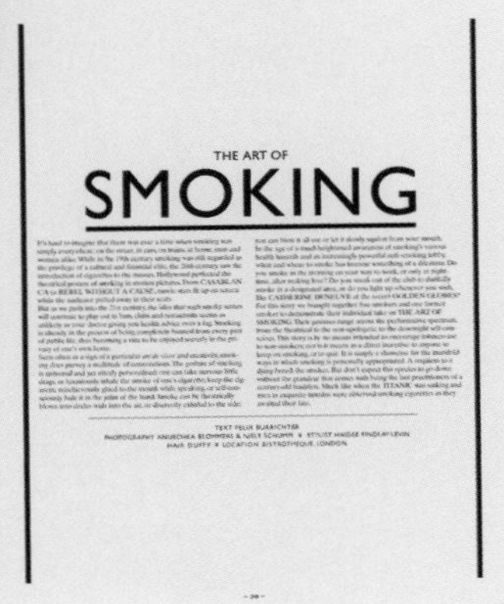
THE ART OF

SMOKING

1. The choice of the title: "50sept" (fifty-seven) in letters and numbers is significant, and represents the combination of two worlds, one mathematical and the other literate. The *page numbers* adopt this principle.
The title at the top of a simple box moves unexpectedly around the front cover, depending on the cover image and because it should never be in the same place as the previous issue.

The large *format magazine* is published by the General Council of the French department of Moselle (this department has the number 57). The graphic designer inserted the name of the department in the strapline of the magazine: "Art, Culture, Moselle et Patrimoine". This demonstrates that the department is an active player in the cultural program.

The journal is conceived as a kind of memory, a space where an image-conscious department shows its commitment to culture. It reports on past projects, about happenings, exhibitions, restorations, historic events, and exceptional personalities from the Moselle region.

The *layout* is deliberately restrained, both in the choice of *typefaces* and in terms of *graphic elements*, but here and there the designer places some characteristic details throughout the *pages* and in different issues that distinguish this publication. The main focus of the *layout* is on the images. The *headlines* set in *uppercase* are deliberately hard-edged, and texts are set in black and gray which emphasizes the *color* images.

The designer plays with the quality and type of each image to create new *compositions* on every page. The *compositions'* balance demonstrates the graphic designer's sensitivity and know-how.

Small differences in *layout* distinguish three types of content: bibliographies, articles, histories. The notes "fall" from the top of the *page* to emphasize their importance, and encouraging the editors to change their otherwise overly academic writing style.

1. *50sept*, magazine
«Art, Culture, Moselle et Patrimoine»
Le Petit Didier

1

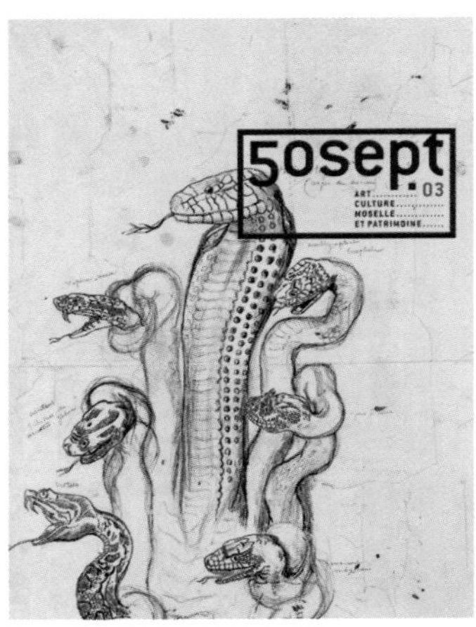

Christian Sell (1831 - 1883),
La Charge
de la brigade Bredow,
1878.

GRAVELOTTE
MUSÉE
DE LA GUERRE DE 1870 :
UN PREMIER PAS

Éric **Necker**

Rénover ou créer un musée obéit à des procédures définies et à une démarche particulière, encadrée par la loi n° 2002-5 du 4 janvier 2002 relative aux musées de France et par ses différents décrets.
La rénovation – il vaudrait mieux parler de re-création ! – de l'ancien petit musée militaire de Gravelotte par le Conseil général de la Moselle est en cours d'étude et la validation du Projet scientifique et culturel du musée par l'assemblée départementale en juin 2003 marque la première étape officielle de ce long processus.
Le Projet scientifique et culturel vise à définir la politique globale du musée en matière de conservation des collections et de diffusion auprès du public. Il précise les différentes orientations et fonctions du musée et définit les moyens nécessaires à leur mise en œuvre.
Dans le cas du projet de Gravelotte, cette étude insiste évidemment sur le concept du musée et sur le cadre thématique et historique de l'exposition permanente.
Quelques points importants sont à souligner pour bien comprendre ce que sera le futur musée.
Il s'agit tout d'abord de réaliser un musée d'histoire et non pas un « musée militaire », la simple présentation de collections militaires ne pouvant suffire. Il apparaît comme indispensable de donner une vision historique globale de la guerre de 1870 et de ses conséquences pour le département de la Moselle, mais aussi de la situer dans le cadre des relations internationales de cette époque. Le cadre thématique du musée s'élargit donc. Le musée doit présenter et faire comprendre :

— les causes de la guerre de 1870 ;
— la guerre de 1870 et plus particulièrement autour de Metz (siège de Metz compris) ;
— les conséquences immédiates, le traité de Francfort ;
— les deux mémoires de la guerre, française et allemande (fêtes du souvenir, commémorations, champs de bataille et monuments, etc.) ;
— la nouvelle frontière et ses conséquences politiques (l'histoire et la notion de frontière dans la région, la création du Reichsland Elsass-Lothringen) et militaires (l'organisation militaire, les fortifications, etc.).

Il faut aussi évoquer un aspect original du projet. La définition du cadre thématique et historique qui vient d'être esquissée ne peut se contenter d'une vision purement française. La guerre fut fondatrice d'une Allemagne politiquement unie et la Moselle, avec l'Alsace, partagea son destin de 1870 à 1918. Il est donc nécessaire de présenter cette histoire mêlée qui reste une partie de l'identité mosellane.
L'objet ne prend de sens que mis dans un contexte, affirmait un muséologue. Même si les collections restent les principaux acteurs du musée, elles ne se suffisent pas à elles-mêmes, elles ont besoin de médias.
L'utilisation de nombreuses techniques paraît donc plus que nécessaire dans un musée d'histoire comme celui de Gravelotte. Si l'on songe naturellement aux techniques audiovisuelles et informatiques, offrant aujourd'hui de larges possibilités, il faut aussi penser aux décors, à l'effet scénographique, à l'architecture même de l'exposition. Ce futur musée de Gravelotte ne se veut donc pas un conservatoire d'objets, il veut expliquer, démontrer, sensibiliser. L'objet ne sera pas seulement présenté à l'admiration de tous, mais il sera aussi témoin et vecteur d'un savoir, d'un événement. Voilà toute l'ambition du futur musée !

La Conservation départementale des Musées et de l'Inventaire (03 87 37 59 66) recherche tous objets ayant trait à la période 1870-1914 en Moselle : affiches, livres et matériels scolaires, souvenirs, témoignages, objets de la vie quotidienne militaire, photographies, journaux, objets en rapport avec le siège de Metz, etc.

50trois

AFRICA IS IN MY MIND, DE L'AVENTURE À LA CULTURE AFRI—CAINE

Des statues monumentales d'Ousmane Sow aux collections privées de Reinhard Klimmt, nul doute que le Conseil général de la Moselle a rendu, durant l'année 2004, un bel hommage à un vaste continent et à son patrimoine artistique : l'Afrique. Africa is in my mind, ce credo affirmé est la traduction d'une passion et d'un amour, ceux de Reinhard Klimmt ancien ministre-président du Land de Sarre et ministre fédéral d'Allemagne, non seulement pour l'art africain traditionnel, mais aussi pour ces artistes anonymes originaires du Mali, du Bénin, du Burkina Faso, du Nigeria, des rives du Niger, de la Volta, du Bénoué, de l'Ogowe ou du Kasaï.

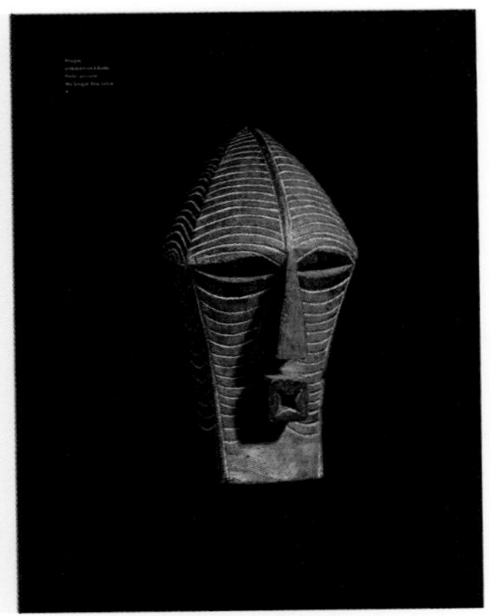

ÉMILE FRIANT ET LA PEINTURE

Émile Friant, auquel le musée départemental Georges de La Tour de Vic-sur-Seille rend hommage[1], est né à Dieuze le 16 avril 1863. Il est le fils unique de Pierre Félix Virgile, chef d'atelier à la maréchalerie de la saline et de Marie Catherine Tortetin, employée chez les Parisot, pharmaciens de la cité. Ces derniers, restés sans enfants, prennent le petit Émile en affection et se lient d'amitié avec les parents. Les deux couples quittent Dieuze après le désastre de 1870 pour s'installer à Nancy en 1872. Émile fréquente l'école Loritz. À l'enseignement général, auquel il ne porte guère d'intérêt, il préfère les cours de dessin dispensés par deux disciples de Charles Sellier : Jules Larcher, élève de Léon Bonnat et Ernest Charbonnier, élève d'Alexandre Cabanel.

LE MÉMORIAL DE L'ALSACE—MOSELLE

Ouvert le 18 juin 2005 et inauguré par Jacques Chirac, Président de la République, le 3 novembre de la même année, le Mémorial de l'Alsace-Moselle, perché sur une colline vosgienne à Schirmeck, dans le Bas-Rhin, présente, au travers d'une scénographie et d'une muséographie résolument novatrices, l'histoire de l'Alsace et de la Moselle de 1870 à nos jours.

1. Printed on a rotary press, this *newspaper* plays with the principle of economy: two-*color* printing, thin paper, and austere design due to the black and white images and choice of *typefaces*.

The *layout* is deliberately simple: a solid block of type – set in two *columns*, *uppercase headlines*, etc. The efficient graphic rules nevertheless leave room for the playful placement of images. The cover of each issue shows a symbol, repeated as a pattern on the inside *pages*, in the *color* of that particular issue.

The *typefaces* used – Brothers by John Downer, Fairplex Narrow and Hypnopaedia by Zuzana Licko – give the *composition* a strong personality. The reader feels a certain modernity in a design that at first seems classic.
The angular or broken character of the *typeface* Brothers reflects the name of the *magazine*: Crac.
Like the *typeface* Fairplex, it is well adapted to the *rotary printing* process, which is rather low quality printing.
The individual *glyphs* of the *typeface* Hypnopaedia are made up of letters from different *fonts* published by Emigre (www.emigre.com).

1. *Crac*, newspaper
Trafik + In medias res

1

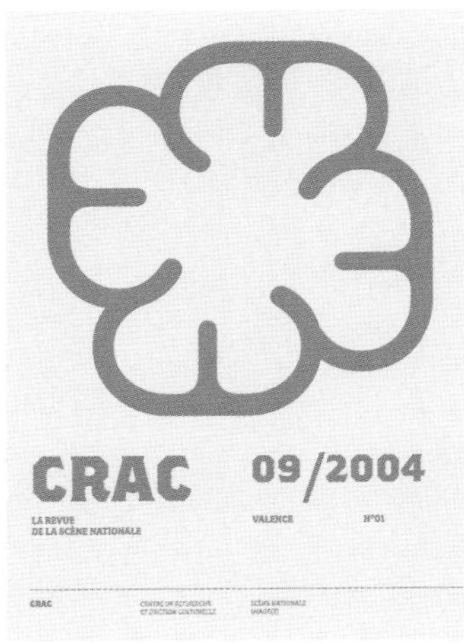

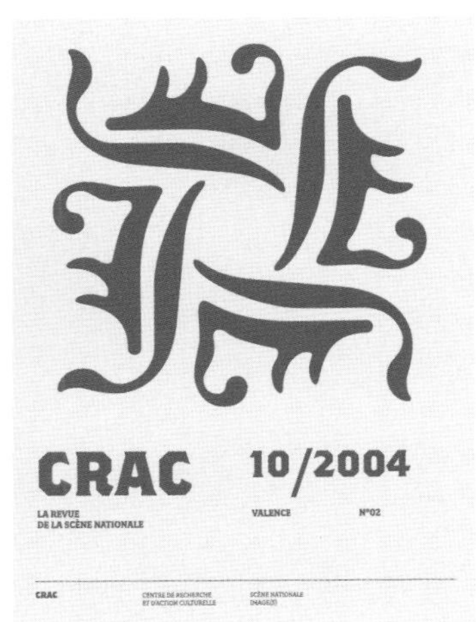

8
CINÉMA

1 – Eleni, la terre qui pleure
2 – Goodbye, Dragon Inn

Mélancolie
GOODBYE, DRAGON INN
Tsai Ming-liang avait tourné des scènes de *Et là-bas, quelle heure est-il ?* dans un vieux cinéma qui devait fermer ses portes trois mois plus tard. En hommage à cette salle et aux cinémas disparus de son enfance, il a réalisé cet émouvant témoignage chargé de souvenirs, réflexion mélancolique sur la mémoire et la solitude.
Un jeune homme d'origine japonaise entre à l'intérieur d'un cinéma pour se protéger de la pluie. C'est la dernière séance, la dernière projection avant que cette vieille salle de Taipei ne ferme ses portes à tout jamais. Sur l'écran est projeté *Dragon Inn*, film de sabre à succès des années soixante. Dans la salle, deux individus ressemblent aux acteurs du film. Uniques spectateurs, ils regardent et se souviennent…
« Lieu d'ébats furtifs, refuge des perdants, des vieux et des fantômes, cet endroit se transforme sous l'œil de Tsai Ming-liang en tombeau poignant, en théâtre du vide existentiel, de la vie projetée, effleurée, jamais empoignée. C'est d'une tristesse infinie, souvent très belle, le cinéaste magnifiant chaque recoin décrépit de ce vaste dédale et orchestrant des correspondances lumineuses entre le film à l'écran et le chassé-croisé dans la salle. »
Louis Guichard et Jacques Morice (Télérama, 2003)

Réalisation : Tsai Ming-liang
Interprètes : Lee Kang-sheng, Chen Shiang-chyi, Mitamura Kiyonobu, Miao Tien.
Durée : 1 h 23
Titre original : Bu san
Pays, version : Taiwan, VOST.
Année de sortie : 2004

Du 1er au 14 septembre 2004

Histoire grecque
ELENI, LA TERRE QUI PLEURE
Théo Angelopoulos est le plus grand ambassadeur du cinéma grec à l'étranger. Son dernier film, premier volet d'une trilogie, fait écho à l'ensemble de son œuvre. L'occasion d'en saisir l'essence et d'en arpenter les contours.
Enfant, adolescente, épouse, mère et femme isolée, Eleni va affronter la mort, l'exil, mais aussi l'amour et la passion tragique. De l'entrée de l'Armée rouge à Odessa en 1919 à la guerre civile en 1949, le film suit le destin des réfugiés tel qu'il a été décrit par les gens qui ont « vécu les peines et les épreuves de l'hellénisme et l'histoire du xxe siècle ». Pour l'auteur de cette trilogie où il est question « d'exil, de séparation, d'errance, de la fin des idéologies et des épreuves constantes de l'histoire », Eleni s'inspire de la mythologie grecque. On retrouve « des traces d'*Œdipe roi* et des *Sept contre Thèbes* dans le récit de cette histoire d'amour et le destin de cette femme ».
« Angelopoulos ne s'intéresse au passé que dans la mesure où il annonce et reflète le présent. Conflits sanglants, luttes fratricides, populations déplacées, récits d'exil et de mort : le cinéaste, une fois de plus poète et philosophe, chante et évoque, à travers la destinée d'une femme marquée par les disparitions et les dévastations, les illusions perdues d'un monde qui était né il y a cent ans avec l'espoir et ne suscite plus aujourd'hui qu'un cri de révolte et des pleurs face à la fin de l'utopie. »
Michel Ciment, critique de la revue Positif (2004).

Réalisation : Théo Angelopoulos
Interprètes : Ewa Kotamanidou, Wassilis Kolowós.
Durée : 2 h 50
Titre original : Eleni
Pays, version : Grèce, VOST.
Année de sortie : 2004

Du 15 au 28 septembre 2004

9

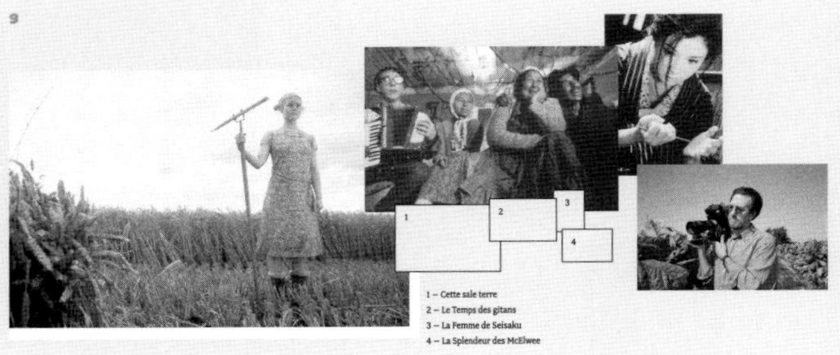

1 – Cette sale terre
2 – Le Temps des gitans
3 – La Femme de Seisaku
4 – La Splendeur des McElwee

Fabuleux Kusturica
LE TEMPS DES GITANS
Perhan, fils bâtard d'un soldat slovène et d'une Tzigane, vit dans un taudis avec sa grand-mère. Il est prêt à tout pour épouser son amour d'enfance, la jeune Azra, et faire soigner sa sœur infirme, même à partir en Italie avec Ahmed Dzida, truand notoire qui achète et revend de jeunes enfants…
« La force qui s'en dégage est celle de la poésie mêlée au surnaturel, quelque chose de tellurique, de primitif, qui naît de la rencontre entre ces personnages et les éléments qui les entourent. »
Serge Toubiana (Les Cahiers du cinéma, 1989)

Réalisation : Emir Kusturica
Musique : Goran Bregovic
Interprètes : Davor Dujmovic, Bora Todorovic, Ljubica Adzovic, Husnija Hasimovic.
Durée : 2 h 22
Titre original : Dom za vesanje
Pays, version : Yougoslavie, VOST.
Année de sortie : 1988

Du 1er au 14 septembre 2004

Documentaire enfumé
LA SPLENDEUR DES MCELWEE
Ross McElwee s'installe en Caroline du Nord, sur les traces de son histoire familiale. Il découvre qu'un célèbre film hollywoodien raconte celle de son aïeul, riche propriétaire de plantations de tabac ruiné par un concurrent trop habile…
« En tentant de démêler la réalité de la fable, le cinéaste multiplie les rencontres de sa famille autour du film, et explore le rôle de l'industrie du tabac dans son État. […] Entre humour et autodérision, il dévoile l'importance de la cigarette en tant que mode de vie mais également comme moteur économique de la Caroline du Nord. »
Michaël Mélinard (L'Humanité, 2004)

Réalisation : Ross McElwee
Durée : 1 h 47
Titre original : Bright leaves
Pays, version : États-Unis, VOST.
Année de sortie : 2003

Du 15 au 21 septembre 2004

Loufoquerie paysanne
CETTE SALE TERRE
La vie de Kath et de Francine, deux sœurs agricultrices, est troublée par deux hommes : Buto, villageois rustre qui convoite leurs terres, demande Kath en mariage ; Lek, bel étranger, veut offrir à Francine une vie meilleure. Cruauté, rivalité et superstition dans une communauté rurale.
« Kötting et Lock lancent un défi qu'on aimerait bien voir relever par le cinéma britannique. Sa hardiesse, ses qualités qui font penser à une installation artistique, en font une œuvre dont la sauvage brutalité est sans égale parmi les films britanniques de l'année. »
(The Independent, 2001)

Réalisation : Andrew Kötting, d'après La Terre d'Émile Zola.
Interprètes : Shane Attwooll, Rebecca R.Palmer, Demelza Randall.
Durée : 1 h 51
Titre original : This filthy earth
Pays, version : Grande-Bretagne, VOST.
Année de sortie : 2001

Du 29 septembre au 5 octobre 2004

Odyssée tragique
LA FEMME DE SEISAKU
Pour échapper à sa condition misérable, Okane devient la concubine d'un vieillard et subit les railleries de son village. Mais elle est réhabilitée par les attentions inattendues de Seisaku, un jeune soldat de retour du front. Okane épouse Seisaku et refuse de le laisser repartir à la guerre… La révélation d'un cinéaste injustement méconnu, qui fut assistant metteur en scène de réalisateurs prestigieux comme Mizoguchi et Ichikawa.
« Aucune forme sociale n'est épargnée. […] Masumura défend un individualisme forcené, qui ne pense l'accomplissement de l'homme que dans la réalisation violente de ses désirs. »
Stéphane Delorme (Les Cahiers du cinéma, octobre 2000)

Réalisation : Yasuzo Masumura, d'après le roman de Genjiro Yoshida.
Interprètes : Ayako Wakao, Takahiro Tamura, Yuzo Hayakawa, Mikio Narita.
Durée : 1 h 33
Titre original : Seisaku no tsuma
Pays, version : Japon, VOST.
Année de sortie : 1965

Du 29 septembre au 5 octobre 2004

ÉDITO

LE CRAC ET MOI

CRAC SOMMAIRE DU 1ER AOÛT AU 5 OCT. 2004

ACTUALITÉS PAGES 4/5

EXPOSITION PAGE 6

CINÉMA PAGES 7/9

PROGRAMMATION GÉNÉRALE PAGES 8/9

PROGRAMMATION THÉMATIQUE PAGES 10/11

AGENDA PAGE 12/13

CINÉMA DES ENFANTS PAGE 14

ÉVÉNEMENT PAGE 15

INFORMATIONS PRATIQUES PAGE 16

ACTUALITÉ

HISTOIRES DE CINÉMA D'ANIMATION

MARDI 5 OCTOBRE 2004 À 20 H 30

INTERVIEW

VOS RENDEZ-VOUS DE LA SAISON

LES 24 HEURES DE LA TÉLÉ

VOYAGE AU FIL DE LA VOLGA

DU 15 AU 29 SEPTEMBRE EN COLLABORATION AVEC LE FESTIVAL EST-OUEST DE DIE

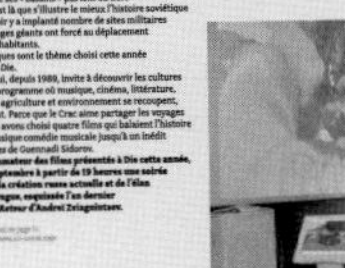

EXPOSITION

FAMILLES D'AGRICULTEURS

PHOTOGRAPHIES DE SYLVIE FRIESS

DU 22 SEPTEMBRE AU 17 NOVEMBRE 2004

LA SUITE

BIOGRAPHIE

INTERVIEW

UNE CERTAINE IDÉE DU CINÉMA

CINÉMA DU 1ER AOÛT AU 5 OCT. 2004

BOLLYWOOD D'HIER À AUJOURD'HUI

MOTHER INDIA

LA FAMILLE INDIENNE

VOYAGE AU FIL DE LA VOLGA

DU 22 AU 28 SEPTEMBRE 2004

AGENDA

AOÛT

SEPTEMBRE

OCTOBRE

JEUNE PUBLIC

VOYAGE INITIATIQUE,

LE CHIEN, LE GÉNÉRAL ET LES OISEAUX

LAPUTA, LE CHÂTEAU DANS LE CIEL

OSEAM, LE TEMPLE

LE LION À LA BARBE BLANCHE

LE DIRIGEABLE VOLÉ

ÉVÉNEMENT

DES FILMS DES ANNÉES 30 TOUJOURS CONTEMPORAINS

HISTOIRES DE CINÉMA D'ANIMATION

MARDI 5 OCTOBRE 2004 À 20 H 30

Periodicals

Viewing and reading time

A publication, whatever it may be (*pocket edition*, art *book*, *periodical*, exhibition catalogue, etc.) is more than a simple series of *pages*. It is a whole, with a beginning, an end and an evolution. As with a movie, one always has to consider the viewing time. *Books*, *magazines*, and *newspapers* can be flipped through (for a quick overview), scanned (looking for information) or read entirely.
The designer has to consider all possibilities.
Like a play, the different parts should be clearly recognizable and memorable to make the contents understandable.

The so-called *content plan* or *flatplan*, a reduced reproduction of double *pages* next to each other, offers an overview of this evolution. It is also an essential tool for evaluating the progress of a *book* or *periodical* (*layout*, ongoing placement of diverse elements, proofreading, corrections).

While the designer respects the publication's *layout*, the *content plan* gives the printed piece weaker or stronger *rhythm*. Each double-*page* spread is seen in relation to the one before and the one after it. He either focuses on the single *page* or takes advantage of the potential that the double *page* offers.

Continuity, break, pause ... the designer shapes the sequence of the *pages* so that the structure of the *book* or *magazine* is visible.

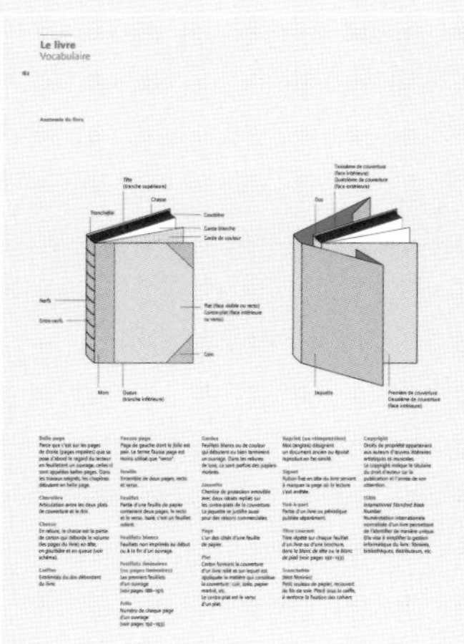

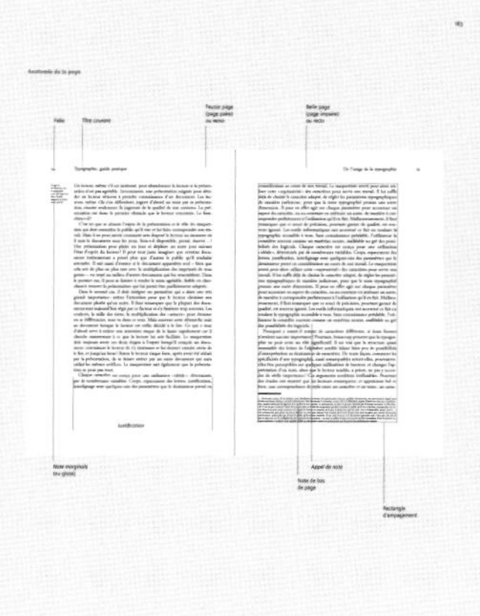

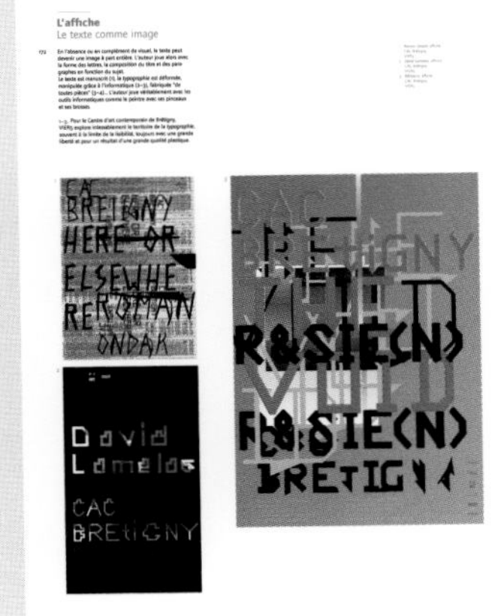

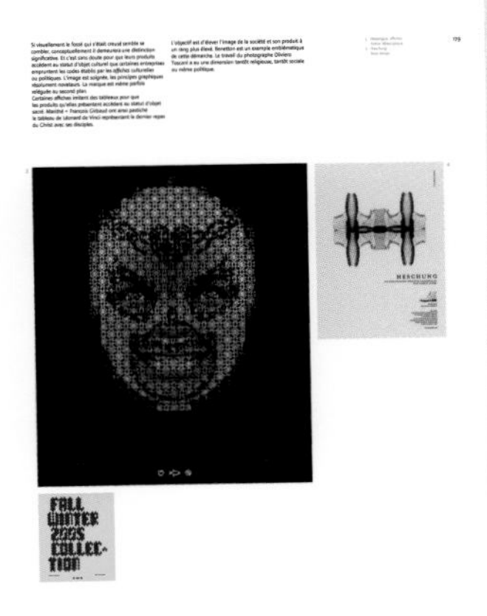

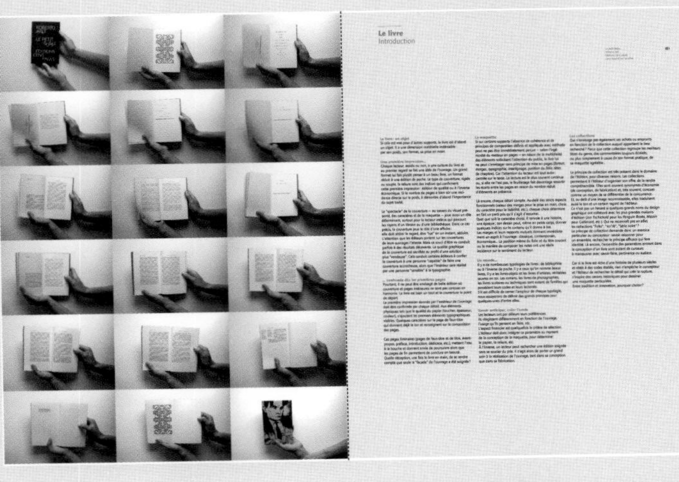

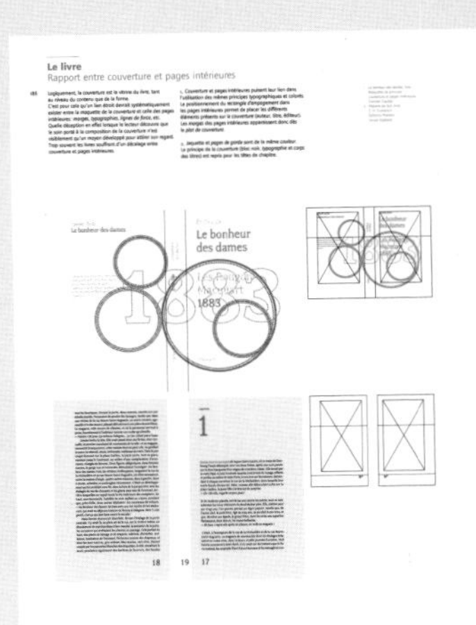

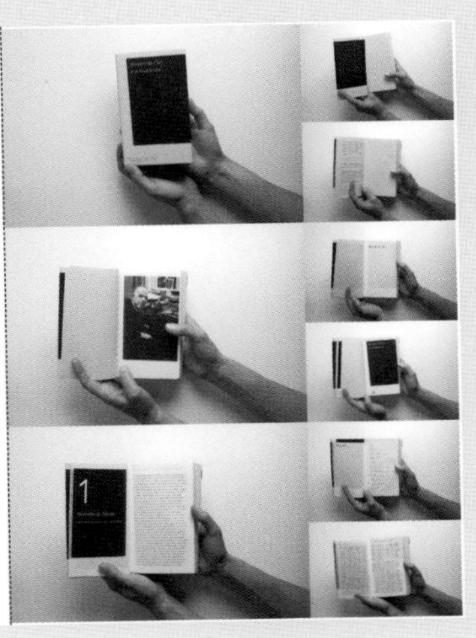

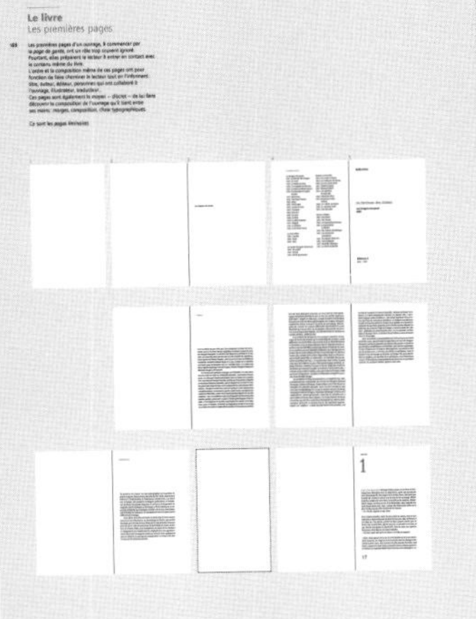

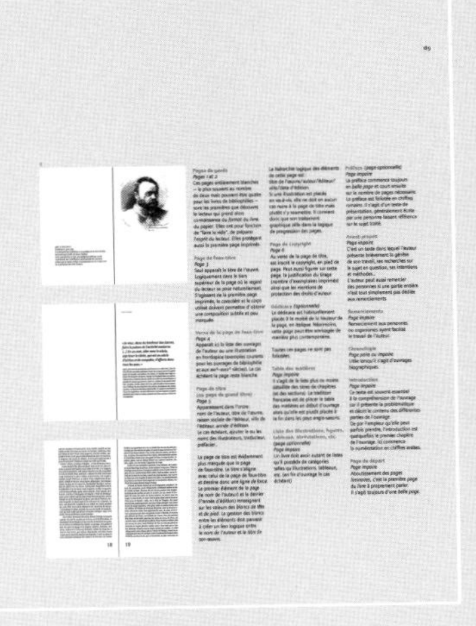

Promotional materials
Introduction

Promotional materials represent an important part of printed matter. Their functions – presentation, information, sales – lead printed advertising to often borrow a *poster*'s codes: to attract attention (because a promotional document is often in a competitive context), and convince quickly. If a promotion is to be read, it needs to be seen first. Most of the time it encounters dismissive readers, and has to somehow impose itself on the target audience. Its functions are: to present an offer, to demonstrate the virtues of a product, praise a company's services, to strengthen the company's image.

The promotion shouldn't be limited to direct mail. It can have many forms that sometimes no longer resemble an advertisement.
Promotional material may assume many forms: postcard, *leaflet*, *flyer*, brochure, catalogue, etc. Its *format* depends on the content, but is designed to fit a mailbox or the pocket. Most of the time before planning the form the production costs need to be assessed. If distributed in large numbers, the unit price is decisive. All design decisions have their effect (*format*, number of *colors*, paper quality, etc.). Weight and *format* will also influence the distribution costs.

A simple *flyer* is quickly read. It should be clear, straightforward and memorable, because it is often abandoned or thrown away. It can also be designed so that one wants to pick it up and to keep it, and even contact the sender to learn more.

Given the immense flood of printed matter, the designer has to find a way of attracting the target audience's attention.
It is naive to think that it is enough to write bigger than the others, to use fake arguments, to surprise with a shocking image to reach the goal. These ideas are tired. The design has to be more creative, especially since the public wants to be taken more seriously, and is no longer seduced by claims of "at cost!", "double your money back!" or "price shock!"

Instead of a noisy promotion, the best way to win the public's interest is to get them involved. The text should leave room for interpretation, instead of pushing the product's qualities. Another means is the *folding* brochure or *flyer*. The front can be designed to show only part of the content, which entices the reader to pick it up and unfold it. Another way of approaching the audience is to surprise them with an unusual form or content. A small document might become a *poster* when unfolded. It might suggest one type of information, yet reveal quite another upon closer examination. One document may hide another, etc.

Promotional materials can also be more elegant. They can also present a concert series or the cultural event program as a luxury product. In this case costs are secondary.
It is all about seducing, reflecting the spirit of the event or of the product, and to fit to a specific audience, to arouse their desire.

To try and present promotional materials in all their diversity would be futile. Nonetheless, here are a few points to contemplate.

Promotional materials
The series principle

A promotional document is often part of a set of other communication media. It can be part of a series of documents, each of which complements the other's content. The principle of the series can be based on a uniform *format*, graphic and typographic codes, identical or complementary *color* palette or a similar organization of information.
The potential reader notices these similarities, and even if he decides not to read the promotion in question, he will have memorized – even unconsciously – the producer's identity. The brand or company is then in an excellent position for a second meeting.

If someone reads the promotion and likes the content, he or she will be very open to the rest of the documents in the series. However, if they are disappointed by the content, it is difficult to regain their confidence.

1. Folded *posters*
A series of five *folding posters* where the number of *pages* depends on the amount of information. The graphic illustration connects all five, and is only recognizable as a whole at the end of the year.

1. Grame, 2004/2005 season, folded poster
Trafik

1

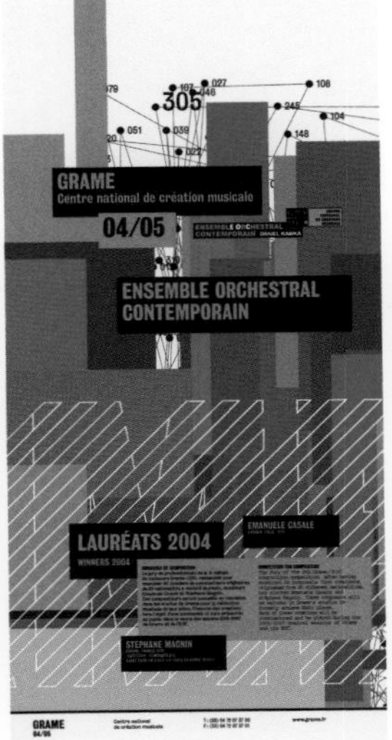

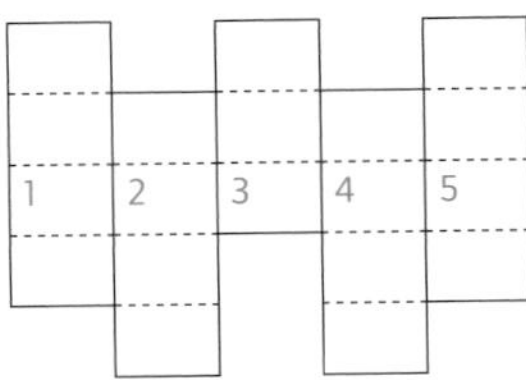

1. This series of brochures is linked by a common *format* and the repeated *composition* (only the *color* and symbol change) on all *covers*. The *page layout* remains constant, and the paper stays the same.
Format 135 × 210 mm, 32 pages, two-color printing, saddle stitched (two staples)

2. These brochures are more differentiated, however, having the same *format* and identical *binding* makes them a cohesive set. They are similar to the previous series issued by the same publisher.
Format 135 × 210 mm, 64 *pages*, two-color or four-color printing, saddle stitched (two staples)

3. All type specimen catalogues have the same *format*, but depending on the *typeface* shown, are designed differently.
Format 215 × 277 mm, 16 *pages*, three-color or four-color printing, saddle stitched (two staples)

1. *The Emigre fonts library*, brochures Emigre
2. ibid.
3. ibid.

1

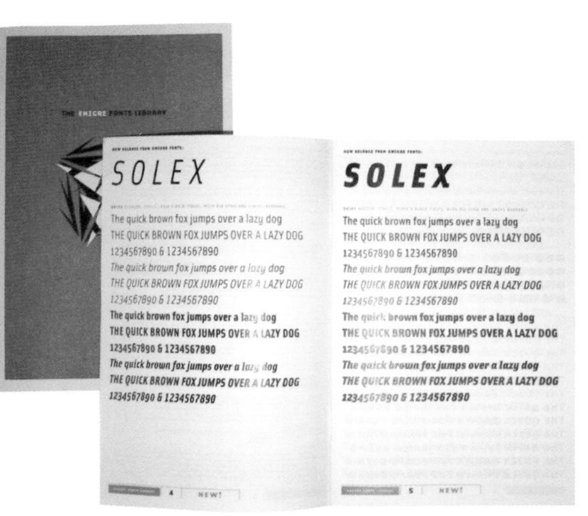

2

3

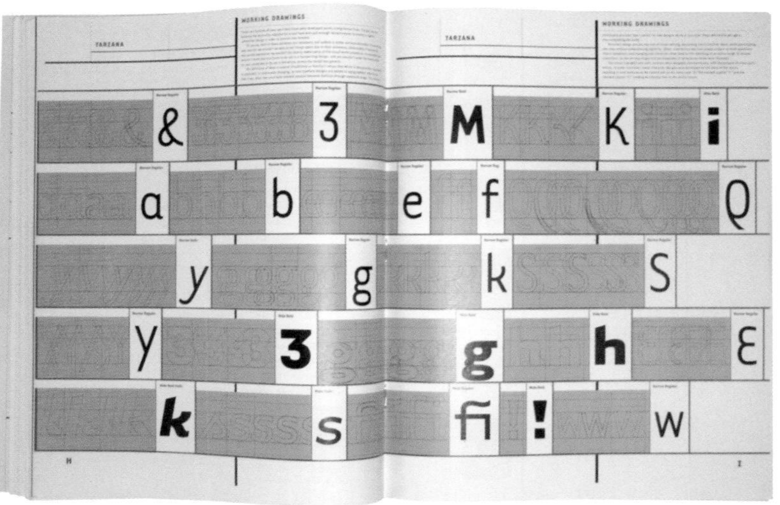

Promotional materials
What kind?

Not only can the *format* change, the form of the promotion itself can also change. Without a doubt, promotions give designers a great deal of freedom.
A priori anything is imaginable, it just has to fit together. Choices may be determined by purely financial criteria, and this economic aspect influences *format*, paper quality and printing.

Next to the economic considerations the practical or functional aspects influence or dictate the design.
For example, the weight of a promotion sent by mail is a definitive criterion. The designer will work on perfecting the relationship between content, *format*, and number of *pages* within a range of inexpensive postage rates.

But a promotion's form can also be exclusively driven by aesthetic or conceptual criteria. These are more difficult to quantify or measure, since it is a matter of using the form to transmit a specific meaning.

The form of the promotion can be decided in isolation or as part of a series. Within the series each piece can also be distinguished from each other by its form.

4. Cards that promote the *typefaces* designed by Wim Crouwel
Format 150 × 210 mm, printing *recto* two color/*verso* one color, black

5. Large *format* type specimen booklet
Format 297 × 420 mm, 8 folded *sheets*, two-color printing

6. Brochure
Format 210 × 297 mm, 16 *pages*, saddle stitched, three-color printing

7. Postcard series, each card presents a typeface
Format 100 × 150 mm, two-color printing

4. Cards (front and back)
FoundryTypes
The Foundry
5. *Ambroise, spécimen d'un nouveau Didot*
Porchez TypoFonderie
6. *Spécimen de caractères et vignettes typographiques*
Porchez TypoFonderie
7. Postcards
Porchez TypoFonderie

4

5

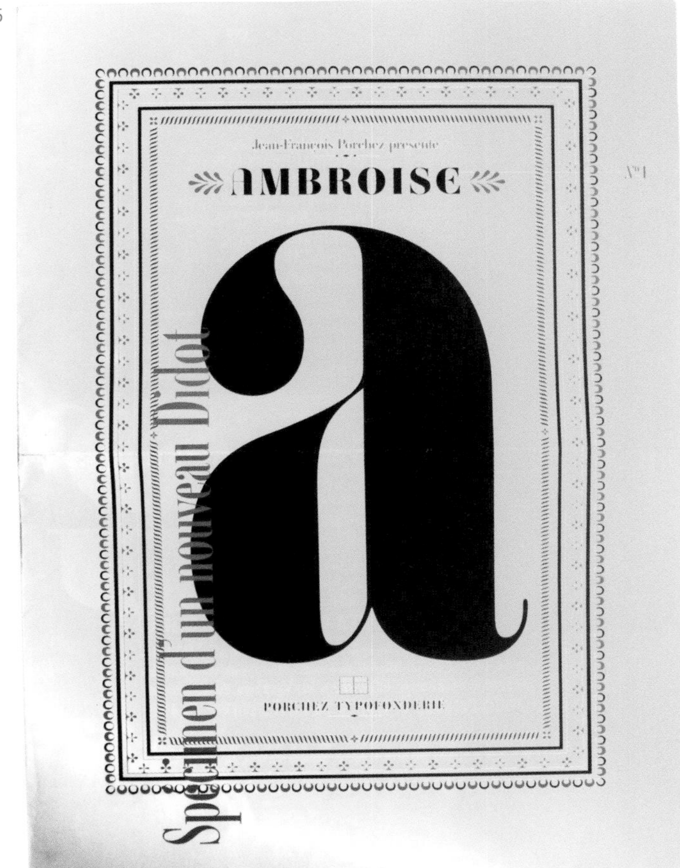

6

7

When designing promotional materials the designer can also be inspired by other media and their particular advantages. He borrows the *graphic elements* to reach his target audience, and to give the piece status that its commercial side lacks. Promotions sometimes appear as *books*, journals, *magazines*, or *newspapers*.

1. The type catalogues issued by Jonathan Hoefler's and Tobias Frere-Jone's type foundry are more like journals in terms of *format* and paper and the cover design. They have many *pages* allowing the *typefaces* to be presented generously.

2. The booklet announcing the "birth" of the *typeface* DTL Paradox designed by Gerard Unger not only presents the typeface, describes its advantages, and its development process. The small *format*, the thread sealing, and the *dust jacket* all make it a real *book*.

3. The Le Monde promotional type specimen that Jean-François Porchez designed for the *newspaper* of the same name adopts its *format* and *layout*.

1. Catalogues Hoefler & Frere-Jones
2. *DTL Paradox*, brochure Gerard Unger
3. *Le Monde*, type specimen Jean-François Porchez

1

2

3

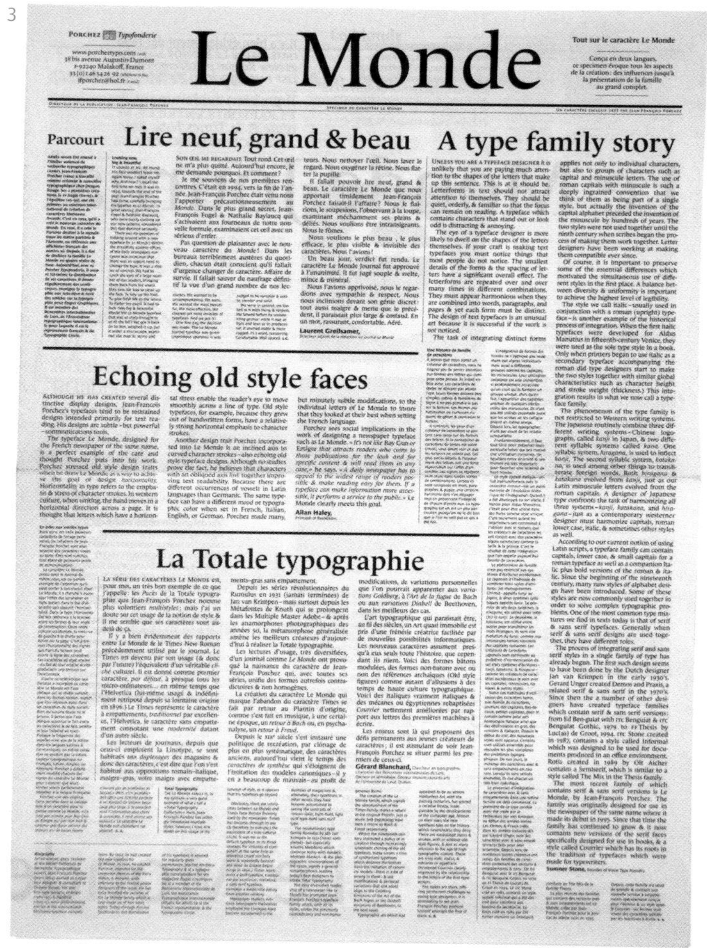

Porchez Typofonderie

Le Monde

Tout sur le caractère Le Monde

Parcourt

Lire neuf, grand & beau

A type family story

Echoing old style faces

La Totale typographie

4–5. The ITC type foundry used to publish a *magazine* that was eagerly awaited by designers. Its *format*, quality (form and content) gave ITC access to the most prestigious agencies, free at first, and then by subscription!
The last issues were smaller before they finally were replaced by the website. Economic reality and media evolution overthrew this unusual venture.

4. *U&LC*, magazine
5. *U&LC*, magazine

4

5

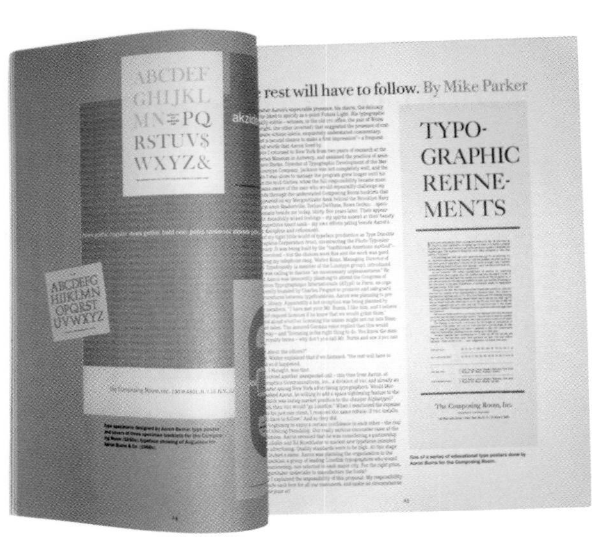

Promotional materials
Advise, inform, organize ...

Every promotional piece, from a simple *leaflet*, brochure to a catalogue aims to present a product or service with the following three goals:

· to inform that the product or service exists
· to provide information on its qualities and characteristics
· to encourage a speedy purchase

The choice of elements (texts, images) and their arrangement is vital to achieve these goals. Capturing the reader's attention in the brief moment devoted to the promotion is crucial. He needs to understand that the contents are intended for him and that he should be interested. Once the reading begins, the piece needs to hold his attention and provide all information needed to understand it.

At this stage the reader isn't fully convinced by what he is reading. That he could stop at any time is an ever-present danger. The chosen elements and their arrangement are therefore very important. Their *hierarchy* has to be studied closely so that the reader, regardless of how long he reads, remembers the essentials.

The means to achieve this are numerous, and range from all kinds of current graphics (to capture attention at all costs) to the greatest restraint (for the objective presentation of the facts).

The designer's choice out of this range of possibilities is based on the product itself, the target clientele, and the context of the product and the context of the promotion.

1. The sober *composition* emphasizes the technical character of the products presented and the company's no-nonsense image.

2. The purely technical and practical information is combined with evocative images. The promotion is not just informative; it also appeals to the reader's senses.

1. *Elan*, catalogue
   Area 17
2. *Marius Aurenti*, poster with color swatch palette
   Damien Gautier

1

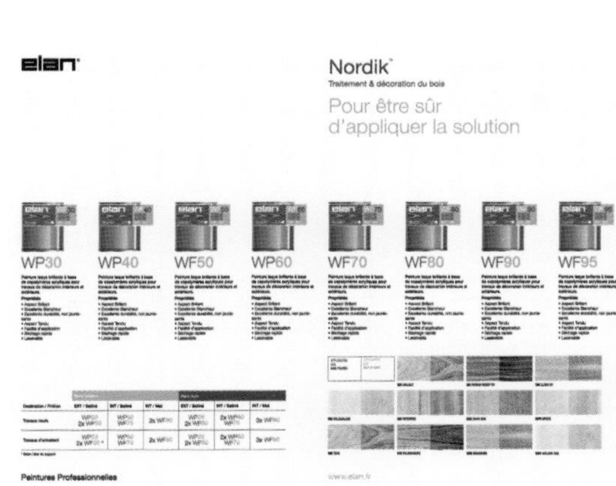

2

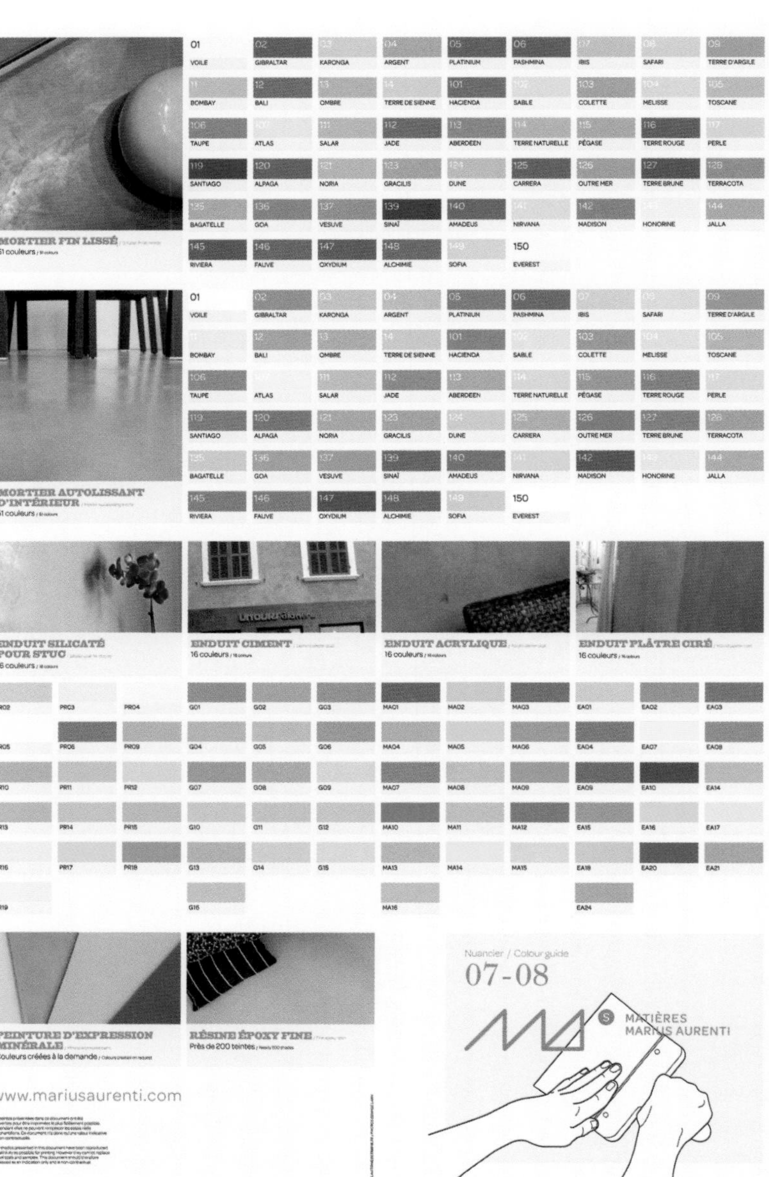

3. This brochure, which presents a collection of clothing and accessories, seems to give the narrative sequences lots of space and importance. This is how the reader learns about, studies and evaluates the products. The *miniature* images are purely informative.

3. Camps, brochure
Trafik

3

CAMPS
CRANTE / CHAUSSURES
DESSUS REMBOURRÉ
PATTES AUTO-AGRIPPANTES
MOUSSE EVA
MALIDA / MAILLOT DE BAIN
80% POLYAMIDE
20% ELASTHANE
EXISTE EN 1 ET 2 PIÈCES
VANNES / SHORT
100% COTON
TRUNKS / SHORT
100% POLYAMIDE
EAGLE / BOB RÉVERSIBLE
100% COTON
DUNCAN / MONTRE CHRONO
FONCTION VIBREUR
ÉTANCHE 10M
CAMPS

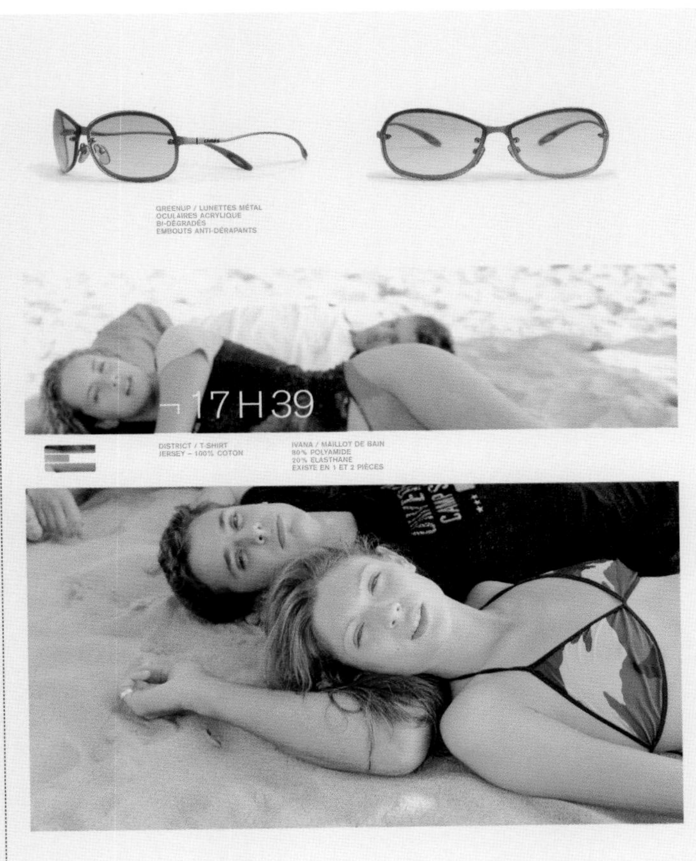

GREENUP / LUNETTES MÉTAL
OCULAIRES ACRYLIQUE
BI-DÉGRADÉS
EMBOUTS ANTI-DÉRAPANTS
17H39
DISTRICT / T-SHIRT
JERSEY – 100% COTON
IVANA / MAILLOT DE BAIN
80% POLYAMIDE
20% ELASTHANE
EXISTE EN 1 ET 2 PIÈCES

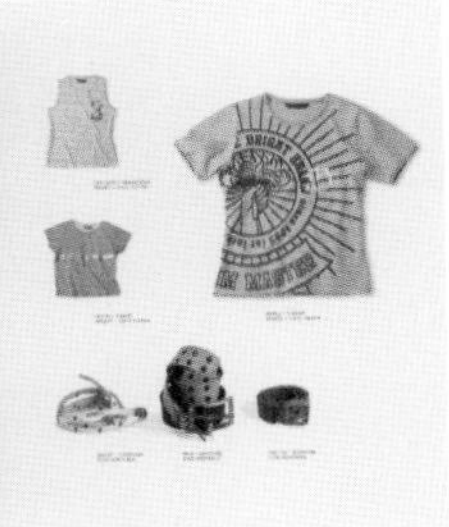

Finishing
Vocabulary

Although this is the last stage in production, *finishing* must be considered during the project planning stage to avoid unexpected additional costs. Some types of paper are better for *finishing* than others, and *page impositioning* depends on the subsequent type of processing.

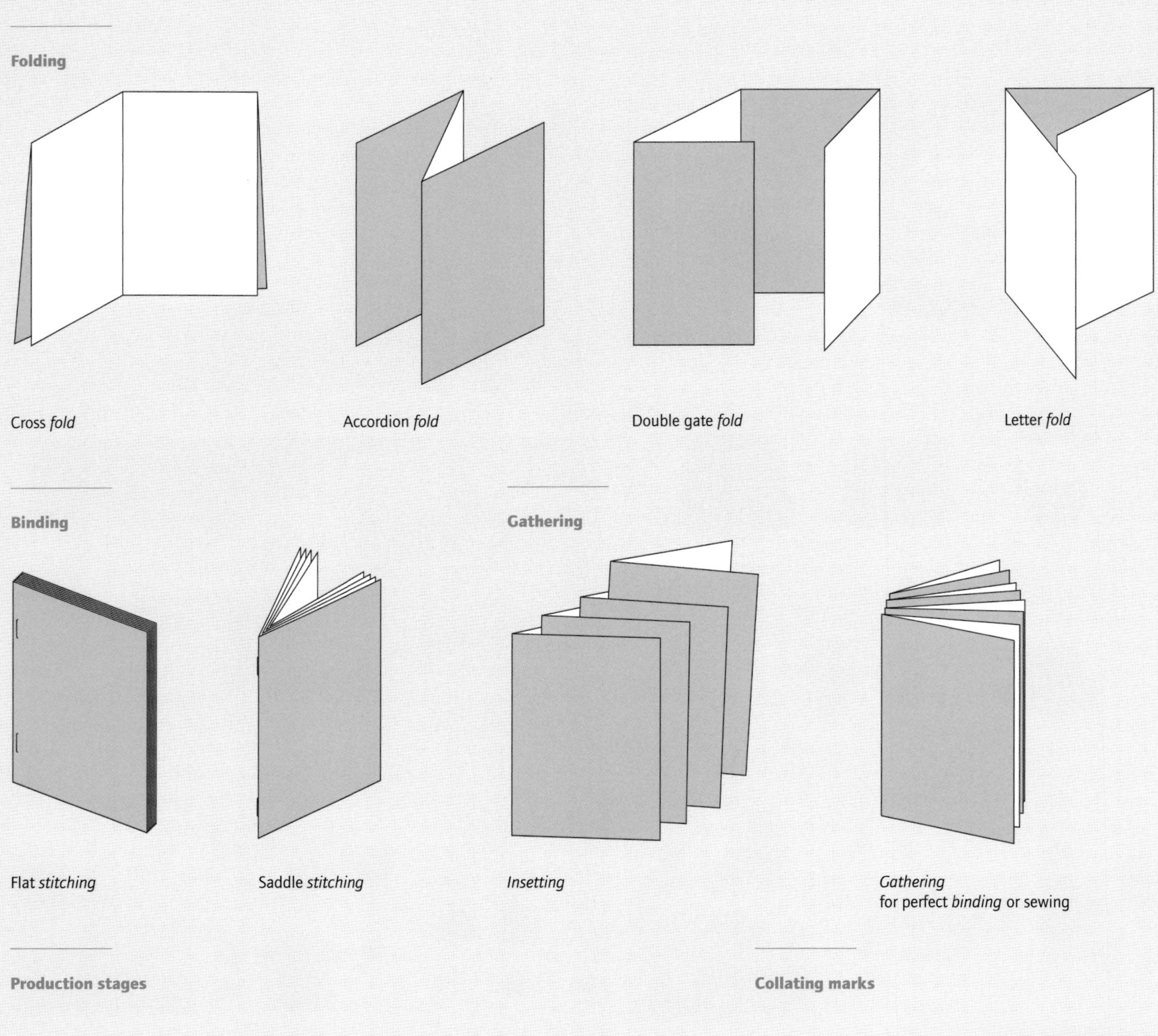

Folding

Cross *fold*

Accordion *fold*

Double gate *fold*

Letter *fold*

Binding

Flat *stitching*

Saddle *stitching*

Gathering

Insetting

Gathering
for perfect *binding* or sewing

Production stages

Gathering

Stapling
and *stitching*

Trimming

Collating marks

These marks are placed during *impositioning*. They help when *gathering* to check if the *signatures* are all there and in the right order.

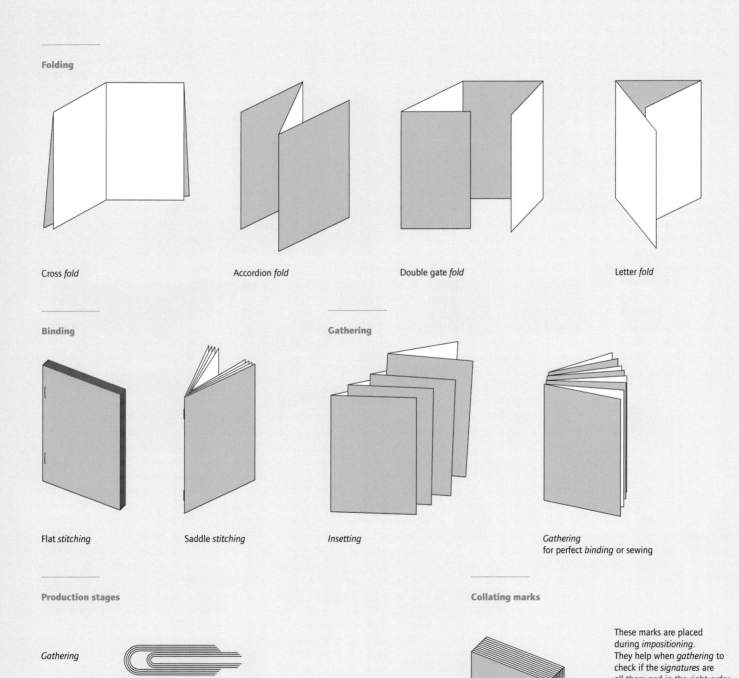

Impositioning

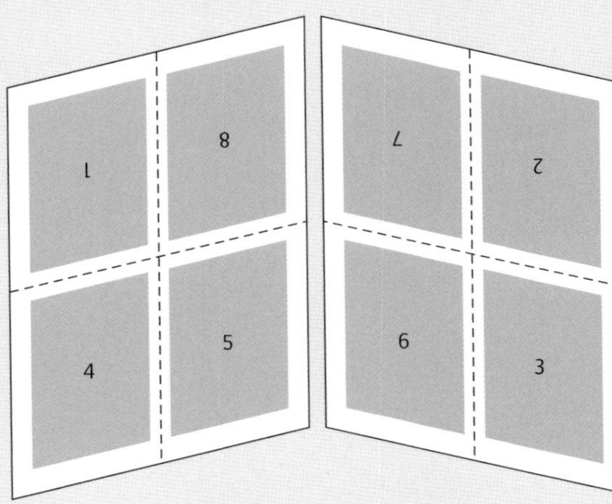

Recto *Verso*

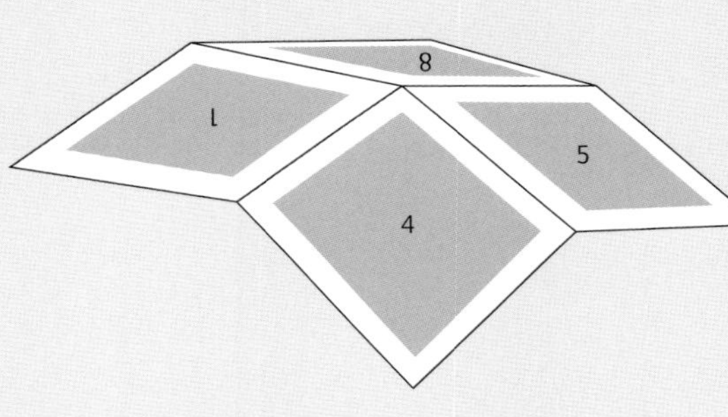

Featherweight paper
Soft, flexible, high volume paper with a rough surface that is very light and results in a thicker *book*. It is often used for readers and novels. Due to its rough surface this paper is not suitable for image reproductions.

Case binding (hardback)
A *book* is a hardback when the *gathered sections* or *book block* is protected by boards covered in linen or leather.

Coated paper
Paper covered with a layer of pigments and/or other *binding* agents in order to increase the quality of printing.

Creep
A cross *fold* pushes the inside *pages* slightly out. This shift is called *creep*. This also happens when folded *pages* are laid within each other. The more *sheets* in a *section* the more the inner *pages* are forced out of the front edge. The amount of *creep* depends on the paper's *grammage*.
The *type area* also moves towards the outer edge the closer one gets to the middle of a *section*.
This phenomenon can be corrected during *impositioning*, by continuously reducing the inner *margin* slightly and according to the paper's thickness.

Cross fold
Folds at 90 degrees to each other, as opposed to the parallel fold.

Edge trimming
The cutting or trimming off the *bleed area* of a printed piece gives it its final *format* and smooth edges.

Folding
The *folding* of a *printed sheet*.

Grammage (paper)
Specific weight or basis weight of paper per unit of area. The value is expressed either in gsm (grams per square meter), or in pounds (lb) per ream (500 or 1000 *pages*).

Impositioning
The placing of *pages* on a *printing sheet* so that after *folding* the *pages* will be in the correct order. An *impositioning* plan or scheme depends on the size of the *printed sheet*, the final *format* and the *folding* machine used in *finishing*.

Insetting
Folded *sheets* are laid in each other to form *sections*.
This method is used together with saddle *stitching*, for example.

Page
A *sheet* of paper has two sides or two *pages*.

Paperback
A *book* is a *paperback* when the *printed sheets* are either *gathered* into *sections* or stacked singly, and then either sewn or glued together. The resulting *book block* is then bound with a flexible cover.

Parallel fold
Folds parallel to one another. This could be an accordion fold, a double gate *fold* or a letter fold.

Recto
Another way of saying the *front* (first) *page* of a *printed sheet*. The back (reverse) side is also called *verso*.

Reprint
The new printing of an old or out-of-print publication as a facsimile.

Routing (binding)
The *collated* unbound *sections* are routed at regular intervals where the threads of the *binding* will be. This *routing* forms a small divot for the thread to rest and the glue to soak into. The resulting *binding* is more durable.

Score, scoring
Thicker or stiffer paper or board is often scored with a tool. This *scoring* makes *folding* easier and cleaner.

Section, signature
The *printed sheet* or part of a *printed sheet* that once folded forms a unit. Each unit is marked (collating marks, *signature* marks) to enable them to be assembled in the correct order. A *section* usually has a multiple of eight *pages*. A *book* (block) is made up of multiple *gathered* and sewn or glued *sections*.

Sewing (section sewing)
The traditional method of *binding*: The *sections* are *gathered* (in the correct order) and then sewn together instead of being glued together.

Sheet
The *sheet* contains two *pages*: *front* and *back page*.

Stapling, wire stapling
Binding with wire or staples. There are two types of *stapling*: side *stitching* or block *stitching* (from the *front page* through the block) or saddle *stitching* (*stapling* through the document's *spine*). This second type of *binding* is only possible with a limited number of *pages*. If there are too many, then there is too much *creep* and the booklet falls open.

Thread sealing (binding)
A combination of *section* sewing and perfect *binding* is used for high quality *paperbacks*.

Top side
The top or face side of a *printed sheet*. The side that is printed first. The reverse side is called the under or *perfecting side*. Double-sided printing – usually different print forms – is called face and back printing, *recto-verso* printing and also printing and perfecting.

Under side, perfecting side
The under, back or reverse side of a *printed sheet* (see top side).

Verso
The back (reverse) side of a *printed sheet* (see *recto*).

Volume
A paper's volume is the ratio of its thickness to its weight. A paper is high volume if it seems thick in relation to its weight. One paper has more volume than another if it is thicker, but both have the same size and weight. A high-volume paper is thick and light, whereas a low-volume paper is thin, heavy and dense.

Wire-O binding
Wire comb *binding*, a kind of spiral wire *binding*.

There are unlimited possibilities for *compositions*; it is impossible to describe all of them here. The examples presented in this last part do show how design concepts and principles can respond to different communication tasks.
These examples also illustrate how some designers have used the tools and principles shown in the previous *sections* to achieve results that are sometimes simple and immediately understandable, at other times are more complex and surprising, but always judicious and relate very well to the context.

Part

05

Headline

Case studies

Contents

Everything you have read so far will be of no help if you don't use it wisely, i.e., if you don't choose a specific principle or approach to achieve the desired result. The theory and mastery of tools and techniques can only form an intelligent basis of a *composition* if it has meaning. It is therefore important to guide the computer's mouse thoughtfully.

The fundamental principles and the essential terms have been presented. You have all the necessary elements to "get down to brass tacks" on your own. There is, however, one essential aspect that needs to be addressed. This is how one makes a choice and sticks to it, how one defines rules and applies them to all documents and *pages*. These choices can't be made purely on aesthetic or visual criteria, as important as these are. The decisions have to be guided by the subject. They also need to be guided by the context, the context of the design commission, the context of where it will be seen, read and used, as well as the technical and financial constraints.

It is not a question of teaching one how to make skillfully composed and aesthetically pleasing designs that are devoid of a clear stance, devoid of a foundation. It is rather a question of finding a link between meaning and form. It should be mentioned that a balanced relationship between the two isn't always the best. Sometimes a project that begins visually has more impact, sometimes a strong concept is better. The worst is not to take a stance at all.

The designer's personality is also relevant, since he is the one who "digests" all these techniques and interprets them in his own way. Again, this is the challenge: to absorb all the principles in this *book* and find an individual style, a style that is steeped in sensitivity and culture. *Composition* and *layout* remain an art and not a science! From the very beginning the client makes the first decision by choosing a particular designer, because he likes her attitude, her approach, her graphic universe.

The following is a detailed list of points to consider when approaching a graphic design project.

Analysis
First of all one needs to know the project's scope. Knowing this scope precisely helps you avoid decisions that can prove impossible in many respects.

1. Context
a. The client:
- their corporate design (graphic and typographic principles, corporate *colors*, etc.)
- their values (positioning, arguments, etc.)
- existing documents (analysis of their content and design)
- their industry (does this sector have its own codes?)
- product identity (if any)

b. Competition
- competing corporate designs (graphic and typographic principles, corporate *colors*, etc.)
- related industries (analysis)

c. Target audience
- Is it defined? If so, what is the target audience?
- How does it "work"?
- What are their expectations? Should they be met?
- What is their cultural background? Should we appeal to it or not? There are many strategies for reaching an audience, some are conventional, others are riskier.

d. Constraints
Don't forget to list the points that must be followed:
- *format*, typeface(s)
- number of *colors*, *binding*, budget
- etc.

2. Subject
A careful, in-depth study of the subject helps you see the semantic and formal relevance of the design decisions made.
It is not uncommon to look beyond the scope of the briefing with the client, to determine if this is too superficial or incomplete to satisfy basic requirements and goals.
A close relationship with the client can be useful to better understand the project's details and circumstances.
This preparatory work is crucial to be able to propose appropriate, efficient and sustainable solutions.

3. The content
- quantity and type of material provided (texts and images)
- texts: Is it one long text or several short texts?
- content structure (chapters, *paragraphs*, numbering, etc.)
- ratio of text to images in terms of quantity
- connections between text and images
- image quality (How large can they be used?)
- relationships between the images (Are all images equally important? Does a *hierarchy* need to be established? etc.)

The designer can know "his" subject intuitively and achieve the relevant objectives without listing the aspects of his analysis clearly. It is nonetheless inescapable in the next step that he justifies these decisions in a structured and well-founded manner. The client will not necessarily share this intuition, nor have the same views on graphic design. A conversation can help the client understand the connection between meaning and form. An intuitive work methodology doesn't absolve a designer from explaining and justifying his decisions.

Planning an approach

1. Stance
Prior to the first phase of analysis you need to define your stance:
- Do you want to support the existing continuity (if it exists), or do you want to break with tradition?
- Do you want to follow the codes (if any) of the industry in which your project is located, or do you want to surprise by adapting certain principles (which can be borrowed from other areas) to differentiate your project? Do you want to reassure with familiar designs, use arguments to convince, or, on the other hand, use the unusual to touch and impress people?

2. Framework
The next step is to define the framework where you will "operate" by considering the following parameters:
- *format*
- *binding*
- paper
- number of *colors*
- etc.

3. Key principles
Now it is time to make the design decisions that give the project its soul:
- typographic choices
- *mass* ratio
- *color* principles
- content organization
- using a *grid*
- etc.

Depending on the piece to be designed and the material provided, you might define a *modular grid*, with two multi-*column grids* cleverly overlapped, with or without *lines of force*, complemented by a principle of arranging texts and images, etc. When these things are defined and tested, this principle, whatever it is, has to guide the design of all *pages* in a publication, or the structure of a *poster* series that you will design.
You must constantly ask yourself if you will always follow this original principle, or if you need to rethink it if the results prove untenable or disappointing. Only with this discipline, which requires you to constantly step back, turn your face from the screen, print and review the current state after a few hours or days will you finally get the high quality that you expect.

You will also have to consider the specifics of the chosen medium:
- The impact of a *poster*, and its direct competition when shown on the *poster* wall.
- The *type area*, the relationship between cover and inside *pages* when dealing with a *book* or *periodical*, or the integration into an existing or newly developed series.
- etc.

Initial sketches and layouts
The approach for a project concept is something very personal. Some make very detailed pencil *sketches*, and even go as far as simulating the *gray value* for type, others will only do quick *sketches* before they start trying things on the computer. For some designers it is unthinkable to start without drawing first. Others claim that their mouse is their pencil, that they feel much more comfortable if they start by using the tools that will be used in the project's execution.

The development process can also be very different depending on the project and its context. It would be arrogant and simplistic to define a single way of doing things. Everyone has to find his own method and find his own tools.

Unity in variety
Planning ahead

1. To create this promotion for a musical event the designer chose a radical graphic system based on the following principles:

- a single medium, the *poster*, always the same *format*
- two *colors*, black and yellow
- white *margins* frame the designs and separate it from its immediate surroundings
- consciously minimal information is given about the venue however, the logotype is always used in the same way in the same position, which increases its impact

These few, clear and simple principles are highly recognizable visually, which allowed the designer to treat the image material very differently for each event: drawings, technical illustrations and playful arrangements of diverse *typefaces*.

1. *Kulturkeller im Schtei*, poster
102 subjects to date since 1997
Erich Brechbühl (Mixer)

1

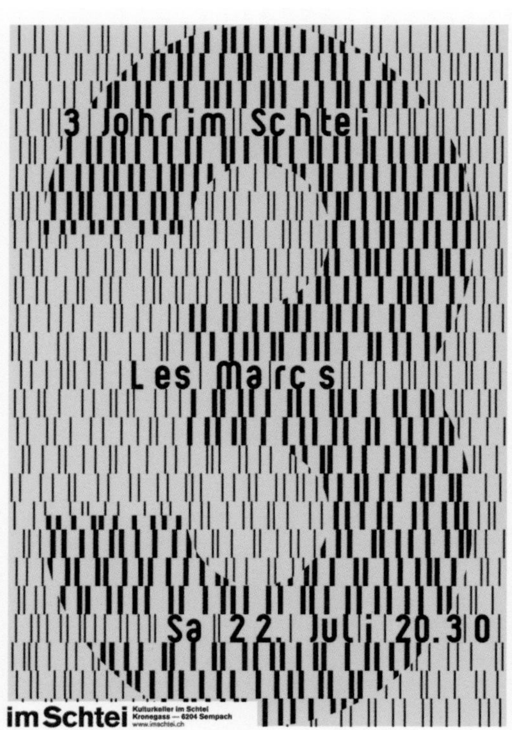

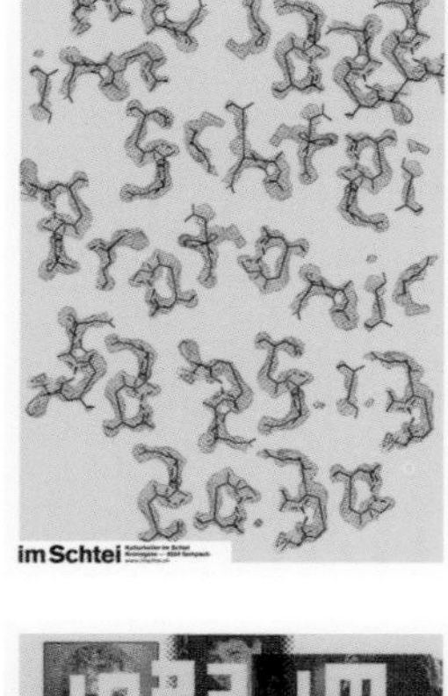

im Schtei

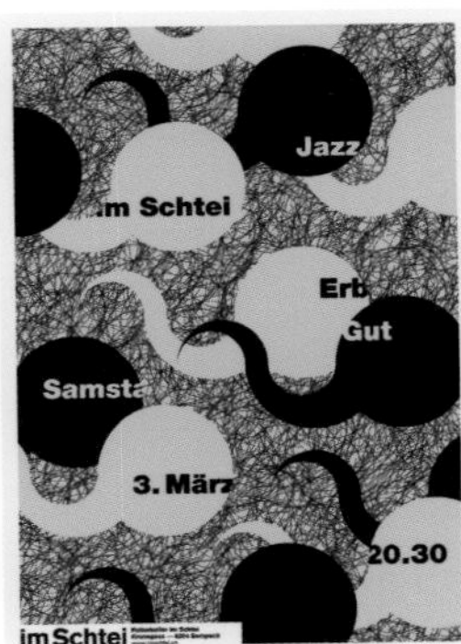
Jazz
im Schtei
Erb
Gut
Samsta
3. März
20.30
im Schtei

Chanson im Schtei
ECOUTES-Moi
l'ombre de ton chien
FR 2. NOV. 20.30
im Schtei

Jazz
im Schtei
Sa 13.4.
20.30
Rond'elle
im Schtei
5 Johr
im Scht
ei: Les Mar
Sa 20. Juli 2002 20.30 Uhr
cs Suprême
im Schtei

Kabarett im Schtei
Andreas Hausheer
im Schtei

im Schtei
Kulturkeller im Schtei
Kronegass — 6204 Sempach
www.imschtei.ch

J.D. ROTH
im Schtei

im Schtei

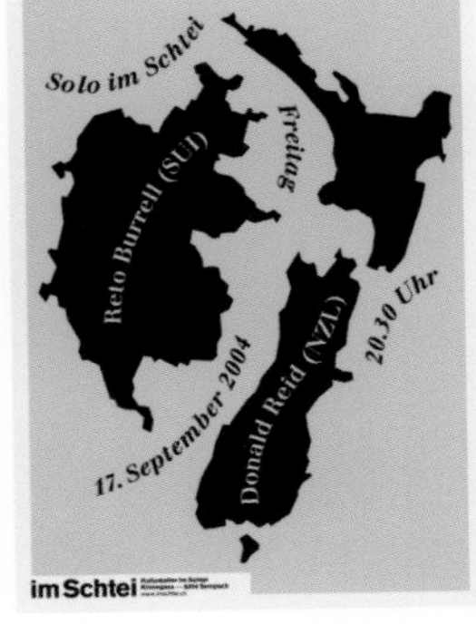
Solo im Schtei
Freitag
Reto Burrell (SUI)
17. September 2004
Donald Reid (NZL)
20.30 Uhr
im Schtei

SOUL/R'N'B
IM SCHTEI
FREITAG
20. MAI 2005
20.30 UHR
im Schtei

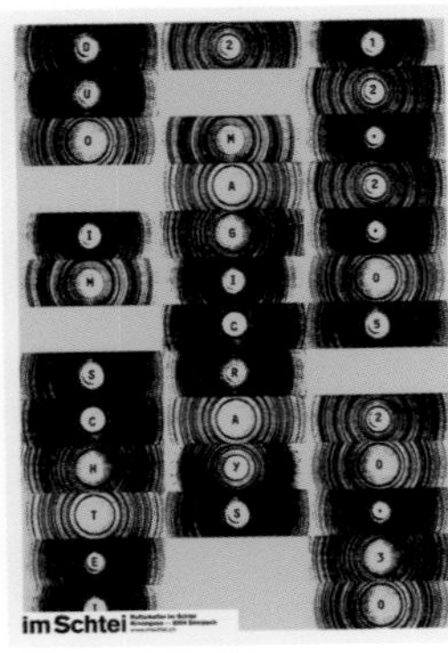
im Schtei

im Schtei

ELECTRONIC COUNTRY IM SCHTEI
MOUNTAINEER
im Schtei
Kulturkeller im Schtei
Kronegass — 6204 Sempach
www.imschtei.ch

A chance to experiment
A few square centimeters are enough

The designer's commitment and quality of work certainly can't be measured in the size of the printed piece. Proof of this can be found in numerous, often small, *flyers*, which are the "playground" of many graphic designers, and place for technical or visual experimentation. This type of promotion, where designers can show off their talents, is the jumping-off point for many careers.

1. For two years four graphic designers organized the Good and Plenty evenings (music, design, dance, film, party, happenings) once a month. The evenings were announced with a series of four *flyers*, each designed around a specific theme (stains, dots, squares, stars, bureaucracy, handwriting, etc.). The four designers each designed one *flyer* for each evening according to the same rules:

- the *format* is set
- uniform *typography*: a single *sans serif typeface* with a set size
- the basic *composition* stays the same
- the illustration must be a vector

Despite these strict – and apparently *binding* – rules the diversity is undeniable. The motifs and the *color* harmonies guarantee the unity of each series, while each of the interpretations is distinguishable from the others. The result demonstrates that rules and freedom are not necessarily contradictory.

1. *Good and Plenty*, flyers
Concept, creative direction:
Sebastian Bissinger (Bank™),
Ian Warner (blotto)
Design: Sebastian Bissinger, Ian Warner,
Willem Stratmann, Ingo Kniest
www.goodandplenty.de

1

Take advantage of the situation

Using the context

The graphic designer Richard Niessen decided to develop a set of stationery simultaneously for five people – who worked together regularly. His idea was to base the design on common geometric shapes and to print them together on the same *sheet*. He also chose an additional element for each individual to distinguish his or her stationery.

The arrangement of the basic elements is different for each person and is inspired by that person's personality or by an element specific to the individual: a drawing by Jennifer Tee, a flag-like graphic for Esther de Vries who likes flags, a construction game, a principle dear to Richard Niessen, and a playful perspective for the designers Raoul de Thouars and Joost Vermeulen.

The stationery for each includes:

- a compliment card with an embossed star made of the basic elements
- a *sheet* of stickers in basic geometric shapes (printed with the basic pattern), which can be used on envelopes or on the letterhead

This way each person can personalize his or her stationery – either subtly or exuberantly. These stickers can also be combined on documents used with one or more of the other five when they collaborate.

The graphic designer chose to work with six *colors*: silver, blue, red, green, yellow and orange in different combinations, depending on the printed piece.

1. Five arabesque stationeries: Esther de Vries, Jennifer Tee, Joost Vermeulen, Raoul de Thouars and Richard Niessen
Richard Niessen

2

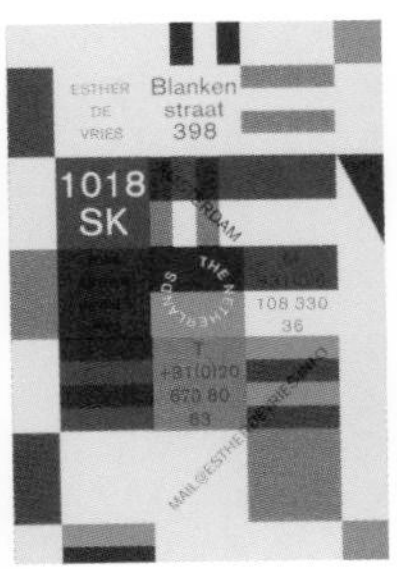

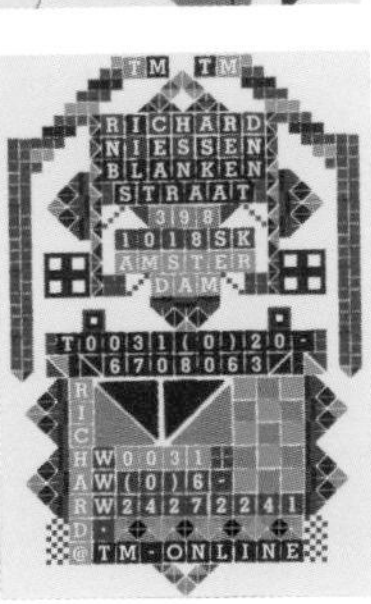

Provoking thought
A way of attracting attention

One of the most difficult tasks is the design of cultural communications. The designer has to find the right balance between the promotion's impact and the respect for the program that the corresponding works display. It is important that the spirit of the place is felt without undermining the spirit of the play. The design has to attract people without being vulgar, and the quality of execution has to be excellent.

The Vienna Theater (Schauspielhaus Wien, Austria) has maintained a working relationship for several years with the same graphic designers. One of the cornerstones of the theater's identity is the uniform use of the *typeface* Times, an archetype of neutral *typography* (due to its widespread availability and use), which lets the image take center stage.

The *posters* present an image that doesn't reveal everything, that provokes thought instead. Each *poster* is a kind of scene, but doesn't illustrate the play. Each image seems to hold a number of clues, whose meaning and connection will only be revealed to the play's audience.

The intent to stimulate a positive or negative public response has been undeniably successful, and each new season offers a new opportunity.

The treatment of photographs is distinct and unchanging. Their apparent neutrality, their constant insinuation of things not seen raise questions, and make the austere *headlines*, which are always set in red, all the more noticeable.

1. Schauspielhaus Wien, posters
Gunter Eder, Roman Breier
Grafisches Büro

1

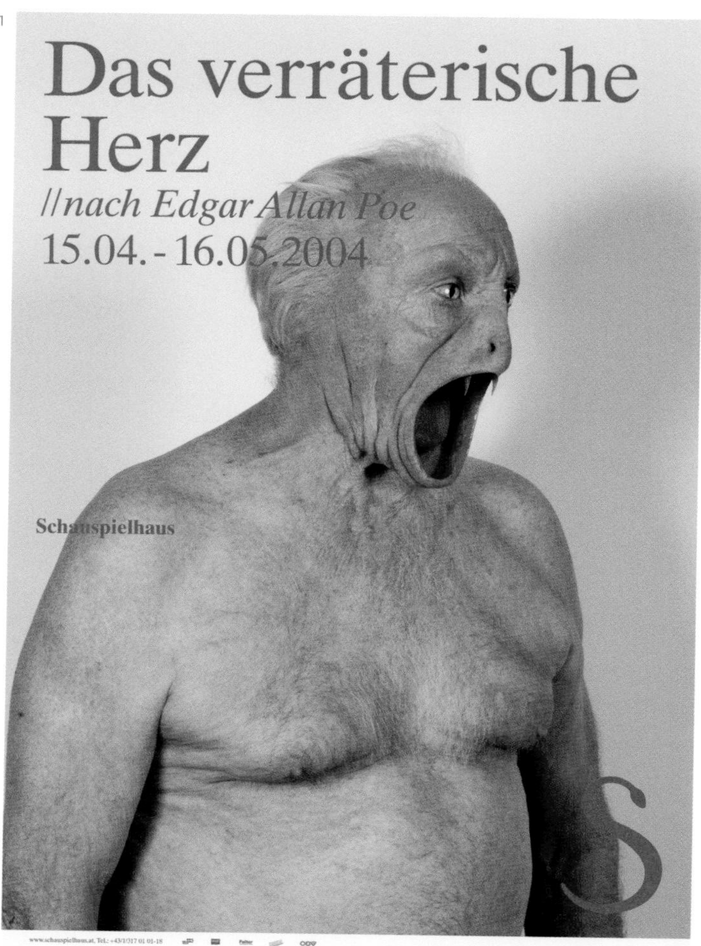

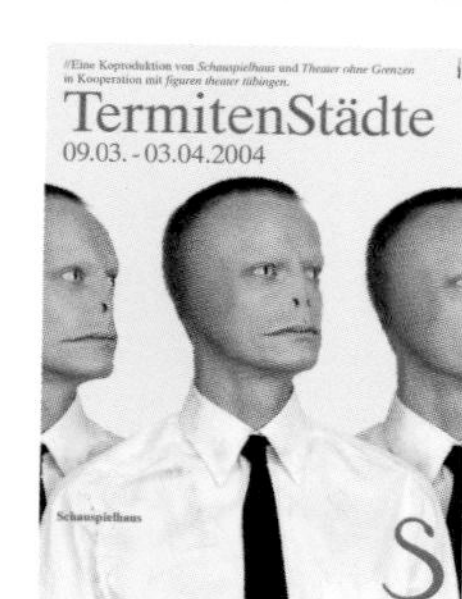

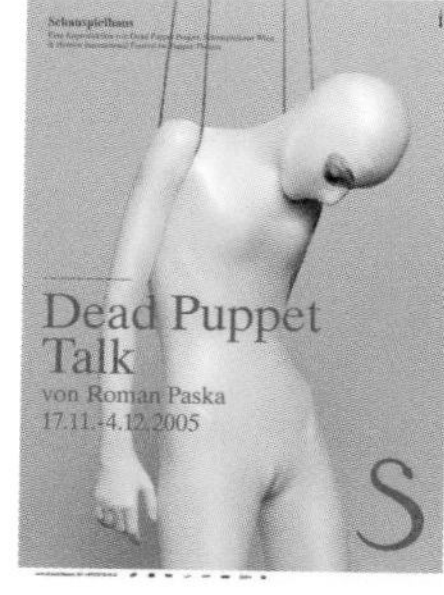

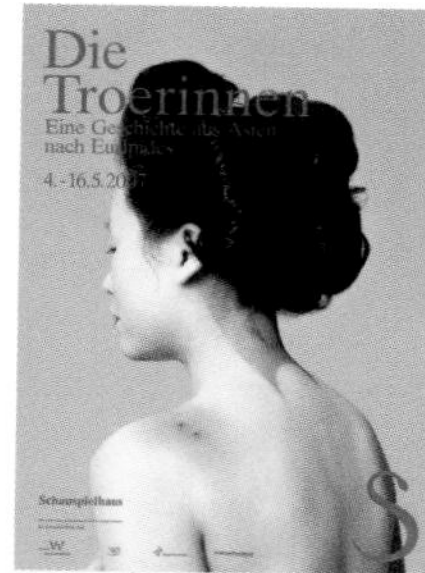

Just enough
Finding the right place

The design office that designed the identity and communications for the Gugging Art/Brut Center (Austria) opted for a minimal design concept because of the expressive power of the images. Nonetheless, the goal was to create a set of recognizable communication materials.

The elements that make up the identity are simple, effective and coherent:

- the background *color* (warm neutral tone)
- the dominant placement of the image, which gives it a strong presence
- *typography*: a *typeface* chosen for its apparent austerity, has been modified to include a diagonal line in the round *counters* (the diagonal line is often synonymous with the forbidden and forgotten and echoes the idea that art brut originated in psychiatric hospitals)

This last detail, despite the minimalist approach, is undoubtedly the most recognizable aspect of these printed pieces so much that it can stand alone as the art center's signature element.

2. Gugging Art/Brut Center, posters, cards, letterhead, tickets
Gunter Eder, Roman Breier
Grafisches Büro

2

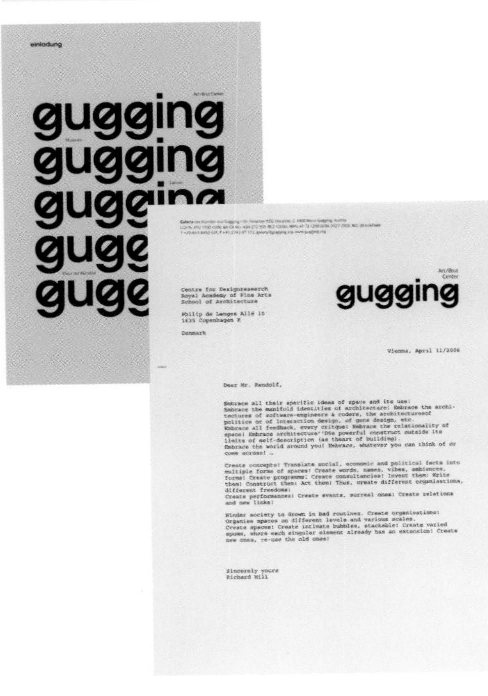

Art/Brut Center
gugging

Centre for Designresearch
Royal Academy of Fine Arts
School of Architecture

Philip de Langes Allé 10
1435 Copenhagen K

Denmark

Vienna, April 11/2006

Dear Mr. Rendolf,

Embrace all their specific ideas of space and its use!
Embrace the manifold identities of architecture! Embrace the architectures of software-engineers & coders, the architecturesof politics or of interaction design, of gene design, etc.
Embrace all feedback, every critque! Embrace the relationality of space! Embrace architecture''Ds powerful construct outside its limits of self-description (as theart of building).
Embrace the world around you! Embrace, whatever you can think of or come across! –

Create concepts! Translate social, economic and political facts into multiple forms of spaces! Create words, names, vibes, ambiences, forms! Create programms! Create consultancies! Invent them! Write them! Construct them! Act them! Thus, create different organisations, different freedoms!
Create performances! Create events, surreal ones! Create relations and new links!

Hinder society to drown in bad routines. Create organisations! Organise spaces on different levels and various scales.
Create spaces! Create intimate bubbles, stackable! Create varied spoms, where each singular element already has an extension! Create new ones, re-use the old ones!

Sincerely yours
Richard Hill

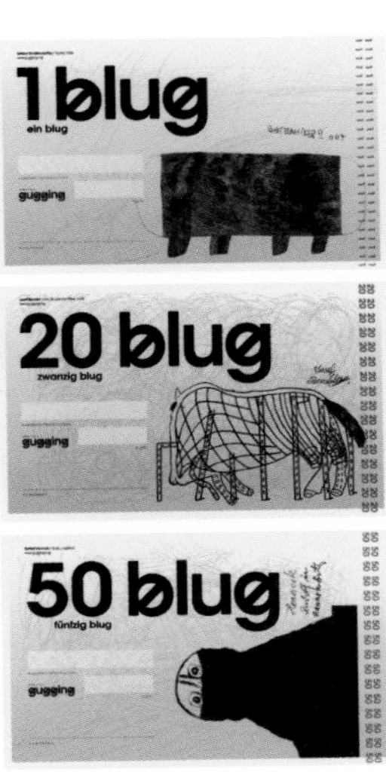

An apparent simplicity
Economy of means, multiple effects

The graphic designer deliberately chose to use restraint while designing the communications for the French cultural center in Algeria. His approach was economical in many ways, not only graphically but also technically.

The eight-*page* journal is actually a single *printed sheet* folded twice (two crossed folds) into four sections. Both *poster* and journal function as a program calendar. The *poster* is also folded into four and printed on both sides.

The designer chose to limit himself to two colours, undoubtedly to create a strong overall identity and remain true to the commission.
But this apparent simplicity conceals an unusual attention to details. *Typography*, patterns, *outlines* are graphically very rich. The choice of *typefaces*, the choice of paper and its pink and blue *colors*, which refer to an aesthetic popular in the Magreb, reinterpret an antiquated graphic style to create something very contemporary.

1. Centre culturel Français d'Alger, program poster, program journal, "Pour Jean Sénac" edition
Christophe Jacquet alias Toffe

1

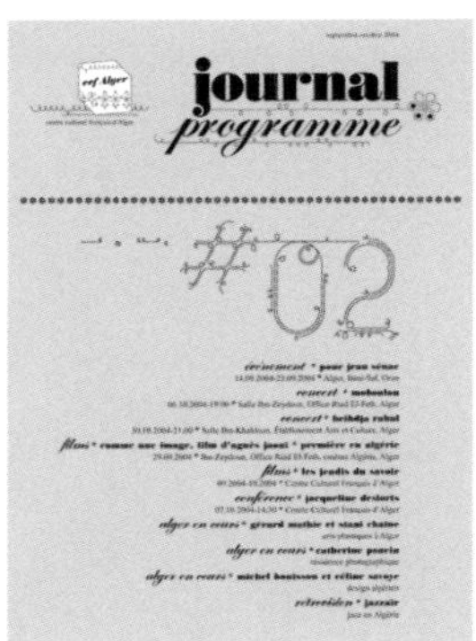

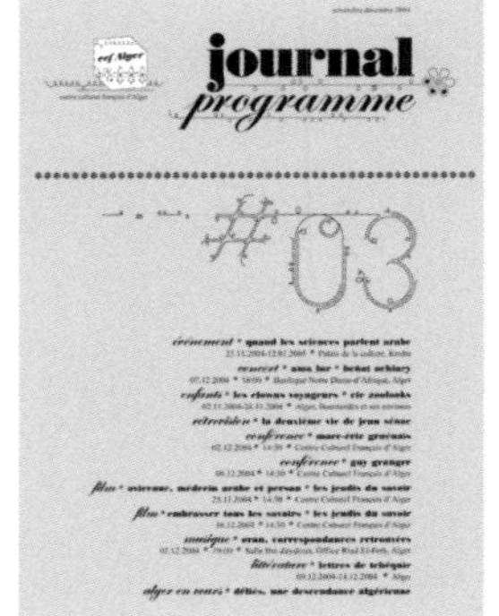

cef Alger
centres culturels français d'Algérie
affiche
programme

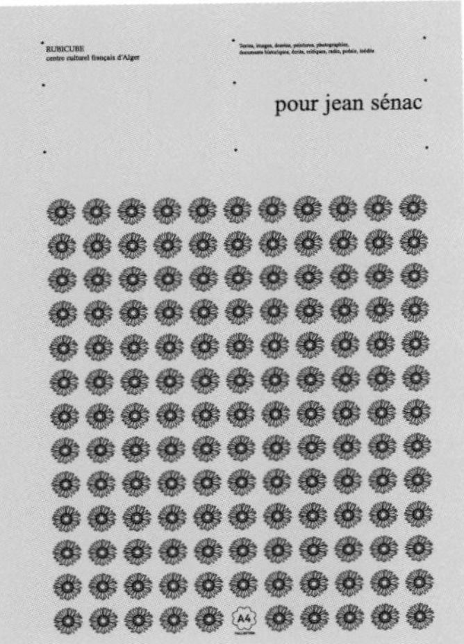

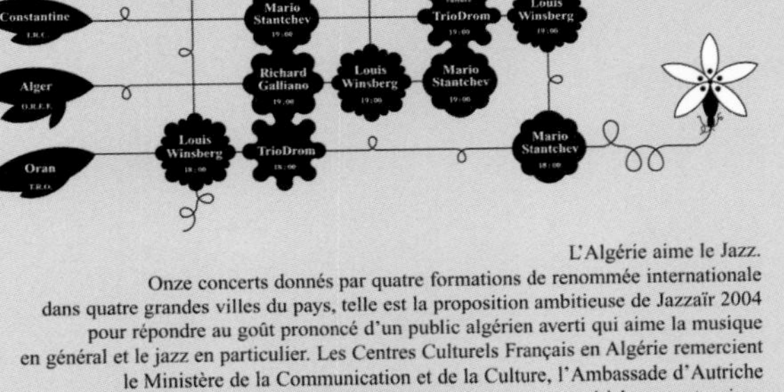

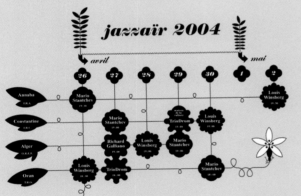

L'Algérie aime le Jazz.
Onze concerts donnés par quatre formations de renommée internationale dans quatre grandes villes du pays, telle est la proposition ambitieuse de Jazzaïr 2004 pour répondre au goût prononcé d'un public algérien averti qui aime la musique en général et le jazz en particulier. Les Centres Culturels Français en Algérie remercient le Ministère de la Communication et de la Culture, l'Ambassade d'Autriche et l'Ambassade de France. Leurs remerciements s'adressent aussi à leurs partenaires, l'Office Riadh El-Feth, le Théâtre Régional d'Oran, le Théâtre Régional d'Annaba, la Maison de la Culture Malek Haddad, le Théâtre Régional de Constantine et Colombine Films pour leur collaboration ainsi qu'à la Compagnie Air France dont le soutien a permis la réalisation de la manifestation.

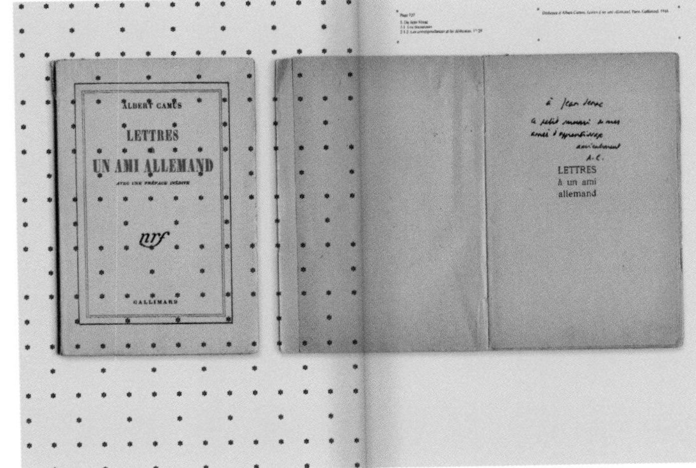

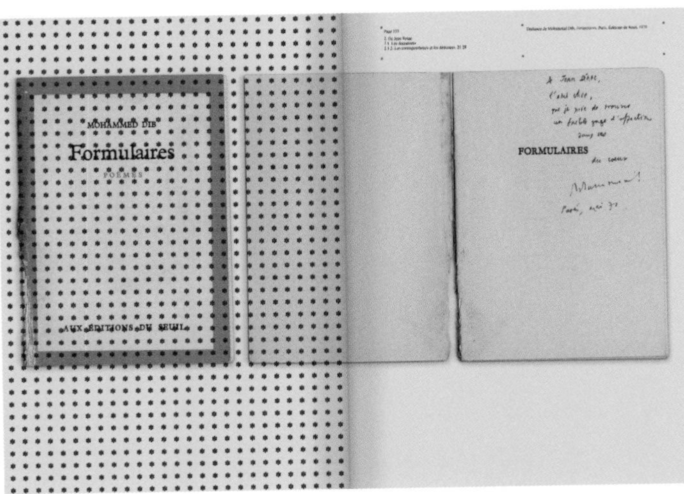

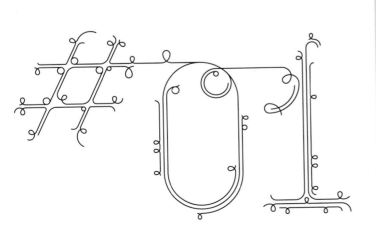

Three in one
Accompany the event

The Wonderland event was initiated by Austria while it was president of the European Union. The event presented young architects from nine countries.
Initially, eleven teams would return to Vienna after two years, and would then exhibit 99 projects by European architect teams.

To present, organize and archive the different stages of the exhibition, the designers decided on a simple principle: one *printed sheet* per country. What began as a *poster* became a folded brochure for the visitors, and after the end of the exhibition it forms a chapter in a *book* with all nine documents.

The *text-image-relationship* is the graphic principle's strongest element. The *typeface* designed especially for the event is superimposed on the images. Each country is identified by a different *color*.

1. *Wonderland*, posters, folded brochures, book
Gunter Eder, Roman Breier
Grafisches Büro

1

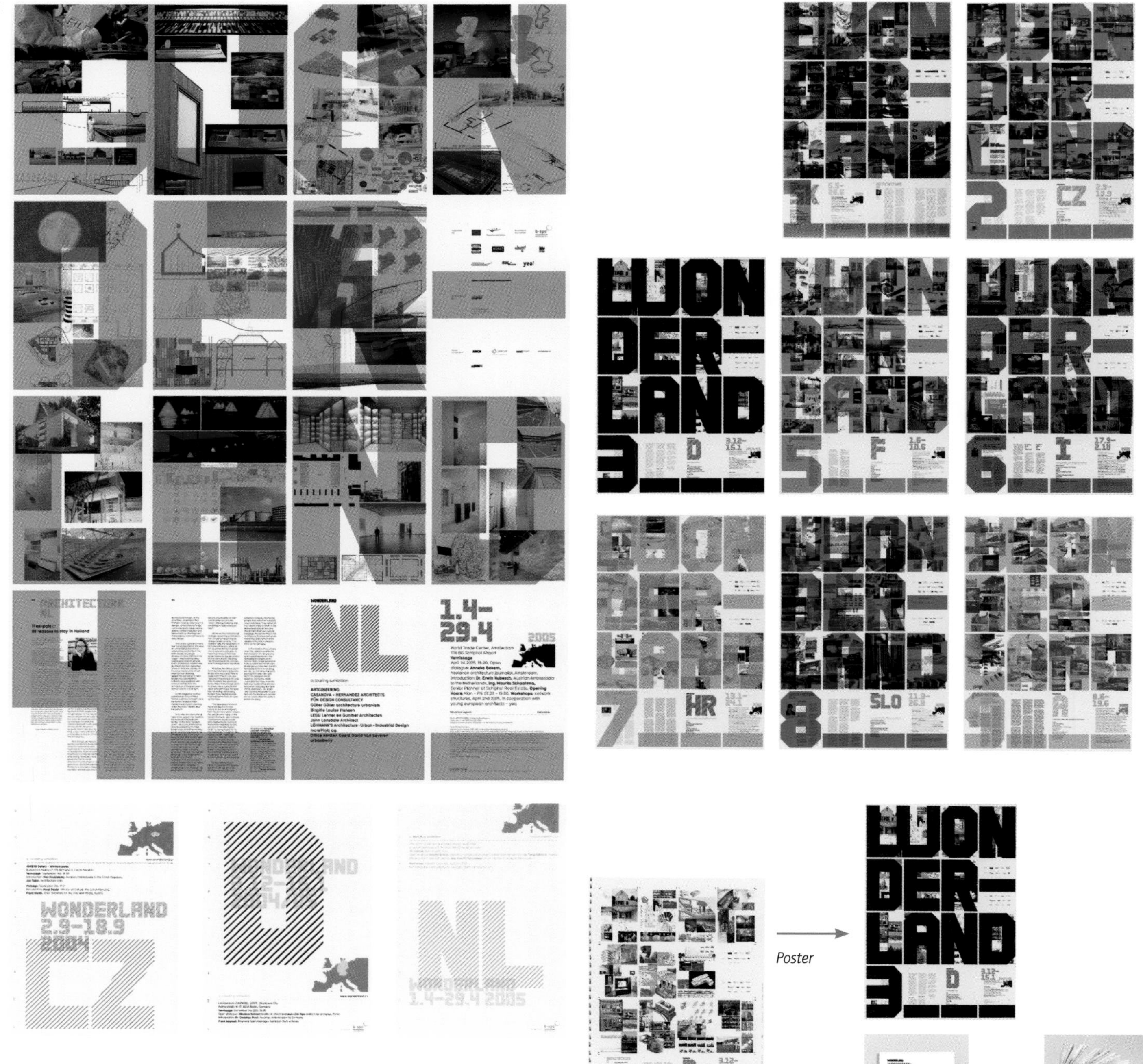

More than asked
An information upgrade

The commission was simple: create the print materials accompanying each exhibition organized by the Camden Arts Center in London. The result could have been a mundane series of *flyers*.
The designers decided on a more intelligent solution, anticipating the fact that visitors need to archive these printed pieces. Each exhibition is accompanied by a "note", a sort of booklet, which can be taken home and filed into a binder using the loop *stitching*.

The tab on the side of each booklet suggests the idea of a series and of filing, and offers the chance to keep these documents instead of throwing them away at the end of each visit.

Format, tab, *typography* and recurring details identify the series, and yet leave some latitude in the design of each piece.

2. *File notes*, binder and "notes"
Camden Arts Centre
Sara De Bondt with James Goggin

2

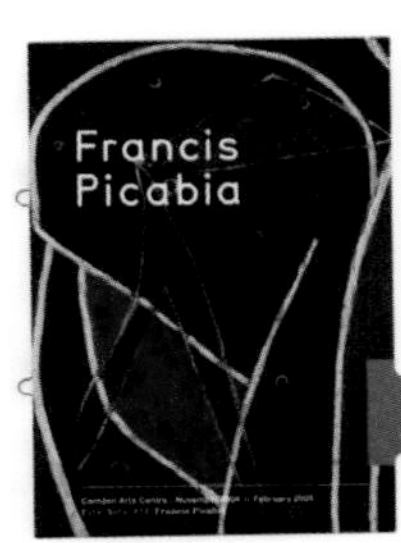

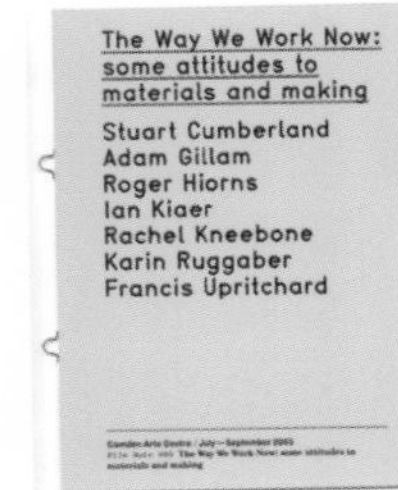

An eye for details

Every element has its purpose

The Dutch design office Experimental Jetset was given the job of designing the identity and all communications for the Stedelijk Museum in Amsterdam. This museum for modern art was being renovated at the time and had to move temporarily into the second and third floors of the old mail sorting building (Post CS) near the central train station.

Every element of the graphic system was carefully defined:

- The *typeface* Univers was chosen for its connection to the museum's logotype designed by Wim Crouwel.
- The oblique blue and red lines clearly refer to the airmail envelopes.

Furthermore, they facilitate four variations of the logotype, which all have a temporary feel – like the museum itself will have over the next four years.

The first pieces designed logically adopted the codes of the existing identity:

- The *color* palette is limited to blue, red and black.
- The type takes a prominent position.
- The logotype is used in different variations (1, 2, 3).

Later, other *colors* associated with the current exhibition were added to the graphic language, without disturbing its overall coherence, however.

The Bulletin is also designed through and through with the *typeface* Univers. Instead of mixing the different elements, the team proposed distributing them onto the different signatures:

- the first has the images, presented on glossy *coated paper*
- the second gathers the texts on offset paper
- the third has the English translations (4)

The printed pieces that were published with the individual exhibitions used *folding* and *embossing* to playfully reveal the title and contents (5, 6).

Invitations were designed as A3 *posters*. These were folded down to A5 *format* and could be mailed without envelopes.

The design here consists almost completely of *typography*. Nonetheless, each invitation has its own individual character, because the playful use of the letterforms and their *composition* on the *page* (*type size*, position, repetition of individual letters, *colors*, etc.) establishes a very spartan graphic principle that varies from show to show (7).

1

4

2

3

5

6

The game played with transparency with some of the printed pieces is also worth noting (6, 7). This isn't a coincidence, quite the opposite. The choice of paper is an important part of the design process; a designer needs to devote special attention to it in order to enrich every piece.

Stedelijk Museum CS,
1. Invitations
2. Leaflets
3. Buttons
4. Bulletins
5. Leaflets
6. Leaflets
7. Posters
Experimental Jetset

7

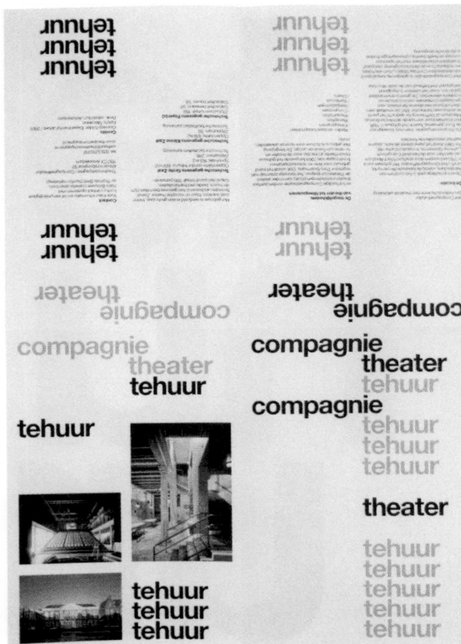

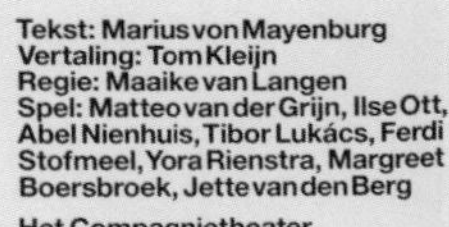

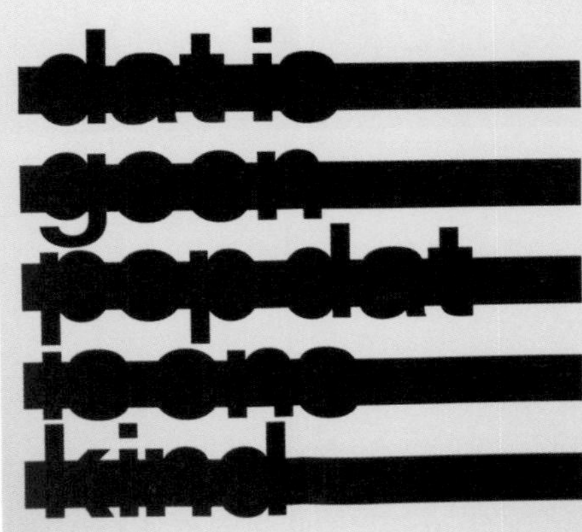

A territory to explore
A "bespoke" response

"Lux, a new territory dedicated to all images." With these words Jérôme Delormas, director of the new cultural center Scène nationale in Valencia presented his project to graphic designers who were invited to create the visual identity for the first season.

The original idea of the chosen project is embedded in this phrase. A "new territory" leads logically to a map that allows you to get oriented, to wander around and to get lost.

To map is to propose a universe of signs, a labyrinth that you can feast your eyes on. A map is an abstract representation that invites you for mental gymnastics that stimulate the imagination.

Every map contains a contradiction that makes it poetic: a coded language, which still opens a vast panorama of interpretation and mental representation. Mapping lux's cultural season meant inventing an "alphabet" of signs specific to each event (exhibition, festival, etc.) (2), on which the designers would base their "imaging" of the territory's geography. Paul Cox, the first guest artist, took part in this game by proposing his own set of signs, which were added to those already developed.

The lux season therefore takes the shape of an imaginary geography. While floating down a river you pass unique and complex signs, wind through synthetic schemes for a festival of digital films, follow the handwritten traces of the graphic designers. The eyes follow one path, then another. Events sometimes mix, the borders are blurred, the transition zones evoke unlikely and promising encounters. The idea of interconnections between the arts, so important to the lux project, takes on visual form in the cartographic representation.

The map has a very large *format* (120 × 180 cm). The public discovers it as a whole, as a *poster* (3) in the city. All printed communications – smaller *posters* (4), *leaflets*, etc. – are cut out of this map. The *front page* of the *newspaper* is about 1/8 of the territory (5). The exhibition catalogues (6) are 1/40 of the territory; postcards and *flyers* (7) are 1/110; the subscription cards are only 1/242.

This scale relationship is a major component of cartography: different *reading levels* overlap each other, from overviews to the smallest details, from the country to the small places. The different printed pieces reframe related image details, because each shows a different image, even if they all originate from the same large image.

A map represents six months of the lux program. A new card unveils the second half-year season. It may be very different from the first, depending on the events planned and the signs that they inspired in the designers. Until then, have a good trip!

Lux ®
1. Cartography
2. Principle of document organization
3. Poster 120 × 176 cm
4. Posters 40 × 60 cm
5. Newspaper
6. Catalogue
7. Postcards, flyer
La bonne merveille

5

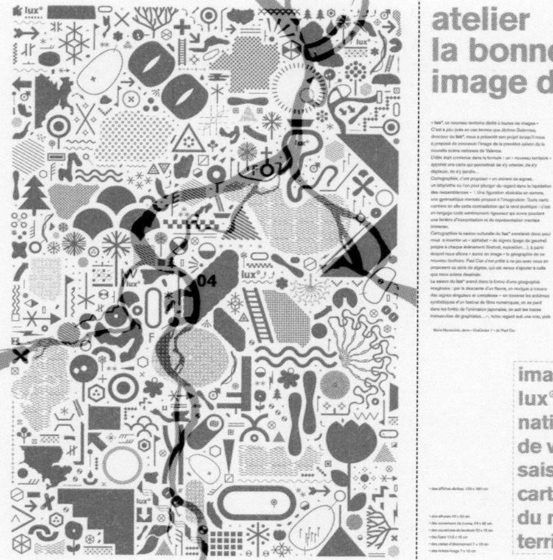

atelier
la bonne merveille,
image de lux®
image de lux®, scène nationale de valence, saison 2007, cartographie du nouveau territoire.

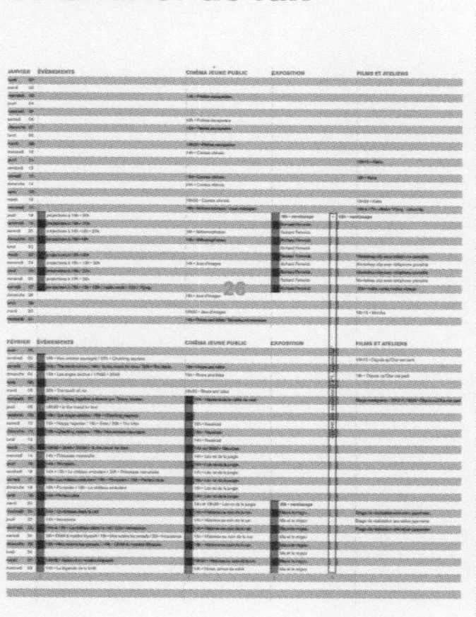

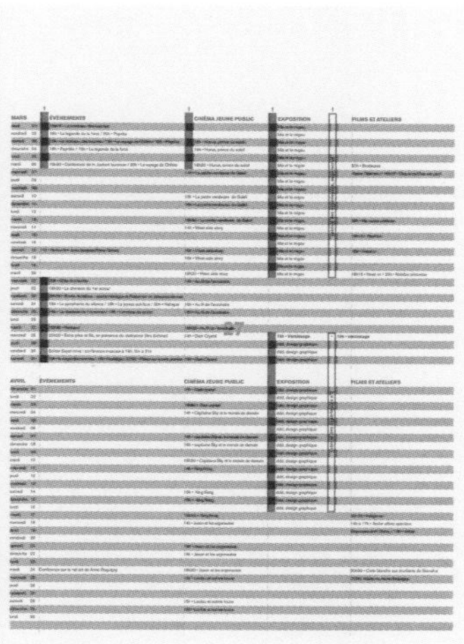

6

7

One rule of the game

Towards an "automatic" layout

A *layout* can also be dictated by a strict rule established at the beginning. The arbitrariness of the rule and strictly obeying it, no matter which elements are encountered throughout the *pages*, leads to unexpected *compositions*.

This approach to *composition* makes it possible to overcome *layouts* that are only based on formal and aesthetic criteria. It also takes a step to more surprising and ever changing *compositions*, because they are based on the original principle. However, this approach is only valid when it is seen as a source of creativity and not as a burden.

1. In the spirit of the Dada movement, the graphic designers decided on an unusual concept for the exhibition catalogue design. The *layout* of the images on the *page* is dictated by the following rules:

- The height of all images is the same. As a result, their widths vary.
- The images are placed side by side with equal spacing.
- The line of images cannot exceed a predefined width. If an image or a *caption* exceeds this limit, it is automatically moved to the next line.

The arrangement of the images and consequently the *page layout* is done without the graphic designer's intervention.

1. *Dada*, exhibition catalogue Centre Georges Pompidou deValence

1

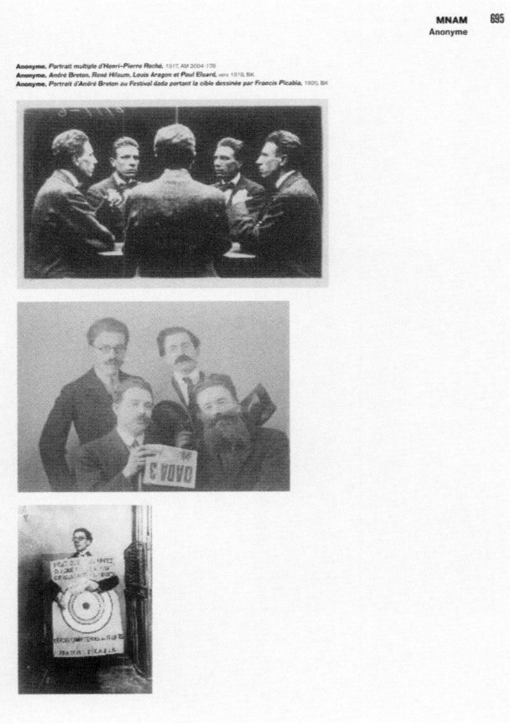

2. The arrangement of texts and images follows a simple rule based on two principles:

- The "primary" exhibitions are placed on a three-*column grid*, the "secondary" exhibitions are placed on a four-*column grid*.
- The exhibitions are organized chronologically and document ten years of events at the Carré d'Art. Whether one, two or three *columns* were used depended on the show's duration.

The superimposition of two *grids* leads to different encounters on each double-*page* spread. The median *line of force* runs through the whole catalogue, forms the chronological axis, and creates a visual guideline.

2. *Le Carré d'Art, 10 ans d'expositions*, exhibition catalogue
Damien Gautier

2

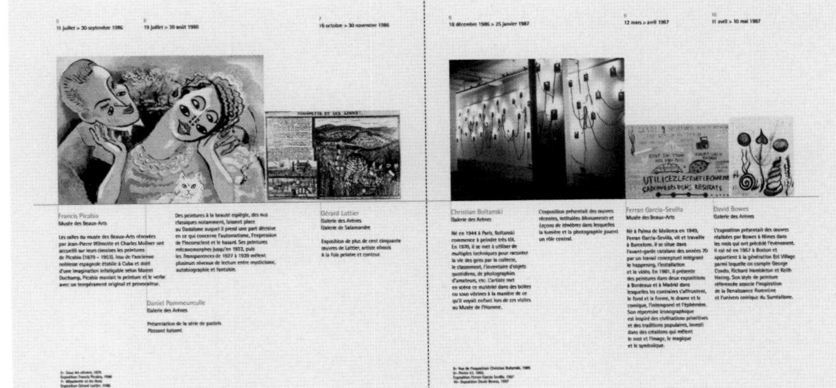

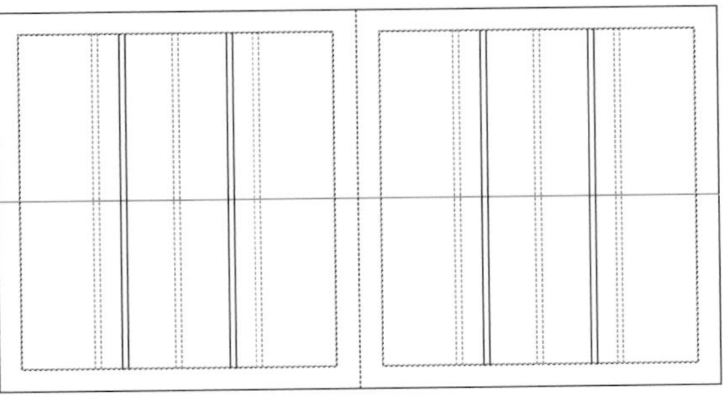

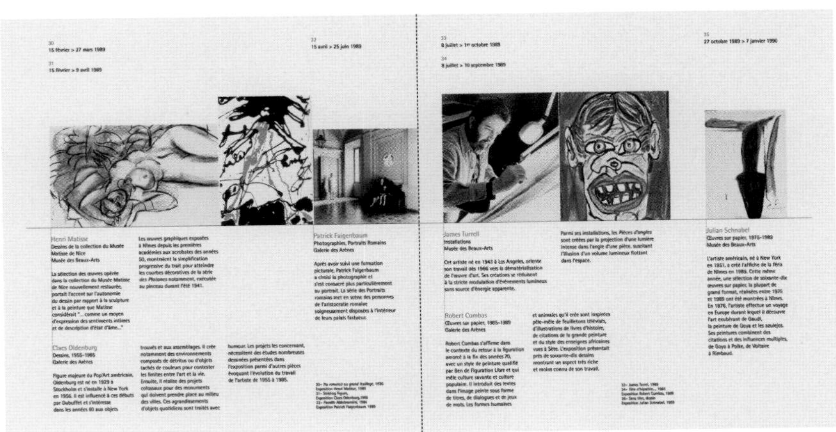

Part

06

Headline

Appendix

Contents

Bibliography

1

Foundations of visual form

Charpentes, la géométrie secrète des peintres
Charles Bouleau
Seuil, 1963

Théorie de l'art moderne
Paul Klee
Gonthier, 1971

La pensée créatrice
Paul Klee
Dessain et Tolra, 1973

L'art du dessin enseigné par les maîtres. De Dürer à Picasso
Bernard Ducourant
Bordas, 1989

Art de la couleur
Abridged edition
Johannes Itten
Dessain et Tolra, 1996

De la loi du contraste simultané des couleurs et de l'assortiment des objets colorés
Michel Eugène Chevreul
Imprimerie Nationale, 1889

Écrits et propos sur l'art
Henri Matisse
Hermann, 2000

L'empire des signes
Roland Barthes
Seuil, 2005

Le petit livre des couleurs
Michel Pastoureau,
Dominique Simonnet
Panama, 2005

Les couleurs de notre temps
Michel Pastoureau
Bonneton, 2005

L'obvie et l'obtus
Roland Barthes
Seuil, 1982

Traité des couleurs
J.W. von Goethe
Triades, 1993

2

Basic elements

À bâtons rompus
Adrian Frutiger
Atelier Perrousseaux éditeurs, 2003

Das Detail in der Typografie
Jost Hochuli
Niggli, 2005

Geometry of Design: Studies in Proportion and Composition
Kimberly Elam
Princeton Architectural Press, 2001

Graphisme. Typographie. Histoire
Roxane Jubert
Flammarion, 2005

Gutenberg-Galaxie 1
Jost Hochuli
Institut für Buchkunst, 2000

La chaîne graphique Prépresse, impression, finition
Kaj Johansson, Peter Lundberg, Robert Ryberg
Eyrolles, 2006

La gestion de la couleur, guide exhaustif à l'usage des graphistes
John T. Drew, Sarah A. Meyer
Pyramyd, 2006

L'aventure des écritures: La page
Under the direction of Anne Zali
Bibliothèque nationale de France, 2002

Lesetypographie
Hans Peter Willberg
Friedrich Forssman
Verlag Hermann Schmidt, 1997

Typographie. Un manuel de Création
Emil Ruder
Niggli, 2002

Typo du xxe siècle
Lewis Blackwell
Flammarion, 2004

Typographic Systems: Rules for Organizing Type
Kimberly Elam
Princeton Architectural Press, 2001

Typographische Gestaltung
Original edition, 1935

Asymmetric Typography
Translation
Jan Tschichold
Faber & Faber, 1967

Une initiation à la typographie
Anne Denastas, Camille Gallet
Niggli, 2006

Visual Grammar: A Design Brief
Christian Leborg
Princeton Architectural Press, 2006

Histoire photographique de la photographie
Henri Van Lier
Les impressions nouvelles, 1992

Histoire de la photographie
Edited by Jean-Claude Lemagny and André Rouillé
Bordas, 1994

Nouvelle histoire de la photographie
Edited by Michel Frizot
Bordas, 1994

Introduction à l'analyse de l'image
Martine Joly
Armand Colin, 2005

Petite fabrique de l'image
Jean-Claude Fozza,
Anne-Marie Garat
and Françoise Parfait
Magnard, 2003

La chambre claire
Roland Barthes
Gallimard, Seuil, 1980

La photographie contemporaine
Michel Poivert
Flammarion, 2002

La photographie contemporaine
Susan Bright
Textuel, 2005

Qu'est-ce que la photographie aujourd'hui?
Beaux-Arts magazine, separate edition

Rhétorique de l'image
Roland Barthes
in: Communication, no. 4, 1964

3

Grid principles

Grid for the Internet and other media
Veruschka Goetz,
Ava Publishing, 2005

Grid systems in graphic design
Josef Müller-Brockmann
4th edition
Niggli, 1996

Grid Systems: Principles of Organizing Type
Kimberly Elam
Princeton Architectural Press, 2004

Typographic Systems: Axial, Radial, Dilatational, Random, Grid, Modular, Transitional, Bilateral
Kimberly Elam
Princeton Architectural Press, 2007

4

The poster

100 beste Plakate
Verlag Hermann Schmidt
(one issue each year)

80+80, photo_graphisme
amaniman, separate edition
Aman Iman Créations/
Filigranes éditions, 2006

Chaumont
Catalogues du Festival d'afiches
Pyramyd
(one issue each year)

Histoire de l'affiche
Josef and Shizuko
Müller-Brockmann
Phaïdon, 2004

L'affiche
Georges Lo Duca in:
Que Sais-je? no. 153, 1969

L'affiche française
Alain Weill in:
Que Sais-je? no. 153 bis, 1982

L'affiche: fonctions, langage et rhétorique
Françoise Enel
Mame, collection Medium, 1971

Le livre de l'affiche
Réjane Bargiel-Harry
and Charles Zagrodski
Éditions Alternatives, 1985

Poster Collection
Museum für Gestaltung Zürich
Lars Müller Publishers
no. 3: Poster for Exhibitions 1980–2000
no. 4: Hors-Sol.
Poster Actions in Switzerland
no. 5: Typotecture. Typography as architectural imagery
no. 6: Visual Strategies against Aids. International Aids Prevention Posters
no. 7: Armin Hofmann
no. 11: Handmade

The book

A book about Special Print Effects
AllRightsReserved Ltd

Book Design
Andrew Haslam
Laurence King, 2006

Designing books – Practice and theory
Jost Hochuli, Robin Kinross
Hyphen Press, 1996

Gutenberg-Galaxie 1
Jost Hochuli
Institut für Buchkunst Leipzig

L'écho d'un langage trouvé. Notes sur le travail de Pierre Faucheux
Samuel Vermeil
in: Marie Louise, no. 2
Éditions F7, 2006

Le livre
Stéphane Darricau
Collection Petit manuel
Pyramyd and CNDP, 2004

Le livre en lettres
Stéphane Darricau
Collection Petit manuel
Pyramyd and CNDP, 2005

Le livre en pages
Stéphane Darricau
Collection Petit manuel
Pyramyd and CNDP, 2006

Le Livre de photographies: une histoire Volumes 1 et 2
Martin Parr and Gerry Badger
Phaïdon, 2005–2007

Les plus beaux livres suisses
Anthology
Office fédéral de la culture
(one issue each year)

Livre et typographie,
Jan Tschichold
Allia, 1999

Massin
Laetitia Wolf
Phaïdon, 2007

Methods of Book Design
Hugh Williamson
Oak Knoll Press, 2nd ed., 1966

On book design
Richard Hendel
Yale University Press, 1998

The design of books
Adrian Wilson
Chronicle Books, 1993

Periodicals

Best of newspaper design
Rockport Publishers
(one issue each year)

Editorial Design
Yolanda Zappaterra
Laurence King, 2007

Le journal tel qu'il est lu
Jacques Douël
Cfpj, 1987

Réussir sa Une
Trade and specialized magazine
Marina Alcaraz
Victoires éditions, 2005

5

Case studies

Altitude: Contemporary Swiss Graphic Design
Claudia Mareis, Robert Klanten,
Nicolas Bourquin
Die Gestalten Verlag, 2006

New Book Design
Roger Fawcett-Tang,
Caroline Roberts
Laurence King, 2004

Recollected Work Mevis & Van Deursen
Paul Elliman, Armand Mevis,
Linda Van Deursen
Artimo, 2005

Serialize Family faces and variety in graphic design
Robert Klanten, Mika Mischler,
Boris Brumnjak
Die Gestalten Verlag, 2006

Glossary

above the fold
The upper half of the *newspaper's front page* that is visible when folded. Some editors refer to the central part of the *front page* as "at the fold". 212f.

annotation
An additional or explanatory (comment) to the main text, placed either below (*footnote*) or in the outside *margin* (marginal note or shoulder note). 71, 96, 109, 181, 183, 194, 195, 226
– see *reference*

artist's book
A special edition *book* often very extravagantly produced. 204

ascender
The part of a letter that extends above the *x-height*. 54, 57, 62f., 68, 142, 211

axis, inclined stress
A more or less inclined (sloped) line that is oriented on the thickness of the strokes. This line (or stress) is one of the factors that determine the *rhythm* of a typeface. 50f., 52, 55, 57

back side, perfecting side
The second *page* (or side) of a *sheet* to be printed. The reverse of the face side. 241
– see *verso*

baseline
The imaginary line on which the lower part of the midsection of a *typeface* rests. (One should note that the "round" or "pointy" letterforms overlap this line in order to optically adjust their form.) 68

baseline grid
The *grid* which defines the *baselines* of the body type. The distance between the *baselines* should be the same as the body type's *leading*. *Layout* programs have a function that makes this *baseline grid* "magnetic", so that text elements are automatically aligned to it. 138, 142

beardline
– see *descender*

below the fold
The part of the *newspaper* that is hidden when folded in half. Also used to refer to the lower section of websites. 213

binding
The *binding* holds the *pages* or multiple *sections* (or *signatures*) together. 45, 71, 109, 144, 181f., 184, 196, 198, 202–204, 209, 234, 236, 240f., 245

binding, stitching
The attaching of *sections* or *signatures* together into a (*book*) block. In the case of single *pages* these are often bound with glue. Thicker products (such as *books*) are usually sewn with a thread (side stitch), whereas brochures and *magazines* are usually bound with wire or staples (saddle stitch, pamphlet stitch, saddle wire). 234, 236, 240f. – see *stapling, wire stapling*

bird's-eye view
The perspective from a higher point of view, this term is commonly used in photography and film. Another term is top view. 78f.

blackletter, gothic
A group of *typefaces* that is part of the *Calligraphics* group. In German referred to "gebrochene" (broken) types due to the interrupted pen strokes. Sometimes incorrectly referred to as "Fraktur", which is, however, a single kind of *typefaces* within this group. 51
– see *type classification*

bleed area, bleed
The outer edge of the *printing sheet* or of the printed piece. The bleed area lies outside the *format* and will be trimmed off. The bleed area allows for small imprecisions in production and allows images, *color* areas, etc. to run off (bleed off) the edge of the page. 89, 241

body (type)
Every letterform or *glyph* has certain amount of space around it. This body size (also called side bearings) is specific to each *typeface* and *glyph*. The width is measured in units called "em" and the height (also called depth) is usually measured in points. Respecting this hidden dimension helps establish a pleasing typographic *rhythm*. 54
– see *body width*

body width (type)
The width of a character including its right and left sidebearings (the space before and after the letterform, originally the width of the block of metal or wood letter). If used to group *typefaces* in a family, then often in terms such as: compressed, condensed, *normal*, extended (listed from narrow to wide). 51, 53, 55–57, 59, 61, 63, 65, 68f., 73, 143
– see *tracking, letterspacing, body*

bold (type)
Bold is a kind or *weight* of type that is thicker than the *normal* or *regular type*. 52, 57f., 62, 64

book
The term originates from the German word "Buch" which *stems* from the beech tree ("Buche"), which was used for making paper and making printing presses. A *book* refers to a bound collection of *printed sheets*. It is one of the oldest forms of preserving and publishing knowledge. 11, 35, 38, 40, 44–46, 48, 50, 56, 71, 82, 89, 92, 100, 104, 109, 112, 124, 139, 158, 166, 170, 181–209, 218, 230, 236, 241, 244f., 254, 265

bookbinding
45 – see *binding*

book block
A stapled, bound or sewn stack of *sheets* (or *sections*) that is trimmed, and when bound to a *book cover*, results in a *book*. 182, 204, 241

book cover
The part of a *book* that is wrapped (or bound) around the *book block* and protects it. 182
– see *book cover board*

book cover board
The (card)board that forms the cover of a *book*. It can be covered with leather, linen or (marbled) paper, etc. The reverse side of the *book cover* board is the inside front cover. 182, 184, 196, 202f., 205 – see *book cover*

book jacket, dust cover, dust jacket
The removable paper cover or jacket that is wrapped around and tucked inside the front and back cover of a bound *book*. It can also be used for marketing the *book*. 182, 184, 204, 236

book series
Books are often grouped thematically and by author into series. A series can be recognized primarily by its design, *format* and production. 109, 181, 196, 198, 200–202, 245

bottom margin, lower margin, footer
The bottom edge of a page. 44–48, 182, 189, 195

bread-and-butter typeface
Typefaces used for the main body of text, in *contrast* to the *typefaces* used for *headlines*. Generally set between 8 and 12 point *type size*. Since typesetters were paid based on the amount of type set, hence the name bread-and-butter typeface. 59f., 62, 220

break line
The last line in a *paragraph* of *justified type* that is narrower than the full *column width*.

brighter color
A lighter *color* achieved by adding white or a lighter *hue*. 24, 26

Calligraphics
Digital *fonts* or *typefaces* with forms that are handwritten, penned or brushed in origin. 51
– see *type classification*

call out, pull quote
A few essential words of an article are set in a block of white space and/or larger to entice the reader to read the whole article. 212f.

canon
A scheme for constructing the *margins* and position of the *type area* on a page. 44, 46, 181

capital, caps
203, 224 – see *capitals, uppercase*

capitals, uppercase
A letter that differs in size and form from the *lowercase* or *minuscule* version. In addition to the *capital* letters, some *fonts* have small *capitals* (or small *caps*) which are approximately the size of the *x-height* of the *lowercase letters*. 55, 62f., 224, 226, 228

caption, cutline
An image must be accompanied by a *caption* that explains the image content and names the source (photographer, illustrator, etc.). It is very important because of its position next to an image, *captions* are almost always read. It needs to contain elements that encourage the audience to read the article. A good *caption* also contains key terms that summarize the main message. 48, 83, 88, 90, 95, 98, 128, 158, 212f., 220, 260
– see *legend*

centered (type)
Text where the lines of type are set to align on a central axis. 66, 199, 224

Classicals
A *type classification* term, one of the categories along with *Blackletter*, Moderns and *Calligraphics*. *Classicals* are roman in origin and are the most commonly used *typefaces* in the Western world. 51, 56–60, 62–64
– see *type classification*

close-up
Shows just the head or face of a person photographed. In the case of still life images, the object fills the image completely. 77, 99
– see *shot, setting*

coated paper
Paper covered with a layer of pigments and/or other *binding* agents in order to increase the quality of printing. 58, 204, 241

collate, gather
The collecting and assembling of folded or single *pages* into a correctly ordered *book block* before this is bound. The sequence of (little) bars on *fold* of *sections* are called collating marks and make this process easier. One also calls this *gathering*. 240f.

collector's edition, artists' books
Books that are lavishly designed and/or illustrated and produced. Often expensive and produced in small numbers. 181, 204–207, 208, 230

color
The eye perceives *color* due to different *light* intensities or wave lengths. 8, 10f., 13f., 17, 20–29, 42, 49, 52, 55, 64, 74f., 78, 81, 84, 98, 101, 103f., 109, 116, 132f., 150, 164, 168–170, 173, 181f., 186, 192, 194, 198f., 202, 204, 208f., 211, 214, 216f., 220, 222, 226, 228, 232, 234f., 245f., 248f., 251f., 254

column
Vertical divisions of the design space are called *columns*. 65, 67, 69, 71, 74, 98, 110–123, 130, 134, 136, 138, 144, 147, 154, 164f., 211–213, 220, 228, 261

column width, line length
The width of a *column* or the length of a line of text. The alignment of the text can be justified, *flush left* or *flush right*. 65, 67, 69, 74, 110f., 115, 117, 120, 147, 164, 211

complementary colors
Complementary colors are opposite of each other on the *color* wheel. 20, 24–27, 233

composition
A *composition* in *layout* means the selecting and placing of different design elements on a page. *Composition* is the art form of harmoniously combining the elements one (or the client) has chosen with one another. 8, 10–39, 44–48, 50, 74–77, 79, 83, 88f., 91–94, 96, 98, 100f., 103, 109, 112, 114, 118f., 122, 124–129, 130, 134–136, 138, 144–146, 152f., 156, 162–164, 169f., 172, 177, 198, 202, 226, 228, 234, 244, 248, 260

content plan, flatplan
The *page* dummy provides an overview of the order of the *pages* and the location of the contents (text, images, adverts) of a planned *magazine* or *newspaper*. 213, 230, 245

contrast
The contradiction between two things in which one aspect calls special attention to the other. 8, 14f., 20f., 24, 26f., 29, 50f., 54, 56–60, 64, 68, 98, 100, 103, 109, 115, 215, 217

cool color
A *color* is referred to as cool due to its association with ice and snow. 20, 26f., 103

copyright
A reference to the intellectual property rights of a work of art, literature or music. The *copyright* indicates the owner and the year the relevant work was published. 182, 189

counter
The white space inside (or negative) form of a letter or *glyph*. 53, 58, 63, 68, 251

cover, book cover, book jacket
The cover of a *book* or *book cover* (hardbound or case-bound *books*) or *book jacket* or jacket (softbound *books*) that wraps the *book block*. 45, 181f., 184–186, 196–205, 208f., 217, 226, 236, 241, 245

creep
When folded *pages* are laid within each other the inner *pages* are forced out of the front edge. This shift is called *creep*. 241

crop, detail
Choosing a *section* of an image. 34, 76f., 80f., 102, 109, 138, 259 – see *cropping*

cropping
Choosing and enlarging a smaller *section* of a photograph. 77, 109

deck, kicker, bank
A *deck* (*kicker*, *bank*) can either be a *headline* or a brief summary of an article's or page's contents. 212f. – see *topline*, *running head*

descender
The lower part of a letterform, located between the *baseline* and the so-called *beardline*. 54, 57, 62, 68, 211

Didones
These *typefaces* are part of the group of Moderns. Their typometry is strictly linear, the letter's *axis* vertical. Also characteristic of these faces is a high *contrast* between the thick and thin (*hairline*) strokes, long horizontal *serifs* with squared ends. 51, 59 – see *type classification*

Didot (typeface)
A *type family* that is in the category of the Moderns. Known for the high *contrast* between the thick and thin strokes and its slender *serifs*. It is the prime example of the *Didone* category of the *Vox-ATypI* classification system (which takes its name from this typeface). 50f., 58f., 235

display type, headline type
Typefaces that, as opposed to *bread-and-butter typefaces*, are intended for use in a *headline*. Some *type families* contain multiple display faces. 59–61, 196, 222

dummy copy
A line (or more) with nonsensical words that symbolizes a missing text or copy line. This is helpful for the designer to get a feel for the amount of text and to see how the line will break. 213

ears, skybox
The space to the left and right of the *newspaper's nameplate* or *flag*. 212f.

Elzévir
A *roman* style printing *type* that is identified by triangular *serifs*. 51 – see *type classification*

embossing, emboss, stamping
Embossing (*debossing*) or stamping is a special form printing that presses a form into a *printed sheet* or paper board. One differentiates between blind *embossing* (no *color*) and foil stamping or foil blocking (with *color*). 21, 196, 198, 204

endpapers, end sheets
White or colored paper *sheets* that mark the end of the *book block* and form the connection to the (hard)cover. Luxury *bindings* sometimes use marbled paper. 182, 186, 188, 191, 202f., 205

face (type)
The visible or printable part of a letterform or *glyph*. The perceived size of the face is dependent on the ratio between the *x-height*, cap-height, and *ascenders* and *descenders*. 54, 57f.

featherweight paper
A soft, flexible and bulky paper with a porous surface that is of very light weight and makes a thicker *book* possible. Commonly used for works of fiction. It is inappropriate for high quality image reproduction due to its irregular surface. 241

finishing
All processes that follow printing – such as: cutting, *scoring*, *folding*, *binding* – on the way to producing a finished piece (*book*, *magazine*, *flyer*, etc.). 240f.

flat color
A uniform *color hue* without shading or variation. 24f., 74

flush left, flush right
A *typesetting* where lines of different length are either aligned to flush to the left or right side of the text *column*. 66 – see *ragged setting*

flush right, right-aligned
66f. – see *flush left*

flyer
A single sheet of paper that is used for advertising. Originally printed on thin paper, this medium has developed to the point where today people design them with great care – on occasion becoming collectible. 145, 148, 166, 232, 248, 255, 259

fold, folding
The way in which a *printed sheet* is folded. There are many different types of folds. 8, 40, 42, 165, 182, 209, 232, 240f.

folio
46, 182f. – see *page number*

footer, foot
The bottom section of a *news-paper* page. 213
see *below the fold*

foredge
This term comes from the craft of bookmaking and means the trimmed front edge of the *book block*. 182

format
The relationship between height and width that defines the *surface* of the page. This ratio is central in determining its *harmony*. The *formats* primarily used today are normed (*ISO* – DIN). 11–14, 20, 34, 36, 38–46, 77, 83, 85f., 91, 96, 102, 110, 112, 133f., 139, 143–146, 150, 154, 156, 161, 165, 169, 181, 184, 189, 196–198, 200, 204, 208, 209, 211, 213, 218, 226, 232–237, 241, 245f., 248, 255, 259

front (face) page [and back]
The front or *face page* is the first of two sides to be printed. The reverse side is called the *back page*. Front and back printing (or printing and perfecting) is the printing of two *pages* of a *sheet* in two separate print runs. 241 – see *recto*

frontispiece
An illustration usually opposite the *title page* of a *book*. 189

front matter, preliminary pages
The first *pages* of a *book*, located before the actual contents. 182, 188–191, 203

front page elements, headline elements
Headline, slug, *subhead*, etc. are all elements of a *front page* (*headline*). 213, 222, 250

full page ad
An advertisement occupying a complete page, often designed and written like a *poster*. 213

Geralde
These are *typefaces* in the *Classicals* category. These *type-faces* have a harmonious look and are highly legible even at smaller *type sizes*. Due to their more squarish form they seem more stable and coherent than the *Humanist typefaces* from Venice. 51, 56f. –see *type classification*

glyph
All typographic elements such as: letterforms, numerals, symbols, etc. that are contained in a single type *weight* or style are called *glyphs*. 20, 50, 181

Glyphic (incise, incised)
Typefaces in the *glyphic* classification are inspired by the early *typefaces* carved in stone. They have clear clean elegant lines and are based on *roman* type forms. There is often an emphasis on the *capital* letters. 51 – see *type classification*

golden ratio, golden mean
The number that sums up proportions pleasing to the human eye. It is indicated as or with the value of 1.618. 16f. – see *golden section*

golden section
A certain relationship between two numbers or measurements that is said to be the ideal in proportion, aesthetics and *harmony*. Two measures are said to have this *golden mean* if the ratio of two is the same as the sum of the two in relationship to the larger one. 16f., 38 – see *golden ratio*

grammage (paper)
Specific weight or basis weight of paper per unit of area. The value is expressed either in gsm (grams per square meter), or in pounds (lb) per ream (500 or 1000 *pages*). 241

graphic elements
Common graphic additions such as lines, borders, *text boxes*, etc. 36, 74, 142

gray value (of type)
The visual *color* of a *monochrome* block of text or area of type. The subjectively perceived *contrast* between the black of the type and the white of the page. 23, 50, 52, 55–58, 61f., 64, 67f., 71, 87, 115, 147, 245

grid
Grids are a system for organizing or rationalizing a design. They divide the area to be designed into zones or units where design elements can be placed. 11, 17, 39, 71, 86, 89, 106, 109–123, 130f., 134, 138–147, 149f., 152, 154ff., 158, 160ff., 164f., 211, 245, 249, 261, 264 – see *baseline grid*, *modular grid*

grid unit, grid spacing
The space between two *grid* lines that is used to size and position elements in a design. 138, 142, 154

gutter
The space between *columns*. 110, 112, 114, 122, 134, 138, 144, 154, 212f.

hairline
The thinnest line or stroke in a letterform. The *contrast* between the thin and thick strokes of a *typeface* or *type family* is one of its key characteristics. 21, 50–52, 54, 56–61 – see *baseline*

harmony
The coherent, successful and pleasing relationship between the different parts of a complex whole is *harmony*. 10f., 16f., 22–25, 27, 38, 44, 81, 109–111, 181, 197, 248

headband
The narrow woven beaded cloth ribbon glued to the head and tail of the *book block* for stability. 182, 204

headcap
The slightly thicker end of the *spine* at the head (and tail) of a (hardbound) *book*. 182

header
The upper *margin* of a page. 44f.

headline
A title set in over a page to indicate a currently recurring topic (e.g. The World Cup, presidential elections). 212f.
see *deck*, *standfirst*, *running head*

heavy stroke, main stroke
The thicker or heavier stroke of a letterform as compared to the *hairline* stroke. The *contrast* between the thick and thin strokes of a *typeface* or *type family* is one of its key characteristics. 21, 50–52, 54, 56f., 59–61 – see *hairline*

hierarchy
A ranking of the information on a *page* gives the content a more understandable appearance. 11, 13, 30f., 74, 77, 109, 245

Honnecourt, Villard de
(about 1230)
A 13th-century French builder, famed for his sketch*book* (portfolio) that contains numerous architectural designs and geometric studies. 109

hue
Another word for *color*. One could refer to a reddish *hue* or to the *color* red. 24f., 27

Humanist
These *typefaces* have very rounded brackets and cupped *serifs*. The *ascenders* are taller – just as the *Geraldes* – than the *capital* letters. From the middle of the 13th century onwards Venice was one of the most important centers of European *typography*. 51, 56 – see *type classification*

hyphenation
The division of words at the end of a line by a short dash (hyphen). *Hyphenation* is unavoidable in *justified type*, they can be avoided (at least in English and French) in the *flush left* ragged right *typesetting*. There are established rules for hyphenating syllables (these differ from language to language). 65–67

image-image-relationship
The arrangement of different image sizes in a *composition*. This relationship is a key design factor. 100–102, 105

impositioning
The placing of *pages* on a *printing sheet*, so that after *folding* the *pages* will be in the correct order. An *impositioning* plan or scheme depends on the size of the *printed sheet*, the final *format* and the *folding* machine used in *finishing*. 240f.

imprint
Information (partly required by law) about production, publishers of the publication (editor, author, editorial staff, company address, printer's information, etc.). *Imprint* is used in *newspapers*, *magazines* and *books*. 189, 212f.

inside margin
The inner *margin* of a *book* nearest to where it will be bound. 44f., 195, 241

insetting
Placing folded *pages* (of a publication) inside each other to form a *section*. 240f., 241 – see *collate*

ISBN
International Standard *Book* Number. This number is a unique permanent identity number for *books*. It is intended to help *book* dealers, libraries, sales departments, etc. organize and manage *books* digitally. 182

ISO
Stands for the International Organization for Standardization. 38

italic
A *type style* with *glyphs* that lean to the right. In general, *italics* have a different appearance than the corresponding *regular type style*. 56f., 63f., 71, 189

jump line
A short instruction at the end of a part of an article that explains where the article continues. 212

justified type
The *typesetting* where all lines except the last fill the space completely. Or in other words, fit flush to both the left and right side of the *column*. 67, 115

justify
In order to set a block of type with all lines having the same length, the type has to be justified. This is done by increasing or decreasing the *word spacing* (and in some cases *letterspacing*). 67 – see *kerning*

kerning
Adjusting the *letterspacing* and in some cases *word spacing* in order to achieve a balanced spacing between the letters (and words). The term comes from when the letters were modified so that one part of a letter extended over another. In some cases it can be used to *justify* lines of *capital* letters into the same *line length*. 65, 67 – see *justify, justified type*

layout
A plan for the design of the *pages* or double-*page* spreads. 7, 11f., 17, 48, 71, 74, 76, 88, 106, 108f., 115, 120, 128, 138, 158, 165f., 181, 186, 192, 196, 200–204, 211–215, 217f., 220, 222, 224, 226, 228, 230, 234, 236, 244f., 257, 260

leading
Leading is the white space between two lines of type. It is measured (generally) in typographic units (e.g. points) from the *baseline* of the one line to the next. 50, 54–56, 65, 68f., 71, 181 – see *line spacing, vertical spacing*

leaflet
A *sheet* that is folded once or multiple times. 232, 259

lede, standfirst
The *lede* (lead) or *standfirst* is the short summary or introduction between the *headline* and the article. It is intended to grab the reader's interest and suggests the article's point of view. This can be used to introduce a set of articles. 212f., 220

legend
The *legend* explains the graphic symbols and graphic language of an information graphic, diagram, or map. It should also contain the source(s) of information. 89, 91, 109, 115, 118, 134, 136f., 158, 212f. – see caption

letterspacing
The space between two letters that during spacing (global) or *kerning* (individual) can be increased or decreased. The normal spacing is predetermined and has the value of zero. The correct understanding and manipulation of this space is essential to the look and feel of a text. 67 – see *tracking, body width*

levels of reading, reading levels
Creating different *levels of reading* (for example through typographic treatment) gives the information a *hierarchy* that makes it easier to understand. 89, 109, 138, 259

ligature
The combination of two (or more) discrete letterforms into a new *glyph* (letterform). These were originally cast in lead to solve problematic letter combinations. Typical *ligatures* are: fi, fl, ff, ffl, ffi. So-called expert *font* sets usually contain these *ligatures*. The newer OpenType format is also useful because it contains *ligatures* (as well as many other additional *glyphs*). 58, 72, 196

light
Light is the visible spectrum of electro-magnetic radiation. It is also an important factor in photography. 11, 13f., 24, 78, 81, 83, 97, 205

Lineals
Also called *sans serif*. The sober neutral look of these *typefaces* led to their popularity during the industrialization. 51, 56, 62 – see *type classification*

line length
65–68 – see *column width*

line of force
A design principle: *Lines of force* can be understood as vanishing lines, guidelines, or axes of *composition*. They can be used to arrange different design elements. 12, 22, 74, 79, 103, 124–136, 164, 186, 189, 245, 261

line spacing, vertical spacing
Line or *vertical spacing* is the white space between two lines of type. It is measured (generally) in typographic units (e.g. points) from the *beardline* of the one line to *topline* of the next. 68 – see *leading*

line system
A system or set of proportions expressed as lines that can be used to establish rules for the *layout* of a page. 109

lowercase letter
The *lowercase letters* or *minuscules* always fill out the *x-height* and have either *ascenders* or *descenders*. 63

magazine
A print (or electronic) product that in *contrast* to a *newspaper* is not necessarily bound to report on the daily events. Most publications are dedicated to theme or particular area. 45, 74, 90f., 93, 96f., 98f., 103, 109, 123, 125, 127, 165f., 174, 178, 182, 211, 213–218, 220, 222, 224, 226, 228, 230, 236f.

majuscule
62, 224 – see *capital letter*

margin
The white space surrounding the *type area*. *Margins* are an integral part of the page's *composition* or design. 34f., 44–49, 66, 88, 96, 110, 112, 126, 135, 138, 144, 156, 181, 184, 186, 188, 192, 194f., 200, 241, 246

mass
In design one understands *mass* to be the optical weight of a graphic (visual) element. This *mass* is defined by parameters such as size, form, *gray value*, *color* intensity. 14f., 20, 103, 109, 143, 147, 245

masthead, masterhead
The upper part of a *newspaper's front page* where the core information is shown (date, logo/ name, price, etc.). 115, 212f., 214, 216, – see *nameplate, titlepiece, flag*

Mechanistic, slab serif
A subgroup of the *Vox*-ATypI *type classification* group Moderns. (Or one of the four groups of the *Thibaudeau type classification*: Égyptienne.) Also known as *slab serif*. These *typefaces* were popular for use in advertising and billboards. 51, 60 – see *type classification*

miniature
A small picture, or extremely reduced reproduction of a *layout*. 87–89, 96, 98–100, 102, 239

miniature format
A very small *format*. 40, 208

minuscule
– see *lowercase*

modular grid
A principle of *composition* where the design space (*surface*) is split into *modules* of identical or different sizes. This type of *grid* may include *columns*. 89, 106, 138–162, 165, 245 – see *grid*

module
A *module* is a single element of a *modular grid* (also called a *grid unit*). 109, 138–144, 147–150, 152–154, 156, 158, 160f.

monochrome
All *color* shades that are derived from a single *color* or based on *colors* that are close to each other on the *color* wheel. 23, 24

muted color
A darker *color*, achieved by adding black or a darker *hue*. 24, 27

nameplate, flag
A *newspaper's* logo and central part of the *masthead*. 212f. – see *masthead*

newspaper
A printed product published periodically (usually daily) that reports on the current events. 38, 41, 45, 60, 82, 109, 115, 120f., 166, 208, 211–216, 228, 230, 236, 245, 252, 259

New Typography
The principles of *New Typography* were taught at the Bauhaus (which was founded by Walter Gropius in 1919; László Moholy-Nagy taught these principles from 1923–1928). *The New Typography* emphasizes functionality and a radically modern aesthetic. 44f., 57, 62

offprint
A special printing of a *magazine* article or *book* contribution. 182

omission
The accidental deletion of a letter or letters, a word or words, or even an entire *paragraph* within an article or text. 32

opacity
Opacity is the opposite of transparency or show-through (in printing). 24

outer margin
The *margin* opposite the inner *margin* and *binding*. 44–46, 48, 96

page
A *sheet* of paper has two sides or two *pages*. 140, 182, 241

page composition
152, 188, 204, 242, 260 – see *composition*

page number, folio
A number on the *page* of a printed piece, which is used to number the *pages* sequentially. 46f., 71, 109, 144, 181–183, 192, 213, 226, 235, 241

paperback, pocket edition
A small softbound *book*, which lends itself for reading while on the go. Pocket sized *books* have been produced since the antiquity. 38, 40, 45, 166, 181, 198, 200–202, 230

paper bulk
A paper's bulk (or volume) is the ratio between its weight and thickness. At the same *grammage* (weight) bulky paper is thicker, and low volume paper is thinner and more compact. 241

paper width
The width of paper in *rotary printing* or offset web printing. This width depends on the type of press being used. 41

paragraph
A unit of meaning within a longer text. 71, 172, 213, 245

periodical
Publications that are issued in a specific *rhythm* (annually, bi-annually, quarterly, bi-monthly, monthly, weekly, daily, etc.) and in a particular form (*newspaper*, *magazine*, etc.) are called *periodicals*. They have content specific to their audience (*readership*). 166, 211ff., 214f., 216f., 218f., 220f., 222f., 224f., 226f., 228f. 230, 265

placard, bill
An older term for a handwritten or printed *poster* that was hung in public spaces and streets in order to announce something. 169 – see full page ad

poster
A printed paper *sheet* which is used to inform, advertise, or promote. *Posters* are hung, pasted or posted in prominent places. 29, 31, 38, 41f., 51, 70, 73, 76, 82, 85, 90, 92, 94f., 109, 122, 148, 166, 168–170, 173, 175–179, 181, 213, 216, 232f., 238, 245–247, 250, 252, 254, 265

primary color
Red, blue and yellow are primary or pure *colors*. They cannot be mixed from other *colors*. 24, 26, 29, 173

printed sheet, printing sheet
The large *sheet* of either printed or to be printed paper. 148, 241, 252

ragged, unjustified (type)
The *typesetting* where the lines are different in length and align to either the left or the right side of the *column*. The uneven edge of the type is said to rag or be ragged. 65f., 69, 115

ragged setting, hand-corrected setting
The original term (in German: "Rauhsatz/Rausatz") indicates type set aligned left ragged right set to a certain line measure with a defined *hyphenation* zone. There are more precise subcategories that should be acknowledged. Hard rag is the *typesetting* with no *hyphenations* other than with words that are hyphenated as a rule (like *sans serif*).
The "Schweizer Rauhsatz" is a *hand-corrected setting*, a very narrow *hyphenation* zone (generally less than five percent) which was popular in the so-called *Swiss School* (of design). Although it is *flush left* ragged right, the setting is very close to a *justified typesetting*. 65f.

readership
A group of readers of a *newspaper* or *magazine*. *Periodicals* try to build their *readership's* loyalty. 166, 181, 196, 211, 214–217

reading rhythm
The speed of reading and the way one's eyes scan across the text is influenced by typographic decisions (orientation, *column width*, typeface, etc.). 8, 53, 55, 65, 66, 89, 115, 120

recto
Another way of saying the front (first) *page* of a *printed sheet* and the opposite of *verso*. Also denotes the right-hand *page* of a double-*page* spread. 182, 241

reference, reference mark (footnote)
A superscripted sign in a text (asterisk, number, letter, symbol, etc.) that indicates or references a *footnote*, endnote or note in the margin. 71, 183, 194
– see *comment*

regular (type)
Regular is the standard or body text *weight* of a *typeface* with a vertical axis (as opposed to the slanted *italic typefaces*). 64

reprint
A new printing of all or part of an older printed piece is called a *reprint*. 182, 241

rhythm (composition)
The *rhythm* of a *composition* depends on the position, size ratio, and number of its design elements. 15, 17, 19, 22, 31f., 74, 85, 90, 100f., 103, 118, 122, 130, 139, 164, 230

rhythm (type, text)
The *letterspacing* determines the typographic *rhythm* of a word. The *leading* determines the text *rhythm* and the *typesetting* (ragged or justified), the type form or *silhouette*. 50, 52, 54f., 64–69, 97, 220

ribbon bookmark, ribbon marker
The narrow cloth band attached to the head of a *book block*'s *spine*, which is used to mark one's place in a *book* when the reading is interrupted. 182

ridge, groove (book)
The hinge between the two hardcovers and the *book*'s *spine*. 182

rivers
An unsightly gap in the text that forms a river of white spaces through many lines. 65, 213

roman, normal
The *roman* or *normal type style* is the upright style or opposite of the *italic type style*. The *normal* proportion or width is the standard width of a *typeface* (as opposed to condensed or extended). 53, 64

Rosarivo, Raúl (1903–1966)
Draftsman, painter, typographer and teacher. In 1940 *Rosarivo* began to examine the proportions of the works of Gutenberg and his contemporaries. 44, 109

rotary printing, offset web printing
In this printing process the press plate is cylindrical and the *sheet* to be printed is wrapped around a cylinder. These two cylinders turn opposite to another and where they meet the ink is transferred. Typically very large printing presses. 41, 168, 211, 228

routing (binding)
The *collated* unbound *sections* are routed at regular intervals where the threads of the *binding* will be. This *routing* forms a small divot for the thread to rest and the glue to soak into. The resulting *binding* is more durable. 241

running head, running title
The recurring information about the *book* set in the upper or *lower margin* (publication title, chapter title, *page number*, date, etc.). 71, 182f., 192, 193 – see *topline*, *overline*, *kicker*, *slug*

sans, sans serif
A *typeface* or *font* whose forms have no little "feet" (*serifs*). 51f., 54, 57, 62f., 65, 69, 248
– see *Lineals*, *type classification*

score, scoring
Thicker or stiffer paper or board is often scored with a tool. This *scoring* makes *folding* easier and cleaner. 241

Script
Part of the *Calligraphics type classification*, these *typefaces* are based on handwritten, penned or brush-lettered forms. 51
– see *type classification*

section, signature
The *printed sheet* or part of a *printed sheet* that once folded forms a unit. Each unit is marked (collating marks, *signature* marks) to enable the correct ordering of the parts of the publication. 240, 241

secondary color
A *secondary color* can be mixed with two *primary colors*. Orange, green and violet are *secondary colors*. The resulting *color* depends on the *primary colors* (red, yellow or blue) chosen. 24

serifs
The (more or less) fine lines that finish the *main stroke* of a letter perpendicular to its orientation. Whether a *font* has *serifs* or not and their form is one of the characteristics of a *typeface* or *type family*. 50–52, 56–58, 61

serif type
Type with small lines at the end of a stroke at the top or bottom of the letterform. 52, 56, 60
see *type classification*, *serifs*

sheet (also leaf)
The *sheet* contains two *pages*: a front and a *back page*. 66, 182, 185, 241

short, NIB (news in brief)
A very short *newspaper* text with just a *headline* and the key information. 115, 120, 212f.

shot, setting
A term from photography and cinematography. One refers to medium *shot*, panorama *shot*, figure *shot*, *close-up shot*, etc. 77, 99
– see *close-up*

silhouette
The (filled) contour of a form. 57, 66, 78, 84, 91, 205, 215
– see *text silhouette*

sketch, layout sketch
The first rough drawing for the *layout* (text and images) on the page. 213

softcover
A *book* is referred to as a *softcover* when the *pages* are either section-sewn or perfect bound. Finally, the *book block* is given a flexible (soft)cover. 241

spine
The narrow side of a *bookbinding* that is attached to the *book block*. With hardcover *books* the *spine* is "hinged" to the *book cover boards*. The width of the *spine* shows the width of the *book* or *magazine*. 109, 182, 184f., 199, 203f., 241

standfirst
90, 134, 212f., 213, 220 – see *lead*

stapling, wire stapling
Binding a publication with wire or staples. 234, 240f.
– see *binding*, *stitching*

stem
The vertical bar of a letterform is called a *stem*. 51, 54

stitching
– see *binding*

subhead(line), crosshead, sidehead
An addition to the main *headline*. This addition gives the reader more information about the article's content. It is also used to offer a different perspective on the *headline*. 212f., 213

surface
This term refers to the *composition's surface*. 8, 11, 14–16, 20f., 23, 25–28, 30, 32, 34–36, 38–40, 42, 44, 49, 68f., 88, 96, 100f., 109, 115–117, 124, 139, 140f., 153, 158, 160, 162, 173, 178, 184, 189, 205, 209, 211, 241, 244

Swiss School
An alternative name for a functionalist style often referred to as "The International Style" for its international application. Originating in the Bauhaus design theories, and pioneered by Josef Müller-Brockmann and Emil Ruder. 45, 106, 109

tabloid
A small *newspaper format* (approximately 12 × 16 inches), can also mean a *newspaper* with sensational (and less serious) content. 38, 41, 211, 213

tail square (head square, foredge square)
The narrow protective flange of cover that extends past the *book block* on top (*head square*), front (*foredge square*) and bottom (*tail square*). 182

teaser
A *short* enticing reference to an article inside the *newspaper*. 212f.

template
Might also be called a *layout sheet*. A plan for the *page* with information on *columns* and reoccurring elements shown. In the past called a "blue line" due to the non-reproducible blue *color* used to make them. 213

tertiary color
A tertiary *color* is made by mixing a *primary color* in equal parts with a neighboring *secondary color* on the *color* wheel: red-orange, yellow-orange, yellow-green, blue-green, blue-violet and red-violet. 24

text box, outline
A line around a text or an illustration. This element often compliments an article with additional information (a reaction, breaking news, etc.). 126, 213

text-image-relationship
An image is often used in connection with text, whether used as a *caption* or a longer text that is illustrated (directly or metaphorically) by the image. One should consider both of these elements carefully and make a connection with both form and content. 73, 83, 88, 90, 92, 94, 211, 254

text silhouette
The outline or contour of a text to show how it would look on a page. 65f., 69

Thibaudeau (type classification)
The system for classifying type – based on the form of their *serifs* – proposed in 1921 by Francis Thibaudeau. 50f.

title page
The first or *front page* of a *magazine* or *newspaper*. 115, 126, 181, 189, 213–215, 228

topline, overline
A *topline* or *overline* is a line of text in the upper part of a *page* that gives information about the page. This information may be the chapter title, *section* title, chapter number, *page number*, etc. 109, 182f., 212f.
– see *running head*

tracking
The amount of space that can be added or subtracted from a word, line or *paragraph* of type. 50, 53, 95, 220 – see *body width*, *kerning*

Transitional
This group of *typefaces* is one of the first to be systematically constructed based on typometry. The *capital* letters have a perfectly vertical axis and solid horizontal base. Unlike the *Humanist* and Garalde *typefaces* they have more rational geometric *serifs*. 51, 58 – see *type classification*

transparence
The degree of *transparence* is equivalent to the amount of *light* a *color* allows to pass through to (and be reflected by) the underlying *color*. 24, 257

Tschichold, Jan (1902–1974)
German typographer (1902–1974), founder of the *New Typography*, before he became a passionate advocate of traditional *typography*. 44, 46, 57, 62, 109, 181, 198, 200

turnover, spill
An article that begins on the (lower right section) *front page* of a *newspaper* and that continues on the second *page* is called a turnover or a spill. 213
– see *jump line*

type area
The area surrounded by the *margins* where the *page* contents are placed. The *page* area minus the *margins* equals the *type area*. 44, 46f., 96, 109, 183, 186, 192, 241

type classification
Typefaces are categorized into different classes or groups based on formal characteristics. Examples of *type classifications* systems are the *Thibaudeau* classification and *Vox* classification for ATypI (Association Typographique Internationale). 50, 56–63

type style
A *font* is usually available in different *weights* and styles (for example: regular, light, *bold*, *italic*, etc.). 60f., 64

typeface
A coherently designed set of forms (*glyphs*), including *uppercase*, *lowercase*, numerals and various signs and symbols with a consistent stroke *weight* makes up a *typeface*. 50–75, 143, 186, 189, 196, 200, 216f., 220, 228, 234

type family (super family)
A group or family of type *weights* and styles that are similar in their core form (*serifs*, stroke ratio, *axis*, etc.) and design. A super family combines multiple *type families*, often with different treatment of the *serifs* (e.g. *sans serif*, *slab serif*, serif). 50f., 56–60, 62

typefont, font
36, 50, 250 – see *typeface*

type scale (size)
A typographic scale is a proportional scale for *type sizes*. This scale can be given in different sizes. Originally given in Didot points (p), *type sizes* are generally measured in Pica points (pt). 50, 53–56, 58, 60, 62, 65, 67–69, 71, 73, 138, 142, 147, 181, 186, 189, 194, 196, 224, 256

typesetting, type alignment
The ordering of lines of text, or setting in relation to a vertical axis. One refers to *flush left*, *flush right*, *centered* and *justified typesettings* or alignments.
8, 46, 66, 71, 126, 135, 199, 224

type size
The size of a type is its body size, and is usually given in points.
61, 248 – see *type scale*, *body size*

typo
A missing or falsely set letter or word is called a typo. 213

typography
In a general sense *typography* is everything that is associated with the *composition* (type selection, *leading* ...) and *layout* of a *page* (*page* proportions, *margins* ...). In a narrower sense *typography* is the art of printing (or the art of type). 15, 20, 36, 44f., 49, 50–71, 73f., 94, 147, 169, 172, 174, 177, 181, 186, 196, 198f., 204, 211, 215, 220, 224, 228, 233, 245, 248, 250–252

Van de Graaf
Dutch typographer who investigated the rules of a harmonious *composition*. 44

verso
Another word for the *back side* of a *printed sheet*. The opposite of *recto*. 182, 241

Vox (type classification)
The French division of *typefaces* into eleven categories based on their formal qualities. It can be seen as an extension of the *Thibaudeau* classification. 50f.

warm color
In addition to *cool colors* the *color* wheel also contains *warm colors* such as: red, orange and yellow tones. 20, 26f., 103

weight (type)
The type *weight* indicates how thick the strokes of the *typeface* are. Many *typefaces* include the *weights* thin (light), regular, medium, *bold* and extra *bold* (heavy). 50, 51, 52, 61, 63f., 71, 73, 143, 181, 222

weight, type style, cut
A *weight* (of type) is a version of a typeface. The thickness of the stroke (*weight*) and the axis or slope of the letterforms (style) are two primary differences. Multiple *weights* and styles together form a so-called *type family*. One refers to a different cut of a *typeface* if another company designs an alternate version (often based on historic originals). 56

Wire-O binding
A type of wire ring *binding*. 241

word spacing
The space between the words in a line of type. Generally, this space is between one third and one quarter of the *type size*. The type designer defines the basic *word spacing*. 67

worm's-eye view
The opposite of the *bird's-eye view* takes a position well below the normal eye level and is directed upwards. Also called the view from below. 78f.

x-height
The height of the *lowercase* letterforms without *ascenders*, *descenders* or overshoot as is most often the case with "x". 54, 56f., 59f., 62f., 68, 211

References